Dedicated to students of policing who endeavor to contribute to society by utilizing contemporary approaches to the field and by promoting ethical and just solutions to community problems.

Further dedicated to those who put up with us through the rigors of writing this textbook:

Arlene and Alyssa;
Jill, Benjamin, Lauren, and Paige;
AnnMarie and Lera.

POLICE
&
SOCIETY

Third Edition

Roy Roberg
San Jose State University

Kenneth Novak
University of Missouri—Kansas City

Gary Cordner
Eastern Kentucky University

A comprehensive **Instructor's M____l/Testing Program** is available

Roxbury Publishing Company
Los Angeles, California

A comprehensive **Instructor's Manual/Testing Program**, a dedicated **Website**, and an **Interactive Student Study Guide** are available.

Library of Congress Cataloging-in-Publication Data

Roberg, Roy.
Police & society / Roy Roberg, Kenneth Novak, Gary Cordner.—3rd ed.
p. cm.
Includes bibliographical references and index.
ISBN 1-931719-19-5
1. Police—United States. 2. Police administration—United
States. 3. Community policing—United States. I. Novak, Kenneth
J. II. Cordner, Gary W. III. Title.

HV8141.R6 2005
363.2'3'0973—dc21

2003043191

CIP

POLICE & SOCIETY, *Third Edition*

Publisher: Claude Teweles
Managing Editor: Dawn VanDercreek
Production Editor: Jim Ballinger
Copy Editor: Pauline Piekarz
Production Assistants: Erin Clemons and Joshua Levine
Proofreaders: Margie Garrett and Arlene Miller
Cover Design: Marnie Kenney
Typography: Jeremiah Lenihan

Printed on acid-free paper in the United States of America. This book meets the standards of recycling of the Environmental Protection Agency.

ISBN 1-931719-19-5

ROXBURY PUBLISHING COMPANY
P.O. Box 491044
Los Angeles, California 90049-9044
Voice: (310) 473-3312 • Fax: (310) 473-4490
Email: roxbury@roxbury.net
Website: www.roxbury.net

Table of Contents

Part I

Policing Foundations

Part II

Police Administration

Part III

Police Behavior

Part IV

Contemporary Issues

Acknowledgements

We extend our sincere appreciation to Claude Teweles, the publisher of Roxbury Publishing Company, whose strong support and non-bureaucratic style have made this process less onerous and certainly more enjoyable. As usual, his wit, humor and insights have been valuable assets and have helped to establish an enjoyable working relationship. We would also like to send our appreciation to the staff at Roxbury, including Jim Ballinger, Phong Ho, and Jill Marcum. Several colleagues have made constructive and helpful comments with respect to the final manuscript, including: James Frank (University of Cincinnati), Tad Hughes (University of Louisville), Gene Paoline (University of Central Florida), and John Szmer (University of South Carolina). Additionally, several reviewers provided insightful comments for the Third Edition, including Elaine Bartgis (Fairmont State College), Charles T. Kelly, Jr. (Southeastern Louisiana University), William Kelly (Auburn University), Gary N. Keveles (University of Wisconsin—Superior), Peter B. Kraska (Eastern Kentucky University), Larry Miller (East Tennessee State University), Albert Sproule (DeSales University), and Gary W. Tucker (Sinclair University).

We would also like to especially thank all of the people who contributed to the *Voices From the Field* offsets throughout the text. These individuals are experts in policing, and have served in policy-making positions in police departments throughout the United States. Their contributions to our discussion on the police are significant, and they have provided a perspective on policing that can not be found in any other forum.

We would also like to acknowledge and extend our appreciation to Jack Kuykendall, one of the foremost early police scholars, who contributed greatly to the initial development of this text and worked tirelessly on the first two editions. As a special note, the lead author would like to personally thank Jack for being a delightful and insightful co-author on numerous projects and publications, as well as a wonderful friend and colleague in the same department for some 25 years. We sincerely wish you all the best in your retirement. ✦

About the Authors

Roy Roberg received his doctorate from the University of Nebraska, Lincoln, where he also taught. Other teaching experiences include Louisiana State University and San Jose State University, where he is currently a Professor of Justice Studies. He has published extensively in the areas of police organizational behavior and change; managerial issues; and higher education in policing. He is the editor of an anthology on policing and co-editor of an anthology in corrections, and is the author or co-author of numerous texts, the latest of which include *Police Management, Third Edition* (2002). He served as a police officer in a large county department of public safety in Washington State.

Kenneth Novak received his Ph.D. in criminal justice from the University of Cincinnati, and has been a faculty member at the University of Missouri—Kansas City since 1999. He has published numerous research articles on a variety of topics in policing, including officer decision-making, citizens' attitudes toward the police, racially biased policing and policy analysis. He has conducted research with a number of criminal justice agencies, including the Kansas City Police Department, the Cincinnati Police Department, and the United States Attorney for the Western District of Missouri. Recently, he co-authored the Third Edition of *Police Management* (2002; Roxbury Publishing). Novak previously worked as an undercover law enforcement officer for the Ohio Department of Public Safety.

Gary Cordner is Professor of Police Studies, Director of the Regional Community Policing Institute, and Director of the International Justice & Safety Institute at Eastern Kentucky University. He received his doctorate from Michigan State University and served as a police officer and police chief in Maryland. Cordner has co-authored textbooks on police administration and criminal justice planning and co-edited several anthologies on policing. He edited the *American Journal of Police* from 1987 to 1992, co-edited *Police Computer Review* from 1992 to 1995, and edited *Police Quarterly* from 1997–2002. Cordner is past-president of the Academy of Criminal Justice Sciences and founder and former chair of that organization's Police Section. He has consulted widely with government and private agencies, including the National Institute of Justice, the COPS Office, the Police Executive Research Forum, Abt Associates, and the Institute for Law and Justice. ✦

Foreword

From the war in Iraq to the war on terror, police have become both more important and less visible. This paradox is unfortunate, since visibility of the police role helps to attract the brightest minds and most committed hearts to the noble task of the police profession: peacemaking. No other profession does more good with less thanks in the task of preventing violence rather than creating it.

The title of this invaluable book is the key to the success—or failure—of the police mission. Police and society are one and the same, two blended parts of a whole. Unlike a military invasion that is blind to the society it invades, policing can only succeed by winning hearts and minds. No society was ever won over to the cause of lawful peace by a police force that failed to understand the values, morals, hopes, and fears of the people being policed. Police may rule by force in a dictatorship, but not in the name of freedom and democracy.

Since September 11, 2001, the word "police" has almost disappeared from the national headlines in the United States. Federal funding for policing—and police research—has been drastically reduced. Both criticism and praise of police has receded into the back pages and small sound bites of the news. The need for police to detect terrorist plots at home, and build democracy abroad, has become greater than ever in the world after 9-11. But the public attention to this need is in steep decline.

In the Third Edition of this influential textbook, Professors Roberg, Novak, and Cordner provide a welcome antidote to the dangerous neglect of policing issues. By keeping police research in the forefront of a generation of college students, we maintain the chance that policing will continue to attract the best and the brightest. Readers of this text are invited to consider seriously a career in policing, or in criminology, law, or related fields. Only a society that takes policing seriously will earn the blessings of a highly competent and accountable police institution.

For any new police manager or police officer, this book is an excellent place to view the police role in broader context. For citizens or taxpayers who want to know whether their own police department is using the best practices available based on research, this book is also an indispensable tool. From patrol to investigations to personnel and politics, **Police & Society** provides a wide-ranging review.

For the student of criminal justice and criminology, this book will help you reflect on the implications of research for a free society. Just because we know things that "work" to reduce crime does not automatically mean we should necessarily do those things. The self-imposed limit to research is values-moral judgments that we as citizens must make about the kind of society we want. Here again, **Police & Society** does an admirable job of laying out the key issues. Any student interested in criminal justice will find much to ponder here about the relationship between research-based policing and democratic policing.

Many who read this book will pursue careers in policing. Others may follow careers in law or politics, in which they may come to make policies affecting policing.

A very few may even go on to conduct research on policing. No matter where this book may lead you, you may trust it to get you off to an excellent start. ✦

—Lawrence W. Sherman
Greenfield Professor and Director
Jerry Lee Center of Criminology
University of Pennsylvania

Preface

P_olice and Society_ offers a comprehensive introduction to policing in the United States. The Third Edition is both descriptive and analytical in nature, covering the process of policing, police behavior, organization, operations, and historical perspectives. Contemporary issues and future prospects are also addressed. Throughout the text, an emphasis is placed on describing the relationship between the police and the community and how this relationship has changed through the years. To adequately explain the complex nature of police operations in a democracy, we have integrated the most important theoretical foundations, research findings, and contemporary practices in a comprehensible, yet analytical, manner. The impact of the continued evolution of society on current police practices is explored, especially with respect to community policing and policing in the post-9/11 era.

The Third Edition has been substantially updated to incorporate the latest research, concepts and practices in policing. All chapters have been significantly revised, and we have added an additional chapter on Legal Issues in policing, where we discuss criminal procedure and civil liabilities of policing in the 21st century.

Important new topics include:

- Police auditor systems.

- Early warning systems.

- New forms of police stressors.

- Officer safety and fatality reduction.

- Terrorism and post-9/11 policing.

- Globalization.

- Policing and the mentally ill.

- Search and seizure.

- Legal issues in interrogations.

- Civil liability.

- Contemporary performance measures.

- Racially biased policing/racial profiling.

In addition, several topics have been expanded from previous editions. These include: broken windows policing; the current status of community policing; gender and racial diversity in police organizations; officer culture; officer discretion; police paramilitary units; Compstat/quality-of-life policing; higher education and policing; demographic changes in America; and police technology.

In order to provide the most realistic and up-to-date view of the police, several types of offsets are provided. *Inside Policing* boxes provide a brief description of real-world police issues and operations as well as biographical sketches that highlight the contributions of important police leaders. In this edition we have added *Voices From the Field* boxes, where nationally recognized police executives provide their insights into contemporary police practices and problems in a thought-provoking Q&A format.

The Third Edition features an expanded glossary of key terms, and each chapter begins with a listing of key terms. Ancillaries to enhance instruction include:

- An **Interactive Student Study Guide** on CD is included with each copy of the book.

- A revised, dedicated **Website.**

- A revised and expanded **Instructor's Manual/Testing Program.**

- Eleven figures and tables in the text are available in PowerPoint on CD.

We would like to thank the many police officers and students with whom we have interacted over the years. Their experiences and insights have given us the basis for many of our ideas, and have provided us a basis for conceptualizing critical issues in policing. We hope that the book increases the understanding and appreciation of policing in society, and encourages thought-provoking dialog among students of the police. ✦

—Roy Roberg
Kenneth Novak
Gary Cordner

Part I

Policing Foundations

## Chapter 1

Police in a Democracy

Chapter Outline

- ☐ The Concept of Democratic Policing
- ☐ The Democracy-Police Conflict
- ☐ Democracy and the Rule of Law
- ☐ Policing, Terrorism, and Homeland Security
- ☐ The Policing System
- ☐ Organizational Structure
  - Other Types of Law Enforcement Organizations
  - Municipal, County, and Regional Police
- ☐ Police in a Democracy
- ☐ The Expectation-Integration Model
  - Community Expectations
  - Organizational Expectations
  - Individual Expectations
- ☐ The Role of the Police
  - Law Enforcement or Politics?
  - Crime Fighter or Social Service Worker?
  - Proactive or Reactive?
  - Police Activities and Patrol Workload
  - Traffic
- ☐ Police Values, Goals, and Strategies
- ☐ Summary
- ☐ Critical Thinking Questions
- ☐ References
- ☐ Suggested Websites for Further Study

Key Terms

case law	organizational expectations
civil law	police
community-policing model	police power
consolidation	political model
contract law enforcement	private police
counterterrorism	proactive
criminal justice system	procedural law
criminal law	public police
discretion	public safety
expectation-integration model	reactive
goals	rule of law
homeland security	special-jurisdiction police
individual expectations	strategies
jurisdiction	substantive law
legal expectations	task-force approach
legalistic model	tribal police
organizational culture	values

The United States is a work in progress as our experiment in democracy continues to unfold. We are all participants in this experiment and by virtue of our studies or experience are well aware that representatives of government, like the police, should never be trusted completely. Before you begin this study of police in society, the authors ask you to answer one question: "If you were a suspect in a criminal case, would you trust the police to report accurately and completely what happened and what you and others involved did and said?" If the answer to that question is no, and from our students it almost always is, then you will begin to understand why the role of the police in a democracy is both complex and controversial.

Why do the police exist? What do they do? What are their problems? How have the police changed? How can the police be made compatible with democratic society? The central theme of this book is to attempt to answer these and related questions about police in the United States.

One note about semantics. Throughout this book the terms *police* and *law enforcement* are used interchangeably. With either term, the intent is to refer to all those who provide police services, whether they work for a police department, sheriff's office, state police, or federal agency.

This book is organized into four sections:

1. Policing foundations, which includes a discussion of the democratic context of policing and the police role, the history of police, and the transition toward community policing.

2. Police administration, which includes a discussion of management and organizational behavior, change and innovation, selection and development, police field operations, and selected problems.

3. Police behavior, which includes a discussion of behavior and discretion, police authority and the use of coercion, and police professionalism and accountability.

4. Contemporary issues, including a discussion of criminal procedure and liability, higher education, cultural diversity, stress and officer safety, and the future of policing.

Most chapters contain special sections called "Voices From the Field" and "Inside Policing." These sections provide brief descriptions of "real world" police issues, excerpts from important research studies, and brief descriptions of the contributions of important historical and contemporary figures in law enforcement.

The Concept of Democratic Policing

The word **police** is related to the Greek words *politeuein*, which means to be a citizen or to engage in political activity, and *polis*, which means a city or state. These definitions emphasize the importance of the individual, the political process, and the state or government. How are individuals to be governed? All governments are vested with **police power** to regulate matters of health, welfare, safety, and morality because a society requires both structure and order if it is to be effective in meeting the safety, economic, and social needs of its members. One important expression of the police power in a society is a police, or law enforcement, organization.

The activities and behavior of the police are determined, in part, by the type of government of which they are a part. In more totalitarian governments, power is exercised by only one person (e.g., a dictator), a small number of individuals, or one political party. Generally, the established laws and policies that control all aspects of life are intended to maintain the interests of those in power; the social order is preserved at the expense of individual freedom. More democratic governments are based on the idea of the "participation of the governed." The members of a democratic society either directly participate in deciding the laws or they elect representatives who make such decisions for them.

Democracies are concerned about the rights and freedoms to be given to individuals and about the limits to be placed on government's use of police power. This concern is usually addressed by creating a constitution. Constitutions may be written or unwritten, but they serve the same basic purpose: to establish the nature and character of government by identifying the basic principles underlying that government. The Constitution of the United States identifies the functions of government and specifies in the Bill of Rights the rights of individuals relative to the government.

The United States has a constitutional democracy in which the exercise of power is based on the premise of the **rule of law,** that is, government by laws and not by individuals or organizations, such as the police. Ideally, laws that are created through a democratic process are more reasonable and more likely to be accepted by citizens than laws created by only a few individuals or by the most influential persons in society. And although democratic government does not always work in this fashion, ours has evolved so that the rule of law in practice has gradually become less tyrannical and more representative of the concerns of all citizens. One of the reasons that the rule of law is considered to be necessary is that proponents of democracy assume that individuals in power will be inclined to abuse their power unless they are controlled by a constitution, democratically developed laws, and the structure or organization of government.

The United States has a republican form of government that is decentralized (e.g., federal, state, and local units of government) to allow more people to participate in the political system and to limit the political power of those individuals elected to political office. Another important organizational feature of the U.S. government involves a "separation of powers," which results in three "branches": executive, judicial, and legislative. This separation exists to provide a system of "checks and balances" so that one branch of government will not become too powerful.

Law enforcement is a responsibility of the executive branch of government in our system. Checks and balances help to constrain the power of the executive branch function of policing in two fundamental ways. First, the police do not get to make the laws that they enforce—the legislature does this, along with appropriating the money that police agencies need to operate. Second, the police do not get to decide what happens to people who violate the law and get arrested—the judicial branch does that, along with continually interpreting and reinterpreting the meaning of laws in our changing society.

Government and laws are created through a political process or system. Being political means becoming involved in attempting to influence the way government resources (i.e., money, technology, and government employees and their knowledge, skills, and decisions) are used and what laws and policies are to be developed to guide governmental decision-making, such as a police use-of-force policy. Voters, special-interest groups (e.g., the National Rifle Association or the National Association for the Advancement of Colored People), and elected officials are active participants in the political process. Theories of political decision-making in a democracy include both pluralistic and elitist, or class, perspectives. The pluralistic perspective argues that debates, bargains, and compromises determine use of resources, laws, and policies. Further, although there are many different interests and groups in a society, no one group dominates. The elitist, or class, perspective argues that only a limited number of persons (e.g., the rich or special-interest groups) have real influence in the political process. This type of politics results in preferential treatment for the most influential and discrimination against those with little or no influence or power.

These perspectives are very important for our understanding of the police. From the pluralist perspective, police can be seen (1) as a benign institution that helps implement the laws and policies that result from the political contest among interest groups, or (2) as one of the interest groups competing in the process to advance its own interests. From the elitist perspective, police are usually characterized as the "iron fist" that helps protect the powerful and repress everyone else. Obviously, policing takes on a more noble connotation within the pluralist framework than the elitist framework. In either perspective, though, the police wield power and thus deserve careful attention.

The Democracy-Police Conflict

"Democracy is always hard on the police" (Berkeley 1969, 1). The police, in both concept and practice, conflict with some of the important characteristics of a democratic society. The police represent the legitimate force of government to compel citizens, if necessary, to obey laws that the majority of citizens, at least theoretically, have participated in creating. Goldstein describes the democracy-police conflict as follows: "The police. . .are an anomaly in a free society. They are invested with a great deal of authority under a system of government in which authority is reluctantly granted and, when granted, sharply curtailed" (1977, 1).

To be successful, a democratic government must be based on a consensus, but when that consensus fails, the police are often the initial representatives of government who respond. For example, one of the common values of U.S. society is the importance of private ownership of property. Yet when one person steals another's property, this action reflects a failure of a consensus on this value. The creation of a police force is based, at least in part, on the idea that consensus cannot be completely achieved.

Another potential democracy-police conflict is related to the role of government. Government exists to represent and serve its citizens. Yet the police provide services that many in the society do not want (e.g., a traffic ticket or an arrest) but cannot avoid. Although citizens, in the abstract, may agree to be governed, in practice they often resist governmental (including police) intervention.

Democracy is also associated with some degree of freedom. While complete freedom is not allowed in any society, at least a democracy permits citizen participation in deciding how and when individual freedom will be restricted. However, the policies and procedures of the police and the decisions of individual police officers do not always include citizen participation. Consequently, the exercise of police authority tends to reflect an authoritarian orientation in an otherwise "free" society. Police are a constant reminder that freedom is limited.

Another important consideration in democracy is equality. The social-contract theory of government rests on the belief that democratic governments are founded on a contract to which all parties agree and in which all parties are equal. Nevertheless, the citizen and the police officer are not equals. Once the contract is established, represented by a constitution and laws, it must be observed. If it is not, the police exist to ensure compliance even if coercion is required (Berkeley 1969, 1–5).

All these factors indicate the reason the opposite of a democratic state is often called a police state. Democracy represents consensus, freedom, participation, and equality; the police represent restriction and the imposition of the authority of government on the individual. That is why the police in a democracy are often confronted with hostility, opposition, and criticism no matter how effective or fair they may be. The democracy-police conflict must be addressed in some manner. As previously noted, democracies have attempted to cope with the exercise of government authority by emphasizing the importance of the rule of law.

Democracy and the Rule of Law

Police accountability to the rule of law is an important tradition in democratic societies. Reith (1938, 188) states that the basis for democratic policing "is to be found in rational and humane laws." The significance of the rule of law to democracy and the police is described in the Royal Commission Report on the British police:

> Liberty does not depend, and never has depended, upon any particular form of police organization. It depends upon the supremacy of. . .the rule of law. The proper criterion [to determine if a police state exists] is whether the police are answerable to the law and ultimately, to a democratically elected [government]. In the countries to which the term police state is applied. . ., police power is controlled by a [totalitarian] government [that] acknowledges no accountability to democratically elected (representatives), and the citizens cannot rely on the [law] to protect them. (1962, 45)

There are a number of ways to categorize laws; for example, laws may be civil or criminal and substantive or procedural (these issues are discussed further in Chapter 11). **Civil laws** are concerned with relationships between individuals (e.g., contracts, many business transactions, family relations); **criminal laws** are concerned with the relationship between the individual and government. Those behaviors that pose a threat to public safety and order (e.g., failure to get a driver's license, theft, rape, murder) are considered crimes. The prosecution of a crime is brought in the name of the people as represented by government officials (e.g., a prosecuting attorney). While police need to be familiar with both civil and criminal law, their primary concern is with criminal law.

In the criminal area, **substantive laws** are those that identify behavior, either required or prohibited, and the punishments for failure to observe these laws. For example, driving under the influence of alcohol is prohibited, and such behavior may be punished by a fine or imprisonment or both, and possibly by suspension of the privilege to drive a motor vehicle. **Procedural laws** govern how the police go about enforcing substantive laws, that is, the democratically determined process for exercising legal authority.

Important frames of reference for procedural criminal laws are the Bill of Rights (first ten amendments), the Fourteenth Amendment (see Table 1.1), and **case law** (the written rulings of state and federal appellate courts) that more specifically define when, and how, each procedure is to be used. When the police enforce substantive laws, their actions represent a restriction on individual behavior. When enforcing substantive laws, officers are supposed to follow procedural laws, which exist to restrict the police power of government and to reduce the possibility that police officers will abuse the power they have been given. The law not only provides the framework for police activity and behavior but is also intended to ensure that the police have a good reason (e.g., "reasonable suspicion" or "probable cause") to intrude into the lives of citizens. The enforcement of laws is considered less important than individual rights and the concern that government may abuse those rights. Procedural laws also balance what would otherwise be an unequal relationship between government and the individual because the government usually has more resources, and often more public support, than a suspect.

Even when the police have legal authority, however, they do not always enforce the law, because of limited resources, public expectations, organizational priorities, and officer preferences. Rather, both the organization and the officer exercise **discretion**; that is, they make a choice concerning what laws will be enforced and how that enforcement will take place. A number of factors influence police discretion; they will be discussed in Chapter 9.

Policing, Terrorism, and Homeland Security

Perhaps there is no greater test of our commitment to freedom, democracy, and the rule of law than the challenge of policing in the post-9/11 era. The events of September 11, 2001, at the World Trade Center, the Pentagon, and in western Pennsylvania suddenly created new top priorities for American law enforcement—**counterterrorism** and **homeland security.** To achieve these new priorities, the U.S. national government has considered and/or adopted a range of responses, including the USA Patriot Act, that impinge on traditional American views about privacy, freedom of movement, and the rights of people accused of crimes. Who is asked to carry out these controversial new responses? The police, of course.

The post-9/11 situation is very challenging for police in several respects. For example, terrorists operate with a different type of motivation than traditional criminals, and often are willing to die to further their cause. Terrorists may employ tools (chemical, biological, or radiological) or explosive weapons of mass destruction that local and state police are ill equipped to resist. Counterterrorism activity engages local and state police with agencies such as the Central Intelligence Agency (CIA) and the National Security Agency (NSA), which they have not traditionally had much interaction with. Homeland security engages the police with the military in a way that has historically been discouraged in America (the military has generally been very restricted in its role within the borders of the United States). Overall, the counterterrorism and homeland security missions tend to thrust federal agencies into the forefront; this is awkward because local and state police have always had the primary responsibility for law enforcement and crime control in the United States.

Table 1.1   Selected Amendments to the U.S. Constitution

Fourth Amendment

The right of the people to be secure in their persons, houses, papers, and effects, against unreasonable searches and seizures, shall not be violated, and no warrants shall be issued but upon probable cause, supported by oath or affirmation, and particularly describing the place to be searched and the persons or things to be seized.

Fifth Amendment

No person shall be held to answer for a capital, or otherwise infamous crime, unless on a presentment or indictment of a grand jury, except in cases arising in the land or naval forces, or in the militia, when in actual service in time of war or public danger; nor shall any person be subject for the same offense to be twice put in jeopardy of life or limb; nor shall be compelled in any criminal case to be a witness against himself, nor be deprived of life, liberty, or property, without due process of law; nor shall private property be taken for public use without just compensation.

Sixth Amendment

In all criminal prosecutions, the accused shall enjoy the right to a speedy and public trial, by an impartial jury of the State and district wherein the crime shall have been committed, which district shall have been previously ascertained by law, and to be informed of the nature and cause of the accusation; to be confronted with the witnesses against him; to have compulsory process for obtaining witnesses in his favor, and to have the assistance of counsel for his defense.

Eighth Amendment

Excessive bail shall not be required, nor excessive fines imposed, nor cruel and unusual punishments inflicted.

Fourteenth Amendment

All persons born or naturalized in the United States, and subject to the jurisdiction thereof, are citizens of the United States and of the State wherein they reside. No State shall make or enforce any law which shall abridge the privileges or immunities of citizens of the United States; nor shall any State deprive any person of life, liberty, or property, without due process of law; nor deny to any person within its jurisdiction the equal protection of the laws. ✦

We will have more to say about the specific challenges of post-9/11 policing in Chapter 15, including the USA Patriot Act and the new Department of Homeland Security. In the big picture, these challenges go to the core issues of democracy and law—how best to ensure safety and order while protecting individual freedoms. Institutions such as Congress, the president, and the courts are responsible for making and reviewing laws and programs designed to support safety with freedom. But there is no more crucial institution than the police when it comes to constructing the reality of safety and freedom on the streets and in our communities. In Voices From the Field, Chief Gil Kerlikowske from Seattle, Washington provides his perspective on blending police strategies in the post-9/11 era.

Voices From the Field
Gil Kerlikowske, Chief of Police
Seattle, Washington

Question: What are the most significant challenges for policing in a free society in the post-9/11 era?

Answer: The next several years will present some of the greatest challenges for police executives since World War II. The number, magnitude, and variety of issues will test our leadership and the resources of our departments. To understand what I am talking about, remember that just a few short years ago we were patting ourselves on the back for our accomplishments: Crime was at a level not seen since the 1960s, we were engaging with the community to a far greater degree than ever before, and we had resources in personnel, training, and technology, largely driven by the federal government, greater than at any other time.

Now we are faced with an increasing crime rate, decreasing resources, and increased demand for additional services related to counterterrorism that have the potential to impact the improvements made in community relations. I believe that today's law enforcement organizations are up to the task of overcoming these challenges and being successful. Why? Because we have come so far so fast and past performance is the best indicator of future success. Community policing, Accreditation, improving the diversity of our forces and our command structure, and demonstrating openness and transparency to those we serve were concepts or only in their infancy just two decades ago. No other private or public sector organization that I am familiar with has demonstrated the flexibility and ability to change and improve that law enforcement has.

The public we serve demands that we be successful. Local police forces are the face of all government, and people in our communities want to know and trust that government is protecting them, ensuring their rights, and responsive to their needs. Now we have to build upon what we learned over the last decade and adapt the principles of community policing and improvements in technology, training, and recruiting in order to hold the line on crime, maintain public trust and confidence, and protect our cities from terrorist threats or attacks. ✦

The Policing System

There are four basic types of policing in the United States: citizen-police officers, private police, public police, and public police who work in a private capacity. While all types of policing are discussed, this book is primarily about public police officers.

It is not uncommon for people in a democracy to participate in the policing process. As citizen-police officers we may make arrests when a felony, or in some states a breach of the peace, is committed in our presence. When we report a crime and cooperate in the subsequent investigation, we are participating in the policing process. Another type of citizen involvement is related to the legal doctrine of *posse comitatus*, in which individuals can be required to assist police officers. This involvement conjures up the image of the posse in Western movies, but it also includes the possibility that any of us, if requested, would be required to aid a police officer.

Vigilantism is another example of citizen participation in law enforcement. Historically, vigilantes were often community members (e.g., civic, business, or religious leaders) or mobs who took the law into their own hands. These groups developed as the result of a public perception that the existing law enforcement system was inadequate and corrupt or that it did not serve the interests of the vigilantes (Walker 1977, 30–31). Although more common in the nineteenth century, this type of citizen involvement in law enforcement still occurs.

There are also both public and private police. **Public police** are employed, trained, and paid by a government agency; their purpose is to serve the general interest of all citizens. **Private police** are those police employed and paid to serve the specific purposes, within the law, of an individual or organization. A municipal police officer is a public police officer; a guard at a bank or department store is a private police officer. Public police may also serve in a private capacity. It is common for public police officers to work part-time in a private capacity, such as at a nightclub or shopping center.

Public police agencies fit into the governmental structure in different ways. Most police chiefs report to an elected official (mayor) or appointed official (city manager) within the executive branch of government, although a few report directly to a city council or quasi-independent police commission. Sheriffs, on the other hand, are elected by the voters and generally report only to them. There is one important caveat to this, however—sheriffs usually have to apply to a county council for at least some of their funding. Thus, while sheriffs are independent elected officials, they are typically dependent on other elected officials for the resources they need to operate. This is another example of checks and balances.

Public police organizations are part of the **criminal justice system,** which includes the courts and correctional institutions. The police function as the "gatekeepers" of the criminal justice system because they determine who will be cited or arrested. The judicial branch and its representatives, including prosecuting and defense attorneys, process the accused to determine guilt or innocence and to sentence those who are convicted. The correctional part of the system (e.g., probation, community treatment programs, jails, prisons, parole) rehabilitates or punishes convicted criminals.

Organizational Structure

The organization of the U.S. police tends to follow the geographical and political structure of the U.S. government. Each of the four levels of government—federal, state, county (or parish or borough), and municipal (city or town)—has police powers and may have its own police forces. The federal and state levels of government have many different police forces that tend to specialize in different types of law enforcement.

Although law enforcement organizations at each level of government are similar in some ways, they may also differ in the types of activities in which they engage. These activities are determined, in part, by their **jurisdiction,** the criminal matters over which they have authority. For example, the Internal Revenue Service's (IRS) jurisdiction is limited to internal revenue violations, which involve federal tax laws. The Federal Bureau of Investigation (FBI) is the generalist law enforcement agency of the federal government. It is charged with the investigation of all federal laws not assigned to some other agency (e.g., the Postal Service or the IRS). Local police enforce all laws that are applicable, including state laws and local ordinances, within the legally incorporated limits of a city or county.

The federal government has more than 60 agencies with law enforcement and investigative powers (see Table 1.2 for a list of the largest federal law enforcement agencies). State governments, in addition to bodies such as the state police or highway patrol (e.g., the Alaska Department of Public Safety or the New York State Police), may also include other governmental agencies (dealing with such matters as revenue collection, parks and recreation, and alcoholic beverage control) that have police powers. The most common type of county law enforcement agency is the county sheriff, but some counties also have investigators who work for prosecuting attorneys and public defenders. In addition, some counties have separate police and sheriff's departments (e.g., city and county of San Francisco). In such situations, the sheriff's department is usually responsible for operating the county jail and for assisting the courts but does not engage in extensive policing activities. Finally, most municipal governments also have their own police force (e.g., Los Angeles Police Department). For the most part, both county sheriffs and local police are involved in patrolling, responding to calls for service, and conducting investigations; however, sheriff's departments also invest substantial resources in managing jails and providing court services.

Table 1.2   Federal Agencies Employing 500 or More Full-time Officers With Authority to Carry Firearms and Make Arrests, June 2002

Agency	Full-time Officers
Immigration and Naturalization Service	19,101
Federal Bureau of Prisons	14,305
U.S. Customs Service	11,634
Federal Bureau of Investigation	11,248
U.S. Secret Service	4,256
Administrative Office of the U.S. Courts[a]	4,090
Drug Enforcement Administration	4,020
U.S. Postal Inspection Service	3,135
Internal Revenue Service, Criminal Investigation	2,855
U.S. Marshals Service	2,646
Bureau of Alcohol, Tobacco, Firearms, and Explosives	2,335
National Park Service[b]	2,139
Veterans Health Administration	1,605
U.S. Capitol Police	1,225
U.S. Fish and Wildlife Service, Division of Law Enforcement	772
General Services Administration, Federal Protective Service	744
USDA Forest Service, Law Enforcement & Investigations	658
Bureau of Diplomatic Security, Diplomatic Security Service	592

Table excludes employees based in U.S. territories or foreign countries.

[a]Includes all Federal probation officers employed in Federal judicial districts that allow officers to carry firearms.

[b]National Park Service total includes 1,549 Park Rangers commissioned as law enforcement officers and 590 U.S. Park Police officers.

Source: B. A. Reaves and L. M. Bauer, *Federal Law Enforcement Officers, 2002* (Washington, D.C.: Bureau of Justice Statistics), 2.

The most distinctive feature of American policing is that it is fragmented and local. There are over 17,000 public police agencies in the United States, far more than can be found in any other country. About 90 percent of these (15,736 agencies) are local (city, town, township, village, borough, parish, county, etc.), whereas the rest are federal, state, or special-purpose law enforcement agencies.

Table 1.3 presents information on state and local law enforcement agencies by size of organization. Clearly, small police departments are most common. Over one-half of all U.S. police agencies have fewer than 10 full-time sworn officers. About 75 percent have fewer than 25 officers, and 90 percent have fewer than 100 officers. This feature of American law enforcement is very important to keep in mind. Although most of us conjure up images of the FBI, NYPD, or LAPD when we think of police organizations, Mayberry RFD is more typical.

Table 1.3	State and Local Law Enforcement Agencies by Size of Agency, June 2000	

Number of Full-time Sworn Personnel	Agencies	
	Number	Percentage
All sizes	17,784	100
1,000 or more	77	0.4
500–999	83	0.5
250–499	203	1.1
100–249	669	3.8
50–99	1,177	6.6
25–49	2,237	12.6
10–24	4,124	23.2
5–9	3,623	20.4
2–4	3,453	19.4
1	1,907	10.7
0	231	1.3

Source: B. A. Reaves and M. J. Hickman, *Census of State and Local Law Enforcement Agencies, 2000* (Washington, DC: Bureau of Justice Statistics, 2002), 3.

The most common type of local law enforcement agency is the municipal (city, town, village, borough) police force. There were 12,409 municipal police departments in the year 2000, the latest census of law enforcement agencies (Reaves and Hickman 2002). The next most common type is the county sheriff's department (3,070). Other common types of local law enforcement agencies are the tribal police department (171), county police department (52), multijurisdictional regional agency (34), and locally elected constable's office (623 in Texas alone).

While the typical police department in the United States is small, there are some very large law enforcement agencies in the country. Over a dozen federal law enforcement agencies have 1,000 or more sworn personnel (the number is somewhat fluid since the creation of the Department of Homeland Security and the reorganization of several federal law enforcement agencies). Each state except Hawaii has a state police or highway patrol agency, all with at least 100 sworn personnel (North Dakota is the smallest with 126 full-time sworn officers, California the largest with 6,678). In addition, there are over 50 local agencies with 1,000 or more sworn police personnel (see Table 1.4). The largest municipal police department is in New York City, with 40,435 full-time sworn personnel. The largest sheriff's department is in Los Angeles County, with 8,438 sworn personnel, 35 percent of whom are assigned primarily to patrol or investigations (Reaves and Hickman 2002).

Table 1.4   Fifty Largest Local Police Departments by Number of Full-time Sworn Personnel, June 2000

City or County	Full-time Sworn, 2000	Percentage Change, 1998–2000
New York (NY)	40,435	9.8
Chicago (IL)	13,466	1.7
Los Angeles (CA)	9,341	3.8
Philadelphia (PA)	7,024	9.8
Houston (TX)	5,343	0.8
Detroit (MI)	4,154	6.4
Washington (DC)	3,612	0.7
Nassau Co. (NY)	3,038	1.0
Baltimore (MD)	3,034	3.4
Miami-Dade Co. (FL)	3,008	6.5
Dallas (TX)	2,862	-0.1
Phoenix (AZ)	2,626	7.9
Suffolk Co. (NY)	2,564	-6.6
San Francisco (CA)	2,227	11.4
Las Vegas-Clark Co. (NV)	2,168	27.8
Boston (MA)	2,164	3.0
San Diego (CA)	2,022	1.8
Milwaukee (WI)	1,998	-5.1
Memphis (TN)	1,904	34.1
San Antonio (TX)	1,882	0.5
Cleveland (OH)	1,822	5.4
Honolulu Co. (HI)	1,792	-9.5
Baltimore Co. (MD)	1,754	14.3
Columbus (OH)	1,744	0.8
New Orleans (LA)	1,664	24.0
Jacksonville-Duval Co. (FL)	1,530	9.8
Denver (CO)	1,489	4.3
St. Louis (MO)	1,489	-8.7
Atlanta (GA)	1,474	0.0
Newark (NJ)	1,466	20.0
Charlotte-Mecklenburg Co. (NC)	1,442	12.1
Prince Georges Co. (MD)	1,431	16.3
San Jose (CA)	1,408	9.9
Seattle (WA)	1,261	1.9
Kansas City (MO)	1,253	6.8

Table 1.4   Fifty Largest Local Police Departments by Number of Full-time Sworn Personnel, June 2000 (continued)

City or County	Full-time Sworn, 2000	Percentage Change, 1998–2000
Nashville-Davidson Co. (TN)	1,249	10.6
Fort Worth (TX)	1,196	2.0
Fairfax Co. (VA)	1,163	9.0
Austin (TX)	1,144	20.9
Miami (FL)	1,110	9.7
El Paso (TX)	1,057	8.0
Indianapolis (IN)	1,045	5.4
Pittsburgh (PA)	1,036	-10.2
Cincinnati (OH)	1,030	7.5
Montgomery Co. (MD)	1,019	8.5
Oklahoma City (OK)	1,011	0.2
Portland (OR)	1,007	2.4
Tampa (FL)	939	5.6
Buffalo (NY)	938	3.3
Tucson (AZ)	928	11.4

Source: B. A. Reaves and M. J. Hickman, *Census of State and Local Law Enforcement Agencies, 2000* (Washington, D.C.: Bureau of Justice Statistics, 2002), 6.

Police agencies are one important aspect of the structure of policing in America—another is *police employment*. Consistent with what has been described above, most police officers work at the local level. About 75 percent of America's 800,000 sworn law enforcement officers work for local agencies, 12 percent for federal agencies, 7 percent for primary state agencies, and 5 percent for special-purpose agencies (Reaves and Hickman 2002; Reaves and Bauer 2003). The proportion of all officers who work for large agencies might be surprising, though, given the preponderance of small police departments. The reason, of course, is that small agencies are just that—small. There are a lot of them (more than 16,000 with fewer than 100 officers), but by definition they do not employ very many personnel. Thus, although about 90 percent of American law enforcement agencies have fewer than 100 officers, those agencies employ only about 36 percent of all sworn police officers in the country. To put it another way, 64 percent of all police officers in the United States (including federal, state, and local) work for agencies with more than 100 sworn officers.

The pattern of police agencies and police employment varies substantially around the United States (Reaves and Hickman 2002; Reaves and Bauer 2003). In general, western states have fewer law enforcement agencies and fewer police officers in proportion to their population than midwestern or eastern states. Hawaii and California have the fewest police agencies per population, South Dakota and North Dakota the most. Washington and Vermont have the fewest police officers per population, Louisiana and New York the most. Rural states tend to rely more on state police than urbanized states—the most "state police-dependent" states are Delaware, Vermont, West Virginia, and Alaska. Sheriff's departments play a very big role in law enforcement in some states and a negligible role in others. The states in which sheriff's departments represent the biggest portion of police employment are Louisiana, Wyoming, Florida, and Idaho. At the other end of the spectrum, the least "sheriff-dependent" states (not counting Alaska and Hawaii, which have no counties and therefore no sheriff's departments at all) are Delaware, Connecticut, New Hampshire, Pennsylvania, and Rhode Island.

One of the more important sources for data about the number of police is ***Crime in the United States*** (or ***Uniform Crime Reports***), which is an annual publication of the FBI and the U.S. Department of Justice. It also includes crime statistics and other police-related information, including the number of officers injured and killed and the number of women and minority officers. Another important data source is the *Municipal Yearbook*, published by the International City Manager's Association, which includes police employee and cost data as well as related management information (e.g., affirmative action programs and collective-bargaining issues).

Some of the most comprehensive data can be found in the publications of the Bureau of Justice Statistics (BJS), which is part of the U.S. Department of Justice. Of particular interest are the Law Enforcement Management and Administrative Statistics (LEMAS) reports published by the BJS. Many states also have agencies that collect and disseminate data about police employment and expenditures, and many law enforcement agencies publish annual reports and have Websites on the Internet.

Other Types of Law Enforcement Organizations

In addition to the basic structure of policing described above, there are other forms of public policing, including tribal police, public safety, consolidation, special-jurisdiction police, contract law enforcement, and task-force arrangements.

Tribal police are law enforcement agencies created and operated by Native Americans. Their jurisdiction is usually, but not always, limited to reservation land. These types of police agencies are separate from those law enforcement organizations operated by the Bureau of Indian Affairs, which is a federal agency.

The **public safety** concept involves the integration of police and firefighting services (and possibly other services like disaster preparedness, hazardous waste disposal, and emergency medical services). This integration can be limited to administrative matters or may include the joint performance of both firefighting and police duties. When the duties or work are integrated, employees are trained to perform both police and firefighting activities.

Consolidation involves the integration of two or more police departments. This integration can be either by function or by organization. Functional, or partial, integration involves the combining of the same activity, perhaps communications or training. For example, two or more police departments may decide to share the same communication system or develop a common training program. Organizational integration involves two or more departments becoming one. This is usually a county and a city department, as in Clark County-Las Vegas, Nevada, or Duval County-Jacksonville, Florida, but it could also involve two or more cities.

Historically, it has been quite common for communities to consider the consolidation of police departments, particularly in urban areas. Supporters of consolidation argue that a larger police force can provide better service at lower cost. Although this argument is not always accurate, it does tend to generate some support for consolidation. Opponents of consolidation argue that if the community maintains control of its own police force, it will be more responsive to the needs of that community. Citizens often want to maintain direct control over the use of the police power in their community. Although functional consolidation of police departments is commonplace in urban areas, the complete consolidation of two or more police departments is rare.

Special-jurisdiction police usually have the same police powers as those officers employed in other police departments, but they tend to have jurisdiction in a specified area believed to require more specialized or separate law enforcement services. Colleges and universities often have their own police force (e.g., San Jose State University Police Department). Other examples include transit police (e.g., Bay Area Rapid Transit in California), park or recreation area police, and public school police. Table 1.5 provides data on the number and types of special-jurisdiction police.

Table 1.5 State and Local Law Enforcement Agencies With Special Jurisdictions by Type of Jurisdiction and Number of Full-time Sworn Personnel, June 2000		
Type of Special Jurisdiction	**Agencies**	**Full-time Sworn Personnel**
Total	1,376	43,413
Government buildings/facilities		
4-year college/university	467	9,308
Public school district	162	3,219
State capitol/government buildings	21	1,121
Medical school/facility	42	978
Public housing	14	673
Other	6	274
Conservation laws/parks and recreation		
Fish and wildlife	66	7,935
Parks and recreational areas	80	3,218
Waterways and boating	13	477
Environmental laws	3	377
Forest resources	5	283
Sanitation laws	2	169
Water resources	5	118
Criminal investigations		
County/city	62	1,838
State bureau	8	692
Arson	31	490
Transportation systems/facilities		
Mass transit system/railroad	21	2,627
Airports	87	2,462
Transportation centers—multiple types	5	1,697
Port facilities	17	940
Commercial vehicle enforcement	3	440
Roadways, bridges, tunnels	5	234

Table 1.5	State and Local Law Enforcement Agencies With Special Jurisdictions by Type of Jurisdiction and Number of Full-time Sworn Personnel, June 2000 (continued)

Type of Special Jurisdiction	Agencies	Full-time Sworn Personnel
Special enforcement		
Alcohol enforcement	17	1,287
Agricultural	3	272
Gaming/racing laws	6	204
Drug enforcement	2	65
Business regulation	1	4

Source: B. A. Reaves and M. J. Hickman, *Census of State and Local Law Enforcement Agencies, 2000* (Washington, DC: Bureau of Justice Statistics, 2002), 12.

Contract law enforcement, or contract policing, involves a contractual arrangement between two units of government in which one agrees to provide law enforcement services for the other. For example, a county sheriff's department might enter into a contract with a municipality to provide a given level of police service for a certain amount of money. The municipality might not wish to pay to establish its own police department or it might believe it would receive better services from the larger organization. Although it is possible to have a contractual relationship between any two governmental units, the most common one is between a county and a city. Contract law enforcement is quite common in many urban areas.

The **task-force approach** to policing is a form of functional consolidation but tends to be temporary (i.e., from a few weeks to years) rather than permanent. Some task forces, however, have lasted more than 20 years. Two or more departments may decide to create a task force to respond to crimes such as auto theft, drugs and related problems, serial rape, or serial murder. Cooperative arrangements can exist at the local level (e.g., several municipal police departments and the county sheriff) or between local and state, or local and federal, law enforcement agencies (e.g., a drug or a gun and gang violence task force). A task force may also include representatives from other criminal justice agencies (e.g., probation and parole) or other governmental and community organizations (e.g., social services). What is unique about this arrangement is that it involves the joint efforts of two or more police departments directed toward common problems.

Municipal, County, and Regional Police

Municipal, county, and regional police, when compared with state and federal law enforcement, have the most employees, cost the most money, respond to a majority of police-related problems, and tend to have a closer relationship with citizens. In addition, a substantial majority of social science research about the police concerns municipal and county agencies.

Although there are similarities, there are also considerable differences among law enforcement agencies. Police departments range in size from more than 40,000 full-time officers to about 2,000 that have only one full- or part-time officer. Some small communities are adjacent to urban areas; others are more isolated. Counties can be densely or sparsely populated. Although it is theoretically possible to create a number of categories or types of local departments using demographic, economic, social, and cultural variables, research has been primarily limited to the study of differences between rural and urban police.

Rural and urban police do not represent discrete categories; rather, both unincorporated areas (in counties) and incorporated areas (cities or smaller communities) vary in population numbers, population density, values, lifestyles, and problems. Consequently, it is often difficult to identify what is a rural or urban area or community. Nevertheless, differences have been noted between larger, more densely populated urban areas and those outside of urban areas in which there are fewer people, usually 2,500 or less.

Although the urban crime rate tends to be higher than the rural crime rate, crime associated with urban areas is often exported to rural areas; for example, urban drug trafficking is a driving force behind the spread of drug use and the development of gangs in rural areas. Some of the crimes associated with rural areas include growing marijuana and manufacturing methamphetamine; theft of crops, timber, and animals; and poaching. Some crimes in rural areas are more easily solved (i.e., an arrest is made) because homicide, rape, and assault are more likely to occur among acquaintances than in urban areas. Also, rural witnesses may be better able to personally identify observed suspects. By contrast, a witness in an urban area is more likely to be describing someone who is a total stranger to them.

Sims describes other differences that exist between urban and rural police:

> Urban police tend not to live where they work, while rural officers do. . . . [R]ural law enforcement is personalistic and non bureaucratic, in contrast to the formality, impersonality and bureaucratization of urban police. Rural law enforcement involves . . . more face-to-face interaction and communication. [It also] . . . includes a greater . . . percentage of police-acquaintance contacts and . . . [fewer] police-stranger contacts. (1996, 45)

In addition, rural law enforcement officers, more than their urban counterparts, often work with lower budgets, less staff, less equipment, and fewer written policies. But they also appear to be more efficient than urban police and more respected by the public. The context in which rural police work takes place also affects their activities. Rural citizens may be more likely to rely on informal social controls (i.e., take care of the problem themselves) rather than report a "private" matter to the police. In addition, rural residents may be more likely to mistrust government and, therefore, may be more reluctant to share information (Weisheit, Falcone, and Wells 1994; McDonald, Wood, and Pflug 1996). Inside Policing 1.1 presents several comments by rural police officers concerning differences between rural and urban police.

The next section begins the discussion of the role of police in a democratic society. First, it provides a conceptual framework that is useful in understanding the police role. Then follows a discussion of recurring debates about the role and several methods used to identify the role of the police.

Inside Policing 1.1   Rural Police Work

Former Rural Police Officer

"The small town police officers are more in tune with the fact that if I'm a member of the Kiwanis, Lions Club or the Jaycees, these people can help me.... [In] New York [if] ... you get into a bind they aren't going to help you as much. [Rural] ... police are very active ... in these types of organizations." (81)

Rural Police Officer

"[When arresting someone] ... you can't act overly high and mighty with them, you won't get any cooperation. In big cities, that's what you do, you come on strong, 'I'm the boss.' That's often a very effective method there but not out here in the rural areas." (82)

Rural Police Officer

"[M]ost ... training academies are geared for large, urban departments. I used to send somebody to the academy and when they came back I would have to ride herd on them for two months to get the academy out of them. At the academy, everything is treated very, very serious. All traffic stops are felonies unless proven other-wise. . . . In a small town, [citizens] are people first and suspects second. In a large town... [it is the reverse]." (84)

Rural Police Officer

"Their [police and citizen's] kids go to the same school. You see [people] . . . on the street, ... in the grocery store. (Big-city cops) the officers are cold. They treat ... [the good and the bad people] . . . the same way." (86)

Small-Town Chief of Police

"I've had people in here to counsel ... [them] on their sex life because they think I'm the almighty, and can do that. I've had people come in here who are having trouble making ends meet, and we [help them] ... get welfare. Somebody needs a ride, like an elderly lady needs a ride to the doctor. We'll take her to the doctor and go get her groceries for her." (87)

Source: R. A. Weisheit, D. N. Falcone, and L. E. Wells, *Crime and Policing in Rural and Small-Town America* (Prospect Heights, IL: Waveland Press, 1996). ✦

Police in a Democracy

The police are the major representatives of the legal system in their transactions with citizens. The police "adapt the universal standards of the law to the requirements of the citizen and the public . . . through their right to exercise discretion." They are also the "major emergency arm of the community in times of personal and public crisis." In carrying out their mandate, the police "possess a virtual monopoly on the legitimate use of force" (Reiss 1971, 1–2).

The police also provide needed governmental and social services. In doing their job, the police often develop an intimate relationship with some citizens in a community:

> Police officers deal with people when they are both most threatening and most vulnerable, when they are angry, when they are frightened, when they are desperate, when they are drunk, when they are violent, or when they are ashamed. Every police action can affect in some way someone's dignity, or self-respect, or sense of privacy, or constitutional rights. (President's Commission 1967, 91–92)

Klockars suggests that there is a tendency to define the police in terms of goals (e.g., reduce crime) rather than the means or methods to achieve those goals (1985, 8–13). Bittner (1970) believes that it is the means used by the police that tend to separate them from ordinary citizens and other government agencies. Specifically, the police are authorized by government to use force (coercion) to compel individuals to comply with the requirements of criminal laws or force them to face the consequences.

The police can be defined as those nonmilitary individuals or organizations that are given the general right by government to use coercion to enforce the law and to respond to individual and group conflict involving illegal behavior. Although the military can be given police powers, this is not the group with which this book is concerned. Of course, the police use methods other than coercion, but this is what distinguishes them from other government agencies and employees. In the remainder of the chapter several aspects of the police role are discussed: compatible and conflicting expectations, recurring debates over roles, and values, goals, and strategies.

The Expectation-Integration Model

The police role is the part they are expected to play in a democratic society. There are three major sources of expectations concerning what the police should do and how they should do it: the community, the police department, and the individual. Figure 1.1 presents a depiction of an **expectation-integration model**. Each box indicates the different possible degrees of integration: substantial, partial, or minimal. The extent of role-related conflict either increases or decreases depending on the degree to which expectations are shared. When expectations from the three sources are compatible, there is minimal difficulty in deciding what the police should do and how they should do it.

Community Expectations

Societal trends and problems—in general and in each community—create an organizational environment of community expectations. Changing social and economic trends and problems in a society or a particular community often affect the police. For instance, there may be a rapid growth in population, an economic recession, a drug problem, or a gang problem. Although trends and problems in themselves do not create environmental expectations, police or citizen awareness of these issues may raise expectations concerning how the police should respond.

The community environment includes problems unique to a particular community, other private and public organizations, other criminal justice agencies, elected and appointed leaders, special-interest groups, identifiable neighborhoods, and the individual citizen. Community has different possible meanings—not only the legally incorporated area of a city or county but also individuals who live in the same area or neighborhood, work for the same organization, or share common concerns (e.g., members of an ethnic or religious group, teenagers, and senior citizens).

As the United States has become increasingly diverse in recent decades, the police relationship with multicultural communities has presented some unique problems. Different languages and cultural perspectives about the police have resulted in substantial changes in some police departments. Not only must the police interact effectively with diverse groups and individuals, they must also attempt to manage the conflicts between different cultural groups.

One of the most important, and recurring, police problems is the relationship between the police and a community that has, from the police point of view, a large number of suspects or individuals who are hostile to and critical of the police. This type of conflict between police and community has often been most pronounced in low-income areas, areas with a high proportion of young people, and areas inhabited by ethnic and racial minorities. Problems of police-community relations in these kinds of areas are indicative of conflicting expectations of the police role.

Figure 1.1   The Police Role: Expectation-Intergration Model

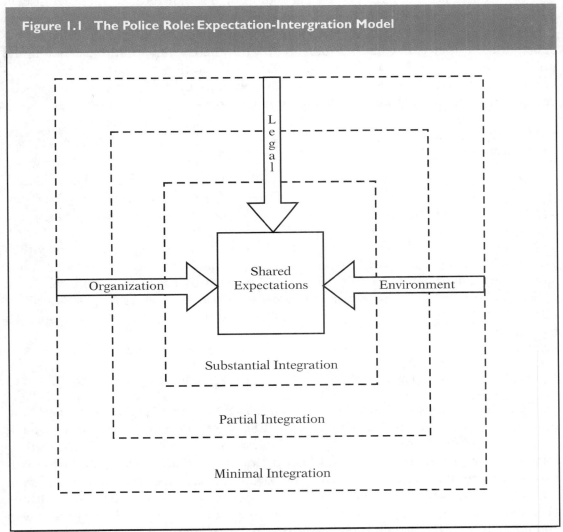

Source: R. R. Roberg, J. Kuykendall, and K. Novak, *Police Management*, 3rd ed. (Los Angeles, CA: Roxbury Publishing Company, 2002), 12.

Each community is also made up of individual citizens, whose expectations of the police are determined by the citizens' educational background, personal experiences, and experiences of family, friends, and the media. Each person can interact with a police officer in at least six ways: as a suspect (including the recipient of a traffic ticket), a victim, a witness, an informer, a bystander, or a citizen interested in influencing police policies and practices. In each of the six roles, the individual's expectations of the police may differ; for example, a victim's expectations differ somewhat from those of a suspect. In addition, citizen expectations may be held by reasonable, well-informed individuals or by people who are uninformed, self-serving, or prejudiced.

The community's **legal expectations** of the police are derived from substantive and procedural criminal laws and legal requirements that have resulted from civil suits. These laws provide the basic framework in which the police are supposed to function. Although the police do not always follow the law, legal expectations have a substantial influence on what they do and how they behave. In addition, as noted, the police do not enforce all laws; rather, they exercise discretion in deciding what laws to enforce and how to enforce them. These discretionary decisions may not always be compatible with what either the formal organization or the community expects.

Organizational Expectations

Organizational expectations come from both the formal and informal aspects of a police department. Formal expectations are derived from leaders, supervisors, training programs, and the goals, objectives, policies, procedures, and regulations of the police department. Informal expectations are derived from officers' peers and work group. Officers are strongly influenced by their work experiences and the way they adjust to the emotional, psychological, intellectual, and physical demands of police work. They must attempt to do their job in a manner that is acceptable to both the police department and their peers; they must try not to be injured or killed or allow other officers or citizens to be injured or killed; and their conduct must not provoke citizen complaints.

Individual Expectations

Police employees' *individual expectations* refer to their perspectives concerning the degree to which their needs are met by the organization and their working environment. All employees expect to be treated fairly and adequately rewarded. Together, formal and informal organizational (departmental) expectations create an **organizational culture** that can be defined as "the pattern of basic assumptions that a given group [the police] has invented, discovered, or developed in learning to cope with its problems of external adaptation and internal integration, [and] that have worked well enough to be considered valid" (Schein 1985, 9). The values and beliefs are concerned with what the police officer considers to be important and with his or her attitudes toward police work and the organization. An officer's norms become his or her basis for discretionary decision-making. Not all formal organizational expectations concerning appropriate police work are incorporated into the values, beliefs, and norms of the officers. The validity of the formal expectations of police officers must first be "tested" in the "reality of the street." Formal expectations do not always pass this reality test. As a result, police behavior is influenced not only by what the department expects but also by the expectations of the organizational culture (Crank 1998).

The Role of the Police

Historically, there have been recurring debates about the role of the police in a democratic society. Although both sides of the debate have been influential in determining the police role, the extent of the influence of any particular perspective varies by community and time period. This is discussed in more detail in Chapter 2.

Law Enforcement or Politics?

What is the most effective way to integrate the role of police into a democratic society? At the extremes there are two alternatives: a rule-oriented way or one that is responsive and individualized. The former is a legalistic (or bureaucratic, quasi-military, professional, or reform) approach, the latter is a political approach. The concept of a law enforcement or legalistic approach assumes that justice is a product of consistent application of laws and departmental policies and procedures. Ideally, these laws, policies, and procedures are rationally developed and free of any bias that would be inconsistent with the fundamental principles of the society.

There are two different variations of the political view of the police role. One is that laws and the police primarily serve the interest of the most influential persons in a community. Such individuals are considered to be above the law, whereas others are treated more harshly. This view leads to politics of preference and discrimination. The second view focuses on responsiveness and individualization. Its advocates argue that strict enforcement of the rules does not take into account the uniqueness of the problems and needs of individuals and neighborhood groups in the community. Complete consistency is not required and preferential treatment and discrimination are not inevitable if police officers are professional. The police response should be lawful and a function of the situational context and community values as these relate to community problems.

This debate between the legalistic and the political approach emphasizes a long-standing tension in democratic societies—the rule of law versus community expectations. At the one extreme is the uncaring bureaucrat who never deviates from the rules and does not seek opinions about which rules are important and when and how they should be applied.

At the other extreme is the tyranny of the majority. However much we subscribe to the rule of law, those who provide government service are often called upon to tailor that service to the needs of a particular community. But how can they do this without providing preferential treatment for some (individuals, groups, neighborhoods) while discriminating against others? The answer to this question remains elusive and varies concerning how, or even if, it can be done.

The legalistic approach and the two variants of the political approach to the role of the police identify three possible types of police-community relationships. The next two chapters discuss three models in the evolution of policing: political, legalistic, and community. The **political model** refers to a police-community relationship that is plagued by problems of preferential treatment, discrimination, and corruption. The **legalistic model** is based on the assumption that political influence has a corrupting influence on policing; therefore, the police-community relationship must be more structured or bureaucratic. The **community-policing model** is based on the desirability of the police being responsive to individuals and groups without engaging in preferential treatment or discrimination.

Crime Fighter or Social Service Worker?

The debate about whether the police should only fight crime or should also provide social services influences the priority given to police activities, the type of personnel selected, the way officers are trained, and the styles of officers. Officers who consider themselves to be crime fighters believe that crime is a function of a rational choice made by criminals and that the primary police purpose is to patrol and conduct investigations to deter crime and apprehend offenders. Officers who consider themselves social service providers believe that crime results from a variety of causes, and that there are other police activities like crime prevention education and community-building that may also reduce the crime rate. The social service orientation tends to result in more police-community involvement and a less aggressive and authoritarian approach to policing.

Police officers checking a suspect for weapons.

There are, of course, no "pure" crime fighters or social service providers; however, the belief that police are, or should be, one or the other influences how the police role in a community will be constructed. Often the role expectations vary by source. Some communities, neighborhoods, or groups may expect police to be crime fighters, whereas others may want a social service orientation. Often, police officers themselves prefer to think of themselves as crime fighters.

Proactive or Reactive?

Proactive police work emphasizes police-initiated activities by the individual officer and the department. **Reactive** police work is more a response to a problem by police when assistance is specifically requested by citizens. Giving a traffic ticket or other citation or conducting a field interrogation is proactive. Developing a response to a crime or other problem that is designed to keep a crime from occurring is also proactive. For example, undercover decoy programs are proactive, as are "stakeouts" (following suspected career criminals) and picking up truants (who may be committing burglaries when absent from school). Responding to specific problems based on citizen requests and following up on those problems are reactive responses.

What can be problematic about proactive responses is that they make the police more intrusive in the community; that is, police are more likely to initiate contacts or programs without being asked, and some proactive programs are potentially dangerous (e.g., stakeout and decoy programs). Being proactive can be associated with good management, but it may also be intrusive and risky.

An officer engaged in a social service activity.

Which is more compatible with democracy—a police force that is primarily reactive or one that is substantially proactive? Although eliminating all proactive policing (e.g., giving traffic tickets) is probably not desirable, it is possible to limit the number of police-initiated contacts and departmental programs. It is also important to distinguish the degree to which proactive police work is a response to community expectations or is entirely the result of the concerns of the police department or individual police officers. In some instances, professional police work has been associated with being proactive. What is clear, however, is that the more proactive, the more intrusive the police, and the more intrusive, the greater the risk to police officers, citizens, and democracy.

In order to define the police role and to attempt to resolve role debates, the police must first integrate diverse expectations by identifying their own values, goals, and strategies. Goals and values are also discussed in Chapter 4.

Police Activities and Patrol Workload

As these debates about the role of the police suggest, police officers perform a variety of different kinds of tasks and activities. Since the 1960s, many studies have attempted to summarize the nature of police work by categorizing different measures of reactive and proactive police work, such as calls to the police, calls dispatched, time consumed, and encounters with citizens (see Cordner 1989 for one review of many of these studies). By the 1980s, it had become widely accepted that actual police work, as contrasted with its depiction in the media, was a rich and varied blend of several types of activities, including crime control (taking crime reports, investigating crimes, inquiring into suspicious circumstances), law enforcement (making arrests, issuing traffic citations), order maintenance (handling disputes, keeping the peace), and service (everything from finding lost children to helping disabled motorists). The actual mix of these different types of activity varies between different jurisdictions (such as between a city and an affluent suburb) and also between different patrol beats within a jurisdiction.

The most comprehensive study of patrol work to date was the Police Services Study conducted in 1977 (Whitaker 1982). This study examined patrol work in 60 different neighborhoods, with observers accompanying patrol officers on all shifts in 24 police departments (including 21 municipal and three county sheriff's departments). The observers collected information on each encounter between a police officer and a citizen, detailing nearly 6,000 encounters in all. The fact that this study included so many different police departments, and police-initiated as well as citizen-initiated activity, makes it very persuasive. In a sophisticated re-analysis of the Police Services Study, Mastrofski (1983) looks at the most frequent incidents encountered by patrol officers. As indicated in Table 1.6, the percentage breakdown of incidents is approximately 29 percent crime-related and 71 percent noncrime-related. The vast majority of crime-related incidents involved nonviolent crimes and suspicious circumstances; only 3 percent of all encounters involved violent crimes. With respect to noncrime-related incidents, an overwhelming majority involved traffic regulation and enforcement, accounting for nearly one-quarter of all patrol incidents, followed by nuisances, assistance, and disputes.

The Police Services Study (Whitaker 1982) also examined the specific actions that police officers took during their encounters with the public. The figures below indicate the proportion of all encounters in which police officers took each kind of action. (The figures add up to more than 100 percent because officers often took more than one type of action in an encounter.)

57%	Interviewed a witness or person requesting service
40%	Interrogated a suspect
29%	Conducted a search or inspection
28%	Lectured or threatened (other than threat of force)
27%	Gave information
23%	Gave reassurance
14%	Used force or threat of force
11%	Gave assistance
9%	Gave a ticket
8%	Used persuasion
5%	Made an arrest
2%	Gave medical help

Table 1.6 Crime and Noncrime Incidents and Their Distribution in Police Services Study

	Percentage of All Encounters*
Crime Incidents	
Violent crimes. Murder, robbery, assault, kidnapping, rape, child abuse.	3.0
Nonviolent crimes. Theft, selling or receiving stolen goods, breaking and entering, burglary, vandalism, arson, fraud, leaving the scene, false report, nonsupport.	15.0
Morals crimes. Drug violations, gambling, prostitution, obscene behavior, pornography.	1.3
Suspicious circumstances. Reports or observations of prowlers, gunshots, screams, suspicious persons or conditions.	9.8
Total	**29.1**
Noncrime Incidents	
Traffic (regulation and enforcement). Violation of traffic laws, traffic flow problem, accidents, abandoned vehicles.	24.1
Disputes. Fights, arguments, disturbances involving interpersonal conflict.	8.6
Nuisances. Annoyance, harassment, noise disturbance, trespassing, minor juvenile problem, ordinance violation.	10.7
Dependent persons. Drunks, missing persons, juvenile runaway, mentally disordered, other person unable to care for self.	3.4
Medical. Injured accident victims, suicide and attempts, deaths, others needing medical attention.	1.9
Information request. Road directions, referral, police or government procedures, miscellaneous requests where no additional police action mentioned.	4.0
Information offer. Return property, missing or stolen property, false alarm report, complaint or compliment about police, general information provision.	2.8
General assistance. Animal problem, lost or damaged property, utility problem, fire or other disaster, assist motorist, lockouts, companionship, irrational or crank call, house check, escort, transportation.	9.2
Miscellaneous. Internal legal procedures, assistance request, officer wants to give information, officer wants information, officer assists, courier.	4.4
Gone on arrival. Dispatched calls where parties to the problem are not at the scene.	1.8
Total	**70.9**

*N = 5,688

Source: S. Mastrofski, "The Police and Noncrime Services," in G. Whitaker and C. Phillips, eds., *Evaluating the Performance of Criminal Justice Agencies* (Beverly Hills, CA: Sage, 1983), 40.

The police invoked the law relatively rarely, making arrests in only 5 percent of the encounters and issuing tickets in less than one of 10 encounters. Officers used force or the threat of force in 14 percent of the encounters (with force actually used in 5 percent, and most of this amounting only to handcuffing or taking a suspect by the arm). The use of force or its threat was about equally likely in situations involving crime, disorder, and traffic encounters, but very rare in service situations.

Perhaps the most interesting characteristic of police work revealed by these figures is the importance of communication skills. Five of the six most common actions taken by officers consisted entirely of talking and listening. These five were interviewing, interrogating, lecturing or threatening, giving information, and giving reassurance. It is primarily by communicating that police officers determine what is going on in any given situation, and it is primarily through communicating that an amicable solution is reached. Enforcing the law and using force often come into play only after communication tactics and informal solutions prove unsuccessful, although it should be noted that serious law violations may require immediate enforcement, and very dangerous suspects may warrant immediate use of force.

Traffic

The traffic function of policing accounts for a sizable portion of all police-citizen encounters and has a significant impact on how the public views the police. According to the most recent study, based on a large sample of U.S. residents, vehicle stops (which may be precipitated by traffic violations or suspicion of a crime) accounted for over half of all police contacts in 1999 (Schmitt, Langan, and Durose 2002). An estimated 19.3 million drivers (about 1 in 10) were pulled over by the police during that year. Of the drivers stopped, 54 percent were ticketed, 6.6 percent were searched, 3 percent were arrested, and 0.7 percent (approximately 139,000 drivers) had some type of force used against them (most of whom felt that the force used had been unnecessary or excessive).

A national study of local police departments (Reaves and Goldberg 2000) indicated the percentage of departments that provide different types of traffic-related functions: traffic law enforcement—99 percent; accident investigation—96 percent; traffic direction and control—91 percent; parking enforcement—84 percent; and school crossing services—43 percent. While all officers in most departments have some responsibility for traffic enforcement, larger departments often have a specialized traffic unit, often utilizing special vehicles, including motorcycles. Officers typically have a great deal of discretion in making stops and issuing citations, and the level of traffic enforcement varies greatly among individual officers and between different departments. Some departments have no formal policies regarding traffic enforcement, although there are often informal policies and expectations. For example, specialized traffic units may have policies requiring officers to generate at least one citation per hour, whereas regular patrol officers may be expected to write one or two citations per shift. Of course, such policies or expectations can lead to unequal traffic enforcement, with officers scrambling at the end of shifts or at the end of the month to "keep their numbers up" or "meet their quotas."

Police Values, Goals, and Strategies

Values are fundamental assumptions that guide the department and the individual officer in the exercise of discretion. The values of the department determine police goals, how resources are used, strategies, and the style of officers. To illustrate the possible influence of values on the police role, two sets of values are listed in Table 1.7. The first listing tends to describe police work as primarily a law enforcement activity in which an officer should be primarily a crime fighter and a legalistic police-community relationship should exist. The second set of values suggests that the police officer is as much, or more, a social-service worker as a crime fighter and supports a politically responsive police-community relationship.

Table 1.7   Police Values

Law Enforcement-Oriented Values	Community-Oriented Values
1. Police authority is based on the law, and law enforcement is the primary police objective.	1. The police will involve the community in all activities, including the development of policies, that affect the quality of community life.
2. Communities can provide police with assistance and information in enforcing the law.	2. The police believe that strategies must preserve and advance democratic values.
3. Responding to calls for service is the highest priority, and calls must receive the fastest response possible.	3. The police must structure the delivery of service so that it will reinforce the strengths of the neighborhoods.
4. Social and neighborhood problems are not the responsibility of the police unless they threaten the breakdown of public order.	4. Employees should have input into matters that influence job satisfaction and effectiveness.
5. Police, as experts, are best suited to determine crime-control priorities and strategies.	

Source: Adapted from R. Wasserman and M. H. Moore, *Perspectives on Policing: Values in Policing* (Washington, D.C.: National Institute of Justice, 1988).

Goals are sometimes called purposes or objectives or aims. When the goals approach is used to define the police role, several goals are usually listed for the police. Table 1.8 provides, in no particular order, several possible police goals.

Once the goals of a police department are identified, the next step is to determine how to achieve those goals most effectively. **Strategies** are those broadly conceptualized police activities that are assumed to have an impact on the attitudes and behavior of individuals. The four basic police strategies are law enforcement, presence, education, and community building.

Law enforcement strategies of the police invoke the formal sanctions of government (e.g., stopping suspicious persons, enforcing truancy and curfew laws, issuing citations, conducting investigations, and making arrests). The *police presence strategy* is that the police are visible, or identifiable, in the community—that is, wearing uniforms, patrolling in marked vehicles, and so on. Both strategies are based on the belief that a concern about the consequences of being caught by the police will deter criminal conduct.

Table 1.8   Possible Goals of the Police

Police Roles

✦ Prevention of crime	✦ Apprehension of offenders
✦ Reduction of the fear of crime	✦ Traffic control
✦ Maintenance of the peace	✦ Responsiveness to community needs
✦ Protection of persons and property	✦ Management of intergroup conflict
✦ Enforcement of laws	✦ Protection of individual rights
✦ Detection of crime	✦ Provision of additional public services

For citizens, the education strategy involves providing knowledge and skills that will reduce the likelihood they will become victimized. The motivation for victims to use such knowledge and skills is based on their concern about, or fear of, the consequences of being the victim of crime. For potential and convicted criminals, education involves both appeals for moral behavior and clarifying the possible consequences of criminal conduct not only for themselves but also for the individuals they victimize; an example might be a program in which criminals and their victims discuss the harm done to the victims.

When the police use a community-building strategy, they are attempting, along with members of the community, to enhance the informal social controls of that community. The police do this by attempting to involve residents in various organizational (e.g., community association, neighborhood cleanup projects) and recreational activities (e.g., block parties, sporting activities). As community members become more active, they may become both more concerned about area problems and more likely to be helpful in attempting to solve those problems. If a sense of community develops, it may have a significant influence on the socialization process and the behavior of residents, who may become more watchful and more concerned about their neighbors, whom they are less likely to betray or victimize.

The law enforcement and presence strategies are more intrusive and punitive; consequently, when emphasized they are more likely to create citizen resentment and anger. The education and community-building strategies are not as likely to result in a negative community reaction.

An important related issue is how to combine strategies to achieve maximum police effectiveness in reducing crime while maintaining widespread community trust, support, and cooperation. When this is done successfully, and police officers follow the law and do not provide preferential treatment or discriminate, the democracy-police conflict is minimized.

The remaining chapters discuss police programs and methods that represent one or more of these strategies in action. The next chapter provides a brief history of the evolution of policing in the United States.

Summary

The word *police* is derived from the Greek words *politeuin* and *polis*. The type of police a society has is determined by its type of government—either totalitarian or democratic. In democratic governments there are a number of democracy-police conflicts. The rule of law is the most important means for dealing with this conflict. Laws represent rules that citizens are supposed to follow and that the police are supposed to follow in their relationship with citizens. In today's world, terrorism has introduced another new challenge for the relationship between democracy, law, and the police.

Police are defined as those nonmilitary individuals or organizations that are given the general right by government to use force to maintain the law, and their primary purpose is to respond to problems of individual and group conflict that involve illegal behavior. The police role, and what is considered to be appropriate activity and behavior, is determined by legal requirements, the police department, and the community. The greater the degree to which individual, organizational, and community expectations are compatible, the less the extent of role conflict for the police in a democratic society.

Conflicting expectations about the police have resulted in three recurring debates over their role: crime fighter or social-service provider, legalistic or political, and proactive or reactive. Three methods that are used to define the police role include the identification of values, the setting of goals, and the development of strategies used to accomplish goals.

Critical Thinking Questions

1. How is policing different in a free and democratic society as contrasted with a totalitarian society?

2. It has been said that "Democracy is always hard on the police." Why do you think this is the case?

3. Why is the rule of law important for policing in a democracy?

4. Discuss the difference between law enforcement and community-oriented values as they relate to the police role.

5. The police system in the United States is very fragmented. Do you think this is a positive or negative feature? Why?

6. What would a police department be like that was proactive and emphasized crime fighting? What would be some pros and cons to this approach to policing?

References

Berkeley, G. E. 1969. *The Democratic Policeman*. Boston: Beacon Press.

Bittner, E. 1970. *The Functions of Police in Modern Society*. Washington, D.C.: U.S. Government Printing Office.

Cordner, G. W. 1989. "The Police on Patrol." In D. J. Kenney (ed.), *Police & Policing: Contemporary Issues*. New York: Praeger, pp. 60–71.

Crank, J. P. 1998. *Understanding Police Culture*. Cincinnati, OH: Anderson Publishing Company.

Goldstein, H. 1977. *Policing a Free Society*. Cambridge, MA: Ballinger Publishing Company.

Klockars, C. B. 1985. *The Idea of Police*. Newbury Park, CA: Sage Publications.

Mastrofski, S. 1983. "The Police and Noncrime Services." In G. Whitaker and C. Phillips (eds.), *Evaluating the Performance of Crime and Criminal Justice Agencies.* Beverly Hills, CA: Sage; pp. 33–61.

McDonald, T. D., Wood, R. A., and Pflug, M. A. (eds.). 1996. *Rural Criminal Justice.* Salem, WI: Sheffield Publishing.

President's Commission on Law Enforcement and Administration of Justice. 1967. *The Challenge of Crime in a Free Society.* Washington, D.C.: U.S. Government Printing Office.

Reaves, B. A., and L. M. Bauer. 2003. *Federal Law Enforcement Officers, 2002.* Washington, D.C.: Bureau of Justice Statistics.

Reaves, B. A., and A. L. Goldberg. 2000. *Law Enforcement Management and Administrative Statistics, 1997.* Washington, D.C.: Bureau of Justice Statistics.

Reaves, B. A., and M. J. Hickman. 2002. *Census of State and Local Law Enforcement Agencies, 2000.* Washington, D.C.: Bureau of Justice Statistics.

Reiss, A. J., Jr. 1971. *The Police and the Public.* New Haven: Yale University Press.

Reith, C. 1938. *The Police Idea.* London: Oxford University Press.

Roberg, R. R., Kuykendall, J., and Novak, K. 2002. *Police Management,* 3rd ed. Los Angeles, CA: Roxbury Publishing Company.

Royal Commission on the Police. 1962. *Report.* London: Her Majesty's Stationery Store.

Schein, E. H. 1985. *Organization Culture and Leadership.* San Francisco: Jossey-Bass.

Schmitt, E. L., Langan, P. A., and Durose, M. R. 2002. *Characteristics of Drivers Stopped by Police, 1999.* Washington, D.C.: Bureau of Justice Statistics.

Sims, V. H. 1996. "The Structural Components of Rural Law Enforcement: Roles and Organizations." In T. D. McDonald, R. A. Wood, and M. A. Pflug (eds.), *Rural Criminal Justice.* Salem, WI: Sheffield Publishing; pp. 41–54.

Walker, S. 1977. *History of Police Reform.* Lexington, MA: Lexington Books.

Wasserman, R., and Moore, M. H. 1988. *Perspective on Policing: Values in Policing. Pamphlet.* Washington, D.C.: National Institute of Justice.

Weisheit, R. A., Falcone, D. N., and Wells, L. E. 1994. "Rural Crime and Rural Policing." *National Institute of Justice: Research in Action.* Washington, D.C.: U.S. Government Printing Office.

Whitaker, G. P. 1982. "What Is Patrol Work?" *Police Studies* 4: 13–22.

Suggested Websites for Further Study

The Official Website of the White House
www.whitehouse.gov
Uniform Crime Reports
www.fbi.gov/ucr/ucr.htm
U.S. Constitution
http://www.access.gpo.gov/congress/senate/constitution/toc.html
U.S. Supreme Court Multimedia Database
www.oyez.org
Bureau of Justice Statistics—Law Enforcement Statistics
www.ojp.usdoj.gov/bjs/lawenf.htm
USA Patriot Act
http://thomas.loc.gov/cgi-bin/bdquery/z?d107:h.r.03162:
U.S. Department of Homeland Security
http://www.dhs.gov/dhspublic/ ✦

## Chapter 2

Police History

Chapter Outline

- Foundations of Policing
    - Early Policing
    - Policing in Nineteenth-Century England
- The Emergence of Modern Policing in the United States
    - The First City Police Forces
    - The County Sheriff
    - Vigilance Committees
- Modern Policing: The Political Model
    - Police Development
    - Criticism in the Progressive Era
- Modern Policing: The Legalistic Model
    - European Developments
    - Changes in the United States
    - Police Reform Movement
- State Police
    - Texas and Massachusetts
    - Pennsylvania
    - Highway Patrol
- Federal Law Enforcement
    - The Revenue Cutter Service and the U.S. Marshal Service
    - Postal Inspectors
    - The Secret Service
    - The Federal Bureau of Investigation
    - Additional Federal Law Enforcement Agencies
- Summary
- Critical Thinking Questions
- References
- Suggested Websites for Further Study

Key Terms

apprehension	marshal
Bertillon system	nightwatch
class-control theory	patronage system
commission approach	political model
constable	posse *comitatus*
constable-nightwatch system	prevention
crime-control theory	professionalization
disorder-control theory	sheriff
frankpledge system	state police
highway patrol	thief catcher
kin policing	urban-dispersion theory
legalistic model	vigilantes

It is important to understand the history of policing for several reasons. Possessing an understanding and appreciation for the history of the police allows one to identify enduring aspects of the police. It also allows for an evaluation of prior police reform efforts. Using this, it provides a basis for anticipating future policing developments (Walker and Katz 2002). Yet despite extensive research into policing since the 1960s, there are still no definitive answers as to what the police role should be or what particular activities are consistently more effective in reducing crime while maintaining widespread community support, particularly among the poor and minority members of society. Is it even possible for the police to be effective in reducing crime without providing preferential treatment for some while discriminating against others?

This question identifies the fundamental police problem in a democracy. The modern approach in responding to this problem is community policing, which is discussed in Chapter 3. Prior to community policing there were other approaches to making police compatible with democracy. These approaches, called models of policing, are briefly discussed in this chapter.

Foundations of Policing

The history of policing begins with a consideration of kin police, Greek and Roman police, and the development of policing in Europe, particularly in England, because of that country's influence on the formation of modern police departments in the United States.

Early Policing

One of the earliest methods of policing is known as **kin policing,** in which the family, clan, or tribe enforced informal and customary rules, or norms, of conduct. Often the response to a deviation from group norms was brutal (e.g., a hand cut off for stealing or a brand on the forehead for being a criminal). In effect, each member of the group had at least some authority to enforce the informal rules (Berg 1992, 15–16).

The kin policing of clans and tribes began to change during the rise of the Greek city-states and Rome. Until about 594 B.C. in Greece and the third century B.C. in Rome, public order was the responsibility of appointed magistrates, who were unpaid, private individuals. The first paid, public police officer was the *praefectus urbi*, a position created in Rome about 27 B.C. By 6 A.D., Rome had a large public police force that patrolled the streets night and day. After the fall of the Roman Empire, anarchy tended to prevail on the European continent until the twelfth and thirteenth centuries, when kings began to assume the responsibility for legal administration.

Their approach included strengthening the **nightwatch,** a group of citizens who patrolled at night looking for fires and other problems, and appointing individuals to conduct investigations, make arrests, and collect taxes. In some countries, such as France, mounted military patrols were also employed.

In the twelfth century in England, **sheriffs** were appointed by the king to levy fines and make sure that the **frankpledge system** worked. This system for keeping order had existed for centuries and was based on an organization of tithings (10 families) and hundreds (10 tithings). Eventually these hundreds became known as parishes, and several hundreds became known as a shire. The area made up of several hundreds was similar to a contemporary county.

In this system, men over the age of 15 formed a **posse** *comitatus,* a group called out to pursue fleeing felons. In 1285 the Statute of Westminster mandated that every hundred citizens appoint two constables to assist the sheriff. Like the sheriff, the **constable** inquired into offenses (conducted investigations), served summonses and warrants, took charge of prisoners, and supervised the nightwatch. By the thirteenth century, law was administered by magistrates, who were appointed by the king, and by sheriffs and constables. In the late 1200s, the office of justice of the peace was established in England. The county sheriff was responsible for policing a county and was assisted by the justice of the peace, who in turn was assisted by constables.

This arrangement was the foundation for a system of law enforcement that was to stay in place until the 1800s. Much of the work of these individuals, however, except the sheriffs, was voluntary and not popular, so the practice of paying for substitutes became commonplace. In many instances, the same person was paid year after year to do the work of those who were appointed to the position but did not wish to serve. Often the substitutes were inadequately paid, elderly, poorly educated, and inefficient. These deficiencies did not help the image or effectiveness of policing in the eyes of the community.

At the end of the 1700s, families by the thousands began to move to newly established factory towns to find work. Patterns of lives were disrupted and unprecedented social disorder resulted. Existing systems of law enforcement, primarily the justice of the peace and the constable, were inadequate to respond to the problems associated with these changes.

In the **constable-nightwatch system** of policing, the constables, who were appointed by the local justices, patrolled their parishes during the day. The constables had limited power, and when they tried to obtain citizen assistance by raising the "hue and cry" to capture a fleeing criminal, they were more likely to be ridiculed than helped. At night, men of the watch were charged with patrolling deserted streets and maintaining street lamps. These individuals, however, were more likely to be found sleeping or in a pub than performing their duties.

In London, criminals had little to fear from this system of law enforcement, and they moved freely about the city streets. Victims of crime, if well-to-do, were protected by their servants and retainers (who formed a bodyguard or type of private police). Poorer citizens had no such protection. When property crimes were committed, the usual procedure was for the victim to employ a **thief catcher.** This person, usually an experienced constable familiar with the criminal underworld, would attempt, for a fee, to secure a return of all, or part, of the stolen property. Often the thief catcher would supplement his fee by keeping part of the stolen property for himself. Thief catchers were not interested in apprehending and prosecuting criminals but only in getting paid and returning all or part of the stolen property.

Critics of this approach to law enforcement began to suggest alternatives as early as the 1730s. In 1748 Henry Fielding wrote *An Enquiry Into the Cause of the Late Increase of Robbers.* Patrick Colquhoun published *A Treatise on the Police of the*

Metropolis in 1795. Both books argued for a more effective approach to law enforcement (Johnson 1988, 173–175).

Policing in Nineteenth-Century England

It is important to focus on the early policing models of nineteenth-century London because this system became a model for policing in England and to some degree for the United States (President's Commission 1967, 3–5). Henry Fielding, the magistrate for Middlesex and Westminster, was among the first to believe police action can prevent crime. From 1754 to 1780, he assisted in the organization of the Bow Street station. This station was organized into three groups that performed specific crime control functions. Men engaged in foot patrol in the inner areas of the city. Additionally, men on horseback allowed for patrol up to 15 miles away from the Bow Street station. Finally, a group of men were responsible for responding to crime scenes to engage in investigations. These plain-clothed men became known as the *Bow Street Runners*, or *"Thief Takers,"* and as such represented the first detective unit (Germann, Day, and Gallati 1978).

In 1822, Sir Robert Peel, the British home secretary, criticized the poor quality of police in London. In 1829 he was able to pass the Act for Improving the Police in and Near the Metropolis, also known as the Metropolitan Police Act. This measure resulted in the creation of the first organized British metropolitan police force and the creation of modern-day police (Germann, Day, and Gallati 1978).

Initially, Charles Rowan and Richard Mayne were appointed to develop the force. They adopted a military structure and sought to employ the most competent personnel possible. There was considerable resistance, however, to this new type of police among the British populace. They feared the abuse of governmental authority, the kind of secret police that existed in other countries such as France, and limitations on individual freedom. Historically, Britain, like other countries, had many problems in this regard. Inside Policing 2.1 provides brief descriptions of the contributions of Peel, Rowan, and Mayne to the development of the British police.

Eventually the police became accepted, largely because Rowan and Mayne were strict about who they employed and how officers were to behave. By the 1850s, every borough and county in England was required to develop its own police force.

One of the most important principles of the Peelian approach was to emphasize the preventive aspects of law enforcement. This attitude resulted in police officers being distributed throughout the city in order to prevent crimes or to be close by when crimes occurred so that officers could make arrests and help victims. This idea was to become an important part of the development of police in the United States. Other principles were also implemented to guide the development of the new police force. Originally there were 12 principles; however, some of them dealt with the same issues. These principles are consolidated, rearranged, and presented in Inside Policing 2.2. As will be discovered later in the text, some of these principles have been called into question in recent decades in the United States, particularly numbers 2 and 4.

The remainder of this chapter is divided into three sections: the development of modern policing at (1) the local (county and municipal) level of government, (2) the state level, and (3) the federal level. The historical discussion of modern policing in this chapter ends in the 1960s, but continues in Chapter 3 with a discussion of the development of community policing between the 1970s and 1990s.

Inside Policing 2.1   Founders of the British Police

Sir Robert Peel

In 1822 Robert Peel was appointed home secretary, the person responsible for internal security in England. One of his most important objectives was to establish an effective police force to respond to riots and crime problems. It took him seven years—until 1829—before he was successful. Because the idea for a new approach to policing was so controversial, Peel initially asked that the new police be established only in metropolitan London. He intended, however, that eventually a similar type of police organization would be established for all of Great Britain. Peel was a strong advocate of the concept of a civilian (rather than a military) police force that did not carry guns and that was put out in the community to patrol to prevent crime. The new police became known as Bobbies, after the founder of the department.

Colonel Charles Rowan

Charles Rowan was one of the first commissioners of the new police in London. He served in that capacity until 1850, when he retired. Rowan had a military background that prepared him for such service. Early in the nineteenth century he served under Major General Sir John Moore, whose approach to dealing with his soldiers probably had a strong influence on how Rowan thought the police should relate to the public. Moore believed that officers should show respect for soldiers and treat them firmly and justly. Rowan wanted the same type of relationship to exist between police officers and citizens. Both he and Mayne encouraged officers to listen to citizen complaints and to be tolerant of verbal abuse by citizens.

Richard Mayne

Richard Mayne, an Irish barrister, served as a police commissioner until 1868. His extended service enabled the London police to develop a force that was well respected by citizens. Together with Rowan, he organized the force into numerous divisions that varied in size depending on the amount of crime in a division's area. Each division had a superintendent in charge, with inspectors, sergeants, and constables, in descending order of rank. Constables were placed in a blue uniform and armed with a short baton and a rattle (for raising an alarm). The uniform was designed so that it would not be similar to military dress. Mayne and Rowan were both concerned that a military-style police would have more difficulty in being accepted by the public.

Sources: Adapted from H. A. Johnson, *History of Criminal Justice* (Cincinnati: Anderson Publishing Company, 1988), 173–175; D. R. Johnson, *American Law Enforcement: A History* (St. Louis: Forum Press, 1981), 20–21. ✦

The Emergence of Modern Policing in the United States

In the 1600s and 1700s the English colonists in America brought with them the system of policing that existed in England. This system included the offices of justice of the peace, sheriff, constable, and nightwatch. Over time, the basic responsibility for law enforcement gradually shifted from volunteer citizens to paid specialists. This process of role specialization was the result of a growing and increasingly complex society attempting to master the physical environment and cope with human problems. One consequence of these economic, social, and technological changes was an increasing public concern about deviant and disruptive behavior.

Inside Policing 2.2   Revised Peelian Principles of Policing

1. The police must be under the control of government.
2. The police must be organized along military lines to ensure stability and efficiency.
3. Police buildings should be located so they are easily accessible to citizens.
4. The public should be informed about the extent and nature of crime. The most appropriate method of evaluating the police is the amount of crime in a community.
5. Police officers should be distributed by time and area. To do this, it is important to keep records of police activities.
6. If a police organization is to be effective, its selection process and training program must be of high quality. New officers should be employed in a probationary status.
7. Police officers who have a good appearance will be more respected by the public.
8. Police officers should be able to control their temper and should emphasize a quiet, determined manner, rather than violent action, in dealing with citizens.
9. To ensure public confidence in the police, all officers must be easily identified; therefore, all officers should be given a number.

Source: Adapted from G. L. Kirkham and L. A. Wollan, *Introduction to Law Enforcement* (New York: Harper and Row, 1980), 29. ✦

Initially, the constable-nightwatch system of policing evolved as a response to the problems of maintaining order and enforcing the law. The system included a limited number of constables who had civil and criminal responsibilities and a patrolling nightwatch staffed with persons who were required to serve as a community obligation. As in England, this obligation was unpopular, and paid substitutes, who were often incompetent, were used until finally the nightwatch became a full-time, paid occupation.

There is a tendency to focus exclusively on the American history of the police as it developed in the northern colonies, but it is important to highlight other areas where different approaches to law enforcement emerged. Two particular areas included the southern colonies and the western American frontier. In the southern colonies, slave patrols represented the first form of modern policing, existing as early as the mid-1700s. Slave patrols were created to apprehend runaway slaves and to ensure that slaves did not revolt against their masters. The need for slave patrols was premised on the fact that slaves represented a dangerous class that the economic elite (e.g., plantation owners) desired to control. Slave patrols relied on private citizens to carry out their duties. Participation in slave patrols was part of a citizen's civil responsibility. This structure often led to great difficulties in accountability to the central government, as well as great variation in the behavior of the various "policing" functions. When disorderly or runaway slaves were encountered, they were often immediately punished by the patrol; thus, recognizable due process was absent from this style of policing. Reichel (1999, 85) comments: "[I]n an ironic sense the resistance by slaves should have been completely understandable to American Patriots. Patrols were allowed search powers that the colonists later found so objectionable in the hands of British authorities." The level of fear and resentment on the part of slaves toward these patrols was great.

In the parts of the West and Southwest that were influenced by Spain, the *alcalde*—a combination of sheriff and justice of the peace—was the most important law enforcement official. This was supplemented in the frontier by the creation of vigilantes. Nevertheless, the law enforcement system that was developed in the northern colonies gradually became the basis for local law enforcement throughout the country.

The First City Police Forces

Between the 1830s and the 1850s, a growing number of cities decided that the constable-nightwatch system of law enforcement was inadequate. As a result, paid daytime police forces were created. Eventually the daytime force joined with the nightwatch to create integrated day-night, modern-type police departments. In 1833 an ordinance was passed in Philadelphia that created a 24-person day force and a 120-person nightwatch, all of whom were to be paid. In 1838 Boston created a daytime force to supplement the nightwatch, and soon other cities followed. This arrangement provided the foundation for the emergence of modern policing: a force of officers in one department available 24 hours a day to respond, often through patrolling, to problems of crime and disorder (Lane 1967; Miller 1977; Johnson 1981).

Four theories have been suggested to explain the development of police departments. The **disorder-control theory** explains development in terms of the need to suppress mob violence. For example, Boston had three major riots in the years preceding the establishment of its police department (Lane 1967). Mob violence also occurred in other cities in the 1830s and 1840s. The **crime-control theory** suggests that increases in criminal activity resulted in a perceived need for a new type of police. Threats to social order, such as highway robbers and violent pickpockets (today called muggers), created a climate of fear. Concern about daring thieves and property offenses was also widespread in cities during this time (Johnson 1981).

The **class-control theory** regards the development of the police as a result of class-based economic exploitation. Its advocates note that urban and industrial growth coincided with the development of the new police. During this period, many persons of different social and ethnic backgrounds competed for opportunities that would improve their economic status. The resulting disruption prompted the middle and upper classes, usually white Anglo-Saxon Protestants, to develop a means to control the people involved, usually poor immigrants, sometimes not Anglo and often not Protestant. This theory holds that modern police forces were merely tools created by the industrial elite to suppress exploited laborers who were being used as fuel for the engine of capitalism (Cooper 1975; Johnson 1981). The last view, **urban-dispersion theory,** holds that many municipal police departments were created because other cities had them, not because there was a real need. Police forces were considered an integral part of the governmental structure needed to provide a stabilizing influence in communities (Mokkonen 1981).

There is some evidence to support all four theories; however, no single theory provides an adequate explanation. Although some cities had major urban disturbances before they established new police departments, others did not. Although there was also a public concern about crime, the degree of concern varied among communities. Some cities established after the 1830s and 1840s did not have mob violence or serious crime. Yet police departments were created because a governmental structure was assumed to include a police component similar to the ones that existed in older, larger cities. Police were also used to control class-based economic unrest, but since many police officers came from the dissident groups, or had friends or family members who were participants, some police officers and departments resisted brutal or excessive responses.

The police departments established from the 1830s to 1850s—Boston in 1837, New York in 1844, Philadelphia in 1854—were loosely based on the Peelian model of the London police. As noted above, this model, designed by Peel, Rowan, and Mayne, emphasized prevention more than apprehension. **Prevention** was to be accomplished by dispersing police throughout the community to keep crime from occurring and to intervene when it did. **Apprehension,** or arrest, was not stressed because it was associated with secrecy, deceit, incitement, and corruption. Chapter 7 discusses the historical development of both the patrol and investigation functions in law enforcement.

The London model also included an elaborate structure based on military principles, strict rules of conduct, and well-defined management practices. Great care was taken in the selection and retention of police officers. Since the creation of a new police force in England was controversial, the most important consideration was control of officer behavior. Community expectations and acceptance were the overriding concerns in the development and management of police.

In the United States, however, the establishment of the new police was not as controversial. Departments were generally based on the Peelian prevention concept, but there were minimal similarities beyond that point. Differences were essentially the result of three factors: social context, political environment, and law enforcement policies. The United States was more violent than Britain, politicians were more meddlesome, and the police were more decentralized and were expected to be locally responsive (Johnson 1981).

The County Sheriff

By the 1870s, most cities had a police department even if it consisted of only one person. In more rural areas, the county sheriff was the dominant law enforcement officer. Inside Policing 2.3 describes the development and role of the sheriff.

Vigilance Committees

Another form of policing that was important during the nineteenth century was the private, organized group known as a vigilance or vigilante committee. The word *vigilante* is of Spanish origin and means "watchman" or "guard." Although the term **vigilante** has several possible meanings, one definition of a vigilante group is a voluntary association of men (they rarely included women) who organized to respond to real or imagined threats to their safety, or to protect their property or power, or to seek revenge.

Inside Policing 2.3   The County Sheriff

The office of sheriff was first established in the eighth century in England. Individuals who occupied this position were both powerful and influential. They served as the chief magistrates of the courts under their jurisdiction, collected taxes, and attempted to apprehend criminals. American colonists adopted the idea of the county sheriff, but by the time all the colonies were settled the duties of the office had been limited primarily to civil matters in the county and criminal law enforcement in areas where municipal police had no jurisdiction.

The sheriff became an elected official in the United States and, for many years, was paid based on fees received for serving summonses, subpoenas, and warrants and for looking after prisoners at the county jail. The sheriff became an important figure in Western states where local law enforcement was the responsibility of the sheriff and of town or city police officers, called marshals. Sheriffs usually were elected to office as representatives of the most influential groups in the county. Only a small portion of the sheriff's time was spent pursuing criminals. Other duties, such as tax collecting, inspecting cattle brands, punishing convicted felons, and serving court orders, proved to be more time consuming.

In 1996 there were 3,088 sheriff's departments in the United States, with 257,712 employees, of which 152,922 were sworn officers. There are also some city sheriffs; for example, in the state of Virginia and in the cities of Baltimore and St. Louis. Three states—Alaska, Hawaii, and New Jersey—do not have the position of sheriff. And in some counties—for example, Dade County, Florida, and Denver County, Colorado—the sheriff is appointed. Many sheriffs' departments are small; almost two-thirds of them employ fewer than 25 deputies. There are 12 sheriff's departments, however, that have more than 1,000 personnel and 25 that have more than 600.

Although the primary responsibilities of the modern sheriff vary somewhat by department, the most typical include the following: (1) collect some types of taxes (in some but not all counties) and serve civil processes; (2) provide personnel (bailiffs) and security for the court system; (3) operate jails and other correctional facilities (such as prison farms); (4) maintain peace and order; (5) provide general law enforcement service in unincorporated areas (that is, those areas not in legally incorporated cities and towns); and (6) in some counties, provide contract law enforcement services.

Sources: B. A. Reaves and A. L. Goldberg, "Census of State and Local Law Enforcement Agencies, 1996" (Washington, D.C.: Bureau of Justice Statistics, 1998); R. D. Pursley, *Introduction to Criminal Justice,* 5th ed. (New York: Macmillan, 1991), 132–135; D. R. Johnson, *American Law Enforcement: A History* (St. Louis: Forum Press, 1981), 100–101; H. Abadinsky, *An Introduction to Criminal Justice* (Chicago: Nelson-Hall, 1987), 155–159. ✦

The behavior associated with vigilante movements ranges from attempts to provide reasonable due process to individuals suspected of criminal acts to arbitrary, discriminatory, and brutal acts of revenge. The term *lynching* was originally used to describe public whippings carried out by a Colonel Lynch, head of a vigilante movement in the late 1700s in Virginia. Later this term was used to mean hanging. In southern states between 1882 and 1951, approximately 4,700 persons were lynched by unorganized mobs, a form of vigilantism. Most of the victims were black (Karmen 1983, 1616–1618).

Vigilante movements were most common in the American West during the nineteenth century. This was in large part due to the fact that the western frontier was undeveloped; hence the need for an established police to engage in social control was not efficient. Vigilantes would form episodically as needed. Yet it is important not to confuse vigilantes with lawless mobs. Often the vigilante was comprised of the social elite from that society, with the purpose of enforcing conservative values of life, property, law and order. Prominent figures who were either part of vigilantes or supported their actions included two U.S. presidents (Andrew Jackson and Theodore Roosevelt), five U.S. senators, and eight governors (Brown 1991).

Interestingly, vigilante movements continue to exist to this day. The Guardian Angels are an example of a vigilante movement that started in New York City in the 1970s and subsequently spread to more than 60 cities. This is a group of teenagers and young males, including college students in some cities, who provide citizen patrols in high-crime areas (Berg 1992, 225). Initially, the police in many cities did not welcome the assistance of the Guardian Angels, but eventually a more cooperative relationship developed.

Any individual action or organized citizen effort that is designed to do something about crime, if not sanctioned by official law enforcement agencies, can be considered a form of vigilantism. Such movements are much less violent today, however, than in the nineteenth century because both law enforcement officers and members of the public are less tolerant of such behavior. And, as is true of the Guardian Angels, the police often cooperate with citizen law enforcement movements. Nevertheless, in some people's opinion, the word vigilante continues to be associated with mob violence and the inappropriate punishment of innocent victims.

The next two sections identify and describe two models of policing: the political and the legalistic (also called the reform, bureaucratic, or quasi-military model). As discussed in Chapter 1, these models indicate different approaches to managing the police-community relationship. Community policing, a third model, is discussed in Chapter 3.

Modern Policing: The Political Model

From about the middle of the eighteenth century to the 1920s, local policing was dominated by politics; consequently, this era saw the development of what was essentially a **political model** of policing oriented to special interests. Politics influenced every aspect of law enforcement during this period: who was employed, who was promoted, who was the chief of police, and who was appointed to the police commission, a group of citizens appointed to "run" the police department in a manner approved by elected officials. To some degree even police arrest practices and services were determined by political considerations.

Police Development

Political and economic corruption was commonplace in police departments during this period. Although some officers were honest and responsible, a large number were neither. Police work during this period became decentralized and neighborhood oriented. Individual officers had a great deal of discretion and tended to handle minor violations of the law on a personal basis. The nature of the offense, whether or not the suspect treated the officer with "respect," what was known about the person's family, and prior activities were all taken into consideration. Standards of enforcement often varied within cities, and local politicians played a more important role in determining enforcement priorities than did the chief of police.

Several trends converged in the mid-1800s that resulted in the creation of political machines that controlled cities, including the police department. As cities grew, there was an increasing need for municipal services, such as police, fire protection, and collection of garbage. Upper-class and middle-class citizens had the political influence to ensure that their needs were met, but many newly arriving immigrants, both native (from rural areas) and foreign born, did not. As the numbers of new arrivals increased, those with political ambition began to try to gain the political support of other newcomers. Often the leaders of these groups were successful and they took political control of many cities. Of course, upper-class and middle-class citizens in these cities did not give up their attempts to influence the political process or get elected to office. Even after they lost power, they played the role of critic of the political machines that emerged (Johnson 1981, 17–55).

In order to be elected to public office, a candidate had to make promises to citizens. One of the most important promises was related to employment. Public jobs served as rewards for some individuals who supported the political party in power. Police jobs became an important part of this political **patronage system.** These types of jobs were popular because they required little or no skill and paid well when compared to other jobs that also required minimal ability. Moreover, many officers did little but frequent bars and pool halls when they were supposed to be working. These officers considered a police job a reward for supporting the political machine more than a real job.

Police departments were also of vital importance to the political machine's boss in his ability to maintain political control. The police were particularly useful during elections because they maintained order at polling booths and were able to determine who voted and who did not. Individuals who became police officers were often avid supporters of the political machine and would do anything to help keep it in power. After all, their jobs depended upon it. But they also supported it because the machine often represented a point of view that was consistent with their own.

The upper class and middle class often criticized the morality of ethnic immigrants and the poor, and they periodically tried to get the police to enforce a white, middle-class standard of morality by supporting legislation that attempted to control drinking, gambling, and prostitution. Nevertheless, even when criminal laws and ordinances were enacted in an attempt to regulate these activities, they were not always enforced, because by the late nineteenth century, many immigrants, particularly the Irish, were working as police officers, and many police officers were tolerant of such "vices" and even participated in them, on and off duty (Johnson 1981, 17–55). Inside Policing 2.4 provides a brief description of what police work was like in the nineteenth century.

Criticism in the Progressive Era

By the 1890s, as cities began to grow larger and become more difficult to manage, the politically dominated, often corrupt, police departments came under increasing criticism. This criticism applied not only to the police but to all city services. All the problems attendant to large cities appeared to become important during this period: an increase in crime, population congestion, inadequate housing, health problems, waste disposal, and so on. The period from the mid-1890s to the mid-1920s became known as the Progressive Era in the United States because many of these types of problems, including poor working conditions and child labor, began to be addressed, not only in the public sector but in private enterprise as well.

Inside Policing 2.4   Policing in the Nineteenth Century

When the new police forces were established, applicants for positions essentially viewed the work as temporary because it was political. For example, in 1880 in Cincinnati 219 of 295 members of the police force were dismissed as the result of a change in elected officials. Police work did, however, have some positive features. When compared with other jobs that applicants might get (i.e., as a common laborer or a craftsman), salaries were attractive, and although temporary, the job still offered some security because once appointed, police officers could usually keep their jobs as long as the politicians they supported stayed in power.

The new police of the nineteenth century were intended to be distributed throughout the community in order to prevent crime. Many police departments, however, simply did not have enough personnel to patrol their communities. Patrol officers, who almost always walked, could cover only a small area. For a time, Chicago was able to patrol only 600 of 651 street miles, Cincinnati was able to patrol only 300 of 402 street miles, and Minneapolis could only patrol 25 of 200 street miles. In fact, in some cities, police did not patrol at all but stayed at the police station waiting to be called.

Patrol officers often encountered resistance to their authority even when making minor arrests. Most arrests (60 to 80 percent) were for drunkenness and disorderly conduct; the person arrested usually did not cooperate and had to be physically subdued. Sometimes bystanders would become involved, particularly when they disagreed with the police officer and tried to free the person being arrested. Once an arrest was made, the patrol officer had to transport the person arrested to the police station. Sometimes the prisoners walked, but some officers used a wheelbarrow to transport "tipsy prisoners." By the 1880s, the call box and horse-drawn patrol wagon were introduced. The patrol officer could "call" the station and a patrol wagon would be sent to transport the prisoner. Interestingly, the patrol wagon was hailed as an important innovation in police work.

The excessive use of force, or police brutality, was rather common during this period. Police work tended to be more personalized, and in some areas of a city police authority was accepted only if they could "back it up" with physical force.

Despite the widespread problems with citizen resistance and police brutality, police officers were not overly concerned with guns. As late as the 1880s there was no common practice regarding the carrying of weapons. In some cities they were authorized for all officers, whereas in other communities only certain officers carried them or they were carried only at night. By the latter part of the century, however, all police began to carry weapons because of the increasing violence in cities, violence that was often directed at the police officer.

One of the more controversial aspects of the police role was their involvement in labor disputes. While there is some evidence to support the idea that police (particularly state police) were used to suppress labor movements, other evidence suggests that many local police forces were sympathetic to the problems of the working class. Employers often complained that they could not depend on the police to break strikes. Many police officers were reluctant to do this because they were former "blue-collar workers" who would probably be returning to that type of work. Moreover, they often had friends and relatives who were involved in the labor dispute.

While nineteenth-century police officers may have been more brutal than their modern counterparts, they were also more likely to be involved in what can be called social-welfare activities. In fact, the police were one of the most important social-welfare institutions in cities. For example, the police were very active in assisting the homeless. Indigents were often given overnight lodging in police stations. In Philadelphia in the 1880s an estimated 127,000 persons per year slept at police stations. And usually these lodgers received some type of food. However, police officers did not allow anyone to make a practice of this, and people who tried were threatened with arrest and told to leave the city.

Source: S. Walker. *A Critical History of Police Reform* (Lexington, MA: D. C. Heath, 1977), 1–25.

Social critics began to argue that political power should change hands. These reformers were made up of religious leaders and civic-minded upper-class and middle-class business and professional people. They argued that government should be managed efficiently, public officials should be honest, and there should be one standard of conduct for everyone. The recommended reform model was based on the principles of industrial management because these principles were given credit for making the United States an economic success. Efficiency meant providing the highest-quality service at the least cost. To become efficient, organizations had to have centralized control under a well-qualified leader, develop a rational set of rules and regulations, and become highly specialized, with duties and performance requirements specified for each specialized position.

The Progressive Era movement touched all aspects of American life. As it applied to government, it was based on three basic ideas: (1) honesty and efficiency in government, (2) more authority for public officials (and less for politicians), and (3) the use of experts to respond to specific problems. This movement and these ideas gained more and more credence as the country moved into the twentieth century. These changes also applied to police departments; gradually they began to shift away from a political orientation to more of a bureaucratic and legalistic approach to law enforcement (Johnson 1981, 17–55).

Modern Policing: The Legalistic Model

By the 1920s, attempts to reform local policing, and to some degree, state and federal law enforcement, were beginning to have an impact. From then to the 1960s was probably the most significant period in the development of policing in the United States because it established the foundations for the professionalization of law enforcement. **Professionalization** has a number of possible definitions. As used here it means an attempt to improve police behavior and performance by adopting a code of ethics and improving selection, training, and management of police departments. Professionalism is discussed in more detail in Chapter 10.

During this period a **legalistic model** (also called the professional, bureaucratic, reform, quasi- or semi-military model) of policing began to dominate thinking about police work. Essentially, it means that the police-community relationship should be based on law and departmental policy because police (both as organizations and as individuals) should not be unduly influenced by politics or personal considerations when making decisions. One of the most important aspects of the legalistic model is related to the mission of the police. Advocates of this model thought that crime fighting should be the primary purpose of the police. They used this idea to mobilize support for their reforms and to improve the public image of the police. The police, in effect, began to emphasize the most dramatic aspects of their work (Johnson 1981, 105–189).

Between about 1920 and the mid-1960s, many police departments changed dramatically in the United States. Political meddling was substantially, but not entirely, replaced by efficient and centralized management and a commitment to professionalism. This change was the result of (1) European developments in criminalistics, (2) changes in American society and politics, and (3) the growth of the police reform movement.

European Developments

The first real attempt to apply the scientific method to police work took place in Europe. In many European police systems, officials were often university graduates, some of whom had been trained in the sciences. One of the most important scientific advances for police work was the **Bertillon system,** created by Alphonse Bertillon for identifying suspects. This system had four components: precise physical measurements, a detailed description of distinguishing features such as scars, a photograph, and later, fingerprints. Such information provided a scientific basis for identifying suspects and for developing a record-keeping system about criminals.

The Bertillon system provided the basis for scientific criminal investigation, which became a cornerstone for the emergence of professionalism in the United States. It was a rational and detached approach to law enforcement that contrasted with the political approach. Moreover, it provided a body of knowledge that could be transmitted to the police in training programs. Such a body of knowledge is crucial to the development of professionalism.

Changes in the United States

American society and politics also began to change in ways that affected the development of policing. As the economy put more emphasis on industrial and consumer goods, and rail and automobile transportation improved, more and more people moved to the suburbs. Many of them were white and middle class. The population of cities began to change as increasing numbers of Spanish-speaking immigrants and blacks from the rural South arrived. Many of these newcomers were unskilled, poor, powerless, and in great need of city services (Johnson 1981, 105–189).

The Spanish-speaking and black neighborhoods were often plagued by extensive crime problems. Many police officers began to think of these neighborhoods as dangerous and troublesome areas in which to work. Given the fact that police forces, beginning with the slave patrols, had a long history of racist behavior, the tension between minority groups and the police increased and became an important factor in the numerous urban riots of the twentieth century. These riots began in East St. Louis in 1917 and were followed by several in 1919, at least seven during World War II, and numerous riots in the 1960s. There were 42 major-to-serious disorders in 1967 alone (National Advisory Commission 1968, 35–206). Although there were many reasons for these riots, a significant factor was the behavior of police officers in minority neighborhoods.

Police Reform Movement

In the newly established suburban communities, the mostly white, middle-class inhabitants expected that government services would be based on the principles of efficiency and quality. The police were expected to be well-trained and courteous, use the best equipment, and employ the latest management techniques. Many of the reform ideas of the Progressive Era and the legalistic model of policing had a positive impact on these communities before they gained influence in larger, older cities, where a tradition of political interference was very difficult to change.

Among the more important developments during this period was the emergence of the **commission approach** to reform. When there was sufficient concern about police behavior in a community, prominent citizens and experts were appointed to commissions to conduct investigations and to make recommendations for change. Commissions were formed at both the local and national level.

In 1919 the Chicago Crime Commission was established to supervise the criminal justice system in Chicago. Unlike most other commissions that were created during the following decade, the one in Chicago became permanent. By 1931, 7 local, 16 state, and 2 national crime commissions had been established to investigate the police. Perhaps the best known of these was the National Commission on Law Observance, established by President Herbert Hoover in 1929. It was also known as the Wickersham Commission, for the man who headed the investigation. In 1931 the commission published 14 volumes, two of which were about the police. The 12 others were concerned with other aspects of crime and the criminal justice system. August Vollmer was the principal police consultant to the Wickersham Commission and author of the major report on the police (Walker 1977, 125–134).

Vollmer's report identified what he thought were the most important problems in law enforcement: excessive political influence, inadequate leadership and management, ineffective recruitment and training, and insufficient use of the latest advances in science and technology. By 1931, it was widely accepted that these were the problems that needed to be addressed in police work. However, another report by the commission, on police lawlessness, overshadowed Vollmer's recommendations. It identified widespread police abuses, including the use of brutality, to secure confessions (Walker 1977, 128–134).

After the Wickersham Commission published its reports, there was at least the beginning of a national consensus on the direction for the professionalization of the police. It was essentially toward a legalistic model in which laws and rules were enforced without regard to politics by well-trained and scientifically proficient, dedicated, honest employees who worked in a centralized department that was primarily concerned with crime fighting. Many police departments, however, remained substantially political well into the 1960s.

One of the most significant events of the twentieth century—the Great Depression of the 1930s—actually made police reform easier. With reduced funds available, there was less opposition to centralizing the police, and in many cities some local precinct stations were closed to save money. Centralization made it easier for chiefs of police to control their officers and also resulted in less meddling by politicians. In addition, for the first time, well-educated, middle-class Americans became interested in police work as a career because it offered job security (Johnson 1981, 105–189).

By the 1930s, the reform themes—centralization, standardization of behavior through the development of policies and procedures, more education and training, selection and promotion based on merit, commitment to the goal of fighting crime, and use of the latest advances in science and technology—were well established.

By the 1960s, however, these reform ideas began to be questioned as a result of three important developments: urban riots, the civil rights movement, and the perception of an increasing crime rate. As minorities, and later women, became increasingly active in trying to change their status in society, and as people began to be more concerned about crime, the police became one focal point for criticism. By the mid-1960s, this concern was so great that two other national commissions were established, in part to address problems concerning the police. These were the President's Commission on Law Enforcement and Administration of Justice (hereinafter called the Crime Commission), established by President Lyndon Baines Johnson in 1965, and the National Advisory Commission on Civil Disorders (hereinafter called the Riot Commission), established in 1967.

Like its predecessor the Wickersham Commission, the Crime Commission focused on crime and the entire criminal justice system. The Riot Commission examined not only the criminal justice system but also many aspects of civil disorders such as poor housing and unemployment. The recommendations of these two commissions concerning the police were a blend of previous reform suggestions plus new ones intended to make the police more responsive to the community. In effect, the legalistic model of policing that had been the basis of reform for several decades began to be challenged. However, this does not mean that its tenets were abandoned, only that some were debated and gradually began to be replaced with new ideas about the role of the police.

Three of the most prominent spokesmen for police reform in the legalistic era were August Vollmer, O. W. Wilson (Inside Policing 2.5), and J. Edgar Hoover (Inside Policing 2.9). They were controversial during their careers and have remained so as historians have provided examples of their abuses of authority and their racist and sexist behaviors. Despite this criticism, their ideas about the police role and police management remain influential and have resulted in improved police performance in many areas.

Inside Policing 2.5   Founders of the U.S. Police

August Vollmer

August Vollmer served first as town marshal and then as chief of police in Berkeley, California, from 1905 until 1932. He became one of the leading spokesmen for police professionalism in the first few decades of the twentieth century. He advocated the principles of merit associated with the Progressive Era, as well as more education and training, adoption of the latest management techniques, and the use of science and technology. Vollmer was an advocate of the police officer as social worker, in the sense that he believed police should act to prevent crime by intervening in the lives of potential criminals, particularly juveniles.

Vollmer is often called the father, or dean, of modern police administration. Some of his important contributions include the early use of motorized patrol and the latest advancements in criminalistics. He suggested the development of a centralized fingerprint system that was established by the F.B.I.; he established the first juvenile unit, was the first to use psychological screening for police applicants, and the first to emphasize the importance of college-educated police officers.

In the area of education Vollmer was instrumental in the establishment of police-training classes and later a criminology degree program at the University of California at Berkeley. He became a professor of police administration at Berkeley in 1929. He helped develop the first degree-granting program in law enforcement at San Jose State College (now University) in 1930. As a result of his efforts, higher education programs became increasingly acceptable.

After he retired as chief of the Berkeley Police Department he continued to serve as a consultant and to write about the police. He also kept in touch with many former employees. He died in 1955.

Inside Policing 2.5   Founders of the U.S. Police (continued)

Orlando Winfield Wilson

O. W. Wilson worked in Berkeley, California, for August Vollmer from 1921 to 1925. At the same time, he completed his degree at the University of California. With Vollmer's recommendation he became chief of police in Fullerton, California, in 1925 but lasted only until 1926 because his ideas about modern law enforcement were not acceptable to many citizens in the community.

Wilson was considering another career when Vollmer recommended him as a possible chief for the Wichita, Kansas, police department in 1928. Wilson was selected for that position and over the next 11 years turned what was considered an inefficient and corrupt department into what some called the West Point of law enforcement. He left Wichita in 1937 because his strict enforcement of vice laws had alienated too many powerful citizens. He resigned under pressure, but not before creating what became a model for other police departments. Visiting dignitaries from other countries, who expressed a desire to visit a police department, were taken to Wichita by the U.S. State Department.

After Wilson left Wichita, he became a professor in the School of Criminology at the University of California at Berkeley from 1939 to 1960. His service was interrupted during World War II when he became a colonel in the U. S. Army. His job was to develop plans to rebuild police departments in countries that had been occupied by Axis Powers. After he left the army he returned to his teaching position.

In 1950 Wilson published the first edition of *Police Administration*, arguably one of the most influential books ever written about police in the United States. It describes in detail how police departments should be organized and managed. It was widely used in training programs, colleges, and universities, and as a basis for organizing and managing police departments in the United States and other countries until the 1970s, when Wilson's ideas began to be criticized. Nevertheless, the basic structure of many present-day police departments is the result of Wilson's ideas.

In 1960, while still teaching at Berkeley, Wilson agreed to serve on the committee to select a new police commissioner in Chicago. When the committee could not find an acceptable candidate, they offered the job to Wilson. He agreed and served until 1967; during that time he made many important changes which received widespread publicity and made Chicago a model of modern policing. One year after he retired, however, the Chicago police performed poorly in their attempts to manage the demonstrations at the 1968 Democratic Convention. This failure raised important questions about Wilson's effectiveness and the difficulty of changing police organizations. After his retirement Wilson moved to California and occupied his time writing and traveling until his death in 1972.

Wilson typified police leadership and management during the legalistic era. He believed politics had no place in policing, he was a strong advocate of centralized police management and strict discipline. He was also an articulate spokesman for police professionalism as it related to more training, and education, better salaries and benefits, and his definition of police management. ✦

Sources: S. Walker, *A Critical History of Police Reform* (Lexington, MA: D. C. Heath, 1977), 21–165; G. E. Caiden, *Police Revitalization* (Lexington, MA: D. C. Heath, 1977), 210–217; G. F. Cole. *The American System of Criminal Justice*, 5th ed. (Pacific Grove, CA: Brooks/Cole Publishing Company, 1989), 178; adapted from W. Bopp, *O. W. Wilson and the Search for a Police Profession* (Port Washington, NY: Kennikat Press, 1977).

Voices From the Field presents a brief historical and personal account of police history from Chief of Police (Ret.) David C. Couper, who was an integral force in implementing quality management and problem solving in Madison, Wisconsin.

Voices From the Field
Historical and Personal Perspectives of Policing
David C. Couper

Question: How has policing changed since the 1960s?

Answer: In the spring of 1960, after serving four years with the marines, I enrolled at the University of Minnesota and started to look for a night job. That's how I began my police career. What changes have I seen? What have I witnessed? When I retired, a good friend of mine, who spent most of her life researching the police, commented on how far the police had come in society. I remember saying, "Improving the police is like stretching a big rubber band. When you let go, it snaps right back to the way it was before you started." In a few words, I would like to share with you why I think that statement is still true.

In the early nineteenth century, when Sir Robert Peel founded the Metropolitan Police Department in London, his basic principle for policing was that, in order for the police to perform their duties, they had to have public approval and that approval would be diminished proportionally by their use of physical force. To Peel, "the police are the public and the public are the police." Even then, 150 years ago, someone knew that if the police were to be successful in preventing crime and disorder, they had to have the goodwill of the people—all the people.

I joined a large-city urban police department in the 1960s. Luckily, I had a four-week recruit academy taught by a police commander who was an unusual cop—he had a college degree. When I got out on the street for duty I met my fellow officers: drunks, shakedown artists, and bullies. But what helped change the culture of that department is that I was among a group of 100 brand new officers joining a 400-man department. It was the young versus the old, and the young had principles the older officers never had. On top of all that, when the Cold War G.I. Bill provided college tuition benefits for many of

us, we worked the night shift and attended college during the day. Around the same period of time, President Lyndon Baines Johnson created a national commission to study crime, the police, and the administration of justice. The report recommended that "police agents" have baccalaureate degrees and made a series of other recommendations on improving the nation's police. In that environment, many of us committed ourselves to changing and improving the police.

When I began police work by walking a beat, there were no portable radios; I "pulled," or checked in with, the dispatcher every hour on our beat. Many of us in that era saw (and often silently condoned) discrimination against blacks and other minorities. It nevertheless impacted us. When our colleges and universities shut down during the days of the Vietnam War protest, we found ourselves on a police line facing our fellow students. And it changed us.

As chief of police of a medium-sized city, a city that wanted change in 1972, I found myself in the forefront of police change. My city found itself in a "war at home"; there was extreme tension not only with university students but with the minority community as well. Many young, college-educated chiefs were able to implement community and problem-oriented policing, total quality management, a "softer" and negotiated approach to public demonstrations and civil disobedience, and effective controls on the use of deadly force. We committed ourselves to bringing women, minorities, and college-educated young people into policing.

Today, in a "post-9/11" world, I see the police in a very precarious position. Yes, they have compact portable radios, cell phones, computers, DNA identification methods, and lightweight body armor, but I believe they have lost the vision that sustained many of us before that treacherous day in 2001. What I believe sustained the police from the 1960s to the 1990s was the understanding that they are the gatekeepers of a great democracy; that they are first and above all things "constitutional officers" committed to preserving and defending, on a daily basis, the Bill of Rights. It is easy to stray from a noble vision and to think that police work is about a life-and-death battle between "them" and "us." Fear has not only permeated our nation, but our nation's police as well. And a police department that is fearful of the public is a dangerous organization.

In the past, the police were uneducated, corrupt, and abusive. They did not have the goodwill or cooperation of the public because of their lack of education, corruption, and use of brutality. This, in part, led to calls for police reform. Today, the police are better educated (yet a college degree is not universally required for employment), corruption is less a problem (but it still exists), and the use of deadly force ha been constrained (although deadly mistakes still occur and police pursuit of fleeing motor vehicles remains a critical issue). But I will contend that the goodwill and cooperation of the public, especially among racial minorities and immigrants, is still severely lacking. ✦

The political era of often corrupt and inefficient policing was somewhat changed by the reforms of the legalistic era, which, in turn, met criticism. The civic problems of the 1960s brought a new set of critics who wanted to overcome the isolation of a professionalized police force from citizen concerns and develop new strategies and methods to respond to crime and order-maintenance problems. These subsequent changes, along with others, resulted in the emergence of what is now called community policing. About the same time (the mid-1970s) that the reforms began to be implemented, the crime rate began a decline that, so far, has lasted about 25 years. In Chapter 3, the development of and controversies about community policing and the extent to which it contributed to a decline in crime are discussed. The next two sections of this chapter briefly trace the development of law enforcement at the state and federal levels.

State Police

Prior to 1900, only two states had a form of state police force—Texas and Massachusetts. The idea was slow to catch on. Not until the 1960s did all states have some form of state police.

Texas and Massachusetts

In early Texas many inhabitants lived in rural isolation and faced dangerous problems such as widespread Indian raids. Consequently, the citizens decided to create a quasi-military force, called the Texas Rangers, to protect themselves. After Texas declared its independence from Mexico in 1836, the Rangers were well established. Originally designed for community defense, by the 1850s they were doing general police work. They pursued robbers, runaway slaves, and illegal immigrants from Mexico. Rangers tended to take the law into their own hands and to be very brutal in their treatment of prisoners, particularly minorities. Such behavior was commonplace well into the twentieth century. In 1935 Texas created a larger state police, the Department of Public Safety, which was given the responsibility of supervising Ranger activity, and their behavioral excesses were gradually reduced (Johnson 1981, 161–162).

A Company of Texas Rangers, circa 1904. (Courtesy of State of Texas Department of Public Safety)

Massachusetts' experiment with a state police force was controversial. Rural residents and prohibitionists were disenchanted with the failure of city police to enforce laws against drinking, so the state legislature created a state police force and gave it general law enforcement responsibilities. Its primary task, however, was to enforce laws against vice. That was what it did in large cities, but in other areas it gradually won a reputation for effective detective work in robbery and murder cases. Nevertheless, controversy about its activities in cities continued, and the state police force was disbanded in 1875. A few state investigators were retained to work in rural areas.

Pennsylvania

The next appearance of a state police force was in 1905, with the establishment of the Pennsylvania State Police. In the Midwest and Northeast, as early as the 1860s, certain problems arose that proved difficult for local police to resolve. These problems were related to economic development, particularly in the areas of mining and industrialization. A combination of an increasing crime problem in affluent rural areas coupled with the exploitation of workers and the workers' demands that such treatment stop resulted in levels of conflict and violence that were difficult to control.

Western Pennsylvania had more than its fair share of such problems. As a major mining region that attracted immigrant labor, it suffered ethnic and labor violence in the latter part of the nineteenth century. The violence became so extensive that President Theodore Roosevelt appointed a commission to look into a major coal strike in 1902. The result was the creation of the Pennsylvania State Police in 1905. This police force was unlike any other in the United States because it emphasized a military approach. All the officers had either national guard or army experience. The state police proved to be evenhanded in handling labor conflict, and the levels of violence began to decline. Like the Texas Rangers, however, state police officers tended to discriminate against "foreigners." In fact, officers were chosen, in part, because they had contempt for foreigners.

Pennsylvania State Police Officers, circa 1900. (Courtesy of Pennsylvania State Police)

Gradually, the Pennsylvania State Police began to expand its duties, and it began to do routine police work in rural areas throughout the state. Between 1908 and 1923, 14 states, mostly in the North, created state police forces based on the Pennsylvania model. Not all state police, however, were as evenhanded as those in Pennsylvania when it came to labor strife. In Nevada, Colorado, and Oregon the state police tended to side with organized business interests (e.g., mining). This bias became such a problem in Colorado that in 1923 the state police were disbanded (Johnson 1981, 161–164).

Highway Patrol

Between the 1920s and the 1960s, state police forces began to take on new responsibilities. One of the most important was enforcement of traffic laws. With the increasing use of automobiles, the number of related problems—the violation of traffic laws, accidents, and the regulatory requirements associated with the registration of vehicles and the licensing of drivers—also increased. As the highway system grew, there was need for a statewide authority because many of the roads were outside the jurisdiction of cities. The automobile also gave criminals more flexibility: They could come and go more easily and avoid capture more readily.

This situation resulted in two approaches to the development of state law enforcement, a **state police** and a **highway patrol.** The former had broad law enforcement powers (similar to municipal police departments), whereas the latter was generally limited to traffic enforcement. The highway patrol approach became more common. For example, in the 1920s, eight state police departments and six highway patrol units were established. In the 1930s, 18 units were created to deal with traffic, but only eight to deal with general law enforcement (Johnson 1981, 161–164). The differences between state police forces and state highway patrols are important. State police have their own criminal investigators, may have their own patrol force, gather criminal intelligence, and usually have a forensic science laboratory. State highway patrols concentrate on traffic and accidents on the state's roads and highways (Borkenstein 1977, 1131–1134).

By the 1960s, nearly all states had some type of state police or highway patrol or a combination of the two. They are usually responsible for traffic regulation on state roads and highways, and about two-thirds also have general police powers. State police often fill a void in rural law enforcement because they provide services where there are none, or their assistance is requested by other law enforcement units (Cole 1989, 120). Inside Policing 2.6 briefly describes the development of the state police in Oregon, which was typical of other states during the 1920s and 1930s. Inside Policing 2.7 describes the evolutionary process of the Missouri State Highway Patrol.

Inside Policing 2.6   The Oregon State Police

Discussions about the possibility of creating a state police force in Oregon began in 1918. During World War I the state had created an Oregon Military Police to protect shipbuilding plants, but it was disbanded after the war ended. Concern about problems associated with state policing continued because responsibilities were fragmented among several state departments. The State Traffic Department had already been established, but it was having a difficult time coping with the increasing number of automobiles on state highways. In 1929 it had only 50 officers to patrol the entire state. Prohibition was also proving to be a difficult problem. Increasingly, criminals were using cars and were able to avoid local police, who had jurisdiction only within city limits.

In response to these concerns, the state senate established the state police force on March 1, 1931. The force was designed by a committee that examined the Royal Canadian Mounted Police, the Texas Rangers, and the state police of New Jersey, Pennsylvania, and Michigan. The new force began operations on August 1. It was given the law enforcement responsibilities of several older state agencies, including the State Highway Commission (which governed the State Traffic Department), the Secretary of State, the Fish and Game Commission, the State Fire Marshals, and the Prohibition Commissioner. The responsibilities of this new police force included the enforcement of traffic laws, game and fish codes, all laws relating to arson and fire prevention, and laws against illegal liquor and drugs. In addition, the department was given law enforcement responsibilities throughout the state so the department could serve as a rural patrol force and assist local police.

The state police department was divided into four districts and 31 patrol stations. The first report of its activities was published in early 1933. Since 1931, the state police had made 415 arrests, written 181 traffic citations, reported on 200 liquor violations, and collected fines totaling about $17,000.

The state police were given additional responsibilities in 1939 and 1941. In 1939 a Crime Detection Laboratory was established at the University of Oregon Medical School; it was sub-

Inside Policing 2.6   The Oregon State Police (continued)

sequently relocated in Portland. By 1989 there were six regional crime detection laboratories, which provided assistance to local police. In 1941 all fingerprint records and criminal photographs were transferred from the state penitentiary to the state police.

In the late 1970s the state police force was reorganized into the present five districts. By 1989 the number of patrol stations had increased from 31 to 45. By 1996, the number of personnel had increased from the original 95 to over 1,200. ✦

Source: Oregon Department of State Police. *Memorandum.* March 15, 1989.

Inside Policing 2.7   Missouri State Highway Patrol

The Missouri State Highway Patrol (MSHP) was officially created in 1931, though it took six years of political compromises to do so. While some states were comfortable with the creation of a state-policing agency, the creation of state level law enforcement was difficult in Missouri due to the general skepticism on the part of local politicians to relinquish control to the state government. State police agencies, in many ways, act in direct competition to lower levels of government, particularly county sheriffs. Yet there was a recognized need for a state-level department in Missouri at the beginning of the 20th Century. This was due in part to the creation of an expanded highway system throughout the largely rural state, the difficulty associated with enforcing Prohibition's bootlegging laws, labor disputes in rural areas, and the decentralization of local law enforcement in the state. Thus in creation of the MSHP represented a significant compromise between local and state politicians: the MSHP would have jurisdiction limited to the enforcement of traffic offenses, and not be empowered to have general policing duties (such as search and seizure). Thus the MSHP had a narrowly defined mission. Slowly, over time, the MSHP did evolve into a full-service state-police agency, though their name remained "highway patrol." This evolutionary process was also experienced in other states, including Mississippi, Nebraska, Ohio and Washington.

Missouri's experience demonstrates another type of state law enforcement evolution. Recognizing the rivalry between state and county level law enforcement, the state initially resisted creating a full-service state police agency. Thus the only way the state was to create a much-needed state-level agency was to limit its power. As social and political conditions changed over time, the mission of the highway patrol was broadened to reflect the general services department it is today. ✦

Source: Falcone, D. N. "The Missouri State Highway Patrol as a Representative Model," *Policing: An International Journal of Police Strategies and Management, 2001* 24: 585–594.

Some states also have other types of law enforcement agencies. Just as with the federal government, any state agency that regulates behavior that is punishable by fine or imprisonment may have a law enforcement component. States that have a park system or environmental laws, any form of legalized gambling, or state income taxes will usually have law enforcement officers associated with that activity. Many states also have an agency whose responsibility is to regulate the selling and distribution of liquor. A few states even have agencies that respond primarily to drug-related problems.

In addition to state police, state highway patrols, and the other types of agencies noted above, many states also provide law enforcement services to local jurisdictions—for example, special investigation assistance and crime labs for the analysis of physical evidence. There may also be a statewide computer system to provide information about wanted persons and stolen property. Many states also gather and analyze crime-related information and provide the results to local police. All states now have some type of organization to set standards for the selection and training of police—for example, the California Commission on Peace Officers Standards and Training (POST).

Federal Law Enforcement

The development of federal agencies tended to lag behind those at the local level because the constitutional mandate for federal law enforcement is not clear. Prior to the Civil War there were three types of federal law enforcement activities.

The Revenue Cutter Service and the U.S. Marshal Service

In 1789 the Revenue Cutter Service was created to respond to problems of smuggling. In that same year the U.S. Marshal Service was established so that the federal courts would have officers to perform police duties. **Marshals** investigated cases of mail theft and crimes against the railroad. They also investigated murders on federal lands, but the majority of their responsibilities were civil. One of the more interesting aspects of the marshal's role was law enforcement in the West, described in Inside Policing 2.8.

Inside Policing 2.8	Federal Marshals in the American West

U.S. Marshals were among the first law enforcement officials in the West. In federal territories they were often the only officials available to deal with criminals. Once a territory became a state, other law enforcement officials, such as the sheriff, town marshal, or city police, assumed responsibility for most law enforcement problems. However, because these local police officers had authority only in one jurisdiction, the U.S. marshal appointed some of them to be deputy marshals, which allowed them to pursue criminals outside the town or county.

Marshals usually had no law enforcement experience but were appointed because of their political connections. Often they were criticized for being inefficient and corrupt, much like city police of the nineteenth century. Their payment—rewards and fees—strongly influenced their priorities. Because rewards for catching criminals were rare, most of a marshal's salary was determined by fees collected from serving civil processes. This system of payment lasted until 1896.

Marshals usually dealt with liquor smugglers, gun runners, and individuals who committed crimes involving the mail. The most infamous criminals were the train robbers. The railroads may well have been the most disliked industry in the nineteenth century. Although railroads played an important role in the development of the United States, the owners treated many citizens in a callous and indifferent manner. Consequently, train robbers were considered to be "heroes" by some people. This status contributed to the rise of romantic legends about outlaws such as the James, Younger, and Dalton brothers

---

Inside Policing 2.8   **Federal Marshals in the American West (continued)**

---

and Bill Doolin. But train robbers were hardly heroes. Jesse James initiated the idea of wrecking a train in order to rob it. Or they might ambush a train at a water stop and use dynamite or gunfire to steal the money or gold it carried.

After a robbery the outlaws would escape to some hideaway and then disperse. U.S. marshals might pursue them with a posse, but full-scale battles between a posse and gang were rare. More often, the outlaws were tracked down individually. Paid informants were very useful in this regard. They resulted in the demise of Bill Doolin and the Wild Bunch, who committed train robberies and bank holdups in the Oklahoma Territory in the early 1890s. Using informants, the local U.S. marshal was able to acquire enough information to track down each member of the gang. Most of the Wild Bunch died in shoot-outs with marshals, their deputies, and members of a posse. These shoot-outs were not in the open but usually during an ambush in which the outlaw was outnumbered and outgunned. Marshals were more inclined to use a shotgun than a "six shooter." When Doolin was finally located, he was killed by a shotgun blast fired by a deputy marshal, one of six hidden posse members who waited for Doolin to walk down the street.

Marshals played an important role in the American West. They were effective in developing informants and isolating outlaws. Perhaps their most important contribution was developing a basis for cooperation between different law enforcement bodies (i.e., town marshal and police, county sheriff) as federal territories became states. ✦

Source: D. R. Johnson, *American Law Enforcement: A History* (St. Louis: Forum Press, 1981), 96–100.

Postal Inspectors

Crimes involving the mail were a significant problem in the nineteenth century. Often these crimes were committed by postal employees because many people sent money through the mail. Swindlers and confidence men also used the mail. Lotteries were a popular "scam" in which people were asked to send a small amount of money to be eligible for an expensive prize; of course, those who sent in money never heard from the lottery sponsors again. In the states, the post office assumed responsibility for all mail-related crimes. At first the postmaster used assistants to investigate crimes, but in 1836 the position of postal inspector was established. By the Civil War, postal inspectors were investigating robberies, embezzlements, and the counterfeiting of stamps, as well as post office employees involved in criminal activities.

The Secret Service

Although counterfeiting money had always been a problem at local and state levels of government, it became a very serious problem nationally when the federal government decided to issue a standard paper currency in 1861, at the time of the Civil War. The first attempts to suppress counterfeiting of national currency occurred in 1864, when the secretary of the treasury employed a few private detectives. In June 1865 the Secret Service was established. The first director, William Wood, distributed his agents among 11 cities and instructed them to work undercover to penetrate counterfeiting rings.

By the late nineteenth century, the Secret Service provided investigative services to other agencies of government that needed them, including the postal service, customs service, and Bureau of Immigration. In 1901 the task of protecting the president was added to the Secret Service's responsibility. In 1908 its role was limited to two major activities: protective services and counterfeiting (Johnson 1981, 73–88).

The Federal Bureau of Investigation

In order to take over some of the duties the Secret Service had been performing for other agencies, the Bureau of Investigation was created within the Justice Department in 1908. This office began its work when the Secret Service transferred eight agents to the new bureau. It later became the Federal Bureau of Investigation (FBI), the general investigative law enforcement agency of the federal government.

The primary reason the FBI eventually became so highly regarded was the publicity surrounding its crime-fighting role in the 1930s. The two most important crimes involving the FBI were the kidnapping of the baby of ace flier Charles Lindbergh and the ambush murders of five people, including one FBI agent, which became known as the Kansas City Massacre. The Lindbergh incident was only one of several such cases in the late 1920s and 1930s. During this period criminals abducted several wealthy individuals or members of their families and held them for ransom. However, the Lindbergh case received the most publicity and the FBI was successful in identifying a suspect who was convicted and executed. In Kansas City, Pretty Boy Floyd and two companions tried to rescue a friend being taken to prison. Four police officers and one federal agent were killed. One of the criminals was captured, convicted, and executed. Floyd was killed by the FBI in a shoot-out, and the third was killed by other criminals.

Another event that added to the prestige and power of the FBI was the election of Franklin Roosevelt as president. He became a strong supporter of J. Edgar Hoover and the FBI and assisted in expanding the bureau's powers. The most important expansion was its responsibility to investigate cases of domestic espionage, counter-espionage, and sabotage (Johnson 1981, 172–181). The federal responsibility for enforcement of laws against drugs began in 1914, when the Harrison Narcotic Act was signed into law. The Bureau of Internal Revenue was given the responsibility for enforcing this act. It created a Narcotics Section, which within a few years became a major division. In 1930 the Federal Bureau of Narcotics was created; it became the Drug Enforcement Administration (DEA) in 1973. In 1982 the DEA became part of the FBI.

By the 1920s, the U.S. Marshals Service, the Federal Bureau of Investigation, the Postal Inspectors, the Secret Service, and the Narcotics Division of the Internal Revenue Service were the established federal law enforcement agencies. The one that received the most attention was the Federal Bureau of Investigation. Between the 1930s and the 1960s, the FBI became the premier law enforcement body in the United States. J. Edgar Hoover was appointed to serve as director in 1924. He became a national law enforcement leader and advocate of police reform in the 1930s and maintained this role into the 1960s. He is profiled in Inside Policing 2.9. Information about the current role and selected activities of the FBI is presented in Inside Policing 2.10.

Inside Policing 2.9   J. Edgar Hoover

J. Edgar Hoover was director of the Federal Bureau of Investigation from 1924 until his death in 1972. He first entered the Department of Justice in 1917, while attending law school. When he took over the bureau in 1924, it had just experienced a scandal and Hoover set out to reform the organization. Like O. W. Wilson and William Parker, he believed in a centralized command structure and improved recruitment and training. Interestingly, Wilson and Parker did not have a high regard for Hoover, and vice versa. This mutual disdain was the result of competition over leadership in the police reform movement and the fact that the FBI under Hoover looked down on local law enforcement.

The FBI began to receive national attention during the 1930s in its well-publicized campaign to catch infamous criminals such as John Dillinger. After some successes, the FBI became a national symbol of effective crime fighting. Hoover enhanced the bureau's reputation by establishing a national fingerprint file, providing assistance to local departments in training their personnel, and providing criminalistics services in some important criminal cases. In the 1960s the bureau also established a national computer system that included important crime-related information.

Perhaps the most important contribution to local law enforcement was the development of the FBI National Academy, which trained police managers from all over the United States. For many years this program was considered, and is still considered by some, to be the most prestigious in law enforcement. Another contribution to policing included the creation of the Uniform Crime Reports. These crime statistics were compiled annually by the FBI, and were used as a method to evaluate the effectiveness of local po-

lice departments. This represented the first systematic attempt to evaluate how effective police were at reducing crime, and the UCR continues to be used for this purpose today.

Hoover enhanced his reputation during World War II as the bureau pursued and arrested several spies. A fervent anticommunist, Hoover was criticized after the war for his involvement with Senator Joseph McCarthy, and in the 1950s and 1960s for his failure to respond effectively to the problems of organized crime. He was also criticized for his tactics in responding to civil rights issues. After Hoover's death it was discovered that the FBI often used illegal methods (e.g., wiretaps) to secure information about such civil rights leaders as Martin Luther King and to gather intelligence on activist groups. Hoover believed that communists had infiltrated the civil rights movement with the intent of using the race issue to destabilize the country.

Hoover is a good example of how a person in law enforcement can become very powerful. As a result of the investigations of his agents, he had access to a large amount of information about many important people in Washington and throughout the United States. Some critics have suggested that such knowledge was a significant factor in his being able to stay in office until his death at the age of 77. Some critics have even suggested that some presidents were fearful of Hoover's power. Nevertheless, despite these criticisms, Hoover did make important contributions to law enforcement in developing the FBI. ✦

Sources: D. R. Johnson, *American Law Enforcement: A History* (St. Louis: Forum Press, 1981), 171–180; G. E. Caiden, *Police Revitalization* (Lexington, MA: D.C. Heath, 1977), 242, 286, 333.

Additional Federal Law Enforcement Agencies

By the 1990s there were many different types of federal law enforcement agencies and agencies that had a law enforcement component, that is, had some employees responsible for law enforcement activities. A listing of federal agencies with at least some law enforcement responsibilities was provided in Chapter 1. Table 2.1 identifies nine federal law enforcement agencies and briefly describes some of their activities.

Inside Policing 2.10   The Federal Bureau of Investigation

Founded in 1908, the Federal Bureau of Investigation is part of the United States Department of Justice. In 1997, it employed more than 11,000 special agents and 16,000 support personnel. The mission of the FBI is to uphold the law through the investigation of violations of federal criminal law; protect the United States from foreign intelligence and terrorist activities; provide leadership and law enforcement assistance to federal, state, local, and international agencies; and perform these tasks in a manner that is responsive to the needs of the public and is faithful to the Constitution of the United States.

The bureau's investigative activities are divided into seven programs: applicant background checks, civil rights issues, counterterrorism, financial crime, foreign counterintelligence, organized crime and drugs, and violent crimes and major offenders. Examples of investigations involving violent crimes and major offenders include searching for fugitives and escaped prisoners involved in FBI investigations; crime on Indian Reservations; assaulting, kidnapping or killing the president, vice-president, and members of Congress; kidnapping and extortion; sexual exploitation of children; and tampering with consumer products.

The headquarters of the FBI is in Washington, D.C. In addition, there are field offices in 56 major cities, including one in Puerto Rico. There are also 400 satellite offices, known as resident agencies, which house from one to 12 special agents. Both field offices and resident agencies are located according to crime trends and available resources. The FBI's role in international investigations (e.g., drugs, terrorism, financial crimes) has resulted in the establishment of 23 legal attaché offices in embassies around the world.

The FBI is also involved in numerous other activities, including managing several computer crime-related data bases, providing crime laboratory services to agents and other law enforcement organizations, and training programs for FBI agents and employees and officers from state and local police. ✦

Source: http:www.fbi.gov.

Summary

The police heritage in the United States can be traced to classical Greece and Rome and to developments in Europe, particularly England. The first form of policing in U.S. cities was the constable-nightwatch system, which existed from the 1600s to the 1930s. When this system proved to be inadequate, it was replaced by modern, integrated day-night police departments. Modern police departments at the local level have moved through three distinct periods of development, each dominated by a different model of policing. These models are political, legalistic, and community policing. Each model has a different conception of the police role and how police officers should interact with members of the community. Two of the models—the political and the legalistic—are discussed in this chapter.

State and federal police forces also have an interesting history. State police forces were created to respond to both law enforcement and traffic problems and to provide related services to local police. Federal law enforcement agencies have existed since the eighteenth century but were not well established until the middle of the nineteenth century. Today there are numerous federal law enforcement agencies and agencies with investigators working in a law enforcement capacity.

Table 2.1   Selected Federal Law Enforcement Agencies

Bureau of Alcohol, Tobacco, Firearms, and Explosives (ATF)

The ATF moved from the Department of the Treasury to the Department of Justice in 2003 and is responsible for the investigation of laws covering the manufacture and sale of alcohol, tobacco, and firearms.

Drug Enforcement Administration (DEA)

The DEA is part of the Department of Justice, reports to the director of the FBI, and is responsible for the enforcement of laws related to the use of narcotics and dangerous drugs. It is primarily concerned with organized groups involved in producing and distributing illegal drugs.

Internal Revenue Service (IRS)

The IRS is a division in the Department of the Treasury. It collects taxes and investigates violations of federal tax laws. The IRS also supervises the legal alcohol industry and enforces certain explosives and firearms laws.

U.S. Customs and Border Protection

The Customs Service is part of the U.S. Department of Homeland Security and is responsible for determining and collecting duties and taxes on goods imported into the United States. Agents work to control smuggling and revenue fraud, among other things. Agents also help to enforce environmental protection laws in coastal waters.

U.S. Marshals Service

The Marshals Service is part of the Department of Justice. Its legal authority is broad and includes such activities as serving federal warrants, locating federal parole and probation violators, investigating fugitives from other countries, providing security for federal courts, and protecting witnesses in federal criminal trials.

U.S. Park Police

The Park Police is part of the Department of the Interior. Most officers are assigned to the Washington, D.C., area, where they are responsible for hosting and providing police services to visitors at the city's parks.

U.S. Park Rangers

The Park Rangers are part of the Department of the Interior and are responsible for law enforcement, among other things, in the national parks.

U.S. Secret Service

The Secret Service is now part of the Department of Homeland Security and is responsible for criminal activities involving counterfeiting and forgery and for protecting the president of the United States, the president's family, and other government officials.

Sources: R. D. Pursley, *Introduction to Criminal Justice,* 5th ed. (New York: Macmillan, 1991); G. E. Rush, ed., *The Dictionary of Criminal Justice* (Guilford, CT: Dushkin, 1986).

Critical Thinking Questions

1. In what way did Sir Robert Peel and his ideas about policing influence the development of policing in the United States? How did English policing differ from early policing in the northern colonies?

2. Identify and explain the characteristics of political policing. Why did political policing develop in the United States?

3. Identify and explain the characteristics of legalistic policing. Why did legalistic policing develop in the United States?

4. Discuss the contributions of August Vollmer and O. W. Wilson to the development and evolution of law enforcement.

5. Briefly discuss the evolution of policing in America, including slave patrols and frontier/vigilante policing.

6. Why is it in America, where there is a desire for local rule, that state and federal law enforcement was able to emerge?

References

Abadinsky, H. 1987. *An Introduction to Criminal Justice.* Chicago: Nelson-Hall.

Berg, B. L. 1992. *Law Enforcement: An Introduction to Police in Society.* Boston: Allyn and Bacon.

Bopp, W. J. 1977. *O. W. Wilson and the Search for a Police Profession.* Port Washington, NY: Kennikat Press.

Borkenstein, R. 1977. "State Police." In S. H. Kadish (ed.), *Encyclopedia of Crime and Justice,* pp. 1131–1135. New York: The Free Press.

Brown, R. M. 1991. "Vigilante Policing." In C. B. Klockars and S. D. Mastrofski (eds.), *Thinking About Police: Contemporary Readings,* 2nd ed., pp. 58–73. New York: McGraw Hill.

Caiden, G. E. 1977. *Police Revitalization.* Lexington, MA: D. C. Heath.

Cole, G. F. 1989. *The American System of Criminal Justice,* 5th ed. Pacific Grove, CA: Brooks/Cole Publishing Co.

Cooper, L. 1975. *The Iron Fist and the Velvet Glove.* Berkeley: Center for Research on Criminal Justice.

Falcone, D. N. 2001. "The Missouri State Highway Patrol as a Representative Model." In *Policing: An International Journal of Police Strategies and Management* 24: 585–594.

Germann, A. C., Day, F. D., and Gallati, R. R. 1978. *Introduction to Law Enforcement and Criminal Justice.* Springfield, IL: Charles C. Thomas.

Johnson, D. R. 1981. *American Law Enforcement: A History.* St. Louis: Forum Press.

Johnson, H. 1988. *History of Criminal Justice.* Cincinnati: Anderson Publishing Co.

Karmen, A. A. 1983. "Vigilantism." In S. H. Kadish (ed.), *Encyclopedia of Crime and Justice,* 4: 1616–1618. New York: Free Press.

Kirkham, G. L., and Wollan, L. A. 1980. *Introduction to Law Enforcement.* New York: Harper and Row.

Lane, R. 1967. *Policing the City: Boston 1822–1882.* Cambridge, MA: Harvard University Press.

Miller, W. 1977. *Cops and Bobbies.* Chicago: University of Chicago Press.

Mokkonen, E. 1981. *Police in Urban America.* Cambridge: Cambridge University Press.

National Advisory Commission on Civil Disorders. 1968. *Report.* New York: New York Times Company.

Oregon Department of State Police. *Memorandum.* March 15, 1989.

President's Commission on Law Enforcement and Administration of Justice. 1967. *Task Force Report: The Police.* Washington, D.C.: U.S. Government Printing Office.

Pursley, R. D. 1991. *Introduction to Criminal Justice.* 5th ed. New York: Macmillan.

Reaves, B. A. 1992. *Sheriff's Departments,* 1990. Washington D.C.: Bureau of Justice Statistics.

Reaves, B. A., and Goldberg, A. L. 1998. *Census of State and Local Law Enforcement Agencies, 1996.* Washington, D.C.: Bureau of Justice Statistics.

Reichel, P. L. 1999. "Southern Slave Patrols as a Transitional Police Type." In L. K. Gaines and G. W. Cordner (eds.), *Policing Perspectives: An Anthology,* pp. 79–92. Los Angeles: Roxbury.

Roberg, R. R., and Kuykendall, J. 1990. *Police Organization and Management: Behavior, Theory and Processes.* Pacific Grove, CA: Brooks/Cole Publishing Company.

Walker, S. 1977. *A Critical History of Police Reform.* Lexington, MA: D. C. Heath.

Walker, S., and Katz, C. M. 2002. *The Police in America: An Introduction.* 4th ed. New York: McGraw-Hill.

Suggested Websites for Further Study

Biosketch of Sir Robert Peel
http://members.tripod.com/kiffg/peel.htm

National Sheriffs' Association (NSA)
http://www.sheriffs.org/

Links to Municipal, County, and State Law Enforcement Agencies Across the United States
http://www.officer.com
http://www.leolinks.com

United States Marshals Service
http://www.usdoj.gov/marshals/

United States Postal Inspection Services
http://www.usps.gov/websites/depart/inspect/

United States Secret Service
http://www.treas.gov/usss/

Federal Bureau of Investigations
http://www.fbi.gov

Kansas City Massacre
http://kansascity.fbi.gov/massacre.htm

Drug Enforcement Agency
http://www.usdoj.gov/dea/index.htm

Bureau of Alcohol, Tobacco and Firearms
http://www.atf.treas.gov/

Department of Homeland Security
http://www.dhs.gov/ ✦

## Chapter 3

Community Policing

Chapter Outline

❐   Transition Toward Community Policing
       Police Research
       Police-Community Relations
       Crime Prevention
       Team Policing
       Foot Patrol and Broken Windows
❐   Community Policing
❐   The Philosophical Dimension
       Citizen Input
       Broad Police Function
       Personal Service
❐   The Strategic Dimension
       Reoriented Operations
       Geographic Focus
       Prevention Emphasis
❐   The Tactical Dimension
       Positive Interaction
       Partnerships
       Problem Solving
❐   Community Policing Today: Rhetoric or Reality?
       Positive Indications
       Questions and Doubts
❐   Summary
❐   Critical Thinking Questions
❐   References
❐   Suggested Websites for Further Study

Key Terms

broad police function
broken windows
citizen input
community crime prevention
community policing
coproduction of public safety
crime prevention through environ-
     mental design (CPTED)
foot patrol
geographic focus
partnerships
personalized service

police-community relations
positive interaction
prevention emphasis
problem analysis triangle
problem-oriented policing
problem solving
reoriented operations
SARA model
situational crime prevention
target hardening
team policing

$\mathbf{T}$he previous chapter described two modern police models and factors that led to the development of a third model, community policing. This chapter will provide a general framework for community policing and describe the transition that has taken place toward this model. Part of the discussion revolves around precursors to community policing, including police-community relations, team policing, and foot patrol. Definitions and philosophy of community policing are described, along with a discussion of where the concept is today in terms of evolution and practice.

Transition Toward Community Policing

The problems of the 1960s and the influence of the legalistic model of policing, as discussed in Chapter 2, continued to be of concern to some police, political leaders, and academics in the 1970s and 1980s. These concerns tended to focus primarily on unsatisfactory relationships between police and their communities, especially minority communities. These issues, together with new information from police research and trial-and-error experience with police tactics and strategies, help account for experimentation with community policing in the 1980s and then its dramatic increase in popularity in the 1990s.

Police Research

Many of the recommendations for changing the police that have been made since the 1970s were the result of increased research into policing practices. During the 1960s, the federal government took several steps that created an innovative climate in law enforcement. In addition to the Crime Commission in 1965 and the Riot Commission in 1967, the federal government created the Office of Law Enforcement Assistance (OLEA) in 1965 and passed the Omnibus Crime Control and Safe Streets Act in 1968. This act increased funding for OLEA, which became known as the Law Enforcement Assistance Administration (LEAA). From the late 1960s through the 1970s, hundreds of millions of dollars were invested to improve the criminal justice system (Caiden 1977, 56–59).

The two most important impacts on the police were the large number of research studies that produced new knowledge about police methods and effectiveness, and financial support for police to pursue higher education. The LEAA made grants and loans available to encourage individuals—both pre-service and in-service—to pursue higher education. With this increase in students came an increase in faculty members specializing in criminal justice and police studies, who also contributed to the growing body of knowledge about the criminal justice system.

Information about the police during the legalistic era was based largely on the experience and publications of classical writers (see Chapter 4), who promoted a paramilitary approach to policing. By the 1970s, such information was being challenged by data derived from systematic research. Many of the challenges were in the areas emphasized by the legalistic model, such as patrol and investigation. Studies cast doubts on the effectiveness of reactive and random (or discretionary) patrol in controlling crime, the need for a rapid response to most citizens' requests for services, and the effectiveness of criminal investigators (detectives) in many cases. Although many of these studies had limitations, the research raised questions concerning the manner in which police invested their energies and the activities in which they engaged. This inquisitive and questioning approach has become ingrained in modern policing, leading to continuous efforts to develop more effective tactics and strategies.

The police were also encouraged to broaden their use of research and the analytical process to solve problems. Goldstein (1990), for example, recommended that the police begin to think in terms of problems rather than incidents; that is, they should change from an incident-based response strategy to a problem-oriented strategy (e.g., viewing a group of incidents as a potential problem). Goldstein argued that officers should not only try to determine the relationship between incidents that might be occurring in the same family, building, or area, but also consider alternatives other than law enforcement to try to solve problems. The key to problem-oriented policing (described later in this chapter) is the use of data to analyze problems in order to discover exactly what they are, why they are occurring, why they are occurring where they are occurring (and not somewhere else), and so forth.

Police-Community Relations

Historically, one of the most persistent and compelling problems confronting the police has been their relationship with minority groups. Depending on the time period, a minority group could be Irish Americans, Italian Americans, Hispanics or Latinos, African Americans, Asian Americans, Native Americans, gays (and lesbians), or other groups. The police have had a long history of discriminating against members of minority groups, whether due to their own prejudice, ignorance, or official responsibility for enforcing laws that restricted the civil rights of some people (such as segregation laws). Numerous civil disturbances in the United States have been precipitated by police behavior considered to be inappropriate by minority groups.

In addition, changes in society and in the routine nature of police work have tended to create more "distance" between the police and the public. The advent of police cars, for example, and later, air conditioning in those cars, led to police officers having bigger patrol beats and less informal contact with citizens. Similarly, the development of 911 telephone systems made it easier for the public to summon the police in an emergency, but also made police patrol units much busier and more closely tethered to their patrol cars, further reducing informal police-public contact. Of course, the police are not alone in having grown busier and more dependent on the automobile over the years—most Americans have had the same experience. Consequently, not only are the police and the community less familiar with each other today—neighbors do not know each other either.

The legalistic model of policing that developed in the United States during the middle part of the twentieth century essentially saw the relationship with the community as a matter of legal and bureaucratic considerations. As tensions developed, this model attempted to be more responsive to the public by diversifying the police force and establishing community-relations programs. In the 1950s and 1960s, many police departments established community relations units in response to perceived problems in police-community relations. Initially, these community relations units engaged mostly in public relations by presenting the police point of view to the community. This one-sided approach was soon recognized as inadequate, though, and was expanded to provide the community with a forum for expressing its views to the police. The two-way **police-community relations** philosophy emphasized the importance of communication and mutual understanding.

In the 1970s it became apparent that a few police-community relations officers or a small unit were not effective in guaranteeing smooth relations between a community and its police department. It was recognized that a community experiences its police department through the actions of patrol officers and detectives more than through the presentations of a few community relations specialists. Efforts were then undertaken to train regular patrol officers in community relations and crime prevention techniques and to make them more knowledgeable about community characteristics and problems (Boydstun and Sherry 1975).

In the 1980s, the public became increasingly fearful of crime, especially violence, gang activity, and drug use, all of which were alarmingly portrayed by the media. Many police departments became more legalistic, proactive, and assertive in an effort to deal with these problems and to satisfy public and political pressure. They

Police and minority relationships have often been confrontational regarding police behaviors, even to the point of precipitating civil disturbances.

tended to rely on aggressive patrol, field interrogations, citations, arrests, and increased undercover activities. These approaches, while applauded by many minority leaders (because crime victimization tends to be disproportionately experienced by minority citizens), also increased the tension between police and minority citizens, particularly African Americans and Hispanics. The perception that some police officers were discriminating against minority citizens became widespread. In fact, this perception was often accurate, particularly as it applied to police use of excessive force. However, the degree to which such behavior was racially motivated or willful was much more difficult to determine. These issues, and how best to deal with them, continue today in the context of racial profiling (Fridell, Lunney, Diamond, and Kubu 2001).

Crime Prevention

Early police efforts at public relations and community relations naturally evolved toward crime prevention, in part because of the public's thirst for information about how to protect themselves and their families. This was ironic in the sense that police efforts to improve community relations led the public to ask for information about how best to control crime. Because of this history, crime prevention as a police strategy refers not so much to preventive patrol as to special programs designed to make citizens, homes, and businesses more difficult to victimize. Organizationally, crime prevention units are often combined with community services and community relations units rather than with patrol or investigations.

Some police departments assign one or more officers to crime prevention duties. These officers then specialize in performing security surveys, giving public crime prevention lectures and presentations, and organizing community participation in crime prevention programs. Other departments have chosen to assign crime prevention duties to all patrol officers. Under this model, each officer is responsible for crime prevention duties on his or her beat.

One method, called **target hardening,** seeks improvements in doors, windows, locks, alarms, lighting, and landscaping that make illegal entry into homes and businesses more difficult and more time-consuming. Another method is to train citizens to avoid threatening situations and to react correctly when attacked or threatened. Still other methods encourage citizens to watch out for their neighbors' property and even to patrol their own neighborhoods.

The basic principles of **crime prevention through environmental design (CPTED)** include target hardening, where access to neighborhoods and buildings is controlled and where specific areas are surveilled to reduce opportunities for crime to occur; and territorial reinforcement, where a sense of security is increased in settings where people live and work through activities that encourage informal control of the environment. CPTED overlaps with community policing by localizing police services, collaborating with other city agencies (e.g., parks or utility departments) to resolve problems, and maintaining regular police-citizen communication about neighborhood problems. Inside Policing 3.1 describes some of the strategies that may be applied through CPTED.

Inside Policing 3.1   CPTED: Strategies and Trends

What Police and Residents Can Do

Police departments, community residents, and local officials all have roles to play in implementing a comprehensive CPTED and community policing strategy to promote public safety in private neighborhoods, business areas, and public housing.

Police can do the following:

- Conduct security surveys for residents and provide security improvements such as adequate lighting and locks.

- Conduct patrols of parks and other public spaces to eliminate crime and drug use.

- Use their substations to inform residents of high-risk locations in the neighborhood.

- Work with urban planners and architects to review the designs and plans in order to enhance community security.

- Prepare educational materials for building owners and managers to deal with problem tenants and improve the livability and security of rental units. These materials are useful because they address not only the design of the physical environment but also how the environment can be more effectively managed to improve safety.

- Control traffic flow to reduce the use of streets by criminals and increase neighborhood cohesion and resident interaction. Streets can be closed or traffic diverted to create residential enclaves that give residents greater control of their environment.

Residents can do the following:

- Engage in cleanup programs to remove trash or graffiti.

- Carry out programs to improve the appearance, safety, and use of public spaces.

- Conduct their own patrols to identify neighborhood problems.

Inside Policing 3.1   CPTED: Strategies and Trends (continued)

- Join an organized block watch program.

Specific crime prevention activities include:

- Security in parks. Parks can be refurbished, lighting can be installed, and opening and closing times can be scheduled to improve security. Adopt-a-park programs can be used to involve residents in cleaning up trash and litter and providing information to police about illegal activities being carried out in recreational areas. Recreational events can be scheduled to increase the community's informal social control of these places.

- Building regulations. Local government can be encouraged to use building codes as well as inspection and enforcement powers to increase environmental security. The owners of deteriorated or abandoned buildings can be required to repair, secure, or demolish them. Provisions related to security can also be incorporated into the city building code. These provisions include target-hardening tactics (e.g., better locks, strengthening of doors, and better lighting) as well as security standards for the design of the structure and site.

Civil Remedies

Civil actions can be used against building owners or tenants to control criminal activity or the inappropriate use of property. These actions may include the following:

- Obtaining title to abandoned property by community-improvement associations.

- Using nuisance abatement, along with inspections by public works, building, fire, housing, or utility authorities, to control criminal behavior or drug use in specific buildings or settings.

- Encouraging leases that contain language that controls illegal activities of tenants.

- Using antitrespassing laws to control unwanted loitering.

- Enforcing liquor laws to control violence and disorderly behavior around bars or liquor stores (especially at closing times).

Trends

One general trend has been for CPTED and community-policing strategies to reinforce each other as they focus on comprehensive problem solving, the promotion of working relationships with the community, and the development of education and orientation programs that can assist residential and business groups as they address specific neighborhood problems—especially those dealing with crime and the environment.

The development of these initiatives affects various factors, such as the level of communication and cooperation among police, city, staff, and residents; the type, amount, and use of community education and orientation programs; and the methods by which crime-prevention programs are described, measured, and evaluated. Currently, these factors apply more to law enforcement agencies because modifying a community-policing model may require changes of significant magnitude. As CPTED evolves, however, its extension from just looking at the manmade environment to looking at how the natural setting is used and managed will also entail significant change for other public agencies involved in promoting safer and more livable communities. ✦

Source: Adapted from D. Fleissner and F. Heinzlemann, "Crime Prevention Through Environmental Design and Community Policing," *Research in Action* (Washington, DC: National Institute of Justice, 1996) 3–4.

In trying to build a more crime-free environment, some cities are requiring police input regarding building designs. In Tempe, Arizona, for example, an ordinance was passed that requires police approval of any commercial building, park, or residential housing development built in the city. Tempe police officers review construction blueprints and visit building sites to ensure that crime-prevention features are built into the designs; officers address issues such as parking lot locations, lighting, and the placement of plants and counters in stores. The goal is to provide employees and residents with a better view of their surroundings and to reduce places where criminals may hide. Getting police involved in building designs for crime prevention is similar to the long-established practice of the city's relying on fire department officials to help determine building codes for fire prevention purposes ("Building a More Crime-Free Environment" 1998).

CPTED is becoming a well-used practice as communities try to determine innovative ways to reduce crime. Police departments in eight of the nation's 10 largest cities have followed Tempe's lead to some degree, including those in New York, Los Angeles, Houston, Detroit, Dallas, Phoenix, San Antonio, and San Diego. For instance, in Los Angeles, police officers have input into any development going up in the city, but their suggestions, unlike those in Tempe, are not binding. Suggestions made by LAPD officers include landscaping with smaller bushes to improve visibility; using curved walls as opposed to sharp edges, which create hiding places; and locating parking lots within plain sight of building occupants. In San Diego, which is moving toward establishing an ordinance similar to Tempe's, officers have been working with city planners regarding building design, but, as in Los Angeles, their suggestions are not yet binding ("Building a More Crime-Free Environment" 1998).

Community crime prevention is based on the assumption that if a community can be changed, so can the behavior of those who live there. Attempts to change communities include the following: (1) organizing the community to improve and strengthen relationships among residents to encourage them to take preventive precautions and to obtain more political and financial resources; (2) changing building and neighborhood design to improve both public and police surveillance, which improves guardianship; (3) improving the appearance of an area to decrease the perception that it is a receptive target for crime; and (4) developing activities and programs that provide a more structured and supervised environment (e.g., recreation programs).

Although community crime prevention is closely associated with the community-policing movement, the evidence of its effectiveness is limited, in part, because of the lack of understanding of social relationships within neighborhoods and of how crime is influenced by both the broader community and societal trends. Perhaps the most promising approach to responding to high-crime areas is to focus on the relationship between the poverty of youth and crime. High-crime areas have a large number of criminals and victims in comparison to other areas; consequently, while developing programs to support, socialize, and supervise youth, it is also important to protect the "fearful, vulnerable, and victimized" (Hope 1995).

The effects of crime prevention programs have not been conclusively established. Many police executives in recent years, however, have attributed crime decreases to community participation in crime prevention programs. Target hardening and increased community participation in crime prevention certainly contribute to crime reduction, and evidence is available that crime prevention programs at least make citizens feel safer and more willing to report suspicious activity (Rosenbaum 1987). On the other hand, the current tendency is to oversell community crime prevention as the solution to every community's crime and fear of crime problems. Yet some communities may not be receptive to such programs; citizen participation is frequently difficult to maintain over extended periods and some programs may have unintended side effects such as increased fear among some participants.

An increasingly popular approach that closely parallels problem-oriented policing is **situational crime prevention** (Clarke 1997). This approach emphasizes the necessity of tailoring crime prevention responses to the specific characteristics of the crime problem being addressed—it rejects any one-size-fits-all thinking. It also focuses primarily on reducing opportunities for crime by, for example, increasing the effort required to commit offenses, increasing the risk of being detected, and reducing the reward should the offense be consummated. Situational crime prevention has achieved substantial success when targeted at a wide variety of types of offenses, including auto theft, shoplifting, thefts from vending machines, assaults at bus stops, and robberies at convenience stores.

Team Policing

The decade of the 1960s was a tumultuous era in the United States, with riots breaking out in many cities. As noted above, in some instances the police actually provided the spark that precipitated these riots. Out of this crisis came the growing recognition that the police lacked responsiveness to, and understanding of, community expectations. Following this urban unrest, it became clear that a different style of police force would be necessary—one that could be more responsive to community needs. Thus, a major reorganization effort toward decentralization and increased community participation, known as **team policing,** was attempted in the early 1970s.

Community policing involves community input and support to help police identify and solve problems.

Team policing in the United States was based primarily on British precedents, especially the Aberdeen system, which originated in Scotland immediately following World War II, and unit beat policing, which was developed in the county of Coventry, England, in 1966 (Sherman, Milton, and Kelley 1973). The Aberdeen system was first established to counteract the low morale and boredom of single officers patrolling quiet streets; it allocated teams of five to 10 men on foot and in cars to move to different parts of the city that had the highest crime rates and numbers of calls for service. The increased workload eliminated boredom and loneliness. Unit beat policing was developed to utilize limited manpower more effectively; constables were organized into teams that remained in one specific area. Although the constables did not work as a team, they all fed information about their area to a central person, or collator, who was responsible for distributing information about the area to the other constables. Thus, by effectively using the collator to coordinate and exchange information, fewer constables could cover a wider geographic area.

Efforts in the United States often had elements similar to both the Aberdeen and unit beat policing systems. Team policing was first used by the Syracuse Police Department in 1968, and by 1974 as many as 60 departments across the country had attempted some form of team policing (Schwartz and Clarren 1977). According to Sherman, Milton, and Kelley (1973), in theory, team policing was based on reorganiz-

ing the patrol force to include one or more quasi-autonomous teams, with a joint purpose of improving police services to the community and increasing job satisfaction of
the officers. The team was normally stationed in a particular neighborhood and was
responsible for all police services in that neighborhood. It was expected to work as a
unit and maintain a close relationship with the community to prevent crime and maintain order.

Sherman and his associates conducted a thorough evaluation of team policing in
seven cities (see Table 3.1). Included in the study were two small cities—Holyoke, Massachusetts, and Richmond, California; two middle-size cities—Dayton, Ohio, and Syracuse, New York; two large cities—Detroit and Los Angeles; and one super-city—New
York City. Although team policing had different meanings in each city, six of the seven
programs attempted to implement three common operational elements: (1) geographic
stability of patrol, that is, permanent assignment of teams of police to small neighborhoods; (2) maximum interaction among team members, including close internal communication among all officers assigned to an area during a 24-hour period, seven days a
week; and (3) maximum communication among team members and the community.

Table 3.1   Summary of Team-Policing Elements by City

Operational Elements	Dayton	Detroit	New York	Syracuse	Holyoke	Los Angeles (Venice)	Rich- mond
Stable geographic assignment	+	+	—	+	+	+	•
Intra-team interaction	—	+	—	—	+	+	+
Formal team conferences	—	+	—	—	+	+	+
Police-community communication	+	+	—	—	+	+	•
Formal community conferences	+	•	•	—	+	+	•
Community participation in police work	+	—	—	•	+	+	•
Referrals to social agencies	+	—	•	•	•	•	+
Organizational Supports							
Unity of supervision	+	+	—	+	+	+	+
Lower-level flexibility	—	—	—	+	+	+	+
Unified delivery of services	+	—	—	+	+	+	•
Combined patrol and investigative functions	+	+	•	+	+	+	+

Key:
+ the element was planned and realized
— the element was planned but not realized
• the element was not planned

Source: L. W. Sherman, C. H. Milton, and T. V. Kelly, *Team Policing: Seven Case Studies, 1973.*
Reprinted by permission of Police Foundation, Washington, D.C.

The departments that were the most successful in implementing these three operational elements also had certain organizational supports in common, including (1) unity of supervision (i.e., one supervisor responsible for a given area at all times), (2) lower-level flexibility in policy making, (3) unified delivery of services, and (4) combined investigative and patrol functions. There was wide variation by city in planning and implementing the various elements. Some programs achieved overwhelming success in certain areas. For example, the Venice (Los Angeles) team developed hundreds of block captains, who exchanged crime information with police on a regular basis; one team in Holyoke virtually abandoned preventive patrol since the citizenry informed them almost immediately of many crimes in progress. In both Dayton and Holyoke, community boards composed of representatives chosen by local groups (e.g., Parent-Teacher Associations, civic associations, tenant organizations) participated in police policy making; the Dayton team also used medical and welfare agencies for referrals most frequently, instead of making arrests (Sherman, Milton, and Kelley 1973).

On the whole, however, most programs differed little from the traditional policing of the past. For instance, in none of the cities studied was a decentralized patrol style realized (i.e., authority and decision making were not delegated down to street officers). There appeared to be three major reasons why team policing either failed or reached only partial success:

1. Departmental middle management, which saw team policing as a threat to their power, subverted and, in some cases, actively sabotaged the plans.

2. The dispatching technology did not permit the patrols to remain in their neighborhoods, despite stated intentions about adjusting that technology to projects.

3. The patrols never received a sufficiently clear definition of how their behavior and role should differ from those of a regular patrol; at the same time, they were considered an elite group by their peers, who often resented not having been chosen for the project (Sherman, Milton, and Kelley 1973, 107–108).

Although it is apparent that team-policing experiments, to a large extent, failed owing to a lack of proper planning and training, it is also true that the amount of change required in switching from a highly bureaucratic, authoritarian structure to a decentralized, democratic one was simply too great—especially in a relatively short period of time. Another hurdle facing those departments attempting such a significant change was that no attempt had been made to establish a departmental climate of innovation. As will be noted in Chapter 5, all these hurdles also confront police departments attempting to move to community policing.

Furthermore, because team policing was based on decentralized decision-making for patrol officers, some police managers became concerned with the problem of accountability. For example, in another well-documented study in Cincinnati, Ohio, known as COMSEC (Community Sector Team Policing Experiment), top administrators had second thoughts about the program as it progressed. Although they wanted the teams to be responsive to the community, they "feared that with the promised autonomy and reduction in central control, their officers might become less productive or even corrupt" (Schwartz and Clarren 1977, 7). Of course, that is precisely why strong, bureaucratic, central control has been a mainstay in police administration over the past several decades (see Chapter 4). The dilemma with such centralized control, however, is not only the lack of community responsiveness but also the reduction of morale among officers (who have fewer decision-making responsibilities).

Despite its drawbacks, team policing became the fad of the 1970s. But it soon became apparent that a "new" approach to policing, one that was attuned to both community needs and officer satisfaction, was needed. In theory, team policing attempted to do both, but, for various reasons, in virtually every city in which it was attempted, the promises could not be fulfilled. Starting in the mid-1980s, new models of policing began to be developed.

Foot Patrol and Broken Windows

Many observers now believe that the abandonment of **foot patrol** by most American police departments by the mid-1900s changed the nature of police work and negatively affected police-citizen relations. Officers assigned to large patrol car beats do not develop the intimate understanding of and cordial relationship with the community that foot patrol officers assigned to small beats develop. Officers on foot are in a position to relate more intimately with citizens than officers driving by in cars.

The results of two research studies, together with the development of small police radios, gave a boost to the resurgence of foot patrol starting in the 1980s. Originally, the police car was needed to house the bulky two-way radio. Today, foot patrol officers carry tiny, lightweight radios that enable them to handle calls promptly and to request information or assistance whenever needed. They are never out of touch and they are always available.

An experimental study conducted in Newark, New Jersey, was unable to demonstrate that either adding or removing foot patrol affected crime in any way (Police Foundation 1981). This finding mirrored what had been found seven years earlier in Kansas City regarding motorized patrol. Citizens involved in the foot patrol study, however, were less fearful of crime and more satisfied with foot patrol service than with motor patrol. Also, citizens were aware of additions and deletions of foot patrol in their neighborhoods, a finding that stands in stark contrast to the results of the Kansas City study, in which citizens did not perceive changes in the levels of motorized patrol. A second major foot patrol research program in Flint, Michigan, reported findings that were similar to the Newark findings, except that crime too decreased (Trojanowicz 1982).

These studies were widely interpreted as demonstrating that, even if foot patrol did not decrease crime, at least it made citizens feel safer and led to improvements in police-community relations. Why the difference between motorized patrol and foot patrol? In what has come to be known as the **broken-windows** thesis, foot patrol officers pay more attention to disorderly behavior and to minor offenses than do motor patrol officers (Wilson and Kelling 1982). Also, they are in a better position to manage their beats, to understand what constitutes threatening or inappropriate behavior, and to observe and correct it. Foot patrol officers are likely to pay more attention to derelicts, petty thieves, disorderly persons, vagrants, panhandlers, noisy juveniles, and street people who, although not committing serious crimes, cause concern and fear among many citizens. Failure to control even the most minor aberrant activities on the street contributes to neighborhood fears. Foot patrol officers have more opportunity than motor patrol officers to control street disorder and reassure ordinary citizens (see Figure 3.1 for a tool that can be used to discuss neighborhood problems with residents).

Figure 3.1 Problem-Identification Interview

Community Foot Patrol Program	PROBLEM IDENTIFICATION INTERVIEW	DATE / / .

RESPONDENT'S PROFILE

☐ Business ☐ Residence Community Name _____

Address: _____ No. of Persons Interviewed _____

Years in Neighborhood: ☐ Less Than 1 ☐ 1 to 2 ☐ 3 to 5 ☐ Over 5

Age Group: ☐ Less Than 18 ☐ 18 – 29 ☐ 30 – 39 ☐ 40 – 49
☐ 50 – 59 ☐ Over 60

Sex: ☐ Male ☐ Female

Race: ☐ White ☐ Black ☐ Oriental ☐ Hispanic ☐ Other

INTERVIEW QUESTIONS

1. When you think of neighborhood problems or crime, what are your concerns? _____
_____
_____

2. How often does this problem occur?
☐ Periodically ☐ Isolated Incident ☐ Constantly ☐ Frequently
_____

3. How has this problem inconvenienced you or changed your daily life? _____
_____
_____

4. What do you feel is the cause of the problem? _____
_____
_____

5. What do you feel could be done to correct the problem? _____
_____
_____

6. Do you feel the police department is responsive to the needs of your neighborhood. (i.e. have the police services been adequate in your neighborhood ?) If not, explain. _____
_____
_____

7. Do you feel the county government has been responsive to your neighborhood's needs? (Do not restrict to crime.) If not, explain. _____
_____
_____

8. _____
9. _____
10. _____

Source: From J. Scannell, *Community Foot Patrol Officer (CFPO) Guidelines and Procedures,* 1998, 36–37. Reprinted by permission of Baltimore County Police Department, Towson, MD.

Geography plays a large role in determining the viability of foot patrol as a police strategy, of course. The more densely populated an area, the more the citizenry will travel on foot and the more street disorder there will be. The more densely populated an area, the more likely that foot patrol can be effectively used as a police strategy. Although foot patrol may never again become the dominant police strategy it once was, it can play a large role in contributing police services to many communities. In Voices From the Field, Chief Darrel Stephens from Charlotte-Mecklenburg, North Carolina presents his perspective on the impact of community policing and problem-oriented policing.

Voices From the Field
Darrel Stephens
Chief of Police, Charlotte-Mecklenburg, North Carolina

Question: What difference has community policing and problem-oriented policing made in American policing?

Answer: Policing in America has changed over my 35-year career. It is not the same institution that was chronicled in the series of Presidential Commission reports on crime and the administration of justice in the late 1960s and early 1970s—it is much better. A great deal more is known about the impact of the fundamental strategies the police have used for many years to address crime problems. We know more about the limitations of the police and how they might be more effective. Police departments are more diverse, educational levels of police officers have significantly increased, and both citizen oversight and community engagement are stronger.

This change has come about for a number of reasons, but two are particularly significant. The first is the advancement of the ideas of community and problem-oriented policing over the past 20 years as better ways of delivering police services to the community. The second is the research that provided the foundation for these ideas to ride the crest of the political wave that invested unprecedented levels of federal funding into local policing.

Prior national efforts to improve the police and address concerns with crime had accepted the basic premise on which the police and criminal justice system rested. Most people believed the best way to deal with crime was to increase the number of police, improve training and equipment, develop systems to reduce response time, build more prison beds, issue harsher sentences, and federalize more crimes that had historically been the responsibility of the states and local government.

The community and problem-oriented policing initiatives took a different approach. These ideas called for a fundamental change in the way the police related to citizens and stakeholders. Citizens are more than the "eyes and ears" of the police to feed the criminal justice system—they are viewed as partners who have ideas, resources, and the ability to do things that can prevent crime as well as solve it. The police use problem-solving techniques to gain deeper insight into the issues that they are called on to address and to develop tailored solutions that have a longer-lasting impact on the problem. Moreover, these solutions are not confined to a law enforcement response. The response might be aimed at prevention or engaging other community or governmental resources that are in a better position to deal with the problem than the police could.

Community and problem-oriented policing has touched most police agencies in America and has significantly improved the quality of policing. ✦

Community Policing

Starting in the 1980s, an even broader approach than community relations and foot patrol began developing. More and more police departments began employing foot patrol as a central component of their operational strategy, rather than as a novelty or an accommodation to downtown business interests. Crime prevention programs became more and more reliant on community involvement, as in neighborhood watch, community patrol, and "crimestoppers" programs. Police departments began making increased use of civilians and volunteers in various aspects of policing and made permanent geographic assignment an important element of patrol deployment. This all came to be called **community policing,** entailing a substantial change in police thinking,

> one where police strategy and tactics are adapted to fit the needs and requirements of the different communities the department serves, where there is a diversification of the kinds of programs and services on the basis of community needs and demands for police services and where there is considerable involvement of the community with police in reaching their objectives. (Reiss 1985, 63)

Community policing is the logical combination of more than 30 years of police effectiveness research and decades of experimentation with police-community relations programs, crime-prevention strategies, and team policing. It can be thought of as an attempt to harness the advantages of foot patrol and generalize them throughout all police field services, with an emphasis on broken-windows theory and its focus on minor crime, disorder, and fear of crime. Still, community policing remains many things to many people. A common refrain among proponents is, "Community policing is a philosophy, not a program." Two equally common refrains among police officers are, "This is what we've always done" and "Just tell me exactly what you want me to do differently." Some critics, echoing concerns similar to those expressed by police officers, argue that if community policing is nothing more than a philosophy, it is merely an empty shell (Goldstein 1987).

It would be easy to list dozens of common characteristics of community policing, starting with foot patrol and mountain bikes and ending with the police as organizers of, and advocates for, the poor and dispossessed. Instead, it may be more helpful to identify three major dimensions of community policing and some of the most common elements within each (Cordner 1999). These three dimensions of community policing are:

- The philosophical dimension.
- The strategic dimension.
- The tactical dimension.

The Philosophical Dimension

Many of its most thoughtful and forceful advocates emphasize that community policing is a new philosophy of policing, perhaps constituting even a paradigm shift away from professional-model policing. The philosophical dimension includes the central ideas and beliefs underlying community policing. Three of the most important of these are citizen input, broad function, and personalized service.

Citizen Input

Community policing takes the view that, in a free society, citizens should have open access to police organizations and input to police policies and decisions. Access and input through elected officials is considered necessary but not sufficient. Individual neighborhoods and communities should have the opportunity to influence how they are policed, and legitimate interest groups in the community should be able to discuss their views and concerns directly with police officials. Police departments, like other agencies of government, should be responsive and accountable.

Mechanisms for achieving greater **citizen input** are varied. Some police agencies use systematic and periodic community surveys to elicit citizen input (Bureau of Justice Assistance 1994a). Others rely on open forums, town meetings, radio and television call-in programs, and similar methods open to all residents. Some police officials meet regularly with citizen advisory boards, ministry alliances, minority group representatives, business leaders, and other formal groups. These techniques have been used by police chief executives, district commanders, and ordinary patrol officers; they can be focused as widely as the entire jurisdiction or as narrowly as a beat or a single neighborhood.

The techniques used to achieve citizen input should be less important than the end result. Community policing emphasizes that police departments should seek and carefully consider citizen input when making policies and decisions that affect the community. Any other alternative would be unthinkable in an agency that is part of a government "of the people, for the people, and by the people."

Broad Police Function

Community policing embraces a broad view of the police function rather than a narrow focus on crime fighting or law enforcement (Kelling and Moore 1988). Historical evidence is often cited to show that the police function was originally quite broad and varied and that it narrowed only in recent decades, perhaps due to the influence of the professional model and popular media representations of police work. Social science data is also frequently cited to show that police officers actually spend relatively little of their time dealing with serious offenders or investigating violent crimes.

This broader view of the police function recognizes the kinds of nonenforcement tasks that police already perform and seeks to give them greater status and legitimacy. These include order maintenance, social service, and general assistance duties. They may also include greater responsibilities in protecting and enhancing "the lives of those who are most vulnerable—juveniles, the elderly, minorities, the poor, the disabled, the homeless" (Trojanowicz and Bucqueroux 1990, xiv). In the bigger picture of the **broad police function,** the police mission is seen to include resolving conflict, helping victims, preventing accidents, solving problems, and reducing fear, as well as reducing crime through apprehension and enforcement.

Personal Service

Community policing supports tailored policing based on local norms and values and individual needs. An argument is made that the criminal law is a very blunt instrument and that police officers inevitably exercise wide discretion when making decisions. Presently, individual officers make arrests and other decisions based on a combination of legal, bureaucratic, and idiosyncratic criteria, while the police department maintains the myth of full or at least uniform enforcement (Goldstein 1977). Under community policing, officers are asked to consider the "will of the community" when deciding which laws to enforce under what circumstances, and police executives are asked to tolerate and even encourage such differential and personalized policing.

Such differential or tailored policing primarily affects police handling of minor criminal offenses, local ordinance violations, public disorder, and service issues. Some kinds of behavior proscribed by state and local law, and some levels of noise and disorder, may be seen as less bothersome in some neighborhoods than in others. Similarly, some police methods, including such aggressive tactics as roadblocks as well as more prevention-oriented programs such as landlord training, may coincide with norms and values in some neighborhoods but not others.

Even the strongest advocates of community policing recognize that a balance must be reached between differential neighborhood-level policing and uniform jurisdiction-wide policing. Striking a healthy and satisfactory balance between competing interests has always been one of the central concerns of policing and police administration. Community policing simply argues that neighborhood-level norms and values should be added to the mix of legal, professional, and organizational considerations that influences decision-making about policies, programs, and resources at the executive level as well as at the enforcement level on the street.

This characteristic of community policing is also aimed at overcoming one of the most common complaints that the public has about government employees in general, including police officers— that they do not seem to care and are more interested in "going by the book" than in providing quality, **personalized service.** Many citizens seem to resent being subjected to "stranger policing" and would rather deal with officers who know them and whom they know. Of course, not every police-citizen encounter can be amicable and friendly. But officers who generally deal with citizens in a friendly, open, and personal manner may be more likely to generate trust and confidence than officers who operate in a narrow, aloof, and/or bureaucratic manner.

The Strategic Dimension

The strategic dimension of community policing includes the key operational concepts that translate philosophy into action. These strategic concepts are the links between the broad ideas and beliefs that underlie community policing and the specific programs and practices by which it is implemented. They ensure that agency policies, priorities, and resource allocation are consistent with a community-oriented philosophy. Three strategic elements of community policing are reoriented operations, geographic focus, and prevention emphasis.

Reoriented Operations

Community policing recommends less reliance on the patrol car and more emphasis on face-to-face interactions through **reoriented operations.** One objective is to replace ineffective or isolating operational practices (e.g., motorized patrol and rapid response to low-priority calls) with more effective and more interactive practices. A related objective is to find ways of performing necessary traditional functions (e.g., handling emergency calls and conducting follow-up investigations) more efficiently in order to save time and resources that can then be devoted to more community-oriented activities.

Many police departments today have increased their use of foot patrol, directed patrol, door-to-door policing, and other alternatives to traditional motorized patrol (Cordner and Trojanowicz 1992). Generally, these alternatives seek more targeted tactical effectiveness, more attention to minor offenses and "incivilities," a greater "felt presence" of police, and/or more police-citizen contact. Other police departments have simply reduced their commitment to any form of continuous patrolling, preferring instead to have their patrol officers engage in problem solving, crime prevention, and similar activities when not handling calls and emergencies.

Many police agencies have also adopted differential responses to calls for service (McEwen, Connors, and Cohen 1986; McEwen, Spence, Wolff, Wartell, and Webster 2003). Rather than attempting to immediately dispatch a sworn officer in response to each and every notification of a crime, disturbance, or other situation, these departments vary their responses depending upon the circumstances. Some crime reports may be taken over the telephone, some service requests may be referred to other government agencies, and some sworn officer responses may be delayed. A particularly interesting alternative is to ask complainants to go in person to a nearby police mini-station or storefront office, where an officer, a civilian employee, or even a volunteer takes a report or provides other in-person assistance. Use of differential responses helps departments cope with the sometimes overwhelming burden of 911 calls and frees up patrol officer time for other activities, such as patrolling, problem solving, and crime prevention.

Traditional criminal investigation has also been reexamined in recent years (Eck 1992). Some departments have despecialized the activity, reducing the size of the detective unit and making patrol officers more responsible for follow-up investigations. Many have also eliminated the practice of conducting an extensive follow-up investigation of every reported crime, focusing instead on the more serious offenses and on more "solvable" cases. Investigative attention has also been expanded to include a focus on offenders as well as on offenses, especially in the form of repeat offender units that target high-frequency serious offenders. A few departments have taken the additional step of trying to get detectives to expand their case-by-case orientation to include problem solving and crime prevention. In this approach, a burglary detective would be as concerned with reducing burglaries through problem solving and crime prevention as he or she was with solving particular burglary cases.

Not all contemporary alternatives to motorized patrol, rapid response, and criminal investigation are closely allied with community policing. Those specific operational alternatives, and those uses of the freed-up time of patrol officers and detectives, that are consistent with the philosophical and strategic foundations of community policing can be distinguished from those that conform to other philosophies and strategies of policing (Moore and Trojanowicz 1988).

Geographic Focus

Community-policing strategy emphasizes the geographic basis of assignment and responsibility by shifting the fundamental unit of patrol accountability from time of day to place. That is, rather than holding patrol officers, supervisors, and shift commanders responsible for wide areas, but only during their eight- or 10-hour shifts, community policing seeks to establish 24-hour responsibility for smaller areas.

Of course, no single officer works 24 hours a day, seven days a week, week in and week out. Community policing usually deals with this limitation in one or a combination of three ways: (1) community-police officers assigned to neighborhoods may be specialists, with most call-handling relegated to a more traditional patrol unit; (2) each individual patrol officer may be held responsible for long-term problem solving in an assigned neighborhood, even though s/he handles calls in a much larger area and, of necessity, many of the calls in the assigned area are handled by other officers; or (3) small teams of officers share both call-handling and problem-solving responsibility in a beat-sized area.

A key ingredient of this **geographic focus,** however it is implemented, is permanency of assignment. Community policing recommends that patrol officers be assigned to the same areas for extended periods of time, to increase their familiarity with the community and the community's familiarity with them. Ideally, this familiarity will build trust, confidence, and cooperation on both sides of the police-citizen interaction. Also, officers will simply become more knowledgeable about the community and its residents, aiding early intervention and timely problem identification and avoiding conflict based on misperception or misunderstanding.

It is important to recognize that most police departments have long used geography as the basis for daily patrol assignment. Many of these departments, however, assign patrol officers to different beats from one day to the next, creating little continuity or permanency. Moreover, even in police agencies with fairly steady beat assignments, patrol officers are held accountable only for handling their calls and maintaining order (keeping things quiet) *during their shift.* The citizen's question, "Who in the police department is responsible for my area, my neighborhood?" can then only truthfully be answered "the chief" or, in large departments, "the precinct commander." Neither patrol officers nor the two or three levels of management above them can be held accountable for dealing with long-term problems in specific locations anywhere in the entire community. Thus, a crucial component of community-policing strategy is to create some degree of geographic accountability at all levels in the police organization but particularly at the level of the patrol officer, who delivers basic police services and is in a position to identify and solve neighborhood problems.

Prevention Emphasis

Community-policing strategy also emphasizes a more proactive and preventive orientation, in contrast to the reactive focus that has characterized much of policing under the professional model. This proactive, preventive orientation takes several forms. One is simply to encourage better use of police officers' time. In many police departments, patrol officers' time not committed to handling calls is either spent simply waiting for the next call or randomly driving around. Under community policing, this substantial resource of free patrol time is devoted to directed enforcement activities, specific crime prevention efforts, problem solving, community engagement, citizen interaction, or similar kinds of activities.

Another aspect of the **prevention emphasis** overlaps with the substantive orientation of community policing and problem-oriented operations. Officers are encouraged to look beyond the individual incidents that they encounter as calls for service and reported crimes in order to discover underlying problems and conditions (Eck and Spelman 1987). If they can discover such underlying conditions and do something to improve them, officers can prevent the future recurrence of incidents and calls. While immediate response to in-progress emergencies and after-the-fact investigation of crimes will always remain important functions of policing, community policing seeks to elevate before-the-fact prevention and problem solving to comparable status.

Closely related to this line of thinking, but deserving of specific mention, is the desire to enhance the status of crime prevention within police organizations. Most police departments devote the vast majority of their personnel to patrol and investigations, primarily for the purposes of rapid response and follow-up investigation *after* something has happened. Granted, some prevention of crime through the visibility, omnipresence, and deterrence created by patrolling, rapid response, and investigating is expected, but the weight of research over the past two decades has greatly diminished these expectations (Kelling, Pate, Dieckman, and Brown 1974; Greenwood and Petersilia 1975; Spelman and Brown 1982). Despite these lowered expectations, however, police departments still typically devote only a few officers specifically to crime prevention programming and do little to encourage patrol officers to engage in any kinds of crime prevention activity beyond routine riding around.

Moreover, within both informal and formal police cultures, crime solving and criminal apprehension are usually more highly valued than crime prevention. An individual officer is more likely to be commended for arresting a bank robber than for initiating actions that prevent such robberies. Detectives usually enjoy higher status than uniformed officers (especially in the eyes of the public), whereas, within many police agencies, crime prevention officers are seen as public relations functionaries, kiddie cops, or worse. To many police officers, crime prevention work is simply not real police work.

The preeminence of reactive crime fighting within police and popular cultures is understandable, given the dramatic nature of emergencies, crimes, and investigations. Much of police work is about responding to trouble and fixing it, about the contest between good and evil. Responding to emergencies and fighting crime have heroic elements that naturally appeal to both police officers and citizens. Given the choice, though, almost all citizens would prefer not being victimized in the first place to being dramatically rescued, to having the police successfully track down their assailant, or to having the police recover their stolen property. Most citizens would agree that "an ounce of prevention is worth a pound of cure." This is not to suggest that police should turn their backs on reactive handling of crimes and emergencies, but only that before-the-fact prevention should be given increased consideration.

A final element of community-policing's preventive focus takes more of a social welfare orientation, particularly toward juveniles. An argument is made that police officers, by serving as mentors and role models, and by providing educational, recreational, and even counseling services, can affect people's behavior in positive ways that ultimately lead to reductions in crime and disorder. In essence, police are asked to support and augment the efforts of families, churches, schools, and other social service agencies. This kind of police activity is seen as particularly necessary by some in order to offset the deficiencies and correct the failures of these other social institutions in modern America.

The Tactical Dimension

The tactical dimension of community policing ultimately translates ideas, philosophies, and strategies into concrete programs, practices, and behaviors. Even those who insist that "community policing is a philosophy, not a program" must concede that unless community policing eventually leads to some action, some new or different behavior, it is all rhetoric and no reality (Greene and Mastrofski 1988). Indeed, many commentators have taken the view that community policing is little more than a new police marketing strategy that has left the core elements of the police role untouched (see, e.g., Klockars 1988; Manning 1988; Weatheritt 1988). Three of the most important tactical elements of community policing are positive interaction, partnerships, and problem solving.

Positive Interaction

Policing inevitably involves some negative contacts between officers and citizens—arrests, tickets, stops for suspicion, orders to desist disruptive behavior, inability to make things much better for victims, and so forth. Community policing recognizes this fact and recommends that officers offset it as much as they can by engaging in positive interactions whenever possible. Positive interactions have further benefits as well, of course: They generally build familiarity, trust, and confidence on both sides; they remind officers that most citizens respect and support them; they make the officer more knowledgeable about people and conditions on the beat; they provide specific information for criminal investigations and problem solving; and they break up the monotony of motorized patrol.

Many opportunities for **positive interaction** arise in the course of call handling. Too many officers rush to clear their calls, however, often in response to workload concerns and pressure from their superiors, peers, and dispatchers. As a result, they typically do a mediocre job of handling the immediate incident and make little or no attempt to identify underlying conditions, secure additional information, or create satisfied customers. The prime directive seems to be to do as little as possible in order to clear the call quickly and get back in the car and on the radio, ready to go and do little or nothing at the next call. Getting there rapidly and then clearing promptly take precedence over actually delivering much service or accomplishing anything. Community policing suggests, instead, that officers should look at calls as opportunities for positive interaction, quality service, and problem identification.

Even more opportunities for positive interaction can be seized during routine patrol, if officers are willing to exit their vehicles and take some initiative. Officers can go in and out of stores, in and out of schools, talk to people on the street, knock on doors, and so forth. They can take the initiative to talk not only with shopkeepers and their customers but also with teenagers, apartment dwellers, tavern patrons, and anybody else they run across in public places or who is approachable in private places. Police should insert themselves wherever people are and talk to those people, not just watch them.

Partnerships

Participation of the community in its own protection is one of the central elements of community policing (Bureau of Justice Assistance 1994c). This participation can run the gamut from watching neighbors' homes to reporting drug dealers to patrolling the streets. It can involve participation in problem identification and problem-solving efforts, in crime-prevention programs, in neighborhood revitalization, and in youth-oriented educational and recreational programs. Citizens may act individually or in groups, they may collaborate with the police, and they may even join the police department by donating their time as police department volunteers, reserves, or auxiliaries.

Under community policing, police agencies are expected not only to cooperate with citizens and communities but also to actively solicit input and participation and build **partnerships** (Bureau of Justice Assistance 1994b). The exact nature of this participation can and should vary from community to community and from situation to situation, in keeping with the problem-oriented approach. As a general rule, though, police should avoid claiming that they alone can handle crime, drug, or disorder problems, and they should encourage individual citizens and community groups to shoulder some responsibility for dealing with such problems.

Police have sometimes found it necessary to engage in community organizing as a means of accomplishing any degree of citizen participation in problem solving or crime prevention. In disorganized and transient neighborhoods, residents are often so distressed, fearful, and suspicious of each other (or just so unfamiliar with their neighbors) that police have literally had to set about creating a sense of community where none previously existed. As difficult as this kind of community organizing can be, and as far from the conventional police role as this may seem, these are often the very communities that most need both enhanced police protection and a greater degree of citizen involvement in crime prevention, order maintenance, and general watchfulness over public spaces.

One vexing aspect of community organizing and community engagement results from the pluralistic nature of our society. Differing and often conflicting interests are found in many communities, and they are sometimes represented by competing interest groups. Thus, the elders in a community may want the police to crack down on juveniles, whereas the youths themselves complain of few opportunities for recreation or entertainment. Tenants may seek police help in organizing a rent strike, whereas landlords want police assistance in screening or managing the same tenants. Finding common interests around which to rally entire communities, or just identifying common interests on which to base police practices, can be very challenging and, at times, impossible.

It is important to recognize that this inherent feature of pluralistic communities does not arise because of community policing. Police have long been caught in the middle between the interests of adults and juveniles, landlords and tenants, and similar groups. Sometimes the law has provided a convenient reference point for handling such conflicts, but just as often police have had to mediate, arbitrate, or just take the side of the party with the best case. Moreover, when the law has offered a solution, it has frequently been a temporary or unpopular one, and one that resulted in the police taking sides, protestations of "we're just enforcing the law" notwithstanding.

Fortunately, nearly all citizens want to be safe from violence, want their property protected, and want some level of orderliness in their neighborhoods. Officers can usually find enough consensus in communities upon which to base cooperative efforts aimed at improving safety and public order. Sometimes, apparently deep conflicts between individuals or groups recede when attention is focused on how best to solve specific neighborhood problems. It would be naive to expect overwhelming community consensus in every situation, but it is equally mistaken to think that conflict is so endemic that widespread community support and participation cannot be achieved in many circumstances.

Problem Solving

Supporters of community policing are convinced that the very nature of police work must be altered from its present incident-by-incident, case-by-case orientation to one that is more problem oriented (Goldstein 1990). Certainly, incidents must still be handled and cases must still be investigated. Whenever possible, however, attention should be directed toward underlying problems and conditions. Following the medical analogy, policing should address causes as well as symptoms and should adopt the epidemiological public health approach as much as the individual doctor's clinical approach.

This **problem-solving** approach should be characterized by several important features: (1) it should be the standard operating method of policing, not an occasional special project; (2) it should be practiced by personnel throughout the ranks, not just by specialists or managers; (3) it should be empirical, in the sense that decisions are made on the basis of information that is gathered systematically; (4) it should involve, whenever possible, collaboration between police and other agencies and institutions; and (5) it should incorporate, whenever possible, community input and participation, so that it is the community's problems that are addressed (not just the police department's) and so that the community shares in the responsibility for its own protection.

The problem-solving process consists of four steps (see Inside Policing 3.2): (1) careful identification of the problem; (2) careful analysis of the problem; (3) a search for alternative solutions to the problem; and (4) implementation and assessment of a response to the problem. Community input can be incorporated within any or all of the steps in the process. Identification, analysis, and assessment should rely on information from multiple sources. A variety of alternative solutions should be considered, including, but not limited to, traditional enforcement methods. Typically, the most effective solutions are those that combine several different responses, including some that draw on more than just the police department's authority and resources.

A crucial characteristic of the problem-oriented approach is that it seeks solutions tailored to specific community problems. Arrests and law enforcement are not abandoned—rather, an effort is made in each situation to determine which alternative responses best fit the problem. Use of criminal law is always considered, as are civil law enforcement, mediation, community mobilization, referral, collaboration, alteration of the physical environment, public education, and a host of other possibilities (see Inside Policing 3.3). The commonsense notion of choosing the tool that best fits the problem, instead of simply grabbing the most convenient or familiar tool in the toolbox, lies close to the heart of the problem-solving method. A carpenter would not use a hammer when a saw would be more effective. Similarly, police should use the criminal law when it is the most effective tool for the situation, but not when some other tool would actually work better.

Inside Policing 3.2   The SARA Model

A commonly used problem-solving method is the **SARA model** (Scanning, Analysis, Response and Assessment). The SARA model contains the following elements:

Scanning:

- Identifying recurring problems of concern to the public and the police.

- Identifying the consequences of the problem for the community and the police.

- Prioritizing those problems.

- Developing broad goals.

- Confirming that the problems exist.

- Determining how frequently the problem occurs and how long it has been taking place.

- Selecting problems for closer examination.

Analysis:

- Identifying and understanding the events and conditions that precede and accompany the problem.

- Identifying relevant data to be collected.

- Researching what is known about the problem type.

- Taking inventory of how the problem is currently addressed and the strengths and limitations of the current response.

- Narrowing the scope of the problem as specifically as possible.

- Identifying a variety of resources that may be of assistance in developing a deeper understanding of the problem.

- Developing a working hypothesis about why the problem is occurring.

Response:

- Brainstorming for new interventions.

- Searching for what other communities with similar problems have done.

- Choosing among the alternative interventions.

- Outlining a response plan and identifying responsible parties.

- Stating the specific objectives for the response plan.

- Carrying out the planned activities.

Assessment:

- Determining whether the plan was implemented (a process evaluation).

- Collecting pre- and post-response qualitative and quantitative data.

- Determining whether broad goals and specific objectives were attained.

- Identifying any new strategies needed to augment the original plan.

- Conducting ongoing assessment to ensure continued effectiveness.

Source: http://www.popcenter.org/about-SARA.htm.

Inside Policing 3.3   The Problem Analysis Triangle

While the SARA model is useful as a way of organizing the approach to recurring problems, it is often very difficult to figure out just exactly what the real problem is. The **problem analysis triangle** (sometimes referred to as the crime triangle) provides a way of thinking about recurring problems of crime and disorder. This idea assumes that crime or disorder results when (1) likely offenders and (2) suitable targets come together in (3) time and space in the absence of capable guardians for that target. A simple version of a problem analysis triangle looks like this:

Offenders can sometimes be controlled by other people: Those people are known as handlers. Targets and victims can sometimes be protected by other people as well: Those people are known as guardians. And places are usually controlled by someone: Those people are known as managers. Thus, effective problem solving requires understanding how offenders and their targets/victims come together in places, and understanding how those offenders, targets/victims, and places are or are not effectively controlled. Understanding the weaknesses in the problem analysis triangle in the context of a particular problem will point the way to new interventions. A complete problem analysis triangle looks like this:

Problems can be understood and described in a variety of ways. No one way is definitive. They should be described in whichever way is most likely to lead to an improved understanding of the problem and effective interventions. Generally, incidents that the police handle cluster in four ways:

- Behavior. Certain behavior(s) is (are) common to the incidents—for example, making excessive noise, robbing people or businesses, driving under the influence, crashing vehicles, dealing drugs, stealing cars. There are many different behaviors that might constitute problems.

- Place. Certain places can be common to incidents. Incidents involving one or more problem behaviors may occur at, for example, a street corner, a house, a business, a park, a neighborhood, or a school. Some incidents occur in abstract places such as cyberspace, on the telephone, or through other information networks.

- Person. Certain individuals or groups of people can be common to incidents. These people could be either offenders or victims. Incidents involving one or more behaviors, occurring in one or more places, may be attributed to, for example, a youth gang, a lone person, a group of prostitutes, a group of chronic inebriates, or a property owner. Or incidents may be causing harm to, for example, residents of a neighborhood, senior citizens, young children, or a lone individual.

- Time. Certain times can be common to incidents. Incidents involving one or more behaviors, in one or more places, caused by or affecting one or more people may happen at, for example, traffic rush hour, bar closing time, the holiday shopping season, or during an annual festival.

There is growing evidence that, in fact, crime and disorder do cluster in these ways. It is not evenly distributed across time, place, or people. Increasingly, police and researchers are recognizing some of these clusters as:

- Repeat offenders attacking different targets at different places.

- Repeat victims repeatedly attacked by different offenders at different places.

- Repeat places (or hot spots) involving different offenders and different targets interacting at the same place.

Source: http://www.popcenter.org/about-triangle.htm.

Community Policing Today: Rhetoric or Reality?

The evidence today about the implementation and the effectiveness of community policing is mixed and somewhat contradictory. This is not really surprising. Because community policing is such a broad and flexible concept, it has been *implemented* differently in different places. In fact, what one jurisdiction calls community policing, another jurisdiction committed to community policing might not even recognize. This has been both the greatest strength and the greatest weakness of community policing.

The *effectiveness* of community policing has been extremely difficult to determine for several interrelated reasons:

- **Programmatic complexity**—There exists no single definition of community policing nor any universal set of program elements. Police agencies around the country (and around the world) have implemented a wide array of organizational and operational innovations under the label "community policing." Because community policing is not one consistent "thing," it is difficult to say whether "it" works.

- **Multiple effects**—The number of intended and unintended effects that might accrue to community policing is considerable. Community policing might affect crime, fear of crime, disorder, community relations, and/or police officer attitudes, to mention just a few plausible impacts. The reality of these multiple effects, as opposed to a single bottom-line criterion, severely reduces the likelihood of a simple yes or no answer to the question, "Does community policing work?"

- **Variation in program scope**—The scope of community-policing projects has varied from single-officer assignments to department-wide efforts. Some of the most positive results have come from projects that involved only a few specialist officers, small special units, or narrowly defined target areas. The generalizability of these positive results to full-scale department-wide implementation is problematic.

- **Research design limitations**—Despite impressive efforts by police officials and researchers, most community-policing studies have had serious research design limitations. These included lack of control groups, failure to randomize treatments, and a ten-

An important duty of community policing officers includes the education of community members.

dency to measure only short-term effects. Consequently, the findings of many community-policing studies do not have as much credibility as we might hope.

Positive Indications

Specific illustrations of successful community-policing implementation are readily available. The Chicago Alternative Policing Strategy (CAPS), which began in 1993, remains the best big-city example of department-wide community policing, with sustained implementation and measurable effects on crime, public opinion, citizen involvement, problem solving, and African Americans' views about neighborhood problems (Chicago Community Policing Evaluation Consortium 2003). Successful implementation in smaller jurisdictions has also been documented (Office of Community Oriented Policing Services 2003). Descriptions of award-winning community policing and problem-oriented policing efforts can be found on the Internet (International Association of Chiefs of Police 2001; Problem-oriented Policing Center 2003; see also Sampson and Scott 2000).

National surveys have consistently found a high level of community-policing implementation among police departments around the country. For example, in 2002 the Police Executive Research Forum (Fridell and Wycoff 2003) surveyed a sample of 282 police departments that had also been surveyed in 1993 and 1997. One way to use these survey data is to identify those community-policing activities that, in 2002, were most commonly adopted. This can provide a kind of snapshot of the current state of community policing.

The 16 *most common* community-policing activities listed below (out of a total of 56 choices offered by the survey) were claimed by at least 75 percent of responding agencies on the 2002 survey:

- Citizens attend police-community meetings.
- Citizens participate in neighborhood watch.
- Citizens help police identify and resolve problems.
- Citizens serve as volunteers within the police agency.
- Citizens attend citizen-police academies.
- Police hold regularly scheduled meetings with community groups.
- Police have interagency involvement in problem solving.
- Police have youth programs.
- Police have victim-assistance programs.
- Police use regulatory codes in problem solving.
- Police work with building-code enforcement.
- Agencies use fixed assignments to specific beats or areas.
- Agencies give special recognition for good community-policing work by employees.

- Agencies classify and prioritize calls.

- Agencies do geographically-based crime analysis.

- Agencies use permanent neighborhood-based offices or stations.

These most common community-policing activities paint a fairly positive picture of citizen participation, partnerships, outreach, problem solving, and organizational change in place in American policing in 2002. Over half of these activities had registered below the 75 percent implementation threshold on the first survey in 1993, indicating that real progress has been made over the decade in the implementation of community policing.

As a measure of that progress, the individual community-policing activities listed below are those that showed a 10 percent or greater increase in implementation between 1993 and 2002 (or between 1997 and 2002, if the item was not included on the 1993 survey). The nature of these community-policing activities, which became more widely adopted over the decade, lends solid support to the positive interpretation of community-policing progress since 1993. (None of the 56 COP activities showed a 10 percent or greater decrease in adoption between 1993 and 2002.)

- Citizens participate in citizen patrols.

- Citizens attend citizen-police academies.

- Police engage in interagency code enforcement.

- Police work with community corrections.

- Police work with alternative dispute resolution.

- Police use regulatory codes in problem solving.

- Police work with building-code enforcement.

- Agencies have a disciplinary system to support problem solving.

- Agencies have a specialized problem-solving unit.

- Agencies have landlord-training programs.

- Agencies provide citizen training in problem solving.

- Agencies classify and prioritize calls.

- Agencies do geographically based crime analysis.

- Agencies have job descriptions that include community policing.

- Agencies do citizen surveys to determine needs and priorities.

- Agencies do citizen surveys to evaluate police services.

- Agencies use fixed shifts.

- Agencies have physical decentralization of field services.

- Agencies use permanent neighborhood-based offices or stations.

- Agencies use employee evaluations to reinforce community policing.

Questions and Doubts

As positive as this picture seems, there is also evidence that community policing is sometimes more rhetoric than reality. For example, the seven *least common* community-policing activities listed below were claimed by less than 25 percent of the responding agencies on the 2002 survey discussed earlier:

- Citizens help prepare work agreements for problem solving.
- Citizens participate in the police promotional process.
- Citizens participate in a court-watch program.
- Citizens help review complaints against the police.
- Citizens participate in the selection process for new officers.
- Citizens help evaluate officers' performance.
- Agencies have decentralized crime analysis.

These least common COP activities illustrate the limited role that the community has thus far taken in police administration and policy-making. Apparently, it has become common for citizens to participate in neighborhood watch and neighborhood problem solving, attend meetings with the police, attend citizen-police academies, and do volunteer work within the police agency. It has not become common for citizens to play a role in evaluating their neighborhood police officers, selecting and promoting police officers, or reviewing complaints against the police. It would seem that police agencies have tended to adopt a relatively modest version of community policing, according to the surveys. Few police agencies have shown much interest in the most "radical" component of community policing, real power-sharing with the community (Brown 1985).

Information from other sources tends to corroborate the sometimes limited or modest nature of community policing as implemented. For example, community-police officers in cities seem to spend relatively little time actually interacting with or engaging citizens (Parks, Mastrofski, DeJong, and Gray 1999). Instead, they spend considerable time in the office doing administration and paperwork, and like their regular patrol colleagues, they spend considerable time on routine patrol and conducting personal business. This pattern of time utilization also holds true for small-town and rural officers (Frank and Liederbach 2003).

It has also been found that everyday problem solving by police officers typically does not conform very closely to the analytical and collaborative problem-solving model promoted by the advocates of **problem-oriented policing** (Cordner and Biebel 2002). Typical street-level problem solving tends to focus on problems that are small in scope; officers analyze those problems primarily through personal observation, and tend to draw on personal experience for responses, which almost always include enforcement, often in concert with one or two other responses (see Figure 3.2). The reality of street-level problem solving seems to be that it is often more thoughtful, analytical, collaborative, and creative than mere knee-jerk enforcement, but it is still a far cry from the ideal model of problem-oriented policing (also see Scott 2000).

Another limitation of community policing is that there is little evidence that it enhances community processes in ways that would be expected to subsequently reduce fear, disorder, and crime (Kerley and Benson 2000). This is probably because most community policing is still *police centered*, with the police more often doing things directly to try to reduce crime and disorder rather than working to strengthen the community so that it might more successfully protect itself. This is not to say that many police agencies have not tried to increase public participation in crime prevention and other activities, but the ideal of police and citizen **coproduction of public safety** has not generally been realized to any significant degree.

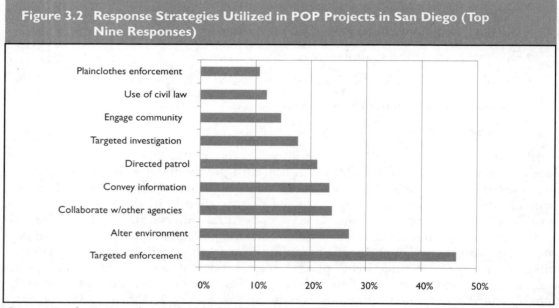

Figure 3.2 Response Strategies Utilized in POP Projects in San Diego (Top Nine Responses)

Source: Cordner, G. and E. P. Biebel, *Problem-Oriented Policing in San Diego: A Study of POP in Practice in a Big-City Police Department*. Report submitted to the National Institute of Justice, Washington, D.C., 2002. Available at http://www.ncjrs.org/pdffiles1/nij/grants/200518.pdf.

Of equal concern is that the adoption of community-policing *strategies* at the managerial level does not always lead to the utilization of community-based *tactics* in the field (Bennett 1998). Implementation of any new program in a complex organization is a management challenge—implementation of such a far-reaching philosophical and strategic change as community policing requires careful planning, systematic attention to detail, leadership, and patience. These capabilities are not always in great supply in police agencies, especially when agencies are buffeted by political pressures and/or frequent changes in top management, both of which are common. Consequently, many police departments have a much stronger commitment to community policing at the top than at the street level.

One of the logical methods for enhancing community-policing implementation is training. A substantial amount of community-policing training has been made available over the past decade by police academies, Regional Community Policing Institutes (see <http://www.cops.usdoj.gov/?Item=229>), the Community Policing Consortium (see <http://www.communitypolicing.org/>), and others. Studies have indicated that this training is often successful in conveying knowledge about community policing, developing skills, and changing attitudes (see, for example, Scarborough, Christiansen, Cordner, and Smith 1998). However, research also indicates that the effects of community-policing training do not survive once the officer leaves training and enters (or reenters) the police culture, where traditional values and practices tend to be held supreme (Haarr 2001). One step that many police agencies have overlooked is the necessity of revising their performance evaluation systems to incorporate community policing and problem-solving activities (see Inside Policing 3.4). A common refrain in many organizations, including police departments, is "if you don't measure it, it won't happen."

Inside Policing 3.4　　**Performance Evaluations of Community Officers**

Building an Evaluation

In order to produce a performance evaluation for the community officer (CO), the kinds of measures used to assess the performance of the traditional patrol officer should be examined. Most patrol officers are evaluated on countable items such as the following:

- Radio calls: number and types of calls, alarm responses; reports written, time spent; follow-up required.

- Arrests: number and types of felony and misdemeanor arrests; warrants served; apprehensions of juveniles.

- Traffic: number and types of traffic stops; accidents and injuries; citations issued; time spent; motorist assists; parking tickets issued.

- Suspicious persons or situations checked or investigated: number and type; number of persons contacted; disposition; time spent.

- Property recovered: type and value of property; time spent.

- Administrative activities: roll call, court appearances, prisoner transport assignments, subpoenas served, reports written or taken, bar checks, and so on.

Statistics for crimes in the CO's beat area are a part of any performance evaluation; it is important to recognize, however, that these may be only indirectly related to the specific officer's performance. Listed below are some outcomes that can be directly related to CO performance:

- Rates of targeted crimes: number and type; monthly and annual trends. (With input from the community, the CO may have prioritized specific crimes—for example, drug dealing or burglary.)

- Neighborhood disorder: social disorder—open use or sales of drugs, panhandlers, runaways, addicts, "winos," truants, curfew violations, prostitution, homeless, mainstreamed mental patients, unlicensed peddlers, gambling, loitering, unsupervised youngsters, youth gangs, and so on.

- Physical disorder: graffiti, abandoned cars, abandoned buildings, potholes, trash in yards, litter on streets, building code violations (residences and businesses), and so on.

The first-line supervisor and the CO can work together to decide which items apply, then develop ways to measure progress. Some items will be countable (see below) but the overall perception of improvement in neighborhood decay will require an on-site assessment from the first-line supervisor. The department can also survey residents periodically to assess their perceptions of progress toward improving the safety and quality of life in the area.

- Calls for service: number and type; monthly and annual trends. New community policing efforts typically result in an increase in the number of calls for service from that area. Most effective CO's discover, however, that in time the number of such calls declines because some

---

Inside Policing 3.4   Performance Evaluations of Community Officers (continued)

---

people tell the CO about problems in person or because residents begin handling more conflicts informally. Monitoring calls for service will help to verify that the CO is doing a good job in the area.

Examples of Quantifiable Problem-Solving Activities for COs:

- Social disorder: number and types of individual and group efforts undertaken by the CO; number of people involved; demographics of participants (e.g., race and income); participation of youth, area businesses, public agencies (e.g., social services), and nonprofit groups (e.g., Salvation Army).

- Physical disorder (beautification): Number and types of individual and group efforts undertaken by the CO; number of people involved; demographics of participants (e.g., race and income); participation of youth, area businesses, public agencies (e.g., code enforcement), and

nonprofit groups (e.g., Boy Scouts and Girl Scouts).

- Innovation: documentable incidents where the CO has demonstrated an imaginative approach toward problem solving; specific initiatives, for example, educational, athletic, and social activities for youth and families.

- Teamwork: if the CO works as part of a team with other officers (e.g., motor patrol or narcotics squad), the number of contacts or joint activities; outcomes; time spent; occasions when the CO's role was specifically to protect the other social-service agents or when the CO was a participant in group problem solving.

Source: Adapted from R. Trojanowicz and B. Bucqueroux, *Toward Development of Meaningful and Effective Performance Evaluations* (East Lansing: National Center for Community Policing, Michigan State University, 1992), 23–27.

It is difficult, if not impossible, to assess the implementation and effectiveness of community policing without taking into account the impact of over $9 billion in federal government support for community policing since 1994, in the form of the Office of Community Oriented Policing Services and the promise of an additional 100,000 "Clinton cops." The *Attorney General's Report to Congress* in the year 2000 claimed that over 105,000 new community-policing officers had been funded during the first six years of the Crime Control Act. An independent evaluation estimated that the actual number of new officers on the street was closer to about 75,000, and some of these were not newly created and filled positions but rather existing sworn personnel who had been "redeployed" to community-policing duties through creative utilization of technology and civilian (nonsworn) personnel (Roth and Ryan 2000).

The attorney general's report also noted that crime had reached its lowest level since 1968, and a COPS Office–funded evaluation similarly credited community policing with making a substantial contribution to crime decreases during the 1990s (Zhao, Scheider, and Thurman 2002). That evaluation has subsequently been sharply criticized on methodological grounds, though (Ekstrand 2003; Muhlhausen 2003). It is very difficult to say at this point how much of the crime decrease was due to community policing versus other police initiatives (such as aggressive enforcement), greatly expanded incarceration of offenders, the waning of the crack cocaine epidemic, economic factors, or demographic changes in society.

Summary

One of the important objectives of police departments is the establishment of good relations with the community. Good police-community relations are desirable in their own right in an open society, and they are also desirable because they help the police obtain the public's cooperation in controlling crime, disorder, and fear. As of the 1960s, if not before, police in America began to recognize that they had police-community relations problems, especially, but not exclusively, with minority groups. Police tried a series of programs and strategies, including police community relations programs, crime prevention programs, team policing, and foot patrol, in an effort to bridge the gap with the community. In the 1980s and 1990s these efforts led to the development and popularity of community policing, which can be understood in terms of a variety of philosophical, strategic, and tactical elements.

During its short history, community policing has proven difficult to measure and evaluate. Clearly, many police departments have implemented some aspects of community policing, but overall the degree of implementation should be considered modest. Although some police officers have embraced community policing wholeheartedly, there is still much resistance at the street level. Evaluations of community policing have been quite promising, especially on the issue of improving police-community relations. However, when serious crime problems arise, both the police and the community still seem more inclined to resort to traditional enforcement responses than to full-fledged community policing.

Critical Thinking Questions

1. The relationship between the police and the community, and especially minority communities, seems to be a chronic problem. Why do you think that is the case?

2. The public seems to react positively to foot patrol. Citizens feel safer and rate the police more highly when served by officers on foot. Why do you think this is the case?

3. A key element of community policing is citizen input. What methods would you suggest the police use in order to get citizen input about priorities and policies? Who needs citizen input the most, the police chief or the beat patrol officer?

4. Getting police officers and police departments to really emphasize crime prevention, as opposed to law enforcement and criminal investigation, has proven to be difficult. Why do you think this is the case?

5. The partnerships element of community policing has been criticized as a mere public relations campaign—an effort to get the public to like the police better. How would you go about establishing meaningful partnerships that accomplish more than just good PR?

6. Many police departments have encountered difficulties in implementing community policing. Why do you think it has been so difficult to translate the rhetoric of community policing into reality?

7. The federal government provided several billion dollars in support of community policing starting in 1994, but that support is waning now. Do you think community policing will survive without federal financial support? Do you think it should? What do you think the federal government should do at this point to help improve American policing?

References

Attorney General. 2000. "Attorney General's Report to Congress: Office of Community Oriented Policing Services." Available at http://www.cops.usdoj.gov/Default.asp?Open=True&Item=289.

Bennett, T. 1998. "Police and Public Involvement in the Delivery of Community Policing." In J. P. Brodeur, ed., *How to Recognize Good Policing: Problems and Issues*. Thousand Oaks, CA: Sage Publications, pp. 107–122.

Boydstun, J. E., and Sherry, M. E. 1975. *San Diego Community Profile: Final Report*. Washington, D.C.: Police Foundation, 1975.

Brown, L. P. 1985. "Police-Community Power Sharing." In W. A. Geller, ed., *Police Leadership in America: Crisis and Opportunity*, pp. 70–83. New York: Praeger.

"Building a More Crime-Free Environment." 1998. *Law Enforcement News*. November 15:5.

Bureau of Justice Assistance. 1994a. *A Police Guide to Surveying Citizens and Their Environment*. Washington, D.C.: Author.

Bureau of Justice Assistance. 1994b. *Neighborhood-oriented Policing in Rural Communities: A Program Planning Guide*. Washington, D.C.: Author.

Bureau of Justice Assistance. 1994c. *Understanding Community Policing: A Framework for Action*. Washington, D.C.: Author.

Caiden, G. E. 1977. *Police Revitalization*. Lexington, MA: D. C. Heath.

Chicago Community Policing Evaluation Consortium. 2003. *Community Policing in Chicago, Years Eight and Nine: An Evaluation of Chicago's Alternative Policing Strategy and Information Technology Initiative*. Springfield, IL: Illinois Criminal Justice Information Authority.

Clarke, R. V., ed. 1997. *Situational Crime Prevention: Successful Case Studies*, 2nd ed. New York: Harrow and Heston.

Cordner, G. 1999. "Elements of Community Policing." In L. K. Gaines and G. Cordner, eds., *Policing Perspectives: An Anthology*, pp. 137–149. Los Angeles: Roxbury,

Cordner, G., and Biebel, E. P. 2002. Problem-oriented Policing in San Diego: A Study of POP in Practice in a Big-City Police Department. Report submitted to the National Institute of Justice, Washington, D.C. Available at http://www.ncjrs.org/pdffiles1/nij/grants/200518.pdf.

Cordner, G., and Trojanowicz, R. C. 1992. "Patrol." In G. Cordner and D. C. Hale, eds., *What Works in Policing? Operations and Administration Examined*, pp. 3–18. Cincinnati, OH: Anderson,

Eck, J. E. 1992. "Criminal Investigation." In G. Cordner and D. C. Hale, eds., *What Works in Policing? Operations and Administration Examined*, pp. 19–34. Cincinnati, OH: Anderson.

Eck, J. E., and Spelman, W. 1987. *Problem-solving: Problem-oriented Policing in Newport News*. Washington, D.C.: Police Executive Research Forum.

Ekstrand, L. E. 2003. "Technical Assessment of Zhao and Thurman's 2001 Evaluation of the Effects of COPS Grants on Crime." Washington, D.C.: U.S. General Accounting Office, GAO-03-867R. Available at http://www.gao.gov/new.items/d03867r.pdf.

Fleissner, D., and Heinzelmann, F. 1996. "Crime Prevention Through Environmental Design and Community Policing." *Research in Action*. Washington, D.C.: National Institute of Justice.

Frank, J., and J. Liederbach. 2003. "The Work Routines and Citizen Interactions of Small-town and Rural Police Officers." In Q. C. Thurman and E. F. McGarrell, eds., *Community Policing in a Rural Setting*, pp. 49–60. Cincinnati, OH: Anderson.

Fridell, L., Lunney, R., Diamond, D., and Kubu, B. 2001. *Racially Biased Policing: A Principled Response*. Washington, D.C.: Police Executive Research Forum.

Fridell, L., and Wycoff, M. A. 2003. "The Future of Community Policing." Washington, D.C.: Police Executive Research Forum. Mimeo.

Goldstein, H. 1977. *Policing a Free Society*. Cambridge, MA: Ballinger.

——. 1987. "Toward Community-oriented Policing: Potential, Basic Requirements and Threshold Questions." *Crime & Delinquency* 33, 1:6–30.

Goldstein, H. 1990. *Problem-oriented Policing*. New York: McGraw-Hill.

Greene, J., and Mastrofski, S., eds. 1988. *Community Policing: Rhetoric or Reality?* New York: Praeger.

Greenwood, P. W., and Petersilia, J. 1975. *The Criminal Investigation Process, Volume I: Summary and Policy Implications*. Santa Monica, CA: Rand Corporation.

Haarr, R. N. 2001. "The Making of a Community Policing Officer: The Impact of Basic Training and Occupational Socialization on Police Recruits." *Police Quarterly* 4, 4:402–433.

Hope, T. 1995. "Community Crime Prevention." In M. Tonry and D. P. Farrington, eds., *Building a Safer Society: Strategic Approaches to Crime Prevention*, pp. 22–89. Chicago: University of Chicago Press.

International Association of Chiefs of Police. 2001. Community Policing Award Winners and Finalists. Available at <http://www.ittnightquest.com/images/itt/finalmonograph2001.pdf>.

Kelling, G. L., Pate, T., Dieckman, D., and Brown, C. E. 1974. *The Kansas City Preventive Patrol Experiment: A Summary Report*. Washington, D.C.: Police Foundation.

Kelling, G., and Moore, M. 1988. "The Evolving Strategy of Policing." *Perspectives on Policing*. Washington, D.C.: National Institute of Justice.

Kerley, K., and Benson, M. 2000. "Does Community-oriented Policing Help Build Stronger Communities?" *Police Quarterly* 3, 1:46–69.

Klockars, C. B. 1988. "The Rhetoric of Community Policing." In J. Greene and S. Mastrofski, eds., *Community Policing: Rhetoric or Reality?*, pp. 239–258. New York: Praeger.

Manning, P. K. 1988. "Community Policing as a Drama of Control." In J. Greene and S. Mastrofski, eds., *Community Policing: Rhetoric or Reality?*, pp. 27–46. New York: Praeger.

McEwen, J. T., Connors, E. F., and Cohen, M. I. 1986. *Evaluation of the Differential Police Responses Field Test*. Washington, D.C.: National Institute of Justice.

McEwen, T., Spence, D., Wolff, R., Wartell, J., and Webster, B. 2003. *Call Management and Community Policing: A Guidebook for Law Enforcement*. Washington, D.C.: Office of Community Oriented Policing Services.

Moore, M. H. and Trojanowicz, R. C. 1988. "Corporate Strategies for Policing." *Perspectives on Policing*. Washington, D.C.: National Institute of Justice.

Muhlhausen, D. B. 2003. "GAO Critiques Research Touting COPS Program Effectiveness," WebMemo #313. Washington, D.C.: Heritage Foundation. Available at <http://www.heritage.org/Research/Crime/wm313.cfm>.

Office of Community-oriented Policing Services. 2002. *Community Policing in Smaller Jurisdictions*. Washington, D.C.: Authors.

Parks, R., Mastrofski, S., DeJong, C., and Gray, K. 1999. "How Officers Spend Their Time with the Community." *Justice Quarterly* 16, 3:483–518.

Police Foundation. 1981. *The Newark Foot Patrol Experiment*. Washington, D.C.: Police Foundation.

Problem-oriented Policing Center. (2003). See www.popcenter.org for winners of the Herman Goldstein Problem-oriented Policing Awards since 1993.

Reiss, A. J., Jr. 1985. "Shaping and Serving the Community: The Role of the Police Chief Executive." In W. A. Geller, ed., *Police Leadership in America: Crisis and Opportunity*, pp. 61–69. New York: Praeger.

Rosenbaum, D. P. 1987. "The Theory and Research Behind Neighborhood Watch: Is It a Sound Fear and Crime Reduction Strategy?" *Crime & Delinquency* 33, 1:103–134.

Roth, J. A., and Ryan, J. F. 2000. "The COPS Program After 4 Years—National Evaluation," Research in Brief. Washington, D.C.: National Institute of Justice. Available at <http://www.urban.org/pdfs/COPS_summary.pdf>.

Sampson, R., and Scott, M. 2000. *Tackling Crime and Other Public-safety Problems: Case Studies in Problem-solving*. Washington, D.C.: Office of Community Oriented Policing Services.

Scarborough, K. E., Christiansen, K., Cordner, G., and Smith, M. 1998. "An Evaluation of Community Oriented Policing Training." *Police Forum* 8, 3:11–15.

Schwartz, A. T., and Clarren, S. N. 1977. *The Cincinnati Team Policing Experiment: A Summary Report*. Washington, D.C.: Police Foundation.

Scott, M. 2000. *Problem-oriented Policing: Reflections on the First 20 Years*. Washington, D.C.: Office of Community Oriented Policing Services.

Sherman, L. W., Milton, C. H., and Kelley, T. V. 1973. *Team Policing: Seven Case Studies*. Washington, D.C.: Police Foundation.

Spelman, W., and Brown, D. K. 1982. *Calling the Police: Citizen Reporting of Serious Crime*. Washington, D.C.: Police Executive Research Forum.

Trojanowicz, R. C. 1982. *An Evaluation of the Neighborhood Foot Patrol Program in Flint, Michigan*. East Lansing, MI: School of Criminal Justice, Michigan State University.

Trojanowicz, R., and Bucqueroux, B. 1990. *Community Policing: A Contemporary Perspective*. Cincinnati, OH: Anderson.

Weatheritt, M. 1988. "Community Policing: Rhetoric or Reality?" In J. Greene and S. Mastrofski, eds., *Community Policing: Rhetoric or Reality?*, pp. 153–176. New York: Praeger.

Wilson, J., and Kelling, G. 1982. "Broken Windows: The Police and Neighborhood Safety." *Atlantic Monthly* 249:29–38.

Zhao, J., Scheider, M. C., and Thurman, Q. 2002. "Funding Community Policing to Reduce Crime: Have COPS Grants Made a Difference?" *Criminology and Public Policy* 2, 1:7–32.

Suggested Websites for Further Study

The Community Policing Consortium
www.communitypolicing.org
Office of Community-Oriented Policing Services
www.cops.usdoj.gov
Crime Prevention
www.ncpc.org
Center for Problem-Oriented Policing
www.popcenter.org
Regional Community Policing Institutes
www.cops.usdoj.gov/Default.asp?Item=115 ✦

Part II
Police Administration

Chapter 4

Police Management

Chapter Outline

Key Terms

aggressive policing	crime clearance rate
arrest rates	crime index
broken-windows theory	decentralization
bureaucracy	disorder index
centralization	flat structure
chain of command	generalists
classical principles	goals
closed system	index crimes
Compstat	job redesign
contingency management	leading
contingency theory	management
controlling	manager's culture
corporate strategy	NCVS

Key Terms (continued)

NIBRS	reinventing government
open system	socialization
organization chart	specialization
organizational design	street cop's culture
organizing	supervision
paramilitary model	SWAT
PPUs	systems theory
planning	tall structure
police union	TQM
private world of policing	UCRs
public world of policing	victim survey
quality-of-life policing	zero-tolerance policing

T he process of policing a democratic society is complex. Indeed, because of this complexity, a police department is probably one of the most difficult public institutions to manage effectively. Consequently, it is important to have a fundamental understanding of both the historical and present-day processes used in managing police departments. Not only are these processes critical to how the police operate and behave in society, but they also contribute to the type of individuals selected to become officers—the subject of Chapter 6.

Management is directing individuals to achieve organizational goals in an efficient and effective manner. The functions carried out by police managers include organizing, leading, planning, and controlling; how well these functions are performed determines, to a large degree, how successful a department will be.

The Managerial Process

Although managers perform each of the functions described above, the time involved in each one varies according to the manager's level in the department. For instance, people at higher levels, such as assistant chiefs, spend a greater proportion of their time in organizing and planning; those at lower levels, such as sergeants, spend more time on **supervision**, which focuses primarily on leading and controlling. The time spent in various functions is also influenced by the size of the department. In a small police department, for instance, a sergeant may function both as an assistant chief and as a supervisor. Each managerial function is briefly described below.

Organizing is the process of arranging personnel and physical resources to carry out plans and accomplish goals and objectives. Organizational design or structure, job design, group working arrangements, and individual work assignments are subject to the organizing process. Although all managers are involved in organizing, once again the degree and scope differ, depending on their level within the department. While the patrol supervisor is more concerned with work assignments, the chief is more concerned with the overall distribution of personnel and physical resources.

Leading is motivating others to perform various tasks that will contribute to the accomplishment of goals and objectives. Motivating others is a difficult and complex process, especially in civil service organizations, where managers have far less control over salaries and pay incentives than in the private sector. Accordingly, police managers must rely more on internal rewards to motivate employees, such as job satisfaction and feelings of accomplishment. This situation suggests that job design is a key ingredient in motivating police personnel (more on this later). It should be noted that the leadership role for top-level managers can also encompass managing the relationship between the police and the community, as well as other important organizations, including criminal justice and government agencies.

A police executive must provide a leadership role within the community, as seen here addressing a town meeting.

Planning is the process of preparing for the future by setting goals and objectives and developing courses of action for accomplishing them. The courses of action involve such activities as determining mission and value statements, conducting research, identifying strategies and methods, developing policies and procedures, and formulating budgets. Although all managers engage in planning, once again the scope and nature of the activity differ considerably, depending on the managerial level within the department. For instance, whereas a patrol supervisor may develop work schedules and operating activities for the upcoming week, police chiefs may plan activities and changes for the upcoming year. In general, the higher the managerial level, the broader the scope of planning and the longer the time frame for the plan.

(**Controlling** is the process by which managers determine how the quality and the quantity of departmental systems and services can be improved, if goals and objectives are being accomplished, if operations are consistent with plans, and if officers follow departmental policies and procedures. Both *efficiency* (relationship between resources and outputs) and *effectiveness* (degree to which goals and objectives are accomplished) are key concepts in this phase of management. If goals or objectives are not realized, or plans, policies, and procedures are not being followed, managers must determine why and take action. Controlling may be the most troublesome managerial function because it may be difficult to determine why performance failures occur and what action to take to improve or correct them. For example, police corruption and brutality continue to be serious problems, despite frequent attempts to determine their causes and correct them.

As noted above, managers at various levels in the department perform their functions differently. Figure 4.1 depicts the various hierarchical levels found in medium to large police departments. Such organizational structures are termed pyramids because the number of personnel decreases as one goes up in the hierarchy (i.e., there are fewer at the top). At the same time, this diminishing group receives increased power, authority, and rewards.

Figure 4.1   Organization Pyramid With Levels of Hierarchy

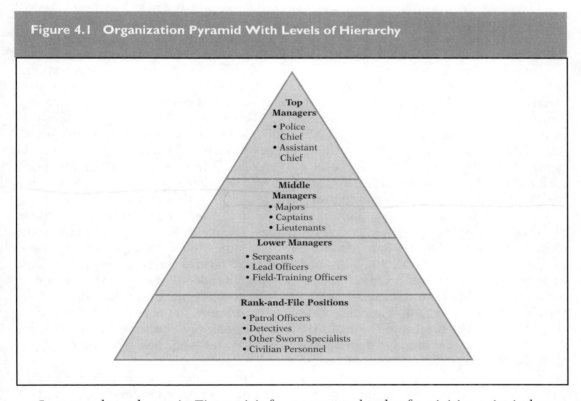

In general, as shown in Figure 4.1, four separate levels of activities exist in larger organizations; smaller organizations may have only two or perhaps three levels. This hierarchical structure is known as the **chain of command,** where the higher the position, the greater the power, authority, and influence. The activities of personnel at each level are as follows: *top managers* conduct overall goal formulation and make policy decisions regarding allocation of resources; *middle managers* formulate objectives and plans for implementing decisions from above and coordinate activities from below; *lower managers* implement decisions made at higher levels and coordinate and direct the work of employees at the lowest level of the organization; and *rank-and-file personnel* carry out specific tasks.

The following discussion of the development of police management theory has relevance to how police departments have been traditionally structured and managed and what impact contemporary developments are having on police management.

The Development of Police Management

The theory and practice of police management have evolved through three major developmental perspectives—classical, behavioral, and contemporary. Each of these perspectives and its impact on police management is described below.

Classical Police Management

The early writers on police management emphasized what is known as a classical approach to organization, including a rigid hierarchical structure, strong centralized control, and authoritarian leadership styles. A cornerstone of this approach was Max Weber's concept of **bureaucracy**, a term he coined at the end of the nineteenth century to identify characteristics that organizations needed to operate on a rational basis. Following the introduction of the bureaucratic model, a number of writers started to develop what have become known as **classical principles** of organization, which were believed to be universal. Some of Weber's administrative principles that reflect this approach include *specialization* (division of work); *authority and responsibility* (right to command and require obedience); *discipline* (necessary for effectiveness); *unity of command* (employees are to receive orders from only one superior); *scalar chain* (hierarchy of authority); and *centralization* (the extent to which decision making is retained by the top organizational levels) (Gerth and Mills 1946).

Early police theorists, in an attempt to create a more professional police force, placed great emphasis on the classical principles. The result was a highly bureaucratic structure, managed and organized along military lines in an attempt to insulate the police from partisan politics. This **paramilitary model** emphasized a legalistic approach and authoritarian managerial practices intended to control officers' behavior in order to improve crime control and lessen corrupt practices. Influential writers promoting these ideals first appeared in the United States in the early 1900s and continued to be influential into the early 1950s. Some editions of the textbooks of these classical writers continued to appear into the 1980s and even the early 1990s and still have an influence on police managerial practices.

A work that had a major impact on police reform was Smith's *Police Systems in the United States* (1940). Smith emphasized that police departments could be significantly improved if they were properly designed and managed according to the "principles of organization," which had won wide acceptance in military and industrial circles. Another significant work that affected police practice was O. W. Wilson's *Police Administration* (1950), followed by later editions with McLaren as coauthor (Wilson and McLaren 1977). The early editions became known as the "bible" of police management, and the prescriptions set forth were, and to some extent still are, followed. Like Smith, Wilson and McLaren suggested that an effective crime-control organization should be designed and managed according to "fundamental" organizational principles, especially with respect to the chain of command and hierarchy of authority.

What became known as the paramilitary model (also referred to as the legalistic, bureaucratic, professional, or reform model) of policing relies heavily on classical theory to reduce the politics commonly associated with police work by making police behavior more objective or bureaucratic and less personal in the political sense. Along with this bureaucratic approach to policing came an increased emphasis on law enforcement as the primary function of the police.

Behavioral Police Management

Beginning in the early 1970s, police management theorists began attacking the classical approach, with its emphasis on bureaucracy and hierarchical structure, authoritarian managerial practices, and a narrow view of the police role. In line with the increased behavioral research (i.e., the scientific study of human behavior) of the 1950s and 1960s, which placed greater emphasis on worker participation and job satisfaction, these writers stressed a more flexible and democratic organizational model, along with a recognition of the complex nature of the police role.

By the 1960s, a considerable amount of behavioral research had also been completed on what police actually do on the job, indicating that the majority of police work was not directly related to law enforcement, but rather to maintaining order and providing social services (e.g., see Bercal 1970; Cumming, Cumming, and Edell 1965; Goldstein 1968; Parnas 1967; and Wilson 1968). Perhaps just as important, it was becoming clear that the police role was broader and more *complex* than many had originally suspected. This research provided the impetus for a new perspective on police work by suggesting that adherence to a legalistic and technical approach to the job would not be effective. In short, effective policing required qualified personnel who could *use discretion wisely* to deal with a wide range of complex problems and situations.

These findings had serious implications for the well-entrenched paramilitary model. As Bittner noted, "The core of the police mandate is profoundly incompatible with the military posture. On balance, the military bureaucratic organization of the police is a serious handicap" (1970, 51). Bittner viewed the proper use of discretion as central to the professional development of the police role, and he believed that overreliance on regulations and bureaucratic routine seriously inhibited such development. Furthermore, he suggested that although the paramilitary model helped to secure internal discipline, it continued to hinder the development of the police role because "recognition is given for doing well in the department, not outside where all the real duties are located" (54–55). In other words, attention to a neat appearance and conformance to bureaucratic routine were more highly regarded than work methods and performance in the community (i.e., interacting and dealing with the public).

Goldstein (1977) suggested that the *organizational climate* in police departments must change if the objective is to retain highly qualified (and educated) officers and thus operate effectively in a democratic society. Officers should be more involved in policy making and in determining methods of operation; they should be able to realize their "full potential" in ways other than promotion. Although Goldstein believes that a movement toward a more collegial model is in order, he does not believe that a police department should be run as a democracy. He emphasizes that some situations, such as mobilizing a large number of officers to deal with an emergency, will always require authoritarian management practices. What is called for, according to Goldstein, "is not a substitution of some radical new style of management, but instead, a gradual movement away from the extremely authoritarian climate that currently pervades police agencies toward a more democratic form of organization" (264).

The "extremely authoritarian climate" noted by Goldstein had become a common characteristic of many police departments by the 1960s. The police were criticized for discriminatory behavior and ineffectiveness in responding to crime, and they were also considered to be using inappropriate management practices. It was suggested that there was even a connection between authoritarian management practices and authoritarian police behavior. Consequently, the knowledge gained from the behavioral science research of the period gradually began to influence the police and help them to understand the importance of increased employee involvement in decision making, of recognizing a broader police role, and of working in partnerships with the community. However, this new knowledge and the required managerial skills were not always embraced by the police, and to some extent, still are not.

Contemporary Police Management

The increased level of sophistication and findings from behavioral science research led to the development of systems theory and contingency theory and the movement toward private sector influences, including corporate strategy, total quality management, and reinventing government. These developments allowed not only for improved managerial practices but also for an understanding of the importance of community relationships to the police.

Systems and contingency theory. Conceptually, **systems theory** means that all parts of a system (organization) are interrelated and dependent on one another. The importance of applying systems theory to police departments is that it allows managers to understand that any changes made in their unit will have a corresponding impact on other units. Thus, police managers should continually be in contact with one another to make sure that the activities of their units are in agreement with the overall needs and goals of the department.

Police managers should be aware that systems can be viewed as either open or closed. An **open system** interacts with, and adapts to, its environment; a **closed system** does not. In general, all organizations interact with their environment to some degree, but the degree of interaction varies greatly. Essentially, those systems that are more open function more effectively because of their environmental adaptability. The environment for police departments is essentially the community in which they operate; those departments that are relatively more open are more effective because they are aware of community needs and expectations and thus can adapt their practices accordingly. In the past, a lack of interaction with the environment, and thus a lack of understanding of community concerns, has led to serious problems in police-community relations.

If police departments are not managed from an open-systems perspective, they cannot adapt to changing environmental influences and forces and thus will be ineffective, or certainly less effective, in their levels of operation. When this happens, the department will inevitably be forced to change, as external critics make demands that ultimately cannot be ignored. This point has been supported by Zhao's (1996) study of 228 police departments, in which he found that changes toward innovative community-policing strategies were more likely to be forced on departments by external environmental demands (e.g., affirmative action programs and community makeup), rather than by consciously chosen internal considerations.

Contingency theory is based on open-systems theory and recognizes that there are many internal and external factors that influence organizational behavior. Because these factors differ according to different organizational circumstances, there is no one "best" way to organize and manage diverse types of police departments. The underlying theme for **contingency management** is that *it all depends* on the particular situation. For example, why does a certain type of leadership work in one type of department but not in other types, or in one part of a department but not in other parts? The answer is simply because situations differ. The task for managers, then, is to try to determine in which situations and at what times certain methods and techniques are the most effective.

In the late 1970s, Roberg (1979) applied contingency theory to policing. He emphasized contingency concepts and the necessity of identifying *both* internal and external variables that affect police departmental behavior. Accordingly, such factors as the complex nature of the role, increasing educational levels of employees, and the relatively unstable nature of the environment (e.g., changing laws, cultural diversity, political influences) must be considered in attempting to determine the most effective police management methods. It has become obvious that when such factors are considered, "many of the simplistic classical prescriptions which have been applied to police organization design are clearly inadequate" (190). It was concluded that a less bureaucratic, less centralized design was necessary for police to perform effectively.

Private sector influences. In the late 1980s, the use of a private-sector process, known as **corporate strategy**, was applied to policing by Moore and Trojanowicz (1988). They suggested that like private-sector managers, police managers should define "the principal financial and social goals the organization will pursue, and the principal products, technologies, and production processes on which it will rely to achieve its goals" (2). A corporate strategy is developed through a process that examines how the organization's capabilities fit the current and future environmental demands, then defines the best strategy to meet the demands. While this process can be complicated, the authors note that such strategies can be captured in relatively simple phrases or slogans; for example, they cite the mission of the U.S. Environmental Protection Agency (EPA) as "pollution abatement." Many police departments began to develop corporate strategies based on newly defined mission statements, which often included terms and phrases dealing with community partnerships, dignity and sensitivity, problem solving, and the provision of quality services.

Total quality management (TQM) was developed in Japan in an effort to help revitalize Japanese industries following World War II. The foundation for this approach lies in *quality-control* techniques and the process of *continuous improvement*. This management process helped turn around the entire Japanese industry, in which "Made in Japan" had become a symbol for inferior products, to become synonymous with the highest-quality products in the world. TQM (also referred to as *quality* *management*) is a customer-oriented approach that emphasizes human resources and quantitative methods in an attempt to strive toward continuous improvement. In order to maximize the use of human resources, quality management stresses the importance of employee participation, teamwork, and continuous learning and improvement. The quantitative dimension involves the use of research and statistical techniques to evaluate and improve the processes in an organization and to link those processes to results. First introduced in the private sector, this approach has spread rapidly to the public sector as well—including the police. It has been estimated that approximately 25 percent of governmental agencies use TQM in at least one functional area of management (West, Berman, and Milakovich 1994).

In a survey of approximately 200 Texas police managers, Hoover (1996) indicated that various components of TQM were being utilized. Three primary concepts were measured: (1) culture (i.e., are lower-level employees empowered, is there teamwork and cooperation, are rewards equitable, is there a sense of work ownership?); (2) customers (i.e., are services to the customers measured with respect to what they want, including surveys and complaints?); and (3) counting (i.e., are quality-versus-quantity indicators of police productivity being measured, such as problem solving versus arrests?). He found that the departments were making reasonable application of culture principles, moderate application of customer-orientation techniques, and sparse application of measurement efforts. Thus, although quality-management concepts are being implemented, work remains to be done (especially with respect to implementing quality-performance measures) if police departments are to improve substantially.

Because of its emphasis on quality service to customers (citizens) and attention to continuous improvement, quality management should prove useful to police departments in the transition to community policing. Possibly the first department to utilize quality-management principles for this purpose was in Madison, Wisconsin. In *Quality Policing: The Madison Experience* (Couper and Lobitz 1991), the police chief of Madison at the time (Couper) and a colleague have written about the experiences of this department's change away from a highly traditional, bureaucratic organization toward a quality-oriented organization. The principles of quality management or "quality leadership" used by this chief in transforming the department are listed in Inside Policing 4.1.

The process that the Madison Police Department went through in changing to a quality-oriented organization, emphasizing participation and teamwork, was time-consuming and demanding. It took approximately 20 years from the start of the change process in the department to reach a state of general implementation of community policing and quality management (Wycoff and Skogan 1993). If traditional paramilitary departments are to implement similar significant changes, this is the type of long-term sustained effort they must be willing to put forth.

A national study of police middle managers' receptivity to the principles of **reinventing government**—that is, improving organizational performance through reorganization, downsizing, and TQM—was undertaken by Vito and Kunselman (2000). As some may remember, *Reinventing Government* (Osborne and Gaebler 1992) was on the *New York Times* bestseller list and influenced the *National Performance Review* (1994), spearheaded at the federal level by then Vice President Al Gore to improve the operations of federal agencies. The top-ranked idea selected by the middle managers, representing municipal, county, and state agencies, was community-owned government (66 percent), or empowering communities to participate in government agencies and ensure accountability. The second most popular idea was customer-driven government (54 percent); that is, empowering citizens as customers to participate in government agencies (e.g., through the use of surveys and other forms of feedback to the department). The third most popular idea was decentralized government, or empowering workers to be responsible and accountable in decision-making processes and program procedures. These findings indicate that the elements of reinvention that reflect the ideals of community policing were supported, particularly the empowerment of citizens to establish a partnership with the police and decentralization of decision-making to line personnel. Whereas additional research is necessary to determine how far-reaching these findings may be, this study suggests that the ideals of community policing may be reaching police middle management.

Inside Policing 4.1   **Principles of Quality Leadership in Madison**

1. Believe in, foster, and support teamwork.
2. Make a commitment to the problem-solving process, use it, and let data (not emotions) drive decisions.
3. Seek employees' input before making key decisions.
4. Believe that the best way to improve work quality or service is to ask and listen to employees who are doing the work.
5. Strive to develop mutual respect and trust among employees.
6. Have a customer orientation and focus toward employees and citizens.
7. Manage on the behavior of 95 percent of employees, not on the 5 percent who cause problems; deal with the 5 percent promptly and fairly.
8. Improve systems and examine processes before placing blame on people.
9. Avoid "top down," power-oriented decision making whenever possible.
10. Encourage creativity through risk taking, and be tolerant of honest mistakes.
11. Be a facilitator and coach; develop an open atmosphere that encourages providing for and accepting feedback.
12. With teamwork, develop with employees agreed-upon goals and a plan to achieve them.

Source: D. C. Couper and S. H. Lobitz, *Quality Policing: The Madison Experience* (Washington, D.C.: Police Executive Research Forum, 1991), 48.

Organizational Design

Organizational design is concerned with the formal patterns of arrangements and relationships developed by police management to link people together in order to accomplish organizational goals. It was traditionally assumed by the classical school of thought that a pyramidal design was the most appropriate for police departments. Even today, some departments that are moving toward community policing, which requires a less bureaucratic approach, steadfastly cling to a pyramidal design.

The classical design, characterized by many hierarchical levels and narrow spans of control (i.e., a small number of employees per supervisor) allowing for close supervision and control of employees and operations, is known as a **tall structure**. Conversely, a **flat structure** is characterized by few hierarchical levels with wide spans of control (i.e., a large number of employees per supervisor), allowing for greater employee autonomy and less control of operations. These differences between tall and flat structures are shown in Figure 4.2. It is easy to see that the tall structure has two extra levels of hierarchy and narrower spans of control for closer supervision and control over subordinates.

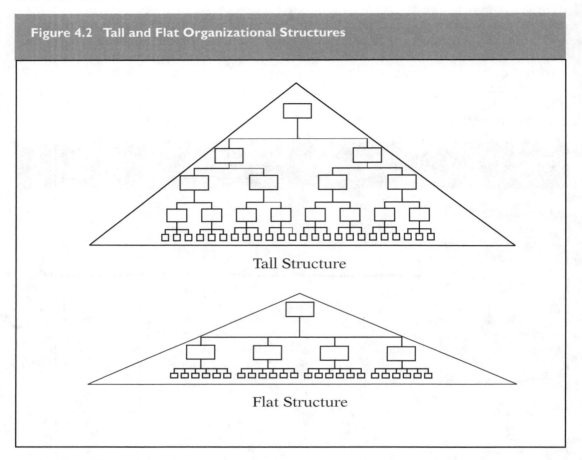

Figure 4.2 Tall and Flat Organizational Structures

Tall Structure

Flat Structure

In general, organizations with tall structures attempt to coordinate their activities through **centralization**; that is, authority and decision-making are retained by the top organizational levels. And, in general, organizations with flat structures tend to use **decentralization,** wherein authority and decision-making are delegated to lower organizational levels, as a mechanism to control their activities. Tall structures also tend to have a greater degree of specialization with respect to the division of labor of personnel or the number of activities or tasks each individual performs. In other words, the fewer the number of tasks performed, the greater the level of specialization; conversely, the greater the number of tasks performed, the lower the level of specialization. For example, in Figure 4.3 of the Portland (Oregon) Police Department, under the Operations Branch, many types of specialized activities can be observed that are supportive of patrol work, including mounted patrol, detectives, response teams, canine units, and traffic. Patrol officers are generally classified as **generalists** because they have a broad range of activities.

In order to make police departments more flexible and to improve decentralized decision-making, many departments moving toward community policing are flattening their structures (i.e., reducing hierarchical levels). For example, in Austin, Texas, it was decided to gradually eliminate the rank of deputy chief and one-third of the positions of captain. There were several reasons, but, for the most part there was a need for more street-level officers to handle calls and be available for the expanded-role concept (i.e., officers as generalists) of the patrol force (Watson, Stone, and DeLuca 1998). In moving their agency toward community policing, the Cedar Rapids, Iowa, police department is reducing the number of ranked officers by eliminating the rank of detective; see Inside Policing 4.2. Instead, patrol officers can qualify to become investigators, but after a period of time they will automatically rotate back into patrol. In this way, officers will have broadened their skill levels to help them better perform their community-policing roles.

Inside Policing 4.2   Detectives May Be an Endangered Species

In the Cedar Rapids, Iowa, police department, officials are moving forward with the portion of a reorganization plan that calls for elimination of the rank of detective. The proposal, which reduces the number of ranked officers, is in keeping with the department's community-policing philosophy. In the last five years, the department has not promoted anyone to the rank of detective. Instead, officers will go through a selection process whereby they apply for a spot in the unit, get a commander's recommendation, and are interviewed by a functional management team.

Under the plan, investigators would be patrol officers who rotate into the division as they would any other specialization, such as narcotics. The officers would remain in the investigative unit for up to a year, gaining experience they would then take back with them into the field. "The whole idea," said Public Safety Commissioner David Zahn, "is to move investigation, with community oriented policing, out onto the street."

Source: Adapted from "Detectives May Be an Endangered Species for One Iowa Department." 2000. *Law Enforcement News,* October, 15: 1, 8.

Formal Organizations

One of the ways to learn about a police department is to look at how it is formally arranged or organized. This is most easily done through an **organizational chart**, which depicts the intended functions, relationships, and flow of communication among designated groups. Such charts tell about the relative status of employees, the authority they have, the chain of command, the formal lines of communication, the job activities throughout the organization, and organizational values and priorities (e.g., is it bureaucratic [tall] or more democratic [flat]? Does it allow for decentralized decision making? Is it highly specialized or more generalist?). For example, one can learn much about the Portland Department, which was adopting a community-policing approach in the mid-1990s, by examining its organization chart in Figure 4.3.

In its transformation toward community policing, the department made some conscious efforts to involve both community and employee participation with respect to "policy issues, public review, and setting priorities for community-policing objectives" (Williams 1995, 159). Thus, both a chief's forum unit and an advisory committee unit, reporting directly to the chief, were added. There is also an assistant chief with a support unit, who is responsible for the daily operation of the department. This arrangement allows the chief greater flexibility to interact with the public, as well as to manage internal change. A public information unit also reports to the chief, conveying additional input from the community.

Figure 4.3 Organization Chart—Portland Police Department

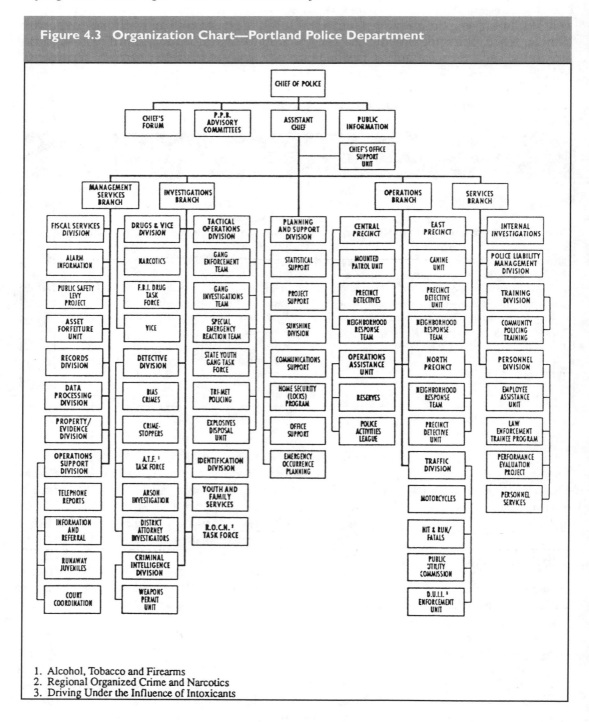

1. Alcohol, Tobacco and Firearms
2. Regional Organized Crime and Narcotics
3. Driving Under the Influence of Intoxicants

Other organizational values and priorities—with a concern for community policing and a concern for the public—can be observed. For instance, under the Services Branch, the Training Division has a specific Community Policing Training unit (in addition to the regular Training Division), and the Personnel Division has a Performance Evaluation Project unit (for determining measurable "quality" police performance indicators); in addition, the Internal Investigations unit is under the Services Branch (it is traditionally located under the Investigations Branch), which suggests that the department was concerned about public perception of fair and impartial investigations of its members. Furthermore, a move toward decentralization can be identified by noting that there are detective units at each of the precinct stations (central, north, and east), rather than one large centralized unit, and by the use of precinct neighborhood response teams, or teams of officers who "use nontraditional methods to focus on chronic neighborhood problems that are perceived by the residents to interfere with the livability of the neighborhood" (Williams 1995, 160).

Organizational design and community policing. It is interesting to observe that although a community-policing approach has been reported in Portland (Williams 1995), the organization chart indicates that a classic, pyramidal design is still in place. This is not too surprising, as large traditional police departments may allow for structural "tweaking" (e.g., decentralizing some operational activities), but major structural changes (e.g., flattening the structure by significantly reducing levels and command ranks) are far more difficult and time-consuming. This is not to suggest that the Portland department has not made progress toward community policing but rather to point out that a substantial, long-term effort is required for significant structural changes to occur. One study by Maguire (1997), which analyzed the structural characteristics of 236 large municipal departments (with 100 or more sworn members), strongly supports this observation. Maguire found no significant structural differences among those departments that reported that they had adopted community policing (44 percent), those that reported they were in the planning or implementation stages (47 percent), and those that reported having no plans for community policing (9 percent).

These and other findings draw attention to whether departments that claim to be doing community policing really are. It is one thing, of course, to report in a survey that one's department has implemented (or is implementing) community policing and quite another to actually practice it. For instance, is it being practiced throughout the entire department, or in part of the department, or in one unit made up of volunteers? Or, is a department reporting—perhaps even believing—that it is implementing community policing in order to gain professional status, community support, or even federal funding? (For example, some departments have used federal money to pay volunteer officers overtime in order to practice "community policing," with little or no additional training.) These are legitimate questions, but there really is no way of knowing for sure until a valid model of community policing is developed and tested on a large sample of departments (Maguire 1997). Nevertheless, Maguire's research will undoubtedly pique the interest of scholars who have suspected that at least some, if not many, of the reports of community-policing "adoptions" are premature or even manipulative. The following discussion on the continued strong influence of the paramilitary model and aggressive police tactics may only further muddy the debate on the "real" level of community-policing practices.

Criticisms of the paramilitary design. As police departments attempt to move toward community policing, including the decentralization of operations and decision making, becoming less specialized, and flattening the hierarchy, the effectiveness of the paramilitary design is increasingly being questioned. Auten (1981), for instance, suggests that the paramilitary organization treats the patrol officer like a *soldier* and thus is based on inappropriate assumptions about patrol work and democracy. He notes that soldiers are expected to obey orders and to show little, if any, initiative or discretion. They work as part of a larger unit; they perform tasks in a precisely prescribed manner; and they must be uniform in appearance, conduct, and behavior. The nature of the police role is quite different from these expectations. First, strict rules cannot be applied to policing because of the nature of the work. Second, orders are rarely required because most of the work by patrol personnel takes place on the street and out of the purview of supervisors. In addition, if the job is to be performed properly, a great amount of initiative and discretion are required. This is particularly true of organizations implementing community policing, where line-level discretion in decision making is seen as a virtue, not a vice. Finally, the managerial philosophy reflected by the paramilitary organization is characterized by an attitude of distrust, control, and punishment.

Although such criticisms and charges of ineffectiveness are not new and continue to grow, there has been surprisingly little research conducted either supporting or refuting them. However, a study conducted by Franz and Jones (1987) lends empirical support to the critics' charges. In this study, police officers were compared with employees in other city departments that had not been exposed to the paramilitary design. The researchers found that police employees perceived (1) greater problems with communications, (2) greater amounts of distrust, (3) lower levels of morale, and (4) lower levels of organizational performance. Franz and Jones concluded that "the data presented seriously question the capability of the quasi-military police organizational model to meet today's needs" (161).

Increasing influence of police paramilitary units. Auten's analogy with the paramilitary model, being based on inappropriate role assumptions about patrol work and the treatment of patrol officers like soldiers, is an interesting perspective when combined with some present-day research on the increasing emphasis on highly specialized **police paramilitary units (PPUs)**. PPUs are a generic term for units that have traditionally been known as SWAT (special weapons and tactics) teams and more recently referred to as SRTs (special response teams) and ERUs (emergency response units). This section will briefly describe the units, their activities, and how an even stronger paramilitary police culture and community presence may be developing.

These units function as military special-operations teams—often gaining expertise and training from the Navy's Seals and the Army's Rangers—and have as a primary function the threat or use of collective force, not always as a function of last resort. The teams frequently wear full regalia, including black or camouflage battle dress uniforms (BDUs), with boots, body armor, and helmets, are armed with submachine guns, sniper rifles, percussion grenades, tear gas, pepper gas, and surveillance equipment, and sometimes employ armored personnel carriers. Two separate national surveys provide a developing picture on how these specialized units are increasingly being used. One study by Kraska and Cubellis (1997) consisted of small-locality police departments (municipal and county) with under 100 sworn officers; the second study by Kraska and Kappeler (1997) consisted of medium to large departments with over 100 sworn officers. The total sample included 473 small-locality departments and 548 medium to large departments.

By combining the data from both surveys, the results indicated that over 77 percent of the police departments had paramilitary units, an increase of 48 percent since 1985 (with a continued growth rate expected). The early formulation of SWAT teams in the 1970s and early 1980s was for the primary purpose of reacting to emergency situations *beyond the scope of patrol*, including civil disturbances, terrorism, hostage situations, and barricaded persons. Today, a much different perspective is emerging. The surveys documented 29,962 paramilitary deployments in 1995, a 939 percent increase over the 2,884 call-outs in 1980 (Kraska and Cubellis 1997). The significant increase in PPU call-outs can be attributed to their increasing emphasis on executing search and arrest warrants and to their use as a proactive patrol force (often in full regalia) in high-crime areas. These activities consisted almost exclusively of proactive, no-knock raids, aggressive field interviews, and car stops and searches. Such activities are frequently carried out with a great deal of intimidation and often lead to increased police-community tensions. As one survey respondent described his department's use of SWAT teams:

> We're into saturation patrols in hot spots. We do a lot of our work with the SWAT unit because we have bigger guns. We send out two, two-to-four-men cars, *we look for minor violations* and do jump-outs, either on people on the street or automobiles. After we jump-out the second car provides periphery cover with an ostentatious display of weaponry. We're sending a clear message: if the shootings don't stop, we'll shoot someone. (Kraska and Kappeler 1997, 10, italics added)

The authors conclude that PPUs are thus becoming a *normal part of routine patrol work*, by moving away from their more traditional emergency roles and into more routine patrol activities.

Another study on the use of a PPU in a self-proclaimed community-policing department (although its approach seemed to favor a paramilitary style) in the Southeast found similar results to those described above (Kraska and Paulsen 1997), that is, the increased use of the PPU as a normal part of mainstream policing functions. Several themes emerged that are unique to these types of units, including a pronounced military culture, a preoccupation with danger, a high level of pleasure from engaging in paramilitary activities, and the viewing of the PPU team as a group of "elite" officers.

This integration of PPUs into patrol work appears to delineate a parallel trend with, but in opposition to, community policing: from less militaristic to more militaristic, from generalist to specialist, and from service- and problem-oriented to aggressive crime fighting. While the potential usefulness of PPUs in *bona fide emergencies* is well established, their use in mainstream policing appears unwarranted, especially in small-locality departments, which tend to be oriented toward crime prevention and service.

Countering an argument that this buildup and increased use of PPUs simply reflects a rational response to crime-rate changes, Kraska and Cubellis (1997) compared call-out rates with the rates of violent crimes (i.e., homicide, robbery, and rape) from 1980 through 1995 for each small-locality jurisdiction and found no significant relationship between violent crime and call-outs. Therefore, they concluded that changes in the rate of violent crime were not an important factor in explaining the increased level of PPU activities. Instead, they argued that:

The increasing use of PPUs in routine patrol work, in full combat gear and weaponry, is indicative of the strong influence paramilitary units continue to have in policing.

> . . . we must first recognize that the specter of the military model still haunts the real world of contemporary policing, despite the recent rhetoric of democratic reforms. . . . [W]e find strong support for the thesis that the military model is still a powerful force guiding the ideology and activities of American police. This should not be surprising considering the war/military paradigm remains an authoritative framework for crime-control thinking and action by politicians, bureaucrats, the media, and much of the public. (622)

It is prudent to keep in mind that the significant increase in the use of PPUs and greater push toward militarism in policing, occurred prior to the terrorist attacks of September 11, 2001. Consequently, it is likely that such growth will continue to increase, and even flourish, in the near term; the implications for community policing, in general, and civil rights, in particular, appear more important than ever. In this regard, below is a discussion on the increasing use of aggressive police strategies and their impacts, including broken-windows, zero-tolerance, and quality-of-life policing.

Broken-windows, aggressive/zero-tolerance, and quality-of-life policing. James Q. Wilson and George Kelling (1982) introduced the **broken-windows** theory of law enforcement in the early 1980s. The theory is based on a hypothesis that a vigorous enforcement of low-level crimes, including physical disorder (e.g., graffiti) and social disorder (e.g., prostitution), will prevent more serious crimes from occurring. They claimed that when signs of disorder (e.g., broken windows) are ignored, incidents of violence and delinquency will erupt and become serious crime problems. Although the merits of the broken-windows theory have been debated at length by law enforcement officials, researchers, and politicians, little empirical research exists regarding the effectiveness of such strategies to reduce serious crime. The research studies that do exist have mixed results.

One method of policing that finds support for the broken-windows theory is so-called **aggressive policing** (more currently known as **zero-tolerance policing**), a police strategy in which officers "aggressively" (some say "heavy-handedly") target minor crime in order to send a signal that such behavior will not be tolerated in the community. Aggressive policing was first studied by Wilson and Boland (1978), prior to the development of broken windows, who found that as the number of traffic citations increased, the serious crime rate decreased. Sherman, Gartin, and Buerger (1989) found that vigorous enforcement of the laws in crime "hot spots" caused serious violent crime to decline. Worrall (2002), in his analysis of arrests, found that as the number of misdemeanor arrests relative to total arrests increases, the felony property crime rate decreases. Conversely, research on **quality-of-life policing,** which targets the reduction of physical and social disorder so that community members will work together to promote neighborhood safety, and concomitantly reduce crime, has not been so successful. Sherman (1990) found that increased enforcement of public drinking laws and parking regulations had an initial impact on citizens' feelings of safety but no apparent impact on serious crime. Similar conclusions were reached by Novak, Hartman, Holsinger, and Turner (1999), who reported that increased enforcement of liquor laws had no effect on robbery or burglar rates, and Katz, Webb, and Schaefer (2001), who measured the effects of quality-of-life strategies on calls for service in numerous categories (e.g., person and property crime, drug crime, public morals, physical disorder, nuisance and disorderly conduct, traffic), and found a reduction in physical disorder and public morals (e.g., prostitution), but not in serious crime.

Harcourt (2001) critiques broken-windows theory from empirical, methodological, theoretical, and rhetorical perspectives. Although broken-windows theory has existed since the early 1980s, it has yet to be empirically verified, and Harcourt argues that the prominent existing data suggest it is false. He suggests that New York City's large drop in crime (see Compstat below) tells us little about broken-windows theory. For instance, many large cities—including Boston, Houston, Los Angeles, St. Louis, San Diego, San Antonio, San Francisco, and Washington, D.C.—have experienced significant declines in crime, some proportionally larger than New York's. And many of these cities have not implemented the aggressive, zero-tolerance strategies of New York. Harcourt argues that a large number of factors in combination—such as a large increase in the number of officers hired, a shift in drug use patterns from crack cocaine to heroin, favorable economic conditions in the 1990s, a decrease in the number of 18-to-24-year-olds, and the arrest of several big drug gangs—have led to the drop in crime in New York City. Another critique of broken windows is offered by Herbert (2001), who suggests that broken-windows (zero-tolerance) policing is essentially replacing community policing as the primary reform model of the day, not because it works to reduce crime but because it fits more comfortably within established cultural and political frameworks (see Inside Policing 4.3). This is one explanation for the belief of some that community policing is more rhetoric than reality.

In line with the above discussion, even though broken-windows theory has been used as the basis for zero-tolerance policing, it is worth noting that zero tolerance is an oversimplification of broken-windows theory as described by Wilson and Kelling (1982). Broken-windows theory encourages aggressive enforcement of less-serious offenses, as long as they are in line with community wishes. Communities are to set thresholds for disorderly public behavior, and the police are responsible for law enforcement in accordance with these norms. Since communities will differ in their tolerance for disorderly behavior, policing will qualitatively differ from community to community. In contrast, the zero-tolerance approach applies the law equally in all environments in which it is applied and thus is not a true reflection of broken-windows theory.

Inside Policing 4.3   Broken Windows Policing Subsuming Community Policing?

Part of the explanation for a lack of genuine reform (in policing today) is the unfortunate popular combining of community policing with broken-windows (zero-tolerance) policing; not because it works to reduce crime but because it's easier for police, citizens, and politicians to understand and accept the *status quo*. This development suggests that we can expect little by way of significant change on the part of police departments. In some cities, like New York, broken-windows policing is merely the professional (legalistic) model on steroids: aggressive, arrest-oriented policing. To embrace this approach is to diminish the potential role of citizens in overseeing police activity, because such oversight is now overshadowed by the energy devoted to disorder. This is important because aggressive policing causes undue harm to far too many citizens. When police too willingly understand themselves as gladiators in a noble fight against crime, they may be too willing to abuse force (and intimidation) in the process. To mandate more and more arrests is to invite officers to cast suspicion on those who may not warrant it and to arrest or abuse those who should be left alone. Such suspicion will inevitably fall disproportionately on minority citizens, further enflaming police-community relations in minority-dominated neighborhoods.

Adapted from S. Herbert. 2001. "Policing the Contemporary City: Fixing Broken Windows or Shoring Up Neo-Liberalism?" *Theoretical Criminology* 5: 459.

Compstat. From 1990 to 1995, the rate of serious, violent crime declined by 37.4 percent in New York City; however, from 1993 to 1996, the number of total arrests rose by 23 percent. Reflecting a zero-tolerance strategy based on broken-windows theory, and directed by a process introduced by Police Commissioner William Bratton, known as Compstat, misdemeanor arrests rose by 40 percent—led by drug arrests, which increased by 97 percent during the period. **Compstat**, an acronym for compare statistics, was developed as a process that utilizes current crime data to analyze crime patterns and to respond quickly with "appropriate" resources and crime strategies. As arrests became more frequent, the annual number of complaints of police misconduct filed with the Civilian Complaint Review Board (CCRB) in New York also increased by more than 60 percent from 1992 to 1996 (see Inside Policing 4.4). The increases in arrests in New York were accompanied by nearly a 40 percent increase in the number of sworn police officers between 1990 and 1995. By contrast, San Diego enjoyed a 36.8 percent reduction in serious, violent crime from 1990 to 1995, while increasing its police force by only 6.2 percent.

Significantly, citizen complaints about police misconduct decreased in San Diego by 9 percent from 1993 to 1996. It has been suggested that San Diego was able to accomplish these crime reductions more effectively and far more cost efficiently (i.e., with fewer police hires) than New York by implementing community policing, which emphasized "creating problem-solving partnerships and fostering connections between police and community for sharing information, working with citizens to address crime and disorder problems, and tapping other public and private agencies for resources to help solve them" (Greene 1999, 183).

It is noteworthy that due to the increased complaints and publicity by the community over New York's zero-tolerance program, a new police chief (Howard Safir) implemented a policy directed at improving officer behavior known as **"courtesy, professionalism, and respect,"** or *CPR*. This new code of behavior may be working, since citizen complaints filed against NYPD officers dropped 21 percent in the first half of 1997, compared with the same period a year earlier. More specifically, complaints of police brutality dropped 20 percent (from 1,278 to 1,021) and complaints of abuse of authority fell almost 29 percent (from 1,166 to 829). In addition, charges of discourtesy fell 32 percent, and charges of profanity by police dropped almost 40 percent. These drops are impressive; nevertheless, some observers (such as the New York Civil Liberties Union) suggest that while *CPR* might be working, it could also mean that citizens have lost confidence in the Civilian Complaint Review Board and simply do not complain anymore ("Good News Just Gets Better" 1997, 18).

Police utilizing aggressive tactics to take back the streets.

Whatever the cause, it is important to note that the department is taking steps to improve officer behavior and is keeping track of the situation in order to determine the progress being made. It is further apparent, however, that with complaints numbering in the thousands in New York, community-police interactions require continuous attention and improvement. Inside Policing 4.4 takes a closer look at the potential problems of this aggressive approach to policing.

Inside Policing 4.4   NYPD's Zero-Tolerance Policing

Diane Saarinen regularly hosted community forums at which police officials described how they were fighting drug dealers who had sometimes taken over entire blocks. As crime began to drop, she wrote strong letters of support to the local police, thanking them for their work. Now, however, she is writing a different kind of letter, strongly complaining of police abuse. She says she has heard too many stories of overly rough police conduct, including dragging people out of cars at gunpoint, of abusive tactics, of roughing up people who do not speak English, and of shooting civilians. "In the beginning we all wanted the police to bomb the crack houses," she says, "but now it's backfiring at the cost of the community. I think the cops have been given free rein to intimidate people at large."

Although most experts agree that the NYPD's aggressive zero-tolerance style has played a role in lowering the crime rate, the question remains whether or not this style of policing comes at too high a price. Opinion polls indicate that most New Yorkers approve of the crime strategy (of course, most citizens are not experts in police tactics or civil rights), but in some communities the heavy-handedness is straining already poor relations with young African Americans and Hispanics. In New York, for example, the city's civilian review board has reported a 50 percent increase in complaints over the past two years. That appears to be true in other cities that are implementing similar aggressive police tactics; for ex-

Inside Policing 4.4   NYPD's Zero-Tolerance Policing (continued)

ample, in Pittsburgh residents voted to establish a civilian review board and Charlotte, N.C., is expected to do the same, following a rash of complaints and disputed shootings.

Are increased complaints an appropriate trade-off for reduced crime? William Bratton, the former New York police commissioner who implemented the aggressive strategy, believes it is not surprising that complaints would increase, as the police are making more arrests and coming into contact with more citizens. He acknowledges that some police go too far, but contends that the reduction in crimes and victimizations is worth it. "In a city of 7.5 million people, 30 million tourists, and 38,000 police, is the level of complaints an appropriate trade-off?" he asked. "I think so, and the people seem satisfied." However, critics wonder if that sort of trade-off is ap-

propriate in a democracy. If there is zero tolerance for lower-level street crimes, why is there not zero tolerance for heavy-handed cops? And the critics are not just from the criminal class or certain neighborhoods. For instance, George Kelling, the Rutgers University professor of criminal justice who coauthored the broken-windows theory and helped Bratton implement it, is worried that his ideas are not being implemented appropriately. "There's an enormous potential for abuse," he says. He criticizes departments that demand IDs from residents or conduct neighborhood drug sweeps, indiscriminately stopping and frisking people, often using excessive force.

Source: Adapted from L. Reibstein. 1997. "NYPD Black and Blue." *Newsweek*, June 2: 66, 68.

As noted above, the Compstat process allows top-level police managers to share information about crime (both inside and outside the department) and essentially holds them accountable for the crime rate in their jurisdictions. Although it makes sound managerial sense to use a Compstat-type strategy to analyze crime, to share information about crime (and related problems), to respond to identified crime patterns, and to hold managers accountable for officer performance, it is potentially troublesome to hold command personnel responsible for crime rates. Since there are a number of complex social and economic factors affecting crime that are outside the purview of police, the police by themselves generally have a short-term impact on crime. (That is why establishing a partnership with the community and other social and governmental agencies is the foundation for true community-policing efforts; together, these institutions can have a long-term impact on crime). Moore suggests in his analysis of Compstat that while the system picked up one of the important ideas that emerged from community policing:

> . . . the focus on disorder offenses as a way of reducing fear, mobilizing forces of informal social control, and reducing serious crime, it left in the background two other big ideas—the idea that both the *legitimacy* and *effectiveness* of police could be increased by reaching out for effecting working partnerships with community groups, and focusing attention on community-nominated problems that might or might not include serious crime problems. (2002, 159, emphasis added)

In addition, holding police managers accountable for the crime rate can lead, and in the past has led, to the manipulation of crime statistics (i.e., underreporting of crime). Underreporting could be especially troublesome in departments where upper-level police managers are rewarded or punished on how well they keep the crime rate down; for instance, the commander of the 41st Precinct in the Bronx (N.Y.) was forced to retire after he was caught underreporting results (Kocieniewski 1998).

It is interesting that Compstat, which started out as an innocuous computer program to compare crime statistics, is now a label for a strategic process that has been described as the NYPD's "all out, attention getting war on crime, fear and disorder" that "some believe will eventually be the *dominant approach* to policing in the United States" (Dodenhoff 1996, 4, emphasis added). Undoubtedly, the continued analogy in American society of police work to "wars" on crime and drugs helps strengthen the hold of the paramilitary organization and its influences on the police. As Roberg, Kuykendall, and Novak (2002) have noted elsewhere, traditional departments have a hard time fighting the allure of incident-based law enforcement actions (i.e., reactive versus preventive measures). Whereas such actions are appropriate in some situations, departments will "drift" toward this traditional paramilitary approach unless checked. This type of response provides the most immediate gratification, is more "romantic," and is more in keeping with the "dangerous and dramatic" self-image of many police officers, as well as the expectations of many in the community (including politicians).

It appears, however, that some departments are beginning to adopt a Compstat-like approach primarily for managerial accountability, which, in turn, may impact the crime rate due to better managerial practices and use of resources. For example, the Hernando County, Florida, Sheriff's Department has recently launched a program termed STARCOM (Sheriff's Tracking Accountability and Responsiveness to Crime Oppression Management), in which responsibility for district problems will be assigned to district commanders and midlevel managers. Although lieutenants will not be held accountable for increases in crime, they will be asked to explain what they are doing about it. For instance, if shoplifting is a continual problem, they will be responsible for developing a strategy to combat it. Top brass from each of the districts will come up for review every six weeks; with some restrictions, the reviews will be open to the public (*Law Enforcement News* 2003).

Police Goals

Like all organizations, police departments are oriented toward the attainment of goals. In a democracy, it is crucial that police managers, employees, and private citizens have an understanding of what these goals are and how they are to be accomplished (measured). As described in Chapter 1, **goals** are general statements of long-term purpose. Goals are often used to identify the role of the police—for instance, to prevent crime, maintain order, or help solve community problems. They are also often used in mission statements. Goals are important because they help to identify expectations of what the police are doing and their levels of performance. Unrealistic and unreasonable goals make the job of managers and employees more difficult and can even ensure failure. When police overpromise or claim to be able to reduce crime or to solve problems that are largely outside police control, the public is usually disappointed and critical. When employees fail to behave in accordance with unreasonable managerial expectations, managers are often critical, and employees are resentful and may even become less productive. These unreasonable expectations can and often do create an adversarial relationship between the police and the community and between managers and employees (e.g., see the discussion on managers' and street cops' cultures in the next section).

Three major influences affect the development of police goals: community, organizational, and individual. *Community influences* consist of the legal framework in which police function and the community's input into departmental priorities. As has been stressed, however, there is no such thing as a "single" community constituency. Police managers, therefore, must be aware of the various communities they serve and their differing expectations. Thus, departments within a heterogeneous geographic area, or even precincts or units within the same department, may need to establish different goals or use different methods to attain goals. *Organizational influences* are those of powerful members, especially top-level managers, who seek certain goals primarily for the efficiency and perpetuation of the department but also to satisfy its members. Finally, *individual influences* generally benefit members (e.g., job security, pay, or fringe benefits).

It is clear, as the expectation-integration model discussed in Chapter 1 suggests, that the closer police managers come to integrating individual and community goals with those of the organization, the more likely it is that the goals will be accomplished. And organizational goals are more likely to be accomplished if they are aligned with supervisory practices. In a study of the effects of 64 sergeants' supervisory styles on the behavior of 239 patrol officers in the Indianapolis, Indiana, and St. Petersburg, Florida, police departments, Engel (2003) found that the *style* of field supervision can significantly influence patrol officer behavior. Although four supervisory styles were discovered (traditional, innovative, supportive, and active), it was the active style that was more likely to have an influence on officer behavior. However, this influence can be either positive or negative; for instance, it can inspire officers to engage in more problem-solving activities, or it can result in more frequent use of force. The active style was also the most conducive to implementing community-policing goals. This research suggests that leading by example is an effective supervisory method, if the example supports the goals of the organization.

Measuring police performance. The performance levels of police departments are, in general, difficult to measure. Performance indicators, such as making arrests, maintaining order, solving problems, providing services, and using discretion, are difficult to define in a meaningful and valid manner. That is to say, although it may be relatively easy to count the number of arrests that are made by the police *(quantity)*, it is much more difficult to get a handle on how "good" the arrests are *(quality)*. For example, was the arrest necessary? Was there violence prior to the arrest that could have been prevented? Did the arrest lead to a conviction? To date, the police have made very little effort to develop qualitative measures of performance. Therefore, officers may be performing activities that are supported within the department while incurring the wrath of the community.

To properly evaluate a police department's overall effectiveness, both *external* and *internal* goals should be assessed. From an external perspective, the department needs to know the extent to which it is satisfying the community it serves. For instance, are there conflicts between departmental and community goals? If the goals are similar, are the methods used to accomplish the goals acceptable? From an internal perspective, the department needs to know whether its goals are compatible with those of its employees. Is there conflict between what employees think the goals should be and what the department actually stresses, or do conflicts exist between operating units in the department? If they are to be meaningful, these goals need to be honest enough to be achievable and specific enough to be measurable. In general, attainable and generally satisfactory evaluation methods for the police include three major areas:

1. ***Crime and disorder measures.*** Crime and disorder statistics should be compared over time (in order to establish reliable trends and patterns). Criminal statistics may include the Uniform Crime Reports and victimization surveys. Measures of community disorder can be taken from the department's calls for service (e.g., complaints about noise, domestic violence, prostitution, or same-location repeat calls).

2. ***Community measures.*** Community measures may include surveys, interviews, and feedback from community meetings regarding such factors as identifying and solving important community problems relative to crime, fear of crime, and general satisfaction with the police. In addition, representative community boards and police advisory committees that participate in departmental goal setting and performance feedback can be included.

3. ***Individual and team measures.*** Evaluation of individual performance (e.g., performance ratings or evaluations by supervisors) and group performance (e.g., team projects) should be conducted at appropriate intervals—that is, biannually or yearly. In addition, employee opinions regarding operating procedures and policies, or concerns with management, can be measured by surveys and interviews.

With respect to crime and disorder measures, police departments often rely solely on the FBI's **Uniform Crime Reports** (Part I crimes, or **index crimes**) as their crime-rate measure. This crime index is the rate per 100,000 population of eight common violent and property crimes—including murder and nonnegligent manslaughter, forcible rape, robbery, aggravated assault, burglary, larceny or theft, motor vehicle theft, and arson—reported to the police. *UCRs*, however, are not a very precise measure of actual crime rates, with estimates of less than 50 percent of criminal acts being reported. The FBI has redesigned the UCR program to form a new program, the **National Incident-Based Reporting System (NIBRS)**, which will help improve the quantity, quality, and accuracy of the statistics (Bureau of Justice Statistics 1997). NIBRS includes 52 data elements on 22 offense categories in the Part A classification. In addition, there are 11 offenses in a Group B category, for which only arrestee data are to be reported, since most of these offenses come to police attention only when arrests are made (see Figure 4.4).

In addition to providing significantly more crime data, the NIBRS (1) distinguishes between attempted and completed crimes, (2) provides additional information on victim/offender relationships and characteristics, and (3) includes the location of crimes. Further, it eliminates the "hierarchy rule" of the UCR, which limits reporting to the most serious offense even though multiple offenses were committed within the course of a single criminal incident (e.g., during a robbery, if a murder and an assault are committed, only the murder is recorded). Thus, those departments that have adopted NIBRS have a much more accurate understanding of crime and disorder in their community and therefore can better plan how to deal with it. The new system, however, has not been widely adopted; as of 2001, 22 states have been "certified" by the FBI to collect and submit NIBRS data. Within these 22 states, some 3,479 agencies are submitting all of their crime data to the FBI in the NIBRS format; this represents approximately 20 percent of the crime volume in the United States (Moore 2002, 120).

Figure 4.4   National Incident-Based Reporting System

Group A Offenses
1. Arson
2. Assault Offenses
   Aggravated Assault
   Simple Assault
   Intimidation
3. Bribery
4. Burglary/Breaking and Entering
5. Counterfeiting/Forgery
6. Destruction/Damage Vandalism of Property
7. Drug/Narcotic Offenses
   Drug/Narcotic Violations
   Drug Equipment Violations
8. Embezzlement
9. Extortion/Blackmail
10. Fraud Offenses
    False Pretenses/Swindle/Confidence Game
    Credit Card/Automatic Teller Machine
       Fraud
    Impersonation
    Welfare Fraud
    Wire Fraud
11. Gambling Offenses
    Betting/Wagering
    Operating/Promoting/Assisting Gambling
    Gambling Equipment Violations
    Sports Tampering
12. Homicide Offenses
    Murder and Nonnegligent Manslaughter
    Negligent Manslaughter
    Justifiable Homicide
13. Kidnapping/Abduction
14. Larceny/Theft Offenses
    Pocket-picking
    Purse-snatching
    Shoplifting
    Theft from Building
    Theft from Coin-operated Machine
       or Device
    Theft from Motor Vehicle
    Theft of Motor Vehicle Parts or
       Accessories
    All Other Larceny
15. Motor Vehicle Theft
16. Pornography/Obscene Material
17. Prostitution Offenses
    Prostitution
    Assisting or Promoting Prostitution
18. Robbery
19. Sex Offenses, Forcible
    Forcible Rape
    Forcible Sodomy
    Sexual Assault with an Object
    Forcible Fondling
20. Sex Offenses, Nonforcible
    Incest
    Statutory Rape
21. Stolen Property Offenses
       (Receiving, etc.)
22. Weapon Law Violations

Group B Offences
1. Bad Checks
2. Curfew/Loitering/Vagrancy Violations
3. Disorderly Conduct
4. Driving Under the Influence
5. Drunkenness
6. Family Offenses, Nonviolent
7. Liquor Law Violations
8. Peeping Tom
9. Runaway
10. Trespass of Real Property
11. All Other Offenses

Source: Adapted from L. T. Hoover, "Why the Drop in Crime? Part I, Measuring Crime," *Texas Law Enforcement Management and Administrative Statistics Program Bulletin* (Huntsville, TX: Sam Houston State University, 1999), 5.

Another source of crime data that has become part of many departments' assessment of crime is the use of **victim surveys,** in which scientifically selected samples of the population are asked about being victims of crime. Victimization data tend to provide a more accurate reflection of a community's incidence of crime. Currently the most widely used and extensive victim survey is the **National Crime Victimization Survey (NCVS),** which asks a national sample of approximately 120,000 individuals over 12 years of age specific questions regarding criminal victimizations. Obviously, by combining UCR data or, better yet, NIBRS data, with victimization data, a department will have an even better understanding of crime and disorder and what to do about it.

Other performance measures that police departments traditionally use to record crime levels include arrest rates and the crime clearance rate. **Arrest rates** are calculated as the number of persons arrested for all crimes known to the police. Arrest rates are an extremely poor measure of performance for several reasons. For example, they rely on UCR measures of crimes reported and police discretion regarding when to make arrests (officer levels of quality and quantity of arrests vary significantly). A further problem is that police make substantially more arrests for minor violations than for serious violations, whereas the crime index is essentially based on serious crime. A final problem is the fact that the majority of police work does not even involve law enforcement activities, including arrests. The **crime clearance rate** is calculated as the number of Part I crimes reported to the police divided by the number of crimes for which the police have arrested a suspect. The crime clearance rate is another poor indicator of police performance for several reasons. For instance, the police usually consider a case to be "solved" even if the suspect is acquitted of the crime charged; furthermore, multiple crimes are often "cleared" by associating them with an arrested suspect who has admitted to similar or other crimes.

Changing performance measures. With all of their problems, the primary measures of police performance remain the frequency of serious crime (UCRs) and the number of arrests made by the police. However, other important and potentially more valid indicators are being discussed. For example, it has been suggested that the police should consider having a UCR-like **disorder index** as a companion to the crime index on major felonies (National Institute of Justice 1997). By developing a set of standardized measures for calls for service, over time, the public's perceptions of community disorder could be measured. As Greene (2000, 359) points out, "these data may more accurately reflect community concerns about crime and disorder or other things that disturb the social fabric." Interestingly, this is precisely what was discovered in the beat meetings in Chicago's community-policing program known as CAPS (Chicago Alternative Policing Strategy); that is, what the police thought the major neighborhood problems were (i.e., serious crime) differed substantially from the community's major concerns, which turned out to be relatively minor quality-of-life problems (Skogan and Hartnett 1997).

Because *problem solving* is such an integral part of community policing, being able to adequately respond to community problems becomes a critical criterion for adequate organization performance. According to Goldstein (1990), evaluating police response to problems requires the following:

- A clear understanding of the problem.

- Agreement on the interest(s) to be served in dealing with the problem and their order of interest.

- Agreement on the method used to determine the extent to which these interests (goals) are reached.

- A realistic assessment of what might be expected of the police; that is, solving the problem versus improving the quality of the management of it.

- Determination of the relative importance of short-term versus long-term impact.

- A clear understanding of the legality and fairness of the response; that is, recognizing that reducing a problem through improper use of authority is not only wrong, but likely to be counterproductive.

Goldstein cautions against defining success as the literal solving of a problem, since many police and community problems, by their very nature, are unmanageable due to their magnitude. Instead, he suggests that officers should be involved in identifying the measurable conditions they would like to see changed and attempt to improve these conditions. The bottom line with respect to how successfully a police department handles problem solving can be measured in any of the following ways (Spelman and Eck 1987):

- Total elimination of the problem.

- Reducing the number of incidents the problem creates.

- Reducing the seriousness of the incidents the problem creates.

- Designing methods for better handling of the incidents.

- Removing the problem from police consideration, assuming it can be handled more effectively by another agency.

Based on research within the Houston Police Department on performance evaluations relating to community policing, a task force identified new performance criteria for tasks and activities officers performed within their neighborhoods (Oettmeier and Wycoff 1997). These tasks and activities are depicted in Table 4.1.

Table 4.1   Community-Policing Tasks and Activities

Activities are listed beneath the tasks they are intended to accomplish. Several activities could be used to accomplish a number of different tasks.

1. **Learn characteristics of area, residents, businesses**
   a. Study beat books
   b. Analyze crime and calls-for-service data
   c. Drive, walk area and make notes
   d. Talk with community representatives
   e. Conduct area surveys
   f. Maintain area/suspect logs
   g. Read area papers (e.g., "shopper" papers)
   h. Discuss area with citizens when answering calls
   i. Talk with private security personnel in area
   j. Talk with area business owners/managers

2. **Become acquainted with leaders in area**
   a. Attend community meetings, including service club meetings
   b. Ask questions in survey about who formal and informal area leaders are
   c. Ask area leaders for names of other leaders

3. **Make residents aware of who officer is and what s/he is trying to accomplish in area**
   a. Initiate citizen contacts
   b. Distribute business cards
   c. Discuss purpose at community meeting

Table 4.1   Community-Policing Tasks and Activities (continued)

d. Discuss purpose when answering calls
e. Write article for local paper
f. Contact home-bound elderly
g. Encourage citizens to contact officer directly

4. **Identify area problems**
   a. Attend community meetings
   b. Analyze crime and calls-for-service data
   c. Contact citizens and businesses
   d. Conduct business and residential surveys
   e. Ask about other problems when answering calls

5. **Communicate with supervisors, other officers and citizens about the nature of the area and its problems**
   a. Maintain beat bulletin board in station
   b. Leave notes in boxes of other officers
   c. Discuss area with supervisor

6. **Investigate/do research to deter-mine sources of problems**
   a. Talk to people involved
   b. Analyze crime data
   c. Observe situation if possible (stakeout)

7. **Plan ways of dealing with problem**
   a. Analyze resources
   b. Discuss with supervisor, other officers
   c. Wrile Patrol Management Plan, review with supervisor

8. **Provide citizens information about ways they can handle problems (educate/empower)**
   a. Distribute crime prevention information
   b. Provide names and number of other responsible agencies; tell citizens how to approach these agencies

9. **Help citizens develop appropriate expectations about what police can do and teach them how to interact effectively with police**
   a. Attend community meetings/ make presentations
   b. Present school programs
   c. Write article for area paper
   d. Hold discussions with community leaders

10. **Develop resources for responding to problem**
    a. Talk with other officers, detectives, supervisors
    b. Talk with other agencies or individuals who could help

11. **Implement problem solution**
    a. Take whatever actions are called for

12. **Assess effectiveness of solution**
    a. Use data. feedback from persons who experienced the problem, and/or personal observation to determine whether problem has been solved

13. **Keep citizens informed**
    a. Officers tell citizens what steps have been taken to address a problem and with what results
    b. Detectives tell citizens what is happening with their cases

Source: T. N. Oettmeier and M. N. Wycoff, *Personnel Performance Evaluations in the Community Policing Context* (Washington, D.C.: Community Policing Consortium, 1997), 22.

With respect to the ways an officer's performance may be measured in an era of community policing, see one chief's opinion in Voices From the Field (next page).

In his analysis of police performance measurement, Moore (2002) makes a valuable distinction between police *production* (e.g., making arrests, reducing fear of crime) and production *costs* (i.e., how much it costs to produce these things). He suggests two important dimensions with respect to how much it costs for the police to accomplish their goals: First is the fair, efficient, and effective use of *financial resources* and second is the fair, efficient, and effective use of *force and authority*. It is suggested that the police need to account for the ways they spend the public's money and use force and authority. As Moore states:

The fact that the police themselves report on their *accomplishments* (reducing crime, making arrests) while outsiders focus on the police *use of authority* suggests that the police are not really owning up to the costs they impose on the pub-

Voices From the Field
Edward Davis, Chief
Lowell, Massachusetts, Police Department

Question: How do you measure police officer performance in a community-policing environment?

Answer: Police leaders of the twenty-first century confront significant challenges, especially in light of the changes our profession has experienced over the past decade. Community policing, once a rarity, has become an expectation. But how does this community expectation translate into measurable dimensions of the individual officer on the street? Mark Moore addresses this important question in his book *Recognizing Value in Policing*, where he makes a compelling argument that crime reductions are an important but only one-dimensional view of the true value that community policing brings. According to Moore, today's police department must hold offenders to account, reduce fear, enhance security, structure a community-wide defense against crime, regulate public spaces, and control traffic. Police, in addition, are responsible for emergency medical and social services of all kinds.

At its core, policing is a paradoxical profession: above all else, police seek to prevent violence. To accomplish this task, we authorize them to use violence. A police officer responds to a military-like command structure and, at the same time, is expected to build relationships with nearly every type of person in the community where he or she works. It is vital that we clearly define our expectations for the patrol officer so that we do not simply send police officers from one emergency to another, giving them little time to build relationships or solve underlying problems.

Courage is an important trait for a police officer. Clearly a police officer must have the courage to venture into physically dangerous incidents. Police defend the weak and may confront danger at risk to personal safety. Good police officers, however, must also be courageous in a more subtle way. They must speak for justice on the street corner and in the locker room. Their courage must include the willingness to stand up to colleagues who do things that are harmful to their organization and the community. This personal courage and commitment to justice must be built upon an internalized understanding of right and wrong.

Police officers must be technically proficient in their work. Obviously, they must understand the law, respect the Constitution, and never abuse the authority with which society entrusts them. But this isn't enough: they also need to solve problems. They must be vigilant in crime-generating places and take necessary action against people and situations. They must be cognizant of the fact that preventing crime is their primary job. The failure to prevent requires a prompt response to apprehend and prosecute the offender. This dimension requires flexibility in attitude and a willingness to try new, unconventional solutions. They must understand the changing role of the police function and how that applies to their individual work.

Police officers have always required good communication skills. This skill becomes more important in a community-policing environment. It is not easy to engage people in conversation. It requires self-esteem, fortitude, and practice. Police today must be sufficiently skilled in this dimension to engage the community individually and in groups. A kind word or a simple greeting on the part of a uniformed officer sends a powerful message of openness and desire to help to the community. Presentations to community groups accomplish the same goal with a wider audience. Officers use these skills to enable their organization to become equal partners with the community. They must respect the growing diversity of police organizations themselves and the country where they live. They must never, ever discriminate against anybody on the basis of race, sex, cultural background, religion, or any other factor that an individual cannot control.

No matter how many mayors, community leaders, and even police chiefs endorse the idea of community policing, it will not be successful until individual officers actively engage the community and work to overcome problems. The expectations of the first line supervisor for his or her officers are of the greatest consequence to the officer on the street. There are few positions in government that play such a pivotal role to the everyday life of our citizens and to the future of our neighborhoods than that of the beat officer. ✦

lic in doing their work. They act as though they are not responsible for the way that they are using both money and force and authority. (127–128)

In general, it is suggested that police departments should begin to routinely measure and report on their use of force and authority as well as the amount of money they spend. The report should then be audited by an outside agency rather than be produced by the agency itself.

Attributes of healthy police departments. The above discussion on police goals and measurement provides a framework for what a police department needs to do to become and remain healthy in a democratic society. The following list, put together by a panel of experts for the National Institute of Justice (Travis and Brann 1997), examines this concept further by describing six attributes that a healthy police department should incorporate into its operational practices:

Attribute One. The healthy police organization knows what it wants to accomplish. It has articulated goals that can be expressed in an operational form, not as general as "To serve and protect." These goals can be appreciated by the people who have to carry them out. The goals can be assessed, meaning that there are measures of things that are reflective of the goals.

Attribute Two. The healthy police organization needs to know its citizens. Are they getting what they want? What they are entitled to? These citizens are not just those who call and complain, who summon the police, but residents in a neighborhood, businesses, and so on. Finally, there are those whom we often think of as the objects of police control: the offenders. They, too, are people who need to be considered in terms of their experiences with the police. There are a variety of user surveys that could measure transactions with citizens—for example, periodic citizen surveys of the community.

Attribute Three. The healthy police organization knows its business, the demands that are placed upon it. Calls for service are a readily available source of information in this regard. The department needs to know why "business" is increasing or decreasing, and knowing more about business is not to be limited to relying on calls for service. There are a variety of other ways that business comes to police. For example, problem-oriented policing requires not just random responses or responses to individual incidents but responses that are planned and coordinated to accomplish some objectives.

Attribute Four. The healthy police organization knows what it's doing about the demands of business. It has the ability to monitor resource allocations and officer activities. In terms of community policing, it knows what other agencies and organizations are doing that are pertinent to problems it's trying to deal with.

Attribute Five. A healthy police organization knows things about its people—things that would tell us what people get from jobs, what they are looking for from their jobs, what motivates them about their work, and what demoralizes them. Knowing these things would help drive decisions about supervision, training, recruitment, and job design. The obvious implication in terms of measurement here is conducting surveys within the organization.

Attribute Six. The healthy police organization feeds back information to people and groups who need to know, whether these are neighborhood groups that need to know more about the kind of service that they're getting, victim's groups, or its constituents within the organization.

Managing Group Behavior

Police managers need to be well informed about managing group behavior and possible conflict between and among groups. Because today's police departments tend to be relatively diverse in cultural background and level of skills, it is natural that different groups will have different—often conflicting—demands on management levels. The remainder of this chapter will discuss the varied nature and impact of these groups—both formal and informal—on management and how management must constructively deal with them.

Police Subcultures

Although the organization chart in Figure 4.3 depicts the formal structure of a police department, the way a department operates actually depends more on *informal* organizational arrangements. Individual beliefs, values, and norms in police departments are strongly influenced by group behavior, especially by experienced officers. As will be discussed in greater detail in subsequent chapters, **socialization** in policing occurs when recruits learn the values and behavioral patterns of experienced officers. From this early socialization, police officers tend to develop a different view of their job from that of their managers. For example, Reuss-Ianni (1983), in her study of New York

Police subcultures develop when younger, less experienced officers learn and inculcate the attitudes and behaviors of older, more experienced officers.

police, observed that these divergent views result in two distinct subcultures within the same organization, namely a **manager's culture** and a **street cop's culture**.

This differing perspective of the patrol officer's job develops because the manager's view is often shaped by experiences that remove him or her from the street reality of officers. One example common to police work is the *ends-means dilemma*. Police managers must be concerned with both ends (i.e., results) and means (i.e., how the results are achieved), whereas officers may be concerned primarily with ends (i.e., making an arrest is more important than protecting constitutional rights). Managers are concerned with departmental priorities, policies, and procedures, whereas officers are concerned with doing the job "according to the street," often acquired not from the department's view of reality but from the officer's perspective, determined by trying to "survive." These differing perspectives can result in an adversarial relationship, where street cops maintain their own "code," which can include the set of rules described in Inside Policing 4.5.

Inside Policing 4.5   Street Cop's Code

1. Take care of your partner first, then the other officers.
2. Don't "give up" (inform on) another cop; be secretive about the behavior of other officers.
3. Show balls; take control of a situation and don't back down.
4. Be aggressive when necessary, but don't go looking for trouble.
5. Don't interfere in another officer's sector or work area.
6. Do your fair share of work and don't leave work for the next shift; however, don't do too much work.
7. If you get caught making a mistake, don't implicate anybody else.
8. Other cops, but not necessarily managers, should be told if another officer is dangerous or "crazy."
9. Don't trust new officers until they have been checked out.
10. Don't volunteer information; tell others only what they need to know.
11. Avoid talking too much or too little; both are suspicious.
12. Protect your ass; don't give managers of the system an opportunity to get you.
13. Don't make waves; don't make problems for the system or managers.
14. Don't "suck up" to supervisors.
15. Know what your supervisor and other managers expect.
16. Don't trust managers; they may not look out for your interests.

Source: Adapted from E. Reuss-Ianni, *Two Cultures of Policing: Street Cops and Management Cops* (New Brunswick, CT: Transaction Books, 1983), 13–16.

Because both the manager's and the street cop's cultures must relate to the expectations of the communities they serve, there are both public and private worlds of policing. The **public world of policing** is presented to the public as the essence of police work: dedicated public servants performing dangerous work for our safety. Although the managers' and officers' perspectives of police work may differ, neither group tends to be completely candid because both have a vested interest in maintaining an image that avoids controversy. For example, if officers use excessive force to make an arrest, they will probably not admit it because of the street-culture norm to be secretive about illegal or inappropriate behavior. Managers may attempt to uncover inappropriate behavior, but they may not disclose it or they may disclose only parts of it. There may be potentially serious adverse consequences to the department, or they may be willing to disregard illegal tactics if a desirable result is obtained. Police managers, if they are to be effective leaders, however, must be willing to deal with such situations, both formally and informally, as the need arises.

In general, the **private world of policing** has been characterized as politically conservative, closed, or secretive, with a high degree of cynicism and an emphasis on loyalty, solidarity, and respect for authority (Doyle 1980). Undoubtedly, this private world of the patrol officer's culture has the strongest influence on the socialization process throughout the department and most likely the greatest impact on police behavior. A significant problem for managers is when the behavior dictated by the worker's culture conflicts with both departmental and community interests. This conflict is most apparent when a certain degree of deviant behavior (e.g., excessive force, racism, free meals, or gratuities) becomes acceptable, or at least tolerated, at the street level. Police managers must be willing to deal strongly with such behavior from both ethical and legal perspectives. Accordingly, police managers need to be aware of group pressures—especially with respect to the street culture—and how they influence officer behavior either positively or negatively.

Employee Organizations

Historically, the best-known police employee organization has been the **police union**, which is made up of police officers and is their official representative in collective bargaining with the employer. Because police departments operate on a local level, there is no single national police union. Instead, local departments may belong to one of many national unions. The largest include the Fraternal Order of Police (FOP) and the International Union of Police Associations (IUPA), which is affiliated with the AFL-CIO. Other local police unions are affiliated with the Teamsters; the American Federation of State, County, and Municipal Employees (AFSCME); and other smaller national unions.

Although a union is an employee organization, not all employee organizations are unions. As Walker (1992) has pointed out, police officers have historically belonged to *fraternal organizations*. These groups are generally organized along ethnic lines. Nationally, for example, Latino officers are represented by the Latino Police Officers Association and Asian officers by the Asian Police Officers Association. Employee groups may also form their own local organizations. In San Francisco, for example, the African American officers' association is known as Officers for Justice (OFJ); in San Jose, California, it is known as the South Bay Association of Black Law Enforcement Officers (SABLE).

As departments become more diverse in their makeup, additional employee organizations develop. For instance, many departments have women's organizations (e.g., the Women's Police Officer Association), and gay and lesbian officers are represented in California by the Golden State Peace Officers Association. Furthermore, police officers and supervisors are often represented by their own associations. It is apparent that if departments are to maintain a healthy work environment, police managers must deal effectively with the diverse needs, expectations, and conflicts of these employee organizations. In general, it is best to establish a working relationship with each group and to share with them the department's expectations. Then, if there are conflicts, they can be dealt with in an open and honest manner.

Police Unions

The police labor movement has gone through several stages. Police associations were evident as early as the 1890s but did not establish themselves until the mid-1960s. Two previous attempts made to unionize police employees failed. The first attempt failed after the Boston police strike of 1919, which created a backlash against police unions throughout the country. The second, between 1943 and 1947, failed because of unfavorable court decisions and strong resistance by police chiefs.

Despite the importance of the structure of police unions in understanding policing in America, there exists little systematic information about them. Kadleck (2003) examined 648 police unions from across the country and found that the typical union was founded after 1960 and consists of a voluntary group of police officers headed by an officer who is elected to that position. Leaders of unions also report having influence over policy creation and indicate a general lack of trust among police managers.

Since the mid-1960s, police unionization has had a great deal of success. Several developments contributed toward this success, including the following:

1. ***Lagging salaries and benefits.*** Officers were angry over the fact that their salaries and benefits had fallen behind those available in other equivalent positions.

2. ***Poor police management.*** Officers were angry and alienated over the way their departments were managed. At the time, police chiefs had virtually unlimited power in managing their departments, and many operated in an arbitrary and vindictive manner. Officers who were critical of management were often punished with frequent transfers and assignments to low-status jobs. Officer participation in any form of decision making was virtually nonexistent.

3. ***Social and political alienation.*** During the social unrest of the 1960s and 1970s, police officers felt that they were being attacked from all sides; for example, they resented accusations of discrimination from civil rights groups and felt that Supreme Court decisions were "handcuffing" them in fighting crime.

4. ***A new generation of officers.*** The movement toward unionization was led by a new generation of officers; they were generally younger and more assertive than the established leaders of police fraternal groups.

5. ***The law-and-order mood.*** Unionization succeeded, in part, because unlike the earlier two periods, there was little opposition to them. Because there was great concern over "law and order," mayors and council members did not want to appear hostile toward the police; thus, they were less likely to become involved in matters of unionization.

6. ***A new legal climate.*** Unions also succeeded because the attitudes of the courts changed dramatically. Previously, they held that police and public employees had no right to unionize, but by the 1960s, they had adopted the position that employees did have that right. (Adapted from Walker 1992, 371)

The early development of police unionization was controversial and often shrouded in conflict, especially with police management. Once established, unions demanded higher salaries; better fringe benefits; more participation in how, when, and where officers worked; and more elaborate disciplinary procedures to protect employees. They also tended to fight back against the charges of critics. In many police departments, employee organizations have become major obstacles to effecting change. What began as an attempt to improve the lot of the working police officer has often become a barrier to improving standards and performance. Of course, members of police unions may not agree with this perspective; from their point of view, they are simply acting to preserve "hard won" gains. In addition, some unions are vocal proponents of organizational change that will improve performance. In some cases, police unions may be more progressive than police managers.

The issues that are negotiated between police unions and management tend to fall into three categories: salaries and benefits, conditions of work, and grievance procedures.

Salaries and benefits are influenced by a number of factors, including the economic health of a community, the inflation rate, salaries in comparable police departments (or in comparable positions in other occupations), management's resistance, the militancy of the union, and the amount of public support for either labor or management.

Conditions of work include a broad range of possible issues, many of which have traditionally been considered management prerogatives, such as the procedures used for evaluation, reassignment, and promotions; equipment and uniforms; number of officers assigned to a car or section of the community; how seniority and education will be used in assignments and promotions; hours worked and off-duty employment; and training and professional development. Critics argue that this kind of union activity is detrimental to the effective management of the department and the provision of quality services to the community (see Bouza 1985). Others, however, blame the poor management and treatment of employees for promoting such union activity; they view employee influence over management prerogatives in positive terms, potentially leading to improved managerial practices (see Kleismet 1985).

Grievance procedures are concerned with the process to be used in accusing an officer of a violation of departmental policies and procedures of law. Usually, this process involves an identification of officer rights (which may even be codified in state law), how the complaints must be filed, how evidence is obtained and processed, how disciplinary decisions will be made, and what appeals, if any, will be allowed. Quite often, police unions, in an effort to protect employees from arbitrary treatment by managers, will demand elaborate grievance mechanisms that frustrate attempts to respond to almost any type of inappropriate police behavior. However, grievance procedures may also be a useful way of clarifying work rules and of understanding and agreeing on performance expectations.

Significant input in the managerial process by police unions is here to stay. It is important to recognize that union leaders often have a strong informal influence over departmental members. Consequently, these leaders should be treated with respect by police managers, and they should be kept abreast of managerial decisions in order that they can share this information with the membership. To facilitate this process, union representatives should be encouraged to serve on task forces and participate in management meetings. An open and participative relationship with the union may help to avoid the costly and unpleasant effects that often result from strikes, job actions (i.e., work slowdowns or speedups), refusals to negotiate, media attention, and perhaps most important, may create an improved working environment.

Summary

The managerial process is concerned with organizing, leading, planning, and controlling. The history of police management theory begins with the classical theorists, who stressed a bureaucratic, paramilitary approach to organizational design. Beginning in the early 1970s, behavioral theorists began attacking the classical approach, placing greater emphasis on worker participation, job satisfaction, more flexible designs, and recognition of the complex nature of the police role. The final theoretical development, contemporary police theory, emphasized police departments as open systems and the use of contingency theory. Private sector processes also became influential, including the use of corporate strategy, total quality management, and principles of reinventing government. There has been much criticism of the traditional paramilitary design, which continues to be influential. Part of this influence includes increased use of PPUs, aggressive police methods, and the manner in which Compstat is utilized.

It is important to establish realistic and measurable police goals, including both quantitative and qualitative indicators. In order to properly evaluate a department's overall performance, both external (community) and internal (departmental) goals should be assessed. New dimensions of organization performance might include various "costs" of policing, including reporting how much money is spent and the use of force and authority. Because today's police departments are culturally diverse and vary widely with respect to skill levels, the managing of group behavior becomes important. From this perspective, both formal and informal groups (including police subcultures) are involved. Finally, police unions, despite being controversial, have improved benefits and job conditions. It is important for management to develop a working relationship with union leaders.

Critical Thinking Questions

1. What aspects of classical and behavioral management theories have contributed the most to today's police organizations?

2. Provide an example of why police managers need to be aware of both systems and contingency theory and how these theories may help them to develop appropriate operating policies for their organizations.

3. With respect to contemporary police management theories, what impact do you think private sector approaches have had, and will have, in the future?

4. What influence does the paramilitary organization design have on present-day policing. Is it still necessary?

5. What impact has broken-windows theory had on policing? What about the future?

6. How would you use the Compstat process if you were a high-level police manager?

7. What is your opinion of Moore's proposal for measuring police performance? As a police chief, how would you attempt to implement these measures?

8. How would you, as a first-line supervisor, handle the difference between the manager's and street cop's culture?

References

Auten, J. H. 1981. "The Paramilitary Model of Police and Police Professionalism." *Police Studies* 4: 67–78.

Bercal, T. E. 1970. "Calls for Police Assistance." *American Behavioral Scientist* 13: 681–691.

Bittner, E. 1970. *The Function of the Police in Modern Society.* Washington, D.C.: U.S. Government Printing Office.

Bouza, A. V. 1985. "Police Unions: Paper Tigers or Roaring Lions?" In W. A. Geller (ed.), *Police Leadership in America: Crises and Opportunity,* pp. 241–280. New York: Praeger.

Bureau of Justice Statistics. 1997. *Implementing the National Incident-Based Reporting System: A Project Status Report.* Washington, D.C.: Department of Justice.

Cacioppo, R. L., and P. Mock. 1985. "The Relationship of Self-actualization, Stress and Quality of Work Experience in Senior Level Australian Police Officers." *Police Studies* 8: 173–186.

Cordner, G. W. 1978. "Review of Work Motivation Theory and Research for the Police Manager." *Journal of Police Science and Administration* 6: 186–292.

Couper, D. C., and Lobitz, S. H. 1991. *Quality Policing: The Madison Experience.* Washington, D.C.: Police Executive Research Forum.

Cumming, E., Cumming, I., and Edell, L. 1965. "Policeman as Philosopher, Guide and Friend." *Social Problems* 12: 276–286.

Dodenhoff, P. C. 1996. "LEN Salutes its 1996 People of the Year, the NYPD and Its Compstat Process." *Law Enforcement News, December: 1, 4.*

Doyle, M. A. 1980. "Police Culture: Open or Closed." In V. A. Leonard (ed.), *Fundamentals of Law Enforcement: Problems and Issues,* pp. 61–83. St. Paul, MN: West.

Engel, R. S. 2003. *How Police Supervisory Styles Influence Patrol Officer Behavior.* Washington, D.C.: National Institute of Justice.

Franz, V., and Jones, D. M. 1987. "Perceptions of Organizational Performance in Suburban Police Departments: A Critique of the Military Model." *Journal of Police Science and Administration* 15: 153–161.

Gerth, H. H., and Mills, C. W. 1946. *From Max Weber: Essays in Sociology.* New York: Oxford University Press.

Goldstein, H. 1968. "Police Response to Urban Crisis." *Public Administration Review* 28: 417–418.

———. 1977. *Policing a Free Society.* Cambridge, MA: Ballinger.

———. 1987. "Toward Community-oriented Policing: Potential, Basic Requirements, and Threshold Questions." *Crime & Delinquency* 33: 6–30.

———. 1990. *Problem-oriented Policing.* Philadelphia: Temple University Press.

"Good News Just Gets Better for NYPD." 1997. *Law Enforcement News* July/August: 18.

Gore, A. 1994. *Common Sense Government Works Better and Costs Less: Third Report of the National Performance Review.* Washington, D.C.: Government Printing Office.

Greene, J. A. 1999. "Zero Tolerance: A Case Study of Police Policies and Practices in New York City." *Crime & Delinquency* 45: 171–187.

Greene, J. R. 1989. "Police Officer Job Satisfaction and Community Perceptions: Implications for Community-oriented Policing." *Journal of Research in Crime and Delinquency* 26: 168–183.

———, 2000. "Community Policing in America: Changing Nature, Structure and Function of the Police." In *Criminal Justice 2000, Volume 3: Policies, Processes, and Decisions for the Criminal Justice System,* pp. 299–370. Washington, D.C.: National Institute of Justice.

Griffin, G. R., Dunbar, R. L. M., and McGill, M. E. 1978. "Factors Associated with Job Satisfaction Among Police Personnel." *Journal of Police Science and Administration* 6: 77–85.

Harcourt, B. E. 2001. *Illusions of Order: The False Promise of Broken Windows Policing.* Cambridge, MA: Harvard University Press.

Hayeslip, P. W., and Cordner, G. W. 1987. "The Effects of Community-oriented Patrol on Police Officer Attitudes." *American Journal of Police* 6: 95–119.

Herbert, S. 2001. "Policing the Contemporary City: Fixing Broken Windows or Shoring up Neo-Liberalism?" *Theoretical Criminology* 5: 445–466.

Hoover, L. T. 1996. "Translating Total Quality Management from the Private Sector to Policing." In L. T. Hoover (ed.), *Quantifying Quality in Policing*. Washington, D.C.: Police Executive Research Forum.

Hornick, J. P., Burrows, B. A., and Phillips, D. M. 1989. "An Impact Evaluation of the Edmonton Neighborhood Foot Patrol Program," November. Paper presented at the annual meeting of the American Society of Criminology, Reno, NV. .

Kadleck, C. 2003. "Police Employee Organizations". *Policing: An International Journal of Police Strategies and Management* 26: 341–351.

Katz, C. M., Webb, V. J. and Schaefer, D. R. 2001. "An Assessment of the Impact of Quality-of-Life Policing on Crime and Disorder." *Justice Quarterly* 18: 825–876.

Kleismet, R. B. 1985. "The Chief and the Union: May the Force Be with You." In W. A. Geller (ed.), *Police Leadership in America: Crisis and Opportunity*, pp. 281–285. New York: Praeger.

Kocieniewski, D. 1998. "Police Official's Ouster Sought in Case of Doctored Statistics." *New York Times* February 28: A11.

Kraska, P. B., and Cubellis, L. J. 1997. "Militarizing Mayberry and Beyond: Making Sense of American Paramilitary Policing." *Justice Quarterly* 14: 607–629.

Kraska, P. B., and Kappeler, V. E. 1997. "Militarizing American Police: The Rise and Normalization of Paramilitary Units." *Social Problems* 44: 1–18.

Kraska, P. B., and Paulsen, D. J. 1997. "Grounded Research into U.S. Paramilitary Policing: Forging the Iron Fist Inside the Velvet Glove." *Policing and Society* 7: 253–270.

Law Enforcement News. 2003. "Compstat-type Anticrime Programs Put Down New Roots Far from New York." *Law Enforcement News* February 28: 1.

Lefkowitz, J. 1973. "Attitudes of Police Toward Their Job." In J. R. Snibbe and H. M. Snibbe (eds.), *The Urban Policeman in Transition*, pp. 203–232. Springfield, IL: C. C. Thomas.

——. 1974. "Job Attitudes of Police: Overall Description and Demographic Correlates." *Journal of Vocational Behavior* 5: 221–230.

Maguire, E. R. 1997. "Structural Change in Large Municipal Police Organizations During the Community Policing Era." *Justice Quarterly* 14: 547–576.

Mastrofski, S. D. 1992. "What Does Community Policing Mean for Daily Police Work?" *National Institute of Justice Journal* August: 23–27.

McElroy, J. E., Cosgrove, C. A., and Sadd, S. 1993. *Community Policing: The CPOP in New York*. Newbury Park, CA: Sage.

Moore, M. H. 2002. *Recognizing Value in Policing: The Challenge of Measuring Police Performance*. Washington, D.C.: Police Executive Research Forum.

Moore, M. H., and Trojanowicz, R. 1988. "Corporate Strategies for Policing." *Perspectives on Policing*. Washington, D.C.: National Institute of Justice.

Mottaz, C. 1983. "Alienation Among Police Officers." *Journal of Police Science and Administration* 11: 23–30.

National Institute of Justice. 1997. *Measuring What Matters. Part Two: Developing Measures of What the Police Do*. Washington, D.C.: Department of Justice.

Novak, K., Hartman, J., Holsinger, A., and Turner, M. 1999. "The Effects of Aggressive Policing of Disorder on Serious Crime." *Policing* 22: 171–190.

Oettmeier, T. N., and Wycoff, M. A. 1997. *Personnel Performance Evaluations in the Community Policing Context*. Washington, D.C.: Community Policing Consortium.

Osborne, D., and Gaebler, T. 1992. *Reinventing Government: How the Entrepreneurial Spirit Is Transforming the Public Sector from Schoolhouse to Statehouse, City Hall to Pentagon*. Reading, MA: Addison-Wesley.

Parnas, R. 1967. "The Police Response to the Domestic Disturbance." *Wisconsin Law Review* Fall: 914–960.

Reibstein, L. 1997. "NYPD Black and Blue." *Newsweek* June 2: 66, 68.

Reuss-Ianni, E. 1983. *Two Cultures of Policing: Street Cops and Management Cops.* New Brunswick, CT: Transaction Books.

Roberg, R. R. 1979. *Police Management and Organizational Behavior: A Contingency Approach.* St. Paul, MN: West.

Roberg, R. R., Kuykendall, J., and Novak, K. 2002. *Police Management,* 3rd ed. Los Angeles: Roxbury.

Rosenbaum, D. P., Yeh, S., and Wilkinson, D. L. 1994. "Impact of Community Policing on Police Personnel: A Quasi-Experimental Test." *Crime & Delinquency* 40: 331–353.

Sandler, G. B., and Mintz, E. 1974. "Police Organizations: Their Changing Internal and External Relationships." *Journal of Police Science and Administration* 2: 458–463.

Sherman, L. 1990. "Police Crackdowns: Initial and Residual Deterrence." In M. Tonry and N. Morris, eds., *Crime and Justice: A Review of Research* 1–48. Chicago, IL: University of Chicago Press.

Sherman, L. W., Gartin, P. R. and Buerger, M. E. 1989. "Hot Spots of Predatory Crime: Routine Activities and the Criminology of Place." *Criminology* 27: 27–55.

Skogan, W. G., and Hartnett, S. M. 1997. *Community Policing, Chicago Style.* New York: Oxford University Press.

Smith, B. 1940. *Police Systems in the United States.* New York: Harper & Row.

Spelman, W., and Eck, J. E. 1987. "Newport News Tests Problem-oriented Policing." *NIJ Reports* January–February: 2–8.

Travis, J., and Brann, J. E. 1997. *Measuring What Matters, Part Two: Developing Measures of What the Police Do.* Washington, D.C.: National Institute of Justice.

Vito, G. F., and Kunselman, J. 2000. "Reinventing Government: The Views of Police Middle Managers." *Police Quarterly* 3: 315–330.

Walker, S. 1992. *The Police in America: An Introduction, 2nd ed.* New York: McGraw-Hill.

Watson, E. M., Stone, A. R., and DeLuca, S. T. 1998. *Strategies for Community Policing.* Upper Saddle River, NJ: Prentice-Hall.

West, J. P., Berman, E. M., and Milakovich, M. W. 1994. "Implementing TQM in Local Government: The Leadership Challenge." *Public Productivity and Management Review* 17: 195–192.

Weisburd, D., and McElroy, J. E. 1988. "Enacting the CPO Role: Findings from the New York City Pilot Program in Community Policing." In J. R. Greene and S. D. Mastrofski (eds.), *Community Policing: Rhetoric or Reality?,* pp. 89–102. New York: Praeger.

Williams, E. J. 1995. *Implementing Community Policing: A Documentation and Assessment of Organizational Change.* Ph.D. dissertation. Portland, OR: Portland State University.

Wilson, D. G., and Bennett, S. F. 1994. "Officers' Response to Community Policing: Variations on a Theme." *Crime & Delinquency* 40: 354–370.

Wilson, J. Q. 1968. *Varieties of Police Behavior.* Cambridge, MA: Harvard University.

Wilson, J. Q., and Boland, B. 1978. "The Effect of Police on Crime." *Law and Society Review* 12: 367–390.

Wilson, J. Q., and Kelling, G. 1982. "Broken Windows: The Police and Neighborhood Safety." *Atlantic Monthly* March: 29–38.

Wilson, O. W. 1950. *Police Administration.* New York: McGraw-Hill.

Wilson, O. W., and McLaren, R. C. 1977. *Police Administration,* 4th ed. New York: McGraw-Hill.

Worral, J. L. 2002. *Does "Broken Windows" Law Enforcement Reduce Serious Crime?* Sacramento, CA: The California Institute for County Government.

Wycoff, M. A., and Skogan, W. G. 1993. *Community Policing in Madison: Quality from the Inside Out.* Washington, D.C.: National Institute of Justice.

Zhao, J. 1996. *Why Police Organizations Change: A Study of Community-oriented Policing.* Washington, D.C.: Police Executive Research Forum.

Suggested Websites for Further Study

Learn More About Total Quality Management
http://www.skyenet.net/~leg/tqm.htm
Bureau of Justice Statistics, U.S. Department of Justice
http://www.ojp.usdoj.gov/bjs/welcome.html
Fraternal Order of Police
http://www.grandlodgefop.org
International Union of Police Associations
http://www.sddi.com/iupa
Detroit Police Department
http://www.ci.detroit.mi.us/police.compstat.html
Philadelphia Police Department
http://www.ppdonline.org/ppd_compstat.html
New York Police Department
http://www.nyc.gov/htm/nypd/html/chfdept/compstat-process.html ✦

## Chapter 5

Police Organization and Change

Chapter Outline

Key Terms

balance of power	job redesign
beat teams	learning organization
CAPS	organizational change
change strategies	quality circle
EPD	quality leadership
group norms	rapid-response units
inertia	R & D
innovation	WHAM
INOP	

As discussed previously, the police have traditionally been organized and managed according to classical prescriptions. In other words, a department is structurally designed in a hierarchical, bureaucratic manner, where the leadership style is authoritarian and employees are tightly controlled. It is extremely difficult to make significant and sustained changes to such traditional, paramilitary departments. As past discussions have indicated, a less bureaucratic, decentralized orientation allows a department to more readily adapt to community needs and expectations. The purpose of this chapter is to describe how the change process and police strategies, especially toward community policing, can be applied in a constructive manner. Furthermore, the importance of developing a climate of innovation (and learning) will be discussed; without such a climate, the amount of effort required to implement new programs cannot be sustained.

Organizational Change

Organizational change occurs when an organization adopts new ideas or behaviors (Pierce and Delbeq 1977). Usually, an innovative idea, such as a new patrol strategy or job design, is introduced and employee behavioral changes are supposed to follow. Consequently, the ultimate success of any organizational change effort depends on how well the organization can alter the behavioral patterns of its personnel—that is, change old behavior patterns to new behavioral patterns to "fit" the new strategy or method. Of course, the greater the degree of change required, the more significant will be the behavioral changes required. For instance, community policing requires a substantial change in the role and job design not only of police officers but also of their supervisors and managers. Thus, a transition toward community policing requires substantially greater behavioral change by personnel than would simply changing a patrol tactic or procedure. The corollary to this behavioral change process is that the greater the degree of planned change, the greater will be the resistance to it. A discussion follows of how resistance to change in policing develops.

Resistance to Change

Probably the most common characteristic of change is people's resistance to it. In general, people do not like to change their behavior. Adapting to a new environment or learning a new work method often results in feelings of stress and fear of the unknown (e.g., will I like it? Will I be able to do it well?). The following is a discussion of the major reasons why resistance to change—using community policing as an example—is so common in police departments.

Inertia. A great deal of **inertia,** or "doing things as they have always been done," is strongly associated with paramilitary departments. People have what is known as "sunk costs" in their jobs and routines, including time, energy, and experience; these are powerful forces in resisting change. Individuals or groups with many such "investments" sunk into a particular department or job may not want changes, regardless of their merit. Community policing, for example, requires officers to do many of their old tasks in new ways and to take on new tasks with which they are not familiar. They may be "asked to identify and solve a broad range of problems; reach out to elements of the community that previously were outside their orbit; and put their careers at risk by taking on unfamiliar and challenging responsibilities" (Skogan and Hartnett 1997, 71). These expectations are often beyond the officers' capabilities and the traditional roles for which they were initially selected and trained (Lurigio and Rosenbaum 1994). There is little doubt that most officers would rather do what they believe they were hired for and what they perceive to be the "real" police role: crime fighting. Consequently, community policing is often dismissed as "social work," which takes important time away from their crime-fighting activities.

Management personnel will have the same inertia factor at work because they also have been selected and trained to do traditional policing. Although inertia occurs at all managerial levels, except possibly at the very top when a new police chief is brought in to implement community policing, the attitudes of sergeants are especially important. Because sergeants have the most direct influence over the day-to-day activities of street officers, it is crucial that they "buy into" the new program, promoting the department's new policies and procedures. In order to do so, sergeants will need to act as facilitators and trainers as well as supervisors (see discussion in previous chapter on supervisory styles). Mitigating against this facilitating and training role, however, is the newness of community policing; most sergeants have never experienced it themselves. They too must learn new skills and behaviors and what is expected of them.

Misunderstandings. Resistance to change is likely to occur when officers do not clearly understand the purpose, techniques, or consequences of a planned change because of inadequate or misunderstood communication. A major problem concerns the uncertainty about consequences of change. If employees are not told how they will be affected by change, rumors and speculation will follow, and resistance and even sabotage may be strong enough to severely limit the change effort. When change is imposed on officers, instead of occurring as a result of their participation, misunderstandings are more likely.

When police departments are attempting to move to community policing, they frequently make the mistake of not clearly articulating what new roles will be created and the effect of those new roles on all involved. For instance, in Houston when evaluators interviewed officers who were assigned to the innovative neighborhood-oriented policing program (often referred to by the officers as "nobody on patrol"), they discovered that officers frequently had no idea what the program was about or what they should be doing differently (Sadd and Grinc 1994). In addition, departments often do not allow officers to participate in the planning and development of the new program in order to gain a sense of "ownership."

Group norms. As discussed in the previous chapter, groups have an important impact on the behavior and attitudes of their members. **Group norms,** or expected behavior from group members, can be a powerful factor in resistance to change. If individual officers follow the norms strictly (e.g., that only law enforcement activities are important), they will not easily perceive the need for change. If significant departmental changes are to occur, police managers must consider group norms and influences and involve group consensus and decision-making in planning for change. The major way to achieve such involvement is to allow for participatory management (discussed below).

Balance of power. Changes that are perceived to threaten the autonomy, authority, power, or status of a group or unit will most likely encounter resistance, regardless of their merit. For instance, such resistance was well documented in the team-policing experiments of the 1970s, when departments attempted to decentralize their operations into neighborhood teams (see Sherman, Milton, and Kelley 1973). Because this approach provided more control and autonomy for lower-level management (sergeants), middle management (lieutenants and captains) resisted the change (by subverting and, in some cases, sabotaging the plans) for fear that they would lose authority, power, and status. Because the failure of most team-policing efforts can be traced, at least in part, to the lack of support by mid-level managers, it is crucial that police executives plan for their role in the change process.

Inside Policing 5.1 provides a glimpse as to the reasons officers resisted change in New York in that city's attempt to make a transition to community policing. Notice how virtually every reason overlaps, to some degree, with the major reasons for resistance discussed above. These reasons for resistance would be similar in most, if not all, traditional paramilitary police departments in the country.

Inside Policing 5.1   Resistance to Organizational Change in New York

The following are examples of reasons that some police officers in the New York City Police Department resisted change toward a community policing philosophy. These examples are based on informal discussions with officers. [Author's note: The department reduced its emphasis on community policing, at least in part, because of this resistance.]

Failure to see the need for change. Some officers believe that community policing is merely a result of the commissioner (chief) wanting to try out his ideas in New York. They see this as a grand management experiment attempted at their expense.

Confusion over new roles and fear of the unknown. Many officers do not fully understand their new roles or what the department expects of them. Some officers perceive a conflict between their new role, where they are asked to "serve the public," and their traditional role, in which they exerted coercive control over the community.

Fear of loss of status, security, and power. Many officers in New York believe they are doing a credible job in controlling crime and see themselves as having achieved a reasonable status in society; they have earned this status by being brave. Community policing, with its reduced emphasis on adventure and bravery and its enhanced focus on public service, has some officers fearing that their status will be diminished.

Lack of involvement with change. Some officers feel that they are simply being told this is the new philosophy and have no sense of participation in the decision. One superior officer stated after a training seminar, "Community policing is the new train—get on or get off." This attitude encourages the feeling that this program is being forced upon them, and they have no more intention of changing their philosophy of policing because the commissioner tells them to than they would change their political philosophy if the president told them to.

Threat to existing social relationships. While foot patrol officers are getting acquainted with merchants and other citizens who live and work in their assigned communities, the radio car cops are busy responding to calls and, as they say, "busting their butts." They are beginning to resent the department's preferential attitude toward the beat cops, and to resent the beat cops themselves, who they feel are not pulling their load and spend their time "schmoozing" with the public. One officer explained, "While I'm out here doing all the grunt work and risking my life, they're playing with the neighborhood kids or attending some community meeting."

Conflicting personal and organizational objectives. The police department is interested in getting officers to work with the citizens toward solving social problems, thereby improving the quality of life and making their streets safer. Some officers believe, however, that many of the problems brought forth by the public are not worthy of police attention and have little to do with crime. Although proponents of community policing believe that resolving such problems will create an environment less conducive to crime and thus lower the crime rate, to many officers this is a waste of their time, since the causes of crime go far beyond esthetic fixes to the immediate neighborhood. Some officers are also candid about their aversion to performing what they perceive as "social work." And they complain that after awhile, other officers do not see them as "real cops."

Source: Adapted from S. L. Pisani. 1992. "Dissecting Community Policing: Part 2." *Law Enforcement News*, May 31: 8, 10.

Overcoming Resistance to Change

The research to date provides some important lessons to help police managers overcome resistance to organizational change in moving toward community policing. For instance, in a national survey of more than 1,600 agencies (Wycoff 1995), police chiefs and sheriffs were asked about the lessons they learned from their experiences with community policing. The most frequently mentioned lessons were (1) the need for pre-implementation training of personnel, (2) the importance of taking a long view of the change process, (3) the need for support from elected officials and other city agencies, and (4) the importance of listening to and involving the community. In addition, 48 percent thought that implementation would require major changes in departmental policies or goals, 56 percent anticipated that rank-and-file employees would resist such changes, and 83 percent strongly supported the need for training in community policing and believed that existing training efforts were inadequate.

Evaluations of major programs in New York and Houston, in which attempts at community policing failed, and the concept has since been deemphasized, provide evidence of the difficulty of attempting to implement significant change—especially in large departments. Even after 10 years of experience with various aspects of community policing in New York, many officers "contended that there was little support among the rank and file" (Sadd and Grinc 1996, 8). In Houston, an independent report by Cresap Management Consultants pointed out a number of operational problems, including officers being torn between immediate reports of crime and preventive work required by community policing, officers being unprepared for their new tasks, and skepticism, even hostility, of many officers about the program's aims. The report further pointed out that it was unlikely that the department could recruit enough officers with the level of complex skills required to do community policing, particularly at current pay levels. The president of the Police Officers' Association stated that "most officers feel it's a hoax, renaming things and using a lot of buzz words and the like," and that "a lot of officers probably feel they're expected to be more like social workers than police officers" ("Study Criticizes Community Policing" 1991, B2).

A group of supervisors addressing common implementation problems with new policies and procedures.

Other major cities have also encountered critical problems in their attempts to implement community policing. For example, in both Los Angeles and Atlanta, officers could not sustain community-oriented projects unless they were freed from the draining effects of responding to frequent, and unpredictable, 911 calls. It takes a considerable amount of time and effort to set up and meet with the public, help define and research problems, and coordinate community and interagency involvement in attempting to solve defined problems. In Los Angeles, community policing officers were also dissatisfied over the conflict between what they were told to do (which was new) and how their performance was actually evaluated (by the old standards, including how many arrests they made) (Booz, Allen, and Hamilton 1992). Common implementation problems with community policing have been documented in a study of eight jurisdictions (Sadd and Grinc 1994, 1996), known as **innovative neighborhood-oriented policing (INOP).** These common implementation problems are discussed in Inside Policing 5.2.

Inside Policing 5.2   INOP: Implementation Challenges

The innovative neighborhood-oriented policing programs evaluated were Hayward, California; Houston, Texas; Louisville, Kentucky; New York; Norfolk, Virginia; Portland, Oregon; Prince George's County, Maryland; and Tempe, Arizona. The INOP jurisdictions varied greatly, as did the prior experiences of each department with community policing. Perhaps the most important contribution of the findings was that each of the sites experienced common implementation problems that hampered their ability to have the desired impacts, including:

1. There was minimal involvement of police officers, city agencies, and community residents in program design; consequently, knowledge of the structure and goals of the program and of community policing in general was lacking in all of these groups.

2. Often, community policing is defined and implemented solely as a police initiative to the virtual exclusion of other city agencies and to the communities it hopes to serve. One of the most important findings of the INOP research is that the education and

training of community residents regarding their roles in community policing is almost nonexistent.

3. The INOP research suggests that among the most difficult tasks of implementation are (a) educating and training police officers and administrators about the goals and techniques of community policing, (b) obtaining the cooperation of other city agencies in the community policing effort, (c) building trust between the police and residents of communities (particularly where there is a history of antagonistic relationships), and (d) stimulating from the outset community involvement in the planning and implementation of community policing.

Source: Adapted from S. Sadd and R. Grinc. *Implementation Challenges in Community Policing: Innovative Neighborhood-Oriented Policing in Eight Cities* (Washington, D.C.: National Institute of Justice, 1996).

As suggested by the above discussion, and by Inside Policing 5.1 and 5.2, a major factor in overcoming resistance to community policing is officer involvement and participation in the change process and program design. In a study of community-policing implementation and officer attitudes in six small-to-midsize agencies in North Carolina (Adams, Roche, and Arcury 2002), a major finding was that those who perceive a participatory management style were more supportive of the change toward community policing. Importantly, the strongest support for a move toward community policing was found among officers in one city that allowed for the most involvement in designing the program and showed the clearest support for community policing by the command staff. In addition, it was found that, compared to traditional officers, community-policing officers were significantly more satisfied with their jobs.

Although it may be a less onerous task for management to allow for high levels of participation in small or midsized departments, the importance of participatory management in bringing about constructive change is strongly supported in the research and should be utilized by departments of all sizes.

The Madison Experience

Possibly the earliest transition from traditional to community policing was in the Madison (Wisconsin) Police Department. The use of what was called quality leadership, including participation at all levels, smoothed the transition process and helped to overcome initial resistance to the new developments. The change process started in earnest within the department in the early 1980s, well before most of the present-day knowledge gained through research and evaluation was available. Thus, much of what the department accomplished in the way of change was groundbreaking. At the time, the department had approximately 280 commissioned personnel serving a community of approximately 175,000 (Couper and Lobitz 1991).

Laying the Foundation

In the early 1970s, with the appointment of a new chief, the Madison Police Department was operating on a high-control, central-authority model. This traditional style of police management continued through the early years of the chief's tenure but not without costs to the department and its members in terms of a high level of distrust, grievances, complaining, and confrontations. In 1981, after a four-month leave of absence, the chief decided that something had to be done regarding the department's internal problems. After discussions with rank-and-file officers, it became clear that a "lack of communication" was a primary concern and a new management or leadership style was necessary. Consequently, the chief decided to let employees participate more in organizational decisions and to take on the role of facilitator for himself. This decision led to the establishment of the Officers' Advisory Council (OAC) to provide advice to the chief.

The development of the OAC was critical in clearing the way for a major change in leadership style. The council consisted of 12 peer-selected employees who served for a two-year period. The OAC over time was given increased responsibility; it developed its ability to gather data and make recommendations using a problem-solving approach. The council learned that if it obtained data to support its recommendations, the recommendations would be put into practice; thus, it had significant input in departmental policies and procedures. The OAC's actions reflected the problem-solving and research orientation of the department's quality-improvement effort.

Key Elements to Change

Following development of the OAC, several key developments took place, including the formation of a committee on the future, a change in leadership style, the implementation of a new operating (experimental) district, and citizen involvement (Couper and Lobitz 1991; Wycoff and Skogan 1993). Each is described below.

1. Committee on the Future.

In 1984, a Committee on the Future was formed to look at trends and how they might affect the police department in the coming years. The committee was composed of a diverse group of members who had at least 15 years of service remaining; the intent was to have members who had a vested interest in the future of the department. A member of the OAC was appointed to serve on this committee in order to link the two groups. After a year of meeting two to four times a month, the committee released a report of its findings listing three major recommendations:

1. Get closer to the people we serve.

2. Make better use of available technology.

3. Develop and improve health and wellness in the workplace.

This thinking about the future caused the department to reexamine its structure, internal practices, and the direction in which it was moving.

2. Quality Leadership.

Early in 1985, almost parallel with the developments in the department, the mayor's office initiated a citywide effort to improve the Quality/Productivity (QP)—now known as TQM—of the city's departments. A four-day seminar conducted by W. Edwards Deming, at the time the leader of the quality movement in this country, was followed by a 15-day training seminar in QP principles and procedures for city employees. Five police employees attended the sessions, which covered team building, group processes, facilitator skills, and the gathering and use of data.

Following the QP training, the department articulated the management philosophy of **quality leadership,** to be used throughout the department, which included the following principles: teamwork for planning and goal setting; data-based problem solving; a customer orientation; employee input in decisions; policies to support productive employees; encouragement for risk taking and tolerance for mistakes; and the manager as facilitator rather than commander. Quality leadership, and its emphasis on employee input, became the means to the goal of a healthier workplace and a necessary prelude to community policing.

3. Experimental Police District (EPD).

A decision was made to develop a prototype of the new design in one part of the department before attempting to redesign the entire organization; see Inside Policing 5.3 for discussion on the development and operation of the **Experimental Police District (EPD).** The result was that the EPD was the first decentralized police facility in the department. Opened in 1988, the EPD housed approximately one-sixth of the department's personnel and served approximately one-sixth of Madison's population. The charge of the EPD was to promote innovation and experimentation in three areas:

1. Employee participation in decision making about the conditions of work and the delivery of police services.

2. Management and supervisory styles supportive of employee participation and of community-oriented and problem-oriented policing.

3. The implementation of community-oriented and problem-oriented policing.

4. *Citizen Involvement.*

To get citizens involved, eight community meetings were held in the project area, two in each alderman's (city counsel) district. The first set of meetings in each district was for people whom the department and alderman designated as community leaders. The second set of meetings was open to all concerned citizens. At the meetings, citizens were questioned about their knowledge of and satisfaction with police services, about neighborhood problems and concerns, and about how they felt police could work with them in responding to problems. The group process used at the meetings resulted in a listing of problems rated by priority.

Inside Policing 5.3   Development and Operation of the Experimental Police District (EPD)

Planning

As a first step in the planning process, project-team members identified departmental problems that they thought needed to be corrected, such as a lack of meaningful involvement with the community, lack of teamwork or team identity among officers, inflexible management styles and resulting loss of creativity, and lack of communications and information exchange among ranks. Project-team members also conducted department-wide interviews in which team members met in small groups with all employees to find out what they thought needed to be corrected. The top preferences were voted on by the group and published in an EPD newsletter and sent to all employees. This was the first time that management had allowed employees to survey other employees on issues that heretofore were considered to be strictly management's concern.

Operation

The goal of the EPD managers was to become facilitators and coaches who allow and encourage creativity and risk taking among officers. They have given officers substantial latitude to decide their own schedules, their own work conditions, and how to address neighborhood problems. Managers also consider the input of officers before making decisions; they try to encourage problem solving by offering ideas, information, and scheduling alternatives. Although things moved slowly at the beginning, the managers began to see increased use of problem solving as a tool.

Source: Adapted from: D. C. Couper and S. H. Lobitz. 1991. *Quality Policing: The Madison Experience.* Washington, D.C.: Police Executive Research Forum, pp. 36–37; and M. A. Wycoff and W. G. Skogan. 1993. *Community Policing from the Inside Out.* Washington, D.C.: National Institute of Justice, pp. 26–27.

Results From Madison

In their evaluation of the Madison Police Department's change process, Wycoff and Skogan (1994) found that "It is possible to change a traditional, control-oriented police organization into one in which employees become members of work teams and participants in decision making processes" (88–89). Further, some of the lessons learned in Madison for overcoming obstacles to change include the following:

1. It is possible to implement participatory management in a police department, and doing so is very likely to produce more satisfied workers. Many managers and employees in Madison believe that such an approach, which they call quality leadership, is a necessary condition for the implementation of community policing.

2. Decentralization contributed significantly to the creation of the new management style. It also contributed to the development of team spirit and processes, conditions that should facilitate community policing. Officers who work in the experimental police district (EPD) believe the decentralized station improved relationships with the public; they report increased numbers of contacts with citizens in the community and an ever-increasing number of citizens who come to the station for assistance.

3. The managers of the Madison Police Department also thought that the best way to move toward decentralization and community policing was to change one part of the organization (i.e., the EPD) before proceeding with department-wide implementation. Furthermore, it was evident that special attention paid to one part of the department did not block change elsewhere (i.e., other changes in the department were not affected by the attention received by the EPD).

4. During the long time frame for undergoing change and experimentation (over two decades), Madison continued to make efforts to recruit highly educated officers whose backgrounds, life experiences, and attitudes increased the likelihood that they would be supportive of change. This may be an important observation as a caution against unrealistic expectations for departments attempting major change efforts whose personnel are not relatively highly educated. (Adapted from Wycoff and Skogan 1994, 89–90)

Based on the research reviewed above, it appears that the bottom line with respect to the successful implementation of community policing can be tied directly to the amount of change made toward the following: (a) decentralized organization, (b) participatory management, (c) higher educational standards, (d) redefinition of the police role, and (e) involvement of a representative body of citizens.

The Chicago Experience

This section will take an inside look at the overall plan for change, as well as the **change strategies,** used by the Chicago Police Department in its attempt to move to community policing (Chicago's attempt at organizational change has been the largest-scale effort to date (Skogan and Hartnett 1997). The experimental program consisted of five of the 25 police districts in the city, including 54 experimental beats; the experimental districts were referred to as "prototypes," since the program

Successful organizational change toward community policing requires the involvement of a representative body of citizens.

would eventually be expanded to include the 20 remaining traditional districts. The program became labeled as the **Chicago Alternative Policing Strategy (CAPS),** thus giving the department and city its own style of community policing. A total of 1,500 police personnel of all ranks went through orientation and skill-building sessions, and close to 700 beat meetings, attended by 15,000 people, were held during the first year and one-half of the program.

Laying the Foundation

The department developed a mission statement and a 30-page supporting report describing the basic philosophy of community policing and identifying, step by step, many of the key components of change that were needed for the program to succeed. The report opened with a "rationale for change" that reviewed the limits of the traditional model of policing and argued for a "smarter" approach that would capitalize on the strengths of the city's neighborhoods. It further argued that the department had to be "reinvented" in order to form a partnership with the community, one that stressed crime prevention, customer service, and honest and ethical conduct. As noted in the last chapter, the elements of "reinvention," reflecting the ideals of community policing, are becoming more accepted among police middle managers. The report was mailed to every departmental member; to help ensure that it would be read, it was included on the reading list from which questions would be drawn for the next promotional exam. It became the basis for planning the eventual citywide implementation of CAPS.

It should also be mentioned that the department had a traditional paramilitary structure, with many managerial levels. The mayor favored the idea of compressing the rank structure and freeing up more personnel for street-level work; he once exclaimed to the researchers, studying the organization, "Captains! Nobody can tell me what they do!" (Skogan and Hartnett 1997, 34). The rank of captain was thus eliminated (although, as we shall see, it was eventually restored), flattening the hierarchy by one level. Such a flattening of the rank structure parallels the need to decentralize community-policing departments by helping to push decision-making authority down to the street and neighborhood levels.

Key Elements to Change

The organizational change process incorporated six key elements, briefly described below:

1. ***The entire department and the city were to be involved.*** Rather than forming special community-policing units, the whole department would change. Thus, community-policing roles were developed for all of the units, including the detective, tactical, gangs, and narcotics divisions, rather than just for uniformed officers. Only patrol would be utilized, however, until the program had proven to be effective. The commitment to citywide involvement was reflected in the decision to use diverse districts spread throughout the city as prototypes for the program (several of which had high rates of crime), as well as existing personnel in the districts. As one executive put it, the department did not "stack the deck in favor of success."

2. *Officers were to have permanent beat assignments.* In order to develop partnerships with the community and to learn about the neighborhood, officers had to be assigned to one place long enough for residents to know them and learn to trust them. Additionally, officers had to have enough free time to allow them to engage in community work. In attempting to resolve the conflict between working with the public and responding promptly to calls for service, officers in each prototype district were divided into beat teams and rapid-response units (see Inside Policing 5.4). Beat teams were to be dispatched less frequently in order to have time to work on community projects. The rapid-response units (i.e., traditional patrols) and other teams that worked throughout the district were to be assigned to other calls.

3. *The department was to have a strong commitment to training.* The department invested a significant effort in training officers and their supervisors in the skills required to identify and solve problems in working with the community. The lesson learned from other cities that did not pay proper attention to a strong training component was that they never developed serious community-policing programs. By emphasizing training, a message would be sent to the rank and file that community policing was real and upper management was committed to the program. A test would be administered at the end of the training program, which they had to pass; participants who did not pass would have to repeat the course. This appeared "to have a salutary effect on their attentiveness" (Skogan and Hartnett 1997, 101).

4. *The community was to play a significant role in the program.* The foundation of CAPS was the formation of police-community partnerships, focused on identifying and solving problems at the neighborhood level. One of the major problem-solving roles for the police was to engage community resources by drawing other city agencies into identifying and responding to local concerns. This community involvement was developed in two ways. First, *beat meetings* began, usually monthly, involving small groups of residents and beat officers. The meetings were held in church basements and park buildings throughout the city. Second, *advisory committees* were formed at the district level to meet with upper management and district staff; committees included community leaders, school council members, ministers, business operators, and other institutional representatives.

5. *Policing was to be linked to the delivery of city services.* Community policing inevitably involves the expansion of the police role to include a broad range of concerns that are outside the scope of traditional policing. Such expansion was considered necessary by management because they realized that although the police could put a lid on many crime-related problems, they could never eliminate them. They wanted to develop problem-solving systems that could keep the lid on even after they had moved on. In addition, the delivery of city services in the prototype districts was linked to community policing through the use of service-request forms. The requests for service generated by officers were closely tracked by city hall, which developed a system to prioritize and track each case.

6. ***There was to be an emphasis on crime analysis.*** The geographic analysis of crime was considered a key element of the program. Computer technology was to be used to speed up the collection and analysis of data, which would be used to identify crime problems in the beat area. A user-friendly crime-mapping system was developed for use on computers (see chapter 7), with print-outs to be distributed at beat meetings and made accessible to the public at each district station. Other planned analytic tools included "beat planners," which were beat officers' notebooks filled with local information. New roll-call procedures were also developed to encourage officers on various shifts to share information about their beats and community resources.

In addition to the six key elements developed in the organizational plan, Chicago also used a number of methods to help facilitate the organization-wide change process, especially with respect to "winning the hearts and minds" (WHAM) of rank-and-file members (see Inside Policing 5.4).

Inside Policing 5.4   WHAM in Chicago

Management knew that there could be no real change without the support of rank-and-file members at the bottom of the organization. This became known as the "winning hearts and minds" (WHAM) component of organizational change. In order to win the hearts and minds of street officers, the following change strategies were used.

Changing the Job

Jobs were changed for the officers who served each prototype district by dividing them into beat teams and rapid-response teams. The department took this approach rather than forming what is known as a split-force of community policing officers and regular ("real") policing officers into separate units; such an approach has been shown to create tension between the two units and ultimately to undermine community policing. By using beat teams, a majority of their time could be spent within their assigned geographical area. This new beat integrity, including the freedom from responding to 911 calls, was accomplished by increasing the number of officers who served in the prototype districts by about 13 percent. In addition, a radio-dispatch plan was implemented that allocated selected calls to beat teams. Beat officers were to work with schools, businesses, and residents to identify and solve problems and to serve as coordinators for service requests to other city agencies. They attended various neighborhood meetings to work with existing community organizations, as well as regularly held public beat meetings, to increase communications between residents and beat officers. Over time, officers would alternate between beat work and rapid-response cars in order to ensure that community policing did not become confined to special units.

Changing Supervision

The role of sergeants was crucial to CAPS, as prototype beat officers needed direction and mentoring in their new roles; sergeants were also responsible for supervising rapid-response officers as well. Although the sergeants were given some initial CAPS training, it soon became apparent that their role was not clearly defined, and they often felt unsure about what was expected of them. The prototype sergeants were told that their job was to coach officers in their new community roles, but, in reality, they knew as little as the street officers about what that entailed. They soon became disgruntled and felt overworked. Additional training attempted to alleviate this role confusion; it was designed to encourage them to become teachers, coaches, and mentors. The additional training consisted of several skill-building sessions with respect to leadership styles, building partnerships, problem solving, and team building.

Inside Policing 5.4   WHAM in Chicago (continued)

Avoiding the Social-Work Image

One of the lessons learned from other cities was that separate community-policing units did not work. Members of these units inevitably were looked down on by their colleagues as "empty holsters" doing "wave-and-smiling" policing. The prototype districts that were selected joined the program as a unit, "warts and all"; they were not staffed by volunteers, or specially selected officers, supervisors, or even district-level managers (two of whom—out of five—never supported the program). Management also made a concerted effort to assure all sworn personnel that commu-

nity policing was not a "soft on crime" approach. They stressed that officers would not become social workers, but rather, referral specialists who could help solve problems at the neighborhood level. In addition, it was emphasized that traditional police work would continue to be important and would be rewarded, with a strong emphasis on making arrests where appropriate.

Source: Adapted from W. G. Skogan and S. M. Hartnett, *Community Policing, Chicago Style* (New York: Oxford University Press, 1997), 89–95.

Results From Chicago

Findings reported below are from the eight- and nine-year evaluation of the CAPS program (seventh overall) of the Chicago Community Policing Evaluation Consortium (2003). It should be noted that the continuing evaluation of CAPS is paid for by city funding (versus federal funding, which ebbs and flows), thus signaling the value the city has placed on evaluating the progress of this program. Since 1991, crime has declined in almost all areas of the city, but it has declined most dramatically in African American communities. Crime rates have declined the least in predominantly white areas, where they were not very high in the first place. The conclusion drawn was that Chicago was a substantially safer place than it was 11 years prior to CAPS, especially in African American neighborhoods. We should point out, however, that this decline in the crime rate is undoubtedly due, in part, to economic trends and other factors beyond control of the police and may not be primarily associated with CAPS.

Before CAPS was launched, public opinion of the police was not very positive, but had improved substantially after eight years of community policing. Three key trends in the quality of police service were measured by the consortium: performance (preventing crime, keeping order), demeanor (being polite and helpful), and responsiveness (to public concerns). Prior to CAPS, citizens were most negative in their views of how well the police performed; favorable ratings increased from 36 percent in 1993 to nearly 50 percent in 2001. With respect to demeanor, by 2001 more than 70 percent of those surveyed gave the police a favorable rating in this area, compared to a little over 60 percent in 1993. Responsiveness to community concern increased to about 55 percent in 2001 from about 38 percent in 1993. These appear to be solid gains associated with the CAPS program.

The consortium found that beat-meeting attendance rates are often highest in high-crime areas. Taking population into account, it was found that attendance rates are highest in the city's predominantly African American beats and lowest in predominantly white areas, with Latino communities attending at rates between those of African Americans and whites. Because Latinos were the most underrepresented racial or ethnic group, a publicity campaign aimed at Spanish-speaking residents has been established. Interestingly, the primary concerns of the residents in beat meetings were not the types of serious crime problems traditionally associated with the police. For instance, the most commonly discussed problem, at 89 percent of the meetings, was *social disorder,* including a long list of minor offenses and conditions that are not criminal but frequently disturb neighborhood residents. These types of problems included prostitution, public drinking, panhandling, curfew or truancy violations, disturbances by teenagers, public exposure, gambling, trespassing, and landlords who lose control of their buildings. *Drug problems* were discussed at 62 percent of the meetings, followed by *physical dilapidation* (e.g., abandoned buildings and cars, graffiti) at 47 percent; *parking and traffic problems* at 44 percent, *policing problems* (e.g., negative comments or complaints); *property crime problems* at 38 percent (e.g., home and garage burglary, auto theft); and *gang problems* at 29 percent.

The 2000 consortium report (Chicago Community Policing Evaluation Consortium 2000) indicated that there were problems with CAPS implementation, especially in the problem solving area. Many management layers remained untouched by CAPS. Additionally, the rank of captain, which had been abolished at the launch of CAPS, was resurrected, signaling to many a retreat from the department's commitment to organization reform. By 2000, several organization changes within the department were made to increase district accountability and responsiveness in problem solving. Charged with reorganizing CAPS implementation, the newly established CAPS Project Office (1999) conducted an assessment of the true level of CAPS implementation in the districts. It concluded that no one above the level of sergeant was in charge of many important elements of CAPS, and no one was overseeing how well they were carrying out their CAPS responsibilities. In 2000, the Office of Management Accountability (OMA) was created to develop and implement a new accountability process; in this process each district is responsible for defining problems and choosing strategies, and based on an analysis of its data, concentrating its resources on them.

In its oversight role, OMA asks, "Are you implementing the strategies you choose?" If the district is doing what it planned, the question becomes, "Is it working?" Along the way, OMA asks questions such as, "Are you managing efficiently?" "Are the community and city services involved?" and "Are outside units involved?" Because the accountability process is a departure for Chicago, it was introduced slowly. Some have described the process as a "kinder, gentler" version of New York's Compstat process. The accountability meetings—especially those at headquarters—were never intended to be a "gotcha" experience (Chicago Community Policing Evaluation Consortium 2003, 66–67). They were intended, however, to hold district commanders accountable for implementing various problem solving strategies with respect to crime and community concerns.

Lessons Learned From Madison and Chicago

Two of the most comprehensive organizational change efforts, from traditional policing to community policing, have taken place in Madison and Chicago. The change processes utilized had many similarities and some significant differences. While each relied on a report developed by departmental personnel to lay the foundation for change and to guide the change process, each attempted to improve communication with rank-and-file officers. Madison, however, spent significantly more time developing a true participatory (quality) leadership style. A comprehensive committee structure was developed, staffed with personnel throughout the department, whose recommendations were generally adopted. This level of employee participation in policing is unparalleled. It is also important to understand that both departments had strong support from their cities' top political leadership. In Madison, quality improvement was a citywide movement, whereas in Chicago, the mayor used the CAPS program to shore up city hall's provision of services throughout the city. Both cities recognized the importance of, and relied heavily upon, the training of their personnel. Finally, both cities started with experimental programs, which, over time, were expanded throughout the department.

One significant difference was that Chicago used regular officers and supervisors ("warts and all") in its prototype districts, whereas Madison selected personnel who were "interested" in the program (effectively volunteers) for its experimental police district; EPD personnel could also decide their own schedules and work conditions. An important consideration regarding the use of regular officers, supervisors, and established beats is that the experimental or prototype programs will not be as likely to generate a "we-versus-they" mentality between experimental and regular officers. Such an approach can go a long way toward reducing the types of resistance to change discussed earlier and documented in Inside Policing 5.1.

One additional caveat should be noted. In Madison, a concerted effort had been made for approximately two decades to recruit highly educated officers who would be more likely to support change. If a true commitment to community policing is to take place, and if the police role is to be significantly broadened to carry it out, the level of higher education required for police may be an important factor (although the research is mixed in this area; see Chapter 14). In Madison, however, it appears that the history of promoting higher education contributed significantly to establishing a more conducive atmosphere for large-scale organizational change.

Although both departments sought input from the community, the level of participation from each community differed significantly. Madison developed feedback mechanisms only (mainly surveys), whereas Chicago took the development of citizen communication and input to a new level for police departments. The involvement of beat officers who were geographically stable, and generally free from 911 response calls, allowed them to work closely with the community in problem solving. By conducting regularly scheduled, public beat meetings, in a way that identified problems and made action plans, they could determine what residents considered to be the important problems in their areas and work to alleviate them. Trends in the assessment of police service quality through 2001, including performance, demeanor, and responsiveness, all have made solid gains since CAPS began in the early 1990s.

It would appear that both departments have made significant progress toward implementing community policing, but they have done it in different ways. In Madison, employee participation in the change process was a strong point (internal change), whereas in Chicago, the development of partnerships with the community through beat teams was the strong suit (external change). Perhaps the most effective change approach to community policing would be to mix the internal practices from Madison with the external practices from Chicago while raising the educational standards for recruits. See Voices from the Field below for a former chief's perspective on bringing about major organization change in a constructive fashion.

Voices From the Field

Lorne Kramer
Former Chief, Colorado Springs Police Department
Current Assistant City Manager of Colorado Springs

Question: One of the biggest challenges for a chief is to promote organizational change emphasizing quality and productivity without losing the battle for the hearts and minds of officers on the street. You have been widely credited with achieving both in Colorado Springs. How did you successfully accomplish this change process?

Answer: There are many reasons why organizations change. In the private sector it's usually related to retaining or improving competitive edge, market share, or profit. In public organizations the reasons for change are more complex and generally related to the culture of the organization or some external force. A police chief must understand the change process and why people will instinctively resist it.

Organizational change is a journey, not an event. Lasting, meaningful change will occur only if the purpose and benefit are communicated and understood. To be successful, the chief must have a trusting relationship within the organization. Leadership behavior, knowing and being interested in employees, fairness, good labor relations, dependability, and keeping your word are all critical to earning and maintaining trust. In addition, the chief needs to ensure that he never forgets what it's like to be a police officer. He needs to be an active listener and maintain a sense of humor. ✦

The redesign and enrichment of traditional police jobs, such as conducting surveys of citizens above, may improve officer satisfaction and performance.

Job Redesign and Community Policing

Just as police departments have been criticized for overreliance on traditional, paramilitary organization, so too has the traditional design of police jobs. Historically, many agencies have stressed a narrow perspective on the role of the police and the community and have consequently designed their jobs from a narrow, legalistic perspective. However, as the complexity of the police role has been recognized, the police have become better educated, and community policing has developed, it has become clear that traditional job designs are not meeting the needs of many police personnel, the department, or the community.

In attempting to enhance community livability through problem solving and crime-prevention efforts, community-policing jobs are substantially redesigned by increasing the use of officer discretion and power, especially with respect to utilizing alternatives other than those available primarily through the criminal justice system. The enriched nature of a community-police officer's day is depicted below.

A Community Police Officer's Day

In addition to traditional law enforcement activities, such as patrol and responding to calls for service, the day might include the following:

+ Operating neighborhood substations.
+ Meeting with community groups.
+ Analyzing and solving neighborhood problems.
+ Working with citizens on crime-prevention programs.
+ Conducting door-to-door surveys of residents.
+ Talking with students in school.

+ Meeting with local merchants.
+ Making security checks of businesses.
+ Dealing with disorderly people.

S. D. Mastrofski. 1992. "What Does Community Policing Mean for Daily Police Work?" *National Institute of Justice Journal,* August, 24.

An observational study in Cincinnati by Frank, Brandl, and Watkins (1997) measured the average amount of time beat officers (traditional) and neighborhood officers (community policing) spent on their daily activities. Significant differences were found on seven of eight activity categories. For example, neighborhood officers spent a substantial amount of their time engaged in community-based service activities, especially meeting-related activities (11 percent), compared to beat officers (0 percent). Only routine patrol (22 percent) accounted for more of their time. In addition, service and problem-solving activities were performed to a much greater extent by neighborhood officers than by beat officers.

As expected, traditional police activities associated with patrol work made up a substantial majority of beat officer workloads (71 percent), including random patrol (33 percent) responding to noncrime calls (20 percent), and crime-related tasks, such as arrests, tickets/citations, and criminal reports (18 percent). These tasks were of much less significance for neighborhood officers; for example, only 5 percent of their time was spent on crime-related activities. This research shows that the content of community policing can be substantially different from the content of traditional policing. The authors suggest that police agencies now need to develop performance measures that are consistent with the activities performed by officers performing community-policing duties and, we might add, recognizing and rewarding them for such activities.

The research on the impact of community-policing activities on officer attitudes and performance is mixed. On the one hand, it appears that in programs with a high level of implementation, such activities can significantly increase levels of personal growth and job satisfaction, as well as improve attitudes toward the department, supervision, the community, and community policing (see Hayeslip and Cordner 1987; Hornick, Burrows, and Phillips 1989; Wycoff and Skogan 1993; Skogan and Hartnett 1997; Zhao, Thurman, and He 1999; Adams, Roche, and Arcury 2002). On the other hand, in programs that were either partially or poorly implemented, officers' attitudes and job satisfaction levels were not so positive, usually with no discernable differences between experimental and comparison groups (see Weisburd and

McElroy 1995; Greene and Decker 1989; McElroy, Cosgrove, and Sadd 1993; Rosenbaum, Yeh, and Wilkinson, 1994; Wilson and Bennett 1994).

With respect to the above findings, one study (Brody, Demarco, and Lovrich 2002) compared job satisfaction of city employees in 12 local jurisdictions—including both police and nonpolice personnel—with respect to the level of community-policing implementation. The results were twofold with respect to departments with a *high level* of community-policing implementation: (1) in each of the areas of job satisfaction examined—training, innovation, teamwork, and job performance—job satisfaction scores increased, and (2) these increased levels of job satisfaction closed the gap between police employees and nonpolice employees in their respective jurisdictions. Further, the results indicated that in departments with a *medium level* of community-policing implementation, the mean job satisfaction scores were at times lower than those departments with a *low implementation* level of community policing. This suggests that to some degree, having a medium level of community policing did more harm than good to employees' job satisfaction. The authors suggest that this result may reflect the fact that because medium implementation departments only made a half-hearted approach to a community-policing philosophy, this led to confusion and resentment among some officers and managers. In conclusion, whereas community policing was shown to increase police officers' job satisfaction, it may not be beneficial unless it is implemented at a fairly high level.

The above findings suggest that not only did job satisfaction increase with the implementation of community policing at a high level, but that satisfaction compared favorably with city personnel not working in traditionally paramilitary organizations. This latter finding tends to support earlier research by Franz and Jones (1987), reviewed in the last chapter, who compared police officers with other city employees who had not been exposed to the "quasi-military police organizational model." They found that police employees perceived greater problems in several important areas, including communication, morale, and performance.

In general, research results with respect to a high level of community-policing implementation and **job redesign** are threefold: (1) officers who value *internal needs* for personal growth and have a service orientation (Cochran, Bromley, and Swando 2002), are more likely to benefit from a community-policing-enriched job design; (2) more traditionally oriented officers or "careerists" (Greene 1989) who value *extrinsic rewards*, such as recognition and security, likely will not benefit from a job redesign; and (3) less clearly, in some departments with organization-wide community policing, all officers appeared to benefit from a job redesign.

These results suggest that *individual differences* of police officers have an impact on how well job redesign efforts toward community policing will be received, and therefore should be taken into consideration when planning for change. As Greene notes:

> Community policing for some officers may represent a personal growth challenge, the chance to meaningfully participate in work decisions, and the enlightened work environment suggested by these programs. But for other officers, community policing can be something completely different; it can be more work to be done at the same pay, it can be added responsibility without commensurate authority or autonomy, and it can mean that officer autonomy is actually restricted by an observant and activated community. For officers who may value these concerns, community policing may be perceived as more detrimental than beneficial. (1989, 181)

Greene further adds that because innovative programs in policing have been criticized for "creaming" off the "better" officers, it is not clear that community policing will "work with all or even the majority of officers currently policing American communities." This is a valid and important point, considering that there are over 17,000 police agencies of various sizes and makeups throughout the country. This point has long-term implications for the field and for whether community-policing programs can, or should, be implemented throughout an organization. For police managers currently moving toward community policing, however, it may be wise to identify those officers who desire a change into community-oriented jobs; as noted above, these officers will normally have service or social activist orientations and high personal growth needs.

Innovation

If constructive and timely change is to take place in police departments, mid-level and top-level managers must develop an organizational climate that fosters and encourages innovation. **Innovation** refers to the development and use of new ideas and methods. Such a climate should be relatively open, trustworthy, and forward looking. In their study on police innovation in six American cities, Skolnick and Bayley (1986) made several recommendations for improving police effectiveness. As you read the recommendations, try to keep in mind how each does or does not apply to the experiences of Madison and Chicago.

First, and most important to successful innovation, is *effective and energetic leadership from the office of the chief.* Although executive leadership is vital to any enterprise, it is essential to traditional paramilitary police departments. Because such departments tend not to be democratically run, most members are aware of the chief's preferences, demands, and expectations. It is not enough, however, simply to espouse certain ideals and values; the chief must become an active, committed exponent of them.

The second requirement for successful innovation is that *the chief must be able to motivate* (and sometimes manipulate) *departmental personnel* into supporting the values that the chief espouses. Some resistance from the "old guard," who have strong ties to the status quo, is likely. Because these individuals may retain much influence, police executives often attempt to keep or enlist their support. As a result, chiefs may actually affirm conflicting norms, telling different audiences what each wants to hear. Consequently, nobody in the department knows what the chief stands for and everyone is confused. Preferably, a majority of the officers can be persuaded that the new values are superior. Persuasion is seldom easy, however, especially in departments that have associations and unions resistant to change. Nevertheless, innovatively inclined chiefs should be able to work with such associations and unions in order to gain the support of the rank and file.

Skolnick and Bayley noted that one of the ways of potentially lessening resistance from the old guard is to first implement change in one part of the department. In this way, the department can learn how best to change with the least amount of disruption, and those who are resistant have a chance to observe the potential benefits of the change. If the change is ultimately considered not to be beneficial for the entire department, it would not be implemented throughout the department.

A third requirement is that *integrity of innovation must be defended.* Once a new value system (one dedicated to the development of new concepts and methods) has been established, it will need to be protected from the pull to return to the status quo. Such protection is especially necessary in policing because police departments tend to be heavily tied to the traditional ways of doing things.

The fourth requirement for innovation is *public support*. Innovative crime-prevention programs that are implemented with community input enjoy strong, often unexpected, support from the public. If properly introduced and explained to the community, police innovations will most likely be widely supported.

Inside Policing 5.5   Sustaining Innovation in Madison

In promoting and sustaining innovation, a vision was created for the department, asking what it wanted to be, how it could get there, and how it would know when it was making continuous improvement. Some of the techniques used in carrying out the plan are described briefly below.

Training

The management team completed seven days of quality-productivity and quality-leadership training; during the last hour of each training day the chief appeared in order to answer questions and address concerns. Thus, he showed support for the new philosophy and served as a role model for the new leadership style. This training was followed by three similar six-day sessions for sergeants. Quality-improvement training then began for all departmental employees, both civilian and commissioned. A three-day training session covering systems thinking, group skills, interpersonal skills, and quality leadership was developed. At the end of the final training day, the chief and deputy chief were on hand to answer questions and clarify some of the principles of quality leadership.

Promotions

The first effort beyond training to start running the department in accord with the new philosophy involved implementing a new promotion policy. This was an important step because who is promoted sends a stronger message than any words from management. Consequently, the chief sent out a memorandum establishing the importance of the new promotion policy, which stated, in part:

I strongly believe that if we are to "practice what we preach" in our Mission Statement to achieve excellence (i.e., teamwork, respect, problem solving, openness, sensi-

tive and community-oriented policing) . . . we will have to alter the way in which we lead. . . . The promotions I make from now on are going to people who have strong interpersonal and facilitative skills and who can adjust and adapt to the new needs and demands. . . . In addition to being totally committed to the Mission of the organization [supervisors and managers] will have to be able to work in a team, become coaches, accept feedback, ask and listen to others in the team, and facilitate their employees' input and growth in the workplace.

Accordingly, subsequent promotions went to those officers who were peer-group leaders and who wished to adopt a quality-leadership style. Some of those promoted would not have been selected in the past; thus, new leaders who would help to implement and sustain innovative policing were being selected.

Customer Surveys

In order to establish baseline data and to assess the quality and customer satisfaction of the department, a survey was developed. The survey asked citizens to rate police services from poor (1) to excellent (5) in seven areas: (1) concern, (2) helpfulness, (3) knowledge, (4) quality of service, (5) solving the problem, (6) putting citizens at ease, and (7) professional conduct. An open-ended question at the end asked: How can we improve? About 25 percent of the responses include feedback on this question.

Surveys were mailed each month (with a stamped, self-addressed return envelope) to all persons identified in every 50th case-numbered report, including victims, witnesses, complainants, and arrestees. The results are periodically published in the department's newsletter, in which both positive and negative comments re-

---

| Inside Policing 5.5 | Sustaining Innovation in Madison (continued) |

garding improvement are summarized. The newsletter also provides statistical results for the seven areas, including demographic data on respondents, and tabulates satisfaction levels in relationship to the age, race, income, and gender of the respondent.

Managing by Wandering Around

The department believes that leadership involves being seen, and that leaders cannot be seen very well if they spend all their time behind a desk. Accordingly, the department has found that a very simple technique of managing by walking around (MBWA) is a powerful one. For most police managers, MBWA means getting out on the "street" (where the action is) and observing and asking or answering questions. In this way, managers learn what their employees need from them to do a quality job, as well as letting them know that managers care about quality work and are looking for ways to improve conditions and processes.

Source: Adapted from D. C. Couper and S. H. Lobitz, *Quality Policing: The Madison Experience* (Washington, D.C.: Police Executive Research Forum, 1991), 59, 62–63, 66–67, 73–74, 80.

As Skolnick and Bayley (1986) pointed out, the need to sustain or defend innovation is critical, since the tendency to regress toward the traditional way of doing things is strong. What methods can police managers use to keep the department on the path toward innovation? Inside Policing 5.5 examines several types of management techniques that the Madison Police Department employed to gain momentum and sustain innovation in its organizational change process.

Quality Circles

As most of the research has revealed, police chiefs can help promote innovation by more directly involving line officers in department decision-making and problem solving. In this way, the officers develop a greater understanding of the possible need for innovation and are more likely to become active participants in the change process. Originally developed in Japan in the mid-1950s to accentuate the Japanese emphasis on participatory management and decentralized decision-making in business, the use of quality circles has grown in U.S. organizations, including police departments. A **quality circle** consists of a group of employees from the same work area who meet on a regular basis for the purpose of identifying and solving common work problems.

The use of quality circles in policing can be illustrated by the Dallas Police Department (Melancon 1984), which originally had one of the most extensive programs in the country. Team leaders, generally sergeants, attend seminars to learn about the philosophy, techniques, and fundamentals of the operation. Team members are volunteers from various work groups, who must attend several meetings prior to determining if they wish to participate. Members attend meetings in both on-duty and off-duty status and may drop out at any time. Over the years, the department has had numerous quality circles in operation at any one time, covering many units, including patrol, detectives, traffic, dispatching, property, records, legal services, community services, training, personnel, and tactics (Hatry and Greiner 1986). Melancon (1984) reported improved morale and worker satisfaction for participating employees. A survey of team leaders indicated that quality circles were beneficial in solving problems in the work area and that management supported the program. The survey further discovered that officers felt that through the program the department exhibited more openness, trust, and support toward the employees.

An early national survey of 300 police departments found that 48 (16 percent) were using quality circles (Hatry and Greiner 1986). One interesting finding was that although police departments with paramilitary structures and authoritarian managerial styles were more likely to have problems implementing quality circle programs, a surprising number of police executives were willing to try participatory techniques. The researchers concluded that management style may be less of a problem than was originally antici- pated; this bodes well for departments attempting to move toward community policing. While quality circles appeared to improve employee morale, there was no significant improvement in department performance. It was believed this situation was due, in part, to the selection of topics that were too narrow in scope and, in part, because the circles involved only a small proportion of the work force in any one department. Finally, it was suggested that if quality circles spent more time emphasizing substantive service-delivery problems confronting individual police work units, their impact on departmental perfor- mance and long-term viability would be greatly strengthened.

Police Departments as Learning Organizations

The discussion of quality-management principles in the last chapter included the concept of continuous improvement. Continuous improvement cannot be accomplished without continuous learning, which is another way to sustain innovation in police departments. In other words, if management can develop an environment that promotes continuous learning, the department (and its members) would benefit from its own and other's experiences, including both success and failure. Such a learning environment leads to a **learning organization,** which is able to process what it has learned and adapt accordingly. According to Geller (1997), there are many structural and process ideas that would help police departments to become learning organizations. One idea is to create a **research and development (R&D)** unit that *actually does* research and development instead of only statistical descriptions of departmental inputs and outputs. Such a unit would be run by someone who understands R&D and be supported by a respectable bud- get (also not the norm). Such a unit might help foster an appreciation for the practical benefits of prior research in the field. It is virtually impossible to be a learning organiza- tion if the use of recent research findings is not part of departmental processes.

Another idea along these lines is to continue to expand *police-researcher partner- ships,* such as those sponsored by the National Institute of Justice. Such partnerships allow the department to get involved in a research project without all the necessary expertise or budget restraints, while learning something about itself. The innovative neighborhood-oriented policing (INOP) project discussed previously would be an example of how such a research project might work. Additionally, if a department finds a researcher it really trusts, it could contract with him or her to serve as a part-time research "broker," helping the department to become a better consumer and user of research. Some police departments have acquired this kind of capacity by hir- ing a criminologist to head their planning or R&D units.

A further idea that would help foster learning would be to *organize police work around problem solving* and to take seriously the *SARA process* for confronting problems. Managers and groups of problem-focused officers, who would be working with the community, could develop procedures to guide their work. For example, checklists could be developed for both police supervisors and community organizers to help ensure that corners are not cut and that the most viable solutions are sought.

One interesting structural suggestion is to *use middle managers to facilitate critical thinking*. Since middle managers in police departments (i.e., lieutenants and captains) are continually coming under fire in reorganization plans as being unproductive and even counterproductive, it may be constructive to give them something useful to do. Because they are between the policymakers above and the policy implementers below, why not charge them "with facilitating critical thinking about the efficacy of policies and implementation" (Geller 1997, 6)? If departments were to do this (assuming proper training and ability levels), the performance ratings of middle managers might reflect how well they enable their units and communities to constructively criticize and improve departmental operations. A concomitant idea would be explicitly to include, as part of individual and unit performance ratings, a *comparison of employee accomplishments with respect to industry standards*, and helping to promote organizational progress.

This idea of matching police performance levels to present-day industry standards and promoting organizational progress is an interesting concept whose time may have already arrived. One municipal police chief in Scottsdale, Arizona, for example, supports the idea that every community should require a "stockholders" report of its local police department. The report would focus on 12 fundamental questions that should be asked by the community and answered by the department (Heidingsfield 1996). Inside Policing 5.6 takes a look at these questions.

Inside Policing 5.6   Community Stockholders' Report on Local PDs

Question 1. Has your police department been willing to examine its inner workings by comparing the local way of doing business with the most progressive national standards of the law enforcement industry? This is the rigorous three-year process of national accreditation.

Question 2. Does your local police department have a simple, easily understood statement of values that are known throughout the department and embody the fundamental notion of ethical behavior and principled decision making?

Question 3. Has your police department been rigorous in its effort to diversify itself by representing community cultures and instilling broad confidence in the police services being delivered?

Question 4. Has your police department embraced the concepts of community policing that imply openness, citizen partnership, and joint responsibility for public safety?

Question 5. Does the leadership of your local police department consistently and passionately carry the message to the community and its police officers that disparate treatment for individuals, heavy-handedness and racism are absolutely not tolerated?

Question 6. Is the maintenance of dignity and respect a theme that is recurrent throughout the police department's culture?

Question 7. Is the police department willing to be formally evaluated by the community on its ability to deliver service in the best manner possible?

Inside Policing 5.6   Community Stockholders' Report on Local PDs (continued)

Question 8. Has your local department embarked on an organizational campaign to reinforce the concepts and premises of ethics in policing?

Question 9. Does your police department have in place an open, formal system to ferret out misconduct and to deal with it decisively and promptly?

Question 10. In its hiring standards, does your department highly value college education and community service, as well as commitment to ideals and strength of character?

Question 11. Does your police department consistently enjoy the nonpartisan support of its elected and appointed leadership?

Question 12. Does your impression and assessment of your community's police officers include characterizations such as compassionate, skilled, fair, available, and open?

When you as a citizen can answer yes to these questions, you then have a dramatic statement about a community's relationship with its police department—one that speaks of properly placed confidence, mutual respect, vigilance, and reassurance.

Source: Adapted from M. J. Heidingsfield, 1996, "Pointed Questions About Your Police Agency," *Law Enforcement News,* September 30: 8.

Summary

The process of organizational change in policing requires the development of a culture that encourages innovation. The primary obstacles to change include inertia, misunderstandings, group norms, and the balance of power. Each of these obstacles makes the change process more difficult and requires a sustained effort by management if it is to be overcome. In general, ways to overcome obstacles to change in the direction of community policing include taking a long-term view of the change process, preliminary training of personnel, gaining support from elected officials and city agencies, and involving the community.

Two relatively successful examples of large-scale organizational change efforts are Madison and Chicago. Many of the reasons for the success of these departments overlap; for example, both improved communication with their personnel; both had political support; both relied on training; both started out with experimental or prototype districts; and both involved the community, especially in Chicago, where regularly scheduled beat meetings were held. Unique to Madison was its concentrated effort to recruit highly educated officers who were believed to be more supportive of change.

Job redesign is also an important consideration in changing a department toward community policing; it was suggested that individual differences need to be considered when planning for job enrichment. Two examples of techniques that can be used to sustain innovation include the use of quality circles and the development of a learning environment.

Critical Thinking Questions

1. Discuss four reasons why police officers tend to resist organizational change. Of the four obstacles described regarding why officers may resist

organizational change, which do you believe is the most serious? How would you attempt to overcome this obstacle?

2. Why do you think the change process in Madison was so successful?

3. What key strategies were used in Chicago's plan for organizational change? Which do you believe are, and continue to be, the most crucial?

4. Discuss the major differences in the change processes used in Madison and Chicago. Which process do you believe will be more effective in the long run, and why?

5. With respect to job redesign and individual differences, what change strategy or approach would you use in attempting to implement community policing?

6. Why is innovation important to the organizational change process? What management techniques would you use to sustain it?

7. What is meant by a learning organization? Discuss several ideas that would help police departments to become learning organizations.

8. With respect to the 12 questions listed in the Stockholders' Report on Local Police Departments (Inside Policing 5.6), what do you believe to be the strengths and weaknesses of your local department? What could be done to improve it?

References

Adams, R. E., Roche, W. M., and Arcury, T. A. 2002. "Implementing Community-Oriented Policing: Organizational Change and Street Officer Attitudes." *Crime & Delinquency* 48: 399–430.

Booz, Allen & Hamilton, Inc. 1992. *Improving Police Service: Summary of Findings To-Date.* Consulting report for the city of Chicago.

Brody, D. C., DeMarco, C., and Lovrich, N. R. 2002. "Community Policing and Job Satisfaction: Suggestive Evidence of Positive Workforce Effects from a Multijurisdictional Comparison in Washington State." *Police Quarterly* 5: 181–205.

Chicago Community Policing Evaluation Consortium. 2000. *Community Policing in Chicago, Year Seven: An Interim Report.* Chicago: Illinois Criminal Justice Information Authority.

Chicago Community Policing Evaluation Consortium. 2003. *Community Policing in Chicago, Years Eight and Nine.* Chicago: Illinois Criminal Justice Information Authority.

Cochran, J. K., Bromley, M. L. and Swando, M. J. 2002. "Sheriff's Deputies' Receptivity to Organizational Change." *Policing: An International Journal of Police Strategies & Management* 25: 507–529.

"Community Policing Strategies." 1995. *Research Preview.* Washington, D.C.: National Institute of Justice.

Couper, D. C., and Lobitz, S. H. 1991. *Quality Policing: The Madison Experience.* Washington, D.C.: Police Executive Research Forum.

Frank, J., Brandl, S. G., and Watkins, R. C. 1997. "The Content of Community Policing: A Comparison of the Daily Activities of Community and 'Beat' Officers." *Policing: An International Journal of Police Strategy and Management* 20: 716–728.

Franz, V., and Jones, D. M. 1987. "Perceptions of Organizational Performance in Suburban Police Departments: A Critique of the Military Model." *Journal of Police Science and Administration* 15: 153–161.

Geller, W. A. 1997. "Suppose We Were Really Serious About Police Departments Becoming 'Learning Organizations'?" *National Institute of Justice Journal*, December: 2–8.

Greene, J. R. 1989. "Police Officer Job Satisfaction and Community Perceptions: Implications for Community-oriented Policing." *Journal of Research in Crime and Delinquency* 26: 168–183.

Greene, J. R., and Decker, S. H. 1989. "Policy and Community Perceptions of the Community Role in Policing: The Philadelphia Experience." *Howard Journal of Criminal Justice* 26: 168–183.

Hartnett, S. M., and Skogan, W. G. 1999. "Community Policing: Chicago's Experience." *National Institute of Justice Journal*, April: 3–11.

Hatry, H. P., and Greiner, J. M. 1986. *Improving the Use of Quality Circles in Police Departments*. Washington, D.C.: National Institute of Justice.

Hayeslip, P. W., and Cordner, G. W. 1987. "The Effects of Community-oriented Patrol on Police Officer Attitudes." *American Journal of Police* 6: 95–119.

Heidingsfield, M. J. 1996. "Pointed Questions About Your Police Agency." *Law Enforcement News*, September 30: 8.

Hornick, J.P., and Burrows, B. A., and Phillips, D. M. (1989). *An Impact Evaluation of the Edmonton Neighborhood Foot Patrol Program*, November. Paper presented at the annual meeting of the American Society of Criminology, Reno, NV.

Lurigio, A. J., and Rosenbaum, D. P. 1994. "The Impact of Community Policing on Police Personnel: A Review of the Literature." In D. P. Rosenbaum (ed.), *The Challenge of Community Policing*, pp. 147–166. Thousand Oaks, CA: Sage.

Melancon, D. D. 1984. "Quality Circles: The Shape of Things to Come?" *The Police Chief*, November: 54–55.

McElroy, J. E., Cosgrove, C. A., and Sadd, S. 1993. *Community Policing: The CPOP in New York*. Newbury Park, CA.: Sage.

Pierce, J. L., and Delbeq, A. L. 1977. "Organization Structure, Individual Attitudes and Innovation." *Academy of Management Review* 2: 27–37.

Pisani, S. L. 1992. "Dissecting Community Policing: Part 2." *Law Enforcement News*, May 31: 8, 10.

Rosenbaum, D. P., Yeh, S., and Wilkinson, D. L. 1994. "Impact of Community Policing on Police Personnel: A Quasi-Experimental Test." *Crime & Delinquency* 40: 331–353.

Sadd, S., and Grinc, R. M. 1994. "Innovative Neighborhood Oriented Policing: An Evaluation of Community Policing Programs in Eight Cities." In D. P. Rosenbaum (ed.), *The Challenge of Community Policing: Testing the Promises*, pp. 27–52. Thousand Oaks, CA: Sage.

——. 1996. *Implementation Challenges in Community Policing: Innovative Neighborhood-oriented Policing in Eight Cities*. Washington, D.C.: National Institute of Justice.

Sherman, L. W., Milton, C. W., and Kelley, T. V. 1973. *Team Policing: Seven Case Studies*. Washington, D.C.: Police Foundation.

Skogan, W. G., and Hartnett, S. M. 1997. *Community Policing, Chicago Style*. New York: Oxford University Press.

Skolnick, J. H., and Bayley, D. H. 1986. *The New Blue Line: Police Innovation in Six American Cities*. New York: Free Press.

"Study Criticizes Community Policing," 1991. *New York Times*, August 8: B2.

VanderVegt, G., Emans, B., and VandeVliet, E. 1998. "Motivating Effects of Task and Outcome Interdependence." *Group & Organization Management* 23: 124–143.

Weisburd, D., McElroy, J., and Hardyman, P. 1988. "Challenges to Supervision in Community Policing." *American Journal of Police* 7: 29–50.

Weisburd, D., and McElroy, J. E. 1995. "Enacting the CPO Role: Findings from New York City Pilot Program in Community Policing." In J. R. Greene and S. D. Mastrofski (eds.), *Community Policing: Rhetoric or Reality?*, pp. 89–102. New York: Praeger.

Wilson, D. G., and Bennett, S. F. 1994. "Officers' Response to Community Policing: Variations on a Theme." *Crime & Delinquency* 40: 354–370.

Wycoff, M. A., and Skogan, W. G. 1993. *Community Policing in Madison: Quality from the Inside Out.* Washington, D.C.: National Institute of Justice, December.

——. 1994. "Community Policing in Madison: An Analysis of Implementation and Impact." In D. P. Rosenbaum (ed.), *The Challenge of Community Policing: Testing the Promises*, pp. 75–91. Thousand Oaks, CA: Sage.

Wycoff, M. A. 1995. *Community Policing Strategies.* Washington, D.C.: National Institute of Justice.

Zhao, J., Thurman, Q., and He, N. 1999. "Sources of Job Satisfaction Among Police Officers: A Test of Demographic and Work Environment Models." *Justice Quarterly* 16: 153–172.

Suggested Websites for Further Study

Houston Police Department
http://www.ci.houston.tx.us/departme/police/index.html

Chicago Police Department
http://www.ci.chi.il.us/CommunityPolicing/CPDhome.html

Madison (WI) Police Department
http://www.ci.madison.wi.us/police/

International Association of Law Enforcement Planners
http://www.ialep.org

California Office of Criminal Justice Planning
http://www.ocjp.ca.gov/ ✦

## Chapter 6

Selection and Development

Chapter Outline

Key Terms

andragogy	disparate impact
assessment center	education
BFOQ	field-training officer (FTO)
career path	four-fifths rule
cognitive learning	in-service training
community-service officer (CSO)	job analysis

Key Terms (continued)

job related	reliability
lateral entry	Reno model
macho orientation	screening in
management training	screening out
pedagogy	specialized training
Police Cadet Corps	supervisory training
police image	task analysis
POST	training
promotion	validity
recruitment strategies	

As noted in the previous chapters, the nature of policing and police departments is changing—becoming more complex and challenging—necessitating the importance of hiring and developing the highest-quality personnel available. Although the quality of police personnel has always been important, with the increased complexity of the police role and the movement toward community policing, the quality of personnel has perhaps become the key element in effective police operation.

The debate over the meaning of "quality," however, is not easy to resolve. For instance, does an individual need a certain level of intelligence, and how is that measured? Are certain physical characteristics a factor? Should higher education be required? What about ethical values? Considerations of quality also suggest that departments should select personnel, including women, who are representative of the communities they serve because they help provide a greater understanding of issues related to gender, race, and ethnicity. Cultural diversity in policing is discussed in depth in Chapter 12.

Police selection and development are also influenced by a city or county civil service system. For instance, civil service requirements may have a significant impact on a department's criteria for selection, promotion, and discipline. Civil service provisions were enacted in 1883 with the passage of the Pendleton Civil Service Act, which tried to eliminate the spoils system, in which politicians could simply hire and fire police personnel based on their political affiliation or friendship. By establishing hiring standards that had to be met by all applicants, police departments gained considerable autonomy and freedom against political influence. But civil service also had a number of negative side effects. For instance, O. W. Wilson and McLaren, who were early critics of the civil service, believed that civil service rules provided too much security for "incompetent and untrustworthy" officers, who are virtually impossible to "weed out" (1977, 28). Today, although it is possible to terminate incompetent or dishonest police employees, as a result of civil service provisions it is an onerous and time-consuming effort.

A police department makes essentially three selection decisions: **entry, reassignment,** and **promotion.** Decisions about police entrance are usually for the lowest level position (patrol), but supervisory and managerial-level entry is also possible. A few departments recruit for lower-level and middle-level managers (e.g., sergeants, lieutenants, and captains) from outside the department; this practice is known as lateral entry (discussed in the final section of this chapter). Some departments also select their chief of police from the outside. Because most sheriffs are elected, potential candidates may include persons outside the sheriff's department or even outside the law enforcement field.

All states have created statewide standards for parts of the personnel process (e.g., selection, training, and promotion). For example, many states now have an organization called Peace Officer Standards and Training (POST). There is still considerable variation among states, however, and some departments do not adhere to the personnel standards that are established because they are not obligated by law to do so.

Hiring recruits who can become effective patrol officers is the primary purpose of the selection process. The importance of this process cannot be overstated, since after a probationary period, officers essentially receive tenure and may be with the department for 20 years or longer. Although incompetent or dishonest officers can be disciplined, reassigned, or in some cases, terminated, it makes more sense to start by hiring high-quality personnel who will be contributing members of the department throughout their careers.

If high-quality police recruits are to be chosen, the selection process should be designed to screen in, rather than screen out, applicants. **Screening out** identifies applicants who are unqualified and removes them from consideration, while leaving all those who are minimally qualified still in the applicant pool. Recruits who may not be well qualified for police work are then selected from this pool. **Screening in** applicants, in contrast, identifies only the best-qualified candidates for the applicant pool. The department will select its recruits from these applicants, thus ensuring a relatively high-quality candidate. Interestingly, many police departments still rely on screening out applicants, but the process has been under attack since at least 1973, when the National Advisory Commission on Criminal Justice Standards and Goals noted:

> The selection of police personnel should be approached positively; police agencies should seek to identify and employ the best candidates available rather than being content with disqualifying the unfit. The policy of merely eliminating the least qualified results in mediocrity because it allows marginal applicants to be employed along with the most qualified. (1973, 20)

Recruitment

The initial step in the selection process is recruiting well-qualified candidates. The relationship of the number of applicants to those who qualify for positions is often a major factor in the quality of the personnel employed. The most common recruitment methods in policing include (1) advertisement, including brochures, newspapers, television, radio, mass mailings, and journals; (2) requests to special-interest groups, including neighborhood, social, political, and minority groups; (3) public announcements, including public-service announcements on television and radio; (4) requests to university career-planning and career-placement offices (campus recruiting is essential if educational requirements are to be increased); and (5) referrals from current employees (Chapman 1982; International City Management Association 1986; Langworthy, Hughes, and Sanders 1995). In addition, many police departments maintain a home page on the Internet containing recruitment information and materials, and some maintain a toll-free 800 number for their recruiting division (TELEMASP 1996). In some police departments, officers are given such incentives as extra days off or a pay bonus if they recruit someone into the department. In some cases, departments send their recruiters to other cities and states in an attempt to enlarge the applicant pool.

One of the major problems with advertising has been the **police image** that has been portrayed. Advertisements often present only the most favorable self-image of both the department and the police role, especially highlighting an ethnically and sexually diverse organization that continually performs adventurous and exciting work. Although this image, from a recruitment perspective, may be effective, it may also be deceitful. The recruits' perception of reality in the department after employment rarely matches the advertised image. There is a strong possibility that such discrepancies lead to employee disenchantment and frustration. Consequently, although the department needs to present an effective image for recruitment purposes, that image should be accurate and realistic.

In attempting to recruit the best-qualified applicants, it is important that departments recognize that different **recruitment strategies** may be necessary. For example, Meagher and Yentes (1986) found a high degree of consensus between male and female officers in their personal reasons for entering policing; the top two choices for both groups were helping people and job security. Women, however, were found to be substantially less interested in "fighting crime" than were men. These findings suggest that although recruitment strategies for both men and women can be essentially the same, to attract women candidates, recruiters should emphasize the helping nature of the role, including community service and problem-solving activities. In a national study of recruitment, selection, and training practices (Langworthy, Hughes, and Sanders 1995), based on 60 departments with over 500 sworn personnel, 52.5 percent responded that they use recruiting strategies to target women.

Another study, by Slater and Reiser (1988) found ethnic groups differed in their reasons for entering policing. The three main reasons selected by each group in rank order were as follows: Blacks—variety, serve the public, responsibility; Hispanic—variety, responsibility and pay, serve the public; Asian—responsibility, serve the public, variety; Caucasians—variety, adventure, responsibility. These findings suggest that departments may need to vary their recruitment efforts somewhat, depending on the particular group. The study by Langworthy, Hughes, and Sanders (1995) indicated that 90 percent of the surveyed departments use recruitment strategies to attract minorities.

In order to improve recruitment practices in today's competitive market, departments may need to consider nontraditional recruitment methods. For example, in New York, the use of a **Police Cadet Corps,** designed to increase applicants with college degrees, may also increase the number of women and minority applicants. The New York cadet corps, in operation since 1986, is used to recruit college seniors who are interested in joining the force after graduation; they receive scholarship money and agree to serve as police officers for two years. While attending college, the students work part-time as police cadets, thus gaining valuable field experience (*Law Enforcement News* 1989). After completing the two-year program, the cadet is promoted to police officer status while completing a college degree (Zecca 1993).

Another nontraditional recruitment method utilizes **community-service officers (CSOs)** who are assigned support duties that do not require sworn authority or a weapon. The Sacramento Police Department in California uses CSOs to help attract minority candidates out of high school, who, after graduating from the police academy, attend college while working for the department. After earning at least 60 college credits and attaining age 21, the CSO is eligible to become a sworn officer (Carter, Sapp, and Stephens 1989).

Another recruitment strategy that departments are using to attract minorities, women, and college graduates is granting *special entry conditions* for these groups. Such conditions may include lower fitness and education standards, exemptions from examinations, faster promotion, higher pay, and waiting list preferences. Langworthy, Hughes, and Sanders (1995) reported that approximately 40 percent of the surveyed departments have special entry conditions for minorities, 32 percent for women, and 28 percent for college graduates.

Selection

Following recruitment, the selection process attempts to determine which candidates are best suited to the needs of the department. The process must decide whether candidates have the requisite skills and abilities to perform effectively. In order to make such judgments, various selection criteria are used, including preemployment standards and preemployment testing, to establish a ranking system from which candidates are hired. It is crucial that these standards and tests be valid and reliable indicators of job performance. **Validity** is the degree to which a measure actually assesses the attribute it is designed to measure. For example, are the physical strength and agility criteria traditionally used for selection related to the ability to perform the job satisfactorily? If not, they are not valid criteria for selection. **Reliability** is a measure's ability to yield consistent results over time. In the physical strength and agility example, the measure would be reliable if a candidate taking the test on more than one occasion received the same or a similar score. Departments attempt to use criteria that are both valid and reliable; of course, it is possible to have selection criteria that are valid but not reliable, or reliable but not valid. For instance, although a physical strength score may be reliable, it may not be a valid criterion if it cannot be shown to be job related.

In addition, validity is important because invalid criteria may have adverse impact on groups that are protected by equal employment opportunity (EEO) laws and regulations. The Equal Employment Opportunity Act of 1972 extended to public agencies the "antidiscrimination in employment" provision of Title VII of the 1964 Civil Rights Act. Title VII prohibits any discrimination in the workplace based on race, color, religion, national origin, or sex. In *Griggs v. Duke Power Company* (1971) the Supreme Court held that an employer's requirement of a high school diploma and two standardized written tests for a position disqualified a higher percentage of blacks than whites and could not be shown to be related to job performance. Consequently, the standards had a **disparate impact** on *Griggs* specifically and on blacks in general. A selection method can be considered to have a legally disparate impact when the selection rate of a group is less than 80 percent of the most successful group; this is also known as the **four-fifths rule.** Prior to *Griggs*, selection standards could be used as long they did not intentionally discriminate; after *Griggs,* standards could not be used that were intended to be impartial but in fact were discriminatory in practice.

In another important decision, *Albemarle Paper Company v. Moody* (1975), the Supreme Court found that selection and promotion tests or standards must be shown to be related to job performance; that is, the standard must be **job related.** This decision had far-reaching implications for police selection because all selection criteria must be shown to be related to on-the-job performance. It is important to note, however, that departments can require a standard, even though it may have a disparate impact, if the standard can be shown to be a valid predictor of job performance. For example, in *Davis v. City of Dallas* (1985), the Supreme Court upheld the Dallas Police Department's requirement of 45 hours of college credit, even though it discriminated against minorities, because of the professional and complex nature of police work. Legal precedent for higher educational requirements had previously been established by other professions. Such a job-related standard, known as a **bona fide occupational qualification (BFOQ),** is permissible under Title VII, even though it may exclude members of a protected group.

Police departments, of course, should attempt to use selection methods that not only are valid but also have no adverse impact. This means that departments must commit resources to validating their selection and testing methods, a task usually accomplished through a job analysis. A **job analysis** identifies the behaviors necessary for adequate job performance. Based on such identification, the *knowledge, skills, and abilities (KSAs)* required for on-the-job behaviors are formulated; procedures (e.g., tests and interviews) are then developed to identify candidates who meet these requirements. The procedures are tested relative to their effectiveness in predicting job performance (Schneider and Schmitt 1986). Because job analysis can be quite complex, it is often conducted by an industrial or organizational psychologist or some professional with similar qualifications. Although the job-validation process is a rigorous undertaking for any department, it should not be looked upon merely as a legal obligation; selection systems that can be scientifically shown to produce high-quality candidates in a fair manner will withstand legal scrutiny and produce the candidates most likely to serve the community effectively (Sauls 1995, 31).

Preemployment Standards

Candidates are measured against a department's view of what is required to become an effective police officer. A number of minimum standards are established that must be met prior to employment. These standards are usually quite rigid and establish certain finite qualifications, which, if not met, will most likely eliminate the candidate from further consideration. Such standards may include age, height and weight, vision, physical agility and strength, residency, education, background, psychological condition, and medical condition. Although not all departments have all of these requirements, they are common to many. The standards themselves, however, vary considerably.

Age. Traditionally, police departments have allowed applicants to be between the ages of 21 and 32 to 38, with some accepting applicants as young as 18. Many police experts and police managers believe that 18- to 21-year-olds may not be mature enough to perform police work satisfactorily, and if hired should only be assigned service duties, much like the Police Cadet Corps and CSO programs described above. Along these lines, in 1997 the Chicago Police Department raised their minimum age for hiring from 21 to 23. And, although Wisconsin state law requires the Madison Police Department to consider applicants who are 18, new training classes typically include a number of individuals changing careers, with an average age of 27 to 28 years (Decker and Huckabee 2002). There have been legal challenges to age requirements, primarily at the upper limits. The Age Discrimination in Employment Act (ADEA) of 1967 and the amendment of 1974 have extended equal employment opportunity to apply to age, specifically to people 40 or older. Police departments have traditionally set maximum age limits for hiring because they also had mandatory retirement ages; many departments were temporarily exempt from the ADEA and were allowed to retain minimum-maximum age policies for a period of time (March 3, 1983, to December 31, 1993). Since January 1, 1994, however, this exemption has not applied, and today departments must be in compliance with the ADEA. Any recruiting or hiring practices that tend to discourage persons over 40 from applying might be deemed discriminatory. In compliance with the ADEA, departments are now hiring recruits over 40 and even 50; for example, the Los Angeles Police Department hired a 59-year-old male recruit as a probationary officer ("Rookie Cop, 59 . . ." 1994).

Height and weight. Stringent minimum and maximum height and weight requirements were standards for most departments in the past. As with age requirements, however, these requirements have been changing over the past several decades due to legal challenges. For instance, minimum height requirements have been challenged successfully as being discriminatory against both women and minority groups, especially Asians and Hispanics. For example, in *Vanguard Justice Society v. Hughes* (1979), the court noted that a 5-foot, 7-inch height requirement excluded 95 percent of the female population but only 32 percent of the male population, and found this to be evidence of sex discrimination. Because of such rulings, the general standard has now become weight in proportion to height.

Vision. Vision requirements were also traditionally very stringent, ranging from 20/20 to 20/70 uncorrected in both eyes, or 20/20 corrected with contacts or glasses. This standard too has been relaxed over the years, because such a requirement cannot be job validated and eliminates otherwise potentially strong candidates. Virtually all police departments, however, still maintain certain corrected and uncorrected vision requirements.

Physical agility and strength. Testing of physical agility and strength has been related to an assumed need for physical strength and endurance. For example, candidates would be required to drag a dummy, scale a wall, perform an agility run, or run a certain timed distance (a half-mile to two miles); if they fell below a certain minimum, they would be eliminated. According to national surveys by the Bureau of Justice Statistics (BJS) of nearly 3,000 state and local police departments and sheriff's offices, in local departments of all sizes, 44 percent use some form of physical agility testing; however, for departments representing populations of over 250,000 (i.e., medium- to large-sized agencies), approximately 90 percent use it (Hickman and Reaves 2003a). For sheriff's offices of all sizes, 35 percent use a physical agility test; for agencies representing more than 100,000 people, over 50 percent use this screening method (Hickman and Reaves 2003b).

Since many of these standards cannot be shown to be job related, they tend to be discriminatory in nature, especially against women. For example, Birzer and Craig (1996) reported that 93 percent of the male, but only 28 percent of the female, applicants passed the physical agility test for a midwestern city department for a nine-year period of time. Further, data collected by the Police Foundation suggests that agencies with physical agility tests have a relatively lower representation of women on the force (Townsey 1992). In her national study of 62 police departments (38 city, 21 county, and 3 state agencies), Lonsway (2003) lends strong support to the Police Foundation concept of lower female representation. She found that the vast majority of agencies (89 percent) use some form of physical agility testing for selection; however, in those agencies that did not use such a test, the representation of sworn women officers was 45 percent higher (15.8 percent to 10.9 percent). The research further indicated a wide range of physical activities used in tests across the country, as well as a wide variation in the standards of

Many police departments use physical agility and strength tests—such as climbing a rope or pole—as pre-employment standards. Some of these standards cannot be shown to be job related and are discriminatory in nature, especially against women

performance required (e.g., cutoff points for pass/fail). This lack of uniformity suggests both consistency and validity problems with this type of testing process, which, when combined with the effect of significantly reducing the number of women applicants who can be considered, is an important discriminatory issue that departments must address. As Lonsway notes:

> Voluminous research has documented that women are capable of performing the job of police officer, that they bring unique and necessary skills to that task, and that they employ less excessive force. It therefore becomes increasingly important to review the various alternatives that are available to reduce the negative effect on women applicants. Furthermore, as a legal matter, a selection device may be successfully challenged if the plaintiff shows that less discriminatory alternatives exist. (2003; 265)

Accordingly, some of the less discriminatory alternatives include either no physical testing or health-based screening (Lonsway 2003). *No physical agility testing* would eliminate the negative impact on female applicants from the selection process. Furthermore, there has been no evidence of an adverse impact on policing where this has been done. In Florida, for example, over one-half of the local police agencies and sheriff's departments use no physical agility test, and no entry-level physical agility test is used by the FBI or the Bureau of Alcohol, Tobacco, and Firearms. When no physical testing is used, departments typically require a medical examination and do the physical training in the academy. With this approach, the physical performance of recruits is tested after they participate in a conditioning program as part of the training academy (i.e., post-academy testing), which not only mitigates the risk of discriminatory impact by allowing recruits to train for successful performance, but may also allow for better assessment of job-related tasks such as defense tactics (Gaines, Falkenberg, and Gambino 1993).

Health-based screening also tends to eliminate the negative effect on women applicants because appropriate norms are used; that is, passing standards are generally normed by gender and/or age (Hoover 1992). This gender norming of health-based standards has also been repeatedly upheld by the courts, both for hiring and testing of police incumbents. The purpose of health-based screening is not based on any attempt to predict successful job performance, but rather on general physical fitness that may have an impact on employee levels of physical and mental health, morale, job efficiency, absenteeism, injuries, and turnover (Mealey 1979; Shepard 1986).

To ensure that police recruits are physically capable of completing academy training, perhaps the best approach would be to use post-academy physical testing combined with health screening. However, physical training programs in the academy should not use physical exercise as a way to discipline or weed out recruits or as a way to establish "macho" status (Charles 1982). Such "physicality" problems are common within academy training and undermine the goals of selecting successful police officer candidates and encouraging lifetime fitness maintenance (Charles 1983), as well as promote an inaccurate police role and image.

Stringent height and weight requirements in policing have been declared discriminatory.

***Residency*.** Whether or not a department has a residency requirement has a strong impact on those who may be recruited. There are essentially two types of requirements: (1) an applicant must reside within a geographic area (state, county, or city) for a specific period of time (one year is common) prior to application (preemployment), or (2) an applicant must relocate after he or she is selected (postemployment). Reaves and Goldberg (1999) reported in their national survey of local police departments with 100 or more sworn personnel that 92 percent of the 49 state agencies, and approximately 60 percent of the local police departments, required some type of residency requirement for new officers. Proponents of such a requirement argue that it is important for individuals to have an understanding of the community in which they work and that those who live in the community have a greater stake in and concern for the community.

Opponents of residency requirements argue that they unnecessarily restrict the applicant pool because the best candidates may not live within the geographic limits; they can also have a negative impact on minority recruitment. It seems clear, however, that if departments wish to hire the best available personnel, then it makes little sense to establish policies that severely restrict the applicant pool; thus, departments should *not* have preemployment residency requirements. Additionally, a national study of large departments found that residency requirements affect citizens' perceptions of the police in a negative way—especially with respect to their ability to protect them (Murphy and Worrall 1999). However, if a residency requirement is necessary for political or other reasons, then a post-employment policy that allows the recruit a reasonable period of time to relocate appears to be reasonable.

Education. Advances in raising educational requirements for police have been slow and sporadic. Until the 1980s, in many police departments an officer with a college degree was often viewed with contempt or resentment; it was not understood why anyone with a degree would want to enter policing. Although times have changed considerably, college requirements for the job have not kept pace. The Bureau of Justice Statistics national surveys indicate that in 2000, only 1 percent of departments required a college degree for employment, 8 percent required a 2-year degree, and 86 percent required only a high school diploma (Hickman and Reaves 2003a). The percentage of officers employed by a department with some type of college requirement for new officers, however, has increased from 10 percent in 1990 to 32 percent in 2000 (Hickman and Reaves 2003a); in sheriffs' offices, some type of college requirement has increased from 4 percent in 1990 to 13 percent in 2000 (Hickman and Reaves 2003b).

A thorough discussion of higher education in policing can be found in Chapter 14. For our purposes here, suffice it to say that the slow progress in the development of higher education standards is puzzling, especially since the preponderance of evidence indicates that college education has a positive effect on officer attitudes, behavior, and performance. In reality, there is much a department can do to recruit college graduates. For instance, in a study of 37 Texas police departments (TELEMASP 1996), it was found that the median number of recruiting trips to college campuses was six and that 21 departments (56 percent) have educational-incentive pay, providing additional pay for officers who have attained certain levels of higher education. In addition, some departments grant bonus points on hiring tests or use an accelerated career ladder for those with a college education. Still others provide tuition-assistance programs and flexible-duty shifts for officers who are still working on their degrees.

One of the departments reported that it has had some success in recruiting college-educated officers through participation in a college internship program.

General Suitability

Departments usually conduct an extensive investigation of an applicant's past experience, behavior, and work history in an attempt to assess his or her character and general suitability for police work. In general, this process is composed of a background investigation and a polygraph examination.

Background investigation. A thorough background investigation, based on the extensive personal history provided by the candidate, is one of the most important aspects of the selection process. The investigator attempts to determine if the person is honest and reliable and would make a contribution to the department. Family background, employment and credit history, employment and personal references, friends and neighbors, education records, criminal and possibly juvenile records, drug use, and, when appropriate, military records, are all checked to develop a general assessment of the person's lifestyle prior to applying for police work. Cohen and Chaiken (1972), in their study of New York police applicants, found that applicants who were rated as excellent by the background investigators had the lowest incidence of misconduct (some 36 percent had personal complaints filed), whereas the applicants rated as poor had the highest incidence of misconduct (some 68 percent). Because these investigations are time-consuming and expensive, some police departments, especially smaller ones with limited resources, may not be very thorough. Snowden and Fuss (2000) found this to be true; that is, in larger departments more time was spent on training and background investigations, including greater use of secondary references and procedures. Because background investigations appear to be a good predictor of future police behavior, it is important that departments take no shortcuts at this stage.

Two important aspects of the background investigation relate to a candidate's criminal record and history of drug use. Generally, a criminal record does not automatically disqualify one from police service. One survey found that 96 percent of departments would reject an applicant with a felony conviction and that 90 percent would reject one with a juvenile felony conviction (Eisenberg, Kent, and Wall 1973). With respect to misdemeanor convictions, departments vary widely, but the trend is to examine the type and extent of violations and make a determination based on the candidate's overall record. Some research suggests that preemployment use of illegal drugs is one of the best indicators of postemployment drug use by police officers (Kraska and Kappeler 1988). Several court cases have laid the foundation for what is a permissible drug use standard for police employment practices. For instance, a Dallas Police Department standard requiring police applicants not to have recent or excessive histories of marijuana use was upheld (*Davis v. City of Dallas*, 1985). In *Shield Club v. City of Cleveland* (1986), the court upheld drug-testing requirements and the rejection of applicants who tested positive for narcotics, amphetamines, or hallucinogenics. In both these rulings, the courts indicated that such requirements were job related and therefore not discriminatory. It is also important to note that each of the departments utilized an objective testing system that prevented any form of individual discrimination. Inside Policing 6.1

provides examples of different departments' prior drug-use policies, which have become more lenient over the past decade or two.

Inside Policing 6.1　　　**Police Departments More Tolerant Regarding Past Drug Use**

Prior use of drugs by recruits has become more prevalent during the past two decades, and police agencies have had to wrestle with adopting more tolerant policies in order to attract candidates. This is also an interesting ethical debate, since it is possible that if officers who have used or abused drugs in the past are hired, they may need to arrest someone for acts they themselves have committed. Listed below are some departments that have recently changed their drug-use policies.

- The Virginia State Police recently changed their guidelines to consider those who have tried (once) any Schedule I (heroin, mescaline, LSD) or Schedule II drug (cocaine, opium, barbiturates) more than five years before applying. However, any use of LSD or PCP would mean disqualification; marijuana may have been used more than once, but not in the past 12 months. People convicted of driving under the influence (DUI) once, more than five years prior to applying, are also eligible.

- In Loveland, Colorado, approximately 10 years ago when it was difficult for the department to find anyone who had not experimented with pot, the department changed its policy to consider a recruit who had not used an illegal substance in the past three years (or more than 20 times) or sold or used any kind of illicit drug that is still a prosecutable offense. The department required its applicants to have some college; they believe there might be a correlation between attending college and admitting to using marijuana (this is an interesting dilemma for departments requiring higher education).

- In San Jose, California, applicants will not necessarily be disqualified for using any particular drug once; in essence, the effect of a history of drug use is determined on a case-by-case basis.

- The Metro-Dade Police Department, in Florida, allows for one-time use and some juvenile drug experimentation but bars outright all Schedule I and Schedule II drugs.

- The FBI has one of the more stringent prior-drug-use standards, barring hard drugs for a period of 10 years prior to hiring, and marijuana for up to five years.

Sources: Adapted from: J. Katz, 2000. "Prior Drug Use OK for Cops Nowadays," *San Francisco Examiner* June 18: A1; "Youthful Indiscretions," 2002, *Law Enforcement News*, March 15/31: 7; "Getting the Inside Dope," 1996, *Law Enforcement News*, October 31: 1; 14.

Polygraph examination. The polygraph, or lie detector, is used to check the accuracy of background information and to determine if there has been any inappropriate behavior, past or present, on the applicant's part (e.g., criminal acts, illegal drug use). Although the polygraph has been touted by some as an effective tool in discovering problems with applicants, some research has suggested that it is not a reliable method to determine truth or falsehood of an individual's statements (see Hodes, Hunt, and Raskin 1985; Kleinmuntz and Szucko 1982; Rafky and Sussman 1985). One problem with the polygraph is the amount of stress it puts on a candidate and the resulting false positives that result, that is, when a candidate is falsely accused of lying. Therefore, some jurisdictions have made such testing illegal. Furthermore, some departments still ask questions about an applicant's lifestyle or sexual practices that are private matters. If a polygraph examination is administered, all questions relating to the applicant's background should be job related. Finally, the polygraph should never be used as a substitute for the background investigation but only as a supplement to it.

Psychological condition. Psychological screening to determine a candidate's suitability for police work has become more common over the past decade; this screening may be written, oral, or both. The most commonly used written tests are the Minnesota Multiphasic Personality Inventory (MMPI); California Personality Inventory (CPI) (Johnson 1990); and the Inwald Personality Inventory (IPI), developed specifically for police screening (TELEMASP 1994). After the tests are administered, they are usually scored by a psychologist, who is looking for serious emotional problems that would disqualify a candidate, or for a profile of a person who would make a "good" police officer. There is considerable controversy surrounding the use of psychological testing for police screening; for example, research has indicated that some tests are racially biased (Winters 1989) or not job related (Dwyer, Prien, and Bernard 1990). After reviewing the literature, Burbeck and Furnham (1985) suggested that such tests may be useful for screening out people suffering from some mental abnormality but not for predicting job performance. Metchik (1999) also cautions that the "screening out" model has questionable validity and reliability , since it cannot differentiate individuals who will become mediocre officers from those who will become superior officers, and the potential for false positives (i.e., incorrectly eliminating good candidates) is high.

Because of these problems with psychological testing, it has been argued by some critics (e.g., Dwyer, Prien, and Bernard 1990) that until such time that predictors identifying job relatedness are developed, clinical assessments for screening police candidates should be eliminated. In the interim, it is suggested that because the best predictor of future behavior is past behavior, background investigation should be more thorough in order to identify candidates with tendencies toward morally unacceptable or violent behavior. Police departments should consider increasing their utilization and scope of background investigation for screening purposes and rely less on clinical judgments.

Part of the problem of selection revolves around the changing nature of policing (i.e., toward community policing) and the perception of what makes a good officer (Grant and Grant 1995). For instance, the Independent Commission on the LAPD (1991) found that prior violent behavior of applicants appeared not to be a negative factor in selection in the Los Angeles Police Department. Such a finding suggests, at least at that time, that a "rough and aggressive" demeanor was perceived to be an asset to police performance rather than a warning signal for potential abusive violent behavior. Metchik (1999) suggests that among the primary goals of community policing is the ability of officers and citizens to work in partnership to improve neighborhood quality of life. Thus, the role of the officer is changing and the "thin blue line" between the police and public is vanishing. Accordingly, the traditional screening model may not be suitable, since it may eliminate individuals who would make very good officers in the community-policing era.

Medical condition. Virtually all police departments have certain medical requirements that an individual must meet before being hired. A medical examination is given by a physician either designated by the department or chosen by the candidate. The exam attempts to determine the general health of the candidate and identify specific conditions, such as heart, back, or knee problems. In general, any "weaknesses" that may be aggravated by the requirements of police work will eliminate the candidate from further consideration. The reason is that the costs of losing an officer to injury or illness, often with long-term disability compensation or a lawsuit, are too great. If a department requires some form of drug testing, it usually takes place during this phase of the process.

Preemployment Testing

The preemployment standards for police departments, and the legal justifications, change periodically. This is an area in which departments need specific, and the most current, information in order to select the best qualified candidates. Although preemployment standards are usually scored on a pass-fail basis and are used to eliminate candidates, preemployment tests are generally used to place candidates in order of rank. The two most commonly used tests are some form of written test and the oral interview. Some departments use the written test simply as a qualifier (i.e., on a pass-fail basis) and the oral interview as the only criterion for rank order.

Written and cognitive tests. Traditionally, departments have used some types of written and cognitive tests, usually some form of standardized intelligence test or jurisdictionally specific knowledge test to screen and rank-order candidates. Few attempts were made, however, to determine if these tests had any impact on the applicant's ability to be a successful police officer. Although it is easy to argue that police officers should be intelligent and knowledgeable, it is difficult to determine what kind of intelligence or knowledge is being measured and what level should be required.

In addition, some research suggests that minorities tend to score lower on police-entry exams (e.g., see Sproule 1984; Gaines, Costello, and Crabtree 1989). Thus, if a simple rank ordering of candidates is used, it will generally create an adverse impact. These problems have led to attempts to validate police written tests empirically since at least the late 1970s (e.g., see Crosby, Rosenfield, and Thornton 1979), and for departments to seek exams that are more objective and job related (Law Enforcement Assistance Administration 1973).0

In a more recent study, Gaines and Falkenberg (1998) examined the written exams of over 400 police applicants in one jurisdiction and found that while males and females did not score differently, African Americans had significantly lower scores than whites. It was determined that exam scores were primarily a function of the *educational level* of the applicant and also unrelated to oral board scores. The exam had questionable validity in that it did not discriminate between highly qualified and less qualified applicants. Since the exam primarily measured educational level, the authors recommended simply adopting a minimum educational requirement. Interestingly, they argued that a more racially diverse pool of candidates would emerge using a two-year college requirement in lieu of the exam. Alternatively, police departments could institute a written exam aimed at the level of a two-year college student.

Although written tests have limitations, departments must have a way of distinguishing among a large pool of candidates and therefore will continue to use such testing. A primary concern is that the tests be objective. Objective testing standards can be defined as measures of relevant knowledge, skills, and abilities (KSAs) used in a neutral manner without regard to the individual's membership in any group (Pynes 1994). There also appears to be a consensus building that *cognitive employment tests* (i.e., tests of the ability to synthesize and analyze material) are an important selection criterion and are equally valid for virtually all jobs (Schmidt 1988). J. Hunter (1986), for instance, found the following with respect to cognitive-ability tests: (1) general cognitive ability predicts performance ratings in all lines of work, although validity is higher for complex jobs than for simple jobs; (2) general cognitive ability predicts training success at a uniformly high level for all jobs; (3) data on job knowledge show that cognitive ability determines how much and how quickly a person learns; and (4) cognitive ability predicts the ability to react in innovative ways to situations in which knowledge does not specify exactly what to do.

Oral interview. Almost all police departments use some form of oral interview, usually at the end of the selection process. The interview allows police representatives (and sometimes community members) to observe the candidates directly with respect to their suitability for the department and to clear up any inconsistencies that may have developed in the earlier stages of the process. Candidates are measured on attributes that generally are not measured elsewhere, including motivation, verbal skills, confidence, potential for violence, decision-making skills, and overall demeanor. The interview is not usually substantive, that is, with specific questions about police policy or the department, but it can be. Typical questions might include these: Why do you want to be a police officer? How have you prepared yourself for a career in law enforcement? What types of books or magazines do you read? Why do you want to work for this department? There will usually be a few questions about hypothetical situations and how the person would respond (i.e., make decisions) to them. For community-policing departments, Campbelis (1999) proposes in-depth interviews designed to identify problem-solving skills and techniques that the candidate might possess. DeLong (1999) further recommends the use of problem-solving scenarios to enable the evaluator(s) to determine if candidates have the needed attributes to adequately perform community-policing activities.

Often, there is an oral board that includes at least three persons: a departmental representative (e.g., a police officer with the rank of sergeant or above), a civil service representative, and a representative from the community. In many departments the interview is highly structured, using specific questions and evaluation forms in an attempt to make the interview job valid. A score is assigned to each candidate, which when combined with the written score, provides a total score; candidates are then rank ordered with respect to hiring priority (though some departments may assign more weight to either the written test or the oral interview).

Some departments use only the oral interview to rank order candidates. This method has been useful in helping departments to overcome potentially adverse impacts of other selection criteria and to increase the employment of women and minorities. Although the interview is more flexible, it is also more subjective, and there is no strong evidence that it is a useful predictor of future police performance (Burbeck and Furnham 1985). Other research indicates that the validity of the oral interview is also suspect and that the characteristics of the raters influence the ratings and ultimately the rankings of the candidates (Falkenberg, Gaines, and Cox 1990; Doerner 1997). Methods that help to improve the validity of the oral interview include using only those rating factors that are critical components of the job, training the raters so that they clearly understand the process and the way responses should be graded, and using set standards that raters can compare with candidate responses (Gaines and Kappeler 1992).

Table 6.1 presents a summary of the general steps of the police selection process and the most important concerns at each step.

Table 6.1 Process Summary of Police Selection	
Steps	**Related Issues**
Recruitment	Advertising, requests, and referrals
Selection criteria	Age, height, weight, vision, criminal record, and possible residency requirement
Written examination	General intelligence or job content
Physical examination	Agility and endurance
Oral interview	Communication skills, interpersonal style, and decision-making ability
Psychological testing	Emotional stability and psychological profiles
Background investigation	Character, employment/credit history, education, references, and criminal record
Polygraph examination	Character and background information
Medical examination	General health and specific problems

Source: R. Roberg, J. Kuykendall, and K. Novak, *Police Management,* 3rd ed. (Los Angeles: Roxbury, 2002), 133.

Table 6.2 represents the findings of the BJS national survey of state and local police department screening methods for new officer applicants in 2000 (Hickman and Reaves 2003a). As indicated in Table 6.2, nearly all used background investigations (96 percent) and personal interviews (96 percent), and a majority used medical exams (81 percent), drug tests (67 percent), and psychological evaluations (61 percent). Among departments serving 25,000 or more residents (i.e., the medium- to large-size agencies), about 8 in10 used physical agility tests and written aptitude tests. More than half of the departments in these population categories used personality inventories and polygraph exams. Sheriff's offices, in comparison with local departments, required substantially fewer psychological evaluations, physical agility tests, written aptitude tests, and personality inventories; the remaining screening criteria were similar to local departments (Hickman and Reaves 2003b).

The selection of candidates for police departments is time-consuming and expensive. Given the costs, the steps of the process are normally arranged from the least costly and most likely to eliminate the most candidates to the most expensive. Accordingly, the written and physical agility tests are usually given at the beginning, followed by the medical exam, polygraph examination (if used), psychological testing (if used), background investigation, and finally the oral interview. The passage of the Americans with Disabilities Act (ADA) in 1990, however, will have a substantial impact on this traditional sequencing.

Americans With Disabilities Act. The purpose of the ADA is to eliminate barriers to equal employment opportunity and to provide equal access to individuals with disabilities to the programs, services, and activities delivered by government entities (Rubin 1994). Thus, the ADA prohibits discrimination against qualified individuals with a disability; it does not mean that by having a disability, one is entitled to protection under the law, but if a person meets the selection criteria for a job and has a disability, he or she cannot be discriminated against for the job. Generally, blanket exclusions of individuals with a particular disability are not permissible. For instance, to exclude all persons with diabetes would ignore the varying degrees of severity and the ability to control the symptoms (Rubin 1994). Also, standards that tend to screen out individuals or groups of individuals on the basis of disability must be related to functions that are essential to the job.

Table 6.2   Screening Methods Used in Selection of New Officers Recruits in Local Police Departments, by Size of Population Served, 2000

Interviews, Tests, and Examinations Used to Select New Officer Recruits

Population served	Background investigation	Personal Interview	Medical exam	Drug Test	Psychological evaluation	Physical agility test	Written aptitude test	Personality inventory	Polygraph exam
All sizes	96%	96%	81%	67%	61%	44%	43%	31%	21%
1,000,000 or more	100	100	100	100	93	87	73	47	73
500,000–999,999	94	94	94	85	94	88	91	71	61
250,000–499,999	98	95	100	90	93	90	80	60	80
100,000–249,999	99	95	96	89	94	83	84	62	72
50,000–99,999	99	99	98	87	97	81	78	60	53
25,000–49,999	99	98	99	87	95	81	79	54	50
10,000–24,999	98	98	98	78	86	69	68	45	32
2,500–9,999	97	96	87	74	65	48	48	29	23
Under 2,500	95	94	65	52	41	24	21	20	7

Source: Adapted from M. J. Hickman and B. A. Reaves, *Local Police Departments, 2000* (Washington, DC: Bureau of Justice Statistics, 2003a), 5.

The ADA requires that applicants be given a conditional offer of employment prior to taking an exam or a test that may be disability related, including background investigations, psychological and medical exams, and polygraph tests. A good rule of thumb is that questions that would disclose information regarding a disability, whether asked on an application or during an interview, may be construed as a disability-related inquiries. That holds true for any selection procedure that would disclose information regarding a disability. If any of these tests are to be administered prior to a conditional offer of employment, no questions may be asked relating to disabilities unless they are essential to police performance. Although the full impact of the ADA on police selection is complicated and ongoing, departments will need to change many of their current procedures to ensure that selection criteria that screen out persons with disabilities are job related and that questions relating to disabilities (unless job related) are asked only after a conditional offer of employment has been made.

Once candidates are selected, they are usually rank ordered and employed based on need. This ranking lasts for a given period, usually from six months to two years, before retesting is undertaken. Once selected, candidates start their developmental phase by attending a recruit training program.

Development

Development of a police department's human resources for successful careers in police work begins with the training of the newly hired recruits, moves to a second phase of field training and evaluation, and continues into a third phase of long-term development, or career growth.

Recruit Training

The initial training of the recruit is generally conducted through a police training academy, where the program content is determined by a state standards organization, often known as **Peace Officer Standards and Training (POST)**. Although all police departments must meet minimum standards, some departments provide substantially more training than is minimally required. Larger departments often maintain their own academies, whereas smaller departments tend to send their recruits to regional or county academies.

Some states now require that people complete one of these basic training programs prior to being considered for employment. As a result, the department hires an already trained employee and does not have to pay for the cost of the training, including the recruit's salary while attending the academy. Another recent development in preemployment screening is testing for literacy. Because literacy skills in police applicants have been markedly declining, and written civil service tests do not adequately screen for literacy, some states (e.g., Michigan and California) require all candidates to pass one of any number of tests designed to measure reading and writing skills before they begin the academy (Clark 1992). Since 1988, for example, the regional training center for Miami-area police departments has required participants in its preservice program to take a test to make sure that they can read at a tenth-grade level. The requirement was imposed because, according to the training center, earning a high school diploma does not guarantee that the graduate can read beyond the junior high school level (Clark 1992). Because the Miami example is undoubtedly reflective of a national concern, the arguments for moving toward requiring a college degree become even more evident.

Recruit training is influenced by program design and delivery. Some of the more important considerations in the design and delivery of a recruit training program include program orientation, philosophy and instructional methods, course content, and field training.

Program orientation. One of the important issues in police training is whether the orientation should be stressful or nonstressful. *Stressful training* is like a military boot camp or basic training; *nonstressful training* has a more academic environment. Many recruit programs continue to have a stressful orientation, expecting recruits to be obedient and subjecting them to both intellectual and physical demands in a highly structured environment. Discipline and even harassment have been an integral part of many of these programs. For in-service training (i.e., training after employment) with more experienced officers, a more academic environment is the norm.

Although stressful recruit training has a long tradition, no evidence exists that this approach is a valid way to train recruits (Berg 1990) or that it is any more or less effective than a nonstressful approach. Probably the most comprehensive study in this area

(Earle 1973) indicated that nonstressful training produces officers who receive higher performance evaluations, like their work more, and get along better with the public. Given the trend toward community policing, problem solving, and higher educational requirements, a stress-oriented approach is likely to be counterproductive and should be eliminated from training programs, replaced by a more academic approach.

Philosophy and instructional methods. The philosophy of a program revolves around two primary approaches: training and education. **Training** can be defined as the process of instructing the individual *how* to do the job by providing relevant information about the job; **education** can be defined as the process of providing a general body of knowledge on which decisions can be based as to *why* something is being done while performing the job. Training deals with specific facts and procedures, whereas education is broader in scope and is concerned with theories, concepts, issues, and alternatives. Many police training programs are heavily oriented toward teaching facts and procedures to the exclusion of theories, concepts, and analytical reasoning. A strict reliance on this approach is problematic, because so much police work requires analysis and reasoning instead of application of specific procedures that supposedly fit all circumstances. Therefore, many academies are attempting to increase the percentage of time spent on an educational approach by employing professionals in the social sciences, especially criminal justice and criminology, psychology, and sociology, as instructors.

Another important aspect of program development is the type of instructional methods to be used. In large part, this is determined by what teaching philosophy is going to be emphasized; two contrasting teaching philosophies are pedagogy and andragogy (Knowles 1970). Pedagogy involves a one-way transfer of knowledge, usually in the form of facts and procedures, from the instructor to the student (recruit). The primary concern is to promote "absolute solutions" to particular situations. An alternative teaching philosophy, which promotes the mutual involvement of students and instructors in the learning process and stresses analytical and conceptual skills, is known as andragogy.

Knowles (1970) describes **pedagogy** as the art and science of teaching children, and **andragogy** as the art and science of helping adults learn. While he does not suggest any fundamental differences between the way adults and children learn, he believes that there are significant differences that emerge in the learning process as maturation takes place. Thus, where pedagogy involves lectures, use of visual aids, student note taking, rote memorization, and taking factual tests, andragogy involves problem analysis, role playing, group discussion and projects, independent student learning, and "acting out" to learn required skills in simulated situations. As administrators continue to recognize the complex nature of the police role and the need to use discretion wisely, increased emphasis should be placed on using andragogical methods of instruction (Roberg 1979). At the same time, pedagogical teaching methods are also necessary, especially with respect to those activities that require memorization (e.g., laws and policies) and behavioral techniques (e.g., traffic stops and approaching a suspect).

The types of instructional methods used in the academy are also critical to the development of community policing. Even though the relevance of an andragogical approach to police training has been recognized since at least the late 1970s (Roberg 1979), programs still tend to emphasize how to do a job rather than why, or why one method may be more effective than another. Recruits would most likely benefit from such an approach with respect to topics that are relevant to community policing, including problem solving, cultural diversity, sexual harassment, conflict resolution,

An instructor presents an idea utilizing pedagogical methods in a typical recruit training class.

communication, and community organization skills (Birzer 1999). In addition, by becoming more actively involved in the learning process, officers may also become more self-directed, another important ingredient of community policing (Birzer and Tannehill 2001).

While an andragogical approach to recruit training offers the potential to improve learning, practice, and self-direction, Birzer (2003) notes that it may be difficult to implement. For instance, management may offer resistance or have trouble implementing the new methods. Also, those responsible for implementing the training curriculum may be limited due to mandated guidelines from training commissions and legal requirements. In addition, because the andragogical approach is a natural complement to community policing, and thus may become associated with it, those who oppose community policing would most likely also resist a new learning-training approach as well. This proved to be the case in the Chicago Police Department, for example, where an evaluation (Skogan and Hartnett 1997) of new training modules to support community policing discovered several problems, including lack of time for curriculum revision and preparation, lack of unity among officers, and hostility toward the new curriculum.

Course content. Police training programs and curricula should be based on two common assumptions: first, the programs should incorporate the *mission statement* of the department and *ethical considerations,* and second, training should be based on what an officer *actually does* on a daily basis (Alpert and Smith 1990; Bayley and Bittner 1989). The subject matter should be based on a **task analysis** of the jobs to be performed by the recruits; such task analysis, however, still tends to be more the exception than the rule, with training based more on legal requirements and experience. Nevertheless, some departments have tried to identify police tasks that are important to the job and to base their training on them.

The increased use of role playing in police training should help to improve decision-making in dangerous situations.

Some states have conducted comprehensive task-analysis studies of several police positions (e.g., entry-level and various managerial positions).

The importance of basing training on what an officer actually does cannot be overstated: that is, to what degree is reality presented and discussed? What image of the police is presented? Traditionally, training has underrepresented order maintenance and social-service aspects of the police role while overrepresenting law enforcement activities; such an emphasis has undoubtedly contributed toward a **macho orientation** of policing that is still evident. Of course, the particular image presented can have a significant impact on the way recruits view their role as police officers. Because the training program is seen as representing the department's view of police work, an unrealistic presentation of policing will not only send the wrong message to recruits, but most likely make initial occupational adjustments more difficult as well.

As the complex nature of the police role has become recognized (Roberg 1976), training requirements, including the number of hours trained and the number of subjects covered, has increased significantly. According to the BJS national survey (Hickman and Reaves 2003a), local police recruits, in 2000, were required to complete an average of about 1,600 hours of academy and field training in departments serving 100,000 or more residents, compared to about 800 hours in those serving a population of less than 2,500. As Table 6.3 indicates, however, there are significant differences among departments in the number of hours required for both academy and field training. On average, about 70 percent of these training hours were state-mandated, with the remainder being a departmental requirement. The number of hours of academy and field training by department size are not significantly different for sheriffs' officers (Hickman and Reaves 2003b).

Table 6.3   Training Requirements for New Officer Recruits in Local Police Departments, by Size of Population Served, 2000

| | Average Number of Hours Required | | | | | |
| | Academy | | | Field | | |
Population Served	Total	State-Mandated	Other Required	Total	State-Mandated	Other Required
All sizes	637	514	123	417	228	189
1,000,000 or more	1,051	564	487	534	189	345
500,000–999,999	950	586	364	784	425	359
250,000–499,999	991	577	414	659	336	323
100,000–249,999	853	601	252	757	425	322
50,000–99,999	790	604	186	689	414	275
25,000–49,999	763	586	177	537	297	240
10,000–24,999	751	574	177	537	297	240
2,500–9,999	611	514	97	389	235	154
Under 2,500	532	469	63	244	153	91

Note: Average number of training hours excludes departments not required training.

Source: M. J. Hickman, and B. A. Reaves, *Local Police Departments, 2000* (Washington, D.C.: Bureau of Justice Statistics, 2003a), 6.

An example of the diverse topics covered in recruit training can be seen in California's curriculum (mandated by the Commission on Peace Officer Standards and Training, or POST), which includes 41 domains (topics). These are to be covered in a minimum of 599 hours of training—larger departments require more hours—with an additional 65 hours of testing. The testing includes both scenarios (where simulated field situations are presented and recruits respond to them) and written exams. In addition, once a recruit becomes a sworn officer, he or she must also complete a minimum of 24 hours of POST-certified training once every two years. Table 6.4 provides a list of the topics covered and the minimum number of hours required on each topic.

Table 6.4   California Police Academy Training Curriculum Content and Minimum Hourly Requirements

	Domain Description	Minimum Number of Hours
01	History, Professionalism, and Ethics	8
02	Criminal Justice System	4
03	Community Relations	12
04	Victimology/Crisis Interventions	6
05	Introduction to Criminal Law	6
06	Crimes Against Property	10
07	Crimes Against Persons	10
08	General Crimes Statutes	4
09	Crimes Against Children	6
10	Sex Crimes	6
11	Juvenile Law and Procedure	6
12	Controlled Substances	12
13	ABC (Alcohol, Beverage Code) Law	4
14	Laws of Arrest	12
15	Search and Seizure	12
16	Presentation of Evidence	8
17	Investigative Report Writing	40
18	Vehicle Operations	24
19	Use of Force	12
20	Patrol Techniques	12
21	Vehicle Pullovers	14
22	Crimes in Progress	16
23	Handling Disputes/Crowd Control	12
24	Domestic Violence	8
25	Unusual Occurrences	4
26	Missing Persons	4
27	Traffic Enforcement	22
28	Traffic Accident Investigation	12
29	Preliminary Investigation	42
30	Custody	4
31	Physical Fitness/Officer Stress	40
32	Person Searches/Baton, etc.	60
33	First Aid and CPR	21

Table 6.4   California Police Academy Training Curriculum Content and Minimum Hourly Requirements (continued)

Domain Description		Minimum Number of Hours
34	Firearms/Chemical Agents	72
35	Information Systems	4
36	Persons with Disabilities	6
37	Gang Awareness	8
38	Crimes Against the Justice System	4
39	Weapons Violations	4
40	Hazardous Materials	4
41	Cultural Diversity/Discrimination	24
	Minimum Instructional Hours	599
Types of Testing		**Hours**
	Scenario Tests	40
	POST-Constructed Knowledge Tests	25
	Total Minimum Required Hours	646

Source: Adapted from Commission on Peace Officer Standards and Training. 1995. *Bulletin 95–9: Regular Basic Course Required Minimum Hours Increases From 560 to 646.* Sacramento, CA: POST, May 12.

Departments must determine what subject matter is most important, because programs are constrained by time and resources. The amount of time devoted to any particular subject emphasizes to recruits the importance attached to that subject by the department. Table 6.4 shows the varying amounts of hours devoted to certain topics, from a low of four hours to a high of 72 hours. It should be noted that in police training there will always be debate regarding what topics should be covered and for how much time. For example, given its importance to effective and just policing, should the area of professionalism and ethics receive more time? What about the use of force? And, as new developments occur in policing, what new topics should be added to the curriculum (such as problem solving and community policing)? Answering such questions is the reason why it is so important that the training for any particular job be based on task analysis; the importance attached to the subject matter is then based on scientific evidence rather than on a few individuals' experience, intuition, or guesswork.

Keeping up: Changing curriculum content. Based on the above discussion, there is likely a need in most police academies to change curricula content by expanding or adding new topics, or by trying new methods. For instance, in one national survey on *police ethics* of 874 members of the International Association of Chiefs of Police (IACP 1998), it was found that while 83 percent of the departments provided some form of ethics training for their recruits, 71 percent provided only four classroom hours or less, whereas 17 percent provided eight hours of training for ethics. For supervisors, although 65 percent of the departments provided some kind of ethics training, it was generally for four hours or less. The report concluded that although most saw a high need for ethics training, the amount of time earmarked for it was far less than might be expected. In another study by Marion (1998) of a regional training academy in

Ohio, it was discovered that ethics was not even included in the curriculum. If officers are to be properly trained and socialized to perform their jobs in an ethical manner, they will be more likely to observe the law and departmental policies. This is why, as discussed in Inside Policing 6.2, ethics must be inculcated throughout the entire academy and field training experience.

Inside Policing 6.2   An Interview on Ethics With Professor Edwin Delattre Author of *Character & Cops*

Question: When it comes to training and ethics, what kind of program would you recommend? Do you think a special course in ethics is the way to go in police academy training?

Delattre: If such a course is expected to stand all by itself, it's doomed to failure because the newcomers get the impression that it has nothing really to do with the rest of their training and the responsibilities they'll have on a daily basis. There has to be a resonance between what you did in any course on ethics and what's done in all the other courses in programs of education. So, for example, when you explain to people that you're trying to make them competent with respect to policy and practice as it relates, say, to traffic chases, it's worth making the point that when you voluntarily accept responsibilities that affect the lives of others, you also accept the duty to become good at the fulfillment of those responsibilities. That kind of resonance is essential to affecting the culture of the institution and the expectations of the people who work in it in the right way.

Question: What about the role of supervisory officers when it comes to making sure that the officers under them are kept at a pretty high level of ethics and integrity?

Delattre: It means forging a department in which the voice of recruitment, the voice of academy training, the voice of field training, the voice of supervision all the way to the top is one voice, and the ways of behaving are one way of behaving with respect to matters of character and integrity. This is how I do things here in the interest of justice and public service that can be trusted. You have to set an example that others will look to you and say "Yeah, this person really rings true when he says, 'We don't take, we don't beat up on suspects in custody, we don't falsify reports.' That's just exactly the way the person really is." There's no other way to achieve that I've ever heard of.

Source: Adapted from: M. Simnetti Rosen, 1997. "A LEN Interview with Prof. Edwin J. Delattre of Boston University." *Law Enforcement News,* May 15: 11–12.

Another topic that appears in need of significant expansion is the *deescalation of force* to reduce violence between police and citizens. While some departments may cover this area briefly under a use-of-force topic, Alpert and Moore (1993) propose that *nonaggressive behavior that reduces violence* needs to be reinforced, rewarded, and established as the model for other officers to copy. Such training would need to recognize and emphasize the use of nonaggressive behavior that, when appropriate, does not lead to an arrest. This understanding would in turn lead to the recognition that many problems in the community can be solved without the use of force. In this vein, officers need to develop skills in *anger management* and *conflict resolution,* so that when faced with verbal challenges they can deescalate the situation without risking First Amendment liability of free expression rights (see Vaughn 1996; Vaughn and Kappeler 1999).

A topic that has long been neglected in recruit training is *policing and teenagers,* who may need to be dealt with differently than adults (see Inside Policing 6.3). One study, for example, on the perceptions of inner-city children and teenagers in Athens, Georgia, found that officers need to be trained to be aware of the potential impact of their "unnecessarily negative, threatening, and impersonal contacts with children and teenagers" (Williams 1999). In another study of juveniles' attitudes toward the police, Hurst and Frank (2000) found that juveniles generally had less favorable perceptions of the police than adults. This was particularly true for nonwhite juveniles.

Inside Policing 6.3   **Teens to Help Write Section of Department's Manual in Effort to Improve Relations**

In what may be the first program of its kind in the state, Pleasanton, California, police have invited teens to help write a new section of the department's police training manual. The section will be "teen specific" and the new regulations will likely help guide officers on how teens should be approached differently on the street than adults. For example, teens may need more explanation than an adult of what law may have been violated.

Teens voiced concerns about their relationship with police at a "Youth Speak Out" event hosted by the Pleasanton Youth Commission. They said they often feel harassed and unfairly singled out by police. Teens say they want officers to be firm but not condescending, and they want explanations of what they did wrong and of the consequences. The police manual's new sections will be required training for new officers and will be part of the annual recertification training for current officers.

Source: Adapted from M. Mendoza, 2000, "A New Program Calls on Teens to Help Write a Section of the Pleasanton Department's Manual in an Effort to Improve Relations," *Valley Times*, February 6: A3, A4.

Community-policing training will need to be significantly expanded as it becomes more widespread. According to the BJS national survey (Hickman and Reaves 2003a), just over one-half of local police departments trained at least some new recruits for eight or more hours in community-policing skills such as problem solving, the SARA process, and developing community partnerships (see Table 6.5). The proportion of departments that trained all recruits ranged from nearly eight in 10 among those serving 50,000 or more residents, to two in 10 among those serving fewer than 2,500 residents. The percent of sheriff's offices utilizing community-policing training, by population size, either for some or for all recruits, was substantially lower than for local police departments—approximately five in 10 for over 50,000 residents and less than two in 10 for under 10,000 residents (Hickman and Reaves 2003b).

For community policing to be successful, it is clear that training will need to emphasize not only problem solving but also critical thinking, analytical skills, decision-making (i.e., using discretion wisely), and communication skills. This suggests that substantially more time will need to be devoted to cognitive versus task training (andragogical teaching methods will likely be most effective). **Cognitive learning** can be defined as training that goes beyond learning a specific skill or task and instead focuses on the process that establishes correct and valid thinking patterns. If valid thinking patterns can be established, officers will have the tools to become effective problem solvers and not just report takers or law enforcers (Bradford and Pynes 1999). In a national survey of training academies, Bradford and Pynes (1999) analyzed course syllabi in an effort to determine the degree of cognitive versus task-oriented training. They found that less than 3 percent of basic-training time listed in the curricula was spent in the cognitive and decision-making domain, with the remaining time spent in task-oriented activities. One exception to this finding was the Common-wealth of Massachusetts, where all subjects are taught in the cognitive domain, encompassing 90 percent of the curricula (720 out of 800 hours).

Table 6.5   Community Policing Training in Local Police Departments, by Size of Population Served, 2000

Population Served	Percent of Agencies That Trained Personnel for 8 or More Hours in Community Policing		
	Total	All	Some
New officer recruits			
All sizes	51	38	13
1,000,000 or more	87	80	7
500,000–999,999	90	90	0
250,000–499,999	95	85	10
100,000–249,999	86	77	9
50,000–99,999	87	75	12
25,000–49,999	81	67	14
10,000–24,999	70	53	17
2,500–9,999	54	40	14
Under 2,500	32	21	11

Source: M. J. Hickman, and B. A. Reaves, *Local Police Departments, 2000* (Washington, D.C.: Bureau of Justice Statistics, 2003a), 14.

In 1997 the Massachusetts Criminal Justice Training Council realized that the goals of community policing required new teaching methods and strategies. A new training curriculum was designed with a greater cognitive focus. Five fundamental objectives of the training program were identified:

- Incorporate community-neighborhood policing throughout the curriculum.

- Adopt a values-driven model of police training (e.g., ethics and law as a constitutional basis for law enforcement).

- Integrate training and education.

- Train as a collaboration of police organizations with a shared history, a common body of knowledge, and an equal share in self-evaluation.

- Enhance character by examining the complexities of society and the choices of police officers.

Task skills and methodology are still taught, but from a cognitive perspective. According to the Massachusetts Criminal Justice Training Council, the objective of cognitive training is getting the officer to "understand how to speak to, reason with, and listen to people and learn to use communication skills to manage a wide range of problematic situations. Physical tactics and tools, though readily available, are secondary to the primary response of communication" (Bradford and Pynes 1999, 289).

Some mention should also be made regarding *terrorism training*. While the following chapter discusses some of the implications of heightened attention to potential terrorist acts with respect to patrol and investigative work, the overriding implication for recruit training is to avoid an "us versus them" attitude that could develop or intensify between the community and the police. This is why a community-policing approach combined with cognitive training is important. Critical thinking, analytical, and decision-making skills, for instance, may ultimately make the difference in implementing "tighter controls" in a legal and ethical manner, instead of violating constitutional rights and lessening police legitimacy. The police need the trust and input of the citizens to gain information with respect to potential terrorist activities; community policing can help to further develop and maintain this trust and input.

Finally, one interesting breakthrough in training methodology that may have important implications is the developing area of *virtual reality training*. Although this method of training is essentially untapped, it would appear to have great potential as far as providing a safe training experience. It works by programming data into computers to generate three-dimensional images to create virtual (lifelike) environments. These are usually viewed through a head-mounted device (goggles or a helmet) that provides users with a sense of depth. Users remain stationary and use a joystick or track ball to move through the environment; they may wear a special glove to manipulate objects or employ virtual weapons to confront virtual aggressors. Recruits can make decisions and act on them without risk to themselves or others; these actions can then be critiqued, allowing trainees to learn from their mistakes. It appears that virtual reality can offer law enforcement benefits in a number of areas, including pursuit driving, firearms training, high-risk-incident management, incident re-creation, and processing crime scenes (Hormann 1995).

Effectiveness of recruit training. How effective is the training provided to the recruits? One means of evaluating it is to follow up on field performance to determine the areas in which recruits are having the most difficulty; methods used can include observation of recruits, the evaluation of recruit performance, and surveys of recruits, trainers, and supervisors. In general, the validity of the measurement will be higher if more than one of these methods is used. Once problems are identified, a determination can be made as to how to improve the program. In addition, as new knowledge and skills become available, they should be incorporated into the program.

Although it is necessary to keep academy curricula abreast of changes in the field with new or expanded topics, one study indicates how important it is for police agencies to incorporate these newly acquired skills and attitudes into the *organization culture*. For example, Haarr (2001), in a 16-month study, examined the attitudinal changes of recruits toward community policing, problem solving, and public relations through basic training, field training, and their first year of probation. The training curriculum of the Phoenix Regional Police Training Academy was revised to educate officers in the theories and practices of community policing and problem solving. The results indicated that the training academy had an initial positive impact on recruits' attitudes toward community policing and problem solving. However, over time these positive attitudes dissipated as recruits returned to their respective departments for field training and were exposed to the work environment and organizational culture. In other words, field training processes and organizational environment factors (e.g., shifts, coworker attitudes, and whether the department requires officers to engage in community policing), were more powerful forces than basic training, suggesting that police agencies failed to reinforce the positive impacts that the training provided. In order to retain these positive attitudes, departments must make sure that recruits continue to utilize the skills learned in basic training and by practicing community policing and problem solving throughout field training and probation. Further, and just as important, police leadership must provide for organizational arrangements, programs, and rewards to set the tone for community-policing efforts.

Field Training

After successfully completing their work at the academy, recruits generally go through a final field-training program to prepare them for the real world of policing. This on-the-job, or apprentice, training has been an integral aspect of the recruit training process for some time, but it has become much more sophisticated since the mid-1970s. As the BJS national survey (Hickman and Reaves 2003a) of training requirements indicates (see Table 6.3), for those departments requiring field training in 2000, the average number of hours was 417. For those departments serving more than 25,0000 but less than one million, however, the average number of hours was over 700; interestingly, for the largest departments—those serving over one million—the number of hours (534) was substantially less.

The traditional method of new officers being broken in by experienced old-timers is giving way to highly structured programs using **field-training officers (FTOs)**—that is, experienced officers especially trained to act as mentors to new recruits. The importance of FTOs cannot be overstated because they will have a significant impact not only on the training of the recruit but on imparting demeanor, values, and the department's culture as well. Up to this point, recruits have learned in the academy how to behave like police officers, but under the guidance of the FTO, the officer is exposed to the "real world" of policing. At this time, the FTO has the opportunity to subvert what has been taught by advising the rookie to "forget what you learned in the academy, I'll show you how we do it out here on the street."

Because of the importance of the position, one would think that police agencies would have a rigorous selection process, with high standards. Unfortunately, this is not always the case. In a national study of 60 departments with more than 500 sworn officers (Langworthy, Hughes, and Sanders 1995), it was observed that the mean number of years required to become an FTO had decreased significantly from 2.6 in 1990 to 1.9 in 1994. It was felt that this reduction was most likely due to departments having difficulty recruiting officers for FTO assignments. Much can be learned about the importance of maintaining high standards in the selection of FTOs from the independent commission on the Los Angeles Police Department, known as the Christopher Commission Report (1991), in the wake of the Rodney King beating. Inside Policing 6.4 is an excerpt from the commission report, investigating the process then in use by the LAPD to select and train FTOs and the discovery of a "siege" mentality passed on to the trainees by many FTOs. As the commission notes, not only should rigorous selection standards be established, but officers with an aptitude for and interest in training junior officers should be encouraged to apply.

Inside Policing 6.4   Los Angeles Police Department: Selection and Training of FTOs

Upon graduation [from the academy] the new officer works as a "probationary officer" assigned to various field-training officers. The FTOs guide new officers' first contacts with citizens and have primary responsibility for introducing the probationers to the culture and traditions of the department. The commission's interviews of FTOs in four representative divisions revealed that many FTOs openly perpetuate the siege mentality that alienates patrol officers from the community and pass on to their trainees confrontational attitudes of hostility and disrespect for the public. This problem is in part the result of flaws in the way FTOs are selected and trained. The hiring of a very large number of new officers in 1989, which required the use of less-experienced FTOs, greatly exacerbated the problem.

Any officer promoted to Police Officer III by passing a written examination covering departmental policies and procedures is eligible to serve as an FTO. At present there are no formal eligibility or disqualification criteria for the FTO position based on an applicant's disciplinary records. Fourteen of the FTOs in the four divisions the commission studied had been disciplined for use of excessive force or use of improper tactics.

There also appears to be little emphasis on selecting FTOs who have an interest in training junior officers, and an FTO's training ability is given little weight in his or her evaluation.

The commission believes that, to become FTOs, officers should be required to pass written and oral tests designed to measure communication skills, teaching aptitude, and knowledge of departmental policies regarding appropriate use of force, cultural sensitivity, community relations, and nondiscrimination. Officers with an aptitude for and interest in training junior officers should be encouraged by effective incentives to apply for FTO positions. In addition, the training program for FTOs should be modified to place greater emphasis on communication skills and the appropriate use of force. Successful completion of FTO school should be required before an FTO begins teaching probationers.

Source: Adapted from Independent Commission on the Los Angeles Police Department, *Report of the Independent Commission on the Los Angeles Police Department* (Los Angeles: California Public Management Institute, 1991), xvi–xvii.

With FTO programs, the probationary period is usually a highly structured experience in which new officers must demonstrate specific knowledge and skills. Frequent evaluations are made of the recruits' performance, usually by several FTOs who supervise their work in different areas and different shifts. In general, there are three phases in an FTO program (McCampbell 1986, 4–5):

Phase 1: The first weeks (eight to 20 or more) are for regional academy training; if the recruit passes, there may be additional weeks of classroom training provided by the department.

Phase 2: In the second phase (12 or more weeks), the recruit is assigned to the first FTO for several weeks, followed by a second FTO on a different shift, and then a third FTO on another shift. The officer then returns to the original FTO. During each tour, there are daily observation reports by the FTOs and weekly evaluation reports by supervisors (usually sergeants). At the end of this phase, the recruit either moves on to the third phase, is given remedial training, or is dismissed. Figure 6.1 is an example of the San Jose, California, Police Department's Daily Observation Report form, which is used to rate the daily performance of recruits. Extensive training is provided to FTOs in how to evaluate and provide guidance to recruits.

Phase 3: In the third phase (16 or more weeks), the recruit is assigned a solo beat outside the training district and evaluated every couple of weeks by the supervisor. After

Figure 6.1 San Jose Police Department's Daily Observation Report Form

SMARTFORM® FORM NO. 23652-CSJ

© SCANTRON CORPORATION 1990
ALL RIGHTS RESERVED IN THE USA 2-391-2-391-2-390-040

1-00-0074-4-3-2-1

FEED THIS DIRECTION

SAN JOSE POLICE DEPARTMENT

RECRUIT'S LAST NAME

FTO'S LAST NAME

TEAM ☐   BEAT # ☐   DAILY OBSERVATION REPORT NO. ☐

RECRUIT BADGE NO.   FTO BADGE NO.   TODAY'S DATE   MONTH   DAY   YEAR

INSTRUCTIONS

RATE OBSERVED BEHAVIOR ON THE SCALE BELOW, USING THE NUMERICAL VALUE DEFINITIONS IN THE FTO PROGRAM STANDARDIZED GUIDELINES.

CHECK "N.O." FOR NOT OBSERVED, "N.R.T." FOR NOT RESPONDING TO TRAINING, "NAR" FOR NARRATIVE COMMENT, AND "REM" FOR REMEDIAL TRAINING.

YOU MUST COMMENT ON THE MOST AND LEAST ACCEPTABLE PERFORMANCE OF THE DAY, AND ON ALL RATINGS OF "2" OR LESS, "6" OR MORE, AND "N.R.T." YOU ARE ALSO ENCOURAGED TO COMMENT ON ANY OTHER BEHAVIOR YOU WISH. REFER TO THE CATEGORY NUMBER IN YOUR COMMENTS.

RATING SCALE

NOT ACCEPTABLE BY FTO PROGRAM STANDARDS   ACCEPTABLE LEVEL   SUPERIOR BY FTO PROGRAM STANDARDS

→ 1   2   3 <4> 5   6   7 ←

TRAINING ☐
SICK ☐
SPECIAL ASSGNMT ☐
DISABILITY ☐
OTHER ABSENCE ☐

USE THE STANDARDIZED GUIDE LINES

CRITICAL PERFORMANCE TASKS

#	Task	N.O.	NRT	NAR.	REM.	TIME
1	DRIVING SKILL: STRESS CONDITIONS					
2	ORIENTATION SKILL: STRESS CONDITIONS					
3	FIELD PERFORMANCE: STRESS CONDITIONS					
4	OFFICER SAFETY: GENERAL					
5	OFFICER SAFETY: W/SUSPICIOUS PERSONS & PRISONERS					
6	CONTROL OF CONFLICT: VOICE COMMAND					
7	CONTROL OF CONFLICT: PHYSICAL SKILL					

FREQUENT AND OTHER PERFORMANCE TASKS

#	Task	N.O.	NRT	NAR.	REM.	TIME
8	DRIVING SKILL: NON-STRESS CONDITIONS					
9	ORIENTATION SKILL: NON-STRESS CONDITIONS					
10	PROPER FORM SELECTION: ACCURACY/COMPLETENESS					
11	REPORT WRITING: ORGANIZATION/DETAILS					
12	REPORT WRITING: GRAMMAR/SPELLING/NEATNESS					
13	REPORT WRITING: APPROPRIATE TIME USED?					
14	FIELD PERFORMANCE: NON-STRESS CONDITIONS					
15	SELF-INITIATED FIELD ACTIVITY					
16	PROBLEM SOLVING/DECISION MAKING					
17	RADIO: USE OF COMMUNICATION CODES/PROCEDURES					
18	RADIO: LISTENS & COMPREHENDS TRANSMISSIONS					
19	RADIO: ARTICULATION OF TRANSMISSIONS					

KNOWLEDGE

KNOWLEDGE OF DEPARTMENT POLICIES & PROCEDURES

#	Task	N.O.	NRT	NAR.	REM.	TIME
20	REFLECTED BY VERBAL/WRITTEN/SIMULATED TESTING					
21	REFLECTED IN FIELD PERFORMANCE					

KNOWLEDGE OF THE PENAL CODE

#	Task	N.O.	NRT	NAR.	REM.	TIME
22	REFLECTED BY VERBAL/WRITTEN/SIMULATED TESTING					
23	REFLECTED IN FIELD PERFORMANCE					

KNOWLEDGE OF THE VEHICLE CODE

#	Task	N.O.	NRT	NAR.	REM.	TIME
24	REFLECTED BY VERBAL/WRITTEN/SIMULATED TESTING					
25	REFLECTED IN FIELD PERFORMANCE					

ATTITUDE/RELATIONS

#	Task	N.O.	NRT	NAR.	REM.	TIME
26	ACCEPTANCE OF FEEDBACK: VERBAL/BEHAVIOR					
27	ATTITUDE TOWARD POLICE WORK					
28	RELATIONSHIPS WITH CITIZENS: SPECIFY					
29	OTHER RELATIONSHIPS: FTO/SGT/LT/DEPT MEMBERS					

APPEARANCE

#	Task	N.O.	NRT	NAR.	REM.	TIME
30	GENERAL APPEARANCE: SPECIFY IF NECESSARY					

Source: Reprinted by permission of San Jose Police Department, San Jose, CA, and Scantron Corporation, Tustin, CA.

about 10 months, a review board determines whether the recruit is certified to continue Phase 3; if so, he or she continues to work the solo beat (with monthly evaluations); if not, he or she returns for remedial training. In the final two weeks, an FTO in plainclothes rides along and observes the recruit. At the end of this phase, the recruit is either certified as a permanent employee, or Phase 3 is extended, or he or she is dismissed.

With respect to community policing, a new type of field-training program has been developed by the Reno, Nevada, police department for the purpose of training officers in the principles and concepts of community policing (see Voices From the Field below). This training, known as the **Reno model,** is new not just because it emphasizes aspects of community policing, but also because it is based on andragogical (versus pedagogical) learning methods and places heavy emphasis on problem-based learning exercises. Training officers in this program develop competency in 15 core areas that represent specific activities police officers engage in while on patrol, including problem solving, communication and community specific skills, conflict resolution, ethics, cultural diversity, leadership, and civil rights. In addition, trainers assign "street" problems to trainees allowing them to learn about policing in the context of solving those problems (Hoover, Pitts, and Ponte 2003). In order for community-policing skills and attitudes to be incorporated into the organizational culture (Haarr 2001), this is the type of field-training program that would be necessary in order for departments to adopt a community-policing model. In Voices From the Field, the Reno chief who was primarily responsible for development of this model discusses how it is adapted for community policing.

Voices From the Field
The Reno PTO Model
Former Chief Jerry Hoover, Reno Police Department

Question: How has your department changed the FTO program to reflect community-policing concepts?

Answer: We have designed and implemented a completely different model of field training at the Reno Police Department. The original training model, which was designed by the San Jose, California, Police Department in 1968, was the result of a changing police environment and numerous litigations regarding hiring and termination procedures. It was based on behavior modification and was a leading innovation in law enforcement training for decades. Since the advent of community-oriented policing and problem solving (COPPS), police administrators have expressed disappointment in their ability to imprint this philosophy on new officers using the San Jose Model.

I worked for five years trying to alter the San Jose Model so that it could be used to train under the COPPS philosophy, but with little success. After receiving a large grant from the Office of Community Oriented Policing Services (COPS), U.S.

Department of Justice, the Reno Police Department created a partnership with the Police Executive Research Forum to create a new model. The Reno Model, as it has come to be called, is founded on adult-learning theory and practice. The model uses a problem-based learning method as the fundamental engine that drives the learning experience of the new officer. Trainees are taught to solve problems, not just respond to calls for service. They become risk-takers because a primary concept of the program allows them to learn from their mistakes. There are no checklists, nor numerical daily evaluations. Instead, the evaluation process is designed on principles of andragogy. The trainee and the police training officer (PTO) work together to create a positive learning environment. This is not to say, however, that trainee performance is not evaluated. A learning matrix consisting of 60 topical areas is used to evaluate trainee performance. These evaluations are in the form of weekly coaching and training reports, problem-based learning exercises, neighborhood portfolio exercises, and prescriptive training plans (remedial training). These evaluation methods produce enough documentation to support decisions to either maintain or terminate a trainee's employment. The attrition rate of trainees in the Reno Model mirrors that of the San Jose Model: 10 percent to 15 percent generally fail the program.

We have had amazing success with this program in Reno and have received hundreds of requests for information from law enforcement agencies across the nation. Police administrators are very interested in the Reno Model, not only for its adult-learning approach and emphasis on COPPS, philosophy, but because we included leadership and ethics as founding principles in the design of the program. While the process is founded in problem-based and adult-learning strategies, more importantly the outcome can be seen in new police officers who understand community policing and provide leadership to their communities at the beginning of their careers. ✦

FTO programs have not always been as effective as was hoped. Although monetary incentives (usually minimal) and special training are generally provided, many officers believe that being an FTO is both burdensome and stressful and not worth the amount of increased pay. The Christopher Commission report noted that the best applicants tended not to apply for the position, in part because it was too much extra work and responsibility and not enough reward. Evaluation is undoubtedly one of the most difficult managerial tasks to perform, and many managers do not do it well. FTOs frequently engage in evaluation activity on a daily basis. Their evaluations may be challenged, and if a trainee is terminated, the FTO may be sued. Unless the stress of being an FTO is lessened substantially, it may be difficult to encourage the best officers to participate. In order for high-quality officers to apply for the FTO position, it is necessary to increase both the status and pay of the position; the position should be considered a promotion, with pay and prestige perhaps equaling that of a first-level supervisor (usually a sergeant). In addition, evaluations should be conducted less frequently and, for the most part, determined by a group of FTOs, rather than by an individual. In other words, a recruit should work with several FTOs over a period of several weeks or months, and a group evaluation of each recruit's performance should be used instead of the daily evaluations by individual FTOs. Of course, each FTO should still give daily feedback and guidance to the recruit while also keeping a daily evaluation log that would be used in determining group FTO evaluations. Such a procedure should not only increase the validity of the evaluation but also help to reduce FTO stress.

After the recruit has passed the FTO program, he or she may become a permanent, sworn police officer or work for an additional period in the field on probationary status. During this time, officers are evaluated several more times, and if their performance is acceptable, they become permanent employees.

Career Growth

Once a person is recruited, selected, trained, and has completed probation in a police department, his or her career begins, and career growth becomes important. **Career growth** can be for individual development as well as for a specific position within the department; it can involve training within or outside the department, and it attempts to match the needs of the individual with those of the department.

Managers must not only be concerned with upgrading the knowledge and skills of officers in their current positions, but they must also plan to incorporate officers' interests with **career paths** that involve position enhancement, new assignments, and promotion. For instance, assume Officer Nancy Brown has worked in a medium-to-large police department for 25 years and has the following career path:

- Assigned to patrol for five years.

- Transferred to traffic unit for two years, where she worked as an enforcement specialist.

- Promoted to sergeant and transferred back to patrol for two years.

- Transferred to detective unit for three years, where she worked as a robbery and homicide investigator.

- Promoted to lieutenant and transferred to a training unit, where she supervised for three years.

- Promoted to captain and supervised the patrol division for three years.

- Transferred to the detective unit again and placed in charge for three years.

- Promoted to assistant chief and served for four years prior to retirement.

An effective career-path program must be able to provide for the improvement of the officer's knowledge and skills in each area of assignment. There is also a need to develop career-path programs that will financially reward officers for staying in patrol and performing well. In many departments, the only way to obtain a pay increase after five or six years of service (other than cost-of-living adjustments) is to be promoted or transferred to a specialized position. This is not an effective system because good performers, even though they may wish to stay in patrol, must be promoted or become specialists to receive increased compensation. Since the 1970s, the Los Angeles Police Department, for example, has had a career-path program that builds in several career-path levels below the rank of lieutenant, each with its own pay scale. This program allows officers to pursue police careers below the command level. All police departments should have overlapping pay scales in which patrol officers and investigators, if highly competent, could be paid at levels equal to those of management. Such a system would encourage many excellent officers to stay in patrol and investigations. This is the system in academe, for example, where the most highly regarded professors are often paid more than their managers (e.g., chairs and deans) and possibly even more than the college president.

Advanced training. Police officers and managers must be kept up to date on changing laws, community needs and expectations, and police methods and technologies, and must be prepared for reassignment or promotion. Large departments often have sufficient resources to allow them to develop and maintain their own advanced training programs. Midsized and smaller departments usually must find outside programs. Many states, as a result of statewide training and standards commissions, have developed extensive career-growth programs for the police. For instance, it is often possible for these departments to send their officers to programs that assist in preparing them for almost any assignment or promotion. Many departments also use private trainers or consultants, as well as university programs, to upgrade their personnel, and many departments allow for flexible schedules or provide incentives for officers to attend college. In general, experienced older officers and managers want to be treated more as peers than as students and usually prefer a more academic approach to a stress-related one. This fact suggests that experienced officers would most likely prefer, and benefit from, an andragogical approach to training.

In-service training. The primary purpose of **in-service training** is the regular updating of all members of the department in a wide variety of subjects. It usually involves subject matter that all department members must know in order to function well. For example, officers must continually be aware of changing laws and ordinances, newly developed techniques, operating policies and procedures, and departmental changes and expectations. In general, in-service training courses last from one to two weeks, and therefore tend to offer relatively limited coverage of their subject matter. An interesting development in Kentucky, which requires 40 hours of approved in-service training each year, allows a college-level course to fulfill the requirement under the following conditions: (1) the course is taken from a regionally accredited college or university; (2) a minimum of 3 semester credit hours is earned; (3) a grade of C or higher is received; (4) approval is granted from the head of the officer's agency; and (5) a college course can be used only once every three years. Such a development is an important step in recognizing the benefit that college courses can offer in verbal and written skills, as well as the advancement of general knowledge. Such a requirement may have a side benefit of enticing officers to enroll in college, or to continue, their college educations.

The BJS national survey (Hickman and Reaves 2003a) indicates that the average annual in-service training requirement for sworn officers in 2000 was 69 hours, including 26 state-mandated hours (see Table 6.6). It is interesting to note, however, that the larger agencies (serving populations over 250,000) require only a little over 40 hours, whereas smaller departments (serving under 250,000 population) require from the low 50s to over 90 hours of in-service training (except for the smallest departments, serving under 2,500 citizens). Surprisingly, those departments requiring the most in-service training are the second smallest, serving populations from 2,500 to below 10,000, with 91 total hours. For sheriff's offices, the amount of hours provided for in-service training was about the same as for local police departments (Hickman and Reaves 2003b).

Specialized training. **Specialized training** attempts to prepare officers for specific tasks (e.g., stakeouts or decoy work) or for different jobs throughout the department (e.g., homicide investigator or supervisor). Specialized training is essential if officers are to perform effectively outside the role of patrol officer.

Officers promoted to first-line supervisory positions (e.g., sergeant) should be provided with some form of **supervisory training.** Such training may be in-house or external and usually covers leadership behavior, specific job requirements, and policies and procedures. Once an officer is promoted to a managerial or executive-level position (e.g., lieutenant or higher), additional *management training* is necessary. The role of the police manager is even more complex than that of first-level supervisor and requires not only increased knowledge regarding management's role in the department but also long-range planning, policy development, and resource allocation. In California, for example, each of these types of training is required: Police chiefs must complete an 80-hour executive-development course within two years of appointment; captains must complete an 80-hour management course within 12 months; lieutenants must complete an 80-hour management course (different in content from the captain's course) within 12 months; and sergeants must complete an 80-hour supervisory course within 12 months.

Table 6.6	Annual In-service Training Requirements for Nonprobationary Officers in Local Police Departments, by Size of Population Served, 2000

| | Average Number of Hours Required Annually | |
Population Served	State-Mandated	Other
All sizes	26	43
1,000,000 or more	24	16
500,000–999,999	28	15
250,000–499,999	21	24
100,000–249,999	23	30
50,000–99,999	28	34
25,000–49,999	27	34
10,000–24,999	27	28
2,500–9,999	27	64
Under 2,500	25	20

Source: M. J. Hickman, and B. A. Reaves, *Local Police Departments, 2000* (Washington, D.C.: Bureau of Justice Statistics, 2003), 6.

In addition, in those departments using community policing, some training relating to the concepts, processes, and new role requirements for managers is necessary. In San Diego, for example, a 16-hour Problem Oriented Policing (POP) training program for supervisors has been implemented. The course includes the basic course in POP (eight hours), issues and concerns for supervisors regarding the analysis of problems, supervision of problem solving, and performance evaluations. The department also has an executive-level POP orientation course (four hours), which emphasizes the history and methods of community and problem-solving policing and discusses the issues and concerns of implementation and operational strategies. Finally, the department has developed training courses in POP for investigators (eight hours) and for trainers (40 hours) (San Diego Police Department 1993).

One national survey of 144 police departments, including the two largest in each state, found that 97 percent provided in-house supervisory training and that 78 percent make the training mandatory (Armstrong and Longenecker 1992). This training was conducted prior to, or at the time of, promotion by 51 percent of the departments; 49 percent provided the training following the promotion. The subjects most frequently taught included supervisory techniques (95 percent), use of the disciplinary process (92 percent), counseling techniques (80 percent), employee evaluation and review (79 percent), and motivational techniques (73 percent).

Management training was provided by 81 percent of the departments. Of those, 37 percent offered the training in-house, and the remaining 63 percent sent their managers outside the department (e.g., to state agencies, contract agencies, or the FBI). The most common subject areas included management strategy (77 percent), budgeting (70 percent), management by objectives (63 percent), labor negotiations and contract administration (63 percent), administration of discipline (58 percent), police planning (52 percent), and work-force allocation and patrol strategy (45 percent).

One of the most troublesome aspects of supervisory and management training for police is the evaluation procedure, or lack thereof. Although recruit training is often rigorously evaluated, training for experienced officers and managers rarely includes any meaningful evaluation. This lack of evaluation can be a serious problem because many of the participants may not take the training seriously and thus will not attain the skills and knowledge necessary to be effective. Consequently, departments should require all supervisory and managerial training programs to include meaningful performance evaluations, because only in this way can they be sure that their future supervisors and managers are effectively trained for their new roles.

Promotion and assessment centers. **Promotion** in police departments is usually based on one or more of several evaluative criteria, including an officer's (1) time on the job (seniority) or time in rank, (2) past performance, (3) written examination, (4) oral interview, and (5) college hours or degrees. In general, a percentage weight is assigned to each evaluative criterion used and an overall promotional score is assigned. As openings at the next level of rank occur, individuals are promoted according to their score. Which criteria are used and what weight is assigned varies by department, according to what the department or civil service commission regards as the most important. Often, police departments use only one or two criteria, even though the criteria may have little, if any, relationship to the supervisory or managerial position for which the candidate is applying. Such a process can lead to the selection of the wrong candidate for the position, which may have a long-term negative impact on the department and the officers being supervised.

In one of the few studies in this area, Roberg and Laramy (1980) analyzed the promotional results of a large midwestern police department that used a written exam (70 percent), performance evaluation (11.25 percent), seniority (10 percent), and college credits (8.75 percent) as criteria for promotion to sergeant. In general, the results indicated that seniority (above the minimum requirement) should not be used as a criterion, and that those with college hours scored higher on the written exam. The study concluded that the department needed to carefully assess and validate the content of its promotional process through analysis of the type of behavior required for effective job performance (e.g., supervisory ability). Because it is difficult to measure supervisory or managerial potential based only on the type of criteria used in the above study, many departments are now using an assessment center approach, which is perhaps the most promising method for selecting officers for promotion.

An **assessment center** is a process that attempts to measure a candidate's potential for a particular managerial position. It uses multiple assessment strategies, typically spread over a two- or three-day period, which include different types of job-related simulations and possibly the use of interviews and psychological tests. Common forms of job simulations include in-basket exercises (e.g., carrying out simulated supervisory or managerial assignments, such as writing memos or reports and responding to letters or personnel matters), simulations of interviews with subordinates, oral presentations, group discussions, and fact-finding exercises (Filer 1977). The candidate's behavior on all relevant criteria is evaluated by trained assessors, who reach a consensus on each participant. The primary advantage of this approach is that it evaluates all candidates in a simulated environment under standardized conditions, thus adding significantly to the validity and reliability of the selection process.

Lateral entry. **Lateral entry** refers to the ability of a police officer, at the patrol or supervisory level, to transfer from one department to another, usually without losing seniority. This concept is viewed by many as an important step toward increased professionalism through the improvement of career growth. Lateral entry is not a new concept, having been strongly endorsed by the 1967 President's Commission Task Force on Police:

> To improve police service, competition for all advanced positions should be opened to qualified persons from both within and outside of the department. This would enable a department to obtain the best available talent for positions of leadership. . . . If candidates from within an agency are unable to meet the competition from other applicants, it should be recognized that the influx of more highly qualified personnel would greatly improve the quality of the services. (1967, 142)

Implicitly, this recommendation increases the competition for leadership positions; if those already within the department are not as well qualified, they will need to upgrade their skills and educational levels. Of course, this need is one of the primary obstacles to implementing lateral entry; older officers within the department feel that they should be provided the opportunity for advancement, not an "outsider." Although this resistance can be a problem, probably of greater significance are the restrictions of civil service limitations, including retirement systems, which generally are not transferable. Because of these restrictions, and lack of departmental support, lateral entry is still used sparingly today. Some legislative reforms that contribute to its implementation have been made; before lateral entry can become widely adopted, however, individual departments will need to openly, and perhaps aggressively, become its proponent. Undoubtedly, the expanded use of lateral entry would increase the quality of the applicant pool for most police departments, thus improving the selection of police supervisors and managers.

The next chapter will discuss the results of the selection and development process—namely, police field operations. These include primarily patrol and investigative work. Generally, recruits are assigned to patrol after leaving the training academy, whereas veteran officers, at some point in their careers, may choose to become detectives and specialize in investigations.

Summary

With the increasing complexity of the police role and the movement toward community policing, the quality of police personnel has become perhaps the key factor to the effective operation of police departments. Thus, screening in, as opposed to screening out, candidates should be used in order that only the best qualified are selected for the applicant pool. Candidates must meet a number of preemployment standards that attempt to depict a department's view of what is required to become an effective officer—for example, physical agility; educational, psychological, and background qualifications; and polygraph examinations. Preemployment selection tests are also used and usually include written tests, oral interviews, or both. Some departments, however, also require reading exams because the reading ability of applicants has declined in recent years.

In preparing recruits for the job, decisions must be made about program orientation, philosophy, instructional methods, course content, and program evaluation. Following academy training, recruits generally go through an on-the-job field-training program prior to job assignment; many departments use a field-training officer (FTO) program for this purpose. The career growth of officers is important because they must be prepared for changes not only in their current jobs but also changes in job assignments and promotions. Departments should establish career paths that allow for employees at all levels to remain motivated throughout their careers. Finally, because promotions have long-term implications for the departments, administrators should carefully analyze the process and criteria used. Assessment centers may offer the greatest potential in this area.

Critical Thinking Questions

1. Describe the meaning of "quality" with respect to police personnel. Explain what you consider to be the most important criteria with respect to quality in police recruits.

2. Why is the process of "screening in" police applicants important? How might this process relate to the potential for community policing?

3. In screening for community-policing officers, what type of written tests would you recommend, and what type of procedure would you use for the oral interview?

4. Can a college-degree requirement for recruit selection be defended as a bona fide occupational qualification (BFOQ)? Why or why not?

5. Discuss whether or not you think that andragogical teaching and cognitive learning can become an integral part of recruit training in the near future.

6. What percentage of the recruit academy curricula do you think should be devoted to community-policing training? Why?

7. Discuss what you believe to be the most important criteria in the selection of FTOs. What process would you put in place to ensure that those selected meet these criteria?

8. What types of in-service training programs or seminars would be most useful in your local or college police department?

References

Albermarle Paper v. Moody. 1975. 10 FEP 1181.

Alpert, G. P., and Moore, M. H. 1993. "Measuring Police Performance in the New Paradigm of Policing." In *Performance Measures for the Criminal Justice System*, pp. 109–140. Washington, D.C.: Bureau of Justice Statistics.

Alpert, G., and Smith, W. 1990. "Defensibility of Law Enforcement Training." *Criminal Law Bulletin* 26: 452–458.

Armstrong, L. D., and Longenecker, C. O. 1992. "Police Management Training: A National Survey." *FBI Law Enforcement Bulletin* 61: 22–26.

Bayley, D., and Bittner, E. 1989. "Learning the Skills of Policing." In R. Dunham and G. Alpert (eds.), *Critical Issues in Policing: Contemporary Readings*, pp. 87–110. Prospect Heights, IL: Waveland Press.

Bayley, D., and Mendelsohn, H. 1969. *Minorities and the Police.* New York: Free Press.

Berg, B. L. 1990. "First Day at the Police Academy: Stress-Reaction Training as a Screening-out Technique." *Journal of Contemporary Criminal Justice* 6: 89–105.

Birzer, M. L. 1999. "Police Training in the 21st Century." *FBI Law Enforcement Bulletin* July: 16–19.

——. 2003. "The Theory of Andragogy Applied to Police Training." *Policing: An International Journal of Police Strategies & Management* 26: 29–42.

Birzer, M. L., and Craig, D. E. 1996. "Gender Differences in Police Physical Ability Test Performance." *American Journal of Police* 15: 93–108.

Birzer, M. L., and Tannehill, R. 2001. "A More Effective Training Approach for Contemporary Policing." *Police Quarterly* 4: 233–252.

Bradford, D., and Pynes, J. E. 1999. "Police Academy Training: Why Hasn't It Kept Up with Practice?" *Police Quarterly* 2: 283–301.

Burbeck, E., and Furnham, A. 1985. "Police Officer Selection: A Critical Review of the Literature." *Journal of Police Science and Administration* 13: 58–69.

Carter, D. L., Sapp, A. D., and Stephens, D. W. 1989. *The State of Police Education: Policy Direction for the 21st Century.* Washington, D.C.:Police Executive Research Forum.

Campbelis, C. 1999. "Selecting a New Breed of Officer: The Customer-oriented Cop." *Community Policing Exchange* 25: 1, 4–5.

Chang, J. 2003. "Police Learn About Sikhs." *San Jose Mercury News* June 7: 1B, 6B.

Chapman, S. G. 1982. "Personnel Management." In B. L. Garmire (ed.), *Local Government Police Management, 2nd ed.*, pp. 241–273. Washington, D.C.: International City Management Association.

Charles, T. M. 1982. "Women in Policing: The Physical Aspect." *Journal of Police Science and Administration* 10: 194–205.

Charles, T. M. 1983. "Police Training: A Contemporary Approach." *Journal of Police Science and Administration* 11: 251–263.

Clark, J. R. 1992. "Why Officer Johnny Can't Read." *Law Enforcement News* May 15: 1, 16–17.

Cohen, B., and Chaiken, J. M. 1972. *Police Background Characteristics and Performance.* New York: Rand Institute.

Commission on Peace Officer Standards and Training. 1995 (May 12). *Bulletin 95–9: Regular Basic Course Required Minimum Hours Increases From 560 to 664.* Sacramento, CA: POST.

Crosby, A., Rosenfield, M., and Thornton, R. F. 1979. "The Development of a Written Test for Police Applicant Selection." In C. D. Spielberger (ed.), *Police Selection and Evaluation*, pp. 143–153. New York: Praeger.

Davis v. City of Dallas. 1985. 777 F.2d 205 (5th Cir.).

Decker, L. K., and Huckabee, R. G. 2002. "Raising the Age and Education Requirements for Police Officers: Will Too Many Women and Minority Candidates be Excluded? *Policing: An International Journal of Police Strategies & Management*, 25: 789–802.

De Long, R. 1999. "Problem Solvers Wanted: How to Tailor Your Agency's Recruiting Approach." *Community Policing Exchange, Phase VI* 25, 2: 6.

Doerner, W. G. 1997. "The Utility of the Oral Interview Board in Selecting Police Academy Admissions." *Policing: An International Journal of Police Strategies and Management* 20: 777–785.

Dowling, K. W. 1999. "Arresting the Arresting Response: Training Community Police Officers to be Problem-solvers." *Community Policing Exchange* 25: 5.

Dwyer, W. O., Prien, E. P., and Bernard, J. L. 1990. "Psychological Screening of Law Enforcement Officers: A Case for Job Relatedness." *Journal of Police Science and Administration* 17: 176–182.

Earle, H. H. 1973. *Police Recruit Training: Stress vs. Non-Stress.* Springfield, IL: C. C. Thomas.

Eisenberg, S., Kent, D. A., and Wall, C. 1973. *Police Personnel Practice in State and Local Government.* Washington, D.C.: Police Foundation.

Falkenberg, S., Gaines, L. K., and Cox, T. C. 1990. "The Oral Interview Board: What Does It Measure?" *Journal of Police Science and Administration* 17: 32–39.

Filer, R. J. 1977. "Assessment Centers in Police Selection." In C. D. Spielberger and H. C. Spaulding (eds.), *Proceedings of the National Working Conference on the Selection of Law Enforcement Officers.* Tampa: University of South Florida.

Gaines, L. K., Costello, P., and Crabtree, A. 1989. "Police Selection Testing: Balancing Legal Requirements and Employer Needs." *American Journal of Police* 8: 137–152.

Gaines, L. K., Falkenberg, S., and Gambino, J. A. 1993. "Police Physical Activity Testing: An Historical and Legal Analysis." *American Journal of Police* 12: 47–66.

Gaines, L. K., and Falkenberg, S. 1998. "An Evaluation of the Written Selection Test: Effectiveness and Alternatives." *Journal of Criminal Justice* 26: 175–183.

Gaines, L. K., and Kappeler, V. E. 1992. "Selection and Testing." In G. W. Cordner and D. C. Hale (eds.), *What Works in Policing: Operations and Administration Examined*, pp. 107–123. Cincinnati, OH: Anderson.

"Getting the Inside Dope." 1996. *Law Enforcement News* October 31: 1, 14.

Grant, J. D., and Grant, J. 1995. "Officer Selection and the Prevention of Abuse of Force." In W. A. Geller and H. Toch (eds.), *And Justice for All: Understanding and Controlling Police Abuse of Force*, pp. 151–162. Washington, D.C.: Police Executive Research Forum.

Griggs v. Duke Power Company. 1971. 401 U.S. 424.

Haarr, R. 2001. "The Making of a Community Policing Officer: The Impact of Basic Training and Occupational Socialization on Police Recruits." *Police Quarterly* 4: 420–433.

Hickman, M. J., and Reaves, B. A. 2003a. *Local Police Departments, 2000.* Washington, D.C.: Bureau of Justice Statistics.

Hickman, M. J., and Reaves, B. A. 2003b. *Sheriffs' Offices, 2000.* Washington, D.C.: Bureau of Justice Statistics.

Hodes, C. R., Hunt, R. L., and Raskin, D. C. 1985. "Effects of Physical Countermeasures on the Physiological Detection of Deception." *Journal of Applied Psychology* 70: 177–187.

Hoover, J., Pitts, S., and Ponte, D. 2003. *Reno Police PTO Manual.* Reno: Reno Police Department.

Hoover, L. T. 1992. "Trends in Police Physical Ability Selection Testing." *Public Personnel Management* 21: 29–40.

Hormann, J. S. 1995. "Virtual Reality: The Future of Law Enforcement Training." *Police Chief* July: 7–12.

Hunter, J. 1986. "Cognitive Ability, Cognitive Aptitude, Job Knowledge, and Job Performance." *Journal of Vocational Behavior* 29: 340–362.

Hurst, Y. G. and Frank J. 2000. "How Kids View Cops: The Nature of Juvenile Attitudes Toward the Police." *Journal of Criminal Justice* 28: 189–202.

Independent Commission on the Los Angeles Police Department. 1991. *Report of the Independent Commission on the Los Angeles Police Department.* Los Angeles: California Public Management Institute.

International Association of Chiefs of Police. 1998. "Ethics Training in Law Enforcement." *Police Chief* January: 14–24.

International City Management Association. 1986. *Municipal Yearbook.* Washington, D.C.: International City Management Association.

Johnson, E. E. 1990. "Psychological Tests Used in Assessing a Sample of Police and Firefighter Candidates: An Update." *American Journal of Police* 9: 85–92.

Katz, J. 2000. "Prior Drug Use OK for Cops Nowadays." *San Francisco Examiner* June 18: A1; A18.

Kleinmuntz, B., and Szucko, J. J. 1982. "Is the Lie Detector Valid?" *Law and Society Review* 16: 105–122.

Knowles, M. S. 1970. *The Modern Practice of Adult Education: Andragogy Versus Pedagogy.* New York: Association Press.

Kraskan, P. B., and Kappeler, V. E. 1988. "Police On-duty Drug Use: A Theoretical and Descriptive Examination." *American Journal of Police* 7: 1–28.

Langworthy, R., Hughes, T., and Sanders, B. 1995. *Law Enforcement Recruitment, Selection and Training: A Survey of Major Police Departments in the U.S.* Highland Heights, KY: Academy of Criminal Justice Sciences—Police Section. 1995.

Law Enforcement Assistance Administration. 1973. *Equal Employment Opportunity Program Development Manual.* Washington, D.C.: U.S. Government Printing Office.

Law Enforcement News. 1989.

Lonsway, K. A. 2003. "Tearing Down the Wall: Problems with Consistency, Validity, and Adverse Impact of Physical Agility Testing in Police Selection." *Police Quarterly* 6: 237–277.

Marion, N. 1998. "Police Academy Training: Are We Teaching Recruits What They Need to Know?" *Policing: An International Journal of Police Strategies & Management* 21: 54–79.

McCampbell, M. S. 1986. *Field Training for Police Officers: State of the Art.* Washington, D.C.: National Institute of Justice.

McNamara, J. H. 1967. "Uncertainties in Police Work: The Relevance of Police Recruits' Background and Training." In D. J. Bordua (ed.), *The Police: Six Sociological Essays,* pp. 207–215. New York: Wiley.

Meagher, M. S., and Yentes, N. A. 1986. "Choosing a Career in Policing: A Comparison of Male and Female Perceptions." *Journal of Police Science and Administration* 14: 320–327.

Mealey, M. 1979. "New Fitness for Police and Firefighters." *Physician and Sports Medicine* 7: 96–100.

Metchik, E. 1999. "An Analysis of the 'Screening Out' Model of Police Officer Selection." *Police Quarterly* 2: 279–95.

Murphy, D. W., and Worrall, J. L. 1999. "Residency Requirement and Public Perceptions of the Police in Large Municipalities." *Policing: An International Journal of Police Strategies & Management* 22: 327–342,

National Advisory Commission on Criminal Justice Standards and Goals. 1973. *Report on Police.* Washington, D.C.: U.S. Government Printing Office.

"Police Corps Ride Again." *Law Enforcement News* September 1: 13, 14.

President's Commission on Law Enforcement and Administration of Justice. 1967. *Task Force Report: The Police.* Washington, D.C.: U.S. Government Printing Office.

Pynes, J. E. 1994. "Police Officer Selection Procedures: Speculation on the Future." *American Journal of Police* 13: 103–112.

Rafky, J., and Sussman, F. 1985. "An Evaluation of Field Techniques in Detection of Deception." *Psychophysiology* 12: 121–130.

Reaves, B. A., and Goldberg, A. L. 1999. *Law Enforcement Management and Administrative Statistics, 1997: Data for Individual and Local Agencies with 100 or More Officers.* Washington, D.C.: Bureau of Justice Statistics.

Roberg, R. R. (ed.) 1976. *The Changing Police Role: New Dimensions and New Perspectives.* San Jose, CA: Justice Systems Development.

——. 1979. "Police Training and Andragogy: A New Perspective." *Police Chief* 46: 32–34.

Roberg, R. R., and Laramy, J. E. 1980. "An Empirical Assessment of the Criteria Utilized for Promoting Police Personnel: A Secondary Analysis." *Journal of Police Science and Administration* 8: 183–187.

Roberg, R., Kuykendall, and Novak, K. (2002). *Police Management,* 3rd ed. Los Angeles, CA.: Roxbury.

Romano, B., and Gonzales, S. 1991. "Police Striving for Cultural Sensitivity" *San Jose Mercury News,* November 10: B1, B2.

"Rookie Cop, 59, Can't Escape Media." 1994. *San Jose Mercury News,* November 29: 3B.

Rubin, P. N. 1994. *The Americans with Disabilities Act and Criminal Justice: Hiring New Employees.* Washington, D.C.: National Institute of Justice.

Sanders, B., Hughes, T., and Langworthy, R. 1995. "Police Officer Recruitment and Selection: A Survey of Major Departments in the U.S." *Police Forum.* Richmond, KY: Academy of Criminal Justice Sciences.

San Diego Police Department, 1993. *Neighborhood Policing.* San Diego, CA: San Diego Police Department.

Sauls, J. G. 1995. "Establishing the Validity of Employment Standards." *FBI Law Enforcement Bulletin,* August: 27–32.

Schmidt, F. 1988. "The Problem of Group Differences in Ability Test Scores in Employment Selection." *Journal of Vocational Behavior* 33: 272–292.

Schneider, B., and Schmitt, N. 1986. *Staffing Organizations, 2nd ed.* Glenview, IL: Scott, Foreman.

Schofield, D. L. 1989. "Establishing Health and Fitness Standards: Legal Considerations." *FBI Law Enforcement Bulletin,* June: 25–31.

Shephard, R. J. 1986. *Fitness and Health in Industry.* New York: Karger.

Shield Club v. City of Cleveland, 1986. 647 R.Supp. 274 (N.D. Ohio).

Simonetti Rosen, M. 1997. "A LEN Interview with Professor Edwin J. Delattre of Boston University." *Law Enforcement News* May 15: 11–12.

Skogan, W. G., and Hartnett, S. M. 1997. *Community Policing, Chicago Style.* New York: Oxford University Press.

Slater, H. R., and Reiser, M. 1988. "A Comparative Study of Factors Influencing Police Recruitment." *Journal of Police Science and Administration* 16: 168–176.

Snowden, L., and Fuss, T. 2000. "A Costly Mistake: Inadequate Police Background Investigations." *The Justice Professional* 13: 359–375.

"Solid Corps for Policing's Future." 1994. *Law Enforcement News,* April, 15: 4.

Sproule, C. F. 1984. "Should Personnel Selection Tests be Used on a Pass-Fail, Grouping, or Ranking Basis?" *Public Personnel Management Journal* 13: 375–394.

TELEMASP. 1994. "Background Investigation and Psychological Screening of New Officers: Effect of the Americans With Disabilities Act." *Texas Law Enforcement Management and Administrative Statistics Program.* October.

——. 1996. "Recruitment Practices." *Texas Law Enforcement Management and Administrative Statistics Program.* September.

Townsey, R. D. 1992. "Female Patrol Officers: A Review of the Physical Capacity Issue." In B. R. Price and N. J. Sokoloff (eds.), *The Criminal Justice System and Women: Women Offenders, Victims, and Workers,* pp. 413–425. New York: Clark Bourdman.

Vanguard Justice Society v. Hughes. 1979. 471 F. Supp. 670.

Vaughn. M. S. 1996. " Police Civil Liability and the First Amendment: Retaliation Against Citizens Who Criticize and Challenge the Police." *Crime & Delinquency* 42: 50–67.

Vaughn, M. J., and Kappeler, V. E. 1999. "Law Enforcement: Pissing Off the Police—Civil Liability Under the First Amendment and the Fighting Words Doctrine." *Criminal Law Bulletin* 35: 594–624.

Wilson, O. W., and McLaren, R. C. 1977. *Police Administration, 4th ed.* New York: McGraw-Hill.

Williams, B. N. 1999. "Perceptions of Children and Teenagers on Community Policing: Implications for Law Enforcement Leadership, Training, and Citizen Evaluations." *Police Quarterly* 2: 151–173.

Winters, C. A. 1989. "Psychology Tests, Suits, and Minority Applicants." *Police Journal* 62: 22–30.

"Youthful Indiscretions: Doors Open Wider to Police Recruits with Prior Drug Use." (2002). *Law Enforcement News,* March 15/31: 7.

Zecca, J. M. 1993. "The CUNY/NYPD Cadet Corps." *ACJS Today,* May/June: 5.

Suggested Websites for Further Study

Los Angeles Police Department
http://www.lapdonline.org/index.htm

Equal Employment Opportunity Act of 1972
http://www4.law.cornell.edu/uscode/42/2000e.html

Age Discrimination in Employment Act of 1967
http://www4.law.cornell.edu/uscode/29/621.html

Minnesota Multiphasic Personality Inventory-2 (Revised Edition)
http://assessments.ncs.com/assessments/tests/mmpi_2.htm

Americans With Disabilities Act Home Page
http://www.usdoj.gov/crt/ada/adahom1.htm

Law Enforcement Employment
http://www.officer.com/jobs.htm

Careers in Law Enforcement
http://www.policeemployment.com

Reno Police Department
http://www.cityofreno.com/pub_ safety/police (note underscore between pub and safety) http://www.fbijobs.com/

Learn more about State POST programs
http://www.iadlest.org ✦

## Chapter 7

Field Operations

Chapter Outline

❐   The Patrol Function
Historical Development
Terrorism and Patrol
Patrol Methods
Use of Patrol Resources
Resource Determination
Resource Allocation
Computerized Crime Mapping
❐   Selected Research on Patrol Operations
Random Patrol
Response Time
Differential Response to Calls
❐   Directed Patrol, Drug Hot Spots, and Enforcement
Proactive Arrests and Crackdowns
Drunk-Driving Enforcement
Guns, Violence, and Gang Control
Zero-Tolerance Arrests
❐   Reactive Arrests and Domestic Violence
Police Pursuits
Foot Pursuits
❐   The Investigative Function
Historical Development
Terrorism and Investigation
Resource Determination and Allocation
❐   Selected Research on Investigative Operations
Investigative Effectiveness
Career Criminal Programs
Bias Crime Programs
Detective-Patrol Relationships
Enticement and Entrapment
❐   Summary
❐   Discussion Questions
❐   References
❐   Suggested Websites for Further Study

Key Terms

announcement effect	crime repression
beat	detective
bias crime	differential police response
Bow Street Runners	directed patrol
cease-fire strategy	domestic violence
computerized crime mapping	due process revolution
crackdowns	enticement

Key Terms (continued)	
entrapment	preliminary investigation
event analysis	proactive approach
field operations	proactive arrests
follow-up investigation	quality-of-life crimes
general deterrence	random patrol
generalist	reactive arrests
hot spots	ROP
hot times	shift
ICAM	SMART
investigators	social services
law enforcement	specialist
order maintenance	specific deterrence
police legitimacy	sting operation
police field operations	target oriented
police pursuit	zero-tolerance policing

Police field operations consist of two primary functions: patrol and investigations. Although most departments have other operational functions (e.g., traffic, vice, juvenile, crime prevention), a substantial majority of all police work involves either patrol or investigations. In local police departments, for example, about 65 percent of full-time officers performed patrol duties, while 16 percent primarily handled criminal investigations. In sheriff's departments, 41 percent of full-time deputies were assigned to patrol duty and 12 percent were assigned to investigative duties; in addition, because most sheriff's offices operate jail facilities and have court-related functions, 24 percent were assigned to jail-related duties and 17 percent primarily performed court-related duties (Reaves and Hickman 2002). These two operational units deal with the greatest diversity of problems and have the most influence on the public's perception of the police. Accordingly, the focus of this chapter is on patrol work and secondarily on investigative or detective work.

In relatively small departments, patrol and investigations typically do not exist as separate units because the police are generalists. A **generalist** is an officer who performs a variety of activities—for example, conducting investigations that result from calls while on patrol that otherwise could be assigned to a **specialist**. In contrast, most medium or large departments tend to *specialize* their investigative activities. In these departments, once a patrol officer is dispatched to the scene of a crime, he or she may conduct a preliminary investigation and then call in the detectives for follow-up and further case development. In highly specialized departments, the patrol officer may call in the detectives as soon as it is ascertained that an investigation is necessary; once the detectives arrive, the officer returns to patrol duty.

As discussed in earlier chapters, in those departments moving toward community policing, the patrol job is being redesigned to define police work more broadly (i.e., to be more general), with increased decision-making powers and problem-solving and investigative capabilities. It should be noted, however, that there will always be a need for detectives in policing. Patrol officers simply cannot receive enough training or have enough time to investigate highly complex and specialized crimes such as homicides, serial killings, or terrorist acts. Even small departments attempt to train a few officers to become proficient in investigating such crimes. When a crime occurs that is out of their realm of expertise, such departments may use investigators from other departments.

The Patrol Function

Police patrol has been referred to as the "backbone of policing" (Wilson and McLaren 1977) because the vast majority of police officers are assigned to patrol and thus provide the greatest bulk of services to the community. Because patrol officers are also the most highly visible personnel in the department, the patrol unit forms the public's primary perception of any particular department. Thus, it is clear why patrol work is considered to be the backbone of policing.

In general, the goals of patrol include (1) crime prevention and deterrence, (2) apprehension of offenders, (3) creation of a sense of community security and satisfaction, (4) provision of noncrime-related services, and (5) traffic control. For departments practicing community policing, another important goal is (6) identifying and solving community problems with respect to crime and disorder. In attempting to achieve these goals, patrol officers perform essentially three functions: law enforcement, order maintenance, and social services. **Law enforcement** involves activities in which police make arrests, issue citations, conduct investigations, and in general attempt to prevent or deter criminal activity. **Order maintenance** may or may not involve a violation of the law (usually minor), during which officers tend to use alternatives other than arrest. Examples include loud parties, teenagers consuming alcohol, or minor neighborhood disputes. **Social services** involve taking reports and providing information and assistance to the public, everything from helping a stranded motorist to checking grandma's house to make sure she is all right. It is important to understand (as discussed in Chapter 1) that while police work is often viewed from a narrow, law-enforcement perspective, research has continuously shown patrol work to be much broader in scope, and in practice, is more likely to involve the order-maintenance and social service activities (for discussion, see Roberg 1976).

Some of these activities may overlap functional areas. For example, traffic control can fall under any of the categories; although traffic enforcement would be a law-enforcement function, directing traffic at the scene of an accident or providing medical assistance would be a service function. Interestingly, traffic control accounts for the most contacts with the public (Schmitt, Langon, and Durose 2002) and therefore has an important impact on how the public view the police. Attempting to solve community problems could also fall under different functions; for instance, planning with a citizen's group to establish a recreation center to keep at-risk juveniles off the street could be considered order maintenance, but may relate to law enforcement as well through crime prevention activities. Based on one of the few observational analyses of patrol work, Inside Policing 7.1 provides an abbreviated description of the diverse and complex nature of a patrol officer's job.

Inside Policing 7.1   Police Patrol: A Job Description

Based on extensive field observations, this behavioral analysis of a patrol officer's job describes the attributes required for successful performance in the field. Although completed almost four decades ago, the findings are still pertinent today, concluding that a patrol officer must do the following:

1. Endure long periods of monotony in routine patrol yet react quickly and effectively to problem situations observed on the street, or to orders issued by the dispatcher.

2. Exhibit initiative, problem-solving capacity, effective judgment, and imagination in coping with the numerous complex situations he or she is called upon to face (e.g. a family disturbance, a potential suicide, a robbery in progress, an accident, or a disaster).

3. Demonstrate mature judgment, as in deciding whether an arrest is warranted by the circumstances or a warning is sufficient, or in a situation where the use of force may be needed.

4. Exhibit a number of complex psychomotor skills, such as driving a vehicle in emergency situations, firing a weapon accurately under varied conditions, and showing facility in self-defense and apprehension, as in taking a person into custody with a minimum of force.

5. Adequately perform the communication and record-keeping functions of the job, including oral reports, formal case reports, and departmental and court forms.

6. Endure verbal and physical abuse from citizens and offenders while using only necessary force in the performance of his or her function.

7. Exhibit a professional, self-assured presence and a self-confident manner in his or her conduct when dealing with offenders, the public, and the courts.

8. Be capable of restoring equilibrium to social groups, e.g., restoring order in a family fight, a disagreement between neighbors, or a clash between rival youth groups.

9. Tolerate stress in a multitude of forms, such as in a high-speed chase, a weapon being fired, or dealing with a woman bearing a child.

10. Exhibit a high level of personal integrity and ethical conduct, e.g., refrain from accepting bribes or favors and provide impartial law enforcement.

Source: Adapted from M. E. Baehr, J. E. Furcon, and E. C. Froemel, *Psychological Assessment of Patrolman Qualifications in Relation to Field Performance* (Washington, D.C.: Department of Justice, 1968), II-3–II-5.

Historical Development

Two of the most important activities of patrol officers are *watching* and *being watched*. In preindustrial societies, watching took place as a means of social control. The nightwatch system was originally the responsibility of the private citizen and service was a form of community obligation. Eventually, the citizen watcher became the paid watchman, who became the nineteenth-century patrol officer. Patrol officers in the political model were dispersed throughout the community in the hopes of preventing crime. However, given their availability, the lack of other government services, and political expediency, the patrol function was expanded beyond crime prevention to become an all-purpose governmental service. Even today, patrol remains the least specialized and most diverse function of police work.

Two critical developments of the 1930s helped change the nature of the patrol officer from a "neighborhood" cop who knew and who was known by the people on his beat: (1) the greatly increased use of the patrol car and (2) the development of the Uniform Crime Reports. By adopting the UCRs (i.e., Part I Crimes reported to the FBI) as their primary measurement of performance, the police tended to stress the crime-fighting dimension of their role and became less interested in what they defined as noncrime-related activities.

These two developments, along with the influence of O. W. Wilson's bureaucratic or paramilitary approach to police management, led to the new professionalized police department. This increased level of "professionalization" was concerned with portraying a proper police image and running things by the book—literally, Wilson's influential *Police Administration* (1950). The image of the patrol officer was one of a nonpolitical, noncorruptible fighter of crime. It was felt that the increased use of the car would increase police efficiency through **crime repression**, which had traditionally been regarded as the most important patrol function. In other words, because more area could be covered and response time would be shortened, crime could be better controlled or suppressed. According to Wilson and McLaren, patrol procedures should be designed to create the impression of a police "omnipresence," which would eliminate "the actual opportunity (or the belief that the opportunity exists) for successful misconduct" (1977, 320). The increased use of patrol cars, however, further isolated the officer from the community. A series of anonymous "beat assignments" replaced officers' intimate knowledge of neighborhoods. Interestingly, some of the more "professionalized" departments took extra measures to depersonalize policing. For example, one strategy adopted to combat corruption was the frequent rotation of beat assignments.

The development of the radio and the telephone also had a strong impact on the relationship between the police and the community. Being able to call police and dispatch them to help citizens changed patrol from essentially watching to prevent crime to waiting to respond to crime; that is, from a **proactive** (police-initiated) to a **reactive** (citizen-initiated) **approach**. As a result, citizens tended to request police assistance more often (the development of an emergency telephone number—911—has significantly contributed to this tendency), and this reinforced the all-purpose service orientation of the patrol function. Because police have often become deluged with 911 calls—many of which are not emergencies and do not necessarily require the response of an officer—some cities are developing and promoting the use of a *311 nonemergency number*. In the Baltimore, Maryland, Police Department, for example, the use of the 311 call system is credited with a 34 percent decrease in unnecessary calls to the 911 number, which represented a decrease of approximately 5,000 911 calls per week. Further, implementation of the dual call system resulted in an absolute reduction in calls (to both 311 and 911) by over 7 percent. Citizens had favorable views of the system, indicating that the 311 call system improved city services and police-community relations, and reduced nonemergency calls to 911. The 311 call system ultimately resulted in more free time for patrol officers to implement community policing (Mazerolle, Rogan, Frank, Famega, and Eck 2002). It appears implementation of a supplemental nonemergency call system can have beneficial returns on effectively managing patrol resources.

Poor people, in particular, began to use the police as lawyers, doctors, psychologists, and social workers. As Walker notes, "While the patrol car did isolate the police in some respects, the telephone brought about a more intimate form of contact between police and citizen by allowing the police officer to enter private residences and involving him in private disputes and problems" (1984, 88). What this meant was that the "professional" officer, who now knew less about the neighborhoods and people, was often ill equipped to perform non-crime-related functions and did not tend to like the order-maintenance and public-service aspects of police work (Sherman 1983).

From the above discussion, it is not difficult to conclude that patrol work has come full circle and is attempting once again to regain knowledge and awareness of the neighborhood context, although in a much more sophisticated fashion than in the past. As community policing continues to develop, patrol officers must become increasingly aware of the neighborhood context by working with citizens and community groups in the coproduction of public safety to identify and solve crime and disorder problems. Some practitioners in the field (Stephens 1996) believe that working with the community to solve problems is so vital to the effective role of policing that an officer's (or detective's) time should eventually be evenly split—at a minimum—between traditional police activities (i.e., responding to calls, administrative activities, and criminal investigation) and working with the community to solve problems. Along with this change in role emphasis, it is further suggested (Stephens 1996) that attitudes must change concerning the amount of time police spend on calls, including taking the time to ask a different set of questions on each crime report: Have we been here before? What is causing this situation to occur or reoccur? How can it be prevented? What should the police do? The callers? The victims? The community? The government? In this way, the police change their emphasis from *incident oriented* to *problem oriented* and from *responding to problems* to *solving problems* that relate to or cause crime.

Terrorism and patrol. In contemporary society, with a heightened awareness of potential terrorist acts, patrol work may need to change as well. De Guzman (2002), for instance, argues that patrol work will need to be more "target oriented," with greater emphasis placed on "event" analysis in addition to crime analysis. **Target oriented** is the concept used by officers to assess likely targets in their districts; that is, they should not only be watching over obvious places and persons who might be of danger but also where disruption in "safe places" might occur. This suggests that the police should be able to "deconstruct the obvious" (Crank 1999). In other words, they should attempt to determine the vulnerability of people and places and how they may become targets of terrorism. **Event analysis** suggests that the police should be aware of important celebrations, ideologies, and anniversaries of known activists, terrorists, or groups and attempt to determine whether these events may be connected to a possible terrorist act. Because one of the central themes of community policing is problem solving, many departments are already familiar with one method of analysis that could be used for this purpose, known as SARA (Scanning, Analysis, Response, and Assessment). The SARA process would be appropriate for analyzing events in the community and their relationships to possible terrorist acts.

Another change De Guzman believes may significantly impact terrorist acts is to intensify traffic enforcement. It is believed that no-nonsense (or even zero-tolerance) policies regarding traffic violations will limit the movement of terrorists. A number of Supreme Court decisions have expanded the use of traffic stops for the purpose of stopping, searching, and investigating. Thus, it is suggested that the previously unreliable "hunch" or "sixth sense" of the police is slowly being acknowledged by the courts as legitimate grounds for police intervention. And, given the social climate of the time, it is unlikely that the courts will strictly interpret the requirements of the exclusionary rule (against unreasonable searches and seizures) as originally set out in *Mapp v. Ohio* (1961). Of course, while such an approach may, at least on the surface, appear better able to track and investigate certain people, there are important constitutional issues with respect to profiling, and perhaps just as important, police legitimacy (i.e., trust in the police). As we have discussed previously, "sixth-sense discretion" and zero-tolerance policies have led to serious problems among minority groups, with a concomitant loss of police legitimacy.

Based on the above discussion, De Guzman (2002) suggests that these activities call for the police to return to, or "lean" toward, a legalistic style and begin "to apply their innate talent for sensing change" (89). While undoubtedly more emphasis will need to be placed on antiterrorist activities in the future, the police need to be careful not to develop a "we versus they" attitude with respect to these activities. Thus, it seems more crucial than ever to promote a community-policing approach, where vital information can be gained through improved relationships with the community. In this way, the public plays an important role in helping to combat not only traditional criminal activity but potential terrorist acts as well. Additionally, this should also lead to gains in police legitimacy, which, in turn, will lead to additional help and information in preventing crime and terrorism.

Patrol Methods

The two most dominant methods of patrol are by automobile and by foot. As noted, the automobile had a revolutionary impact on policing—and today is the most dominant method of patrol. Because it offers the greatest coverage and most rapid response to calls, it is also usually considered to be the most cost-effective method of patrol. Along with this increased coverage, however, came a trade-off in terms of isolation from the community. All of a sudden, police officers lost contact with citizens in nonconflict and nonadversarial situations. The police, in the name of efficiency, essentially became "outsiders" in the communities they served. The urban riots of the early 1960s emphasized the problems that had developed in police-community relations. For instance, the President's Commission on Law Enforcement and Administration of Justice suggested that "The most significant weakness in American motor patrol operations today is the general lack of contact with citizens except when an officer has responded to a call" (1967, 53).

When automobiles first began to be used for patrol purposes, two or more officers were often assigned to a car. Since the 1940s, however, many departments have begun to use single-person cars. There has been considerable controversy surrounding this issue. Do *one-* or *two-officer cars* do more work? Which method is safer for the officer? Which is safer for the citizen? The most comprehensive study on this debate was undertaken in San Diego in the mid-1970s (Boydstun, Sherry, and Moelter 1977). The findings indicated that one-person units produced more arrests, filed more formal crime reports, received fewer citizen complaints, and were clearly less expensive. A second study replicating the San Diego analysis (Kessler 1985) found the same results and further indicated that two one-officer cars responded to the scene of an incident faster than one two-officer car. One-officer units also had a safety advantage. Even considering the danger of the area and shift assignment, one-officer units had fewer resisting-arrest problems and about an equal involvement in assaults on officers. A study of over 1,000 officers in three Australian state police forces (Wilson and Brewer 2001) indicated that in all 12 patrol activities measured, two-officer cars encountered more resistance from citizens than one-officer cars; this suggests that officers working together may handle interactions with the public in a qualitatively different—perhaps less cordial—manner than single officers. Finally, a study of the perceptions of 50 officers in a North Texas police department (del Carmon and Guevara 2003) found that they believed that two-officer units could observe more, were as safe as single-officer cars, could respond more quickly to calls, and should be used at night or in areas where people mistrust police. However, the possibility of distractions, disagreements, and intrusion of privacy into an officer's role or duty was also noted.

In recognition of the loss of contact with the community, there has been a resurgence of *foot patrol* in the 1970s and 1980s, especially in downtown areas. The development of the portable walkie-talkie radio vastly improved the capabilities of foot patrol officers because they can now be in constant communication with headquarters regarding conditions on their beat. Of course, foot patrol officers are severely limited in terms of mobility and response to calls. Consequently, they are sometimes paired with other forms of patrol, such as car, horse, or motor scooter. Some departments use a combination of foot and car, or foot and motor scooter; that is, they allocate approximately one-half of their time to walking their beat and the other half to motor patrol. Departments that utilize such a patrol method feel that they are getting the best out of both forms of patrol—that is, a greater degree of citizen contact than provided by motor patrol alone and greater mobility than provided by foot patrol alone.

In recognition of the loss of contact with the community, there has been an increase in the use of foot patrol, especially in downtown districts.

Two comprehensive evaluations of foot patrol, or "walking a beat," revealed that although foot patrol may effect a slight reduction in crime, it primarily reduces citizens' fear of crime and changes the nature of police-citizen interactions—toward more positive and nonadversarial exchanges. The major studies were the Newark Foot Patrol Experiment, which included data on foot patrol in Newark and 28 additional cities in New Jersey (Police Foundation 1981), and the Neighborhood Foot Patrol Program, which was conducted in 14 neighborhoods of Flint, Michigan (Trojanowicz 1982). Later reports of the Flint study (Trojanowicz and Banas 1985a) discovered a decrease in the disparity between black and white perceptions of crime and policing and an increased positive acceptance of the program and confidence in police services by black members of the community.

In general, it appears that for foot patrol to be successful, it must be implemented in areas in which officers can interact with citizens—shopping centers, neighborhoods, or areas with businesses or outside citizen activity—and be able to see those citizens frequently. The size of a foot-patrol beat should be small enough that it can be covered at least once or twice per shift. Research has indicated that such coverage is necessary in order to obtain the benefits of improved police-community interaction and a reduction in the fear of crime (Greene 1987; Payne and Trojanowicz 1985; Trojanowicz and Banas 1985a; and Sherman 1983).

Departments may use numerous other patrol methods, depending on their particular needs and budgetary constraints. In general, *motorcycle patrol* is used for traffic control and enforcement in highly congested areas. One of the major problems with this form of patrol, however, is that it is extremely dangerous to the officer; just about any type of accident tends to cause harm to the rider. Wilson and McClaren stated that the hazard of motorcycle operation "is sufficient to condemn its use, and fairness to the officer and his family forbids it" (1977, 33). *Motor scooters* and *three-wheeled vehicles* are primarily used for traffic enforcement and in parks; they may also be used as part of "park and walk" programs, thus extending officers' mobility. *Bicycles* are often used in parks and beach areas and in conjunction with stakeouts; they offer good mobility and interaction with the public. Because of these assets, bicycle patrols have increased in departments implementing community policing. During the 1960s, *horse patrol* was used mainly for crowd control but today is being increasingly used in both downtown and park areas. *Planes* and *helicopters* are used primarily for traffic control, surveillance, and rescues; their mobility and observation capabilities are great, but so are their cost and noise levels. Helicopters are increasingly being used in both automobile and foot pursuits. Cities surrounded by large bodies of water use *boat patrol* for the enforcement of boating rules, emergency assistance, and other law enforcement activities, including surveillance and narcotics control. In deciding what form of patrol should be used, police managers need to consider speed, access, density of population, visibility, cost, and community support.

Table 7.1 indicates different types of patrol methods and their utilization in large police departments. This table shows departments' diverse attempts to meet needs (e.g., parks, lakes, downtown areas, freeways) with different patrol staffing levels and types of patrol; for example, Detroit and Los Angeles staff over 60 percent of their patrol units with two officers, whereas Atlanta and Baltimore have no two-officer units. In addition, Atlanta, Chicago, and Houston commit over 25 percent of their officers to patrol per 24 hours, whereas the remaining cities commit less than 20 percent. In addition, there are vast differences with respect to how departments use different types of patrol; for instance, while 50 percent of the departments assign 80 to 90 percent of their patrol resources to automobiles, Los Angeles, New York, and Seattle (with only 42 percent) assign 60 percent or less. Leaders in other types of patrol include motorcycle patrol (Seattle, 14 percent and Los Angeles, 6 percent); foot patrol (New York, 39 percent, Chicago, 15 percent, and Atlanta, 14 percent); bicycle patrol (Seattle, 16 percent and Los Angeles, 15 percent); horse patrol (Seattle, 4 percent); and marine patrol (Detroit, 4 percent and Seattle, 3 percent).

Use of Patrol Resources

This section discusses how police resources are used, including resource determination (how many officers a department

Patrol on bicycles offers good mobility and interaction with the public, and is increasingly being used in departments implementing community policing.

should have), resource allocation (how officers should be distributed), and computerized crime mapping (how to concentrate patrol activities).

Table 7.1   Patrol Allocation in Selected, Large Police Departments, 1997

| Department | Departments Using Patrol Type and Percent of All Patrol Units Accounted For | | | | | | Percent of Officers on Patrol Per 24 Hours | Percent of Units with Two Officers |
	Auto	Motorcycle	Foot	Bicycle	Horse	Marine		
Atlanta	77%	1%	14%	3%	1%	0%	31%	0%
Baltimore	96	1	2	0	1	0	16	0
Chicago	82	1	15	1	0	0	26	52
Detroit	84	1	7	3	1	4	16	68
Houston	95	1	1	1	1	0	27	11
Los Angeles	64	6	5	15	0	0	19	63
New York City	54	1	39	5	1	0	19	57
Seattle	42	14	8	16	4	3	16	31

Source: Adapted from B. A. Reaves and A. L. Goldberg, *Law Enforcement Management and Administrative Statistics, 1997* (Washington, D.C.: Department of Justice, 1999), 71–80.

Resource Determination. Essentially two methods are used to determine the "appropriate" number of police personnel for a city: intuition and comparison. The *intuitive approach* is little more than an educated guess by police managers of how many human resources a department needs to police a city "effectively." Today, the figure arrived at is usually based on tradition (i.e., personnel numbers from past years) and increased by a certain percentage deemed appropriate to keep up with the increasing crime rate or level of services provided. As noted earlier, with the implementation of the Uniform Crime Reports, most police departments tied their levels of effectiveness to the index crimes. This development created a vicious cycle: When crime is going "down" (according to the UCRs), departments take the credit for reducing crime, and when it is on the increase, they ask for additional personnel with which to "fight crime" more effectively.

Probably the most frequently used method for resource determination is the *comparative approach*, which involves comparing one or more cities, using a ratio of police officers per 10,000 population unit; if the comparison city(ies) has (have) a higher ratio of police-to-population, it is assumed that an increase in personnel is justified, at least to the level of the comparison city. Table 7.2 indicates the significant differences in police-citizen ratios between selected major cities. Although comparison is frequently used, it is not a valid indicator of needed strength, since individual cities are extremely diverse in their needs for police services, expectations, crime rates, and levels of violence. For example, the diversity of major cities in the same state can be observed by comparing San Jose with a police-citizen ratio of 16 to Los Angeles with a ration of 27, or San Antonio with 19 to Houston with 31. In addition, police departments vary widely in managerial effectiveness, use of technology, competency of officers, and policing styles. For example, because Washington, D.C., has nearly three times the police protection of Seattle, and nearly four times as much as San Jose, one might assume that it would be the safest of the three cities, which is not the case.

It should be noted that the comparison method is perhaps most useful to a department and the community's political structure as a yearly gauge for its own needs and progress. In other words, compared with last year's (or that of several years ago) level of police services provided to the city, how does the department measure up? If, for example, it can be shown that a department significantly increased its services to the community, a strong case could be made to the mayor or city manager and the city council that the ratio, and thus the resources for the department, should be increased.

Another area of debate over police resources is whether or not adding *more police* has an impact on the crime rate. A review of 36 studies found little evidence that more police reduce crime (Marvell and Moody 1996). The same authors, however, provided their own 20-year analysis of 56 cities of over 250,000 population and of 49 states. Using complex statistical techniques, they found consistent results that as the number of police in a jurisdiction increased, the level of crime was reduced the following year. Since this study is the most sophisticated to date—even though its findings are contradictory to an overwhelming majority of the research—it provides the clearest indication that modest increases in police numbers do appear to affect the crime rate (at least for the following year).

Additional experimental research on this topic is necessary, however, before too much emphasis is placed on the quick fix of simply adding more police to reduce crime, even though it may be the most politically expedient thing to do. The above discussion clearly shows that police-to-population ratios, have little, if any, direct impact on crime rates. In general, managerial effectiveness, competency of officers, policing methods, and technology all appear to be factors in how the police affect crime. Accordingly, how the police are used and what they do are probably more important than adding a limited number of new officers to a department.

Table 7.2 Police-Population Ratios of Selected Major Cities, 1999	
City	**Sworn Officers per 10,000 Citizens**
District of Columbia	63
Chicago	49
Baltimore	44
Detroit	40
New York	53
Houston	31
Los Angeles	27
Seattle	24
San Antonio	19
San Jose, CA	16

Source: Adapted from B. A. Reaves and T. C. Hart, *Law Enforcement Management and Administrative Statistics, 1999* (Washington, D.C.: Department of Justice, 2000), 1–12.

Resource allocation. Traditionally, police resources have been allocated equally over a 24-hour time period of three 8-hour shifts—for example, day shift: 8 A.M. to 4 P.M.; evening or "swing" shift: 4 P.M. to midnight; and "graveyard" shift: midnight to 8 A.M. During these shifts, officers patrol geographic areas of approximately equal size. Of course, such an allocation method does not take into account the fact that police calls vary by time of day, day of week, area of the community, and even time of year.

Because the workload distribution is not equal across time periods, days, or patrol areas, it is apparent that the equal allocation of police resources would mean that some officers were being overused (some would say overworked) while others were being underused. Such an arrangement presents operational problems, not only in attempting to respond to calls for service but also in not being able to perform directed or preventive patrol duties. Underused officers are quite likely to become bored and unmotivated, whereas overworked officers are likely to become fatigued and stressed. Accordingly, allocation plans should be based on need rather than resource equalization.

In these plans, the two most important variables for determining allocation are *location* and *time*. Knowing the location of problems assists departments in dividing up a community into **beats** (sectors or districts), or geographic areas, of approximately equal workload. Time of occurrence is critical because it determines how officers will be grouped into working time periods, or **shifts.** As a general rule, the greater the number of problems or calls for service, the *smaller* the size of the beat and thus the more concentrated the resources. The time it takes to service a call is also important, since the resource being allocated is a skilled officer's time, which needs to be managed as effectively as possible. Once data on these variables have been collected and analyzed, beat boundaries, number of officers, and shift times are determined. Because of population shifts and changes in demand for service, it is important that departments continually reevaluate patrol beat boundaries and assignment of personnel.

As Figure 7.1 of the Kansas City, Missouri, Police Department's dispatched calls for service by time of day indicates, the evening shift has the greatest number of calls with approximately 45 percent, followed by the day shift with approximately 35 percent, and the graveyard shift with approximately 20 percent. Figure 7.1 further depicts the wide variation of calls with respect to the time of day. For example, the evening shift has a range of calls from about 45 at 9 P.M. to 30 at midnight, while the graveyard shift ranges from about 30 calls at midnight to about 10 at 2 A.M.. Because of such wide variation of calls by time of day, departments often develop an "overlapping" shift to cover the increased workload; for instance, in Figure 7.1, such a shift might overlap the evening and graveyard shifts from approximately 2 P.M. to 10 P.M. when the workload for calls is the highest.

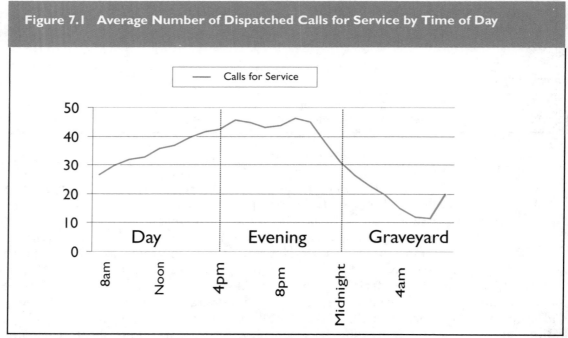

Figure 7.1   Average Number of Dispatched Calls for Service by Time of Day

Source: Kansas City (Missouri) Police Department. *Annual Report 2002.*

To overcome the inherent problems in the equal allocation of resources, many medium and large departments have adopted alternate scheduling, such as a 4-10 plan; smaller departments generally do not have adequate personnel to utilize this schedule. With such a plan, officers work four days a week, 10 hours per day, with three days off in a row. Officers tend to like the 4-10 plan because it allows for increased leisure time, while the department gains increased coverage due to overlapping shifts, although there may be fatigue problems with such a compacted schedule. Another method that has been used to increase patrol coverage is the creation of an additional permanent shift. This additional shift would overlap other shifts during high workload periods, as noted above in Kansas City, this would be from 2 P.M. to 10 P.M.

Computerized crime mapping. One of the important recent breakthroughs with respect to resource utilization has been the development of **computerized crime mapping** to assist officers about where to concentrate their patrol activities. Data obtained through a department's computer-aided dispatch and records-management systems (which store and maintain calls for service, records of incidents, and arrests) are matched with addresses and other geographic information such as beats and districts; maps can then be computer generated for a geographic area to be overlaid with specific information (Rich 1996). The Bureau of Justice Statistics national survey of nearly 3,000 state and local police departments in 2000 indicated that 15 percent of local departments, including over 80 percent of those serving 100,000 or more residents utilized crime mapping; overall, this included 59 percent of all officers (Hickman and Reaves 2003a). In sheriff's offices, 13 percent used crime mapping, including 44 percent of those serving 1 million or more residents; overall, this included 37 percent of all personnel (Hickman and Reaves 2003b).

In conjunction with the Chicago Police Department's development of its community-policing strategy (see Chapter 5), where beat officers focus on problem solving, a crime-mapping system known as **ICAM (information collection for automated mapping)** was developed to help beat officers focus on problem solving. The system was developed from the beginning to be user friendly in order that all officers throughout the department could have access to the system and be provided with information to help them better understand the problems in their assigned areas and develop strategies to address them. Officers also share the ICAM maps with residents through their beat meetings, thus giving them a chance to help the police cut down on crime through joint problem-solving efforts (Rich 1996).

The ICAM main screen is depicted in Figure 7.2 and appears automatically when the computer is turned on. ICAM can perform two main tasks, indicated in the boxes containing the "Do It" buttons: (1) it can produce a map of reported offenses of a particular type in an area, or (2) it can generate a list of the 10 most frequently reported offenses in a beat.

Although no determinations can be made regarding the number of crimes ICAM has helped to resolve, some anecdotes of ICAM's effectiveness as a crime-solving tool for Chicago are available (see Inside Policing 7.2). ICAM also helps officers to make decisions regarding their work plans. For example, one beat officer in the 24th District said she uses ICAM as an aid in deciding where to concentrate her foot-patrol activities (Rich 1996).

Selected Research on Patrol Operations

Prior to the 1960s, there was only a limited amount of research about the patrol function. During the last several decades, however, a significant amount of research has been conducted on various aspects of patrol, much of it containing important policy implications. Except for team policing and community policing, covered in Chapter 3, some of the better controlled, more important studies are discussed in this section.

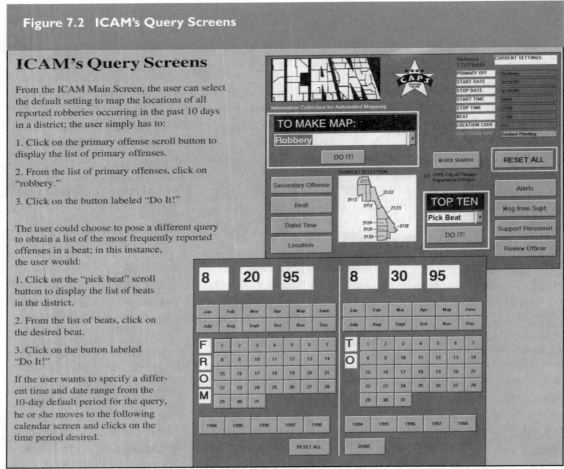

Source: T. F. Rich. 1996. *The Chicago Police Department's Information Collection for Automation Mapping (ICAM) Program* (Washington, D.C.: National Institute of Justice), 7.

Random Patrol

Possibly the most influential early study on police operations, both for its breakthrough in initiating large-scale experimental research in police departments and the general impact of its findings, was the Kansas City Preventive Patrol Experiment (Kelling, Pate, Dieckman, and Brown 1974).

Up until this time, police departments had little interest in scientific observation or intellectual inquiry; many, in fact, were antiresearch (Caiden 1977). The purpose of the one-year experiment was to determine the effect of **random patrol** (i.e., officers patrolling "randomly" in their beats when not on assignment) on crime rates and citizens' feelings of security. For study purposes, one part of the city was divided into 15 areas, which were randomly divided into five beats, each containing three groups. Each group was matched with respect to crime data, population characteristics, and calls for service, and assigned different levels of patrol as follows: *reactive beats* had no preventive patrol activities; *proactive beats* were assigned two to three times the normal number of

Inside Policing 7.2   ICAM in Action

Anecdotes of how the Information Collection for Automated Mapping program has been used to help solve crimes include the following:

- In the 10th district three officers caught three teenagers in the act of burglarizing a home. The surrounding area recently had experienced a rash of burglaries, and the officers suspected that the teenagers were responsible for many of them. The teenagers confessed to committing several of the burglaries but could not remember the addresses of the homes. The officers used ICAM to generate a map and a list of all burglaries occurring in the past six months in the general vicinity where they were operating. The officers then drove the teenagers to specific homes to determine which ones they had burglarized. With just a few hours' work, 11 burglaries were cleared, and residents were able to recover their stolen property, which had been stored in the home of one teenager.

- In the 22nd District, officers learned of a rash of burglaries occurring at schools and used ICAM to map the exact locations of these burglaries and determine patterns about the times they were occurring. Officers then established surveillance at the appropriate times and locations and soon arrested a burglar as he was fleeing a school.

- In the 7th District, an ICAM map showed that the locations of recovered stolen vehicles were clustered around specific abandoned buildings. Armed with this information, police officials worked with the city's Department of Planning to expedite demolition of the buildings.

Source: T. F. Rich, *The Chicago Police Department's Information Collection for Automated Mapping (ICAM) Program* (Washington, D.C.: National Institute of Justice, 1996), 12.

patrol units; and *control beats* maintained the normal level of patrol (i.e., one car per beat). Figure 7.3 is a schematic representation of the 15-beat experimental area.

The results indicated that the three patrol conditions appeared not to affect (1) crime rates suppressible by patrol (these included burglaries, auto thefts, larcenies involving auto accessories, robberies, and vandalism), (2) citizens' attitudes toward police, (3) feelings of security, or (4) rates of reported crime. Since most police departments had routinely based decisions on requests for personnel and resource allocation on having a certain percentage of an officer's time devoted to random patrol (normally 40 to 60 percent), this research raised important questions about the effectiveness of routine pre-

An officer using a laptop computer; the use of computers by patrol officers is going to become more sophisticated and widespread in the near future.

ventive patrol and the resource needs of police. The conclusions of the Kansas City study suggested that traditional preventive patrol was not effective and that this uncommitted time devoted to random patrol could be used more effectively.

Although there are several reasons why differing levels of patrol had no impact on either crime rates or citizens' attitudes (Larson 1975; Feinberg, Kinley, and Reiss 1976), the most likely reason is because normal patrol is spread so thin to begin with that simply adding another car or two to a relatively large area is unlikely to have any measurable impact. And because patrol strength cannot be increased to higher levels for any length of time, due to manpower and budgetary constraints, the Kansas City findings are as relevant today as they were in the 1970s. Much of the research reviewed below relates to how police can better manage their time or restructure their activities to reduce crime and provide better service to the community.

Figure 7.3 Kansas City Preventive Patrol Experiment: Fifteen-Beat Area

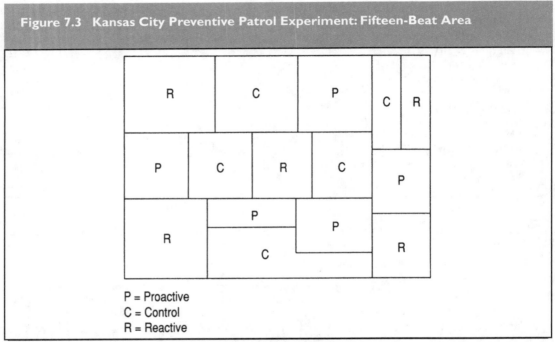

P = Proactive
C = Control
R = Reactive

Source: G. L. Kelling, T. Pate, D. Dieckman, and C. E. Brown, *The Kansas City Preventive Patrol Experiment* (Washington, D.C.: Police Foundation, 1974), 9.

Response Time

Shortly after the preventive-patrol study, a follow-up investigation in the Kansas City Police Department raised serious questions about another common assumption of patrol: the effectiveness of *rapid response* times (Pate, Bowers, Ferrara, and Lorence 1976). Until this time, the assumption was that the faster the response to calls, the more satisfied citizens would be and the more likely that suspects would be apprehended. Based on these assumptions, police departments have spent considerable money in attempting to reduce response times by introducing new technology (e.g., the 911 telephone number, vehicle-location console monitors, and computer-aided dispatchers) and sophisticated beat models (Caiden 1977). Overall, the results found that because the average citizen waits so long (approximately six minutes) to call the police—he or she often calls a friend or relative first—there is virtually no chance to make an arrest at the crime scene, regardless of how quickly police respond. Furthermore, it was discovered that citizen satisfaction with police departments depends less on quick response than on knowing approximately when the officer will arrive. Other studies have found similar results (Spelman and Brown 1982; Sherman 1983).

The impact of this study was that the police began to realize that they could respond differentially to calls; that is, because not all calls have the same level of importance, they can be assigned different priority levels. For example, noncritical calls can be responded to less quickly than critical calls. As long as citizens are informed of approximate arrival times, their satisfaction levels with the police remain high, even though they may not actually see an officer for an extended period of time or, in some cases, not at all. Of course, for critical calls (e.g., crimes in progress, injuries), it remains important for the police to respond as quickly as possible.

Differential Response to Calls

The findings about response time led to investigations attempting to determine how the police can best manage demand for services. Essentially, managing demand requires categorizing requests for service and matching those requests with differential police responses. Differential response programs classify calls according their degree of seriousness and are then responded to by (1) an immediate response by a sworn officer; (2) a delayed response by a sworn officer; (3) no direct police response, but with reports taken by telephone, mail, or having the citizen to come to the police station (McEwen, Connors, and Cohen 1986). A substantial body of research on **differential police response (DPR)** indicates that alternative response strategies significantly reduced costs and improved effectiveness, did not affect citizens' levels of satisfaction, and did not increase crime (Cahn and Tien 1981; Cohen and McEwen 1984; McEwen, Connors, and Cohen 1986; Won-Jae 2002; and Worden 1993).

In Greensboro, North Carolina (McEwen et al. 1986), citizens expressed satisfaction with 90 percent of the alternative responses, except for walk-ins. With respect to a delayed officer response, satisfaction was directly related to whether or not the caller was told that a delay might occur. In Lansing, Michigan, Worden (1993) found differential responses to be both efficient and equitable. Low-priority crimes receiving a delayed response had a median response time of 16 minutes, and received a citizen satisfaction rate of over 90 percent. DPR was also shown to be equitable in that whites and racial and ethnic minorities were just as likely to be satisfied. In a more recent study of twenty Texas police departments using DPR, Won-Jae (2002) found that about 80 percent of all citizen calls were noncritical, of which 15 percent simply requested information. The remaining 20 percent of calls required immediate dispatch; the response time was approximately twice as fast (8 minutes) as delayed response time (17 minutes). It was concluded that the Texas departments drew the following benefits from DPR strategies: (1) a decrease in operating costs; (2) a decrease in the number of calls that needed immediate response; and (3) an increase in patrol officers' available time for community policing and crime prevention.

Directed Patrol, Drug Hot Spots, and Enforcement

Directing what officers do rather than allowing uncommitted random patrol time became increasingly popular after the Kansas City experiment. The development of computerized crime analysis and, more recently, computerized mapping allows the police to identify more precisely patterns of crime and disorder. This increased precision allows patrols to be directed to primary crime areas at primary crime times. As such, **directed patrol** is more proactive, uses uncommitted time for a specified activity, and is based on crime and problem analysis. Of particular importance is the proactive dimension of the directed activity, be it making arrests, issuing citations, conducting field interrogations, or educating the public about crime. Proactivity produces more information, heightens citizen awareness of police, perhaps creates an impression of greater police watchfulness, and most certainly requires police to be more alert and active.

An early study (Cordner 1981) in Pontiac, Michigan, over a period of nearly 18 months found some evidence that *targeted crimes* could be decreased through the use of directed patrol based on crime analysis. The findings, however, indicated that the tactics employed during directed assignments, rather than the amount of time devoted to directed patrol, had the greater effect on crime. This was perhaps due to the relatively limited number of "opportunities" in any particular target area for "aggressive patrol efforts."

Targeting **hot spots** for crime developed out of research analyzing 911 calls in Minneapolis (Sherman, Gartin, and Buerger 1989), in which it was discovered that 5 percent of the addresses in the city accounted for 64 percent of all 911 calls. Thus only a few locations, which were labeled hot spots, required a highly disproportionate amount of police time and resources. Following this research, the Minneapolis Hot Spots Patrol Experiment was designed to test the crime-prevention effects of extra patrol officers directed at hot spots for crime during **hot times** for crime over a one-year period (Sherman and Weisburd 1995). Increased police presence was directed to a randomly selected 55 of the worst 110 hot spot street corners in the city. The remaining 55 received normal patrol coverage, primarily in response to citizen calls for service. Results indicated that increased police presence failed to reduce serious crime but did have a "modest" effect on disorder. Mere visibility seemed to have caused the modest effect on disorder, as the officers' activities at the hot spots were unstructured and not very substantial.

A study of *drug hot spots* in Jersey City, New Jersey (Weisburd and Green 1995), found that these areas included a disproportionate share of arrests not only for drug-related crime but for crime and disorder overall. Almost one-half of all arrests for narcotics (47.8 percent) were found in 56 drug hot spots, which made up only 4.4 percent of Jersey City streets. Interestingly, for violent crimes, the drug hot spots accounted for about one-fifth of the total arrests, which is more than four times what would be expected if arrests were evenly distributed throughout the city. Other offenses, such as burglary and theft, vandalism, and drunk driving, also occurred relatively more frequently in the drug hot spots compared with other places in the city. Since it appears that drug hot spot areas also contain a disproportionate amount of overall crime (including violent crime) and disorder problems, these problems will most likely be reduced by removing much of the illicit drug market traffic (Weisburd and Green 1995).

A multistrategy approach to drug control is the *Beat Health Program* of the Oakland, California, Police Department, which emphasizes *civil remedies* to control drug and disorder problems by focusing on the physical decay and property management conditions of specific hot spot locations; thus, program staff interact primarily with nonoffending third parties—landlords, business owners, and private property owners—responsible for the property. A special unit made up of Beat Health officers coordinates site visits by a group of city inspectors, known as **SMART (Specialized Multi-Agency Response Team)**. Depending on preliminary assessments made by Beat Health officers, representatives from agencies such as housing, fire, public works, and Pacific Gas and Electric are invited to inspect a problem location and to enforce local safety codes (see Inside Policing 7.3 for an example of the program). A training program for landlords, which helped them to screen prospective tenants and evict those who violated rules, was also initiated. An evaluation of the Beat Health program and SMART (Green Mazerolle, and Roehl 1999) found during the 12-month postevaluation period that the number of drug calls for service per square miles decreased by 16.2 percent in the Beat Health residential sites while increasing by 5.4 percent in the control residential sites. It appears that the key component of this type of program is a combination of increased police activity and the cooperative working arrangement with other governmental agencies to enforce civil code violations.

Inside Policing 7.3   Beat Health Program: A Case Study

An anonymous caller to the Oakland Police Department drug hotline reported narcotics trafficking, abandoned vehicles, and trash at a single-family home in a nice area of the city. The Beat Health team contacted the owner, who said the problems were probably due to an illegal tenant staying at the house with the permission of the legal tenant. Police records revealed that the illegal tenant was on probation for drug charges.

An inspection of the property was conducted by the SMART team, each city agency inspector found violations—missing stair banisters, broken windows, possible electrical tampering, overgrown weeds, trash, dog waste, abandoned vehicles, engine parts in the yard, and two pit bulls. The Beat Health officer then arranged for the code-compliance officer to inspect the inside of the residence, which resulted in the discovery of numerous citations for violations. Within 3 months, the illegal tenant was evicted, the yard cleared of abandoned vehicles and trash, and code violations fixed. The case was closed 6 months after it was opened with the property being restored and no new calls or complaints received.

Source: L. Green Mazerolle and J. Roehl, *Controlling Drug and Disorder Problems: Oakland's Beat Health Program* (Washington, D. C.: National Institute of Justice, 1999), 3.

Another multistrategy hot spot study in Jersey City, New Jersey (Braga, Weisburd, Waring, Green Mazerolle, Spelman, and Gajewski 1999), evaluated the impact of using a *problem-oriented* approach in violent crime areas. The experiment included violent crime locations that made up 6 percent of the total of Jersey City but which accounted for 24 percent of the assaults and 20 percent of the robberies. The violent crime locations were matched in pairs of treatment and control groups. The treatment areas were analyzed according to need and received a number of interventions that could be categorized as a "policing-disorder" strategy; almost all areas, however, received (1) a number of aggressive order-maintenance tactics, including repeat foot and radio car patrols, dispersing loiterers, issuing summonses for public drinking, and "stop and frisks" of suspicious persons, and (2) investigations into drug sales and drug enforcement. A little less than one-half required storefront cleanups by owners and removal of trash on streets by the public works department; several areas also used increased lighting and housing-code enforcement.

The effects of the intervention were measured by analyzing six crime incident categories (robbery, nondomestic assault, property, disorder/vandalism, narcotics arrests, and total incidents) and six citizen-call categories (robbery, street fighting, property, disorder/nuisance, narcotics, and total calls). The findings indicated that the total number of both criminal incidents and calls for service were significantly reduced at the treatment areas relative to the control areas. The results of this experiment indicate that a problem-oriented approach, focusing on aggressive patrol and drug enforcement, may have a significant impact on reducing violent behavior.

These studies appear to have important implications for reducing drug problems and, concomitantly, for reducing violent and other crime and disorder problems by using multiple patrol strategies and working with other government officials to enforce civil code violations.

Proactive Arrests and Crackdowns

Proactive arrests, which are initiated by the police, focus on a narrow set of high-risk targets. The theory is that a high certainty of arrest for a narrowly defined set of offenses or offenders will have a greater deterrent effect than will a low certainty of arrest for a broad range of targets (Sherman 1997). One of the most widespread developments in the use of proactive arrests in the mid-1980s was the use of police crackdowns. **Crackdowns** can be defined as intensive, short-term increases in officer presence and arrests for specific types of offenses or for all offenses in specific areas. Drunk driving, public drug markets, streetwalking prostitutes, domestic violence, illegal parking, and even unsafe bicycle riding have all been targets for publicly announced crackdowns (Sherman 1990a). The theory behind this approach is that the use of such crackdowns makes the risks of apprehension far more uncertain than in any fixed level of police-patrol activity. Most of the controversy centers on the effectiveness of the crackdown; that is, are they worth the increased cost and public inconvenience (Sherman 1990a)?

One of the early investigations of crackdowns covered 18 case studies of various target problems and attempted to analyze what is known to date regarding crackdowns (Sherman 1990b). The evidence appears to support the notion of an initial deterrent effect on some offenses, as well as support for the notion of *residual deterrence*; that is, some crime reduction continues even after the crackdown has ended. Interestingly, the case studies revealed that short-term crackdowns suffered less from *deterrence decay* (i.e., a lessening of the crime deterrent effect) than did longer-term crackdowns. This suggests that the use of crackdowns might be more effective if they are limited in duration and rotated across crime targets or target areas. Koper (1995), for instance, found that a hot spot was free of crime or disorder for about a 15-minute interval, at which point a negative effect developed. With respect to deterrence decay, the cost-effectiveness of crackdown strategies should also be evaluated. For example, in an experimental study of raids on crackhouses (Sherman and Rogan 1995), it was found that although crime on the block dropped sharply after the raid, the deterrent effect decayed after only seven days. Due to the labor-intensive nature of drug crackdowns, the strategy appears not to be cost-effective in the long run.

Drunk-Driving Enforcement

In the 1980s, drunk driving or *driving under the influence (DUI)* became a major public and political concern. A national crusade ensued, pushed in particular by an organization called Mothers Against Drunk Driving (MADD), established by the mother of a child who lost her life to a drunk driver. Police departments reacted by intensifying enforcement actions through crackdowns on drunk drivers and roadblocks checking for drunk drivers. Some departments even posted when and where the roadblocks would be in an attempt to publicize their efforts. In general, the research on these crackdowns suggests that they tend to produce an initial reduction in traffic accidents and fatalities, but once the publicity wears off, traffic accidents and fatalities increase (Andenaes 1974; Ross 1992). It appears that an **announcement effect** may take place; that is, the initial publicity surrounding a crackdown may cause a change in people's drinking and driving behavior, but as the publicity wanes, people return to their previous levels of drinking and driving. Interestingly, although drunk-driving crackdowns have had a limited impact, the actual rate of alcohol-related driving fatalities has been decreasing for some time. Essentially, safer cars equipped with seat belts and air bags, better engineered roads and safety measures, and an increase in the legal drinking age have all contributed to this reduction (Ross 1992). While it appears that drunk-driving crackdowns will always have a sporadic effect, increased social control efforts—especially with respect to education (including driver education type programs), traffic safety measures, and safer vehicles—will undoubtedly have a greater and longer-lasting impact.

Guns, Violence, and Gang Control

Several proactive arrest strategies have been applied to the impact of increased police presence and activity on reducing guns, gun crimes, and gang violence.

The Kansas City Gun Experiment (Sherman, Shaw, and Rogan 1995) indicated that increased seizures of illegal guns in a high-crime precinct can reduce violent gun crimes. The experimental area contained extra gun-unit officers, working overtime shifts, who concentrated on detecting and seizing illegally possessed guns, while a control area had only regular levels of activity. Over a 29-week period, the number of gun crimes in the experimental area declined by 49 percent but by only 4 percent in the control area. There appeared to be little evidence of a displacement effect to neighboring beats. While these results appear promising, such a program is extremely expensive and may not be able to be maintained by a department.

Using the Kansas City Gun Experiment as a model, McGarrel, Chermak and Weiss (2001) evaluated a 90-day patrol project in Indianapolis that was intended to reduce violent crime involving firearms. This study compared two opposing police strategies:

specific deterrence, where the goal was to focus on the seizure of illegal weapons from targeted offenders (i.e., suspicious-looking pedestrians and motorists), and **general deterrence,** where the goal was to maximize motor vehicle stops as a sign of increased police presence. A third comparison group area, where police activity was unchanged, was also evaluated. Significantly, gun-related crime declined by 29 percent compared to the prior year in the targeted offender/specific deterrence area, while increases occurred in the general deterrence and comparison areas. Further, there was little indication of displacement of violent crime to the five beats surrounding the targeted area.

Cohen and Ludwig (2003) reported on the impact of *firearm suppression patrol (FSP)* in Pittsburgh. FSP was focused on specific target areas, where officers were relieved from responding to calls for service to focus on proactively seizing guns from citizens. Similar to Kansas City, police did this by engaging in traffic enforcement and pedestrian stops. The researchers found that FSP reduced shots fired by as much as 34 percent in the target areas and reduced gunshot-related injuries by 71 percent in these areas. This was found despite a modest number of guns actually seized, suggesting the impact was realized not due to incapacitation but due to the deterrent value of this type of patrol activity.

These findings suggest that specific deterrence strategies appear to be more effective than general deterrence strategies. Importantly, in Kansas City there was also a high degree of community support for the use of aggressive patrol tactics. This support was attributed to two important considerations: (1) police managers met with community leaders prior to implementation and secured their endorsement, and (2) police officers were told by their supervisors to treat citizens with respect and to explain the reasons for vehicle stops. This finding has important implications for virtually all strategies of police patrol.

The Boston Gun Project (Kennedy, Piehl, and Braga 1996) is an approach in which the police used a mix of strategies in an attempt to prevent gun violence, especially by gang members, many of whom were on probation. What became known as the **cease-fire strategy** was an attempt to deter the particular problem of gang-related violence. If gangs refrained from violent activity but committed other crimes, the normal approach of police, prosecutors, and the rest of the criminal justice system came into play. If the gangs hurt people, however, cease-fire members got involved (Kennedy 1998).

Cease-fire included criminal justice strategies such as joint patrols of police and probation officers (who teamed up to make sure convicted young adult offenders were not roaming the streets and were abiding by the law); federal and local prosecutors; school police and youth corrections; and joint ventures were carried out with various federal agencies, including the Bureau of Alcohol, Tobacco and Firearms (ATF)—which can help track firearms linked to violent crimes and determine patterns that could lead to suppliers of illegal guns—the Drug Enforcement Administration (DEA), and the Immigration and Naturalization Service (INS). Direct meetings between gang members and authorities also took place, with warnings of severe sanctions if violence continued.

Cease-fire also included community and private sector strategies, such as educational and employment opportunities. Community centers, the clergy, and gang-outreach workers also played a role in spreading the antiviolence message to young offenders and attempted to help them to enter mainstream society. The results were startling, with gang and gun-related homicides in the 24-and-under age category cut by 70 percent from 1990 to 1995; during one 28-month period there were no homicides in this age group (Clark 1997).

The apparent success of the program likely rests on the specific deterrence effect of identifying and focusing on a particular problem and sustaining a cooperative effort among federal and local criminal justice and public social-service agencies. Because of the initial positive results, other police departments have become interested in adopting or replicating the cease-fire deterrence strategy. Inside Policing 7.4 takes a look at the Minneapolis program.

Inside Policing 7.4   **Minneapolis Homicide Reduction Project**

The first replication of the Boston effort was launched in Minneapolis in the spring of 1997, and the city's homicide rate fell by 80 percent during the summer months. Analyzing the city's murder rate from 1994 to May 1997, it was found that nearly 45 percent of all city homicides appeared to be gang related and were clustered in a few neighborhoods; nearly one-third of suspects and arrestees had probation histories and nearly 75 percent of suspects had arrest records. Armed with this data, officials decided to set up joint police-probation officer patrols; increase collaboration between federal, state, and local law enforcement agencies; beef up foot patrol on high-crime beats; and aggressively enforce quality-of-life crimes as well as the city's curfew. Authorities also spread the word to members of the city's 30 known gangs that it would no longer be business as usual.

It has also not gone unnoticed that the program has increased police morale. Officers have not been this excited about their jobs in 20 or 25 years; they feel they're actually saving lives by intervening when an incident is about to happen. Due to its apparent success, the program will remain in place indefinitely. Officials are so heartened by the decline in violence that elements of the project will most likely be adapted to drug enforcement operations as well.

Source: J. R. Clark, 1997, "LEN Salutes Its 1997 People of the Year, the Boston Gun Project Working Group," *Law Enforcement News*, December 31: 1, 4, 5.

Zero-Tolerance Arrests

Another strategy of proactive arrests has become known as **zero-tolerance policing,** based on the broken-windows theory (Wilson and Kelling 1982) of crime causation (see Chapter 4). In practice, this theory suggests that if police aggressively pursue minor **quality-of-life crimes** (e.g., panhandling, public urination, rowdy behavior), the improvement in the quality of life in an area will indirectly lead to a lower rate of serious crime (Kelling and Coles 1996).

New York City's zero-tolerance policies, where, in designated areas, many stops were made for minor violations of traffic laws, ordinances, and misdemeanors, have been credited with significant crime reduction (Bratton 1996; Kelling and Bratton 1998). Questions remain, however, with respect to how much of this reduction can be attributed to *zero-tolerance arrests* and whether the cost was worth it (citizen complaints of police abuse increased 60 percent). Upon closer scrutiny, the evidence suggests that crime had been decreasing, sometimes as dramatically but without the use of zero-tolerance arrests and tactics, in other major cities over the same time period (see Greene 1999; Harcourt 2001; Herbert 2001; Witkin 1998).

Sherman (1997) suggests that the larger concern about **zero-tolerance policing** is its long-term effect on people arrested for minor offenses. Even while massive increases in arrests may reduce violence in the short run, they may also increase crime in the long run (as arrestees may become more defiant and aggressive). Furthermore, the effects of an arrest experience over minor offenses may permanently lower **police legitimacy**—the public's confidence in the police as fair and equitable—both for the arrested person and for his or her social network of family and friends. In addition, program development to foster greater police legitimacy in the course of making arrests is suggested, for example, providing arrested minor offenders an opportunity to meet with a police supervisor who would explain the program to them, answer questions about why they are being arrested, and give them a chance to express their views. An early study on police field interrogations in San Diego backs this up. Boydstun (1975) discovered that field interrogations not only had some apparent crime prevention effects, but if conducted with civility and an explanation for the reason, there was no adverse impact on citizen attitudes, even in minority communities. Thus, with respect to crime prevention, focusing on police "style" may be as important as focusing on police "substance" (Sherman 1997). As noted above, this appeared to be one of the lessons learned from the Kansas City Gun Experiment.

With respect to the types of patrol strategies described above, Voices From the Field relates one chief's opinion regarding the most effective strategies currently available to police.

Voices From the Field
Former Chief Paul F. Evans
Boston Police Department

Question: What have 30 years of research and development taught us about the most effective police patrol strategies and tactics?

Answer: Profound shifts in police practice have been pushed forward by the groundbreaking research of the past three decades. We have learned a huge amount about specific problems. But more important, the research has bred a new approach of basing strategy on information and knowledge. Research has taught us how to align resources with the actual nature of the problems we seek to address. In turn, it has pushed us to measure effectiveness in terms of prevention of harm and disorder and improvement in quality of life in our communities. It has moved us away, finally, from reliance solely on internal measures of effort and process.

The value of research has been borne out for me in the course of 10 years of leading the Boston Police Department. There are three operating principles that I have seen at work in the fabric of our innovations and that have been pushed forward by research:

- First is the importance of shared ownership and accountability, between community and police and among all the stakeholders in public safety process.

- Second, and closely related, is the importance of collaboration.

- Finally, I have seen the importance of getting everyone onto the same page with a shared mission and a collaborative, shared strategy for accomplishing the mission.

At the time I took over at Boston PD, the practice of the policing and justice process in Boston was characterized by fragmentation and limited accountability. This fragmented approach also prevailed inside the police department. My favorite example is the area of drug investigations. When I took over, Boston was like most departments in the country when it came to antidrug strategy. We committed a lot of resources to a centralized drug unit. Then, at the end of 1993 and the beginning of 1994, we saw a frightening rash of drug-related homicides that cut across three police districts in the geographic center of the city. In response, we brought front-line personnel together to analyze the problem and propose solutions. Here, for the first time in a long time, the mission of drug control was revised. Each of the three districts was assigned a drug squad to work under the control not of a headquarters boss but the local commander. Further, the three affected commanders were directed to collaborate across district lines. The results were dramatic, as the commanders responded. We saw a 50 percent drop right away in violent crime associated with these street drug markets. We saw the power of investing resources in those closest to the problem, authorizing our local personnel to direct resources as the problem dictated. A real sense of ownership began to grow among local police and between police and community. They saw the results every day on their own streets and sidewalks.

The second major principle to emerge from our work is the importance of collaboration, which we developed in Boston between police and probation. As firearm crime reached its highest point in the city in 1990, and faced with the dramatic inability of our old "crimefighting" strategy to have much impact on crime and fear, line-level cops and probation officers began to compare notes. They confirmed what they knew instinctively. They were all dealing with the same players. They set a new goal among themselves: to prevent the next shooting from happening. That meant new roles for both police and probation. Probation officers began to get out of the courthouses and start supervising their probationers in the community. This new behavior helped bring offending under control, as offenders

adjusted to new rules on the street. Thus, probation officers assumed a new and profound role in crime reduction. By going beyond occasional cooperation to formal collaboration, they changed the atmosphere and the rules on the street. The effort became Operation Nite Lite. The new approach forced offenders to change their behavior in ways that would have been impossible under the old regime of official fragmentation and informal cooperation.

Finally, effective performance demands that everyone involved in the effort operate with a sense of mission that is both correct and shared. With that in place, we proceeded to develop a collaborative strategy to make our communities safe and secure places to live and work. Prevention of crime has to become the strategic mission of the policing process. For decades, especially in the U.S., our mission was of reaction, of the "three R's" of random patrol, rapid response, and retrospective investigation. Once the reactive approach collapsed under its own weight of crime and fear, the new mission of prevention took its place.

We saw this happen most profoundly in the changed relationship between the police and communities of color. When the mission shifted to prevention of the next shooting, a relationship with key community leaders—especially African-American clergy—became not only important but also indispensable. We found that we reinforced one another's credibility, and this became an important aspect of our effectiveness. The willingness of each party to collaborate with each other began to improve how others in minority communities viewed the police. These ministers put their reputations on the line. At the same time, police were willing to step out of their shells and take a risk at working with a body of leaders who had been quite vocal in their negative opinions of police practices. The risks paid off. ✦

Reactive Arrests and Domestic Violence

Reactive arrests are made in response to citizen complaints, are random, and are generally for minor offenses. Although little value is given to the general preventive nature of reactive arrests, one set of studies looked at the specific effects of arrest for misdemeanor **domestic violence** (i.e., assault on or battery of a domestic partner).

The *Minneapolis Domestic Violence Experiment* (Sherman and Berk 1984) was the first study on the use of arrest in misdemeanor domestic violence, comparing arrest responses to nonarrest responses (either mediation or separation). The results indicated that suspects who were arrested were significantly less likely to become violent over the next six months. Subsequent replication studies, however, produced mixed, and often conflicting, results. For example, in Omaha, Charlotte, and Milwaukee, arrests appeared actually to increase domestic violence, but in Omaha, arrest warrants issued for offenders who fled the scene had a substantial deterrent effect. The results were mixed in two other cities, Colorado Springs and Miami, although some evidence of a deterrent effect of arrest was found. All four of the experiments that analyzed data by employment status of offenders found that arrests increase assaults among unemployed offenders, while reducing it among employed offenders. Other research (Marciniak 1994) has indicated that the type of community in which one lives may have an impact as well.

In response to the Minneapolis results and political pressure—especially from women's groups—police departments across the country implemented *mandatory-arrest* policies in cases of misdemeanor domestic violence. The replication experiments indicate clearly, however, that such a response was premature (ironically, in the past the police have not paid enough attention to important research findings; in this case, they may have paid too much). Taken as a whole, these experiments have produced several findings that should be considered in formulating arrest policy in cases of domestic violence: (1) arrest generally increases violence among unemployed suspects while decreasing it among employed suspects; (2) arrest increases violence, regardless of individual employment status, in communities with high levels of unemployment and single-parent households; and (3) offenders who flee before police arrive (approximately 50 percent) are substantially deterred when warrants are issued for their arrest.

Police Pursuits

Police can chase suspects either on foot or by motor vehicle. A **police pursuit** is an event in which a suspect attempts to flee from police in order to avoid arrest. Alpert and Friedell (1992) suggest that a vehicle pursuit is at least as dangerous to the public as the use of a firearm. Estimates on the number of police pursuits yearly run as high as 50,000, with the number of injuries they cause at approximately 20,000 (Charles, Falcone, and Wells 1992). A national survey of some 436 police departments (Alpert 1997), which also included case studies of approximately 1,250 pursuits in three departments (Metro-Dade, Miami; Omaha, Nebraska; and Aiken County, South Carolina), found that most pursuits are initiated for traffic violations: in Miami, 45 percent (448), in Omaha, 51 percent (112), and in Aiken County, 36 percent (5). A large percentage of pursuits, however, were also initiated for felonies: in Miami, 35 percent (344), in Omaha, 40 percent (89), and in Aiken County, 43 percent (6).

In addition, the national survey indicated that 41 percent of the chases in Miami ended in personal injury (428) and 20 percent ended in property damage (213); in Omaha,14 percent ended in personal injury (31) and 40 percent in property damage (91); in Aiken County, 12 percent ended in personal injury (2) and 24 percent in property damage (4). Arrests were made in 75 percent of the chases in Miami (784), 52 percent in Omaha (118), and 82 percent in Aiken County (14). Finally, in separate studies, it was found that the pursuits led to deaths of at least one person in 0.7 percent of all chases (a little less than one-in-a-hundred chases) in the Miami area (Alpert and Dunham 1988) and 0.2 percent in Minnesota (Alpert and Fridell 1992).

These are significant numbers and suggest that the police must pay careful attention to the development of proper policy, training, and enforcement of guidelines. In this regard, the national survey revealed that while 91 percent of the responding departments had written policies governing pursuits (meaning nearly 10 percent did not), many of them were implemented in the 1970s. Forty-eight percent of the departments reported having modified their pursuit policy within the past two years, with most of those (87 percent) making the modifications more restrictive than previously. The strong effects of policy changes were evident in the findings from both the Metro-Dade and Omaha departments.

In 1992 Metro-Dade adopted a *violent felony only* pursuit policy, and the number of pursuits decreased by 82 percent (from 279 to 51) the following year. In 1993 Omaha changed to a more permissive policy, allowing pursuits for offenses that were previously prohibited, and pursuits increased over 600 percent the following year (from 17 to 122). In a follow-up study analyzing 1,049 pursuit-driving reports over a four-year period from the Metro-Dade Police Department, Alpert and Madden (1999) discovered that the more police cars that were involved, the more likely the pursuit was to result in a dangerous crash. Further, the odds of injury increased at higher speeds, at night, and in commercial rather than residential areas. They used the results to develop a "pursuit decision calculus" that police administrators can use to determine when the ultimate costs of a pursuit may outweigh its benefits.

The Bureau of Justice Statistics national survey found with respect to pursuit-driving policies in local departments that nearly all (93 percent) had a written policy; 57 percent had a *restrictive policy* (i.e., based on criteria such as offense type or maximum speed); 27 percent had a *judgmental policy*, leaving the decision to the officer's discretion; and 5 percent discouraged all vehicle pursuits (Hickman and Reaves 2003a). With respect to sheriff's offices, 92 percent had a written policy; 47 percent had a restrictive policy; 36 percent had a judgmental policy; and 5 percent discouraged pursuits (Hickman and Reaves 2003b).

In addition, in the national survey by Alpert (1997), most departments reported that routine follow-ups to pursuits were mandated (89 percent). Most also indicated that they were either informal supervisory reviews (33 percent) or incident reports prepared by pursuing officers (47 percent). With respect to training, while 60 percent of the departments reported providing entry-level driver training at their academies, virtually all the training focused on the mechanics of defensive and pursuit driving rather than on questions of when or why to pursue. The findings of the national survey included the following implications for state and local departments:

1. Create and maintain systems to collect information on pursuit driving.

2. Review and update pursuit policies.

3. Evaluate the need for pursuit-specific training.

4. Support written policies with training and supervision.

5. Require that officers justify their actions or have a supervisor evaluate the pursuit (i.e., after-action reports and meaningful discipline for problem pursuits).

The national study concluded that a balance needs to exist between the need to enforce the law and the safety of the public, and that an appropriate policy balancing these perspectives would limit chases to the pursuit of violent felons. Geoffrey Alpert, the author of the study, believes that officers need more training and direction through policy in order to know when they can and cannot pursue. He suggests that pursuit policies should be similar to shooting policies, in which it has become reasonably clear when one can and cannot fire a weapon ("NIJ Study Sees Police Pursuit Policies Changing" 1997b, 14).

A study of statewide police agencies in nine Western states by the Pursuit Management Task Force (PMTF 1998) of law enforcement line officers indicated that the officers strongly supported reasonable pursuits and effective supervision of such pursuits. The officers also expressed a preference for using spiked strips (tire-deflating devices) and electrical vehicle-stopping technologies. PMTF found that more than 50 percent of all pursuit collisions in their survey occurred during the first two minutes of a pursuit, and that more than 70 percent of all collisions occurred before the sixth minute of a pursuit. This suggests the importance of training (whether to pursue and how to pursue) and that any pursuit technology (e.g., electrical or mechanical) must be able to be deployed very rapidly to have any significant impact in preventing pursuit-related collisions. The task force made several recommendations, including that states should consider legislation that fleeing from a lawful stop in a motor vehicle is a serious crime with significant penalties, and research should be conducted to improve methods of interagency communications technology.

In an interesting twist on the study of pursuit driving, Dunham, Alpert, Kenney and Cromwell (1998) explored the law violators' perspective about why they fled. A sample of jail inmates from three locations was interviewed regarding their admitted recent experience in a vehicular pursuit. The inmates most frequently fled from police because they were driving a stolen car (32 percent); 27 percent were driving with a suspended license; another 27 percent were fleeing from a crime scene. About one-quarter were also afraid of being beaten by the police (21 percent) or were under the influence of alcohol or drugs (21 percent). Thirty percent of the pursuits terminated when the suspect stopped and either ran on foot or gave up; another 30 percent ended when the suspect's vehicle crashed. In 25 percent of the chases, the suspect outran the police and got away, at least temporarily. These findings may be helpful in determining pursuit policies by providing a better understanding of the suspect's thought processes.

Foot pursuits. Until recently, foot pursuits of suspects have received very little attention; however, as the Dunham et al. (1998) study above indicates, approximately one-third (30 percent) of the vehicle pursuits ended when the suspect stopped and either ran on foot or gave up. And, as an examination of assaults on officers (Pinizzotto, Davis, and Miller 1997) indicates, a significant number of officers assaulted during foot pursuits had no plan of action other than arresting the suspect (see Inside Policing 7.5). One department, in Collingswood, New Jersey, however, developed a foot pursuit policy as a result of an annual safety committee review indicating several officers had been injured during foot chases (Bohrer, Davis, and Garrity 2000). Subsequently, the department established restrictions delineating when officers should not conduct foot pursuits; a review procedure for compliance with foot-pursuit policy; and a twice-yearly foot pursuit training coinciding with use-of-force training and the firearms requalification process. Within two years after the new policies were established, significant changes in how officers handled foot pursuits were noted—especially with respect to improved communications and using a team concept to set up a perimeter area rather than simply chasing fleeing suspects—which has led to fewer injuries.

Inside Policing 7.5	Officer Injured During Foot Pursuit

While on vehicle patrol, the victim officer and his partner saw two individuals in a car that matched the description of two suspects wanted for possessing a handgun. When the officers stopped the car, the passenger immediately fled on foot and the victim officer chased him for several blocks. After the victim officer lost sight of the suspect, he began searching an area in front of a building. The suspect, hiding in nearby bushes, opened fire with a small-caliber handgun, wounding the officer in the head and legs, causing extensive injury. The assailant escaped from the scene but surrendered to authorities two days later. The victim officer survived the attack but could not resume his duties and retired from the department.

Source: Adapted from A. J. Pinizzotto, E. F. Davis, and C. E. Miller III, *In the Line of Fire: A Study of Selected Felonious Assaults on Law Enforcement Officers* (Washington, D. C.: Department of Justice, 1997), 59.

The Investigative Function

Investigators, or **detectives** (the terms can be used interchangeably), are essentially specialists in responding to crimes serious enough to warrant an investigation. The primary goal of the criminal investigation is to increase the number of arrests for crimes that are prosecutable and will result in a conviction. As by-products of this goal, detectives recover stolen property and produce information that may be useful in other crimes, often through the development and manipulation of informants (Cawley, Miron, and Araujo 1977; Forst 1982; Waegel 1982; and Wycoff 1982). As discussed previously, crime investigation responsibilities are usually specialized, especially in medium to large police departments. Patrol officers conduct the initial, or **preliminary investigation,** which is generally for the purpose of establishing that a crime has been committed and for protecting the scene of the crime from those not involved in the investigation. Once this has been done, detectives generally conduct **follow-up investigations** and develop the case. In some jurisdictions, the development phase involves working with the prosecuting attorney to prepare a case for trial. In others, this phase is the responsibility of investigators employed by the prosecuting attorney's office.

The basic responsibility of the detective is to (1) determine if a crime has been committed; (2) identify the perpetrator; (3) apprehend the perpetrator; and (4) provide evidence to support a conviction in court. The case can be considered *solved* if the first three objectives are successfully attained. Other outcomes, such as recovering stolen property, deterring criminal behavior, and satisfying crime victims, may also be part of the process (Brandl 2002). The disposal phase may or may not involve a prosecution or a conviction. Investigations can be terminated if the police determine that no crime has been committed, if they have insufficient evidence to proceed, or if there is no longer a suspect available (e.g., a murder-suicide).

Historical Development

Henry Fielding is credited with developing the first police investigators, known as the **Bow Street Runners,** a special section of the Bow Street Station developed in London between 1749 and 1750. This section was made up of carefully selected personnel who would move swiftly to the scene of a crime to begin an investigation (Germann, Day, and Gallati 1978). Investigative work, however, did not become primarily a public function in America until the early 1900s. Until that time, private detectives were hired to recover stolen property, often in unscrupulous and violent ways, rather than to apprehend criminals. The transition to a public policing activity took place because of a desire to prosecute suspected criminals and a general disapproval of the methods employed by private detectives. In addition, the emergence of insurance companies tended gradually to lessen the victim's concern about the return of stolen property.

Kuykendall (1986) analyzed the historical role of the police detective, who, in the mid-1850s to early 1900s, was more like a "secretive rogue" whose methods were as unscrupulous as those of the private detectives preceding them. Although some of their exploits were romanticized, the detectives were mostly inefficient and corrupt. They often had a close association with criminals, used and manipulated stool pigeons, and even had "deadlines" that established areas of a city in which detectives and criminals agreed that crime could be committed. Nineteenth- and early-twentieth-century detectives believed that their work should be essentially clandestine. They were considered to be members of a "secret service" whose identity should remain unknown lest the criminal become wary and flee. Some detectives wore disguises, submitted court testimony in writing, and even used masks when looking at suspects. Although they did investigate crimes, detectives functioned primarily as a nonuniformed patrol force. They tended to go where persons congregated (e.g., beer gardens and steamboat docks) to look for pickpockets, gamblers, and troublemakers.

Just as police reformers of the early twentieth century hoped to replace the "neighbor" patrol officer with the "soldier" crime fighter, they also hoped to replace secretive rogues with a scientific criminal investigator. The detective's relationships with criminals and stool pigeons were criticized as corrupting and undesirable for a professional police officer. It was further believed that the use of science would make such relationships unnecessary. The reformers stressed the importance of the detective as a perceptive, rational analyst, much like Sherlock Holmes; they also emphasized reorganization of departments to improve efficiency.

Like their colleagues on patrol, detectives gradually began to be more reactive than proactive. By the 1920s and 1930s, detectives were mostly investigating crimes after the fact rather than using clandestine tactics. Although many were ill prepared to utilize the newly developed scientific methods, this was less of a problem than it first appeared because the use of scientific evidence proved to be of value in only a few cases and rarely aided the police in identifying suspects. Consequently, the information that became most important in making arrests and ensuring successful prosecutions was derived from witnesses, informers, and suspects. As detectives stopped being secretive rogues, they gradually became inquisitors, who often coerced information from suspects to make cases.

By the 1960s, important changes in criminal procedural laws (e.g., search and seizure, evidence, Miranda)—known as the **due process revolution**—and the continuing emphasis on reorganization and efficiency in police departments had created a detective who had become essentially a bureaucrat, or case processor. Although some detectives continued to work undercover, the majority were reactive and infrequently identified suspects who were not obvious. These detectives spent a greater proportion of their time processing information and coordinating with other criminal justice agencies than looking for suspects.

All the elements of the detective's role described above are present to some degree today. Some detectives are secretive, some are skillful in obtaining confessions without coercion, and all must invest considerable time in processing information. Whereas the emergence of the legalistic model of policing tended to produce a detective who was more bureaucrat than sleuth, subsequent approaches and models of policing (e.g., team and community) tend to have a broader view of the detective's role. As a result of crime-analysis techniques, the detective has continued to evolve, becoming somewhat less reactive (since the 1960s) and more proactive, with an emphasis on criminals rather than on crimes. Of course, this is not a new role for the detective, and thus far police departments have been able to make these changes without the extensive corruption problems historically associated with them (Kuykendall 1986).

Detectives begin an investigation of a crime scene. Today, the detective's primary role is that of a case processor.

Detectives today have multifaceted roles: they work undercover, they may operate sting programs, they may be involved in career-criminal programs, they may be involved in breaking up organized gang activity, and they may be involved in intelligence-gathering operations. Detectives involved in such activities, however, constitute a relatively small percentage of those involved in investigative work, with the substantial majority functioning more as bureaucrats than sleuths. To characterize the detective as a bureaucrat is not intended to demean the role but rather to suggest the perspective from which most detectives should be viewed. They are primarily information processors, not Sherlock Holmeses or Dirty "Make My Day" Harry's.

Terrorism and investigation. Just as patrol work may need to change to some extent with respect to the contemporary threat of terrorism, so too may investigative work. De Guzman (2002) suggests two potential areas of concern regarding investigation and terrorism. First, as noted above, police investigation has become primarily reactive in nature; it may need to again become more proactive. This means that evidence of a crime should not only be connected to a certain suspect, but also determine whether or not the evidence may have some connection to a possible terrorist activity. This would be especially true if there were evidence that seemed not to fit with the nature of the crime committed; that is, could there be other motives attached to the offense under investigation? Second, for the most part, investigation remains highly individualized and disjointed from the rest of the department. Investigation units themselves tend to be highly fragmented. And, just as community policing is being implemented in many departments, investigation remains virtually untouched by the process. These conditions hamper the effectiveness of solving cases and will be especially troublesome in cases involving terrorism. Consequently, it seems prudent for investigative units to integrate themselves with the rest of the department and redirect their functional focus, especially with respect to community-policing practices.

Resource Determination and Allocation

The ideal number of personnel to be assigned to investigative units has never been precisely determined. Traditionally, many departments have used a "10 percent of total sworn personnel" criterion; the range in medium to large police departments is from 8 percent to approximately 20 percent of sworn personnel. The criteria most often used to determine a department's needs for investigative personnel include whether detectives work in pairs or alone; the extent of patrol participation in investigations; level of training, experience, and competency of investigators; and the technological assistance available.

One-person assignments, as in patrol, generally appear to be the most appropriate for the vast majority of investigative work. Exceptions include particularly dangerous assignments, some interrogations, and meeting suspicious informers. Even in these areas, however, as in investigations in general, there is less direct evidence concerning the relative effectiveness of one- and two-person assignments in criminal investigation (Bloch and Weidman 1975).

The investigative workload generally requires some degree of specialization in medium to large departments. The most common specialization is to have separate detective units for crimes against persons (e.g., homicide, robbery and assault, sex crimes, vice, and narcotics) and crimes against property (e.g., arson, auto theft and burglary and larceny) (Greenwood and Petersilia 1975). Many departments today also have specialized detective units for juveniles, gangs, intelligence, arson, computer, and bias crimes.

Selected Research on Investigative Operations

Several important investigative issues are discussed in this section, including investigative effectiveness and how investigative work can be improved, career criminal programs, bias crimes, detective-patrol relationships, and the twin issues of enticement and entrapment as applied to covert operations.

Investigative Effectiveness

In the mid-1970s, as a result of an in-depth study by Greenwood and Petersilia (1975), investigative units were criticized as ineffective and inefficient. In this study, operations in 25 detective units were observed and surveys were completed in 156 units. The major findings of this study indicated that (1) most serious crimes are solved through information obtained from victims rather than through leads developed by detectives; (2) in 75 percent of the cases, the suspect's identity is known or easily determined at the time the crime is reported to the police; and (3) the major block of detective time is devoted to reviewing reports, documenting files, and attempting to locate and interview victims for cases that experience has shown are unlikely to be solved but are carried out to satisfy victims' expectations. William and Snortum (1984), who replicated the study, reported similar findings but concluded that detectives make a valuable contribution to the investigative process through skilled interrogation and case-processing techniques.

In an extensive study of burglary and robbery investigations, Eck (1984) found that preliminary investigations by patrol officers and follow-up investigations by detectives are equally important for solving crimes. He further discovered that even in situations where the preliminary investigation by patrol officers did not develop any leads, detectives were able to identify a suspect in approximately 14 percent of the cases and make an arrest in 8 percent. Thus, Eck concluded that investigators do, in fact, make a meaningful contribution to the solution of criminal cases. To improve the effectiveness of investigations, it was recommended that increased emphasis be placed on collecting physical evidence at the scene of a crime, identifying witnesses, using informants, and utilizing police records. It was further noted that successfully disposing of a case can be improved if (1) patrol officers carefully gather evidence at the crime scene and communicate that information to the detectives on the case; (2) cases are more carefully screened for further development (i.e., deciding which cases can be ignored or given only minimal attention); (3) productivity measures are developed to ascertain if individual detectives or detective units are meeting their goals; and (4) investigations are targeted (e.g., toward career criminals, who are known to have engaged in the behavior under investigation).

Finally, Farmer (1984) maintains that a broader approach to the study of the investigative function is needed. He notes that "the notion of case clearance as the sole objective of detective work is as inadequate as is the idea that the principal function of a detective is to solve crime" (49). In addition, there is proactive investigative work to be considered: "Investigators may pursue other equally important goals to aid citizens—including increasing citizen satisfaction, reducing fear, counseling victims, and deterring further crime" (50). In line with this reasoning, Eck suggests that criminal investigation can be improved by detectives focusing on justice and crime prevention: "If detective work were more than tracking down and arresting offenders, detectives would have to interact with communities . . . work more with other sections of the police force and other public and private groups to achieve their objectives" (1996, 181). Eck suggests four guiding principles to improve investigative effectiveness:

1. *Abandon crime control through apprehension as a principal goal* of investigations. There is little evidence that increased apprehensions by detectives make much of a difference in crime levels, except under special circumstances (see below).

2. Detectives should *focus on justice.* Offenders should be arrested because they violated the law. Detectives should find out who the offenders are and bring their evidence forward.

3. The special circumstances mentioned in item 1 are clear crime patterns. Obviously, arresting a repeat rapist or killer prevents crimes. As noted in point 4, *focusing on patterns* allows detectives to combine enforcement powers with many other techniques.

4. *Crime prevention through problem solving* should be emphasized. Detectives should look for patterns of crimes, determine why the patterns exist, and implement programs that stop the patterns (see Inside Policing 7.6).

Inside Policing 7.6   **Improving Criminal Investigation Through Problem Solving**

Although problem solving has generally been related to patrol officers, there have been many cases in which detectives have applied this approach. Because detectives are not tied to a radio and have more control over how their time is used, they may find it easier to address problems than would patrol officers. Problem solving requires the examination of crime patterns, of which there are three basic types: (1) *common offenders*, the most usual approach to applying crime analysis to investigations; (2) *common victims or targets*, how are they similar and how do they differ from nonvictims and nontargets; and (3) *repeat places*, which asks the question, why are crimes occurring here instead of at other, similar places. Two examples of how detectives have used problem solving are described below.

Domestic Homicides

In Newport News, Virginia, one of the homicide detectives felt that as satisfying as it was to solve murders, it would be more satisfying to prevent them from occurring. He noticed that half of the homicides the department had investigated in the previous year were related to domestic violence, and in half of these cases, the police had previously been to the address. This suggested the possibility of attempting early intervention with the couples involved.

The detective brought together representatives from many public and private organizations, including the prosecutor's office, women's advocates, hospitals, the local newspaper, the military, and others. In cooperation they developed a program that forced the couples involved in domestic violence into mandatory counseling. When certain conditions were present in an assault case (e.g., serious injury or presence of a gun), an arrest was mandatory. In such circumstances, it was decided that the prosecutor would not drop charges unless the abuser and the victim entered into counseling. If they completed counseling and if the victim agreed, the charges would then be dropped. Although no formal evaluation of this program has been conducted, the department reports that both domestic homicides and repeat domestic violence declined in the first years following implementation.

Gas Station Robberies

In Edmonton (Alberta, Canada), a robbery detective noted that one particular chain of gas stations had a very high robbery rate. Because of a high cigarette tax in Canada, there is a large black market for cigarettes, and cigarette theft can be lucrative. By reviewing crime reports, the detective noted that many of the robberies only involved the theft of cigarettes. He visited those stations and found that there was a single attendant in a small booth stocked with cigarettes, candy, and other small items. The detective worked with the managers of the gas station

Inside Policing 7.6   **Improving Criminal Investigation Through Problem Solving (continued)**

chain, and they identified a number of simple changes that could be made to the booth itself, to cigarette displays, and to various operating procedures. The gas station chain made the recommended changes. Since the changes were made, the police department reports a major decline in the robberies of this chain of gas stations.

Source: Adapted from J. E. Eck, "Rethinking Detective Management." In L. T. Hoover, ed., *Quantifying Quality in Policing* (Washington, D.C.: Police Executive Research Forum, 1996), 178–180.

Two relatively recent developments in physical evidence are likely to have a significant impact on investigative effectiveness. First is the *automated fingerprint identification system (AFIS)*, which allows for fingerprints recovered at a crime scene to be compared with thousands of other prints on file in a department's computer system. The computer will match fingerprints that are close to those found at the scene and a suspect can be identified. Second, *DNA testing* allows for the comparison of human cell materials found at the crime scene (usually blood, semen, or hair) in an attempt to find a match between two samples. Since no two individuals, except for identical twins, have the same DNA makeup, it is essentially irrefutable evidence—that is, if properly collected, stored, and analyzed (serious mistakes in all of these areas have occurred). As with fingerprint identification, it used to be that the police first needed to identify a suspect in order to make a match; however, technology has allowed for the development of DNA (and fingerprint) banks through which comparison matches can be made, thus potentially saving the police enormous amounts of time in investigative follow-ups. In a democracy it is important to keep in mind that while the development of both fingerprint and DNA banks are significant breakthroughs, we must be careful not to interfere with individual rights (i.e., the Fourth and Fifth Amendments) when collecting samples for these banks.

Career Criminal Programs

Some police departments have begun implementing programs that attempt to arrest, prosecute, and convict repeat offenders (career criminals) at a significantly higher rate than normal police practices would allow. The theory behind such programs is that since a small proportion of criminals commit a disproportionate number of crimes (i.e., some research suggests that between 7 to 10 percent of individuals are responsible for committing 50 to 60 percent of crimes), if these offenders are convicted and subsequently incarcerated, there will be a significant reduction in the crime rate.

One of the most highly developed programs of this type is the **repeat offender project (ROP)** (known as "rope") of the Washington, D.C., Police Department. The proactive ROP unit, consisting of approximately 60 officers, would target a small number of career criminals believed to be committing five or more index crimes a week. To arrest persons not wanted on a warrant, ROP officers had to develop evidence about specific crimes in which their targets had participated. This effort involved a number of activities, including "buy and bust" techniques, cultivating informants, investigating tips, and placing targets under surveillance.

Prior to program implementation, ROP's proposed procedures were evaluated by the local American Civil Liberties Union (ACLU). The ACLU was concerned that ROP would be used as a "dragnet" operation that harassed and entrapped people. These concerns were alleviated when it was explained that ROP would use no formulas or "profiles" for target selection. Furthermore, the department made it clear that places where citizens have a right to privacy would be put under surveillance only with court permission (Epstein 1983). Target selection for ROP was based on informal understandings about what makes a "good" target. Common characteristics included the target's "catchability," deservedness, and longer-term yield (Martin and Sherman 1986).

A two-year evaluation of the program concluded that by most measures used, the ROP unit achieved its goals of selecting, arresting, and contributing to the incarceration of repeat offenders. For example, targeted offenders were eight times more likely to be arrested, and while ROP officers made fewer arrests relative to other officers, the arrests were of high quality with respect to felony, drug, and weapons crimes. While the ROP program appears to have been successful, the authors of the study are cautious in their interpretations of the findings (Martin and Sherman 1986). They suggest that before other departments implement such programs they should recognize the potential side effects and dangers of "perpetrator-oriented proactive policing." For instance, the program is extremely costly in terms of time, resources, and expenses to equip the unit; thus, it may not be cost-effective in the long term. Additionally, ROP decreased its officers' arrest productivity and most likely other aspects of police service as well, especially with respect to reduced order maintenance activities. The unorthodox tactics used by ROP-type programs further create potential dangers to civil liberties. Although due to careful program planning and supervision such problems appear to have been avoided by this particular ROP program, other departments would need to be just as cautious in their development of similar programs.

Bias Crime Programs

Although there is little accurate information regarding **bias crimes** (i.e., crimes that are racially or sexually motivated), they are a continuing concern for the police. Blacks, Hispanics, Jews, homosexuals, and other minority groups that are targets of criminal activity because of their race, ethnicity, or sexual orientation are potential victims of bias crimes. Police departments need a mechanism to identify and record these crimes, and develop a specific response. The training of officers about the possibility of such "hate" crimes is an important first step. When such crimes occur, the department must make a concerted response involving investigation, traditional patrol, and communication with the group that has been the target of the crime.

One study on bias crimes (Garofalo and Martin 1995) found that bias crime clearances were higher in departments where police responses to these crimes emphasized specialized investigations and arrest. It was further suggested that departments must provide some type of motivation for inducing patrol officers to recognize and report bias crime when they encounter it. Concerning the manner in which bias crimes are handled, a study of 19 departments in the central United States by Walker and Katz

(1995) found that four (25 percent) had separate bias crime units with written procedures for handling bias crimes. Six of the departments (37.5 percent) did not have a separate bias-crime unit, but either designated specific officers in an investigative unit to handle bias crimes or had special policies and procedures that all officers would follow. Six of the departments (37.5 percent) had neither a special unit nor special procedures. Of the 12 departments that did not have a special bias-crime unit, eight provided no special training regarding hate crimes. Projecting the findings from this sample to the national level, it was estimated that special bias-crime units exist in only about 13 percent of municipal police departments. Clearly, more effort needs to be exerted in this area of law enforcement, especially with respect to developing specialized investigative units or personnel.

Detective-Patrol Relationships

The relationship in a police department between detectives and patrol officers is both extremely important and a source of potential conflict. This potential conflict must be addressed by the department because effective communication between the two is vital to the success of many investigations. It is crucial that investigators make an effort to develop and maintain a good rapport with patrol officers. This relationship should be based on frequent personal contacts, the acknowledgment of patrol officers' contribution to investigations, seeking out patrol officer advice when appropriate, and keeping officers informed as to the status of cases.

One of the major problems that continues to exist in many departments is related to the different status of detectives and patrol officers. Investigators tend to dress in civilian clothes, are often perceived to have more status in the department, and may even be of a higher rank or receive a higher salary. There are several ways to address this problem. One possible solution relates to the basic structure of the department—that is, using a community-policing model, in which detectives and patrol personnel work together as a team. Another solution is to create a personnel system that gives equal status and financial rewards to both patrol officers and investigators. Rotating personnel through various investigative slots, so that the position is not thought of as being "owned" by anyone, is also a constructive approach. As noted in Chapter 4 (see Inside Policing 4.2), the Cedar Rapids, Iowa, Police Department has eliminated the position of detective and instead selects qualified patrol officers to rotate into the investigative division as they would any other specialty. Police departments must also be alert to the manner in which detectives and patrol officers are treated. It is essential that patrol officers not be given the impression that, when compared to investigators, they are second-class citizens (Bloch and Weidman 1975).

Enticement and Entrapment

In the course of using covert or undercover investigations, the police must be extremely careful that they do not violate citizen rights and therefore harm police-community relations even though they increase arrest rates. Do certain investigative activities involve **enticement**? That is, by their existence do these activities encourage the commission of crimes? When does **entrapment** occur? That is, when are individuals provided by the police with both the opportunity and the intent to commit a crime? Whether the police play the role of victim or criminal, covert activities have the potential of enticing and entrapping. The differences between enticement and entrapment are subtle, but the implications for the citizen are profound. Creating opportunities for crime by the police is a legitimate police practice, and assist the police to target offenses in a proactive manner. However, if the behavior of law enforcement officers causes an otherwise innocent person to commit a crime, then that person has a legitimate defense in court to have the charges dismissed.

In **sting operations,** undercover detectives set up their own fencing outlets and encourage thieves to sell them stolen merchandise; the transaction is generally videotaped for later use in court. Can such programs actually result in more victims? If criminals can easily sell stolen property for a competitive or higher price, will they steal more while the outlet is available? Does the cost-to-benefit ratio of such programs (e.g., more arrests, more useful information, or the development of informants) outweigh the potential hazards? What about a police officer playing an inebriated decoy on the street, waiting to be mugged? Can this practice cause an individual, who otherwise might not be inclined to steal, to take advantage of such an easy mark? Do career-criminal programs unfairly target certain individuals or groups for arrest? Does the random selection of targets for the undercover selling of drugs provide the intent to buy drugs? These are some of the questions that police departments face with respect to undercover operations. Extensive legal guidelines provide the framework for acceptable policies and procedures, but once again, the importance of community satisfaction should play an integral role in determining the extent and type of undercover activities a police department should use.

Summary

The primary goals, activities, and historical development of police field operations are patrol, the "backbone of policing," and investigative work. Recent research has indicated that patrol activities related to law enforcement are more substantial than research over the past few decades has indicated, whereas detective work is primarily concerned with information processing rather than sleuthing. Patrol work is attempting to regain the neighborhood contextual knowledge that was lost in an attempt to "professionalize" the police in the early 1960s and 1970s, working with citizens and community groups in the coproduction of public safety to identify and solve problems of crime and disorder. Since the 1960s, as a result of crime-analysis techniques, investigative work has become more proactive, with an emphasis on criminals rather than on crimes. Patrol methods are chiefly by foot or automobile. Resources are determined by intuition and comparison. A new method of allocation is by computerized crime mapping.

Selected research on patrol and investigative operations emphasizes effectiveness relating to cost and crime reduction. Although research suggests that some patrol strategies are effective in reducing crime, they may also produce negative community relations. Thus, the more sensitive of these strategies should be carefully implemented but not without community acceptance. For example, differential response, directed patrol, different types of proactive arrests, covert patrol, and career criminal programs must have strong community support if they are to be of mutual benefit to both the police and the public.

Critical Thinking Questions

1. Describe the primary goals of patrol, including community-policing departments, and provide an example of each.

2. What is computerized crime mapping? How might such mapping improve patrol work?

3. Why was the Kansas City preventive patrol study important to policing at the time it was conducted. Are the implications still important today?

4. Describe several strategies of directed patrol and the potential negative impact of such strategies. Which strategies might be applicable to your local police department?

5. Describe the Kansas City gun experiment and the Boston gun project. Why do you think these patrol strategies were successful?

6. With respect to the research on the use of arrests in misdemeanor domestic violence cases, what patrol policies would you formulate?

7. What major policies would you formulate for vehicle pursuits? For foot pursuits?

8. Discuss the general level of effectiveness of investigators. What policies might you implement in order to improve effectiveness?

References

Alpert, G. P. 1997. *Police Pursuit: Policies and Training, May.* Washington, D.C.: National Institute of Justice.

Alpert, G. P., and Dunham, R. 1988. "Research on Police Pursuits: Applications for Law Enforcement." *American Journal of Police* 7: 123–131.

Alpert, G. P., and Fridell, L. 1992. *Police Vehicles and Firearms: Instruments of Deadly Force.* Prospect Heights, IL: Waveland Press.

Alpert, G. P., and Madden, T. J. 1999 "Toward the Development of a Pursuit Decision Calculus; Pursuit Benefits Versus Pursuit Costs." *Justice Research and Policy* 1: 23–41.

Andenaes, J. 1974. *Punishment and Deterrence.* Ann Arbor, MI: University of Michigan Press.

Baehr, M. E., Furcon, J. E., and Froemel, E. C. 1968. *Psychological Assessment of Patrolman Qualifications in Relation to Field Performance.* Washington, D.C.: Department of Justice.

Bloch, P. B., and Weidman, D. R. 1975. *Managing Criminal Investigations.* Washington, D.C.: U.S. Government Printing Office.

Bohrer, S., Davis, E. F., and Garrity, T. J. 2000. "Establishing a Foot Pursuit Policy: Running into Danger." *FBI Law Enforcement Bulletin.* Washington, D.C.: Department of Justice.

Boydstun, J. E. 1975. *San Diego Field Interrogation: Final Report.* Washington, D.C.: Police Foundation.

Boydstun, J. E., Sherry, M. E., and Moelter, N. P. 1977. *Patrol Staffing in San Diego.* Washington, D.C.: Police Foundation.

Braga, A. A., Weisburd, D. L., Waring, E. J., Green Mazerolle, L., Spelman, W., and Gajewski, F. 1999. "Problem-oriented Policing in Violent Crime Places: A Randomized Controlled Experiment." *Criminology* 37: 541–581.

Brandl, S. G. (2002). "Police: Criminal Investigations." In J. Dressler (ed.), *Encyclopedia of Crime & Justice*: 1068–1073. New York: Thomson.

Bratton, W. 1996. "Remark: New Strategies for Combating Crime in New York City." *Fordham Urban Journal* 23: 781–785.

Brooks, L. W., Piquero, A., and Cronin, J. 1994. "Workload Rites and Police Officer Attitudes: An Examination of Busy and Slow Precincts." *Journal of Criminal Justice* 22: 277–286.

Cahn, M. F., and Tien, J. 1981. *An Alternative Approach in Police Response: Wilmington Management of Demand Program.* Cambridge, MA: Public Systems Evaluation, Inc.

Caiden, G. E. 1977. *Police Revitalization.* Lexington, MA: Lexington Books.

Cawley, D. F., Miron, H. J., and Araujo, W. J. 1977. *Managing Criminal Investigations: Trainer's Handbook.* Washington, D.C.: University Research Corporation.

Charles, M. T., Falcone, D. N., and Wells, E. 1992. *Police Pursuit in Pursuit of a Policy: The Pursuit Issue, Legal and Literature Review, and an Empirical Study.* Washington, D.C.: AAA Foundation for Traffic Safety.

Clark, J. R. 1997. "LEN Salutes Its 1997 People of the Year, the Boston Gun Project Working Group." *Law Enforcement News* December 31: 1, 4, and 5.

Cohen, J., and Ludwig, J. 2003. "Policing Crime Guns." In J. Ludwig and P. J. Cook (eds.), *Evaluating Gun Policy: Effects on Crime and Violence.* Washington, D.C.: Brookings Institution Press.

Cohen, M., and McEwen, J. T. 1984. "Handling Calls for Service: Alternatives to Traditional Policing." *NIJ Reports* September: 4–8.

Cordner, G. W. 1981. "The Effects of Directed Patrol: A Natural Quasi-Experiment in Pontiac." In J. J. Fyfe (ed.), *Contemporary Issues in Law Enforcement* pp. 37–58. Beverly Hills: Sage

Crank, J. 1999. *Understanding Police Culture.* Cincinnati: Anderson.

de Guzman, M. C. 2002. The Changing Roles and Strategies of the Police in Time of Terror." *ACJS Today* 22(3): 8–13. Greenbelt, MD: Academy of Criminal Justice Sciences.

del Carmon, A., and Guevara, L. 2003. "Police Officers on Two-officer Units: A Study of Attitudinal Responses Toward a Patrol Experiment." *Policing: An International Journal of Police Strategies & Management* 26: 144–161.

Dunham, R. G., Alpert, G. P., Kenney, D. J., and Cromwell, P. 1998. "High-speed Pursuit." *Criminal Justice and Behavior* 25: 30–45.

Eck, J. 1984. *Solving Crimes.* Washington, D.C.: Police Executive Research Forum.

——. 1996. "Rethinking Detective Management." In L T. Hoover (ed.), *Quantifying Quality in Policing,* pp. 167–184. Washington, D.C.: Police Executive Research Forum.

Epstein, A. 1983. "Spurlock's Raiders." *Regardies* 3: 41–42.

Farmer, D. J. 1984. *Crime Control: The Use and Misuse of Police Resources.* New York: Plenum.

Federal Bureau of Investigation 1991. *Uniform Crime Reports, Crime in the United States.* Washington, D.C.: Department of Justice.

Feinberg, S. E., Kinley, L. and Reiss, Jr., A. J. 1976. "Redesigning the Kansas City Preventive Patrol Experiment." *Evaluation* 3: 124–131.

Finn, P. E., and Sullivan, M. 1988. "Police Response to Special Populations: Handling the Mentally Ill, Public Inebriate, and the Homeless." *Research in Action.* Washington, D.C.: National Institute of Justice.

Forst, B. 1982. *Arrest Convictability as a Measure of Police Performance.* Washington, D.C.: U.S. Government Printing Office.

Garofalo, J., and Martin, S. E. 1995. *Bias-motivated Crimes: Their Characteristics and the Law Enforcement Response.* Carbondale, IL: Southern Illinois University.

Germann, A. C., Day, F. D. and Gallati, R. R. 1978. *Introduction to Law Enforcement and Criminal Justice.* Springfield, IL: Charles C. Thomas.

Greene, J. 1999. "Zero Tolerance: A Case Study of Police Policies and Practices in New York City." *Crime and Delinquency* 45: 171–187.

Greene, J. R. 1987. "Foot Patrol and Community Policing: Past Practices and Future Prospects." *American Journal of Police* 6: 1–15.

Green Mazerolle, L., and Roehl, J. 1999. *Controlling Drug and Disorder Problems: Oakland's Beat Health Program.* Washington, D.C.: National Institute of Justice.

Greenwood, P., and Petersilia, J. 1975. *The Criminal Investigation Process.* Santa Monica, CA: Rand.

Hammer, T. M. 1987. "AIDS and the Law Enforcement Officer." *NIJ Reports.* Washington, D.C.: National Institute of Justice, pp. 2–7.

Harcourt, B. 2001. *Illusion of Order: The False Promise of Broken Windows Policing.* Cambridge, MA: Harvard University Press.

Herbert, S. 2001. "Policing the Contemporary City: Fixing Broken Windows or ShoringUp Neo-Liberalism?" *Theoretical Criminology* 5: 445–466.

Hickman, M. J., and Reaves, B. A. 2003a. *Local Police Departments, 2000.* Washington, D.C.: Bureau of Justice Statistics.

Hickman, M. J., and Reaves, B. A. 2003b. *Sheriffs' Offices, 2000.* Washington, D.C.: Bureau of Justice Statistics.

Kansas City Missouri Police Department. 2002. *Annual Report.* Kansas City, MO: Police Department.

Kelling, G. L., and Bratton, W. 1998. "Declining Crime Rates: Insiders' Views of the New York City Story." *Journal of Criminal Law and Criminology* 88:1217–1231.

Kelling, G. L., and Coles, C. M. 1996. *Fixing Broken Windows.* New York: Kessler Books.

Kelling, G. L., Pate, T., Dieckman, D., and Brown, C. E. 1974. *The Kansas City Preventive Patrol Experiment: A Summary Report.* Washington, D.C.: Police Foundation.

Kennedy, D. 1998. "Pulling Levels: Getting Deterrence Right." *NIJ Journal* July, pp. 2–8. Washington, D.C.: National Institute of Justice.

Kennedy, D., Piehl, A. M., and Braga, A. A. 1996. "Youth Gun Violence in Boston: Gun Markets, Serious Youth Offenders, and a Use Reduction Strategy." *Law and Contemporary Problems* 59: 147–196.

Kessler, D. A. 1985. "One- or Two-officer Cars? A Perspective From Kansas City." *Journal of Criminal Justice* l3: 49–64.

Koper, C. S. 1995. "Just Enough Police Presence: Reducing Crime and Disorderly Behavior by Optimizing Patrol Time in Crime 'Hot Spots': A Randomized, Controlled Trial." *Justice Quarterly* 12: 625–649.

Kuykendall, J. (1986). "The Municipal Police Detective: An Historical Analysis." *Criminology* 24: 175–201.

Larson, R. C. 1975. "What Happened to Patrol Operations in Kansas City? A Review of the Kansas City Preventive Patrol Experiment." *Journal of Criminal Justice* 3: 267–297.

Marciniak, E. 1994. *Community Policing of Domestic Violence: Neighborhood Differences in the Effect of Arrest.* Unpublished Ph.D. dissertation. College Park: University of Maryland.

Martin, S. E., and Sherman, L. W. 1986. *Catching Career Criminals: The Washington, D.C. Repeat Offender Project.* Washington, D.C.: Police Foundation.

Marvell, T. B., and Moody, C. E. 1996. "Specification Problems, Police Levels and Crime Rates." *Criminology* 34: 609–646.

Mazerolle, L., Rogan, D., Frank, J., Famega, C., and Eck, J. E. 2002. "Managing Citizen Calls to the Police: The Impact of Baltimore's 3-1-1 Call System." *Criminology and Public Policy* 2: 97–124.

McEwen, J. T. 1995. "National Assessment Program: 1994 Survey Results." *Research in Action.* Washington, D.C.: National Institute of Justice.

McEwen, J. T., Connors, E. F., and Cohen, M. I. 1986. *Evaluation of the Differential Response Field Test.* Washington, D.C.: U.S. Government Printing Office.

McGarrel, E. F., Chermak, S., and Weiss, A. 2001. "Reducing Firearms Violence Through Directed Police Patrol." *Criminology & Public Policy* 1: 119–148.

"NIJ Study Sees Police Pursuit Policies Changing as Appreciation of Danger Rises." 1997. *Law Enforcement News* July/August: 1, 14.

Pate, T., Bowers, R. A., Ferrara, A., and Lorence, J. 1976. *Police Response Time: Its Determinants and Effects*. Washington, D.C.: Police Foundation.

Payne, D. M., and Trojanowicz, R. C. 1985. *Performance Profiles of Foot Versus Motor Officers*. East Lansing, MI: National Neighborhood Foot Patrol Center, Michigan State University.

Pinizzotto, A. J., Davis, E. F., and Miller III, C. E. 1997. *In the Line of Fire: A Study of Selected Felonious Assaults on Law Enforcement Officers*. Washington, D.C.: Department of Justice.

Police Foundation. 1981. *The Newark Foot Patrol Experiment*. Washington, D.C.: Police Foundation.

President's Commission on Law Enforcement and Administration of Justice. 1967. *Task Report: The Police*. Washington, D.C.: U.S. Government Printing Office.

Pursuit Management Task Force. 1998. *Pursuit Management Task Force: A Summary of the PMST's Report on Police Pursuit Practices and the Role of Technology*. Washington, D.C.: Department of Justice.

Reaves, B. A., and Goldberg, A. L. 1999. *Law Enforcement Management and Administrative Statistics, 1997: Data for Individual State and Local Agencies with 100 or More Officers*. Washington, D.C.: Department of Justice.

Reaves, B. A., and Goldberg, A. L. (2000). *Local Police Departments, 1997*. Washington, D.C.: Bureau of Justice Statistics.

Reaves, B. A., and Hickman, M. J. 2002. Census of State and Local Law Enforcement Agencies, 2000. Washington, D.C.: Department of Justice.

Rich, T. F. 1996. *The Chicago Police Department's Information Collection for Automated Mapping (ICAM) Program*. Washington, D.C.: National Institute of Justice.

Roberg, R. R. 1976. *The Changing Police Role: New Dimensions and New Issues*. San Jose, CA: Justice Systems Development.

Ross, H. L. 1992. *Confronting Drunk Drivers: Social Policy for Saving Lives*. New Haven, CT: Yale University Press.

Shaw, J. W. 1995. "Community Policing Against Guns: Public Opinion of the Kansas City Experiment." *Justice Quarterly* 12: 695–710.

Schmitt, E.L., Langan, P. A., and Durose, M.R. 2002. *Characteristics of Drivers Stopped by Police, 1999*. Washington, D.C.: Bureau of Justice Statistics.

Sherman, L. W. 1983. "Patrol Strategies for Police." In J. Q. Wilson (ed.), *Crime and Public Policy*, pp. 145–163. San Francisco: Institute for Contemporary Studies Press.

——. 1990a. "Police Crackdowns." *NIJ Reports* March/April: 2–6. Washington, D.C.: National Institute of Justice.

——. 1990b. "Police Crackdowns: Initial and Residual Deterrence." In M. Tonry and N. Morris (eds.), *Crime and Justice: A Review of Research*, pp. 1–48. Chicago: University of Chicago Press.

——. 1997. "Policing for Crime Prevention." In L. W. Sherman, D. Gottfredson, D. MacKenzie, J. Eck, P. Reuter, and S. Bushway (eds.), *Preventing Crime: What Works, What Doesn't, What's Promising*, pp. 8/1–8/58. Washington, D.C.: Office of Justice Programs.

Sherman, L. W., and Berk, R. A. 1984. "The Specific Deterrent Effects of Arrest for Domestic Assault." *American Sociological Review* 49: 261–272.

Sherman, L. W., Gartin, P. R., and Buerger, M. E. 1989. "Hot Spots of Predatory Crime: Routine Activities and the Criminology of Place." *Criminology* 27: 27–55.

Sherman, L. W., and Rogan, D. P. 1995. "Deterrent Effects of Police Raids on Crack Houses: A Randomized, Controlled, Experiment." *Justice Quarterly* 12: 755–781.

Sherman, L. W., Shaw, J. W., and Rogan D. P. 1995. *The Kansas City Gun Experiment*. Washington, D.C.: U.S. Government Printing Office.

Sherman, L. W., and Weisburd, D. A. 1995. "General Deterrence Effects of Police Patrol in Crime 'Hot Spots:' A Randomized, Controlled Trial." *Justice Quarterly* 12: 625–648.

Spelman, W., and Brown D. K. 1982. *Calling the Police*. Washington, D.C.: Police Executive Research Forum.

Stephens, D. W. 1996. "Community Problem-oriented Policing: Measuring Impacts." In L. T. Hoover, (ed.), *Quantifying Quality in Policing*, pp. 95–129. Washington, D.C.: Police Executive Research Forum.

Trojanowicz, R. C. 1982. *An Evaluation of the Neighborhood Foot Patrol Program in Flint, Michigan*. East Lansing, MI: National Neighborhood Foot Patrol Center, Michigan State University.

Trojanowicz, R. C., and Banas, D. W. 1985a. *The Impact of Foot Patrol on Black and White Perceptions of Policing*. East Lansing, MI: National Neighborhood Foot Patrol Center, Michigan State University.

——. 1985b. *Job Satisfaction: A Comparison of Foot Patrol Versus Motor Patrol Officers*. East Lansing, MI: National Neighborhood Foot Patrol Center, Michigan State University.

Waegel, W. B. 1982. "Patterns of Police Investigation of Urban Crimes." *Journal of Police Science and Administration* 10: 452–465.

——. 1984. "'Broken Windows' and Fractured History: The Use and Misuse of History in Recent Police Patrol Analysis." *Justice Quarterly* 1: 57–90.

Walker, S., and Katz, C. M. 1995. "Less Than Meets the Eye: Police Department Bias-Crime Units." *American Journal of Police* 16: 29–48.

Weisburd, D., and Green, L. 1995. "Policing Drug Hot Spots: The Jersey City Drug Market Analysis Experiment." *Justice Quarterly* 12:711–735.

William, M., and Snortum, J. 1984. "Detective Work: The Criminal Investigation Process in a Medium-size Police Department." *Criminal Justice Review* 9: 33–39.

Wilson, C., and Brewer, N. 2001. "Working in Teams: Negative Effects on Organizational Performance in Policing." *Policing: An International Journal of Police Strategies and Management* 24: 115–127.

Wilson, J. Q., and Kelling, G. L. 1982. "Broken Windows: The Police and Neighborhood Safety." *Atlantic Monthly* 249: 29–38.

Wilson, O. W. 1950. *Police Administration*. New York: McGraw-Hill.

Wilson, O. W., and McLaren, R. C. 1977. *Police Administration*. 3rd ed. New York: McGraw-Hill.

Witkin, G. 1998. "The Crime Bust." *U.S. News and World Report* May 25: 28–36.

Won-Jae, L. 2002. "Patrol Workload." *Texas Law Enforcement Management and Administrative Statistics Program*. March/April.

Worden, R. E. 1993. "Toward Equity and Efficiency in Law Enforcement: Differential Police Response." *American Journal of Police* 12: 1–32.

Wycoff, M. A. 1982. "Evaluating the Crime Effectiveness of Municipal Police." In J. R. Greene (ed.), *Managing Police Work*, pp. 15–36. Newbury Park, CA: Sage.

Suggested Websites for Further Study

Uniform Crime Reports
http://www.fbi.gov/ucr.htm
San Jose (CA) Police Department
http://www.sjpd.org/
Kansas City (KS) Police Department
http://www.toto.net/kckcops/
Oakland (CA) Police Department

http://www.oaklandpolice.com/
Police Research Through the National Criminal Justice Reference Service
http://www.ncjrs.org/ncjhome.gov
National Institute of Justice: The Research Agency of the U.S. Department of Justice
http://www.ojp.usdoj.gov/nij
United States Department of Justice
http://www.usdoj.gov
Crime Mapping and Analysis
http://everest.hunter.cuny.edu/capse/projects/nij/crime.html
Crime Scene Investigations
http://police2.ucr.edu/csi.html ✦

Part III

Police Behavior

Behavior and Misconduct

Chapter Outline

Key Terms

abuse of authority	police culture
avoiders	police deviance
clean-beat crime fighters	police misconduct
code of silence	police violence
culture	predispositional theory
danger signifiers	professional-style officers
discretion	racial profiling
economic corruption	reciprocators
enforcers	rotten-apple theory of corruption
grass eaters	service style
gratuity	service-style officers
in-group solidarity	slippery-slope theory
legalistic style	socialization theory
meat eaters	subculture
noble-cause corruption	subjugation of defendant's rights
occupational deviance	symbolic assailant
old-style crime fighters	systemic theory of corruption
particularist perspectives	universalistic perspectives
peer group	use corruption
police corruption	watchman style

This chapter provides an introduction to police behavior. It will look at many different perspectives on the conduct of the police, both in terms of the way police make decisions and in the factors that motivate their decisions. It is concerned with a general discussion of both appropriate and inappropriate (deviant) police behavior. Two particular forms of deviance are considered in this chapter: the acceptance of gratuities and police corruption. Chapter 9 will address other forms of police deviance that are related to the exercise of police authority and the use of coercion. Issues and strategies for controlling police behavior will be discussed in Chapter 10.

Perspectives of Police Behavior

Police behavior may be described from universalistic or particularistic perspectives. **Universalistic perspectives** look at the ways officers are similar. They are widely used by police researchers because they provide ways to distinguish police work from other occupations. **Particularistic perspectives** emphasize how police officers differ one from another.

Universalistic Perspectives

A wide variety of research has sought to explain police behavior in universalistic terms. This research takes three perspectives: sociological, psychological, and organizational (Worden 1989).

Sociological perspective. The sociological perspective emphasizes the social context in which police officers are hired and trained and in which police-citizen interactions occur.

Police officers, as a result of their training and work experience, tend to view situations in a certain manner and act accordingly. Most of the research in this area has attempted to identify external or contextual factors that influence an officer's discretion (Black 1980). Research on women in policing has discussed the absence of roles for female officers and the problems women have adapting to male expectations (Martin 1990).

Psychological perspective. The psychological perspective is concerned with the nature of the "police personality." Officers may have a certain type of personality prior to employment, or their personality may change as a result of their police experience. One of the enduring issues in research on police behavior is whether the values and attitudes of police officers stem from their backgrounds and upbringing or are the result of the experience of police work. Between the 1970s and the 1990s, researchers considered experience in police work as the most important determinant of the police personality. Recently, however, research has questioned this assumption, contending that predispositional factors (discussed later) may be more important than previously thought (Caldero 1997).

Organizational perspective. The organizational perspective suggests that organizational (departmental) factors—formal, informal (cultural), and institutional—play an important role in police behavior. Research on the influence of formal factors looks at the ways the department structures police activity. For example, J. R. Greene and C. B. Klockars (1991) studied the caseloads of officers to assess the overall importance of law enforcement, order maintenance, and service activity in the daily work of the police. They discovered that police spend more time on law enforcement than had been previously thought. As discussed in Chapter 7, most of the research in the 1960s and 1970s discovered that law-enforcement activities accounted for only between 10 to 30 percent of an officer's workload. Greene and Klockars, however, found that police officers spend about 43 percent of their time on law enforcement, only 21 percent on maintaining order, and 8 percent on service. The second-largest category, traffic, accounted for 24 percent of their time.

Research on informal factors studies **police culture.** In some ways, policing is both a culture and a subculture. As a **culture,** police work is characterized by its own occupational beliefs and values that are shared by officers across the United States—for example, police everywhere value their assigned beats. Their territories and the way they deal with their territories define to a great extent their reputations in the department (Herbert 1997). Police organizations often have their own local cultures as well, variations of the broader occupational culture (Manning 1989, 1997). As a **subculture,** police work has many values imported from the broader society in which officers live. Subcultures often develop within police organizations among working groups of officers, where values and norms for behavior are set and enforced among subgroups (e.g., a particular police precinct, unit, or officers on a particular shift). Research on institutional factors is concerned with how the department adapts to its environment. Institutional theory recognizes that concerns over efficiency and effectiveness are secondary to values carried by important actors such as a mayor or city council member. Crank and Langworthy (1991) discuss the ways in which various police practices reflect broader values and how the department acts on the values. In several articles, Mastrofski and his colleagues (Mastrofski and Ritti 1996; Mastrofski and Uchida 1993) have discussed institutional processes affecting the behavior of police departments.

Particularistic Perspectives

Instead of emphasizing similarities among police, particularistic perspectives focus on decision-making differences among officers. Particularistic perspectives include typologies and other officer classification schemes, which are perspectives that identify different officer types or styles of policing.

Worden's (1989) research on police behavior suggests that officers, contrary to conventional wisdom, are not psychologically homogeneous—that is, they are not always intensely loyal to one another nor preoccupied with order. Nor are they all suspicious, secretive, cynical, or authoritarian. The police socialization process does not necessarily result in officers having the same outlook.

Worden identified five ways that police officers are different from one another. First is their view of human nature. Cynical police, for example, tend to be pessimistic, suspicious, and distrustful. The important issue here is the extent to which a person is cynical prior to employment, how that cynicism changes over time, and how it influences his or her behavior.

Second, officers have different role orientations. Some see themselves as crime fighters who deter crime by making arrests and issuing citations. Others believe that the police role involves not only fighting crime but problem solving, crime prevention, and community service.

Third, officers have different attitudes toward legal and departmental restrictions. Some officers think that the ends justify the means in policing, often because they think that legal and policy guidelines are too restrictive, resulting in a criminal going free and thereby increasing crime and the suffering of victims. In addition, some officers believe that the criminal justice system is not punitive enough, and it is up to them to guarantee punishment through "street justice."

Fourth, officers' clientele influences their beliefs and their behavior. Preferences of particular judges, for example, or pressure on patrol enforcement practices from Mothers Against Drunk Driving, can influence patterns of police enforcement. The influence of particular groups can lead to selective enforcement of particular laws and alienate other groups with whom the police interact.

Fifth is the relationship between management and peer group support. Theoretically, police departments reward desired behavior and punish undesired behavior. Many observers, however, have noted that police departments are punishment oriented. They do not have many ways to reward good behavior, so they tend to control the behavior of line officers by setting up elaborate standard operating procedures and punishing officers for infractions. Consequently, officers often turn to their **peer group** members for aid—that is, to other officers of the same rank in the department. The peer group is very influential in policing. Officers depend on it for physical protection and emotional comfort. This dependency in turn can result in increased secrecy in the department.

Socialization Versus Predisposition

As it enters the twenty-first century, police work is in the midst of broad change. The most visible changes are occurring under the umbrella of community policing, which emphasizes police discretion, problem solving, decentralization of authority, and community involvement. Departments are increasingly seeking personnel who have the attitudes, values, and skills for community policing.

Community-policing concerns about hiring the "right" kind of officer have rekindled the debate about where officers' attitudes and values come from. If they come from the way officers adapt to their occupational environment, then commanders will have to change the department or the way it does its work. If they come from the background characteristics of officers, then administrators will have to change their hiring policies. These two ways of thinking about police officers' values and attitudes are called the socialization theory and the predispositional theory.

Socialization theory. Beginning in the 1960s, as the body of knowledge about police behavior increased, social scientists suggested that police behavior was determined more by work experiences and peers than by preemployment values and attitudes. This was called the **socialization theory**—that is, individuals are socialized as a result of their occupational experiences. If a police officer becomes corrupt, it is because the police occupation contributes in some way to weaken values; in other words, corruption is learned within the department. This theory applies to any type of police behavior, good or bad.

Two socialization processes take place in a police organizations. *Formal socialization* is the result of what transpires in the selection process, the training program, what is learned about policies and procedures, and what officers are told by supervisors and managers. *Informal socialization* takes place as new recruits interact with older, more experienced officers. One's peers play an important role in determining behavior, not only in the police occupation but in other jobs as well. An understanding of informal socialization processes is important because what one learns on the job and from one's peers may contradict what is learned during the formal socialization process.

In many police departments the selection process attempts to eliminate individuals who may be prone to unnecessary violence or dishonest behavior. Therefore, police behavior—both good and bad—is seen as a consequence of behavior that is learned after employment. The police experience, and how individuals adjust to that experience, is the most important consideration in determining how "good" police behavior is to be achieved and how "bad" police behavior is to be avoided.

Predispositional theory. In recent years there has been a renewal of interest in the **predispositional theory,** which suggests that the behavior of a police officer is primarily explained by the characteristics, values, and attitudes that the individual had before he or she was employed. If an officer is dishonest or honest, brutal or temperate in the use of force, he or she probably had those positive or negative traits before being hired. Predispositional theory focuses on the idea that the policing occupation attracts people with certain attitudes and beliefs, thus socialization has less explanatory value.

The predispositional theory received early support from Rokeach, Miller, and Snyder (1971), who found that police held similar conservative political values. Individuals who wanted to become officers had a particular value focus: belief in the importance of authority together with a high emphasis on professional fulfillment.

Caldero and Larose (2003) extended Rokeach's research. Surprisingly, they found no differences between Rokeach's 1971 findings and the views of respondents in their research in the early and mid 1990s. Their research consequently offers support for the predispositional theory and argues that "individual value systems are more important than occupational socialization" in understanding police behavior (Caldero and Larose 2003, 162). The central principles of these research efforts are presented below.

1. Police have distinctively different values from other groups in American society.

2. Police values are highly similar to the values of the groups they are recruited from.

3. Police values are also determined by particular characteristics of personality that set police officers apart from the groups from which they are recruited.

4. Police values are unaffected by occupational socialization.

5. The values carried by police officers are stable over time.

6. Regardless of racial or ethnic differences, police officers hold similar values.

7. Education has little impact on values held by police officers.

8. The police socialization process has little effect on the values of individual officers.

This research was discussed by Crank and Caldero (1999), who found that values consistent with police culture were already in place when police were hired. Moreover, after hiring, police values were little changed over an individual officer's career. Finally, screening processes ensured that police recruits held similar values, regardless of their ethnicity or gender. The perspectives developed by Crank and Caldero can be described as a "subcultural" theory of police attitudes and behavior, meaning that police values in general are not learned on the job but are already learned when a recruit applies for police work. Police work selectively accents some of these values;

for example, working-class values are reflected and intensified in the strong loyalties officers have for one another.

Studies of Police Behavior

This section will review important studies on police behavior. Many of these studies were written many years ago. Why then, you might wonder, if police work is changing so dramatically, are these old studies discussed here?

These studies are as important today as they were when they were written. In many ways, the fundamental issues facing the police, the problems they confront on their beats, and the people that they must work with have not changed a great deal. Indeed, one of the fundamental problems is that, in spite of truly staggering organizational changes that have occurred over the past half-century, what officers do on the street has changed little. Put an officer into walking beat and he or she will view that work pretty much as officers did 100 years ago, spiced up only by technological gadgets. Keep in mind that it is not the dates that the studies were written that is important; it is the currency of the ideas.

Violence and the Police

The first social science–oriented study of the police, *Violence and the Police* (1970), was conducted by Westley in Gary, Indiana, in 1949. He identified the importance of socialization as a significant factor in police behavior. He found that "old timers" indoctrinated recruits with the belief that if the recruits were to be good cops, they must take charge of situations in which they became involved. Being in charge of a situation meant that citizens, particularly those in the lower classes, had to show the officer respect. If a citizen failed to show respect or challenged an officer's authority, officers felt compelled to react. Officers believed that they could not back down when faced with challenges to their authority. To do so only encouraged citizens to challenge the police more often, thus making the police officer's job more difficult. Many of the officers in Gary stated that it would be appropriate to "punish" the citizen by using some type of physical force.

Westley also found that the police in Gary believed that the public did not support them. They felt isolated from the public and did not believe that the public could be trusted. Consequently, many police officers were secretive about their daily routines. The police hated "stoolies," police officers who took problems outside the department and "washed their dirty linen" in public. A concern for secrecy and protecting fellow officers was grounded in the fundamental belief that the public could not be trusted to fairly evaluate the appropriateness of police behavior.

Westley's research and analysis underscore the importance of in-group solidarity. **In-group solidarity,** or closeness and loyalty among officers, results from a perception that the public cannot be trusted. In-group solidarity and officer secrecy make it difficult to determine what police officers actually do. Solidarity is often accompanied by a **code of silence** in which officers will not discuss inappropriate police behavior or may lie about it in order to protect a brother officer, creating what has been called "the blue wall of silence."

Justice Without Trial

The important study, *Justice Without Trial* (1966), by Skolnick, was an analysis of two police departments, and it provided many important insights about the activities and behavior of police officers. One of these was related to the *production orientation* of a police department, meaning that police behavior was influenced by the goals or objectives that the department emphasized. For example, if a department was concerned about making arrests and issuing traffic citations, then officers were likely to be aggressive in making arrests and issuing tickets.

Skolnick discussed the significance of danger in police work. He coined the phrase **symbolic assailant** to represent the person the police officer thinks is potentially dangerous or troublesome. Who is a dangerous person? Those "types" of people with whom the officer has had the most dangerous or troublesome experiences become, in effect, that officer's "symbolic assailant." From their experiences and from stories told by other officers, police develop a repertoire of **danger signifiers,** such as a person's actual behavior, language, dress, area, and in some situations, age, sex, and ethnicity.

Such signifiers can be interpreted by the police as challenges to their authority. The person who is perceived to challenge their authority may be verbally or physically abused. Of course, such abuse confirms an officer's belief that a particular kind of person or a particular area is troublesome or potentially dangerous. Further, it convinces the person abused, and others who witness the abuse, that the police are repressive and brutal. Finally, the symbolic assailant has implications for the perception that racial minorities may be more dangerous or predisposed for trouble, which can contribute to our understanding of the modern phenomena of racial profiling.

Varieties of Police Behavior

Perhaps the most important study of police behavior conducted in the 1960s was Wilson's *Varieties of Police Behavior* (1968). Wilson studied eight police departments and reported that in many respects they were quite different. He discussed these differences in terms of three styles of policing. Since Wilson's study, there have been many other attempts to identify different styles of police behavior in terms of both departments and individuals. However, what makes Wilson's perspective unique is the fact that he was able to identify and create typologies of behaviors within different organizations. Thus while the individual street officer continued to enjoy a great deal of discretion, their discretionary decisions were influenced by the larger organizational culture of the police department. Organizational culture, in turn, was largely influenced by the political climate of the local city government. Later empirical replications of his theory have supported much of Wilson's observations (Langworthy 1985).

Wilson found that there were two general categories of problems confronting police departments: *Law-enforcement problems* were those behaviors considered serious enough to warrant a citation or arrest, such as serious traffic violations and most felonies and major misdemeanors. *Order-maintenance problems* involved less serious violations of the law such as misdemeanors or problems that police usually handled without resorting to issuing citations or making arrests.

Wilson stated that differences in policing styles were found primarily in how order-maintenance problems were handled. He identified three different organizational styles: the watchman, the service, and the legalistic. To illustrate, assume that police discover a group of teenagers drinking beer in a public park, a problem in maintaining order.

In the **watchman style,** police officers are given a great deal of latitude in how they handle such problems. Often there are no policies or procedures to guide them. Consequently, each officer is free to devise his or her own response or solution. The officers might take the beer and tell the teenagers to go home. They might even provide a lecture about excessive drinking or they might do nothing at all. And if different officers observed the same problem, there would probably be several different responses to that problem.

In the **service style,** police see themselves as providing a product that the community wants. Such departments tend to be found in homogeneous communities with a common idea of public order. They train officers in what to do and how to do it. The police intervene frequently, but many do so informally, and an arrest is not an inevitable outcome. The officers might refer the beer-drinking teenagers to a department program involving teenage drinking or to a community program. Or, they might call the parents to come and get their son or daughter. Of course, police in the service style do not do this with all order-maintenance problems but for those problems the community or the department considers important.

In the **legalistic style,** police try to enforce the law—write a citation or make an arrest—if possible. Police view themselves as law enforcers. They would probably arrest the teenage beer drinkers. Of course, police in the legalistic style do not always make arrests, but they tend to make more arrests and issue more citations than police do in the other two styles.

City Police

Another important study of police behavior was conducted by Rubinstein (1973). Rubinstein, who worked as a patrol officer in Philadelphia, provided numerous important insights about police activity and behavior. His findings support Skolnick's contributions regarding the importance of the perception of danger in police behavior. Rubinstein suggested that a patrol officer's most important concern was physical control of those individuals with whom he or she interacted. Of course, officers do not perceive all persons as requiring physical control, but in general they tend to watch a suspect's hands, are always alert to the possibility of weapons, and may even stand close to suspects to limit their ability to lash out with a swing or a kick.

Whereas Wilson highlighted the importance of understanding organizational culture, Rubinstein's research emphasized the importance of an officer's working environment as a critical factor in police behavior. Officers learn on the job from other officers about what is important and what is not, the types of situations and people that are potentially dangerous, and how to respond to them. The police department can substantially influence how the officer responds, but much is left to the individual officer. Rubinstein's experience provides support for the socialization theory of police behavior.

'Observations on the Making of Policemen'

Also in 1973, Van Maanen reported on his experiences in law enforcement in "Observations on the Making of Policemen." He attended a police academy and then participated in a limited role as a police officer for six months in a small city in California. One of his most interesting findings concerns the process by which an individual is initiated into a police department. He identified four stages, which are briefly described below.

Preentry choice. Most individuals who choose a police career select it from among a variety of career choices. They tend to go into police work believing they are entering an elite occupation. Many already know someone or something about police work and already tend to identify with the goals and values of the police, at least as they understand them. Their motivation for entering police work is often related to doing something important in society.

Admittance: Introduction. The second stage is the police academy experience. All officers, after being hired, must take some form of academy training, where they learn the necessity of adhering to the rules and regulations of the department. The academy Van Maanen attended had a military atmosphere in which officers followed a rigid routine and were punished for deviating from it (e.g., being late). Officers spent much time studying the technical aspects of police work, and instructors elaborated on these aspects with police experiences, or "war stories." These stories provided important insights about the traditions and values of the department and what was considered to be "good" police work. Recruits learned that they must stick together and protect one another. Today, many academies are less stress-oriented, yet many of the lessons Van Maanen described are applicable today.

Change: Encounter. Once the police academy has been completed, new officers enter the third stage, going to work in the patrol division, each being assigned to a training officer.

Once they are in the field, they are taught what the work is really like. It is also during this phase that the new officers are "tested" by the older officers. Can they perform? Can they operate the equipment effectively? Do they have "common sense"? Are they willing to take risks? Officers are always tested about their willingness to "back up" other officers. Perhaps the most crucial "test" an officer must pass is related to his or her dependability in helping fellow officers when they are in trouble.

New officers work with training officers during the 'encounter' phase of socialization.

Continuance: Metamorphosis. In the final stage, new officers adjust to the reality of police work. In effect, this reality involves a large number of routine problems and bureaucratic tasks, with only an occasional exciting or adventurous activity. For some officers, however, the possibility of an exciting or adventurous "call" continues to be an important motivating factor. As they progress in police work, many officers learn that the public does not understand or support them. And they often decide that the police system—meaning managers and supervisors and how they enforce rules and regulations—is unfair. Perhaps the most common adjustment made by officers, at least in the city Van Maanen studied, was to "lie low and hang loose." That is, they did as little work as possible in order to avoid getting into trouble.

Police: Streetcorner Politicians

Another important study of police behavior was conducted in Oakland, California in the 1970s by Muir. The result was a book titled *Police: Streetcorner Politicians* (1977). Muir considered two issues central to police ethical development, namely perspective and passion. ***Perspective*** is the degree to which the officer understood the nature of human suffering, that is, the degree of compassion displayed by the officer. *Passion* is how the officer responded to the contradiction of achieving just ends with coercive means—that is, how comfortable the officer was in exercising authority.

Muir argued that individual officer styles vary according to the officer's perspective and passion, and called these four styles the professional, the reciprocator, the enforcer, and the avoider. **Professional-style officers** are both compassionate and comfortable with their authority. When necessary, these officers will use coercion to accomplish their work. Yet they view coercion from a perspective that would prefer to find other outcomes. Professionals recognize that coercion is sometimes a necessary means, but they will seek other means first.

Enforcers tend to use force when they have the opportunity. They recognize the need to use force, but they lack the "common touch," a sense of sharing a common destiny with those that they police. Enforcers have not integrated their use of force into a philosophy of life. Force is simply the simplest way to solve problems that they confront.

Reciprocators are compassionate but not comfortable with their authority. These officers try to persuade individuals to cooperate without relying on coercion. These officers understand the responsibilities that go with police work but are uncomfortable with coercion, even in circumstances where there are no alternatives. Reciprocators might be thought of as possessing a social-worker approach to policing.

Avoiders are neither compassionate nor comfortable with their authority. They tend to avoid difficult situations and problems. They lack the maturity of perspective to use coercion in a responsible way, and they also lack compassion for ordinary people. Most often, avoiders are officers who have decided the best way to avoid trouble is to do as little work and take as few risks as possible.

Working the Street: Police Discretion

Brown's *Working the Street: Police Discretion* (1981) was a study of policing styles conducted in three southern California cities, and in many ways was very similar to Muir's work. Individual officer styles, Brown suggested, depended on a combination of their aggressiveness and selectivity of crime problems. Aggressiveness was the degree to which they actively seek out problems. Selectivity was the extent to which they were concerned only about serious crime problems.

Using these two variables, Brown identified four styles of police behavior: **Old-style crime fighters** are very aggressive and tend to be selective, concentrating primarily on felonies. These officers develop extensive knowledge of the area in which they work, use informants, and tend to be coercive. They are sometimes willing to act illegally to get "results." **Clean-beat crime fighters** believe in the importance of legal procedures. These officers are proactive and legalistic but do not tend to be selective. Almost all violations of the law are considered to be significant. **Service-style officers** do the minimum amount of work necessary to get by; that is, they are not aggressive but are selective. Only the most serious problems will result in their enforcing the law. Such officers tend to rely on informal solutions to problems rather than legalistic ones. **Professional-style officers** engage in limited proactivity and are not selective. They are situationally oriented, though "tough" when necessary, and at other times they may be service minded. Like Muir, Brown uses the term professional to denote the type of police officer that he considers to be the most desirable. What makes Brown's observations different from Muir's is that he was concerned with highlighting individual nuances of police style; Muir was interested in finding out what makes a "good" police officer.

It should be apparent that the observations by Wilson, Rubinstein, Muir, and Brown contributed to distinct understandings of officer behavior. Each offered different levels of analysis when considering discretion (i.e., organizational factors, situational factors, and individual officer factors). Each perspective is incomplete, as they forsake the other correlates of behavior. Thus a more complete model for understanding police behavior can be found by including each of these levels of analysis when attempting to understand street-level discretionary behavior.

Crank's *Understanding Police Culture* (1998) is included here because it integrates a great deal of writing about police work and shows present-day trends in thinking about the police. It is an effort to develop a "middle-range theory" about the police and to show how this theory can provide new insights into police work. Middle-range theory attempts to integrate findings from a broad body of research into a more general perspective.

Crank suggests that police culture emerges from the daily practice of police work. Culture, he argues, does not make the police different from the public. Rather, it humanizes the police by giving their work meaning. Rejecting the notion that police culture is a "dark force," he argues that culture is carried in police common sense, in the way in which everyday activities are celebrated, and in the way police deal with death and suffering. Consequently, to understand police culture, one must examine the physical setting in which police work occurs and the groups with which police interact, such as wrongdoers, the public, the courts, the press, and the department's administration. Because these groups tend to be similar everywhere, police culture tends to take on similar characteristics in different departments, and one can speak of a police culture generally.

Elements of police culture are organized around four central principles. The first and most central principle is *coercive territorial control*. The police are trained formally and socialized informally to view their work in terms of the use of force to control specific territories to which they are assigned. Police learn about the use of force, both in terms of a use-of-force continuum (see Chapter 9) and in terms of informal tactics that enable them to control the public in police-citizen encounters. The use of force is more than a set of skills, however. Force is acted out as a moral commitment to control their assigned territories. Herbert (1997) echoed the importance of territoriality. In his observations of Los Angeles officers, he found that the ability of the police to control behavior in an assigned geographic area was a central factor that influenced officer behavior.

The second principle is *the unknown.* Police activity routinely puts officers in circumstances that are unpredictable and may have outcomes beyond their control. Such unpredictability makes police work interesting. The common unpredictability of everyday encounters may mask significant danger. Police officers have a wide repertoire of skills to ensure that unknown situations do not deteriorate into dangerous life-threatening encounters.

The third principle is *solidarity,* or the intense bonding and sense of occupational uniqueness that officers feel for one another. It is produced by the dangers and unpredictability of their work and from the intense individualism that is part of the police ethos. Central to solidarity is conflict with other groups: Police officers often feel alienated from the courts and the public and from outsiders and different ethnic groups. The greater the conflict with outside groups, the greater the degree to which the police feel united in a sense of solidarity.

The fourth principle is *loose coupling,* the idea that police develop strategies and tactics to protect themselves when department goals and policies are perceived to undermine their ability to do their work. At the core of the police morality is the idea that they have to do something about "bad guys." Efforts by administrators to control police behavior, as well as by the courts to hold them accountable for due process, are often met with distrust by line officers when such efforts interfere with their sense of occupationally-driven morality. Lying in court, keeping information from administrators, and circumventing due process are all ways some police officers carry out their work in spite of administrative rules limiting what they are permitted to do.

However, it is unclear whether a common police culture actually exists to the degree that Crank has indicated. Paoline (2003) argued that the reality of a single set of police attitudes, values and norms for behavior might be overstated. He identified several arenas where there may be variation in culture within the policing occupation, including variation between organizations, officer styles, and rank within an organization. For example, as Wilson pointed out previously, there exists a great deal of variation between organizations in their style of social control. Therefore it is prudent to assume there may be subtle, yet important, cultural variations between legalistic, watchmen or service-style departments. Also, Muir and Brown indicated separate individual styles of policing, thus cultural norms might vary across these typologies. Paoline also noted there exists cultural variation between ranks within an organization. Specifically, upper management, middle management and line officers may all adhere to different norms, attitudes and values that shape their behavior. His assertions are supported by research that has identified different values between management and street officers (Reuss-Ianni 1983) as well as different supervisory styles among middle managers (Engel 2001). Finally, a "single police culture" might be less prevalent in the future as police departments continue to diversify. With the inclusion of more college-educated officers (see Chapter 14), more racial/ethnic minorities, and more women (see Chapter 12), considering police culture as a monolithic entity may become less useful when describing police behavior.

This section has provided brief summaries of some of the more important studies about police behavior from the 1930s to the 1990s. Inside Policing 8.1 presents quotes of police officers regarding their own behavior. Their statements indicate the importance of some of the variables that are identified in this section.

Inside Policing 8.1   **Police Officer Quotes**

Commitment to the Public. "I know it sounds corny as hell, but I really thought I could help people. I wanted to do something good in the world, you know?" (Baker 1985, 9)

Street Craziness. "The cabby had picked up the naked prostitute and now she couldn't pay. All four of them were screaming at each other. The cabby was screaming for his money, the naked prostitute was screaming that she had been raped by a john, and the other two prostitutes were yelling that the cabby should have known that she had no money when he picked her up naked." (McNulty 1993, 285)

Street Standards. "You have all the instructors up there teaching you the penal law, the study of minority groups. . . . psychology, . . . sociology. Then you got the [other cops]—telling you, 'that's all bullshit. It's either you or him out in the street. Go for the eyes. Kick them in the groin.'" (Baker 1985, 12)

The Perception of Danger. From a training class on actions to take inside a house: "On the page below, you'll see JDLR. That's Just Don't Look Right. Refer to GTHO, p. 5. Turn to p. 5. It says Get the Hell Out."(Crank 1996, 413)

Unpredictability. "The situations that seem to be the most unlikely to be dangerous are the ones that erupt into the most violent. The most tragic incidents have always come from the smallest incidents, usually traffic. . . . When you walk up to a car with a little old lady sitting in it and she pulls a sawed-off shotgun on you, you're completely surprised. Who you're stopping is always the joker in the deck." (Fletcher 1991, 12–13)

Advice to young officers. "Don't drive faster than your guardian angel can fly." (Crank 1996, 415)

Supporting Fellow Officers. "It's a contact sport and if you don't watch my back for me, there's no one else I can count on. If you're not looking out for me, I'm going to get hurt." (Baker 1985, 210)

Fear. "I'd be lying between my teeth if I said I never get scared. I wouldn't want to work with a police officer who said he's never scared. That macho act—can't nothing hurt me, can't nothing touch me—that's all it is, an act. (Fletcher 1991, 276)

Survivors and Police Distrust of Media. "I had just finished shopping when I heard the chilling report of a police shoot-out on the car radio. The reporter was the one who informed me that it was my husband that had been killed. My neighbors found me, crying hysterically, parked in the middle of the road several blocks from home." (Sawyer 1993, 4)

Sources: Adapted from M. Baker, *Cops: Their Lives in Their Own Words* (New York: Simon and Schuster, 1985); C. Fletcher, *What Cops Know* (New York: Pocket Books, 1990); C. Fletcher, *Pure Cop* (New York: St. Martin's Press, 1991); E. McNulty, 1993, "Generating Common Sense Knowledge Among Police Officers," *Symbolic Interaction* 17: 281–294; S. Sawyer, *Support Services to Surviving Families of Line-of-Duty Deaths* (Camdenton, MO: Concerns of Police Survivors, 1993); J. Crank, 1996, "The Construction of Meaning During Training for Parole and Probation," *Justice Quarterly* 31: 277.

Decision-Making and Police Discretion

Police officers make decisions that affect the public in important ways. Yet scholarly knowledge about the way police make decisions is limited. When scholars talk about decision-making, they generally mean decisions involving citizens and questionable behavior. When police see something that is "out of kilter," two important decisions must be made: (1) whether to intervene in a situation (this is not a choice if the officer is sent by the department), and (2) how to intervene (Wilson 1968). What kinds of decisions are available for an officer who makes a routine traffic stop? Bayley and Bittner (1989, 98) note that officers have 10 actions to select from at the initial stop (for example, order the driver out of the car), seven strategies appropriate during the stop (for example, give a roadside sobriety test), and 11 exit strategies (for example, release the driver with a warning). From start to finish, this represents a total of 770 different combinations!

Decision-making is different from the use of discretion. The circumstances above represent decision-making regarding when and how to intervene in situations. **Discretion** is more narrowly defined. The most commonly used definition is the decision not to invoke legal sanctions when circumstances are favorable for them (Goldstein 1998). Davis (1969, 4) described discretion as, "whenever the effective limits on his power leave him free to make a choice among courses of action or inaction." In encounters with suspects, for example, police may be presented with a situation in which they have the legal basis for an arrest. They do not, however, always make an arrest. The decision not to make an arrest when it is legally justifiable is sometimes called nonenforcement discretion.

Discretionary decisions not to arrest occur often in police work. An officer may witness a person drinking beer in a park, which is a violation of local codes. This situation might be handled with a warning rather than a citation or an arrest. Why did the officer not make an arrest? The officer might feel sympathy for the suspect. Or the officer might be waiting to see how the suspect reacts, prepared to arrest him if the suspect resists or gets "smart-mouthed." The officer might view this situation as a problem that can be easily handled without going to the trouble of arresting the suspect. The officer might be about to go off duty and not want to spend time doing paperwork at the end of the shift. Or arrest might be inconsistent with either an officer's "style" (i.e., she or he simply does not arrest beer-drinkers in parks) or the style of the police organization (i.e., officers in a watchman-style organization would be more apt to use nonapplication of the law). Many factors affect officers' decisions about whether they should intervene, and what they should do after intervening, and whether they should make an arrest, even when legal circumstances are favorable.

There has been a considerable amount of research concerning variables that influence police decision-making and discretion. Sherman (1985), Brooks (1989), and Riksheim and Chermak (1993) have analyzed research in this area. Their observations are grouped into four categories of variables: organizational, neighborhood (or community), situational, and officer (or individual). Figure 8.1 provides a visual depiction of how these factors simultaneously impact the discretion and decision making of street-level police officers.

Organizational Variables

There are several organizational (departmental) variables.

Bureaucratic nature. The bureaucratic nature of a police department is an important factor affecting police behavior, as discussed in Chapter 4. It should be emphasized that the purpose of bureaucratic procedure is to guide and direct police behavior (Alpert and Smith 1998; Auten 1988). And, as Wasserman (1992) observes, without written policy, departments relinquish policy decisions to the idiosyncratic judgments of street officers. Nevertheless, various researchers have questioned the effectiveness of the bureaucratic "control principle" (Alpert and Smith 1998). Cordner (1989) challenged the notion that written policy always contributes to the quality of police service. The discretionary demands of street activity may undermine bureaucratic efforts to control behavior (Adams 1990). Bureaucratic controls can backfire, contributing to police secrecy and undermining bureaucratic control. For these reasons, the effectiveness of bureaucracy as a way to stimulate some behaviors and dampen others is certainly limited. Highly bureaucratic departments also tend to be impersonal and may overemphasize punitive discipline in an attempt to control officers' behavior. This tendency may result in officers doing as little as possible in an effort to avoid getting into trouble.

Figure 8.1 Factors That Impact Police Discretion

Work periods and areas. Another important organizational variable is the frequency with which officers change work periods (or shift or tour) and the areas (beat or district or sector) in which they work. The more frequent these types of changes, the more distant the relationship between citizen and officer. There may be less communication and less understanding about community problems. Also important is the size of the area in which the officer works; the smaller the area, the more likely that a service rather than an enforcement orientation will prevail (Mastrofski 1981). A small area with a high quantity of serious crime, however, is more likely to have a law enforcement style (Brooks 1989, 126–130).

There is also some indication that discretionary choices differ based on the assignment of the officer within the organization. Novak et al. (2002) compared the decision making of officers assigned to community-policing tasks to officers assigned to traditional "911" duties. They found that while these officers used similar factors in their decision making, several important differences were observed. They found that community-policing officers were more likely to use victim preference when making an arrest decision than their more traditional counterparts, indicating that community-policing officers may be more responsive to citizens' demands. They also found community-policing officers were less likely to arrest hostile citizens, and that traditional officers were much more likely to arrest intoxicated citizens. This appears to indicate officers assigned to community-policing tasks may be more tolerant of nonconforming behavior than their counterparts.

Neighborhood Variables

To what extent do characteristics of neighborhoods affect police performance? Clearly the kind of beats police patrol affect the work they do. As early as 1968, Wilson noted that, in watchman-style departments, officers adapted their work to the kinds of problems that characterized their beats. This practice resulted in uneven delivery of service. Wilson and Kelling (1982) extended this idea to argue that police should tailor their work to the kinds of problems they encounter, a theme expanded by Skolnick and Bayley (1986).

Characteristics of neighborhoods may also affect police behavior. One of the most interesting characteristics is racial composition. Research tends to support the view that the police write more reports, make more arrests, engage in more abusive behavior, and receive more citizen requests for police intervention in minority areas. As a result of this increased activity, police get to know the people in these areas better than in other areas. In addition, police tend to view minority areas as places where violent crimes are more likely to occur and where they are more likely to have their authority challenged. As a result, police are more suspicious and alert and more concerned for their own safety. Data consistently show that police arrest more individuals in minority areas than in other areas, though arrest rates are highly correlated with criminal activity (Sampson and Lauritsen 1997).

Another aspect of neighborhoods is their racial and ethnic heterogeneity. The greater the racial and ethnic diversity, the more likely the police will become involved in encounters with citizens whom they think are troublesome. Police tend to exercise a great deal of discretion in these areas, may tend to feel more insecure, are often more aggressive, and tend to make more arrests. They are much more likely to arrest and threaten use of force in racially mixed neighborhoods (Smith 1980).

Situational Variables

Many elements in a situation affect police behavior.

Mobilization. The manner in which the police are mobilized, or enter into a situation, is important in determining their conduct. In proactive, or police-initiated, encounters, officers are more likely to face antagonism from citizens. Proactive police behavior is more intrusive and less likely to be supported by victims and bystanders. As a result of the increased likelihood of a negative citizen response, police are more likely to make arrests and treat citizens harshly (Sherman 1985, 187). Consequently, proactive encounters are more likely to result in police-citizen antagonisms and conflict.

Family disturbances require high levels of police discretion.

Demeanor and attitude. The characteristics of both suspects and complainants are important variables in the discretion of police officers. As Inside Policing 8.2 shows, perhaps the most important of these is the demeanor of the suspects. Disrespectful or uncooperative suspects are more likely to be arrested than suspects who are not. The socioeconomic status of individuals is also an important situational factor. Individuals in a lower socioeconomic status are more likely to be treated harshly by the police, and suspects in that status are more likely to be arrested. Klinger (1994) contends that legal factors, specifically the criminal conduct of suspects after coming into contact with police, outweigh demeanor considerations.

The attitude of the complainant is another widely cited factor influencing police decisions to arrest, according to the research of Black (1980), Smith (1987), Worden (1989) and others. Black, for example, observed that arrests were more likely to occur in both felony and misdemeanor situations when the complainant wanted the suspect to be arrested. But officers are less likely to do what the complainant wants if the complainant shows disrespect.

The demeanor of suspects and attitude of complainants may interact with individual officer styles. For example, a widely cited "test" that many police officers apply to suspects is called the attitude, or personality, test. Many officers believe that they cannot allow a citizen to challenge an officer's authority. The challenge can include a question about being stopped, too many questions in general, criticism of the officer, or failing to comply promptly to a police request for information. Of course, any physical resistance would also be included. Research suggests that citizens who flunk such tests are more likely to be verbally and physically abused or given a traffic citation or arrested (Van Maanen 1978). For example, a study by Lersch and Feagin (1996) that analyzed 130 newspaper reports of police brutality found that a citizen was equally likely to be assaulted for a "disrespectful" attitude toward the officer as for posing a serious bodily threat to the officer or another person; they also found that minority group citizens were involved in the vast majority of the incidents.

Race. Research on the importance of race in police behavior is mixed. A large body of research supports the contention that African Americans are treated more harshly than whites or are more likely to be arrested (Kappeler, Sluder, and Alpert 1994; Chambliss 1997; Maurer 1993). Some researchers contend that this situation is the result of the fact that African-Americans, and possibly other minorities, may be more likely to resist police authority or display a "bad" attitude or outright hostility, from an officer's point of view. Others respond that hostility to the police derives from a history of police mistreatment.

Recently the issue of racial profiling has captured the attention of citizens and police administrators. **Racial profiling** refers to proactive police actions that rely on race or ethnicity rather than behavior that leads the police to identify a particular person as being, or having been, engaged in criminal activity (Ramirez, McDevitt, and Farrell 2000). The key component of this concept is that the encounter is police-initiated and not part of some other source of information (such as a wanted person who fits the citizen's description). The second component is that police use race, rather than behavior, to initiate the encounter. Racial profiling might occur in the context of traffic stops, but can also be involved in other arenas (such as pedestrian checks).

There exists a belief among citizens that profiling is common among police agencies. The Gallup Organization conducted a survey of Americans that indicated 59 percent felt racial profiling was widespread; among blacks, 77 percent felt it was widespread (Gallup Organization 1999). Further, 42 percent of blacks indicated that they have been stopped by the police because of their race or ethnicity. This corresponds with lower ratings of citizen satisfaction with police services among racial and ethnic minorities. In fact, in a survey by the Bureau of Justice Statistics, fewer blacks and Hispanics reported police used "legitimate" reasons for stopping them than whites (Langan et al. 2001).

At the same time there have been numerous examinations of police departments conducted across the nation to determine whether there is racial bias in police traffic-enforcement patterns. These inquiries have often been conducted voluntarily by police departments, but they have also been conducted pursuant to lawsuits and mandated by state law. The majority of these investigations have indicated racial and ethnic minorities have a disproportionately high number of contacts with the police, compared to the population characteristics of the jurisdiction. At times it has been found that minorities are only slightly more likely to be stopped; other times the disparity is extreme. Harris (1999) found blacks in large Ohio cities were between 2.3 and 2.7 times more likely to be stopped than whites. Spitzer (1999) found blacks in New York City were 23 percent more likely to be stopped than whites, and Hispanics were 39 percent more likely to be stopped.

What remains largely unknown is exactly why racial and ethnic minorities consistently have disproportionate numbers of police contacts. One possible explanation is bigoted/racist police officers. Another rationale may be differential traffic offending by racial minorities, though upon closer inspection, this reason does not seem to hold up to empirical scrutiny. Perhaps it is cognitive stereotyping, in which officers believe minorities are more likely to possess guns and drugs than whites. It might also be differential officer deployment in predominantly minority communities in accordance with higher rates of crime and calls for police service. Thus it would logically follow there will be disparity in police-minority contacts when examining citywide traffic enforcement patterns. Further research will be necessary in order to determine how widespread these disparities are and what causes them.

Given the importance of identification of racial profiling in America, Voices From the Field discusses what police departments should be doing in response to bias in traffic enforcement. Lorie Fridell is the Director of Research at the Police Executive Forum—a nonprofit agency dedicated to improving policing.

Gender. The effects of gender on police behavior regarding arrests are relatively under-studied. The masculine predispositions of police departments are widely cited (Martin 1980, 1990). Visher (1983) found females were less likely to be arrested than males who engage in similar behavior, especially when females act in an appropriate, "ladylike" fashion. However, the opposite could be true as well. When females act outside of their gender role, they may be more likely to be sanctioned by the police because they are deemed more deserving of arrest. Further, the extent to which these predispositions affect police-citizen encounters is unclear. Kraska and Kappeler (1995) suggest that sexual violence by the police may be more widespread than previously thought. Opportunity, power, authority, and isolation increase the likelihood of sexual harassment of citizens (Sapp 1994). Attractive women are also more likely to be stopped by police officers for traffic violations, and the intent is not to issue a traffic citation but to make personal contact (see Kappeler, Sluder, and Alpert 1994).

Voices From the Field
Racially Biased Policing
Lorie Fridell, Ph.D.
Police Executive Research Forum

Question: What should police departments be doing to respond to racially biased policing?

Answer: "Racial profiling"—increasingly referred to as "racially biased policing" or "bias-based policing"—is not a new concern. It is the most recent manifestation of a long history of sometimes tense, even volatile, police-minority relations. Law-enforcement agencies across the nation are increasingly responding to the issues of racially biased policing and the perceptions of its practice. A comprehensive agency response cuts across six areas of intervention: accountability/supervision, policy, recruitment/hiring, education/training, minority community outreach, and data collection.

Critically important is police agencies' adoption of clear policies that delineate for their officers the circumstances in which a person's race and/or ethnicity can be used as one factor among multiple factors to make a law enforce-

ment decision—such as a decision to approach, detain or arrest. Virtually all agencies allow officers to consider race or ethnicity as one of several factors when given a suspect's description, such as a "be on the lookout for an Asian male, about six feet two inches tall, with red T-shirt and black jeans—suspect in convenience store robbery on the corner of Maple and Vine streets." In these and similar circumstances, the reference to race in the description becomes relevant to police officers' decisions about whom to question, detain, or arrest. There is still much debate in the field, however, regarding whether there are additional circumstances in which race and/or ethnicity might be properly considered for police decision making. These and other considerations are addressed in the Police Executive Research Forum report on racially biased policing. ✦

Age. The age of the citizen encountering the police can influence police-citizen encounters in several ways, particularly when the citizen is a juvenile (or under 18 years old). Black (1976) stated that juveniles are less "respectable" than older people in that they hold a lower social standing in American society. Hence they pose a greater threat to officers and therefore are more likely to receive formal application of law, such as arrest (Novak et al. 2002). If indeed officers treat juveniles more harshly than adults, this observation may explain why juveniles often hold less favorable attitudes toward police than adults (Hurst and Frank 2000). However, the movement toward community policing may impact how officers interact with juveniles. As Mastrofski et al. (1995) noted, officers who expressed negative attitudes toward community policing were more likely to arrest juvenile offenders than their pro-community-policing counterparts. Other researchers found community-policing officers may be more disposed to informal sanctioning when encountering juveniles, and the role of the community-police officer may be seen as mentor and role model rather than law enforcer (Cordner 1995). In short, juveniles may hold a unique position in police-citizen encounters.

Suspect-complainant relationship. Another interesting situational variable is the relationship between the suspect and complainant. In general, if the relationship is close, the police may be reluctant to take official action (i.e., make an arrest) because they believe that it would be difficult to gain testimony from the victim in the courts. But the relationship has been, and remains, influential in the manner in which some police departments respond to calls about domestic violence or a family fight. In addition, when the relationship between the complainant and suspect is close, the complainant may not wish the police to take official action. The preference of the complainant has a substantial influence on the officer's decisions. Although officers do not always do what complainants want, they are more likely to take official action, such as writing a report, if the complainant requests such action.

Seriousness of offense. The type of offense also has an impact on police discretion. The more serious the crime, the greater the possibility of a formal response. Violent crimes are more likely to result in an arrest for a simple reason—the victim is a witness to the crime. Consequently, about 50 percent of all violent crimes result in an arrest; only about 20 percent of property crimes do so. Police are more likely to arrest in felony encounters than in misdemeanor situations. This may seem like common sense, but in fact it is not (Friedrich 1980). As Black (1980) noted, the legal decision to arrest is based on probable cause, not the seriousness of the act. Because the legal standard of proof is probable cause, officers tend to make arrests during situations where there is greater and more prohibitive evidence, regardless of the type of crime. Evidence sufficiency is often more likely to be present for serious offenses.

Mental state of the citizen. Recently greater attention has focused on the treatment of mentally disordered suspects by the police. Some have indicated that suspects who demonstrate symptoms of mental deficiency are treated more harshly by police, while observing a disproportionately higher number of mentally disordered people coming into contact with the criminal justice system. Teplin (1984) found the arrest rates for mentally disordered citizens to be 46.7 percent, compared to 27.9 percent for those not displaying such deficiencies, suggesting arrest was used with this special population to resolve conflict, rather than other discretionary choices available to officers. However, research conducted by Engel and Silver (2001) did not find support for this "criminalization hypothesis." They reported that factors such as seriousness of offense, seriousness of a weapon, and victim-offender relationship offered greater explanatory value than mental capacity of the citizen. In fact, they indicated citizens with mental deficiencies were significantly less likely to be arrested than others—the opposite of what Teplin found. This appears to indicate the relationship between mental deficiencies and police behavior deserves greater examination.

Location. Police are also influenced by the location—public or private—of the call. Police are more likely to respond harshly in public settings than in private settings. This difference is the result of several factors: the type of crime (usually perceived as more serious crimes), the need to appear in control of the situation in public, the ambiguous role of the police in situations that occur in private places, and the fact that there are more police-initiated, or proactive, calls in public. As noted above, proactive police interventions with citizens are more likely to result in arrests and citizen resistance than are reactive police responses. Proactive interventions are usually the result of the police witnessing illegal behavior, usually at the misdemeanor level. Thus, as Black observed, police tend to be more proactive when a crime is not legally serious.

Presence of others. The presence of other police officers and bystanders has a slight influence on what police officers do (Parks 1982). If an officer thinks other police officers expect him or her to be harsh or punitive, or to write a report, or to make an arrest, then the officer is inclined to do so. Behaving in a manner that other officers believe to be appropriate is an important part of being accepted into the police "brotherhood." Crank and Caldero (1999) suggest that officers who "wolf-pack" stops, that is, congregate in high numbers during routine stops, are more likely to create a variety of problems for managers. These problems include due process violations, violence, and increased levels of line-level secrecy.

Officers who work alone also tend to behave differently from officers who work in pairs. There is some support for the belief that officers working by themselves are more likely to make arrests because they are more concerned about taking control of a situation when working alone. Although two-person units may be less likely to make arrests, they are more likely to treat suspects harshly, possibly because each officer is concerned about what his or her partner will think, particularly if a suspect challenges police authority (e.g., asks questions, talks back, fails to follow police direction, or fights) (Brooks 1989, 134–137; Sherman 1985, 189–192).

All the above variables have some influence on police behavior, but some are more important than others. Table 8.1 identifies those variables associated with both the suspect and complainant that appear to have a reliable influence on police behavior—that is, they are found to be influential in several studies.

Discretionary decisions are difficult to bring under departmental control. The ability of the police to use discretion enables them to adapt their responsibilities to the characteristics of public-order problems on their beat (Sykes 1986) and efforts to control discretion have sometimes backfired, creating line-level resistance and secrecy (Crank 1998). Perhaps the best to be hoped for is stated by D. Guyot (1991, 96): "The challenge for departmental leadership is to reduce the vindictive decisions and increase the wise ones."

	Role of Citizen	
Variables	**Suspect**	**Victim**
Race	x	o
Demeanor	x	x
Relation to victim	x	o
Social class	x	o
Age	x	o
Sex	x	o
Complainant's preference	o	x
Public/private setting	x	x
Number of citizens present	x	x
Proactive/reactive	x	o
Number of officers present	x	o

Table 8.1   Critical Variables Influencing Police Behavior

Key: x—consistent relationship found; o—no consistent relationship found

Source: Adapted from L. W. Sherman, "Causes of Police Behavior: The Current State of Quantitative Research." In A. S. Blumberg and E. Niederhoffer, eds., *The Ambivalent Force*, 3rd ed. (New York: Holt, Rinehart and Winston, 1985), 183–195.

Individual (Officer) Variables

Many individual factors influence police behavior.

Education, age, and experience. Education is discussed at length in Chapter 11. It is difficult to separate age and experience because most individuals entering police work are young, typically in their twenties, and grow older as they are gaining experience. In general, younger officers may work harder and are more aggressive and more punitive than older officers. However, the quality of the older officers' work may be superior. While some older, more seasoned officers may do less work and become less punitive, others may actually become more punitive if they become excessively cynical. Older police officers may become frustrated with the department and the legal system and engage in illegal behavior, including the use of excessive force.

Race. The race of the officer is also important. The bulk of the research on race has been about African American officers. Some evidence indicates that they are more respected by the African American community, but they may also be stricter in dealing with African American citizens. When compared with white officers, African American officers tend to be more aggressive and to make more arrests in African American neighborhoods (Brooks 1989, 138–140). This, however, may be in part due to differential assignment of nonwhite officers to African American communities. Overall, the race of the officer has less explanatory power than many might assume, because when individuals don a police uniform they tend to become "blue" versus black or white. This would appear to support the socialization process. Yet, there are also important race-related considerations concerning the police use of force. These are discussed in the next chapter.

Gender. The gender of the officer is also influential in the exercise of police discretion. There is some evidence to suggest that women are less aggressive. The studies that support this observation, however, were conducted in the first decade of women's involvement in patrol work (see Martin 1989, 312–330, for a summary of these studies). One study found that women were less likely than men to use force (Grennan 1988, 78–85). If women as a group tend to be less aggressive or use force less often than men, this finding may either be desirable or undesirable, depending on one's preference in policing styles. For the most part, however, the less aggressive (i.e., less forceful and abusive) the police, the more likely they are to have a positive relationship with the community.

Career orientation and family situation. Other important variables that influence the exercise of an officer's discretion are career orientation and family situation. W. F. Walsh's study (1986), conducted in the New York City Police Department, found that officers in high-arrest categories were ambitious and believed that making arrests increased their chance of being promoted, or they believed that making felony arrests was an important part of police work. Some officers made numerous arrests because it gave them an opportunity to work overtime, which resulted in a higher salary. One of the reasons some of the high-arrest officers wanted to work overtime was because their wives did not work and they needed the money. Conversely, some of the officers in low-arrest categories had "outside work," or their wives worked and supplemented the family income.

There is also some indication that an officer's orientation toward community policing can influence behavior. Mastrofski, Worden and Snipes (1995) examined officers' decisions to arrest citizens in Richmond, Virginia. They found that officers with more favorable attitudes toward community policing were more "selective" in making arrests compared to those officers with less favorable attitudes. They reported that arrest decisions for officers with less favorable views toward community policing were more strongly influenced by offense seriousness and evidence sufficiency compared to those with more positive views toward community policing. They argued that officers who support community policing tend to make different discretionary choices than traditional officers but were unable to thoroughly describe the arrest patterns for officers with positive views of community policing.

The degree to which all these variables influence individual officers varies, but in general the decisions officers make to stop someone, to behave in a certain way when interacting with citizens, and to select a way to solve a problem are determined by numerous factors besides the legality of a citizen's behavior. Yet, in spite of a great deal of research, scholars know little about the relative importance of extralegal factors. All that can be said for certain is that, in some circumstances, the police will make arrests based in part on factors other than whether the law is broken. Yet, even the law is highly interpretive, and officers have wide discretion in the application of punishments for misdemeanors. The contribution of extralegal factors consequently continues to be a topic in need of thoughtful research.

Police Deviance

Unfortunately, not all police behavior is legal or proper. Sometimes police officers engage in acts that are inappropriate, and occasionally they do things that are illegal.

Many people believe that police officers should be held to a higher standard than ordinary citizens. They hold the police as symbols of the moral fabric of society and their behavior as a standard for the public to emulate. Consequently, the police must display the image as well as the substance of propriety. They not only must be above reproach, they must also appear to be above reproach.

Police deviance is behavior that does not conform to the standards of norms or expectations. How are such standards determined? There are three major categories: ethical, organizational, and legal. Ethical standards are principles of appropriate conduct officers carry internally. Ethical behavior is an expression of personal values.

Organizational (departmental) standards can be both formal and informal; they are derived from policy, procedures, rules, and regulations of the department (formal) and from the expectations of one's peers (informal). Legal standards are represented by the laws officers are sworn to uphold and by due process which establishes the means officers may use to achieve good ends.

Clearly, many of these standards carry the potential for conflict with others. Formal departmental policies may clash with informal cultural norms. The expectations surrounding the enforcement of the law may conflict with the principles of due process. And a police officer's personal values may be different from the ethical principles established by the department. In short, the standards expected of a police officer are extraordinarily complicated, and deviance, in one form or another, is almost impossible to avoid.

It is very difficult to determine how frequently police engage in deviant behavior. It is difficult because people are not always forthcoming about their own inappropriate behavior, partly because of the blue code of silence, and partly because it is not always easy to distinguish between inappropriate and appropriate behavior. Given the many conflicting expectations facing police, it is likely that deviance is widespread. Few police officers work even one shift without engaging in some form of behavior that is deviant by one standard or another. In fact, many police departments have so many rules and regulations that it is difficult not to violate some of them. Many of the violations are minor—for example, a requirement that officers wear their hats when not in a car.

Types of Deviance

Kappeler, Sluder, and Alpert (1994) identify four general kinds of police deviance:

1. Police crime. Police crime is different from a criminal act; not every criminal act committed by the police is a police crime. Police crime is the "officer's use of the official powers of his or her job to engage in criminal conduct" (21). In other words, an officer uses police authority to engage in violations of the criminal code.

2. Occupational deviance. **Occupational deviance** is activity that does not conform to standards and is committed during the course of normal work activities or under the guise of the police officer's authority (22; see also Barker and Carter 1994, 6). It is not just that the deviance is job related, but that the deviant act was substantially facilitated by being a police officer.

3. Police corruption. **Police corruption** involves the use of police power and authority for personal gain (see also Sherman 1978; Goldstein 1977). Barker's study of police ethics is instructive here. He defines police corruption as follows: "Whatever the officer receives through the misuse of his or her authority must be of some material reward or gain. Material reward or gain must be some tangible object, either cash, services, or goods that have cash value" (1996, 25).

4. Abuse of authority. Finally, Kappeler and his colleagues observe that Carter's (1985, 22) definition of the term **abuse of authority** contains three different elements:

   • Officers may physically abuse others through the use of excessive force.

   • Officers may psychologically abuse citizens through the use of verbal assault, harassment, or ridicule.

   • Officers may violate a citizen's constitutional, federal, or state rights. (Kappeler, Sluder, and Alpert 1994, 24)

A similar typology was developed by Punch (1985), who identifies four kinds or categories of corruption:

1. Straightforward corruption is done for some reward. In this arrangement, the police may be linked to organized crime and selectively fail to enforce some crimes.

2. Predatory corruption occurs when the police stimulate crime, organize graft, or actively extort money. Here, the police themselves are the organized crime.

3. Combative corruption occurs when the major goal is to make arrests, obtain convictions, and get long sentences. It includes the following practices (see Manning 1980):

   • Flaking: planting evidence on a suspect.

   • Padding: adding evidence to strengthen a case.

   • Verbals: words attributed to a suspect that are actually created by the police to help incriminate the criminal.

   • Intimidating witnesses.

   • Scoring on informants: shaking down informants for money, drugs, and other goods.

   • Burning: revealing the identity of an informant.

   • Paying informants with illegally obtained drugs.

4. Perversion of justice includes lying under oath, intimidating witnesses, and planting evidence on a suspect. It is distinguished from item 3 above by the motive of the police officer. In combative corruption, the motive was to do justice, although it is a "police" conception of justice. Here the motive is revenge.

Punch's typology differs from the others in two ways. First, his category "perversion of justice" recognizes that police behavior can carry sentiments of revenge against felons. Second, his category "combative corruption" clearly recognizes corruption for a perceived noble cause—that is, revision of legal means for perceived good ends. Punch's model is consequently an important contribution to the literature on corruption.

Barker (1996) argues that assessments of police corruption should focus specifically on those activities for which there is a monetary reward. He identifies eight patterns of corrupt practices, which are reproduced in Table 8.2.

Table 8.2   Patterns of Police Corruption

Pattern	Acts	Degree of Organization
Corruption of authority	Free meals, liquor, discounts, rewards	None
Kickbacks	Money, goods, and services from those who serve clients of the police	High
Opportunistic theft	Thefts from arrestees, victims, crime scenes, and unprotected property	None
Shakedowns	Money, goods, or other valuables from criminals or traffic offenders	None
Protection of illegal activities	Protection money from vice operators or companies operating illegally	Often high
Fixes	Quashing of prosecution proceedings or disposing traffic tickets; fixers could be on payroll	Medium, fixers, could be on payroll
Direct criminal activities	Police officers engaged in such crimes as burglary, robbery, etc.	Low, small groups
Internal payoffs	Sale of work assignment, off-days, evidence and promotions	Low to high; depending other forms of corruption present

Source: Tom Barker, *Police Ethics: Crisis in Law Enforcement* (Springfield, IL: Charles C. Thomas, 1996), Table 7-1, 38.

The Trouble With Gratuities

One of the most perplexing areas of police deviance concerns gratuities. A **gratuity** is the acceptance of something of value, such as coffee, meals, discount-buying privileges, free admission to athletic or recreational events or movies, gifts, and small rewards. Most commonly it is coffee, beverages, or meals free or at reduced cost. Gratuities do not seem to be harmful, and they are often offered under the friendliest of circumstances. A beer "on the house" is, for many young people, an indication of their social worth, that they are valued by their friends and colleagues. Yet an officer who accepts gratuities may unknowingly undermine the legitimacy of his or her police department, endanger a future promotion, and possibly lose the job. Though acceptance of gratuities is a common practice in many police departments, it is considered to be unethical by the International Association of Chiefs of Police. Although many departments have an explicit policy that precludes accepting gratuities, these policies are frequently ignored by officers. Many police managers view violations of such policies to be a minor problem and may not enforce departmental regulations against them.

Although a police officer may enjoy gratuities at first, they have a way of unpleasantly complicating life. For example, in a survey of citizens in Reno, Nevada, a majority of citizens polled did not think police should accept any gratuities. Almost half of the respondents stated that if they provided a gratuity they would expect special consideration (e.g., extra patrol, warning instead of citation if stopped for traffic violation) by police officers (Sigler and Dees 1988).

Business owners may offer gratuities in order to encourage the police to spend more time at their establishment. Assume, for example, that an officer goes to the same restaurant every day to eat because a free meal is provided. The value of the meals, over a month's time, is equal to about $180. The restaurant owner likes having police officers around because she thinks it will decrease the likelihood of a robbery or unruly customers. However, if the owner offered to give the officer $180 in cash every month to spend the equivalent amount of time at the restaurant, the officer would probably not accept the money, and the police department would most certainly consider the acceptance of money to be a more serious problem than acceptance of the free meals. But there is no real difference in the two acts; both involve giving something of value for the express purpose of obtaining a private service—extra police protection or preferential treatment—from a public official.

Deleon-Granados and Wells (1998) explored this gratuity exchange principle in a medium-sized midwestern city. An outcome of the acceptance of gratuities is that the business offering the "perk" receives a disproportionate amount of police service, compared to businesses that do not engage in such behavior. After all, in order to receive a free cup of coffee, the officer has to actually be at that location to receive it. Therefore, businesses that provide gratuities to police receive additional police presence, service, and safety compared to their counterparts. Their unique research found, perhaps not surprisingly, that officers were much more likely to be observed at establishments offering gratuities than of those that did not. This raises ethical issues regarding whether police presence should (in any part) be linked to whether the business provides "free stuff" to police officers.

Deviant Officers

Police officers vary in their vulnerability to corruption. Most do not become involved in corrupt activities. They are morally committed to their work and are not psychologically capable of illegal activity. Only a small percentage become "bent" to the extent that they commit illegal activity. What should society think about those who do?

One of the more important insights into police corruption was presented by the Knapp Commission, which conducted an investigation into the activities of the New

olice Department in the late 1960s and early 1970s. Inside Policing 8.2 pro-
ummary of its findings, which remain comprehensive and influential.

Policing 8.2   The Knapp Commission

The Knapp Commission was established in May 1970 by Mayor John V. Lindsay as a result of an article that appeared in the *New York Times* on April 25, which stated that there was widespread corruption in the New York City Police Department. The commission was given the task of determining the extent and nature of police corruption. Judge Whitman Knapp was appointed to head the investigation, which issued its final report in 1972.

The investigation found corruption to be widespread in the police department and many officers, both investigators and patrol officers, to be involved. Corruption was most extensive among investigators (what the commission called plainclothes officers) in the area of gambling. The plainclothes officers participated in what was known as a "pad." For example, each illegal gambling establishment in a precinct would contribute a certain amount of money (as much as $3,500 per establishment once or twice a month) to the officers. The total amount collected would be divided among the officers, each one receiving his "nut" (which was usually $300 to $400 per month, but at least one precinct had a "nut" of $1,200 per officer). Newly assigned officers had to wait two months before receiving a "nut," but all plainclothes officers who left the precinct were given two months' severance pay.

Corruption in the narcotics area was less organized but was also extensive. Many of the payments came from "shakedowns" of narcotics dealers. Such payments were known as "scores"; the highest payoff uncovered was $80,000. There was some evidence to suggest that such large payments to police officers were not uncommon. [Since the 1980s, corruption scandals in police departments have been primarily related to narcotics].

Other plainclothes officers not involved in gambling and narcotics were engaged in other corrupt activities. They attempted to obtain money by engaging in "shakedowns" of the criminals with whom they interacted, for example, auto thieves.

Uniformed patrol officers did not receive the large sums of money that went to plainclothes officers, but many patrol officers were involved in corrupt activities. Some participated in small gambling "pads" and often collected money from construction sites, bars, grocery stores, parking lots, and other business establishments. They could also get money from traffic violators, tow trucks (for business given to the company), prostitutes, and defendants who wanted their court cases "fixed." These types of businesses were subject to a number of city laws, which, if violated, could result in a fine. In order to get around some of these laws, patrol officers were paid to "look the other way." Most often, the payoffs were $20 or less, but many officers were able to collect a large number of such payoffs in a month, adding substantially to their salary.

Ranking officers, sergeants, lieutenants, and even others above this level, participated in corrupt activities, but the evidence was difficult to obtain, above the level of lieutenant. This is because when ranking officers were involved they used a "bagman," usually a patrol officer, to collect the payoffs. He received a percentage of the payoff. If he was discovered, he had to be willing to take the fall.

Although the Knapp Commission was careful to point out that not all police officers in New York City were corrupt, those who were not aware of the corruption problems and, for the most part, did nothing about them.

Source: Adapted from Knapp Commission, *Report on Police Corruption* (New York: George Braziller, 1972), 1–11.

Of particular importance in the inset is the description of grass-eaters and meat-eaters. **Grass-eaters** are police officers who accept graft when it comes their way but do not actively solicit opportunities for graft. **Meat-eaters** are officers who actively solicit opportunities for financial gain and are involved in more widespread and serious corruption (Knapp Commission on Police Corruption 1972).

A casual reader might think that meat-eaters are a more serious problem than grass-eaters. They certainly commit more serious crimes. Yet that is not so. The Knapp Commission found that the grass-eaters were a more significant problem. They outnumbered meat-eaters by a considerable margin, and even though they did not solicit illegal opportunities, they took advantage of them when opportunity provided. Their illegal involvement created a "wall of silence" behind which meat-eaters could operate with impunity. The problem confronting efforts to clean up corruption, the commission found, was the **code of silence,** which they could not penetrate. The code of silence is the secrecy that line-level officers maintain about their activities, both from the public and from police administrators.

Barker (1996) expanded the Knapp Commission's typology of deviant officers, identifying five types. *White knights* are totally honest and may take an extreme stance in ethical issues. These officers are in the minority and are not deviant. *Straight-shooters* are honest but willing to overlook some of the indiscretions of other officers. They suffer in silence or seek out corruption-free assignments. *Grass-eaters* engage in corrupt activities if the opportunity arises. *Meat-eaters* actively seek out opportunities for corruption. Finally, *rogues,* at the far end of the scale, are considered an aberration even by meat eaters. They engage directly in criminal activities and in high-visibility shakedowns of citizens.

The Persistence of Corruption

Corruption has been and continues to be one of the most frequent problems faced by police departments in the United States. In describing early twentieth-century America, Fogelson says:

> The police did not suppress vice; they licensed it. From New York . . . to San Francisco, and from Chicago . . . to New Orleans . . . , they permitted gamblers, prostitutes, and saloon keepers to do business under certain well understood conditions. These entrepreneurs were required to make regular payoffs [to the police]. (1977, 32)

Consider the New York City Police Department. It was found to have serious corruption problems in 1895 (by the Lexow Committee), in 1900 (by the Mazet Committee), in 1913 (as a result of the Curran investigations), in 1932 (by the Seabury Committee), in 1942 (as a result of the Amen investigation), and in 1952 (by the Brooklyn Grand Jury) (Caiden 1977, 159). The Knapp Commission followed with a fresh new corruption exposé in the 1970s. In the mid-1980s, the department was rocked by the Buddy Boys scandal ("Drug Corruption . . ." 1986, 1). In 1993 the Mollen Commission noted widespread drug extortion among members of the 75th Precinct.

New York City has a large police department, with approximately 38,000 officers. It is unreasonable to assume on the one hand that all these officers will be honest, or on the other that any particular incident indicates that the entire department is tainted. Yet New York displays the persistence of corruption that characterizes many American police departments, large and small.

It is remarkable that many police departments have been as successful as they have at controlling corruption problems. As Walker (1984) observed, in the 1800s corruption was the business of many police departments. Today, although many have periodic scandals, they are usually less pervasive than in the past. Generally, present-day investigations tend to uncover only a small number of deviant police officers. They rarely uncover all the corrupt officers, nor do they reveal the officers who know what is taking place and say nothing.

Why does corruption continue to recur in police departments? There are essentially four reasons: First, police officers are very powerful. By virtue of their authority they encounter widespread opportunities for corruption. They are constantly exposed to situations in which the decisions they make can have a positive or negative impact on a person's freedom and well-being. Citizens may try to influence this discretion by offering free coffee and meals, money, sex, property—any item of value that will result in a favorable decision. Sometimes an offer can be extraordinarily tempting. The Knapp Commission identified payoffs as high as $80,000 in drug cases, and that was in the late 1960s. Once officers begin to accept payoffs, they may become "addicted"—that is, they begin to depend on the extra income and spend accordingly.

Second, the community and political environment are influential in establishing attitudes toward corrupt activities. Corruption in other government agencies, among prominent politicians, and in the business world enables police officers to rationalize their own behavior. Murphy and Caplan make this point in the following statement:

> Operating in this larger environment, it is not surprising that police become cynical about their work and feel that "nothing is on the level." When they meet citizens from every walk of life who are willing to pay them to overlook the law . . . some officers come to see themselves as "operating in a world where [money is] constantly floating about, [and they would be] . . . stupid and . . . fainthearted . . . not to allow some of [that money] to stick to their fingers." (1991, 248)

In police departments there are often many standards of behavior for officers to follow. In fact, there are so many standards that it is difficult to adhere to all of them. This multiplicity is also true of society in general. There are many laws, some of which are often violated by citizens, particularly traffic laws. Officers see instances of such behavior all around them, in both the public and private sector, among both the poor and the rich. Many officers even come to believe that if they are to be good police officers (e.g., to help people, maintain order, keep citizens from being afraid, make arrests, ensure a successful prosecution), they have to violate some of the rules they are supposed to follow.

Third, there is widespread tolerance among citizens for some kinds of police deviance. Citizens encourage the police to violate due process and citizens' rights in order to arrest felons. Television regularly displays "good" policing as that which inflicts pain on suspected felons, even when their guilt or innocence is as yet undecided. Businesses encourage small corruptions by giving officers gratuities and other perks for preferential treatment. In sum, it is unclear whether citizens always want police to "play fair," thus encouraging their moral and economic corruption.

Fourth, patterns of deviance can themselves become standards of behavior. Officers may be introduced by their training officers, for example, to restaurants that provide meals discounted for police. When standards encompass deviant behavior, line officers become secretive. Enormous pressure is put on all officers not to discuss police behavior outside police ranks. Even nondeviant officers will not break the code of silence for fear of reprisal. This belief can carry over to the chief executive and managers in the department. In addition, executives and managers may be blamed and lose their jobs if the deviance is exposed, even if they are not involved. Caiden (1977, 165) has identified characteristics of departments that have had widespread corruption problems. He refers to such departments as being systematically corrupt. These characteristics are presented in Inside Policing 8.3.

Inside Policing 8.3   Characteristics of Corrupt Police Departments

1. The department's professional code of ethics is contradicted in practice.
2. Police managers and officers encourage, aid, and hide illegal and unethical behavior.
3. Nonparticipants in corrupt activities are penalized because they do not receive any of the benefits of corruption, and they may have to endure the displeasure of corrupt officers.
4. When corrupt officers are investigated, they will be protected; or if they are found guilty of corrupt practices, they will not be punished severely.
5. Officers who do not like the corruption in the department have no one to assist them within the department, and if they complain to someone outside, they may not be believed.
6. Officers who consider exposing the corrupt practices of other officers may be intimidated, even terrorized, in order to "shut them up." In some cases, such officers may actually have to be protected from bodily harm.
7. The officers who are corrupt develop rationalizations for their behavior. These in-

clude the arguments that "everyone else is doing it," that others [attorneys and judges] are corrupt, that police officers deserve "something extra" because they risk their lives or because the public doesn't appreciate them and pay them enough.

8. Eventually corrupt officers accept their behavior as "normal," as a way of doing business in police work. If and when they are exposed, they may be genuinely surprised that their corrupt behavior is considered deviant. They may even argue that they are being unfairly singled out because such behavior is commonplace for many officers.
9. Those responsible for investigating corruption tend to suggest, in effect, that the corrupt officers are only a few "rotten apples."
10. Following a corruption scandal, efforts to reform the police department have only minimal influence in changing the attitudes of officers toward corruption, and the reforms are intended only to convince the public that something is being done to correct the problems.

Source: Adapted from G. E. Caiden, *Police Revitalization* (Lexington, MA: D.C. Heath and Company, 1977).

Caiden argues that real progress in dealing with corruption was made in the 1950s and 1960s because the police began to understand that the basic problem was systemic, not just the result of a few "rotten apples" (169–171). The **systemic theory of corruption** is that corruption stems from the nature of police work, and if anticorruption protocols are inadequate, corruption will spread throughout a police department. The **rotten-apple theory of corruption** is that corruption is limited to a small number of officers who were probably dishonest prior to their employment. The term *rotten apple* stems from the metaphor that a few rotten apples will spoil the barrel; in other words, a few bad officers can spoil a department. It was the most prevalent theory of corruption prior to the 1960s and 1970s. This explanation is compatible with the predispositional theory of police behavior. A systemic theory of corruption tends to support the sociological perspective of police behavior.

Caiden may be too optimistic about the extent to which police corruption has been controlled. The drug "wars" begun in the 1960s have significantly increased the opportunities for corruption, with the possibility of financial payoffs that far exceed other forms of corruption. And, there is some evidence that the rotten-apple theory is still influential. Dorschner's (1989) description of the Miami Police Department linked corruption to a rapid expansion in the number of personnel and an inadequate screening process. Yet, as he notes, the police department had extensive problems with political corruption even prior to its rapid expansion. Its political atmosphere provided the environment for the development of systemic corruption.

Some research has found support for the rotten-apple theory. Lersch and Mieczkowski (1996) suggested that particular kinds of officers are more likely to be involved in questionable use-of-force incidents. They noted that 7 percent of sworn personnel in a large southeastern police department accounted for over one-third of the use-of-force complaints from 1991 to 1994. These officers were younger than their peers and had less experience, and the incidents were more likely to result from proactive contacts with citizens.

The Prevalence of Police Deviance

It is difficult to gauge the extent of deviant behavior among the police. This is not surprising: People who commit illegal acts tend to keep them secret. In police departments, where peer support and loyalty are high, assessments of the extent of deviance will always be difficult and are likely to underestimate its true extent.

A few authors have assessed the prevalence of deviance in particular departments. Barker (1994) looked at five categories of deviance in what he called "South City." Using a questionnaire, he asked each officer to judge the extent to which individuals in the department engaged in, or had engaged in, each of the five patterns. His findings are presented in Table 8.3.

Table 8.3   Perceived Extent of Police Occupational Deviance in South City

Deviant Pattern	Perceived Extent (%)
Sleeping on duty	39.58
Police brutality	39.19
Sex on duty	31.84
Police perjury	22.95
Drinking on duty	8.05

A review of this table shows that deviance in some categories was quite high. Four of 10 officers were thought to be sleeping on duty by their fellow officers and the same number to be indulging in police brutality. Slightly over one in five were believed to engage in police perjury. It is not reasonable to assume that these numbers represent police everywhere: Generalizing from one research setting to the entire population is bad science. Barker's findings, however, because they represent a seemingly normal department, are troubling. And, there is evidence that other forms of deviance may be widespread.

Crank (1998) discussed two surveys to assess police deviance in one department in Illinois (Knowles 1996) and two in Ohio (Martin 1994). His overview presents two types of deviance not yet considered: racial and sexual harassment. Crank's discussion extends Sykes' (1996) analysis of these two surveys. Officers were asked in both surveys whether they had seen another officer harass a citizen based on race or gender (see Inside Policing 8.4).

Inside Policing 8.4   Perceived Extent of Racial and Sexual Harassment in Illinois and Ohio

Racial Harassment

One out of every four officers in the Illinois survey (26.2 percent) and one in six in the Ohio survey (14.9 percent) stated that they had witnessed racial harassment by their fellow officers. If one extrapolates these percentages back to the base populations from which they were drawn, one can appreciate the magnitude of the harassment and its potential for the alienation of minority citizens. According to the 1994 crime reports, Ohio has 18,721 sworn "local," or municipal, officers, and Illinois, outside the Chicago Police Department (which declined to participate in the Illinois survey), has 16,131. Certainly not all of these officers are active on the streets. One can allow a generous estimate that 50 percent of a police department is in administrative support. This reduces the street-officer populations to 9,360 in Ohio and 8,065 in Illinois. Calculating the population estimates from these reduced figures, one arrives at 2,113 instances of police harassment in Illinois and 1,395 in Ohio in a single year's time, excluding the largest department in either state. Thus, in the two typical states, dominated by smaller police departments but with a sprinkling of big-city departments as well, police racism is by any reasoning a pervasive phenomenon. Nor are these figures in some way inflated by groups that harbor ill will against the police: Keep in mind that these are numbers that the police are reporting about themselves.

Sexual Harassment

Six percent of the officers surveyed in Ohio stated that they had witnessed sexual harassment, and 8.6 percent of the respondents in Ohio agreed. These percentages sound relatively small until one recognizes that they are incidents where one officer (1) witnesses another officer display this behavior, and (2) is willing to tell an interviewer he or she witnessed the behavior. In other words, situations where officers won't come forward, and incidents where officers acted alone—more likely occurrences—aren't reported. Extrapolating back to the original populations, one begins to appreciate the magnitude of this activity. These numbers represent approximately 1,520 incidents in Ohio and 3,175 in Illinois, not including estimates by the state police or the city of Chicago.

Source: Adapted from J. Crank, *Understanding Police Culture* (Cincinnati: Anderson Publishing Co., 1998), 212.

When these three surveys are considered together, they present a disturbing picture of police deviance. In all three departments, the findings suggested that deviance was widespread. In all three, there appeared to be strong peer support to cover up deviant activities. Finally, all three departments were typical—none had a particularly negative record of police corruption. These findings, when compared with findings presented in the previous discussion, suggest that police corruption may indeed be diverse in its types, widespread across departments, and hidden behind the secretive screen of department loyalties.

Police Sexual Misconduct

The research cited above provides insight into a poorly understood area of police behavior in sexual deviance. A similar view is provided by Kappeler (1993). In a review of litigation on police sexual misconduct, he found that the police lost 69 percent of the cases brought against them, a high number when one considers the average 10 percent for all other forms of civil litigation.

Many police have argued that much of this litigation stems from misunderstandings about police work. Many departments tend to justify sexual misconduct as a boys-will-be-boys attitude among their male personnel (see Sapp 1994). Others argue that sexual activity is consensual, a view sharply challenged by Kraska and Kappeler (1995). The image of consensuality, they contend, is an illusion. The substantial power differential that police have in exchanges with the public results in an image of consensuality, when in fact sexual relations may stem from a citizen's fear of the consequences if she or he fails to submit to an officer's implied or direct demands.

Measuring the extent of police sexual misconduct is very difficult because, similar to other forms of deviance, the behavior is rarely reported. However, McGurrin and Kappeler (2002) attempted to generate a greater understanding of the prevalence and characteristics of these incidents by examining newspaper articles over an eight-year period. They found 501 reported cases of police sexual misconduct. The majority of incidents involved rape/attempted rape or sexual assault/attempted sexual assault. Yet they found over 8 percent of cases involved sexual abuse of a child. Officers tended to be male, on-duty, municipal line officers, with a modal age of 25. Numerous officers had been previously convicted of sex offenses. Over 40 percent of the incidents commenced with a traffic stop, and about half of these involved physical force. Of those that involved force, over half indicated that the officer's physical presence was sufficient to coerce the victim. Police departments attempting to deter this type of deviance must make efforts to encourage citizen complaints about misbehavior and take these complaints very seriously.

Drug Wars and Police Deviance

Deviance is a persistent problem. Unfortunately, some forms of deviance may be intensifying. Drug corruption, in many different forms, appears to be on the increase among police in the United States. As a new century begins, the United States is deeply involved in a drug war, carried out by municipal police, federal police, and military troops, aimed at controlling the use and distribution of illegal narcotics. The authors are not going to debate the merits of drug legalization here—suffice it to say that there are persuasive arguments for both the legalization and the criminalization of illegal substances. Our concern is with the negative impact of the current drug interdiction on U.S. police.

Kappeler, Sluder, and Alpert (1994) identify four types of corruption:

(1) When officers use drugs, it is called **use corruption.** Kraska and Kappeler (1988) found that about 20 percent of the officers they studied in a medium-size department admitted that they smoked marijuana.

(2) **Economic corruption** occurs when officers seek personal gain. Officers might, for example, keep drug money confiscated from dealers.

(3) **Police violence** is the use of force to extract confessions.

(4) The **subjugation of a defendant's rights,** to obtain a drug conviction includes police perjury and "flaking," or the planting of drugs on a suspect by a police officer in order to acquire evidence.

A relatively recent tool available to police in the war on drugs is *civil asset forfeiture*. Simply stated, assets may be forfeited to the government if they were used to facilitate a crime or if they are the fruits of criminal behavior. Regarding drug trafficking, assets often include homes, property, vehicles, boats, and aircraft. These assets, or the proceeds from their sale, are (in part) given back to the police to fund their enforcement activities. Additionally, since the legal proceedings are civil rather than criminal in nature, acquisition of assets is quite easy. Civil proceedings often do not afford the property owner the same due process protections as are found in criminal court, and property may be seized without notice or hearing. Further, the standard of proof for civil forfeiture is preponderance of evidence, which is significantly lower than proof beyond a reasonable doubt (Lersch 2002). In practice, assets are forfeited even when the property owner is not charged with a crime, or when an agreement not to contest civil forfeiture is exchanged for dismissal of criminal charges.

This process presents a sticky situation for police organizations, particularly if they derive a significant proportion of their budget from civil asset forfeiture. Lersch (2002) indicates that the property (and not the criminal) may become the true target of investigation. Thus, even though individual officers may not derive direct compensation from these forfeitures, they may benefit from organizational rewards (such as promotion) for making the "big score." It is important to note that civil asset forfeiture is in no way indicative of deviant or corrupt behavior. However, it is important to note that this tool can provide fertile grounds and a legal rationale for engaging in drug-related corrupt behavior by street-level officers.

Use of violence and subjugation of rights have been described by Crank and Caldero (1999) as **noble-cause corruption,** which occurs when police abandon ethical and legal means in order to achieve so-called good ends (see also Delattre 1996, 190–214; Klockars 1983). Both violence and subjugation of rights may be used by police who are more concerned about the "noble cause"—getting bad guys off the street, protecting victims and children—than about the morality of "technically" legal behavior. Noble-cause corruption occurs when officers break the law to do something about the drug problem.

According to Crank and Caldero, noble-cause corruption and economic corruption may be inversely related. They argue that police departments during the twentieth century have been somewhat successful in combating economic corruption among the police. This success has been accomplished in large part by instilling police with a mission to do something about crime. The consequence is that, as police economic corruption decreases, noble-cause corruption seems to increase. Police today may be less likely to commit crime for personal gain, but they also may be more likely to commit crime in order to carry out ends-oriented justice.

Two examples of drug corruption occurred in Philadelphia and Miami in the mid-1980s, as described in Inside Policing 8.5. In these examples, the reader can see the presence of both economic and noble-cause corruption. The severity of some of the corrupt activities, including murder, emphasizes why drug corruption has emerged as a critically important problem in law enforcement.

Inside Policing 8.5   Examples of Corruption

Corruption in Miami

In the 1980s, the Federal Bureau of Investigation began a broad investigation into the Miami Police Department. The FBI believed that there was pervasive corruption in the department. This concern was the result of numerous incidents of illegal police activity, including charges of police officers murdering drug dealers, firing their weapons at drug dealers' homes, conspiring to sell police radios and badges, and being involved in "big time dope dealing." The unit charged with narcotics enforcement had $150,000 and several hundred pounds of marijuana stolen from its safe. By the mid-1980s, 75 police officers had been arrested. The most infamous of these were the seven officers called the Miami River Cops. Three of them were charged with the murder of a drug dealer. All were charged with being involved in selling drugs, including selling drugs from their police cars.

Corruption in Los Angeles

In the late 1990s, the LAPD became embroiled in a corruption scandal that seems as if it could have been written for a Hollywood screenplay. In 1998, officials discovered approximately six pounds of cocaine was missing from the department's evidence room. The investigation focused on Officer Rafael Perez of the Rampart District of the LAPD, and the investigation expanded to the CRASH (Community Resources Against Street Hoodlums) Unit in that district. In a plea agreement, Perez provided investigators with information on widespread corruption within the LAPD. Crimes committed by officers included theft, selling drugs, robbery, perjury, and planting evidence and guns on unarmed citizens to secure conviction in court. For example, Perez testified that he and his partner, Officer Nino Durden, shot Javier Francisco Ovando in the head and chest, only to discover the suspect to be unarmed. The officers planted a "drop gun" on Ovando, who was later convicted and sentenced to 23 years for assaulting the officers. Criminal wrongdoings by officers were even linked to executives at Death Row Records, a popular west-coast label who specialized in "gangsta" rap. Over time, about 70 officers were implicated in the scandal, cases produced by the CRASH Unit were thrown out, and the reputation of the LAPD was significantly tarnished.

Source: *Sources:* Adapted from *Law Enforcement News*, 1985, October 21: 1 and 5; Boyer, P. J. 2001. "Bad Cops," *New Yorker* (retrieved September 1, 2004 from http://www.newyorker.com/fact/content/?010521fa_FACT).

Since the Knapp Commission proceedings, New York has experienced another cycle of corruption and scandal. This time, however, the problems were different from those cited in preceding scandals because of their linkages to drugs. The Mollen Commission, established in 1993, also sought to identify the presence of police corruption. Kappeler, Sluder, and Alpert summarize the commission's findings as follows:

Witnesses told the commission of systematic corruption that was strikingly similar to the [mid-1980s] Buddy-Boys case. Michael Dowd, a former officer in the 75th precinct, bluntly described how he and his peers routinely robbed crime victims, drug dealers, and arrestees of money, drugs, and anything else of value. Dowd revealed that many officers were receiving substantial sums for protecting illegal drug operations; Dowd's share amounted to $4,000 each week. Dowd told of officers routinely using drugs and alcohol while on duty, informing the commission that he regularly snorted lines of cocaine off the dashboard of his police cruiser. Other witnesses told of extensive use of excessive force culminating in the physical and psychological brutalization of many citizens. (Frankel and Stone 1993)

Summary

Universalistic perspectives of police behavior are sociological, psychological, and organizational. Two particularistic theories are predisposition and socialization. The former explains police behavior in terms of the type of individual employed, while the latter is concerned with what happens after employment. Some of the more important studies of police behavior were made by Westley, Banton, Skolnick, Wilson, Muir, and Brown. These studies tend to support the importance of the socialization theory, because the influential factors that they have identified are all related to the experiences of being a police officer. More recent research has suggested that predispositional factors are also important.

There have also been attempts to relate police behavior and discretion to a number of specific variables: organizational, neighborhood, situational, and officer. Legal factors tend to determine the decision to arrest, but extralegal factors also sometimes play a role. In spite of a great deal of research on extralegal factors, their actual contribution to the use of police discretion is unclear.

Police deviance includes abuse of authority and deviant acts (contrary to standards) committed in the normal course of the job. The latter can be misconduct in terms of rules or corruption, such as accepting gratuities, which the authors consider inappropriate. Police corruption is marked by periodic scandals in some departments, and corruption involving drugs appears to be increasing.

Critical Thinking Questions

1. Do you believe the predispositional or socialization theories offer greater explanatory value in understanding police behavior? Why?

2. What contributions have Westley, Skolnick, Wilson, Muir, Brown, and Rubinstein made to understanding police behavior? How do the perspectives of these authors differ?

3. Explain Van Maanen's socialization.

4. Discuss organizational (departmental) and neighborhood variables considered important in police behavior.

5. What are meat-eaters and grass-eaters? Which is the greater problem in controlling police corruption? Why?

6. What is a police gratuity? Is acceptance of gratuities a serious problem for American police? Why (not)?

7. What is meant by noble-cause corruption? Provide an example.

8. Why do you think certain police departments (e.g., the New York City Police Department) have a long legacy of corruption? Do you think some departments are "more corrupt" than others? If so, why do you believe this to be the case?

References

Adams, T. 1990. *Police Field Operations*. Englewood Cliffs, NJ: Prentice-Hall.

Alpert, G., and Smith, W. 1998. "Developing Police Policy: An Evaluation of the Control Principle." In L. Gaines and G. Cordner (eds.), *Policing Perspectives: An Anthology*, pp. 353–362. Los Angeles: Roxbury Publishing Co.

Auten, J. 1988. "Preparing Written Guidelines." *F.B.I. Law Enforcement Bulletin* 57: 1–7.

Baker, M. 1985. *Cops: Their Lives in Their Own Words*. New York: Simon and Schuster.

Banton, M. 1965. *The Policeman in the Community*. New York: Basic Books.

Barker, T. 1994. "Police Deviance Other than Corruption." In T. Barker and D. Carter (eds.), *Police Deviance*, 3rd ed., pp. 123–138. Cincinnati: Anderson Publishing.

——. 1996. *Police Ethics: Crisis in Law Enforcement*. Springfield, IL: Charles Thomas Publishers.

Barker, T., and Carter, D. 1994. "A Typology of Police Deviance." In T. Barker and D. Carter (eds.), *Police Deviance*. 3rd ed., pp. 3–12. Cincinnati: Anderson Publishing.

Bayley, D. H., and Bittner, E. 1989. "Learning the Skills of Policing." In R. G. Dunham and G. P. Alpert (eds.), *Critical Issues in Policing: Contemporary Readings*, pp. 87–110. Prospect Heights, IL: Waveland Press.

Black, D. 1973. "The Mobilization of Law." *Journal of Legal Studies, The University of Chicago Law School* 2: 125–144.

——. 1976. *The Behavior of Law*. New York: Academic Press.

——. 1980. *The Manners and Customs of the Police*. New York: Academic Press.

Brooks, L. W. 1989. "Police Discretionary Behavior: A Study of Style." In R. G. Dunham and G. P. Alpert (eds.), *Critical Issues in Policing: Contemporary Readings*, pp. 121–145. Prospect Heights, IL: Waveland Press.

Brown, M. K. 1981. *Working the Street: Police Discretion*. New York: Russell Sage Foundation.

Caiden, G. E. 1977. *Police Revitalization*. Lexington, MA: D. C. Heath.

Caldero, M. 1997. "Value Consistency Within the Police: The Lack of a Gap." Paper presented at the annual meeting of the Academy of Criminal Justice Sciences, Louisville, KY, March.

Caldero, M., and A. P. Larose. 2003. "Value Consistency Within the Police: The Lack of a Gap." *Policing: An International Journal of Police Strategies and Management* 24(2): 162–180.

Carter, D. 1985. "Police Brutality: A Model for Definition, Perspective, and Control." In A. S. Blumberg and E. Niederhoffer (eds.), *The Ambivalent Force*, pp. 321–330. New York: Holt, Rinehart and Winston.

Chambliss, W. 1997 "Policing the Ghetto Underclass: The Politics of Law and Law Enforcement." In B. Handcock and P. Sharp (eds.), *Public Policy: Crime and Criminal Justice*, pp. 146–165. Upper Saddle River, NJ: Prentice Hall.

Cordner, G. 1989. "Written Rules and Regulations: Are They Necessary?" *F.B.I. Law Enforcement Bulletin* July: 17–21.

——. 1995. "Community Policing: Elements and Effects." *Police Forum* 5: 1–8.

Crank, J. P. 1996. "The Construction of Meaning During Training for Parole and Probation." *Justice Quarterly* 31(2): 401–426.

——. 1998. *Understanding Police Culture*. Cincinnati: Anderson Publishing.

Crank, J., and Caldero, M. 1999. *Police Ethics: The Corruption of Noble Cause*. Cincinnati: Anderson Publishing.

Crank, J., and Langworthy, R. 1991. "An Institutional Perspective of Policing." *Journal of Criminal Law and Criminology* 8: 338–363.

Davis, K. C. 1969. *Discretionary Justice*. Baton Rouge, LA: Louisiana State University Press.

Delattre, E. J. 1996. *Character and Cops: Ethics in Policing*, 3rd ed. Washington, D.C.: American Enterprise Institute.

DeLeon-Granados, W., and W. Wells. 1998. " 'Do You Want Extra Police Coverage with Those Fries?' An Exploratory Analysis of the Relationship Between Patrol Practices and the Gratuity Exchange Principle." *Police Quarterly* 1: 71–85.

Dorschner, J. 1989. "The Dark Side of Force." In R. G. Dunham and G. P. Alpert (eds.), *Critical Issues in Policing: Contemporary Readings*, pp. 250–270. Prospect Heights, IL: Waveland Press.

"Drug Corruption—The Lure of Big Bucks." 1986. *Law Enforcement Journal* December 30: 1, 4.

Engel, R. S. 2001. "The Supervisory Styles of Patrol Sergeants and Lieutenants." *Journal of Criminal Justice* 29: 341–355.

Engel, R. S., and E. Silver. 2001. "Policing Mentally Disordered Suspects: A Reexamination of the Criminalization Hypothesis." *Criminology* 39: 225–252.

Fletcher, C. 1990. *What Cops Know*. New York: Pocket Books.

——. 1991. *Pure Cop*. New York: St. Martin's Press.

Fogelson, R. M. 1977. *Big-city Police*. Cambridge, MA: Harvard University Press.

Frankel, B. 1993. "Ex-NYC Officer Tells Stark Tale of Cops Gone Bad." *USA Today* September 28: A-3.

Frankel, B., and Stone, A. 1993. "You'll Be in the Fold by Breaking the Law." *USA Today*, September 30: A1, A2.

Friedrich, R. J. 1980. "Police Use of Force: Individuals, Situations, and Organizations." *Annals* 452: 82–97.

Gallup Organization. 1999. *Racial Profiling Seen as Widespread, Particularly Among Young Black Men*. Hyperlink <http://www.gallup.com/poll/releasees/pr991209.asp www.gallup.com/poll/releasees/pr991209.asp>, accessed 11-21-01.

Goldstein, H. 1977. *Policing a Free Society*. Cambridge, MA: Ballinger Books.

Goldstein, J. 1998. "Police Discretion Not to Invoke the Criminal Justice Process: Low Visibility Decisions in the Administration of Justice." In G. F. Cole and M. G. Gertz (eds.), *The Criminal Justice: Politics and Policies*, 7th ed., pp. 85–103. Belmont, CA: Wadsworth Publishing Co.

Greene, J. R., and Klockars, C. B. 1991. "What Police Do." In C. B. Klockars and S. Mastrofski (eds.), *Thinking About Police: Contemporary Readings*, pp. 273–285. New York: McGraw-Hill.

Grennan, S. A. 1988. "Findings on the Role of Officer Gender in Violent Encounters with Citizens," *Journal of Police Science and Administration* 15: 78–85.

Guyot, D. 1991. *Policing as Though People Matter*. Philadelphia: Temple University Press.

Harris, D. A. 1999. "The Stories, the Statistics, and the Law: Why 'Driving While Black' Matters." *Minnesota Law Review*, 84: 265–326.

Herbert, S. 1997. *Policing Space: Territoriality and the Los Angeles Police Department*. Minneapolis: University of Minnesota Press.

Hopkins, E. J. 1931. *Our Lawless Police*. New York: Viking.

Hurst, Y. G., and Frank, J. 2000. "How Kids View Cops: The Nature of Juvenile Attitudes Toward the Police." *Journal of Criminal Justice* 28: 189–202.

Johnson, D. R. 1981. *American Law Enforcement*. St. Louis: Forum Press.

Kania, R. 1972. "Police Corruption in New York City." In A. W. Cohn and E. C. Viano (eds.), *Police Community Relations: Images, Roles, Realities*, pp. 330–341. New York: J. B. Lippincott.

——. 1988. "Should We Tell the Police to Say 'Yes' to Gratuities?" *Criminal Justice Ethics* 7: 37–48.

Kappeler, V. E. 1993. *Critical Issues in Police Liability*. Prospect Heights. IL: Waveland Press.

Kappeler, V. E., Sluder, R. D., and Alpert, G. 1994. *Forces of Deviance: Understanding the Dark Side of Policing*. Prospect Heights, IL: Waveland Press.

Klinger, D. 1994. "Demeanor on Crime: Why 'Hostile' Citizens Are More Likely to Be Arrested." *Criminology* 32–3: 475–493.

Klockars, C. 1983. "The Dirty Harry Problem." In C. Klockars, ed., *Thinking About Police: Contemporary Readings*, pp. 428–438. New York: McGraw-Hill.

Knapp Commission on Police Corruption. 1972. *Report on Police Corruption.* New York: George Braziller.

Knowles, J. J. 1996. *The Ohio Police Behavior Study.* Columbus, OH: Office of Criminal Justice Services.

Kraska, P. B., and Kappeler, V. E. 1988. "Police On-duty Drug Use: A Theoretical and Descriptive Explanation." *American Journal of Police* 7 (1): 1–28.

——. 1995. "To Serve and Pursue: Exploring Police Sexual Violence Against Women." *Justice Quarterly* 12-1: 85–112.

——. 1999. "Exploring Police Sexual Violence Against Women." In L. K. Gaines and G. W. Cordner (eds.), *Police Perspectives: An Anthology*, pp. 324–341. Los Angeles: Roxbury Publishing.

Langan, P. A., Greenfeld, L. A., Smith, S. K., Durose, M. R. and Levin, D. J. 2001. *Contacts Between Police and the Public: Findings from the 1999 National Survey.* Washington, D.C.: Bureau of Justice Statistics.

Langworthy, R. H. 1985. "Wilson's Theory of Police Behavior: A Replication of the Constraint Theory." *Justice Quarterly* 3: 89–98.

Lersch, K. 2002. "All's Fair in Love and War" In K. Lersch ed., *Policing and Misconduct.* Upper Saddle River, NJ: Prentice Hall.

Lersch, K. M., and Feagin, J. R. 1996. "Violent Police-citizen Encounters: An Analysis of Major Newspaper Accounts." *Critical Sociology* 22: 29–49.

Lersch, K., and Mieczkowski, T. 1996. "Who Are the Problem-prone Officers? An Analysis of Citizen Complaints." *American Journal of Police* 15(3): 23–44.

Manning, P. 1980. *The Narc's Game.* Cambridge, Mass: MIT Press.

——. 1989. "The Police Occupational Culture in Anglo-American Societies." In L. Hoover and J. Dowling (eds.), *Encyclopedia of Police Science.* New York: Garland Publishing.

——. 1997. *Police Work: The Social Organization of Policing*, 2d ed. Prospect Heights, IL: Waveland Press.

Martin, C. 1994. *Illinois Municipal Officers' Perceptions of Police Ethics.* Chicago: Illinois Criminal Justice Information Authority, Statistical Analysis Center.

Martin, S. E. 1980. *Breaking and Entering: Policewomen on Patrol.* Berkeley: University of California Press.

——. 1989. "Female Officers on the Move?" In R. G. Dunham and G. P. Alpert (eds.), *Critical Issues in Policing: Contemporary Readings*, pp. 312–330. Prospect Heights, IL: Waveland Press.

——. 1990. *On the Move: The Status of Women in Policing.* Washington, D.C.: Police Foundation.

Mastrofski, S. 1981. "Policing the Beat: The Impact of Organizational Scale on Patrol Officer Behavior in Urban Residential Neighborhoods." *Journal of Criminal Justice* 4: 343–358.

Mastrofski, S., and Ritti, R. 1996 "Police Training and the Effects of Organization on Drunk Driving Enforcement." *Justice Quarterly* 13(2): 291–320.

Mastrofski, S., and Uchida, C. 1993 "Transforming the Police." *Crime and Delinquency* 30-3: 330–358.

Mastrofski, S. D., Worden, R. E., and Snipes, J. B. 1995. "Law Enforcement in a Time of Community Policing." *Criminology* 33: 539–563.

Maurer, M. 1993. *Young Black Men and the Criminal Justice System: A Growing National Problem.* Washington, D.C.: The Sentencing Project. U.S. Government Printing Office.

McGurrin, D., and V. E. Kappeler. 2002. "Media Accounts of Police Sexual Violence." In K. Lersch ed., *Policing and Misconduct.* Upper Saddle River, NJ: Prentice Hall.

McNulty, E. 1993 "Generating Common Sense Knowledge Among Police Officers." *Symbolic Interaction* 17: 281–294.

Muir, W. K. 1977. *Police: Streetcorner Politicians.* Chicago: University of Chicago Press.

Murphy, P. V., and G. Caplan. 1991. "Fostering Integrity." In W. A. Geller, ed., *Local Government Police Management,* pp. 239–271. Washington, D.C.: International City Management Association.

Niederhoffer, A. 1967. *Behind the Shield.* New York: Doubleday and Co.

Novak, K. J., Frank, J., Smith, B. W., and Engel, R. S. 2002. "Revisiting the Decision to Arrest: Comparing Beat and Community Officers." *Crime and Delinquency* 48: 70–98.

Paoline, E. A. 2003. "Taking Stock: Toward a Richer Understanding of Police Culture." *Journal of Criminal Justice* 31: 199–214.

Parks, R. 1982. "Citizen Surveys for Police Performance Assessment: Some Issues in Their Use." *Urban Interest* 4: 17–26.

"Philadelphia Unveils Anti-corruption Plan." 1985. *Law Enforcement News* October 21: 1, 5.

Plitt, E. 1983. "Police Discipline Decisions." *Police Chief* March: 95–98.

Punch, M. 1985. *Conduct Unbecoming: The Social Construction of Police Deviance and Control.* London: Tavistock Publications.

Ramirez, D., McDevitt, J., and Farrell, A. 2000. A Resource Guide on Racial Profiling Data Collection Systems: Promising Practices and Lessons Learned. Washington, D.C.: Bureau of Justice Assistance.

Reuss-Ianni, E. 1983. *Two Cultures of Policing.* New Brunswick, NJ: Transaction.

Riksheim, E. C., and Chermak, S. M. 1993. "Causes of Police Behavior Revisited." *Journal of Criminal Justice* 21: 353–382.

Rokeach, M., Miller, M., and Snyder, J. 1971. "The Value Gap Between Police and Policed." *Journal of Social Issues* 27-2: 155–171.

Rubinstein, J. 1973. *City Police.* New York: Farrar, Straus, and Giroux.

Sampson, R., and Lauritsen, J. 1997. "Racial and Ethnic Disparities in Crime and Criminal Justice in the United States." In M. Tonry, ed., *Ethnicity, Crime, and Immigration: Comparative and Cross-National Perspectives,* pp. 311–374. Chicago: University of Chicago Press.

Sapp, A. D. 1994. "Sexual Misconduct by Police Officers." In T. Barker and D. Carter (eds.), *Police Deviance,* 3d ed., pp. 187–200. Cincinnati: Anderson Publishing.

Sherman, L. W. 1978. *Scandal and Reform: Controlling Police Corruption.* Berkeley: University of California Press.

——. 1985. "Causes of Police Behavior: The Current State of Quantitative Research." In A. S. Blumberg and E. Niederhoffer (eds.), *The Ambivalent Force,* 3rd ed., pp. 183–195. New York: Holt, Rinehart and Wilson.

——. 1988. "Becoming Bent." In A. Elliston and M. Feldbert (eds.), *Moral Issues in Police Work,* pp. 253–265. Totowa, NJ: Rowan and Allanheld.

Sigler, R. T., and Dees, T. M. 1988. "Public Perception of Petty Corruption in Law Enforcement," *Journal of Police Science and Administration* 6: 14–19.

Skolnick, J., and Bayley, D. 1986. *The New Blue Line: Police Innovation in 6 American Cities.* New York: The Free Press.

Skolnick, J. H. 1966. *Justice Without Trial.* New York: John Wiley and Sons.

Smith, D. 1987. "Police Response to Interpersonal Violence: Defining the Parameters of Legal Control." *Social Forces* 65: 767–782.

——. 1980. "The Neighborhood Context of Police Behavior." In A. Reiss and M. Tonry (eds.), *Communities and Crime.* Chicago: University of Chicago Press.

Spitzer, E. 1999. *The New York City Police Department's "Stop and Frisk" Practices: A Report to the People of the State of New York from the Office of the Attorney General.* Albany, NY: New York Attorney General's Office, <http://www.oag.state.ny.us/press/reports/stop_frisk/stop_frisk.html http://www.oag.state.ny.us/press/reports/stop_frisk/stop_frisk.html>, accessed 5-19-03.

Sykes, G. 1986. "Street Justice: A Moral Defense of Order-Maintenance Policing." *Justice Quarterly* 3(4): 467–512.

——. 1996. "Police Misconduct: A Different Day and Different Challenges." *Subject to Debate: A Newsletter of the Police Executive Research Forum* March, April. 10-3: 1, 4–5.

Teplin, L. A. 1984. "Criminalizing Mental Disorder: The Comparative Arrest Rates of the Mentally Ill." *American Psychologist* 39: 794–803.

Van Maanen, J. 1973. "Observations on the Making of Policeman." *Human Organization* 32, 407–418.

——. 1978. "The Asshole." In P. K. Manning and J. Van Maanen (eds.), *Policing: A View From the Streets,* pp. 221–238. Santa Monica, CA: Goodyear Publishing.

Visher, Christie A. 1983. "Gender, Police Arrest Decisions, and Notions of Chivalry." *Criminology*

Walker, S. 1984. "Broken Windows' and Fractured History: The Use and Misuse of History in Recent Patrol Analysis." *Justice Quarterly* 1: 57–90.

Walsh, W. F. 1986. "Patrol Officer Arrest Rates." *Justice Quarterly* 3: 271–290.

Wasserman, R. 1992. "Government Setting." In G. Garmire, ed., *Local Government Police Management,* 2nd ed. Washington, D.C.: International City Management Association.

Westley, W. A. 1953. "Violence and the Police," *American Journal of Sociology* 59: 34–42.

——. 1970. *Violence and the Police.* Cambridge, MA: MIT Press.

Wilson, J. Q. 1968. *Varieties of Police Behavior.* Cambridge, MA: Harvard University Press.

Wilson, J. Q., and Kelling, G. 1982. "Broken Windows: The Police and Neighborhood Safety." *Atlantic Monthly* 127: 29–38.

Worden, R. 1989. "Situational and Attitudinal Explanations of Police Behavior: A Theoretical Reappraisal and Empirical Assessment." *Law and Society Review* 23: 667–711.

Suggested Websites for Further Study

Police Subculture in Australia
http://www.ozemail.com.au/~wtmp/cop.html
The International Association of Chiefs of Police
http://www.theiacp.org
The Christopher Commission
http://www.hrw.org/reports98/police/uspo73.htm
Racial Profiling Data Collection Resource Center
http://www.racialprofilinganalysis.neu.edu
Contacts Between Police and Public: Findings from the 1999 National Survey
http://www.ojp.usdoj.gov/bjs/pub/pdf/cpp99.pdf
"Broken Windows" and Police Discretion (by George Kelling)
http://www.ncjrs.org/pdffiles1/nij/178259.pdf ✦

Force and Coercion

Chapter Outline

Key Terms

abuse of authority	deadly force
coercion	excessive force
command voice	firearms training
continuum of force	fleeing-felon rule

Key Terms (continued)

less-than-lethal weapons	psychological force
mere presence	third-degree
officer survival	use of force
physical force	verbal force
police brutality	

Police departments represent the legitimate force of government in internal state matters. Their authority is derived primarily from law. The police are charged with enforcing substantive criminal laws, such as laws against robbery and rape, and they are expected to operate within procedural laws, such as having probable cause to make an arrest and advising suspects of their rights. In addition to these legal guidelines, the police are guided by departmental policies and procedures.

The **use of force** is central to the police craft. Police carry the legal authority to maintain order, to gain compliance, and to kill if need be. They are granted this authority in order to shield victims from dangerous felons; to control unruly, hostile, or physically abusive citizens; and to protect immediate threats to human life.

Use of force is the most controversial aspect of the legal authority of the police. Yet its necessity is inescapable. It is a skill, which means that it is a means to an end—the preservation of orderly social relations as society perceives them. Consequently, police use-of-force in the United States should be considered in the broader context of how it contributes to democratic relations among citizens.

Where does the right to use force come from? How can society reconcile the use of force with the democratic principle of equality? In 1970 Bittner, briefly discussed in Chapter 1, provided important insights into the use of force. According to Bittner, the use of force can be justified in two ways. The first is self-defense: People can use force to defend themselves if they have a realistic belief that they are in danger. The second is based on the inherent police power to address matters of health, welfare, order, and safety; that is, the police are a "mechanism for the distribution of situationally justified force in society" (1995, 129).

Why does society need a police mechanism for the distribution of force? Historically, U.S. society has moved from the use of force to the use of democratic, rational processes for solving problems and disagreements among citizens. Yet it is impossible to abandon altogether the use of force in the pursuit of democratic justice. In order to preserve democratic processes, society grants to police an exclusive right that is not permitted to other citizens: the use of force to achieve democratic ends.

Many students of police behavior think that "force" is violent behavior by the police. That is incorrect. Force, or **coercion,** occurs any time the police attempt to have citizens act in a particular way. Force can be very mild, such as a simple request to see a driver's license. Even a request, though, is a use of force because it carries with it the authority of the state to back up the request with greater force, and the implicit recognition, by citizen and officer alike, that "no" is not an acceptable answer. Because the police carry the governmental authority to intervene in a citizen's activities, all police-citizen interactions carry elements of force, even when officers are not consciously trying to be forceful. Consequently, this section will discuss police-citizen interactions in order to shed light on social contexts in which the use of force emerges.

Police use of force and its justifications are determined by two factors. The first is formal training according to the state code and limits on the use of force determined by local departmental regulations and by due process constraints. The second factor is local police cultures, which represent understandings of police territorial responsibilities, danger, and the control of unpredictable situations.

This chapter will then turn to excessive use of force. At what point does force become excessive, even brutal? Many observers contend that the excessive use of force is increasing in the United States today, although others believe that police are encountering increasing problems that require it. The chapter will review the literature on the overuse of force and then discuss its most controversial aspect, the use of deadly force.

Police-Citizen Interactions

How often do encounters between police and citizens become situations in which force is used? Information is provided by a number of scholarly studies and by a questionnaire provided by the Bureau of Justice Statistics.

Context of Force

One of the most extensive and important studies of police-citizen encounters was conducted by Reiss (1967). He reported on more than 5,000 observations of police-citizen interactions that took place in areas that were racially diverse and had different crime rates. About 86 percent of the encounters were reactive, resulting from citizen requests. About 14 percent of the encounters were proactive, initiated by police officers. Police were more likely to experience antagonism or injury in proactive encounters, primarily because, unlike in reactive situations, the person or persons they stopped did not request assistance from the police.

Reiss also found that approximately 60 percent of citizens behaved in either a detached or civil manner toward police, about 20 percent were agitated (mildly upset), and about 10 percent were antagonistic. Almost all such antagonism came from suspects. Officers behaved in a businesslike or routine manner in about 74 percent of the encounters, were personal (jovial or humorous) in about 15 percent, and were hostile or derisive in about 11 percent. Police were more likely to be hostile or derisive when citizens were agitated or antagonistic. Reiss also noted that police behavior was closely related to citizen behavior; if a citizen was antagonistic, the officer would most likely respond in the same manner. The importance of a citizen's attitude in the exercise of police discretion was noted in Chapter 8.

Of the 5,000-plus encounters, the police made only 225 arrests, less than 5 percent. About 50 percent of the persons arrested openly challenged police authority; the challenge, however, was more likely to be verbal than physical. Of those arrested, 98 (42 percent) were treated "firmly," while only 21 (9 percent) were handled with "gross" force. These figures mean that in all the police-citizen encounters observed, only about 2 percent involved any type of physical force. None involved the use of lethal, or deadly, force.

Reiss' research suggested that police-citizen encounters were most likely to result from citizen requests for help, and that, in most cases, police treated citizens in a businesslike or routine manner. Most encounters were like those of any business providing a service to a client; they involved exchanges of information in a friendly or civil manner. Police were rarely antagonistic toward citizens, and when they were, it was typically in response to citizen-initiated hostilities. Overall, police officers infrequently made arrests, and when they did, they rarely used physical force.

Another important study of police-citizen encounters was conducted by Sykes and Brent (1983), who analyzed more than 3,000 police-citizen encounters. They identified several different types of situations. Three of the most important are listed below:

1. *Hazardous*: Calls that officers believe are potentially risky and personally rewarding but possibly depressing. Examples: assaults and purse snatchings.

2. *Annoying*: Calls that are neither risky nor personally rewarding but possibly depressing. Examples: unwanted guests, loud parties, disturbances involving children, and failure to pay a bill.

3. *Boring*: Calls that are neither risky nor rewarding but possibly slightly depressing for some officers. Examples: taking reports and persons drinking.

Sykes and Brent found that the most common initial police response was definitional, occurring about 83 percent of the time. Police almost always spoke first when dealing with citizens; thus, they had the opportunity to direct the discussion with their questions. The second most common initial response was imperative, occurring in about 17 percent of encounters. Researchers did not find the coercive response to be used initially in any police-citizen encounter. It was eventually used, however, if citizens did not cooperate with the officers. Even then, the most common officer response was to repeat the initial approach one or more times in order to obtain cooperation.

From Sykes and Brent's research, it is clear that officers first try the definitional approach, and if a citizen does not cooperate, will frequently repeat it. If cooperation is not forthcoming, or the citizen's behavior becomes threatening or too abusive, officers will become imperative and coercive. What is not clear, however, is how this sequence should proceed in a given situation. Should the department provide specific guidance, or should it be left to an officer's discretion? For instance, if one officer uses the definitional approach several times with an uncooperative citizen, is this officer "better" than one who uses it only once before making threats or using force? How can one judge which approach is better?

Bayley (1986) studied police interactions with citizens in Denver. He focused on two types of situations in which officers made tactical choices about appropriate actions—domestic disturbances and traffic stops. This discussion will focus only on the traffic stops because of recent changes in the manner in which many police departments respond to domestic violence calls. Bayley divided police-citizen interactions into three stages: The *contact stage* describes tactical choices made when officers first approach citizens. The *processing stage* is concerned with decisions made during the interaction between contact and exit. The *exit stage* describes strategies used to end contact with the citizen.

Bayley identified several contact actions by police officers in traffic stops. In some situations, more than one action was used. These actions are listed in Table 9.1. Many are similar to the findings of Sykes and Brent.

Table 9.1 Actions at a Traffic Stop	
Initial Actions of Police Officers at Traffic Stops	
Action	**Use (%)**
1. Asked driver for documents	88.4
2. Explained reason for stop	28.0
3. Asked driver if he knew reason for stop	25.6
4. Had driver leave the vehicle	20.1
5. Allowed driver to leave vehicle	16.5
6. Asked passengers for documents	15.9
7. Allowed or ordered passengers out of vehicle	9.2
8. Ordered driver and/or passengers to remain in vehicle	4.2
Processing Actions of Police Officers at Traffic Stops	
Action	**Use (%)**
1. Checked whether vehicle and driver were wanted	59.1
2. Discussed nature of traffic violation	27.4
3. Searched vehicle from outside or inside	25.0
4. Gave roadside sobriety test	12.8
5. Body-searched driver and/or passenger	7.3
6. Questioned drivers and/or passengers	3.7
Exit Actions of Police Officers at Traffic Stops	
Action	**Use (%)**
1. Issued traffic citation	43.3
2. Gave admonishment or warning only	20.7
3. Arrested driver (DUI or other offense)	15.8
4. Released without admonishment or warning	13.8
5. Issued citation and gave warning	12.8
6. Completed "contact" card (recorded information about driver)	9.8
7. Transported or arranged transportation for driver	2.4
8. Impounded vehicle	1.8
9. Insisted driver proceed on foot	1.8
10. Arrested passenger	1.8

Totals do not add up to 100% because more than one alternative was used in many traffic stops. In addition, some categories have been combined.

Source: D. H. Bayley. 1986. "The Tactical Choices of Police Patrol Officers." *Journal of Criminal Justice* 14: 329–348.

Asking drivers or passengers questions or for documents (definitional approach) was the initial police action in a large majority of cases. Giving orders (imperative approach) was also sometimes used. Bayley's findings revealed the complicated nature of police-citizen transactions. In the three areas—contact, processing, and exit—officers used at least 28 different actions. By carefully reviewing the first actions, one can see how the use of coercion is part and parcel of police work, even when not directly used. The initial acts all involve various levels of coercion, from the relatively mild, "asked passengers for documents," which is not coercive, but carries the potential for a stronger response, to the more significant "ordered driver to remain in vehicle." Under processing actions, coercive behavior includes "body search." Exit actions range from the mildly coercive "gave admonishment" to the quite serious "arrested driver." Moreover, the original stop itself represents a seizure, an aggressive intervention of the state into the affairs of citizens.

This research gives some understanding of how practical applications of force are integral to police work. This realization may be uncomfortable for citizens. Yet, if they fail to see how force is intertwined with the daily routines of police work, they will not understand what the police are about.

Bayley and Garofalo (1989) studied 62 police officers in New York City to determine the extent to which they used some type of violence, including verbal aggression. They identified 467 potentially violent situations, of which 168 were proactive. Of these situations, although reports suggested possible violence, such as a fight or the reported presence of weapons, only 78 (17 percent) actually involved visible conflict when the police arrived. In 70 of these cases, the violence was not physical but involved only verbal threats or gestures. Police used physical force against citizens 37 times, and citizens used it against the police 11 times. Police force was almost always limited to "grabbing and restraining." Police use of deadly force was not observed.

Most recently, Terrill (2001) studied police use-of-force in 3,544 police encounters with suspected offenders/disputants in Indianapolis and St. Petersburg. He found that police used **verbal force** in nearly 60 percent of encounters, pat-downs and handcuffing in about 10 percent of encounters, and greater levels of force in about 5 percent of encounters.

These studies indicate that, while police work rarely involves the use of significant levels of violence, the use or threat of force is ever-present. The use of violence is one of the most important areas of study. The potential consequences to both the victim and officer can be severe, including emotional trauma and the possibility of either physical injury or death, particularly when the police use physical force.

The Police-Public Contact Survey

In 1995 the Bureau of Justice Statistics prepared the first national questionnaire designed to assess overall use of force by the police during police-citizen contacts (Greenfeld, Langan, and Smith 1997). The Police-Public Contact Survey was conducted of representative American households, which were asked about their contacts with the police during the 12 months prior to the interview. A total of 6,421 households were interviewed over three periods (May, June, and July 1996), with one-third interviewed during each monthly period. The authors looked at the prevalence of citizen contacts with the police, reasons for citizen contacts, and police actions during citizen contacts. It estimated from the interviews that 44.6 million citizens had face-to-face contact with a police officer during the previous year. In most instances, citizens initiated the contact. An estimated 1.2 million people were handcuffed. Although this number may seem large, it represents only 2.6 percent of the citizens police came into contact with. Survey findings are presented in Table 9.2.

Table 9.2   Highlights From the Police-Public Contact Survey

Prevalence of Citizen Contact With Police

- An estimated 44.6 million persons (21 percent of the population age 12 or older) had a face-to-face contact with a police officer during 1996.

- Men, whites, and persons in their 20s were the most likely to have face-to-face contact. Hispanics and African-Americans were about 70 percent as likely whites.

- Nearly three in 10 persons with a contact in 1996 reported multiple contacts with police during the year.

Reasons for Citizen Contact With Police

- An estimated 33 percent of residents who had contact with police had asked for or provided the police with some type of assistance.

- An estimated 32 percent of those who had contact with police had reported a crime, either as a victim or a witness.

- Reporting traffic tickets and being involved in traffic accidents were common reasons for police contacts.

- Just under one-third of those contacts were police initiated; for most, nearly one-half, the citizen initiated the contact. (The remainder were unclear from the data.)

- Teenagers were most likely to have a police-initiated contact, and persons age 60 or older were the likely.

- Persons age 60 or older were the most likely to have a citizen-initiated contact with the police, and teenagers were likely.

- Hispanics had a higher level of police-initiated contacts and a lower level of self-initiated contacts.

Police Actions During Contacts With Citizens

- An estimated 1.2 million persons were handcuffed during 1996, or about 0.6 percent of the population, aged 12 or older.

- Men, minorities, and persons under the age of 30 represented a relatively large percentage of those handcuffed.

- An estimated 500,000 persons (0.2 percent of the population aged 12 or older) were hit, held, pushed, choked, threatened with a flashlight, restrained by a police dog, threatened or actually sprayed with chemical or pepper spray, threatened with a gun, or experienced some other form of force. Of those, about 400,000 were also handcuffed.

Source: Adapted from Lawrence Greenfeld, Patrick Langan, and Steven Smith, *Police Use of Force: Collection of Statistical Data* (Washington, D.C.: Bureau of Justice Statistics, 1997).

As has been shown, the actual or potential use of force is a common occurrence in police-citizen encounters. Some uses of force are mild and may not be noticed by citizens or police officers. In conclusion, there are a wide variety of uses of force to control and direct different kinds of circumstances.

In Voices From the Field, James Fyfe discusses his perspective on use-of-force training. Dr. Fyfe, a former professor and retired NYPD lieutenant, is widely regarded as the nation's leading authority on police use of force.

Voices From the Field

James J. Fyfe
Deputy Commissioner for Training
New York City Police Department

Question: What are some of the guiding principles of training officers in the use or force?

Answer: Training officers to use force should be based on the principle that, since the primary police responsibility is to protect life, they should use as little force as possible, and should do everything reasonably possible to avoid using force at all.

This training should not be confused with the legal standard used by prosecutors in deciding whether to bring criminal charges against officers who have used force. The criminal law test typically is whether, at the instant they used force, officers reasonably feared for their safety. This standard distinguishes only between use of force that is criminal and use of force that is not, but is an inadequate measure of acceptable police conduct. Like doctors, truck drivers, and professors, police officers can do many unprofessional and inappropriate things that do not reach the level of crime. In good police agencies, therefore, the test of whether police have used force reasonably involves examining whether, from the time they became aware that they were likely to encounter someone in an adversarial situation until they actually came face-to-face with the person, officer tried to structure their meeting in ways that made use of force less likely. This is not as confusing as it sounds. In plainer English: a police shooting that occurs because an officer unnecessarily forced a confrontation and then had to shoot his way out of it is unacceptable even if it is not criminal.

Thus, training must emphasize tactics. We do this by encouraging officers to make certain that, before contacting potentially violent persons or groups, that they have enough help on the scene to deter attacks on officers. Officers must also be trained to position themselves in ways that let adversaries know that they can't win any confrontation, and that they have no choice but to submit to the police. For example, we train officers to respond to robbery calls by stopping their cars out of sight of the scene; by approaching covertly on foot; by taking cover behind parked cars or other objects; and by waiting to surprise suspects when they are totally exposed as they walk out of their victims' doors. When a shouted police command causes such bad guys suddenly to find that they are in the gunsights of officers they can hardly see, they virtually always surrender, so that no force is necessary to take them into custody.

This kind of bloodless intimidation is extremely effective with rational offenders who want to live another day. Not all the potentially violent people police contact are so rational, however. When dealing with the mentally ill or emotionally disturbed—something NYPD officers do once every 7.3 minutes—officers must try to avoid intimidation, because it is likely only to make things worse. Consequently, officers must be trained to avoid frightening emotionally disturbed persons. They must also be trained to avoid cultural taboos that may anger, or create confrontation with, members of some new immigrant groups.

Training must be precise, and must put flesh also put flesh onto the vague phrases—like *reasonable and necessary*—found in most legal standards. In most cases, police departments do this by adopting some sort of scale of escalating force, and matching levels of force to the provocation or condition involved. The one included in our NYPD training (see Table 9.3) tells officers that the only legitimate purpose of force is to stop the objectionable types of conduct listed in the scale's left column.

This scale does not mention police canines. This is so because virtually none of our patrol officers are accompanied by dogs. But NYPD's canine officers are trained that dogs—who are easily capable of causing serious injury every time they bite someone—rate only slightly below deadly force on this scale. Our canines, therefore, are deployed only in extremely serious situations that might otherwise make it necessary to use firearms.

Force training must continue throughout officers' careers and, as I have suggested, should focus primarily on teaching officers to avoid force whenever possible. This is no easy task—it's very easy to teach officers to use their batons, sprays, and guns. But the well-trained, *really good street cops*—the role models for their colleagues—almost always can get the job done without having to use any of these devices or techniques. When the circumstances make this impossible, such officers' training causes them instinctively to use no more than the appropriate degree of force from this scale. ✦

The Use of Force

This section will look at two different but related ways police departments provide direction in the use of force. These ways are formal training in levels of force and informal, cultural standards about the use of force in routine encounters.

Training

Officers are trained to use a **continuum of force** (see Inside Policing 9.1), from the least to the greatest, to match the intensity of the suspect's resistance (Terrill 2001). Ideally an officer employs the least force necessary to solve a problem, restrain a suspect, or control a situation. Skolnick and Fyfe's (1993) description of levels of force is presented below. Table 9.3 presents the use-of-force continuum currently in place in the New York City Police Department.

1. *Mere presence.* At the lowest level of force, the simple presence of an officer is usually enough to control most situations. **Mere presence** operates on the assumption that the visible authority of the state is sufficient to deter criminal wrongdoing. As a wide body of research has shown, however, the passive authority of the state alone is insufficient to deter all illegal behavior or gain compliance from everyone. As Wilson (1968) observed 30 years ago, officers have to get personally involved—they have to develop personal skills in the use of coercion in order to control some kinds of problems.

2. *Verbalization.* This stage is sometimes called **verbal force.** When officers speak, they are taught to do so persuasively. Officers verbalize their commands in "adult to adult" communications. That is, they communicate on the presumption that they are talking to adults who will understand and comply with their requests. *Example*: "Sir, would you please step out of the car."

3. *Command voice.* **Command voice** is more vibrant and is issued in the form of an order. Skolnick and Fyfe (1993) provide the following example: "Sir, I asked you for your vehicle papers once. Now I'm *telling* you to give them to me *now.*"

4. *Firm grips.* Physical grasps of the body direct a suspect when and where to move. They are intended to control a suspect's physical movements but not intended to cause pain. They can be restraining, holding, or lifting. *Example*: Two persons are attempting to fight. An officer grabs one person to hold him back, or two or more officers working as a team may separate the two persons or "swarm" one person.

5. *Pain compliance.* A suspect's compliance is gained by causing pain. Various techniques are taught that enable officers to cause pain without lasting injury. *Example*: A person the officer is attempting to handcuff pulls away, and the officer twists the suspect's arm in order to put on the cuffs.

6. *Impact techniques.* Impact techniques involve physical contact between the suspect and an officer's body or nonlethal device. They are intended to knock down or incapacitate a dangerous suspect who has not responded to other techniques. Included among impact techniques are increasingly popular less-than-lethal weapons, including bean bags shot from a shotgun and OC pepper spray. *Example*: A suspect under the influence of drugs resists the police so vigorously that she cannot be controlled. She is struck with a baton, or sprayed in the face, or stunned with an electrical weapon such as the Taser. More technologically advanced **less-than-lethal weapons** are currently being developed. For example, sticky foams may be fired from a large gun from 35 feet away. They act like contact cement, sticking the suspect to the floor or to whatever he or she touches. "Dazzler" light and laser weapons use brilliant pulses of light to distract, disorient, and control violent suspects and potentially violent crowds (Miller 1995, 485–486).

7. *Deadly force.* The highest level is force that is capable of killing a suspect. The purpose is usually to incapacitate a suspect who presents an immediate and potentially deadly threat to another person, not to kill the suspect. Death, however, is a frequent by-product. Skolnick and Fyfe (1993) describe three uses of **deadly force**: the carotid hold (or sleeper hold), which induces unconsciousness in a suspect and can be deadly in practice; the bar arm-control hold, in which the forearm is squeezed against the neck to cut off the flow of air; and the use of a gun. *Example*: A suspect vigorously resists arrest, and the officer gets behind him and "chokes him out" in order to gain control of the suspect and place him in handcuffs.

As discussed earlier, there are often differences of opinion concerning what is and is not appropriate when police force is used. One important factor in determining appropriate use is the actual or perceived threat posed by the person resisting police authority. This threat potential is assessed not only in terms of the nature of the threat or actual resistance but also by the physical size of the person in question and whether he or she is under the influence of drugs or alcohol or might have a weapon. In addition, any prior knowledge about the person and the potential for danger would be important. Also, if the police officer is biased or has had "dangerous" experiences with members of a minority group, then certain types of minority persons (e.g., young, black men) may be perceived to be potentially more dangerous than other people.

Inside Policing 9.1	Use of Force During Arrest

An officer can use whatever force is reasonable and necessary to make the arrest, to overcome resistance, and to prevent escape. The key is that force has to be reasonable. A suspect may legally counter the use of excessive force with force sufficient to fend off the officer's use of force. Further, the officer, the police chief, and the city may be sued. When a police officer encounters resistance, he or she is taught to use escalating levels of force until resistance is overcome. The officer must keep in mind that increasing levels of force have to be reasonable—a police officer cannot meet mild resistance with deadly force. The purpose of force is to effect an arrest. If an officer encounters a suspect who resists, the officer should not necessarily back down.

While it might make sense to back away and wait for assistance, the law says the officer does not lose his or her right to self-defense by using force to effect the arrest, overcome resistance, or prevent the suspect's escape. In almost every case, the suspect's actions will indicate the level of force to be used to arrest him. When a suspect arms himself with a deadly weapon, it is generally reasonable to respond with deadly force.

Even if an arrest is later found to be unlawful, a suspect still has a legal obligation to submit to arrest. A citizen may only resist an excessive use of force. If a citizen resists an arrest, lawful or not, the suspect has committed a separate crime of resisting arrest.

Source: Adapted from Mark R. Miller, *Police Patrol Operations* (Placerville, CA: Copperhouse Publishing, 1995), 298–299.

Areas of Training

The training regimen for the use of force is elaborate. Particular areas of training related to the use of force are discussed below.

Firearms. For most police trainees, the most popular training is in firearms (Marion 1998). It is frequently the highlight of the academy, although continuing (in-service) **firearms training** for veteran officers has been less systematic and probably less effective (Morrison 2003). Traditional firearms training is gradually giving way to situationally-based training, which includes simulated firearms scenarios and the use of mobile targets. "Shoot-don't shoot" scenarios are used to teach officers to exercise restraint when using deadly force. Among the most popular of these are FATS (Firearms Training Systems) and PRISim (Professional Range Instruction Simulator), which present trainees with scenarios whose outcomes are manipulated by a specialist. Scenarios are presented whose outcomes are uncertain and typically call for the unholstering of a weapon. Many outcomes, however, do not call for the discharge of a weapon, and officers learn to react quickly in order *not* to shoot. When they shoot, a laser mounted on the weapon shows the number of target hits and locations of the hits.

OC spray. Officers are required to train in the use of OC (oleoresin) spray. Some departments require that trainees submit to being sprayed; in others, being sprayed is voluntary. OC's location on the force continuum also varies. In the continuum presented above, it is located at level 6 as an impact technique. Some departments, however, consider it less powerful than a baton. The North Carolina Justice Academy, for example, locates OC spray just above mace and below hard hands, the PR-24 (baton), and swarming techniques (Lamb and Friday 1997). According to this perspective, officers are taught to use OC spray when they think a person is about to become belligerent, in order to prevent the escalation of force (Trimmer 1993).

Table 9.3   The New York City Police Department Scale of Escalating Force

Provocation or Condition	Appropriate Force Response
Imminent threat of death or serious physical injury.	Deadly force: Usually the firearm.
Threatened or potential lethal assault.	Drawn and/or displayed firearm
Physical assault likely to cause physical injury.	Impact techniques: Batons, fists and feet.
Threatened or potential physical assault likely to cause physical injury.	Pepper Spray.
Minor physical resistance: grappling, going limp, pulling or pushing away, etc.	Compliance techniques: Wrestling holds and grips designed to physically overpower subjects and/or to inflict physical pain that ends when the technique is stopped and that causes no lasting injury.
Verbal resistance: Failure to comply with directions, etc.	Firm grips on arms, shoulders, etc., that cause no pain, but that are meant to guide people (e.g., away from a fight; toward a police car).
Refusal to comply with requests or attempts at persuasion (see below).	Command voice: Firmly given directions (e.g., "I asked for your license, registration, and proof of insurance, Sir. Now I am telling you that if you don't give them to me, I will have to arrest you."
Minor violations or disorderly conditions involving no apparent threats to officers or others.	Verbal persuasion: Requests for compliance (e.g., "May I see your license, registration and proof of insurance, Sir?").
Orderly public places.	Professional presence: The officer on post deters crime and disorder; the Highway Unit deters speeding.

Self-defense. Officers are taught a variety of techniques for self-defense. Marion (1998) describes self-defense training as follows:

> Recruits may be taught some "come-along" or "hand holds" (Peak 1993) as well as pressure points. . . . By the end of the University Academy, recruits learn the Infra-Orbital [under the base of the nose], the Mandibular Angle [behind the ear] and the Hypoglossal [under the jaw] pressure points (Faulkner 1994). They also learn take-downs and proper handcuffing techniques. The force continuum is stressed in self-defense training, where cadets are taught to use no more force than necessary to subdue a subject. But once again, officer safety is the primary concern of all the training. (1998, 68)

Officer survival. Central to many training programs are classes on **officer survival.** Such classes deal with the major risks faced by police officers—officer stress, suicide, and threats. Officers are taught how to deal with the murder of a partner, about the police officers' memorial in Washington, D.C., and about the federal pension their spouse will receive if they are killed. They are exposed to the bureaucratic paperwork associated with death. Extremely violent encounters, though rare in practice, are central to training. Officer survival is also a component of many other classes. Classes on police procedure instruct officers that concerns about safety provide a legal justification for a wide variety of actions, including pat-downs. Finally, it is not unusual for officers to see training films emphasizing the hazards of police work.

One type of nonlethal force available to the police is the baton.

Flashlights. A flashlight is infrequently thought of as a weapon, yet many officers use flashlights in just that way. For example, about two-thirds of 365 impact weapon incidents in the Los Angeles County Sheriff's Department over a five-year period involved flashlights rather than batons (Anderson 2003). As McEwen (1997) noted, policies on the use of flashlights are often ambiguous. Some departments provide policies forbidding the use of flashlights as weapons. When a flashlight is considered a weapon, it is regarded only in a backup capacity.

The policy in one department McEwen assessed stated that, "The department does not recognize the flashlight as a formal policy weapon." Recognizing that it may be needed in some circumstances, the policy further observed that "when a flashlight is utilized in an application of force, whether to restrain or to effect an arrest, or in defense against an attack, it will be considered a weapon and all requirements pertaining to the use of force and the reporting of such force will be applicable." McEwen concludes that flashlights will be used as less-than-lethal weapons and that policy needs to recognize this fact and bring flashlights under use-of-force policy (1997, 51).

Canines. An emerging area of interest in the use of force is the use of K-9 dog patrols. Many police departments use police canines for a number of purposes: to search for drugs, explosives, and individuals who might be trying to avoid or escape from the police, and to control individuals and crowds (Golden and Walker 2002). Many officers also believe that the use of dogs to search for suspects who might be armed reduces the possibility that the officers will be injured or killed. Although they are not trained to do so, some handlers permit their dogs to bite as a "reward."

The use of canines varies by department. Some departments do not recognize them as a level of force, others do. K-9's are listed by the North Carolina Police Department at a level just above swarm techniques and below deadly force (Lamb and Friday 1997). Campbell, Berk, and Fyfe (1998) argue that the widespread use of canines in some departments requires a revision in thinking about the use of force. In a study of the Los Angeles Police Department and the Los Angeles Sheriff's Department, they found that the use of canines was routine, and encounters often ended with bites, many serious. Inside Policing 9.2 describes the uses associated with canines.

Inside Policing 9.2   Canines and Police Use of Force

Should dogs be thought of as a kind of police use of force?

Campbell, Berk, and Fyfe argue that they should. The use of dogs is common. Moreover, dog bites are frequently severe. Consider the following observations:

> The data show that using police dogs as a means of force has been common in the Los Angeles area. From the middle of 1990 through the middle of 1992, LAPD's (Los Angeles Police Department) police dogs (which varied in number between 13 and 15) bit 44 percent of the 539 suspects they helped to apprehend. A total of 37 percent (n-86) were bitten badly enough that they were admitted to hospitals. As far as we have been able to determine, this was a greater number of hospitalizing injuries than was caused by all the noncanine officers in the department combined during the period. In 1990 alone, this bite-to-use ratio—the LAPD term for the percentage of persons bitten among those apprehended after canines had arrived at the scene—was 81 percent. For the LASD (Los Angeles Sheriffs Department), the bite-to-use ratio was 36 percent (119 bitten of 335 per-

sons apprehended) over the slightly different period we studied. No deaths have resulted in Los Angeles, but some victims were permanently disfigured, whereas others have experienced persistent physiological and/or psychological problems. Indeed, survivors of police shootings in Los Angeles (and the vast majority do survive) typically have injuries less severe and less enduring than are suffered by the LAPD's canine bite victims. (1998, 543)

The study observes that the use of canines frequently lacks the rigor of policy that accompanies the use of other kinds of less-than-lethal and lethal weaponry. When policies were in place, they were enforced in an incomplete and perfunctory way. Moreover, minority-group members suffered a disproportionate number of dog bites, raising the specter that they might be used in a discriminatory way (see also Beers 1992).

The authors concluded that because of the hazardous and injurious consequence of dog bites, the implementation and review of department policy regarding canines should be conducted in a rigorous manner with other uses of force.

Police Culture and the Use of Force

The use of force is also affected by informal standards of police culture. "Culture" refers to what Reuss-Ianni calls "precinct street cop culture," which carries the "values, and thus the ends, towards which officers individually and in task groups strive"

(1983, 8). Although each department has its own culture, Crank (1998) has identified a wide variety of cultural themes, or building blocks of culture, that are so similar across departments that police officers generally can be described as participating in a police culture. As building blocks, these themes have two features. First, they are areas of activity. Second, according to McNulty (1994), they also carry with them ways of commonsense thinking about the activity. Several cultural themes affect how police officers use force. These themes are summarized in Inside Policing 9.3.

Inside Policing 9.3   Cultural Themes Affecting Police Use of Force

1. **Force**. Force is a theme as well as a subject of formal police training. Whether legal, questionable, or illegal, force is bound up in the day-to-day doing of police work. . . . Department policy reflects administrative rather than street imperative and is typically viewed as more organizational "bullshit." It's not that cops don't believe in the necessity of due process in a democracy or the imperatives of the administration, nor is it that, by nature, cops are authoritarian. It's just that when things get wild, when an officer has to maintain the edge and is burning with energy and fear, other considerations become irrelevant. (1998, p. 65)

2. **Stopping Power**. Stopping power is the symbolic and real importance of guns (hand guns) to the police. Guns are central to police culture. Police officers have been raised in families where guns are normal fare, and guns symbolize their sense of traditional individualism. Guns bring to the foreground the idea of personal responsibility. They represent the apex of an officer's street skills and are used at the defining moments of a police officer's career: confrontation with an dangerous and armed offender.

3. **Edge Control**. Edge control means that an officer (1) makes sure that he or she has more firepower, skills, training, or backup than the bad guys and (2) brings decisive force to bear on encounters with bad guys. The idea of always bringing a little more force to bear on encounters than is actually needed is described by C. Shearing and R. Erickson as "taking a four-foot leap over a three-foot ditch" (1991, p. 492).

4. **Deterrence.** Police view deterrence in a specific way. Their ability to halt an adversary comes not by using threats or reason but by using force. "Deterrence is immediate, slamming, final. Deterrence doesn't threaten to bring about punishment; deterrence ends the threat. Nothing else works; all else is weakness" (Crank 1996, 254).

5. **Anticipating Danger.** The anticipation of danger, or the scenting of trouble, is central both to police training and to the police culture (Kappeler, Sluder, and Alpert 1994). Skolnick (1994) describes the anticipation of danger in terms of **symbolic** assailants, people who give signs that they may be dangerous because of their dress, the way they walk, bulges in their clothes that might indicate a weapon, and the way they talk. Officers are leery of individuals who display these indications of trouble. There may be *assailant geographies*, public and private places that show signs of being as potentially perilous, such as playgrounds that appear safe but are known as areas where drugs are exchanged.

These cultural themes are interrelated. For example, if the anticipation of danger is linked to deterrence, it is easy to see how police will sometimes react too forcefully before all information about the potentially dangerous nature of a suspect is known, especially if the suspect is acting in a hostile way. By carefully considering the various themes presented here, the reader can begin to understand how the difference between justified force and excessive force, so important in legal and administrative reviews of police behavior after an incident, is balanced by the ways street officers confront danger and gauge forceful responses.

Hunt (1985) has also described how police rely on informal, cultural standards in the use of force. By focusing too much on legal definitions of force, society tends to overlook the "understandings and standards police officers actively employ in the course of their work" (316). Hunt observed that police have *working notions of normal force,* which are standards of acceptable force learned on the street. They are different from what police learn in training; for example, that they should not hit a person on the head or neck because it could be lethal.

> On the street, in contrast, police conclude that they must hit wherever it causes the most damage in order to incapacitate the suspect before they themselves are harmed. New officers also learn that they will earn the respect of their veteran co-workers by not observing legal niceties in using force, but by being "aggressive" and using whatever force is necessary in a given situation. (1985, 319)

Force is normal, or acceptable, under two circumstances. First, it is normal because it is the natural outcome of strong, even uncontrollable, emotions normally arising from certain routine sorts of police activities. Second, it is justifiable if it establishes police authority in the face of a threat or is morally appropriate for the type of crime encountered by the officer. When officers use too much force, or when they do not use enough, they are the subject of reprimand, gossip, and avoidance. Hunt described how normal levels of force are learned in day-to-day practice and the psychological mechanisms that justify the use of force.

Use-of-Force Conflicts

On occasion, the use of force by police officers may conflict with community standards, legal factors, or departmental policy. These three types of conflicts are considered below.

Type 1: Conflicts with the community. In Type I conflicts, the law and departmental policy may consider the police use of force appropriate, but a substantial segment of the community does not. Such conflict occurs most often in a minority neighborhood. The relationship between police and some minority citizens may be one of suspicion and distrust, so when the police, particularly officers who are not members of that minority group use coercion, they have a substantial burden placed on them to prove that the use was appropriate. In these circumstances, incidents of force, even seemingly minor ones, feed into an accumulated reservoir of grievances in which any additional incident, however justified, can provoke community violence, rioting, and other antipolice activity.

Kappeler, Sluder, and Alpert (1994) describe a case of Type 1 conflict that occurred in Miami in 1979.

> On December 17, 1979, Arthur McDuffie, an African American, was riding his motorcycle on the streets of Miami, Florida. The police officers gave chase and [were] eventually joined by more than a dozen Miami patrol cars. Following a brief pursuit that allegedly reached speeds over one hundred miles per hour, McDuffie stopped his motorcycle. Officers converged on the scene, and at least six white of-

ficers jumped McDuffie. In a matter of minutes, McDuffie lay motionless on the ground with his head split open. He died four days later as a result of police-inflicted injuries. . . . As a result of inconsistencies uncovered by a departmental investigation, the officers were indicted for manslaughter and tried in Tampa. An all-white jury was selected to hear the charges; in May of 1980, the jury acquitted all of the officers.

As a result of the jury's verdict, "one of the ugliest incidents of racial violence in the United States rocked Miami and sent shock waves across the whole country." (1994, 56)

The Miami incident resulted in 18 deaths and three days of rioting. As Kappeler and his colleagues noted, the police pledged to make changes in recruitment, selection, training, complaint management, and supervision (see also Alpert, Smith, and Watters 1992, 472).

Type 2: Conflicts with the law. A Type 2 conflict occurs when there are differences between law and departmental policy. For example, a department might decide to overlook illegal immigration because it thinks that enforcement will lead to loss of public support. Policy-law conflicts tend to involve the public. Some segments may favor the law, others the department. An area of considerable concern has to do with high-speed police chases (Alpert, Kenney, Dunham, and Smith 2000). Consider a description of chase policy in Tampa, Florida.

Tampa, Florida, illustrates the issues surrounding high-speed chases. In 1994, over 11,000 cars were stolen. In 1995, officers began to chase car thieves, and the number of auto thefts was cut in half. Further, the rate of overall crime dropped by 25 percent, and officers attribute this to the use of stolen cars by felons to commit other crimes. However, police involved in chases have been involved in several accidents. In one of these, officers careened into a utility pole. In another, they knocked a house off its foundation. More troubling, a car driven by a suspect crashed into another car and killed the two German tourists inside. This accident happened less than three weeks after a suspected car thief, followed by another sheriff's deputy, hit a car and killed two occupants. (Navarro 1995, 18)

Since the 1980s, departments nationally are increasingly restricting high-speed pursuits. Chases are most troubling—they require a police department to balance public safety with law enforcement. Unfortunately, these two goals move at cross-purposes sometimes, and increases in law enforcement sometimes threaten the public safety. Chases are dangerous; the suspect, police officers, and innocent bystanders are sometimes injured and killed. Police chases are the "most deadly force" (Alpert and Anderson 1986). Yet, many officers balk at the notion that they should withdraw from a chase and permit a suspected felon to escape. As Alpert (1989, 229) observes, "few would argue that police should not initiate a chase, but that is where the consensus disappears." Wide controversy exists regarding if and when a chase should be curtailed.

The consequences of a Type 2 conflict are usually twofold: Some segments of the community would be pleased by the pursuit policy, others would not. In Tampa, residents facing higher insurance costs and economic loss supported the policy restricting pursuits. Within the police department, however, many officers would probably be angry and upset. Brown (1983), in his study of two large police departments, found substantial differences among officers concerning the appropriate policy for the use of deadly force. In fact, in cities in which organizational policies concerning the use of force are more restrictive than state law, officer morale may become an important issue.

Type 3: Conflicts between norms. In a Type 3 conflict, an officer's behavior meets the expectations of some segments of the community but is inconsistent with both law and departmental policy. For example, assume that two police officers are working in a neighborhood that has extensive drug problems. They decide to harass and physically abuse individuals suspected of drug dealing. Such action is clearly illegal and in violation of departmental policy, but it may be applauded by many persons in the neighborhood. In such a situation, the police department might discipline the officers, perhaps even terminate them, and possibly recommend criminal prosecution. But the residents of the neighborhood might protest the action of the department, perhaps vigorously.

Type 3 conflict is most likely to occur when the police department and officers get too close to residents in a particular area and begin to enforce what they consider to be "neighborhood norms" rather than following the law. Community-oriented policing could result in this type of conflict if not carefully monitored. It remains to be seen if the police can "resist" citizen pressure to "go outside the law to get the job done."

The examples provided in the three types of conflict illustrate important problems in determining the appropriateness of police behavior. Officers are sometimes required to make choices that will alienate part of their public. There are also many less dramatic examples concerning the exercise of police authority and the use of coercion. And there are many "gray areas." For example, a police officer might stop a citizen for a traffic ticket. If the citizen refuses to give the officer his or her driver's license, the officer must decide how to treat the citizen. At what point in this police-citizen encounter should the officer begin to use coercion? When should verbal threats be made? In many police departments the guidance provided to police officers in these areas is vague or nonexistent. Officers, police managers, and members of the community are likely to have opinions about appropriate behavior in these situations, and at times there will be conflicting expectations among these groups.

The recognition that some decisions will have no good outcome may be frustrating for young adults interested in a career in policing. Many individuals approach police work with a clear notion of "good-guy vs. bad-guy" fixed in their minds. Unfortunately, policing is not like that, nor can it be. In a democratic society, as Wilson (1968) observed long ago, the use of force will always be controversial.

Inappropriate Force

In a democracy, police authority is constrained by democratic ideas of fair play. On the one hand, due-process laws provide the legalized means that police are permitted to use in order to pursue suspected criminals and to deal with citizens and suspects. Department policy provides the administrative means, such as the use-of-force continuum, that police are supposed to follow in their day-to-day activities (Terrill, Alpert, Dunham, and Smith 2003). On the other hand, many police officers are ends-oriented. They are more focused on the ends of criminal justice—arresting dangerous felons or acquiring information about criminal activity—than on following legally acceptable means to achieve those ends. Also, police culture seems to give more emphasis to "good" ends than to legal means, and it sometimes justifies questionable means in the pursuit of these good ends (Crank 1998; Klockars 1980).

The use of questionable and illegal force, as well as of unacceptably high levels of force and police brutality, has consequently been a problem for the police throughout the twentieth century (see, for example, Inside Policing 9.4). What is meant by inappropriate police behavior? What constitutes brutality? Clearly, these questions have to be at the center of any investigation into police misuse of force and abuse of authority.

Inside Policing 9.4   Use of Force, the Community, and Liability

According to an article in *Law Enforcement News* (1998), in 1998 the Washington D.C. Metropolitan Police unveiled a new use-of-force policy. The policy was developed in response to an escalating number of shooting incidents in recent years. The Metropolitan Police had been involved in 640 shooting incidents during the five-year period from 1992 to 1997. This is more shootings than in either the Los Angeles or the Chicago Police Department for the same period, both of which have double Washington's manpower. Moreover, 85 people had been shot and killed since 1990. Eight police officers had also been shot since 1993. In 1997, three officers were killed in a three-month period.

The shootings had resulted in more than 300 civil suits against the District. One man, armed with a knife, was shot by SWAT team members 12 times and subsequently awarded $6.1 million dollars. Of particular concern was that police were shooting at a large number of cars. Since 1993, "54 cars have been shot at after officers said they had drove at them in 'vehicular attacks.' Nine people had been killed, all of them unarmed, and 19 wounded" (1).

The following is an example of such an incident: A 16-year-old man, wanted for reckless driving and running red lights, was shot through his side window. In two other cases, one individual was shot while he sat at a roadblock. Another was shot while sitting in his vehicle during a traffic stop. Officers involved in these cases stated that they fired to stop a vehicular attack. However, all of these shootings were considered to be unjustified, and the city agreed to pay the families of the victims in out-of-court settlements.

In response to these problems, the police department revised its use-of-force policy, rewrote the continuum of force, and increased annual training requirements.

Officers are trained to use certain measures to prevent an incident from escalating to brutal or deadly force. A suspect's body movement, for instance, will be met by a uniform presence. If a suspect is unresponsive, the officer may respond with verbal force. If threatening words or gestures are used, the officer assumes an escort position to lead the subject. To meet passive resistance, the officer may grab the suspect's wrists and pin his arms behind him. Responses to active resistance range from take-down techniques and pepper spray or other nonlethal weapons to the use of deadly force. (10)

Nightsticks and the use of arms across the front of a person's neck to render the person unconscious were banned. Officers were also prohibited from shooting through doors or windows unless someone was clearly visible and from firing on fleeing cars. Officers were told to get out of the way of cars being used as deadly weapons.

A survey of officers found that 75 percent of those who had used their firearms failed to meet department standards. Consequently, firearms instruction was increased from 8 to 16 hours yearly, and training was expanded to focus on defensive tactics and judgment. Officers were taught how to deescalate situations and reduce the need for deadly force. Finally, shooting review teams were to be sent to the scene of all shootings in order to thoroughly investigate them.

Brutality and Excessive Force

Police brutality is difficult to define. It means different things to different people. Two approaches to defining brutality are recognized in this book. The first distinguishes between brutality and excessive force. Kania and Mackey (1977, 28) define **excessive force** as violence "of a degree that is more than justified to effect a legitimate police function." According to Carter, **police brutality** is excessive force, but to a more extreme degree, and includes violence that does not support a legitimate police function (1994, 270). An officer who beats a suspect who has already been handcuffed, for example, is committing police brutality.

This definition, however, does not fully address some aspects of police behavior that are widely seen as brutal but are not violently forceful. Carter, in dealing with this problem, focused on **abuse of authority**, which is the second approach to defining brutality. He defined abuse of authority with a three-part typology, depending on the nature and effects of police abuse.

> *Physical Abuse/Excessive Force.* Operationally, this classification includes (1) any officer behavior involving the use of more force than is necessary to effect an arrest or search, and/or (2) the wanton use of any degree of physical force against another by a police officer under the color of the officer's office. The key test is whether there was any physical force directly used against an individual with no distinction between injurious and noninjurious incidents with the proposition that the causal variables are the same.

> *Verbal/Psychological Abuse.* These are incidents where police officers verbally assail, ridicule, or harass individuals and/or place persons who are under the actual or constructive dominion of an officer in a situation where the individual's esteem and/or self-image are threatened or diminished. Also included in this category is the threat of physical harm under the supposition that a threat is psychologically coercive and instills fear in the average person.

> *Legal Abuse/Violation of Civil Rights.* This form of abuse occurs with greater frequency than the other categories. Legal abuse is defined as any violation of a person's constitutional, federally or state-protected rights. Although the individual may not suffer any apparent psychological damage in the strictest sense, an abuse of authority has nonetheless occurred. In all cases of physical abuse and in many cases of verbal abuse, there will also be a legal question. However, legal abuse can—and does—occur frequently without the other forms. (Carter 1994, 273)

The underlying premise of the typology is that whenever police officers exercise their authority in a manner inconsistent with law or policy, they have abused their authority. Carter states that this model is useful because each of the different kinds of abuse has different causes, and each has to be treated differently, with different implications for policy.

Physical and Psychological Force

Both physical and **psychological force** were commonplace well into the 1930s. Hopkins (1931, 212–215) reported on a study of the New York City Police Department in 1930 that found in 166 cases (23.4 percent of the total cases studied) some type of **physical force** was employed. The most frequently used method was to strike the suspect one or more times with a fist (67 cases). Other methods included use of a rubber hose (19 cases) and a blackjack (12 cases). One suspect was "hung out the window, kicked and dragged by the hair" (1931, 215). Larson (1932, 95–100) also discussed some of the coercive methods commonly used by police during this period. These methods became associated with the term **third degree**. Various third-degree methods historically employed by the police are listed in Inside Policing 9.5.

Inside Policing 9.5   Historical Methods of Psychological and Physical Force Used by the Police

Psychological Force

- Suspects are placed on "The Loop"—that is, moved from station to station to deny them access to family, friends, and attorneys.

- Suspects are placed in very small, completely dark cells. Rats are placed in women's cells to "exhaust their nervous energy." A prisoner in an adjoining cell is told to "moan" and "yell" during the night. A large stove is placed next to a cell, and the stove is filled with items (e.g., bones, vegetable matter, old tires) designed to give off a foul odor and increase the heat in the cell to unbearable levels (i.e., to create a "sweat box").

- Suspects are interrogated for long periods under bright lights and without food or water, and/or they are denied access to substances like tobacco to which they are addicted. Suspects are threatened with various weapons; for example, a gun with blank shells is fired at the subject.

- Murder suspects are required to touch or hold the hand of the murder victim.

- Police pretend to beat prisoners in an interrogation room adjoining that of the suspect. One police officer is "hard" and "tough" and threatens the suspect; the other officer is sympathetic and supportive and pretends to protect the suspect from harm in exchange for information

or a confession (also known as "good cop, bad cop" and the Mutt and Jeff technique).

- Police officers make false promises about what will happen to the suspect.

Physical Force

- Suspects are beaten on all parts of their body (usually except for the head) with rubber hoses, clubs, blackjacks, fists, telephone books, straps, brass knuckles, pistol butts, and whips. Arms and legs are twisted. Testicles are kicked, twisted, squeezed, and used to lift suspects upward, and testicles are also burned with acid. Suspects are tortured with electric shocks, dental drills, and lighted cigars. Suspects are dragged or pulled by their hair.

- Suspects are drenched with cold water from a hose, their heads are held under water, water is forced into their noses, they are hung out the window, they are choked with neckties and ropes, and they are required to go without shoes until their feet are bleeding. Chemicals such as tear gas, scopolamine, and chloroform are employed.

Sources: Adapted from J. A. Larson, *Lying and Its Detection* (Chicago: University of Chicago Press, 1932), 95–121; E. J. Hopkins, *Our Lawless Police* (New York: Viking Press, 1931), 25, 128, 215.

Most police officers of this period tended to deny any use of physical force. However, Bruce Smith, a prominent police consultant of that era, commented about the third degree in this regard: "In every police station in this country about which I know anything, there is a room remote from the public parts of the building where prisoners are questioned" (Hopkins 1931, 195). The Wickersham Commission (National Commission on Law Observance and Enforcement 1931), discussed in Chapter 2, found that the police use of such methods was widespread.

Continued problems with coercive psychological techniques resulted in famous decisions of the Warren Court in the 1960s. In 1966 the *Miranda v. Arizona* Supreme Court decision observed that psychologically coercive techniques interfered with constitutional ideas of fair play. Consequently, the court issued its now famous requirement that suspects be advised of their right to an attorney and that the police's right to question suspects be restricted, except when that right has been waived or after an attorney has advised the suspect whether to talk to the police. The courts have limited the reach of Miranda, however. In *Illinois v. Perkins* (1990) an undercover officer, placed in a cell with a suspect, acquired information that the suspect had committed a murder. The U.S. Supreme Court ruled that undercover officers did not have to give Miranda warnings to incarcerated suspects prior to eliciting incriminating statements (Kappeler, Sluder, and Alpert 1994). As Vaughn (1992) has noted, other court rulings have expanded the rights of the police to use trickery and deception. By permitting open deception, however, several observers of the police have contended that the courts are encouraging the police to emphasize "good" ends over legal means (Skolnick and Fyfe 1993).

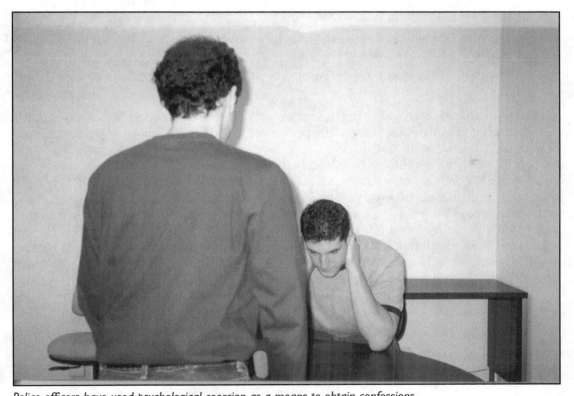

Police officers have used psychological coercion as a means to obtain confessions.

Police today continue to rely on deception, a form of psychological coercion, to secure information. Nor has the use of physical coercion been abandoned. For instance, in 1985 in New York City, several police officers employed stun guns (i.e., a weapon that shoots an electrical charge into a person) to secure confessions ("Stun-Gun Charges. . ." 1985). Similar incidents also took place in San Antonio, Texas, and Los Angeles in the 1980s (Berg 1992, 208). The following are examples of contemporary uses of deception:

1. The person, or suspect, is not told the truth about why he or she is being questioned.

2. The suspect is not told that the person asking the questions is a police officer.

3. The suspect is told that he or she is being interviewed rather than interrogated and that he or she is free to leave at any time.

4. The police misrepresent the circumstances of the crime the suspect is alleged to have committed; for example, a suspect might be told there was an eyewitness or that there is other available evidence that "ties" the suspect to the crime.

5. The police may make the crime seem more serious (carrying a more severe punishment) than it is in order to induce the suspect to make a bargain to confess to a less serious crime.

6. The police provide a justification to the suspect for the act; for example, "the victim got what she deserved."

7. The police may make some type of promise that later can be denied or modified.

These examples illustrate that there are sometimes differences between what is legal and what is ethical. Generally, the police can *legally* use trickery and deception as long as their methods do not involve coercion or improper promises (the police cannot promise a light sentence, since that is the judge's prerogative, but they can promise to speak to the prosecutor on behalf of the suspect). While legal, though, is it right to lie? Is it right for an investigator to tell a suspect that his fingerprints have already been found at the scene of a crime if they have not? Is it right for a police officer to pretend to be a drug dealer and offer to sell drugs to a suspect? These are not clear-cut cases, of course. Such behavior by the police may seem unethical to some but merely clever to others. Some citizens would have their confidence in the police shaken if they thought the police did not use such methods. Others are shocked that they do.

The matter of police ethics, and the role of ethics in guiding and controlling police behavior, is discussed at greater length in Chapter 10.

Frequency of Excessive Force and Brutality

How widespread is police violence? Barker (1986) studied the extent of police brutality, along with other types of police deviant behavior, in a city of moderate size in the southern United States. Based on questionnaire responses from 43 (of 45) officers in that department, he found that about 40 percent used excessive force at times. Officers tended to believe that lying in court (committing perjury), sleeping on duty, and having sex or drinking on duty were more serious forms of deviant police behavior than the use of excessive force. This was particularly true when the excessive force was used against persons in custody. Almost half the officers said they would rarely, if ever, report another officer if he or she used excessive force.

In another study, Carter conducted a survey of 95 police officers in McAllen, Texas. He found that 23 percent believed that excessive force was sometimes necessary to demonstrate an officer's authority, and 62 percent believed that an officer had a right to use excessive force in retaliation against anyone who used force against the officer. In the areas of verbal abuse, slightly over one-half of the officers believed that it was permissible to talk "rough" with citizens and that "rough" talk was the only way to communicate with some citizens.

Friederich (1980), in his comprehensive analysis of research on the use of force, found that police used force in only about 5 percent of encounters with offenders or suspects. In about two-thirds of these encounters, it was considered to be excessive. Because only a small percentage of all police-citizen encounters are with offenders or suspects, and only about 5 percent of these types of encounters involve the use of force, his findings suggest that both the use of force and the use of excessive force are rare events in police work.

Because almost all use-of-force incidents involve suspicious persons, offenders, or suspects who resist police authority, any circumstances that result in an increase in the number of these types of police encounters will likely result in more incidents in which police use force, including excessive force. From the police point of view, the 1980s and 1990s were a period when the police were confronted with greater resistance to their authority and were at greater risk of being injured. Consequently, the police may be using excessive force more now than in the 1970s.

Excessive use of force may be either unintentional or deliberate. Force may be inflicted to secure cooperation, to maintain the officer's authority, or to retaliate. When it is used, the officer believes that many, if not all, of the other officers (including supervisors and managers) who may be aware of this behavior will not report the brutality and will lie about the incident if it is investigated by the department or other individuals.

Perhaps the most infamous case of police brutality in recent years was the attack on Rodney King which took place in Los Angeles in 1991. Inside Policing 9.6 describes this incident and some of the subsequent events connected with it. Interestingly, a comprehensive study of the Los Angeles police just prior to the King incident had indicated widespread officer support for the values and management of the police department (Felkenes 1991). Furthermore, widespread support was found in both white and minority and male and female officers. It was found that, overall, all patrol officers were very satisfied with their jobs and would recommend that their friends consider a job with the department. This research also found that Los Angeles police officers were likely to have a professional outlook concerning their role in society. The conflict between the shortcomings of the Los Angeles Police Department reported in the aftermath of the Rodney King incident and police officer support for the department reported in the Felkenes research vividly illustrates the differences that can exist between community and departmental expectations of the police role in society and the meaning of what is, and is not, police brutality.

Inside Policing 9.6   The Rodney King Incident

On March 3, 1991, Rodney G. King was stopped for a speeding violation and trying to evade the police. What ensued between King and police officers was videotaped by a "home-camera buff." King did not immediately cooperate with police and may have resisted the attempts of officers to arrest him. Several officers hit him with police batons and kicked him over 50 times. Before the incident was over, 27 police officers (two of whom were black and four of whom were Latino), representing three different police agencies, were on the scene, and they stood by as King was brutally beaten and severely injured. The beating appeared to continue even after King had stopped making any meaningful effort to resist police authority. King received 11 skull fractures (including a shattered right cheek bone, shattered right eye socket, and fractured right sinus bones), a broken ankle, and numerous other injuries as a result of the beating. When the videotape was shown on local and national television, it created tremendous outrage across the United States. Other citizens came forward with examples of how they had also been mistreated by the police.

The reports of the officers involved in the incident indicate that they may not have been truthful in describing the events in question. For example, some officers reported that King drove his car in excess of 100 miles an hour in order to avoid the police. However, a tape recording of the conversations between pursuing officers and one police department never indicated a speed in excess of 65 miles an hour. Two of the officers involved were, in fact, charged with submitting a false report.

An independent commission, headed by Warren Christopher, former deputy attorney general and deputy secretary of state of the United States, was appointed to investigate the King incident and related incidents in the department. Information revealed in the investigation indicated that some of the officers involved did not take the King matter seriously and even made jokes about it. One officer said after the incident that he hadn't "beaten anyone this bad in a long time." At the hospital to which King was taken, one police officer reportedly told King that "we played a little hardball tonight and you lost."

The attitudes of some Los Angeles police officers concerning race, excessive force, and the shooting of suspects are illustrated in the police officer statements listed below. These statements were taken from records of computer communications between patrol cars and between patrol cars and police headquarters. These statements are an example of 1,450 similar remarks made in the 16 months preceding the King incident. The language is reported as given, including the spelling errors of the officers. Although the number of such remarks is less than one-tenth of 1 percent of the total communication statements made during the period in question, the fact that such statements were

Inside Policing 9.6   The Rodney King Incident (continued)

made so openly indicates the possibility of both tolerance and support within the department for the values and beliefs represented by these remarks.

Statements Concerning Race

"Don't cry Buckwheat, or is it Willie Lunch Meat?"

"Sounds like monkey slapping time."

"Well . . . I'm back over here in the projects, pissing off the natives."

"If you encounter these Negroes shoot first and ask questions later."

"Just clear its [busy] out hear. This hole is picking up, I almost got me a Mexican last night but he dropped the dam gun to quick, lots of wit."

Statements Concerning Excessive Force

"I'm gonna bk my pursuit suspect . . . hope he gets ugly, so I can vent my hate."

"Capture him, beat him and treat him like dirt . . . Sounds like a job for the dynamic duo."

"After I beat him, what do I book him for and do I have to do a use of force [report]."

"Some of the suspects had big boot marks on their heads, once they were in custody."

"The last load went to a family of illegals living in the brush alongside the Pas frwy. I thought the woman was going to cry . . . so I hit her with my baton."

"I should shoot 'em huh, I missed another chance dammmmmmm. I am getting soft."

Some of the other findings of the Christopher Commission and of research conducted by newspaper reporters are listed below:

1. Supervisors in the department were aware of a "significant number" of officers who used excessive force repeatedly and who also lied in reports about what they had done. Sometimes these officers were even praised by supervisors.

2. The messages sent via the computer that indicated prejudice and a tendency toward violence on the part of some officers were ignored by police supervisors and managers.

3. It was rare for the department to find in favor of citizens who complained about the police use of excessive force. In over 2,000 citizen complaints filed between 1986 and 1990, only 42 were resolved in favor of the complainant. For the same period, the department brought excessive-force charges against officers in 80 cases, and in 53 of these, officers were found guilty as a result of an internal affairs investigation. In some of these 53 cases, more than one officer was involved. In incidents involving several officers, all officers denied the allegations, and none of the officers who had been present at the incident reported another officer for the use of excessive force. The disciplinary action taken against officers for the use of excessive force varied. Some officers were suspended for more than 20 days, but some were treated more leniently than other officers who had been disciplined for kissing a girlfriend while on duty, for the unauthorized use of the department's copying machines, and for sleeping on duty.

The commission stated, however, that it believed that only a small percentage of officers, perhaps 3 to 5 percent, was responsible for most of the racial and excessive-force problems (this figure means that at least several hundred Los Angeles police officers may have engaged in this type of behavior). The Christopher Commission also found serious problems with the police department's management and suggested that the chief of police retire when his term of office was over.

As a result of the King incident, four officers were charged with criminal assault, among other things, and placed on trial. Their defense was that prior to the events depicted on the videotape, King, whom they considered to be a large and potentially dangerous person, violently resisted their attempts to arrest him. They indicated that they believed King was under the influence of liquor or drugs, and from their training and experience, this would make him very difficult to control. When they were unable to control him physically, they used the Taser, but even after he was shocked with electricity, King continued to refuse police orders to lie down in a

> ## Inside Policing 9.6   The Rodney King Incident (continued)
>
> prone position with arms and legs spread; he even got up and "charged" one of the officers. Consequently, the officers began to use their batons and some kicks, as they were trained to do in such situations. The officers tended to perceive every movement by King, even when he was on the ground, as an indication that he continued to pose a threat. Therefore, they continued to beat him until he complied with police orders. Only one of the four officers in question believed that what they had done was excessive or that it constituted "police brutality."
>
> The jury in the criminal trial found the four officers not guilty on all criminal charges except one, on which the jury was divided. Many citizens, who believed that the videotape of the beating was sufficient evidence to convict the officers, were outraged at what they considered to be an unjust verdict. There was widespread violence (more than 50 persons were killed), extensive property damage (numerous buildings were burned down), and looting in Los Angeles and several other cities. Many elected officials expressed their concern and demanded that additional steps be taken to hold the officers accountable for their actions.
>
> Two of the officers were subsequently convicted in federal court for the violation of King's civil rights. Both were sent to federal prison. King also sued the city of Los Angeles and was awarded $3.6 million.
>
> ---
>
> *Sources:* Adapted from "Inside View of L.A. Beating," 1991, *San Jose Mercury News*, March 19: 1A, 9A; "Doubt Shed on Cops Report in L.A. Beating," 1991, *San Jose Mercury News*, March 23: 1F, 4F; "L.A. Fires Only 1% of Officers," 1991, *San Jose Mercury News*, May 5: 4B; "Report Calls For Gates' Ouster," 1991, *San Jose Mercury News*, July 10: 1A, 6A. Used by permission.

Brutality in the Twenty-First Century

The police professionalism movement, discussed in Chapter 10, has placed powerful administrative and ethical controls on the behavior of line officers. Throughout the twentieth century, this and subsequent reform movements have tried to control violent and brutal police behavior. Looking back over the past 100 years, can one say that police brutality has decreased? What are the trends in brutality? Is it a problem that society needs to be concerned about?

This section looks at two opposing views on police violence and brutality. The first argues that brutality is a significant problem in major American cities and is not being dealt with successfully. The second contends that brutality should be considered against the backdrop of increasing levels of violence among the citizenry.

View 1: Brutality is a problem. In 1998 the Human Rights Watch published *Shielded From Justice,* an assessment of brutality in major American cities. It looked at brutality and accountability procedures in 14 large cities, selected to represent different regions and to provide an overall picture of police behavior across the United States. Its assessment of brutality and lax accountability was a harsh indictment of big-city policing.

> Police officers engage in unjustified shootings, severe beatings, fatal chokings, and unnecessarily rough physical treatment in cities throughout the United States, while their police superiors, city officials, and the justice department fail to act decisively to restrain or penalize such acts or even to record the full magnitude of the problem. Habitually brutal offenders—usually a small percentage of officers on a force—may be the subject of repeated complaints but are usually pro-

tected by their fellow officers and by the shoddiness of internal police investigations. A victim seeking redress faces obstacles at every point in the process, ranging from overt intimidation to the reluctance of local and federal prosecutors to take on brutality cases. Severe abuse persists because overwhelming barriers to accountability make it all too likely that officers who commit human rights violations escape due punishment to continue their abusive conduct. (1998, 1)

Prosecution of cases has been infrequent and ineffective. Local prosecutors, the study argues, are frequently closely allied with police and are ineffective in efforts to prosecute police brutality. Indeed, most prosecutions conducted by the Human Rights Watch did not keep a log of police brutality cases. The criminal section of the Civil Rights Division of the U.S. Department of Justice is responsible for prosecution of civil rights violations. This includes the excessive use of force and police brutality. Yet the record of prosecution has been bleak.

In fiscal year 1997, the Civil Rights Division received a total of 10,891 complaints, with 31 grand juries and magistrates to consider law enforcement officers leading to 25 indictments and informations, involving 67 law enforcement agents; nine were convicted, 19 entered guilty pleas, and four were acquitted. (1998, 102)

In other words, of over 10,000 complaints, only 28 resulted in convictions or pleas. This is a conviction rate of 2.6 per 1,000 cases. The data are clear: Citizens hoping for criminal remedies at the federal level for police brutality are virtually certain to be frustrated.

Federal data also show an alarming rise in reports of police brutality over recent years. In 1989, 8,953 cases were forwarded to the FBI. By 1996 the figure had risen to 11,721. Though the time interval is too short to make long-term inferences about trends, the data show an increase of 30 percent in reported cases over the seven-year period.

Human Rights Watch concluded that the most significant problem confronting big-city police departments was the lack of a system of effective accountability (discussed in Chapter 10). However, critics have countered that data collected by Human Rights Watch was derived primarily from high-profile cases. This is a selective bias that, outside of the FBI reports listed above, tells little about the ordinary cases encountered by police departments. Human Rights Watch responded to this concern by observing that it was difficult to obtain information from departments in instances that had not reached public attention, and that prosecution for those cases was consequently even less common than the more visible cases that it discussed.

View 2: Brutality is not a problem. Not all observers of the police believe that there is a brutality problem. Sulc (1995) argued that restraint, rather than brutality, is typical of police behavior toward citizens. He contended that police brutality is less prevalent than it was 20 years ago. Citing the news magazine *New Dimensions*, he observed that

While the FBI's civil rights division reports 2,450 complaints involving law enforcement officers in 1989, during the same period, 62,712 law enforcement officers were victims of assaults. In 1990, there were more than 71,794 assaults against law enforcement officers nationwide, according to the Uniform Crime Reports. Sixty-five officers were killed. (1995, 80)

Sulc attributes the widespread perception of police violence to media attention.

Police violence, although unquestionably a matter of serious import, isn't as bad as it appears. It is exacerbated by warped media treatment both in fiction (network shows) and in reporting (network news). The unusual stress of police work contributes to the overreaction of cops—the overreaction of media and public to the cops contributes to the stress. (1995, 81)

Tucker (1995) argues that the public tends to look at complaints against the police and fails to consider whether the complaints are justified:

The truth, however, is that most complaints are either frivolous or unjustified. This is borne out by the experience of the old New York City board, which the Vera Institute of Justice, a nonpartisan organization, found to be prejudiced neither for nor against civilians or police officers. In 1990, the Board's annual report showed a total of 2,376 complaints for "excessive force," 1,140 for "abuse of authority," 1,618 for "discourtesy," and 420 for "ethnic slurs." Among the 2,376 complaints for excessive force (presumably the most serious charge), injuries were documented in 267 cases. These involved 71 bruises, 92 lacerations requiring stitches, 30 fractures, 22 swellings, and 41 "other." In the 2,286 cases that were pursued, 566 were dropped because the complainant became uncooperative, 234 were dropped because the complainant withdrew the charge, and 1,405 were closed with less than full investigation, usually because the complainants became unavailable. Only 81 cases resulted in a finding against the policeman. (1995, 72)

The "no problem" perspective suffers from a tendency to blame police brutality on the behavior of their victims or on increases in crime, seeming to imply that police officers are not primarily responsible for their own behavior. Nor does the perspective acknowledge the very real problems victims of brutality face when they try to file reports—filing a report in a police department is frequently an intimidating experience, and full follow-up on reports that are filed is not common in many departments. This perspective nevertheless raises important points that should not be overlooked. The following six points summarize central policy issues confronting excessive force and police brutality.

1. The presence of brutality cannot be gleaned only from "official reports," which may be unsubstantiated. Individuals file brutality or excessive-force reports for a variety of reasons, and not all of the reports will accurately tap underlying instances of brutality. Also, scholars know from their studies of crime that official reports vary sharply from true levels, though that same argument suggests that brutality may well be higher than suggested by "official" reports.

2. Citizens may perceive behavior whose purpose is to ensure officer safety as acts of brutality. There is no question but that the experience of being arrested, searched, and cuffed is harsh and unpleasant. But it should not be dealt with in the same way as brutality, which is typically viewed by the public and police officials alike as inappropriate or illegal behavior.

3. The media are widely and correctly perceived to dramatize that which comes to their attention. This applies to the villainy of criminals, and it extends to the brutality of police as well. One should not assume that what is presented in the media is a thorough or accurate portrayal of the facts. Indeed, as Walker (1998, 30–32) has pointed out, what we receive from the

media is the exceptional, not the normal, case. Unfortunately, bad officers are able to hide behind the protective veneer of police loyalty, and the media are frequently the only way that excessive force and brutality are brought to the attention of the public.

4. Police brutality emerges in the context of a police-citizen interaction, and it is unreasonable to believe that police can be wholly dispassionate in the conduct of criminal investigations and in dealing with rude individuals. Although dispassionate police work is a goal of police reformers, the ability to police without the expression of emotion, including anger, is improbable. It is important that police departments seek to control the angry or mean-spirited outbursts of officers against citizens, but it is also inconceivable that they will be wholly successful.

5. Research suggests that some officers exhibit single or rare instances of excessive force, and only a small percentage are rogues in their behavior, accounting for repeated violent acts. These two types of police officers should be dealt with in different ways, the rare or one-time offender subject to interdepartmental review and the repeat offender decertified and prosecuted.

6. The public, widely supportive of a "war on crime" and aggressive anticrime efforts, has created an environment in which police officers feel morally justified in the use of force. It is seemingly unfair to single out officers for the overuse of force when the message they frequently receive from powerful public, media, and political figures is to do just that.

Police executives being interviewed after incident.

Use of Deadly Force

The term *deadly force* is defined as that force used with the intent to cause great bodily injury or death. Such deadly force is almost always limited to those situations when police use firearms in encounters with suspects. As noted, there are certainly other times that citizens may be seriously injured or killed as the result of the use of other types of force, but that is rarely, if ever, the intent of the police. Some police scholars have suggested, however, that choke holds be defined as deadly force because deaths do occur when such holds are employed (Fyfe 1983). When the police engage in a high-speed pursuit that results in an accident and someone dies, this may be seen as use of force in which the outcome involved death. This fact does not mean that deaths that result from this and other police activities are not important, but only that they are not included in the definition and therefore will not be considered.

Based on the definition above, there are three categories for which data are required if the extent of the use of deadly force is to be determined:

Category 1: Death. The police use a deadly weapon, and as a result, the person dies.

Category 2: Injury. The police use a deadly weapon, and the person is wounded but does not die.

Category 3: Noninjury. The police use a deadly weapon, but the person against whom it is directed is not injured.

A fourth possible category, but one that will not be addressed, relates to the total times the officer fires his or her weapon. A person who is shot at and killed, wounded or missed, may be fired at more than once. Research indicates that police officers miss with about 60 to 85 percent of the bullets they fire (Geller and Scott 1992). For example, on the one hand, an officer could shoot at a suspect five times and hit the suspect only once, causing either death or an injury. Or, more than one bullet might strike the victim. On the other hand, an officer might shoot several times and not hit the intended person.

Category 1: Death. Sources of data for Category 1 use-of-deadly-force can be found in three places: the National Center for Health Statistics, FBI reports, and the study of individual cities. The National Center for Health Statistics data are found in the volumes on mortality that are published annually and based on reports from coroners and medical examiners. Under the "homicide" cause-of-death category, there has been a "police or legal" intervention subcategory since 1949. These data provide a very rough estimate of the number of people killed by police as the result of the use of deadly force. In the 42-year period from 1949 to 1990, police killed approximately 13,000 people.

However, the estimate of 13,000 may be low. An analysis of the records of 36 large police departments conducted by Sherman and Langworthy (1979) suggests that the center's statistics are approximately 25 to 50 percent too low because of reporting problems. This means that a more realistic estimate of citizen deaths from Category 1 use-of-deadly-force is between 16,000 and 20,000 since 1949. Although there is no accurate way to determine the number of citizen deaths that have resulted from the use of deadly force since the 1840s when modern police departments were first established, it is not unreasonable to assume that 30,000 to 40,000 citizens, and possibly many more, have been killed by police officers in the United States.

The FBI does not provide data on the police use of deadly force unless requested. The data are based on what are called Supplemental Homicide Reports submitted to the FBI by police departments, and the submission of such reports is voluntary. Although the number of people reported killed by police may give an accurate picture of the use of deadly force in individual cities, the reports do not provide an accurate national overview.

One of the most comprehensive studies conducted in individual police departments was made by Matulia (1985), who studied citizens killed by the police in the 57 largest cities (250,000 population or higher) in the United States between 1975 and 1983. He found that the police had killed a total of 2,336 people, or an average of about 259 per year. He estimated that this figure represented about 70 percent of the total number of citizens killed by police each year in the United States. By using this estimate, the total number of citizens killed during this period would be about 370 per year. This estimate is consistent with National Center data if Sherman and Langworthy's adjustment is taken into consideration, as well as with a recent analysis by the Bureau of Justice Statistics (Brown and Langan 2001), which found annual fluctuations between about 300 and 450 (see Figure 9.1).

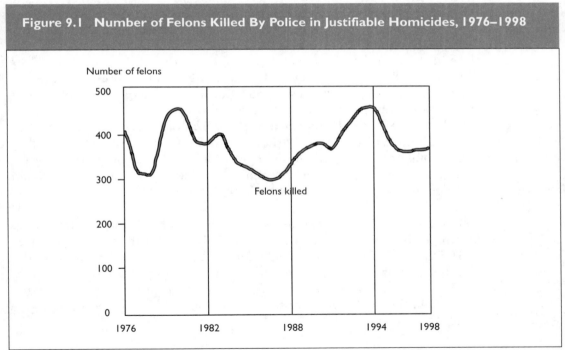

Figure 9.1   Number of Felons Killed By Police in Justifiable Homicides, 1976–1998

Source: J. M. Brown and P. A. Langan, *Policing and Homicide, 1976–1998: Justifiable Homicide By Police, Police Officers Murdered By Felons* (Washington, DC: Bureau of Justice Statistics, 2001), 1.

Category 2: Injury. Category 2 data (i.e., a person is shot and injured) are more difficult to acquire for the entire United States because there is no national reporting requirement. Fyfe (1988), however, provides some interesting insights on this category of data. He summarizes several studies conducted over varying time periods (two to nine years) from a total of 14 large cities in the United States. Although some variation exists among departments, these studies suggest that, in general, when the police shoot an individual, that person is approximately twice as likely to be wounded as killed. If this estimate is accurate for the entire United States, this means that for the period 1949 to 1990, police used deadly force that injured citizens between 32,000 and 40,000 times.

Category 3: Noninjury. Data for Category 3 (i.e., person is shot at but not injured) are even more difficult to obtain. However, there are some indications of the frequency of police actions in this area. In studies of four large cities, the frequency that officers shot and missed, as a percentage of total times they used their firearms, was 48.6 in Los Angeles during the period 1971 to 1975 (Fyfe 1978), 73.1 in Chicago for the period 1975 to 1977 (Geller and Karales 1981), and 74.1 in Detroit for the period 1976 to 1981 (Horvath and Donahue 1982). If these data are indicative of practices throughout the United States, it means that, depending on the city, police officers shoot at and miss two to four times as many people as they shoot at and either injure or kill.

The above discussion includes some very general projections about the use of deadly force in the United States. There is a need to determine how changes in training, departmental policy, programs (like community or problem-oriented policing), and new laws affect frequency of deadly force incidents. For example, as a result of changes in the policies concerning the use of Category 1 deadly force, there was an apparent decline in the number of citizens killed in the early 1980s (Fyfe 1988; "Big Decline in Killings. . ." 1986). These policy and legal changes will be discussed later.

Van Raalte's (1986) research identifies as many as 30,000 officers killed in the line of duty in the twentieth century. However, he does not separate those killed in accidents from those killed by citizens. Historically, there is about a 1:4 or 1:5 ratio when comparing officers killed to citizens killed; that is, about one police officer is killed by a citizen for every four or five citizens killed by the police (Kuykendall 1981). Most recently, though, homicides of police officers have been decreasing at an even faster rate than homicides by officers, so that the ratio in 1998 was about 1:6 (Brown and Langan 2001).

In recent years, there has been substantial research concerning the circumstances in which police use deadly force. Some of the more prominent authorities in this area are Geller (1983), Fyfe (1978, 1979, 1980, 1982, 1983, 1985, 1988), Scharf and Binder (1983), and Blumberg (1985, 1997), among others. The most important research findings for four areas—(1) environmental and departmental variations, (2) factors that influence officers, (3) racial considerations, and (4) changes in law and policy—are summarized below.

Environmental and Departmental Variations

The frequency with which police use Category 1 deadly force varies considerably across the United States. Matulia found that the rates per 1,000 police officers varied from 0.44 in Sacramento, California (about 1 incident for every 2,000 police officers), to 7.17 in Jacksonville, Florida. Overall, the mean rate was 2.24 citizens killed for each 1,000 officers for the period 1975 to 1983. Of the 57 largest cities studied, 29 were below this rate and 27 were above.

Two categories of factors influence the frequency with which police use deadly force: environmental and organizational (departmental). Environmental factors—factors having to do with the community and neighborhood where the police do their work—are the homicide rate, the overall arrest rate, violent-crime arrest rate, and gun density (i.e., ratio of gun ownership to total population). Generally, the police are more likely to confront situations where they think the use of deadly force is necessary in areas with higher crime and more guns. In addition, in any area where there are higher poverty and divorce rates, often the police may be called on more to intervene in potentially dangerous situations (Fyfe 1980, 1988; Kania and Mackey 1977; Sherman and Langworthy 1979). These factors do not by themselves, however, explain all of the variation that may exist.

Departmental values, policies, and practices of political leaders and police managers also affect the frequency with which police use deadly force. Current research suggests that a more restrictive shooting policy would reduce the frequency with which deadly force is employed (discussed in more detail later). In addition, some evidence suggests that the leadership attitude in the city and department influences the frequency of use (Carmichael and Jacobs 2002). For example, the increase in the use of deadly force in Philadelphia in the 1970s appeared to be the result of the aggressive policing attitude of leaders in the city and the department. The training that officers receive may also be influential. Some departments may encourage officers to intervene aggressively in potentially dangerous situations rather than wait until adequate "backup support" is available. Officers, on their own initiative, may also engage in such behavior (Fyfe 1988).

What is not known about neighborhood and department variation is more striking than what is known. Scholars know that often deadly force *fatalities* occur, but they do not know how many deadly force incidents occur (Blumberg 1997). The proportion of deadly force incidents, rates of justifiable homicide, and firearms discharge rates vary dramatically across jurisdictions (Geller and Scott 1992) and departments (Fridell 1989). Blumberg has made the following observations.

> The inescapable conclusion one must draw from the available evidence is that nobody knows how many times each year law enforcement officers in the United States fire their weapons at citizens, how many citizens are wounded, or how many are killed as the result of police bullets. (1997, 521)

Officer Factors

The decision by an officer to use deadly force appears primarily to be the result of his or her perception of whether a threat exists and how frequently the officer is exposed to threats. As used here, "threat" could mean any situation in which the department permitted the use of deadly force. An officer's assignment appears to be a much more important predictor of the use of deadly force than age, intelligence, and educational background. Officers with more risky assignments are more likely to use deadly force.

Off-duty officers are involved in many shootings. As many as 15 to 20 percent of incidents of police use of deadly force involve an officer who is off duty. The more aggressive the off-duty officer is in intervening in potentially violent situations, whether or not encouraged to do so by the department, the higher the rates for the use of deadly force.

The race of the officer also appears to be important, largely because of the assignment and living practices of officers. For example, African American officers are more likely to use deadly force and to be the victims of its use than are other officers because they are more likely to live in, frequent, and be assigned to areas with high crime rates. Therefore, they are exposed to more situations in which they might have to use deadly force or become its victim (Fyfe 1988; Geller and Scott 1992).

There is also some evidence that women police may use deadly force less frequently than men because they may have no ego involvement with suspects. Men may tend to personalize violent encounters to such a degree that the encounter becomes a survival competition governed more by macho rules than by departmental training and policy (Grennan 1987).

Racial Considerations

African American and Hispanic minorities are more likely to be shot by the police than are whites. There are two explanations for this disproportion. The first is that such disparities in shooting incidents simply mirror ethnic and racial involvement in criminal activity. When compared with rates of police-citizen contacts, arrest rates, and resistance to or attacks upon the police, there is no apparent racial disparity in police use of deadly force. That is, in communities in which blacks are shot at a high rate from the percentage of contacts with police, their arrest rates and the likelihood that they will resist the police tend to be similarly high (Fyfe 1988; Geller and Scott 1992). The second explanation is that police disproportionately use deadly force against minority-group members. Fyfe, for example, found that police officers in Memphis were 15 times as likely to shoot at African American offenders who had committed property crimes as at white property-crime offenders.

Because of the sensitivity of the racial issue in the use of deadly force, more restrictive policies have tended to reduce the number of African Americans who have been killed. Sherman and Cohn (1986) found that in the 15-year period between 1970 and 1984, the police use of deadly force declined substantially, largely because fewer African American citizens were killed by police. As Figure 9.2 indicates, this trend reversed itself during the period 1987–1993, probably because of the crack epidemic and the violence associated with it, but then resumed. The rate at which police used deadly force against African Americans in 1998 was about 50 percent lower than it had been in 1976, although still more than twice the rate for whites (Brown and Langan 2001). These trends suggest that prior to the adoption of more restrictive deadly force policies by many police departments, African Americans were more likely to be shot at in certain types of situations (e.g., running away from the scene of a crime) than were whites. Declines in racial disparities in deadly force incidents today are associated with departmental efforts to control discretion in the use of deadly force (Sparger and Giacopassi 1992).

Legal and Policy Changes

Blumberg identifies five changes in present-day laws and departmental policy regulating the use of deadly force.

1. Many states have modified the fleeing-felon rule and have tightened the legal basis for use of deadly force.

2. The shooting of unarmed, nonviolent suspects has been ruled by the Supreme Court to be a violation of the Fourth Amendment of the Constitution.

3. Almost all urban police departments have enacted restrictive administrative policies regarding the use of deadly force.

4. The courts have made it much easier for a citizen to file a lawsuit and collect civil damages as a result of a police action.

5. Social-science research has facilitated the understanding of the reasons for, and policy implications of, the use of deadly force. (1997, 507–508)

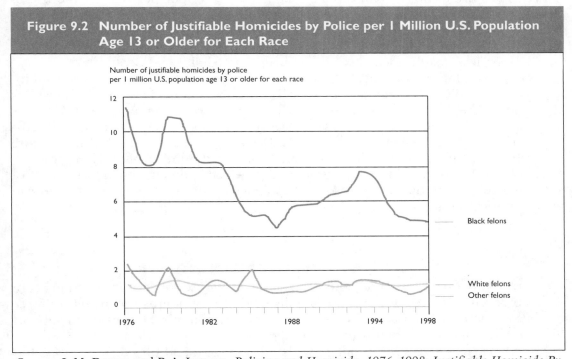

Figure 9.2 Number of Justifiable Homicides by Police per 1 Million U.S. Population Age 13 or Older for Each Race

Source: J. M. Brown and P. A. Langan, *Policing and Homicide, 1976–1998: Justifiable Homicide By Police, Police Officers Murdered By Felons* (Washington, DC: Bureau of Justice Statistics, 2001), iii.

As late as 1967, few police departments had policies to guide officers in the use of deadly force. The state laws that existed at that time and that still exist in many states tended to broadly define occasions when officers could use deadly force. Perhaps the broadest of these legal guidelines was the **fleeing-felon rule**, which authorized the use of deadly force when attempting to apprehend individuals who were fleeing from a suspected serious crime. This rule dates from the early Middle Ages, when almost all crimes considered to be felonies were punishable by the death penalty; consequently, to kill those fleeing from suspected felonies did not seem inappropriate.

An alternative to the fleeing-felon rule was first developed and tested in New York. The New York Police Department, responding to concerns over the high number of officer and civilian shootings, formulated a restricted policy permitting the use of deadly force only under circumstances of immediate danger to an officer or the public. The policy resulted in a nearly 30 percent reduction in shootings of citizens by officers. No increase in the number of officers shot was observed (Fyfe 1979).

Changes in departmental policies have had more influence than changes in the law in determining when police officers use deadly force. Once police departments began to develop policies in this area, they often were more restrictive than state law. Initially, departments limited the number of situations in which police could use deadly force; for example, a policy might indicate that a person who was fleeing from a certain property crime could no longer be shot at.

By the 1980s, more and more police departments began to adopt what is often called a defense-of-life shooting policy. Generally, such policies restrict the use of deadly force situations to those in which the officer's life, or another person's, is in jeopardy or to prevent the escape of a person who is extremely dangerous. In some departments, even under these circumstances, deadly force can be employed only when other, less deadly, means seem inappropriate (Geller and Scott 1992).

Since the adoption of more restrictive deadly-force policies, the number of citizens killed by police has declined. This decline is understandable when one considers that prior to the adoption of a defense-of-life policy, in some communities as many as 25 percent of the victims of police use of deadly force posed no threat to a police officer or another person when they were shot. Despite the fears of many officers, more restrictive guidelines have not resulted in an increased number of police injuries or deaths (Fyfe 1988). In addition, no evidence either confirms or refutes the belief of some police officers that more restrictive policies encourage suspects to try to run away from the police.

Summary

Force is an inherent part of police-citizen interactions. Police are trained to act in terms of levels of force. However, local police cultural standards for the use of force differ considerably from formal departmental policy and are more likely to support greater force than do formal training and policy.

Some use of force is legal, but some is questionable and illegal. The public frequently has different definitions of excessive force and brutality from those of the police. The frequency of illegal police violence or brutality is low. There are two views of police brutality. The first is that brutality is widespread because rogue police officers are permitted to hide behind lax accountability mechanisms. The second is that brutality is not a major problem and has to be considered in the context of overall high levels of violent crime.

Police use-of-deadly-force has been extensively studied, but its frequency is still difficult to determine because of reporting problems. Research has examined the factors that contribute to the use of deadly force and attempted to explain why its frequency varies from community to community. In the last decade, policy guidelines for the use of deadly force have changed, and many police departments have adopted strict policies governing the use of such force. The result has been fewer citizens being killed by the police.

Critical Thinking Questions

1. Why do police exist? To what extent is police use of force and coercion inevitable? To what extent is police brutality inevitable?

2. Describe the type and nature of police-citizen encounters, particularly as they relate to the use of force by police officers.

3. Describe the use-of-force continuum. Where should canines be placed on the continuum? Pepper spray?

4. What are the police cultural themes having to do with force, and how do they influence an officer's use of force?

5. What is meant by normal force?

6. How frequent is the police use of illegal violence? Why do police sometimes use illegal violence?

7. Identify and define the three categories of deadly force. Why is it so difficult to measure the amount of deadly force in each category?

8. Discuss the impact of environmental, departmental, officer, and racial factors on the police use of deadly force.

9. Is police violence in the United States increasing or decreasing? Is it appropriate (necessary) or excessive? Explain your answers.

References

Alpert, G. P. 1989. "Questioning Police Pursuits in Urban Areas." In R. G. Dunham and G. P. Alpert (eds.), *Critical Issues in Policing: Contemporary Readings*, pp. 216–229. Prospect Heights, IL: Waveland.

Alpert, G. P., and Anderson, P. 1986. "The Most Deadly Force: Police Pursuits." *Justice Quarterly* 2: 1–14.

Alpert, G. P., Kenney, D. J., Dunham, R. G., and Smith, W. C. 2000. *Police Pursuits: What We Know*. Washington, DC: Police Executive Research Forum.

Alpert, G. P., Smith, W. C., and Watters, D. 1992. "Implications of the Rodney King Beating." *Criminal Law Bulletin* 28(5): 469–478.

Anderson, D. C. 2003. "Managed Force," Ford Foundation Report. Available at <http://www.fordfound.org/publications/ff_report/view_ff_report_detail.cfm?report_index=452>.

Barker, T. 1986. "Peer Group Support for Police Occupational Deviance." In T. Barker and D. L. Carter (eds.), *Police Deviance*, pp. 9–21. Cincinnati: Pilgrimage.

Bayley, D. H. 1986. "The Tactical Choices of Police Patrol Officers." *Journal of Criminal Justice* 14: 329–348.

Bayley, D. H., and Garofalo, J. 1989. "The Management of Violence by Police Patrol Officers." *Criminology* 27: 1–12.

Beers, D. 1992. "A Biting Controversy." *Los Angeles Times Magazine*, February 9: 23–26, 43–44.

Berg, B. L. 1992. *Law Enforcement: An Introduction to Police in Society.* Needham Heights, MA: Allyn & Bacon.

"Big Decline in Killings of Citizens by Police." 1986. *San Francisco Chronicle* October 20: 23.

Bittner, E. 1995. "The Capacity to Use Force as the Core of the Police Role." In V. Kappeler (ed.), *The Police and Society: Touchstone Readings,* pp. 127–137. Prospect Heights, IL: Waveland. Reprinted from *The Functions of Police in Modern Society.* Washington, DC: National Institute of Mental Health.

Blumberg, M. 1985. "Research on the Police Use of Deadly Force." In A. S. Blumberg and A. Niederhoffer (eds.),*The Ambivalent Force: Perspective on the Police,* pp. 340–350. New York: Holt Rinehart, & Winston.

——. 1997. *Controlling Police Use of Deadly Force: Assessing Two Decades of Progress.* In R. G. Dunham and G. P. Alpert (eds.), *Critical Issues in Policing,* 3rd ed., pp. 507–530. Prospect Heights, IL: Waveland.

Brown, J. M., and Langan, P. A. 2001. *Policing and Homicide, 1976–1998: Justifiable Homicide by Police, Police Officers Murdered by Felons.* Washington, DC: Bureau of Justice Statistics.

Brown, M. F. 1983. "Shooting Policies: What Patrolmen Think." *Police Chief* 50: 35–37.

Campbell, A., Berk, R., and Fyfe, J. 1998. "Deployment of Violence: The Los Angeles Police Department's Use of Dogs." *Policing* 22(4): 535–561.

Carmichael, J. T., and Jacobs, D. 2002. "Violence by and Against the Police." In R. G. Burns and C. E. Crawford (eds.), *Policing and Violence,* pp. 25–51. Upper Saddle River, NJ: Prentice-Hall.

Carter, D. L. 1994. "Theoretical Dimensions on the Abuse of Authority by Police Officers." In T. Barker and D. Carter (eds.), *Police Deviance,* 3rd ed., pp. 269–290. Cincinnati, OH: Anderson.

——. 1985. "Police Brutality: A Model for Definition, Perspective, and Control." In A. S. Blumberg and E. Niederhoffer (eds.), *The Ambivalent Force: Perspective on the Police,* pp. 321–330. New York: Holt, Rinehart & Winston.

Chapman, S. G. and Crockett, T. S. 1964. "Gunsight Dilemma: Police Firearms Policy." In S. G. Chapman (ed.), *Police Patrol Readings,* pp. 311–321. Springfield, IL: Charles C. Thomas.

Crank, J. P. 1996. "The Construction of Meaning During Training for Parole and Probation." *Justice Quarterly* 31(2): 401–426.

——. 1998. *Understanding Police Culture.* Cincinnati: Anderson.

Crank, J. and Caldero, M. 1999. *The Corruption of Noble Cause: Police and the Ethics of Power.* Cincinnati: Anderson.

"Doubt Shed on Cops' Report in L.A. Beating." 1991. *San Jose Mercury News* March 23: 1F, 4F.

Faulkner, S. 1994. "A Ralph Nadar Approach to Law Enforcement Training." *Police Studies* 17(3): 21–32.

Felkenes, G. T. 1991. "Affirmative Action in the Los Angeles Police Department." *Criminal Justice Research Bulletin* 6: 1–9.

Fridell, L. 1989. "Justifiable Use of Measures in Research on Deadly Force." *Journal of Criminal Justice* 17: 157–165.

Friederich, R. J. 1980. "Police Use of Force: Individuals, Situations, and Organizations." *Annals of the American Academy of Political and Social Sciences* 452: 82–97.

Fyfe, J. J. 1978. "Shots Fired: An Examination of New York City Police Firearms Discharges." Ph.D. dissertation, University of New York at Albany.

——. 1979. "Administrative Interventions on Police Shooting Discretion." *Journal of Criminal Justice* 7: 309–323.

——. 1980. "Geographic Correlates of Police Shooting." *Journal of Research in Crime and Delinquency* 17: 101–113.

——. 1982. "Blind Justice." *Journal of Criminal Law and Criminology* 73: 707–722.

——. 1983. "Enforcement Workshop: The Los Angeles Chokehold Controversy." *Criminal Law Bulletin* 1961–1967.

——. 1985. Interview. *Law Enforcement News* June: 9–12.

——. 1988. "Police Use of Deadly Force: Research and Reform." *Justice Quarterly* 5: 165–205.

Geller, W. A. 1983. "Deadly Force: What We Know." In C. Klockars (ed.), *Thinking About Police,* pp. 313–331. New York: McGraw-Hill.

Geller, W. A., and Karales, K. J. 1981. *Split-Second Decisions: Shootings of and by Chicago Police.* Chicago: Chicago Law Enforcement Study Group.

Geller, W., and Scott, M. 1992. *Deadly Force: What We Know.* Washington, DC: Police Executive Research Forum.

Golden, J. W., and Walker, J. T. 2002. "That Dog Will Hunt: Canine-Assisted Search and Seizure." In J. T. Walker (ed.), *Policing and the Law,* pp. 71–89. Upper Saddle River, NJ: Prentice Hall.

Greenfeld, L., Langan, P., and Smith, S. 1997. *Police Use of Force: Collection of Statistical Data.* Washington, DC: Bureau of Justice Statistics.

Grennan, S. A. 1987. "Findings on the Role of Officer Gender in Violent Encounters With Citizens." *Journal of Police Science and Administration* 15: 78–85.

Hopkins, E. J. 1931. *Our Lawless Police.* New York: Viking.

Horvath, F. and Donahue, M. 1982. *Deadly Force: An Analysis of Shootings by Police in Michigan, 1976–1981.* East Lansing: Michigan State University.

"How Much Force Is Enough." 1998. *Law Enforcement News* November 30: 1, 10.

Human Rights Watch. 1998. *Shielded From Justice: Police Brutality and Accountability in the United States.* New York: Human Rights Watch.

Hunt, J. 1985. "Police Accounts of Normal Force." *Urban Life* 13(4): 315–341.

Illinois v. Perkings. 110 S.Ct. 2394 (1990).

"Inside View of L.A. Beating." 1991. *San Jose Mercury News,* March 19: 1A, 9A.

Kania, R. R. E., and Mackey, W. C. 1977. "Police Violence as a Function of Community Characteristics." *Criminology* 15: 27–48.

Kappeler, V. E., Sluder, R. D., and Alpert, G. P. 1994. *Forces of Deviance: Understanding the Dark Side of Policing.* Prospect Heights, IL: Waveland.

Klockars, C. 1980. "The Dirty Harry Problem." *Annals* 452: 33–47.

Knapp Commission, 1972. *Report on Police Corruption.* New York: George Braziller.

Kuykendall, J. 1981. "Trends in the Use of Deadly Force by Police." *Journal of Criminal Justice* 9: 359–L366.

"L.A. Fires Only 1 percent of Officers." 1991. *San Jose Mercury News* May 5: 4B.

Lamb, R., and Friday, P. 1997. "Impact of Pepper Spray Availability on Police Officer Use-of-Force Decisions." *Policing* 20(1): 136–148.

Larson, J. A. 1932. *Lying and Its Detection.* Chicago: University of Chicago Press.

Marion, Nancy. 1998. "Police Academy Training: Are We Teaching Recruits What They Need to Know?" *Policing* 21(1): 54–79.

Matulia, K. R. 1985. *A Balance of Forces,* 2nd ed. Gaithersburg, MD: International Association of Chiefs of Police.

McEwen, T. 1997. "Policies on Less-Than-Lethal Force in Law Enforcement Agencies." *Policing* 20: 39–59.

McNulty, E. 1994. "Generating Common-Sense Knowledge Among Police Officers." *Symbolic Interaction* 17: 281–294.

Miller, M. R. 1995. *Police Patrol Operations.* Placerville, CA: Copperhouse Publishing Company.

Milton, C. H., Halleck, J. W., Lardner, J., and Albrecht, G. L. 1977. *Police Use of Deadly Force.* Washington, DC: Police Foundation.

Miranda v. Arizona. 384 U.S., 436,466 (1966).

Morrison, G. B. 2003. "Police and Correctional Department Firearm Training Frameworks in Washington State." *Police Quarterly* 6(2): 192–221.

Muir, W. K. 1977. *Police: Streetcorner Politicians.* Chicago: University of Chicago Press.

National Commission on Law Observance and Enforcement. 1931. *Report on Lawlessness in Law Enforcement*, no. 11. Washington, DC: Government Printing Office, (Also known as the Wickersham Commission.)

Navarro, M. 1995. "The Debate Over High-Speed Police Chases." *New York Times National* Dec. 17: 18.

Newman, D. J., and Anderson, P. R. 1989. *Introduction to Criminal Justice*, 4th ed. New York: Random House.

Peak, K. 1993. *Policing America: Methods, Issues, Challenges.* Englewood Cliffs, NJ: Prentice Hall.

President's Commission on Law Enforcement and the Administration of Justice. 1967. *Task Force Report: The Police.* Washington, DC: Government Printing Office.

Reiss, A. J., Jr. 1967. *The Police and the Public.* New Haven, CT: Yale University Press.

"Report Calls for Gates' Ouster." 1991. *San Jose Mercury News* July 10: 1A, 6A.

Reuss-Ianni, E. 1983. *The Two Cultures of Policing: Street Cops and Management Cops.* New Brunswick, NJ: Transaction.

Scharf, P., and Binder, A. 1983. *The Badge and the Bullet.* New York: Praeger.

Shearing, C., and Erickson, R. 1991. "Culture as Figurative Action." *British Journal of Sociology* 42: 481–506.

Sherman, L. W., and Cohn, E. G. 1986. *Citizens Killed by Big-City Police: 1974–1984.* Washington, D.C.: Crime Control Institute.

Sherman, L., and Langworthy, R. 1979. "Measuring Homicide by Police Officers." *Journal of Criminal Law and Criminology* 9(4): 317–331.

Skolnick, J. 1994. "A Sketch of the Policeman's Working Personality." In J. Skolnick (ed.), *Justice Without Trial: Law Enforcement in Democratic Society*, 3rd ed., pp. 41–68. New York: Wiley.

Skolnick, J., and Bayley, D. 1986. *The New Blue Line: Police Innovation in Six American Cities.* New York: Free Press.

Skolnick, J., and Fyfe, J. 1993. *Above the Law: Police and the Excessive Use of Force.* New York: Free Press.

Sparger, J., and Giacopassi, D. 1992. "Memphis Revisited: A Reexamination of Police Shootings After the Garner Decision." *Justice Quarterly* 9(2): 211–225.

"Stun-Gun Charges Shake NYPD to the Rafters." 1985. *Law Enforcement News* May: 6, 13.

Sulc, L. B. 1995. "Police Brutality is Not a Widespread Problem." In P. Winters (ed.), *Policing the Police*, pp. 79–85. San Diego: Greenhaven.

Sykes, R. E., and Brent, E. E. 1983. *Policing: A Social Behaviorist Perspective.* New Brunswick, NJ: Rutgers University Press.

Tennessee v. Garner. 471 U.S. 1,105 S. Ct. 1964 (1985).

Terrill, W. 2001. *Police Coercion: Application of the Force Continuum.* New York: LFB Scholarly Publishing.

Terrill, W., Alpert, G. P., Dunham, R. G., and Smith, M. R. 2003. "A Management Tool for Evaluating Police Use of Force: An Application of the Force Factor." *Police Quarterly* 6(2): 150–171.

Trimmer, R. 1993. "Pepper Spray After Concord: Legal Issues for Policy Makers." *North Carolina Justice Academy* July.

Tucker, W. 1995. "Inner-City Crime is a Worse Problem than Police Brutality." In P. Winters, (ed.), *Policing the Police*, pp. 69–78. San Diego: Greenhaven.

Van Raalte, R. 1986. Interview. *Law Enforcement News* March: 9–12.

Vaughn, M. 1992. "The Parameters of Trickery as an Acceptable Police Practice." *American Journal of Police* 11(4): 71–95.

Walker, S. 1998. *Sense and Nonsense About Drugs and Crime: A Policy Guide,* 4th ed. Belmont, CA: West/Wadsworth.

Wilson, J. Q. 1968. *Varieties of Police Behavior: The Management of Law and Order in Eight Communities.* Cambridge, MA: Harvard University Press.

Suggested Websites for Further Study

Bureau of Justice Statistics: Overview of National and Local Data on Use of Force
http://www.ojp.usdoj.gov/bjs/abstract/ufbponld.htm

Human Rights Watch: Police Brutality
http://www.hrw.org/about/initiatives/police.htm

Amnesty International: Race, Rights, and Police Brutality
http://www.amnestyusa.org/countries/usa/document.do?id=133746465C2-D34CA8025690000692D98

Firearms Training Systems for Law Enforcement
http://www.fatsinc.com/html/law/default.htm

Firearms Judgment Training Simulation
http://www.ais-sim.com/prisim.htm

American Civil Liberties Union: Police Practices
http://archive.aclu.org/issues/policepractices/hmpolice.html ✦

Accountability and Ethics

Chapter Outline

Key Terms	
accreditation	external review
CALEA	false complaints
certification	Garrity interview
civilian-review board	grievance arbitration
civil liability	internal affairs
decertification	internal review
early-warning (early-identification) system	police-auditor systems
	professionalism
ethical formalism	reliability
ethical relativism	sustained complaints
ethical utilitarianism	unfounded complaints
exclusionary rule	unsubstantiated complaints
exoneration	validity

The police are the visible representatives of criminal justice processes in the United States. Yet, in important ways, the police stand apart from society. Their special dispensation is the use of force so that citizens can live together in peace. Nevertheless, by virtue of the authority granted to them to use force, they have the potential to undermine due processes of law (Skolnick 1994). This potential may be infrequently utilized, yet citizens are concerned about police abuse of authority.

The police are respected and feared at the same time. They are respected by many citizens who highly regard the commitment police make to their work, but they are also feared because of the enormous life-and-death authority that they carry. The accountability of the police to democratic processes has been and continues to be one of the central issues confronting the police throughout modern times (McMullan 1998).

To whom are the police accountable? One might be tempted to answer that they are accountable to elected and appointed officials, the general public, people who receive police service (e.g., victims, suspects), and other parts of the criminal justice system (e.g., prosecuting attorneys, judges). Yet this answer overlooks important issues of accountability. Do citizens understand police work well enough to judge the behavior of the police? Should police be responsible for assessing the behavior of their own officers? And what happens when the public encourages the police to break the law in order to do something about law-breaking people? In short, the issues of accountability are complicated, and there is little agreement on who has the authority to hold the police accountable, the means by which they should be held accountable, or for what they should be held accountable (Geller 1985).

The control of police behavior occurs in two fundamentally different ways. The first way is through mechanisms of oversight. These are based on the idea that if a police officer's behavior can be tracked, then illegal or inappropriate behavior can be identified, corrected, or punished. Oversight mechanisms are both internal and external to a police department. Internally, oversight is through departmental investigation, early warning systems, and the restraints of bureaucratic organization and management. Externally, oversight occurs through citizen review, external auditing, and legal remedies for police misconduct.

The second way is through standards, which will be considered in the second half of this chapter. According to this view, officers can be hired with, or trained in, standards of conduct by which they can gauge their behavior. Both professional and ethical standards of "right behavior" fortify them with an appropriate way of thinking about their work and thereby control their behavior.

Internal Accountability Mechanisms

Three oversight mechanisms within police departments will be considered here: standard managerial processes, early warning systems, and internal complaint reviews.

Bureaucratic Organization and Management

The most important day-to-day source of accountability for police officers is in the way their department is organized and managed. Accountability is carried out through the design and operation of principles of bureaucratic organization, as extensively discussed in Chapter 4. This idea will be reviewed here primarily in terms of management-employee relations.

Written directives. In police departments, bureaucratic standards are omnipresent. As Alpert and Smith observe, "Law enforcement is a paradigm of operational control. Virtually every aspect of policing is subject to some combination of either policy, guideline, directive, rule, or general order" (1999, 353). The organization of rules and regulations takes on a specific language in a bureaucracy. Principal terms are listed below. These terms provide the statements that guide the behavior of the department and indicate the responsibility of officers within it.

1. *Departmental policies* are not, as often thought, rules but rather statements of guiding principles that should be followed. A policy should be thought of as a guide to thinking rather than a fixed outcome. A policy is a general statement that gives guidance to police officers as to the proper course of action (e.g., a use-of-force policy).

2. A *goal* is a general statement of purpose that is useful in identifying the role and mission of the police (e.g., to apprehend criminals).

3. An *objective* is a more specific and measurable statement of purpose that is related to a goal (e.g., make arrests in 25 percent of burglary cases).

4. A *procedure* identifies a method or series of steps to be taken when performing a task or attempting to solve a problem (e.g., how to investigate a traffic accident).

5. Finally, a *rule*, or *regulation*, is a specific statement that identifies required or prohibited behavior by officers (e.g., all officers must dress in a certain manner). The terms *rule* and *regulation* are often used interchangeably.

Administrative guidance focuses on a wide variety of topics. Under principles of departmental supervision, managers' responsibilities aim at ensuring that officers' behaviors are consistent with bureaucratic policies and standards. Written directives (policies, procedures, rules, regulations), as Carter and Barker (1994, 22–23) have observed, are important for the following reasons:

1. They inform officers of expected standards of behavior.

2. They inform the community of the departmental mission, goals, values, policies, procedures, and expected standards of officer behavior.

3. They establish a common foundation for the execution of the police process to enhance operational consistency, equal protection, and due process.

4. They provide grounds for disciplining and counseling errant officers.

5. They provide standards for officer supervision.

6. They give direction for officer training.

Within a bureaucratic environment, standards are expressed in written terms as departmental policy and guidelines. Yet in a police department, managers may not follow policies and standards to the letter. In practice, managers may react in a variety of ways when officers deviate from those written standards. They may (1) ignore it, (2) act formally or informally, or (3) protect the officer.

A manager's formal responses include counseling or training (advising or teaching the person how to improve) or some type of disciplinary action (reprimand, suspension, demotion, or termination). The more public criticism there is of certain types of police behavior, the more likely managers are to use some form of punitive discipline. Some managers like to make an example of an employee in order to send a signal to other officers that certain types of behavior will not be tolerated. Employees, however, may consider this type of managerial response to be politically motivated and unfair. From the employees' point of view, they are being made a scapegoat to satisfy political interests.

If a manager believes a deviation exists but has insufficient evidence to act formally, he or she might respond informally, perhaps by transferring the employee to a new work area or assignment. Certain types of assignments can be used so often in a department that they become known as punitive assignments (e.g., the jail or foot patrol during the winter). Sometimes, for instance, if the problem is related to the behavior of the officer when interacting with the public, the officer may be assigned to a job with minimal public contact. In addition, the manager may hope that this type of informal, punitive control will result in a resignation or retirement.

A manager may be aware of a deviation but elect to protect the officer for at least five reasons. The manager may (1) approve of the "deviant" activity or behavior, (2) believe that the most likely official departmental response would be too punitive, (3) be influenced by the so-called code-of-silence in policing, (4) believe that acknowledging the deviation would result in criticism of his/her management ability, or (5) simply want to avoid dealing with the problem by denying that it exists.

Limitations of written directives. Policies, procedures, rules, regulations, and objectives are written standards against which an officer's behavior is judged by supervisors. Officers are expected to conform to these standards. In many police departments, standards number in the hundreds and are printed in very thick manuals. Standards tend to accumulate over time as police departments are faced with a wide variety of situations. It is not uncommon for police officers to be unfamiliar with many of these standards because some are rarely used.

Why do police departments have so many policies? Part of the reason lies in the unpredictable nature of the police function. Police work is highly varied and carried out in a diversity of circumstances. Policies provide direction in unclear situations. Auten notes that the absence of policy leaves officers "in the dark in the expectation that they will intuitively divine the right course of action in the performance of their duties" (1988, 1–2).

Policies, while providing a standard for behavior, suffer from significant limitations. In practice, they are sometimes rule-oriented and tell officers what not to do rather than suggest a possible course of action. This can have an alienating effect on individual officers. Some researchers contend that the rigid bureaucracy characteristic of many police departments is principally responsible for the alienation of line officers and the intensification of more secretive elements of police culture. Consider the following statement Manning recorded during an interview:

> "140 years of fuck-ups. Every time something goes wrong, they make a rule about it. All the directions in the force flow from someone's mistake. You can't go eight hours on the job without breaking the disciplinary code . . . the job goes wild on trivialities." (1978, 79)

A related issue is that police work, by its nature, requires officers to make quick discretionary decisions in varied, unpredictable situations. It has proven difficult, if not impossible, for police managers to formulate written guidelines that effectively cover all the varied situations that police officers encounter on the street. Consequently, policing continues to require officers to act based on "an intuitive grasp of situational exigencies" (Bittner 1970). Officers learn much of what they need to know to make good decisions and do good police work on the job, by apprenticeship and trial and error, rather than by referring to the manual of policies, procedures, rules, and regulations. In this context, written guidelines can seem irrelevant at best and, at worst, an impediment to effective policing (Cordner 1989).

Internal Investigation

All police departments have some way of responding to citizen complaints or internal concerns about police behavior. In many small and moderate-size departments, this response may be the part-time responsibility of only one officer, probably a supervisor or manager. In larger departments, it has been the practice to establish a unit, often called **internal affairs,** to respond to complaints. Prior to studying the investigation process itself, this chapter will first consider the ways in which complaints come to the attention of the police department.

In some communities, citizens do not complain about the police because they do not think it will do any good or because they are afraid the police will retaliate. Some departments make it difficult for citizens to complain by creating a cumbersome complaint process and by the negative (e.g., unfriendly, rude, curt, discouraging) behavior of officers when citizens attempt to complain.

The political climate in a community may be particularly important in encouraging or discouraging complaints against the police. On the one hand, a new mayor or other elected official who calls for an aggressive "crackdown" on crime or who talks about the police as the "thin blue line" between citizens and criminal predators may be indicating to citizens that their concerns about police excesses will not be taken seriously. On the other hand, a new mayor or chief of police might encourage citizens to come forward with complaints about the police. Such encouragement, however, may result in an increase in frivolous as well as serious complaints.

A small number of officers receive a disproportionate number of complaints. For instance, Lersch and Mieczkowski (1996), in their study of a large police department in the Southeast, found that 2.9 percent of the officers in their study accounted for about 25 percent of the complaints. This finding may be explained by several factors. The officers' training may have been inferior. They may have had a more aggressive style of policing, which could result in more complaint-generating conflict with citizens. Finally, complaints may have been related to the area in which the officers worked—for instance, an area in which citizens are more likely to resist police authority (Toch 1995). Younger officers probably receive more complaints (Croft 1987) because more younger officers are assigned to patrol duties and, as a result, they are probably more likely than other officers to have disagreements with citizens. It should be noted that research on characteristics of officers receiving complaints is mixed. For example, Alpert (1989) noted that age had no effect on use-of-force problems; similarly, Hayden (1981) found that length of service also had no effect.

Citizens voicing a complaint with an officer.

The investigative process. When police officers are being investigated as suspects in a crime, they have the same legal procedural rights as any other suspect. But what rights should they have when they are being investigated administratively by supervisors, managers, or internal affairs units? States vary in the rights afforded police officers facing discipline. California has enacted into law what is, in effect, a police officer's bill of rights. Inside Policing 10.1 provides a summary of these rights.

Inside Policing 10.1   Police Officer's Bill of Rights

When any police officer is under investigation and subjected to interrogation that could lead to punitive action, the interrogation shall be conducted under the following conditions. These rights do not apply to an interrogation in the normal course of duty, which might involve counseling, instruction, or informal verbal admonishments.

1. The interrogation shall be conducted at a reasonable hour, preferably when the police officer is on duty, or during normal waking hours, unless the seriousness of the investigation requires otherwise. If the interrogation takes place during off-duty time, the officer shall be compensated in accordance with regular departmental procedures.

2. The persons to be present at the interrogation must be identified in advance, and the officer will not be interrogated by more than two investigators at one time.

3. The police officer will be informed of the charges against him or her prior to any interrogation.

4. The interrogation will be for a reasonable period of time.

5. The police officer shall not be subjected to any offensive language or threats of punitive action, except that an officer refusing to respond to questions or submit to interrogation shall be informed that failure to answer questions that are directly related to the investigation may result in punitive action. There will be no promise or reward offered as an inducement to answer any question.

6. The interrogation may be recorded by either the persons conducting the interrogation or the officer under investigation or both. The officer in question is entitled to written or recorded copies of the interrogation if additional action is contemplated by the department or if there is to be a continuing investigation.

7. If prior to, or during, the interrogation it is decided that the officer may be charged with a criminal offense, the officer will immediately be informed of his or her constitutional rights.

8. If a formal written statement of charges is filed against a police officer by the department, the officer has a right to request that a representative of his or her choice be present during any interrogation.

Source: Adapted from the *California Government Code*, Section 3303.

The process for investigating complaints against officers tends to be similar to other types of investigations. The steps used by many police departments are briefly summarized below (D'Arcy et al. 1990):

1. Review the complainant's allegation to determine what departmental standard(s) was violated.

2. Contact and interview all witnesses and reinterview the complainant if necessary.

3. Collect all other evidence, such as photographs, medical reports, police reports, and so on.

4. Obtain background information on the complainant (e.g., criminal history and any prior allegations against officers).

5. Obtain background data concerning the officer (e.g., prior complaints, personnel evaluations, prior disciplinary actions by the department).

6. Interview all departmental members who may be involved.

Although internal investigations and criminal investigations are similar, there are important differences. Carter (1994) identifies several pertinent differences in internal investigations:

1. The Fourth Amendment guarantees apply to police officers at home and off duty, as they do to any citizen.

2. Lockers at the police station, a police car, and other elements of on-duty performance are unlikely to be protected by the Fourth Amendment.

3. If an unlawful search occurs, the fruits of that search may be used during a disciplinary hearing but not in a legal proceeding. This may not apply to departments that have elaborate policies on the internal investigation process.

4. Under *Garrity v. New Jersey* (1967), statements compelled during an internal investigation cannot be used later in a court of law. Such compelled testimony for internal investigations is routine practice and is not protected by the Fifth Amendment from use within administrative processes and hearings, but it cannot be used in a criminal prosecution for the very reason that it was compelled, not voluntary. This type of compelled testimony is frequently referred to as a **Garrity interview**.

Complaint outcomes. Investigations into citizen complaints are typically classified in one of four possible ways: **Sustained complaints** are ones that, as the result of an investigation, are determined to be justified. **Unsubstantiated complaints** are ones that, in the opinion of those making the decision, have no supporting evidence and so cannot be considered either true or false. The majority of citizen complaints against officers are classified in this manner because it is often difficult to determine with reasonable certainty that the complainant's allegation is true. **Unfounded complaints** are those that the investigation determines did not occur as alleged by the complainant. **Exoneration** of an officer occurs when the investigation results in a finding that the alleged complaint is essentially true, but the officer's behavior is considered to be justified, legal, and within organizational policy (Perez 1994).

If an officer is found guilty of the complaint, she or he can appeal the outcome. Avenues of appeal typically include the parent government's civil service system and the courts. If the complaint is sustained, the officer will receive some sort of punishment. Carter identifies several kinds of punishments.

1. *Termination of employment.* This is complete severance, including salary and benefits.

2. *Demotion/loss of rank.* Loss of rank is a significant action because it represents loss of salary and liability in career growth. It may not include "grades," which are salary increments within ranks.

3. *Punitive suspension.* An officer is barred from work without salary for a designated period, usually not exceeding four weeks. In many jurisdictions the officer cannot even work off-duty in positions that require police authority.

4. *Punitive probation.* An officer stays on duty with full salary and benefits. A subsequent sustained misconduct allegation may result in dismissal.

5. *Reassignment.* This is often used in conjunction with some other kind of punishment. An officer may be taken out of a specialized position or moved to another shift or location.

6. *Mandatory training.* An officer may receive training on the issue related to the misconduct.

7. *Reprimand.* An officer is officially admonished for his or her behavior. It is in written form, usually from a division commander, with a copy placed in the personnel file.

8. *Supervisory counseling.* This is a discussion with the officer concerning a problem usually related to some performance factor or procedure. It is intended to be both instructive and corrective. It does not typically become a part of the employee's personnel file (1994, 367–368).

Research concerning the number, types, and dispositions of complaints against police is limited. Several studies, however, provide useful insights. A summary (Independent Commission . . . 1991; Dugan and Breda 1991; "Younger NYC Cops" 1989; Petterson 1991; Walker 1998; Wallace 1990) is presented below:

1. Although less than 1 percent of citizens complain about police methods and behavior, as many as 10 to 15 percent may think that they have something to complain about—either what officers did or failed to do.

2. The rate of complaints varies among police departments, from about 6 to 81 complaints per 100 officers per year.

3. The percentage of sustained complaints also varies among police departments, from about 0 to 50.

4. Complaints concerning the excessive use of police force are usually sustained less often than other types of complaints.

5. It appears that a small number of police officers account for a disproportionate number of complaints. Although the research varies, a reasonable estimate is that approximately 10 percent of the officers in a police department receive at least 25 or 30 percent of the complaints by citizens.

6. It also appears that a disproportionate number of complaints are filed against younger, less-experienced officers. As many as two-thirds or more of all complaints in some departments may involve officers who are 30 years of age or younger and who have five or less years of experience.

Table 10.1 presents the results of a survey of citizen complaints in 10 large cities. This table reveals widespread differences between rates of complaints per 100 officers and the percentage of sustained complaints. The frequency of complaints varies sharply from city to city. To understand these differences, several factors must be considered.

The number and types of complaints against the police, in general, are the result of actual differences in police behavior, the perceived receptivity of a police department to accepting and acting upon complaints, and a political climate that either discourages or encourages citizens to complain.

Table 10.1 Citizen Complaints About Police Misconduct in 1988

City	Number of Complaints	Complaints per 100 Officers	% Sustained
San Francisco	1,146	81.4	1.2
Seattle	412	35.9	7.7
Boston	427	21.8	25.0
Cleveland	376	21.7	8.8
New York	4,179	15.7	2.4
Indianapolis	156	15.3	14.1
Miami	312	13.3	21.4
Los Angeles	702	9.1	17.1
San Jose	91	9.0	16.4
Oakland	47	7.3	0.0

Source: Adapted from B. Wallace, 1990, "S. F. Watchdog Upholds Few Charges," *San Francisco Chronicle*, May 29: 1, 4–6.

The reasons for variations in sustained complaints are also related to the degree to which departments have well-defined standards for police behavior, take those standards seriously, and conduct thorough investigations into complaints. Low rates of sustained complaints may result from a departmental culture that implicitly encourages officers to engage in aggressive police work.

Issues in Internal Investigations

There are several controversies concerning the internal investigation of police officers. These include the physical location of the internal affairs unit, the personnel assigned to work in internal affairs, whether or not complaints should be encouraged, whether or not internal affairs units should be proactive or reactive, what should be done about false complaints, the type and severity of discipline for officers who have sustained complaints, and whether the police can effectively police themselves.

Location and personnel. Does the location of internal affairs units influence the number of citizen complaints? It is possible that a citizen who believes he or she has been abused by the police will be reluctant to go to the police department to file a complaint. As Perez observes,

> The uniforms, badges, guns, and paramilitary carriage of police officers at a station house might be too much to confront for more passive complaints. A system that requires complaints cannot be made exclusively for those citizens having the audacity to confront the government. (1994, 103)

As a result of this possibility, some police departments have placed the internal affairs unit in another location away from police headquarters. This change of location may also have a positive impact on the public perception of the police, because citizens may believe that the police are taking their complaints seriously.

368 Part III ✦ *Police Behavior*

Most often the personnel who conduct internal investigations are sworn police officers, but some departments also use civilians for some investigations on the assumption that some citizens who want to complain will be more comfortable with a civilian than a police investigator. Also, the use of civilians creates the public perception that complaints will be taken more seriously and be more thoroughly investigated. In addition, because a substantial number of complaints are made by minority citizens, internal-affairs units may also be staffed with minority members. This use of civilian (nonsworn) minorities may even be necessary if the police department has no minority officers who can be assigned to the internal affairs unit.

Assignment to internal affairs is often controversial. Internal affairs investigators are rarely popular with other officers. The term headhunter, or some other uncomplimentary nickname, is sometimes used by officers to describe internal affairs investigators. As a result, some police chiefs and sheriffs have made it clear that assignment to, and effective performance in, an internal affairs unit is a "fast track" to advancement/promotion within the agency.

Orientation of internal affairs units. Should citizen complaints against the police be encouraged? Encouraging citizens to come forward—either openly or anonymously—has several possible consequences. On the one hand, it may increase the trust between police and citizens and provide managers with valuable information about officer behavior (Walker and Graham 1998). On the other hand, it may also result in more complaints, justified or otherwise. Unfortunately, in departments that encourage complaints, a morale problem may develop as an increasing number of officers have to endure investigations into complaints. Whether or not complaints are sustained, internal affairs investigations are often stressful for the officers involved and unpleasant for officers throughout the department.

Should internal affairs units be reactive or proactive? A reactive unit investigates only those complaints that are brought to its attention. A proactive unit seeks out officers involved in deviant behavior. For example, an internal-affairs investigator might purposely commit traffic violations and, when stopped by an officer, offer a bribe to avoid a citation. If the officer takes the money, he or she is usually terminated and may be criminally prosecuted. Such a proactive approach may be strongly resented by officers because it creates a climate of mistrust between them and managers. Although some authorities recommend that internal affairs units be proactive (Murphy and Caplan 1991, 261–263), managers must be aware of the possible adverse consequences of such action.

Although it is not clear how often it occurs, citizens make **false complaints** about police officers. How should the police respond? In some jurisdictions, persons suspected of filing a false report can be criminally prosecuted. Police officers can also sue the person for defamation if he or she falsely accuses an officer of criminal conduct, misconduct, or incompetence.

While it is the officer involved who decides whether or not to file a civil suit against a citizen who made a false complaint, the police department decides whether to file criminal charges. Should they have that right? Although filing criminal charges may act as a deterrent against false complaints, it may also have a chilling effect on citizens with legitimate grievances, making this a most difficult question to resolve.

Sustained complaints. When complaints against officers are sustained, what should be done? The alternatives include counseling, retraining, verbal reprimands, written reprimands, demotions, suspension without pay, and termination. Unfortunately, there is no standard to follow. Generally, of course, the more serious the behavior of the officer, the more severe the punishment.

After their examination of 171 sustained complaints involving excessive force or improper police tactics in the Los Angeles Police Department, the Christopher Commission (Independent Commission . . . 1991) concluded that the type of disciplinary measures taken against the officers were too lenient. Only about 12 percent of the officers were terminated, resigned, or retired. Approximately 58 percent were suspended without pay for a period of time, and the remainder received some type of reprimand.

Officers do not have to accept the recommended disciplinary action if they believe it is inappropriate. Many police departments have an appeals process that allows the officer in question to challenge the type of discipline recommended. Officers can challenge in court what they perceive to be extreme forms of discipline. In unionized agencies, another option for officers may be to file for **grievance arbitration**. One recent study found that grievance arbitration typically reduces the amount of discipline that is ultimately imposed by 50 percent (Iris 2002). Consequently, disciplinary actions by managers may be based, at least in part, on an assessment of whether or not the officer will appeal or file a grievance. The authors of this book are aware of instances in which police managers knew of inappropriate behavior but took no action because they believed that the appeals process would undermine any effort to punish the officer.

Another factor affecting the complaint process is the likelihood of civil litigation (discussed in Chapter 11) if the complaint is sustained. Some departments may be reluctant to discipline officers for fear that it will be interpreted as an admission of negligence on the part of the department. In some instances, citizen complaints cannot be investigated because the complainant will not cooperate until the civil suit is resolved. Consequently, the investigation of a citizen complaint may not be completed for a long time, possibly a year or more.

Early-Warning/Early-Identification Systems

A modern approach to police officer accountability that combines the bureaucratic and internal investigation methods is the use of an **early warning system** (EWS), also called an **early identification system** (Walker 2003c). These systems track specific types of officer behaviors and then alert management when individual officers exceed the threshold for such behavior. For example, management might be notified about any officer who receives more than two use-of-force complaints within a year, or who files more than two use-of-force reports in any month. The types of behaviors that are tracked typically include citizen complaints against officers, internal rule violations, use-of-force reports, charging of suspects with resisting arrest, sick days, and accidents. These systems are based on the premise noted above that a small percentage of officers are responsible for a large percentage of improper behavior. They attempt to identify such officers quickly in order that discipline or other corrective action can be taken sooner rather than later.

It goes without saying that an early-warning system must be used with due regard for the rights of officers as well as citizens. An officer might come to the attention of the EWS because of a vindictive citizen (such as a crime suspect), an overcontrolling supervisor, a particularly tough assignment, or just bad luck. All the EWS does is identify officers who might be engaging in a pattern of improper conduct. Investigation and judg-ment are still required to determine if there really is a problem and if corrective action is needed. Also, if intervention is needed, the initial response is often counseling or retraining, unless the improper conduct has been very serious (see Table 10.2).

Table 10.2 Early-intervention Alternatives

- Referral to department employee-assistance program
- Referral to professional family-counseling service
- Referral to credit-counseling services
- Retraining on traffic stop tactics
- Verbal judo training

Source: Samuel Walker, *Early Intervention Systems for Law Enforcement Agencies: A Planning and Management Guide* (Washington, D.C.: Office of Community Oriented Policing Services, 2003), 38.

Effectiveness of Internal Investigations

Can the police effectively regulate the behavior of their own? Historically, there has been a recurring debate on this question.

Proponents of internal (departmental) review argue that **internal review** is neces-sary to maintain police morale, that **external review** interferes with the authority of the chief executive, and that other methods (e.g., elected and appointed officials, the courts) are available to citizens if they are not satisfied. In addition, many police offi-cers do not believe that external review of police conduct is likely to be impartial. They believe that such reviews and recommendations for discipline will often be politically motivated. Furthermore, they believe that, in general, those favoring internal review have been the police themselves and ideological supporters.

Proponents of the external (citizen) review of police behavior (to be discussed in the next section) include individuals with a liberal political ideology, civil rights organiza-tions, minority-group members, and the media (West 1988). Proponents argue that internal investigations of police complaints are the actions of a system closed to outsid-ers and favorably predisposed toward police officers. Furthermore, internal investiga-tions may not be trusted by the public. If the public perceives that the police are unre-sponsive and unfair in their investigation of complaints, public confidence in the police will be eroded. Consequently, involving citizens in the complaints process has the capacity to restore trust and confidence in police-citizen relations (West 1988).

External Accountability Mechanisms

The second set of oversight mechanisms are those outside the police department. They have emerged primarily in response to concerns that police departments do not hold their members sufficiently accountable. Three external oversight mecha-nisms—civilian review, police auditors, and legal remedies—are considered here.

Civilian Review

A **civilian-review board** is an effort to control police behavior by establishing an external form of review for allegations of police misconduct. It should be noted, how-ever, that even in those communities that have some type of external review, the police department usually continues to conduct its own investigations of complaints.

Research indicates that over half of the 50 largest cities in the United States have some type of external review of citizen complaints against the police, and that more than 100 external oversight agencies are now in existence (Walker and Bumphus 1991; Walker 2003a). The creation of an external review board is usually related to a political perception that the police are out of control and typically follows in the wake of a police scandal.

A brief history of civilian review. Citizen participation in the review of com-plaints against the police can be traced to the Progressive Era, when reformers wanted to reduce the influence of corrupt politicians (Caiden 1977). Yet throughout the first half of the twentieth century, there was little progress in establishing citizen review. In its 1967 report, the President's Commission on Law Enforcement and Administration of Justice noted the problems faced by citizens when they tried to complain about police brutality. Such citizens might be arrested, or the police might file criminal charges against them for filing a false report. Many police departments had no formal internal-investigations unit or procedure. The commission found that less than 10 percent of citizen complaints were substantiated, and even when they were, officers were infrequently or too lightly punished.

Both the National Advisory Commission on Civil Disorders (1968) and the National Commission on the Causes and Prevention of Violence (1969) reached similar conclu-sions. These studies found that police departments had inadequate investigative proce-dures and resisted efforts to make complaint procedures more meaningful.

Terrill (1991) divides the discussion about civilian review into three time periods, which he calls "climates of opinion." The first era was the late 1950s and 1960s, during which various forms of civilian review boards were first suggested. These early pro-posals, considered politically controversial, were vigorously resisted by the police. Several cities, such as Chicago and New York, struggled to establish some form of civilian review; only Philadelphia established a review process that lasted for several years, but it too was eventually abandoned, in part for political and legal reasons but also in large measure because the police department's internal affairs unit processed many more cases and meted out much harsher punishments than did the civilian review board (Caiden 1977; Terrill 1991).

The second era, the 1970s, was distinguished by increases in public concern about the criminal justice system. Urban riots, the civil rights movement, the President's Commission on Law Enforcement and Administration of Justice (1967), and the National Advisory Commission on Civil Disorders (1968) all called attention to trou-bling behavior on the part of the police. This period was marked by increased public support for civilian review.

Several communities (e.g., Detroit and Miami-Dade County, Florida) established some type of civilian oversight of the police. However, these civilian-review processes were not without problems and resistance. The city of Detroit, over the opposition of the Detroit Police department, established a five-person Board of Police Commissioners, which continues today. Its role includes the development of policies and procedures in consultation with the chief of police and approval of the police budget. The board also created the Office of Chief Investigator, who was given a staff of both civilian and police investigators. The chief investigator is responsible for coordinating the investigation of complaints and disciplinary matters in the police department. The board has the authority not only to receive complaints but also to review the investigation of complaints undertaken by the police department, and either to affirm or change any disciplinary action taken against officers.

During the third era, the 1980s, several major cities established review processes, including the San Francisco Office of Citizen Complaints, the San Diego Police Review Commission, and the Dallas Citizens' Police Review Board. Police opposition to civilian review did not change, however, nor did their principal arguments. Although the police no longer considered civilian review to be part of a communist plot to overthrow the government, as they had in the 1960s, police executives, departments, and unions continued to argue that it undermined managerial authority and the professionalism of the police. To strengthen their argument, many departments worked hard to improve the internal investigations of citizen complaints.

Petterson's survey (1991) of 19 communities with some type of civilian-review board indicates the diversity of approaches in this area. One of the boards was established in the 1960s, four in the 1970s, and 14 in the 1980s. Fourteen of the boards conduct their own investigations, whereas the others rely on investigations by the police department. Only one of the boards, however, is actually authorized to determine the discipline to be imposed on officers. The others can only recommend disciplinary measures that the police department may or may not use.

Inside Policing 10.2   Organizational Features of Citizen Review

The Nature of Citizen Input

How are citizens involved in the review process? There are three ways.

1. Citizens conduct the initial fact-finding investigation.
2. Citizens have input into the review of complaints but do not conduct the investigation.
3. Citizens monitor the process but do not review individual complaints.

The Complaint-Review Process

Review boards may have two purposes.

1. They review individual complaints. Virtually all boards do this.
2. They review department policies and make recommendations for changes. About 66 percent of the boards also do this.

Jurisdiction

Do boards monitor police officers only or are they also responsible for other public employees? Seventeen percent of the boards studied also set up other boards with the authority to monitor other public employees.

Organizational Structure

1. The majority (85 percent) had a multi-member board. Boards ranged in size from 3 to 24 members. Twenty-seven

Inside Policing 10.2   **Organizational Features of Citizen Review (continued)**

percent of these boards included sworn police officers. This structure deals with one of the most important questions affecting civilian review: Who has representation on the civilian review board? Many minority-group members, while seeking advocacy, are concerned with the issue of tokenism.

2. The remainder (15 percent) are administrative boards with a single administrative director. These boards presume that administrative procedure, rather than representation, is the best way to conduct review of police behavior.

Operating Policies

There are four different policies, each of which has direct implications for police accountability.

1. Independent investigative powers are held by about 33 percent of all review boards.
2. Subpoena power is held by 38 percent.
3. Public hearings are conducted by about half (46.2 percent).
4. About 32 percent provide legal representation for the officer, for the citizen, or both.

Each of these four policies may be described as a different element of a "criminal trial" model. Only 11 percent of the boards studied had all four elements. Two of the review boards had none.

Source: Adapted from S. Walker and B. W. Kreisel 1996: "Varieties of Citizen Review," *American Journal of Police* 15: 65–88.

Today, civilian-review boards encompass many different types of organizational designs and purposes. Walker and Kreisel (1996) identified five dimensions among which civilian-review boards vary. They are discussed in Inside Policing 10.2.

The limits of civilian review. The decision by a community to establish some form of civilian review of police behavior is usually based on the assumption that it will be more effective and fair than an internal investigation by the police. The limited research in this area, however, tends not to support this assumption. Caiden (1977) concluded that attempts to institute civilian review in the 1970s failed because the police resisted such attempts and used both political and legal means to limit their potential effectiveness.

West (1988) found that complaint procedures (internal or external) were not related to the number of complaints filed or the seriousness of those complaints. But when complaints were encouraged by either the police or civilian-review boards, they were less likely to be sustained. It appeared that frivolous and minor complaints occurred more frequently when complaints were encouraged.

Perez (1994) has identified several problems associated with civilian review. First, civilian-review boards do not tend to find problems occurring more frequently than internal affairs units do. He observes that

> No fair system will find the police guilty of misconduct very often because, in a legalistic sense, the police are not guilty of misconduct very often.
> One must also consider a sociological reality. Most civilian-review board members develop an appreciation for the police and for police work. Over time, they are less and less prone to be tough on officers, and they actually begin to find fault with complainants. (1994, 146)

Consequently, civilian review is unlikely to change the efficiency or effectiveness of police review. Finally,

> Members of civilian-review boards . . . seem to have a sort of "boys will be boys" attitude toward truthfulness. . . .When a lie is discovered by civilian systems, it is considered to be a part of the "playing of the game," a natural product of a system designed to investigate misconduct. . . .Thus, while chiefs take lying very seriously, civilian review boards largely do not. (1994, 147)

Perez notes three additional limitations of civilian review. First, it is too far removed from the day-to-day existence of the line officer to understand and respond to the dynamics of illegal behavior. Second, civilian review can take away opportunities for the immediate supervisor to deal creatively with problems. Inadvertently, civilian review undermines the ability of the police department to "generate genuine humility and acceptance of error on the part of young, developing police officers" (161). Finally, civilian review tends to discourage the use of internal socialization processes. Perez believes that the role of peers and their contribution to the socialization of recruits is an inevitable and essential part of police work. It should be encouraged, not discouraged.

Police Auditor Systems

Police auditor systems have developed more recently than civilian review board systems. The most important difference is that police auditors do not usually investigate or even monitor individual citizen complaints—that is left to the internal processes of the police department. Instead, the auditor model focuses on the police organization and its policies and practices. In the fashion of the Government Accounting Office (GAO), police auditors examine different aspects of the ongoing operation of the police department to ensure that legal requirements are being met and that the most efficient and effective practices are being followed. As noted by Walker (2003a, 6–7), the auditor model:

> Seeks to identify problems in the complaint process or other police policies and recommend corrective action to the chief executive. . . . The underlying assumption is that these recommendations will have a preventive effect, reducing the likelihood of certain forms of misconduct occurring in the future.

Jurisdictions with well-established police auditors include the San Jose Police Department (Guerrero-Daley 2003) and the Los Angeles County Sheriff's Department (Bobb 2002). Others include Austin, Boise, Omaha, Philadelphia, Portland, Reno, Sacramento, Seattle, and Tucson. Among the principles that seem to make this model most effective are independence from the law enforcement agency, free access to internal police data and documents, public reporting of findings and recommendations (see Table 10.3), and direct access to the chief/sheriff (Walker 2003b).

Legal Control

Criminal, civil, and administrative laws are important tools in the control of police. Like all citizens, the police are required to obey substantive criminal laws. In addition, some states impose criminal penalties for officers who misuse the verification given them by standards commissions. Such officers can be decertified. Procedural laws, called criminal procedure or due process, provide legal guidelines for the police when enforcing substantive laws. They govern the process of investigating crimes and apprehending suspects. Police officers and departments may also be sued civilly if they fail to act in a responsible manner.

Table 10.3 Police Auditor Recommendations and Results in San Jose, California

Year	Auditor Recommendations		
	Adopted	Not adopted	Pending
1993	5	0	0
1994	13	2	0
1995	6	0	0
1996	9	1	0
1997	4	0	0
1998	1	0	0
1999	7	1	0
2000	11	1	1
2001	13	2	4
Total	**69**	**7**	**5**

Source: Teresa Guerrero-Daley, *2002. Year-End Report* (San Jose, CA: City of San Jose Independent Police Auditor, 2003), 83-92. Available at <http://www.ci.san-jose.ca.us/ipa/reports/02ye.pdf>.

Legal issues affecting police work are examined in depth in Chapter 11. The focus here is specifically on the role played by the law in controlling police behavior as another means of establishing external accountability.

Exclusionary Rule. One method of legal control over police behavior is the **exclusionary rule.** This is a rule imposed by the U.S. Supreme Court that requires that any evidence gathered by the police through improper searches or seizures (including interrogations) must be excluded from trial. The purpose of the exclusionary rule is to take away any incentive that the police might have to "bend the rules" and thereby to encourage them to respect peoples' constitutional rights more closely. This legal principle is explained in more detail in the next chapter.

Criminal Liability. When police officers violate a criminal law, they can be held for criminal prosecution in both state and federal courts. Criminal law prosecution sometimes occurs when excessive use of force is alleged, for example. In these kinds of cases, officers might be charged with assault or, in the case of deadly force, manslaughter or murder. Police officers caught in corruption investigations often face charges of theft, fraud, extortion, or some type of misuse of official authority. As noted, criminal prosecution might take place in a state or federal court. It is not uncommon for federal prosecution to be initiated if state prosecution is declined or unsuccessful, since federal law enforcement agencies and the U.S. Department of Justice bear some responsibility for helping control police abuses at the state and local levels.

Criminal violations of civil rights. Police officers, like anyone else, can also be charged with criminal violations of civil rights, as defined in Title 242, Section 18, of the U.S. Code. It is difficult, however, to prove beyond a reasonable doubt that a police officer committed a crime—either state or federal—as a result of the possible use of excessive or deadly force. To do this, it is usually necessary to establish that the officer had criminal intent to engage in the behavior. The prosecution has to establish that the officer knew and understood the nature and consequences of his or her action, that the officer knew that what he or she was doing was a crime and did it anyway. For this reason, officers who are accused of using excessive force are often prosecuted federally for having violated the civil rights of the victim. This approach has proven successful—in many cases police officers have been found not guilty in a state court of assault or murder but have subsequently been found guilty of civil rights violations in a federal court.

Decertification. Another method of legal control involves the possible **decertification** of officers. About three-fourths of the states have some form of decertification (Goldman and Puro 1987). In Florida, the Criminal Justice Standards and Training Commission is authorized to "decertify" (or suspend or put on probation) officers for (1) violating the legal rights of individuals; (2) the "negligent deprivations of liberty or prop-

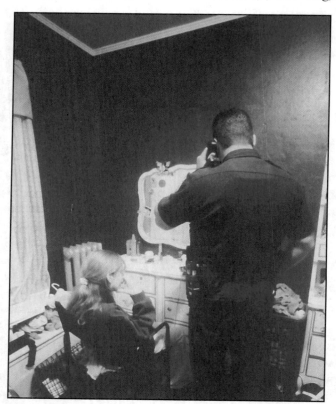

erty"; (3) failing to maintain the required qualifications for the job; (4) falsifying or misrepresenting information during the application process; and (5) "gross insubordination, gross immorality, habitual drunkenness, willful neglect of duty, incompetence, or gross misconduct." Between 1976 and 1983, the commission decertified 132 officers, suspended 14, and put two on probation. In 22 cases, decertification was the result of behavior that involved criminal conduct; in the other cases, it was for departmental or private misconduct (Goldman and Puro 1987, 67–68).

Civil liability. One of the most common legal methods to control police behavior is a **civil liability** suit. This means that a police officer, his or her supervisor, the chief, and the police department (or at least the governmental unit—i.e., the city of

Officer searching a residence. The scope of his search is limited by the Fourth Amendment and related legal cases.

which the department is a part) can be sued for monetary damages for negligent behavior. Civil liability has become a firmly established fact of life for police officers and police departments in recent decades. The threat of being sued is often mentioned by police officers as one of their constant worries (Scogin and Brodsky 1991). Presumably, this threat has the desired effect of discouraging officers from misusing their authority. Civil liability is discussed in much greater detail in Chapter 11.

The Limits of Oversight Mechanisms

Oversight mechanisms, especially those focused on punishment, are in many ways responsible for the development of the more secretive elements of police culture. Crank and Caldero (1999) explain police culture and its relationship to secrecy with the metaphor of an onion:

> Think of police culture as an onion. It has a heart that animates every police officer and gives meaning to police work. The heart is how police officers feel and think about their work, how they celebrate their victories and mourn their losses. It is how they do their work and how it is meaningful to them. The values most central to police, the heart of the onion, are encased by the first layer. . . .The outermost layers of the onion enable police to protect themselves from external influences, particularly the upper-management levels of the organization itself, so that they can maintain their moral control over their territories and protect the inner "heart," the commitment to the noble cause. (146–147)

Chapter 1 defined the organization culture as "the pattern of basic assumptions that a given group has invented, discovered, or developed in learning to cope with its problems of external adaptation and internal integration, [and] that have worked well enough to be considered valid" (Schein 1985, 9). The culture is made up of values that guide the behavior of police officers. This section will discuss these values.

Sparrow, Moore, and Kennedy (1990) have listed what they consider to be some of the most influential values of police officers. These values are summarized in Inside Policing 10.3.

The values that undergird police culture are derived substantially from daily work experiences. The most important elements of police culture reflect how officers adapt to their environment. Culture is the process of adaptation shared, discussed, and finally formed into habits. Cultural values are the meanings associated with those habits.

It is the type and frequency of problems confronted by the police—not the hopes of police reformers or administrators—that determines the way police do their work and what is important to them. Externally imposed control systems, often failing to understand this simple truth, backfire by intensifying resentment and secrecy. Police will not change unless their working environment is in some way changed, but they will become more secretive. As reformers and administrators intensify their efforts to hold the police accountable for an impossible mandate—to police a democracy—the strength of the secretive elements of police culture will also increase (Manning 1998).

The next section looks at moral/ethical standards, as distinct from legal standards, which control behavior by providing officers with an internal gauge for their work. These standards are preventive because officers are expected to anticipate outcomes of their behavior before they act. They can be divided into professional standards and ethical standards.

Inside Policing 10.3   Building Blocks of the Police Culture

1. The public wants the police to be crime fighters, and that is what the police think of themselves as being, the primary crime-fighting organization in government.

2. No one other than another police officer understands the "real" nature of police work and what is necessary to do to get the job done.

3. Police have to stick together; loyalty to one another is more important than anything else because everyone else, including the public, politicians, and police managers, seems to try to make the job of police offi-

cers more difficult. And these individuals are often unfair in their evaluations of the police.

4. Police cannot "win the war" on crime without violating legal, organizational, and ethical standards.

5. The public does not support or appreciate the police, and they expect too much of police officers.

Source: Adapted from M. Sparrow, M. Moore, and D. Kennedy, *Beyond 911: A New Era for Policing* (New York: Basic Books, 1990), 51.

Professional Standards

The concept of **professionalism** in policing is associated with the recurring attempts of reformers to ensure that police officers are honest. More specifically, an occupation, to be considered a profession, must adopt certain criteria. Recognition that such adoption is a prolonged process is called a process-criterion approach. As an occupation becomes a profession, one criterion is the learning of a systematic process that uses the scientific method (Cullen 1978; Geison 1983). Inside Policing 10.4 provides a list of the criteria the authors believe indicate that an occupation has reached professional status.

Inside Policing 10.4   Professional Criteria

1. Professionals are represented by professional associations, which serve the purpose of transmitting knowledge of the field.

2. Professionals are provided autonomy to perform their work. Even in organizations characterized by a bureaucracy, professionals are granted the opportunity to do their work with only limited control by supervisors.

3. A profession encompasses a unique body of knowledge, associated with research, which must be constantly updated.

4. Professionals require lengthy and formal training.

5. Professionals require certification of quality and competence.

6. Professionals have a commitment to service on behalf of a clientele.

Sources: J. B. Cullen, 1978, *The Structure of Professionalism*, Princeton, NJ: Princeton University Press; G. L. Geison, ed., 1983, *Professions and Professional Ideology in America*, Chapel Hill: University of North Carolina Press; R. Hall, 1968, "Professionalization and Bureaucratization," *America Sociological Review* 33: 92–104.

The Police Professionalization Movement

Occupations that adopt the criteria presented in Inside Policing 10.4 are professionalized and are recognized as such by the public and other professional organizations. Their members believe in these criteria and are accorded the status of professionals (Hall 1968). As professionals, they are granted wide latitude to decide how to conduct their work. Even when they work in bureaucratic organizations, they have the autonomy to define problems in their area of expertise, to respond to those problems, and to gauge the success of their work. In a word, they are largely left alone by managers. Members of professions, such as doctors and lawyers, operate on these principles.

These conditions have not been true of the police. The police professionalization movement, begun in 1893 by the International Association of Chiefs of Police (IACP) and central to efforts to reform the police until 1968, sought to bureaucratize the police through specialization of function and intense control of line officers (Fogelson 1977). Rather than fostering independent decision making in line officers, the movement sought centralization of command under the authority of the chief. Individual officers were not admitted to the ranks of professionals but instead were controlled with ever tighter accountability (Fogelson 1977). Police departments, not police officers, became professionalized (Regoli et al. 1988).

As the police professionalization movement unfolded, officers were considered to be the product of a management system controlled by police executives. Police executives blended bureaucratic management and chain-of-command control to attempt to force line officers to go along with the reforms the executives wanted (Kuykendall and Roberg 1990). Consequently, police officers below the executive level were (and continue to be) rarely considered professional colleagues but only a group of individuals that had to be "managed." These police officers were left out of the professionalization process. One consequence of this trend was the development of sharply antagonistic relationships between line personnel and management (Reuss-Ianni 1983). Such antagonisms continued to be a critical issue in the twenty-first century.

As subordinates, police officers have been told what not to do more often than what to do, and they have been laden with rules and policies seeking to control their behavior rather than to expand and sharpen their discretionary skills (Alpert and Smith 1999). Therefore, the professionalization movement itself, except for commitment to service (discussed later), did not contribute toward professionalization of policing. True professionalism did not begin until the professionalization movement declined, and the community-policing movement—with its emphasis on the decentralization of authority and empowerment of line officers—began to gain ground.

Criteria of Police Professionalization

Characteristics of policing as a true profession are described below.

Autonomy. The development of professional autonomy is a central criterion in the process of professionalization. Autonomy provides professionals with the discretion to carry out their work, and its presence shows that society acknowledges their professional status.

Police departments, as previously noted, have historically sought to control the behavior of line officers. The community-policing movement, however, emphasizes increased autonomy and with it the decentralization of authority and the use of creative techniques in solving problems. Each of these items expands the autonomy of police officers and thus represents movement toward professionalism.

Decentralization of authority occurs in two ways. One is the transfer of authority to make tactical decisions down the chain of command. For example, patrol officers may be given the authority to decide what kinds of crime problems they want to focus on. Line officers are expected to make tactical decisions traditionally reserved for sergeants and lieutenants. The second way is geographic decentralization, meaning that officers are assigned to specific areas and take increased responsibility in solving the problems confronted in those areas.

Increased decision-making is a relaxation of traditional constraints on the use of police discretion. Wilson and Kelling (1982) argue that officers should be provided with broad latitude in controlling common public-order problems on their beat. Such problems, if unaddressed, lead to neighborhood degradation and the onset of serious crime. By allowing officers wider latitude to deal with these problems, more effective long-term solutions to crime can be developed.

"Creative, customized police work," according to Skolnick and Bayley (1986), is important in finding creative solutions to recurring public-order problems. Goldstein (1998) suggests that officers engaged in problem-solving analysis redefine problems in noncriminal terms. Tailor-made responses, he contends, are a critical ingredient in finding effective solutions.

A unique body of knowledge. Another criterion of professionalism is that a profession has an area of unique expertise that only its practitioners are qualified to assess. Such expertise can be gained in three ways.

The first way, common especially before the 1960s, is to study the work of experts. These are well-educated, experienced practitioners, usually executives such as O. W. Wilson and August Vollmer, who lectured and wrote journal articles and books. Wilson's famous *Police Administration* (1950) contains many useful ideas about how to manage police departments. Many of his ideas were the result of his extensive experience, but some were taken from writers about general management principles. Many police today continue to depend almost exclusively on the knowledge of experts as a basis for their actions.

The second way to gain expertise is by consulting-modeling. In this method, the management and practices of a police department are analyzed by an expert or consultant who then compares the results to a model of what he or she considers to be desirable—for example, an effective way to select and train officers.

Models come from several sources. One source is the creativity and imagination of the expert or consultant. Another might be a police department that the consultant likes or considers to be progressive. If the consultant has been a police manager, the model might be his or her former department. Or, models may come from books written by other experts in the field.

The third way to acquire expertise is by scientific research. Scientific research is empirical—that is, based on what can be observed. Two conditions apply to scientific observations. The first is that the observation has **validity**, meaning that what the observer sees is what is actually going on. The second is that it has **reliability**, meaning that if other observers conducted the research again in the same setting, they would be likely to come to similar (if not precisely the same) conclusions.

Research conducted by Sherman (1999) and by Sherman and his colleagues (1997), for example, shows how scientific research has had powerful effects on police knowledge. It has dramatically expanded knowledge about what works in policing. It has enabled scholars systematically to compare a wide variety of research on policing. And it has provided a benchmark for thinking about the quality of police research.

Education and training. A further criterion of professionalism is formal preparation. Professionals typically undergo extensive training and education, followed by certification.

Chapter 6 identified the types and extent of police training. Higher education is becoming increasingly important in all aspects of policing, as discussed in Chapter 12. Over the past three decades, the numbers of educated officers and the quantity of education that they possess have increased dramatically. Nevertheless, it does not yet approach the level expected in other professions.

Certification and accreditation. Professionalism also requires **certification** as a criterion of its members to ensure quality and competence. Usually state-level organizations give licenses or certifications. The legal profession, for example, has state bar associations, and all lawyers must pass the bar examinations in their state in order to practice law there.

State standards organizations fulfill this function for the police. They set standards for the selection, training, and certification of police officers. Currently, all states have such organizations—the titles of which vary. For example, in Arizona the state organization is called the Law Enforcement Officer Advisory Council; in Kentucky it is called the Kentucky Law Enforcement Council. The central function is training, defined by Berg (1994) as learning the techniques for particular processes or procedures through example and instruction.

Officers making an arrest. Citizen complaints often result when officers use force when making arrests.

The first standards organization, established in California in 1959, was the Commission on Peace Officer Standards and Training (POST). Its purpose is "to raise the level of competence of local law enforcement officers, to help improve the administration, management, and operation of local law enforcement agencies" (Commission on POST 1990, 4). In attempting to accomplish this mission, the commission engages in four activities:

1. Develops minimum selection standards and minimum required knowledge and skill standards for the training of all levels of police officers (i.e., entry, supervisor, technical, managerial, and executive).

2. Develops and approves training programs that meet POST standards.

3. Provides management and research assistance and services to local law enforcement agencies.

4. Provides financial reimbursement to local agencies for officers who attend some POST-approved training courses. (4)

Today POST commissions exist in nearly every state. They provide a wide diversity of training that focuses on skills, knowledge, cultural diversity, attitudes, and ethics.

An important aspect of licensing is **accreditation.** Professional organizations frequently provide for means of accreditation of member associations. Universities, for example, are periodically reviewed and accredited by regional accreditation boards. The purpose of accreditation for the police is to determine if a department meets general standards of policy and training. This determination is accomplished through self-assessment in an attempt to match national standards set up by the Commission on Accreditation for Law Enforcement Agencies (**CALEA**). If a department is deemed to meet these standards, it is accredited by CALEA for a five-year period, which is renewable on reassessment if the department remains in compliance with the standards (Cole 1992).

CALEA was established in the early 1980s with 944 standards; this number was later reduced to 897 and then to the current 436 (Commission on Accreditation . . . 1995). Proponents of accreditation believe that self-assessment helps to identify departmental strengths and weaknesses and may reduce the exposure to liability. Departments in several states have been offered reduced insurance rates for completing the process (Williams 1989). Accreditation may help departments to address administrative issues and policies, and perhaps by tightening up in these areas, to become more professional and less exposed to liability (McAllister 1987). Nearly all of the accreditation standards, however, require that only a formal policy or procedure be established or that records be maintained. There is no systematic or in-depth monitoring system set up to determine the extent that CALEA-revised policies and procedures are actually implemented and followed.

The 436 standards set by CALEA are extensive, and if all are applied, it is likely that a department would become more, not less, bureaucratic. Also, most of the standards that apply to patrol work focus on law enforcement to the virtual exclusion of order maintenance and service (Mastrofski 1990). This situation is not entirely consistent with community policing. According to Cordner and Williams (1995, 1996, 1999), an examination of these standards regarding their applicability to community policing indicated, for the most part, that these standards are either silent or neutral on the subject. It appears that such standards could be constraining departments that are attempting to implement community policing, especially in the areas of officers' participation, encouraging risk-taking in applications of discretion, and removing organizational barriers to creativity (Cordner and Williams 1996, 256). Cordner and Williams suggest that CALEA and its sponsoring organizations (including the International Association of Chiefs of Police, the National Sheriffs Association, the National Organization of Black Law Enforcement Executives, and the Police Executive Research Forum) address the following concerns in the future:

1. Improve its research and development capacity and establish a more proactive posture toward contemporary changes in policing.

2. Play a more active role in big-picture issues affecting policing.

3. Pay more attention to accreditation issues and participate more actively in CALEA's direction and focus (1996, 378–379).

At this time, it seems prudent to suggest that, in relatively well-developed departments that are in transition to community policing, accreditation could impede managers' efforts to promote change (Oettmeier 1993; Sykes 1994). This conclusion would hold until the accreditation process places significant emphasis on problem solving, innovation, and community input, instead of focusing on bureaucratic rules and regulations. On the other hand, in less well-developed departments that have inadequate policies and procedures, accreditation may be very beneficial.

Commitment to service. One of the most important criteria of a professional is a "commitment to service." Service means a formal obligation to act on behalf of the professional's clientele to render service as needed (Rhoades 1991). This is one area in which the police professionalism movement has contributed to the professionalism of individual officers.

One of the principal objectives of the movement was to instill a sense of calling in police officers. Early twentieth-century reformers, concerned about the lax standards many recruits brought to police work, sought to instill in officers a commitment to law enforcement.

To them, this meant a commitment to a belief in the contribution of police to society. The movement was successful in instilling this sense of commitment in police recruits. Chapters 3 and 4 discussed the service activities of police officers. Indeed, in many departments today, police work is mandated as a 24-hour obligation. In a reversal of direction, some reformers today are concerned about the overcommitment of police to their work, believing that police officers are overzealous in their pursuit of "bad guys" (Chapter 8).

Ethical Standards

The most effective method for controlling a person's behavior is for that person to believe in the standards of conduct he or she is supposed to follow. Ethical standards identify right and wrong behavior in any endeavor in life. Individual ethical standards about integrity, responsible behavior, use of coercion, and compassion provide officers with internal guides for their conduct. If officers do not have an internalized standard of ethics, they are more likely to engage in some form of deviant behavior (e.g., corruption or brutality). Inside Policing 10.5 gives the code of ethics for police officers for the state of California. Part of this code was adopted from the International Association of Chiefs of Police's (IACP) code of ethics, which is utilized by many states.

Inside Policing 10.5   Law Enforcement Code of Ethics

The purpose of the police code of ethics is to ensure that all peace officers are fully aware of their individual responsibility to maintain their own integrity and that of their department. Every peace officer, during basic training, or at the time of appointment, must swear to abide by the following code of ethics. The officer is also expected to abide by certain canons (rules) that embody those ethics.

Code

As a law enforcement officer, my fundamental duty is to serve humanity; to safeguard lives and property; to protect the innocent against deception, the weak against oppression or intimidation, and the peaceful against violence or disorder; and to respect the constitutional rights of all people to liberty, equality, and justice.

I will keep my private life unsullied as an example to all; maintain courageous calm in the face of danger, scorn, or ridicule; develop self-restraint; and be constantly mindful of the welfare of others. Honest in thought and deed in both my personal and official life, I will be exemplary in obeying the laws of the land and the regulations of my department. Whatever I see or hear of a confidential nature or that is confided to me in my official capacity will be kept ever secret unless revelation is necessary in the performance of my duty. I will never act officiously or permit personal feelings, prejudices, animosities, or friendships to influence my decisions. With no compromise for crime and with relentless prosecution of criminals, I will enforce the law courteously and appropriately without fear or favor, malice or ill will, never employing unnecessary force or violence and never accepting gratuities.

I recognize the badge of my office as a symbol of public faith, and I accept it as a public trust to be held so long as I am true to the ethics of the police service. I will constantly strive to achieve these objectives and ideals, dedicating myself to my chosen profession—law enforcement.

Canons

1. The primary responsibility of police officers and departments is the protection of citizens by upholding the law and respecting the legally expressed will of the whole community, not that of a particular political party or clique.

2. Police officers should be aware of the legal limits on their authority and the "genius of the American system," which limits the power of individuals, groups, and institutions.

3. Police officers are responsible for being familiar with the law and not only their responsibilities but also those of other public officials.

4. Police officers should be mindful of the importance of utilizing the proper means to gain proper ends. Officers should not employ illegal means nor should they disregard public safety or property to accomplish a goal.

5. Police officers will cooperate with other public officials in carrying out their duties. However, the officer shall be careful not to use his or her position in an improper or illegal manner when cooperating with other officials.

6. In their private lives, police officers will behave in such a manner that the public will "regard [the officer] as an example of stability, fidelity, and morality." It is necessary that police officers conduct themselves in a "decent and honorable" manner.

7. In their behavior toward members of the public, officers will provide service when possible, require compliance with the law, respond in a manner that inspires confidence and trust, and will be neither overbearing nor subservient.

8. When dealing with violators or making arrests, officers will follow the law; officers have no right to persecute individuals or punish them. Officers should behave in such a manner so that the likelihood of the use of force is minimized.

9. Officers should refuse to accept any gifts, favors, or gratuities that, from a public perspective, could influence the manner in which they discharge their duties.

Inside Policing 10.5   Law Enforcement Code of Ethics (continued)

10. Officers will present evidence in criminal cases impartially because the officer should be equally concerned with the prosecution of criminals and the defense of innocent persons.

Sources: Adapted from California Commission on Peace Officers Standards and Training, 1990, *Administrative Manual*, c-5; J. M. Pollock-Byrne, 1989, *Ethics in Crime and Justice*, Pacific Grove, CA: Brooks/Cole.

Ethical Perspectives

Attempts to identify appropriate ethical standards for the police have proven difficult. Different schools of thought, concerning what is and is not ethical show the difficulty encountered by reformers concerned with police behavior.

Ethical formalism. The school of **ethical formalism** places moral worth on "doing one's duty." An officer who believes that police should "go by the book" is an ethical formalist. Legalistic policing is a kind of ethical formalism. An element of legalistic policing, as noted earlier, was that officers strive for the full enforcement of the law. Police legalism does not provide for fine distinctions in police discretion. On the contrary, legalistic departments justify their presence in terms of their capacity to enforce the law fairly among all groups.

Ethical utilitarianism. According to the school of **ethical utilitarianism,** it is the results of one's actions that determine what is moral or good. Behavior is judged not by the goodness of the acts, but by the consequences that they bring. For example, if an officer thought an illegal search was necessary in order to arrest a serious criminal, a utilitarian argument could be used to justify that search. An officer who says that she or he would sooner be "judged by 12 than carried by 6" is taking a utilitarian point of view—it is wiser to use deadly force in an ambiguous though perilous encounter and take a chance of being convicted of illegal behavior by a jury than to hesitate and possibly be killed by the suspect.

Ethical relativism. Perhaps the most complicated ethical position of all is **ethical relativism.** Relativism means that which is considered good varies with the particular values of groups and individuals. This perspective can be used to justify enforcing certain laws in some neighborhoods but ignoring them in others (Pollock-Byrne 1998, 12–30). Police might object strenuously that they are not relative in their ethics. Yet, the idea of "full enforcement" of the law is neither realistic nor possible (Goldstein 1998). The discretionary nature of police work is widely cited. Consequently, an ethically relativistic approach to policing is probably a more realistic description of day-to-day police ethics than any other.

Inside Policing 10.6, adapted from Pollock (1997), displays in summary form several schools of ethics.

Elements of community policing are consistent with ethical relativism. One of the tenets of community policing is that community values should determine what is "good" in police work. But what a particular neighborhood considers to be "good" police work may result in the police tolerating certain types of illegal behavior or in officers engaging in illegal tactics to solve problems (e.g., conducting illegal searches

---

Inside Policing 10.6   Schools of Ethics

Religion

What is good is that which conforms to God's will.

How do we know God's will?
Bible or other religious document.
Religious authorities.
Faith.

Ethical Formalism (Deontological Ethics)

What is good is that which conforms to doing one's duty and the categorical imperative.

What is the categorical imperative?

Act in such a way that one would will it to be a universal law.

Treat each person as an end and not as a means.

Utilitarianism

What is good is that which results in the greatest benefit for the greatest number.

Act utilitarianism "weighs" the benefits of an act for just those people and just that incident.

Rule utilitarianism "weighs" the benefits after determining the consequences of making that behavior a rule for the future.

Egoism

What is good is that which results in the greatest benefit for me.

Enlightened egoism, however, may allow one to reciprocate favors and may be practiced by a "good" person (because it benefits the self to be nice to others).

Source: Adapted from J. Pollock, "Ethics and Law Enforcement." In R. G. Dunham and G. P. Alpert (eds.), *Critical Issues in Policing*, 3rd ed. (Prospect Heights, IL: Waveland Press, 1997), 348.

---

of suspected drug dealers). Inside Policing 10.7 describes an incident in one Western city in which ethical relativism resulted in police officers tolerating illegal behavior.

Inside Policing 10.7   Ethical Relativism and the Law in Police Work

In Santa Ana, California, in the early 1980s, most of the people who frequented the downtown part of the city at night were "overwhelmingly Mexican." This area, in effect, became a *corso,* a customary part of Spanish life in which mariachi bands play and sing in cafes and bars and then come out onto the street, creating a festive atmosphere. Some of the persons participating in the *corso* were illegal aliens, but police officers made no attempt to determine the status of those individuals who frequented the area. In addition, officers did not usually provide assistance to agents of the Immigration and Naturalization Service (INS), whom many city residents called the "green gestapo" (referring to the green card that legal residents are supposed to have). In fact, the police department had a history of not cooperating with the INS because the police chief did not agree with the methods used by INS agents to identify and arrest illegal aliens (many of whom were otherwise law-abiding). Known prostitutes also frequented the downtown area at night. One prostitute, Sugar, was a drug addict who had four children. Sugar openly solicited young men to have sex. In one incident, Sugar met a young man on the street, then engaged him in a short conversation, and then walked together with him around the corner of a building to a more private area. When the young man returned, a foot patrol officer called out in Spanish, "How was it?" The bystanders, who apparently knew what was going on, laughed at the young man's obvious embar-

Inside Policing 10.7   Ethical Relativism and the Law in Police Work (continued)

rassment. The officer in question said: "We don't arrest these people [because] they are young men . . . who work hard [to] save up money to bring their families from Mexico. . . . They're gonna have sex. There just isn't any point in arresting people for having sex."

Notice that in this example, the community, meaning those individuals who frequented the downtown area at night, openly tolerated the practice of prostitution by drug addicts; consequently, the police ignored this illegal behavior as long as prostitutes did not appear to be under the influence of drugs at the time of the sexual activity. In addition, some officers undoubtedly thought it would be pointless to enforce laws against prostitution in such circumstances. This example also illustrates how community values can be in conflict with laws enforced by other government agencies such as the INS.

Source: Adapted from J. H. Skolnick, and D. H. Bayley, *The New Blue Line* (New York: The Free Press, 1986), 40–43.

Ethical Dilemmas

Police confront profound ethical dilemmas. To fail to recognize this fact is to fail to understand the nature of policing. An ethical dilemma central to the craft of policing is the conflict between means and ends.

In their day-to-day practice, police confront what is widely called the "Dirty Harry" problem, that is, a conflict between means and ends. The end is so obviously good that they feel compelled to pursue it. Yet there are not legal means to do so. Should the officer use illegal or "dirty" means to pursue an unquestionably good end? Klockars notes that police will tend to justify dirty means if "what must be known and, importantly, known before the act is committed, is that it will result in the achievement of the good end" (1991, 414).

Klockars presented a compelling argument that the Dirty Harry problem is at the core of the police role. Police tend to think that they are dealing with people who are factually, if not legally, guilty. Consequently, an officer's belief in the certainty of guilt is not always determined by factual accuracy but by police cultural standards: "Dirty Harry problems," Klockars observes, "can arise wherever restrictions are placed on police methods and are particularly likely to do so when police themselves perceive that those restrictions are undesirable, unreasonable, or unfair" (1991, 414). In other words, Dirty Harry problems are probably more widespread, and less certain in the likelihood of factual guilt, than the police think that they are.

The particular ways that means vs. ends conflicts affect police work are expanded by Crank and Caldero (1991). The core of police work, they argue, is the "noble cause" (see Chapter 8). This is the belief in the absolute rightness of doing something about criminals. It is a compelling commitment to "get bad guys off the street." Police, they note, not only dislike lawbreakers and troublemakers, but they identify intensely with victims of crime and feel a moral responsibility for their assignments. The "noble cause" is corrupted when police consider it justifiable to break the law in order to apprehend or punish suspected wrongdoers. Noble-cause corruption means that officers are willing to violate legal means in order to achieve a noble end (Delattre 1996). Officers, Crank and Caldero contend, are hired into policing already morally committed to the idea of the noble cause. They are frequently hostile to due process ideas at the time they are hired, and police culture reinforces this hostility. Only later in their career, as they move up the departmental ladder and gain broader perspective, do some officers begin to understand how the police are part of a broader system of competing moral values.

Officers confronting demonstrators in Washington, D.C. Civil disorder and civil disobedience create special problems for the police.

Noble-cause corruption takes many different forms. It includes testifying wrongly or testimonial deception (Barker 1996), fluffing up evidence (Barker and Carter 1999), and in more extreme cases, drug corruption (Manning and Redlinger 1977). It encompasses all situations in which police bend the rules in order to sustain an arrest or get a conviction.

The Limits of Professional and Ethical Standards

The idea that codes of conduct can prevent misconduct seems reasonable. Yet prevention has proven to be difficult. First, although professional and ethical standards provide a good model for police work, they may have limited impact on its reality. They tend to be in written form, presented to satisfy external audiences, with little impact on day-to-day police behavior.

Second, the need for controls is driven to a certain extent by the people-based, unpredictable nature of police work. This same unpredictability, however, limits the effectiveness of those controls. And unpredictability cannot be removed from police-citizen interactions (Harmon 1995).

Third, the study of ethics can result in the development of arguments to justify deviating from established ethical or professional standards. Officers who belong to different ethical schools may use those schools to justify their behavior. It is not hard to review the research on police ethics, for example, to find adequate justification for breaking the law in order to get bad guys off the street, if that is what a police officer believes in.

Fourth, the manner in which officers carry out their day-to-day activities is affected as much by informal group ethics—the "ethics of the street"—as by any of the ethical schools discussed. The exercise of discretion, whether or not officers follow departmental standards or the law, use force, lie, accept gratuities, or engage in other corrupt practices, may be affected as much by peer group processes as formal ethical and professional standards.

In Voices From the Field, Deputy Chief Michael Berkow, an recognized expert on police internal affairs, presents his view that a combination of formal and informal mechanisms is the best approach to controlling police behavior.

Voices From the Field
Michael Berkow
Deputy Chief, Los Angeles Police Department

Question: What are the most effective methods for achieving a high level of police integrity and ethics?

Answer: The problems of police corruption and misconduct have been with us since the inception of organized policing. Some argue that these problems are unique to policing. I think that Abraham Lincoln was closer when he said, "Nearly all men can stand adversity, but if you want to test a man's character, give him power." The role of a police officer, the unique and special powers we are given when sworn in, and the manner in which we carry out our job (frequently alone, often at night, constantly in contact with people and situations that can benefit us individually) create ample opportunities to test one's moral character.

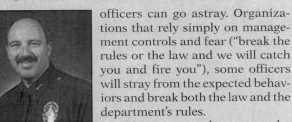

The best methods are a blend of positive measures (strong screening procedures at the time of hire, with integrity a highlighted factor for screening-in as well as screening-out, clear value statements embedded in the organizational culture, solid integrity training throughout one's career) coupled with effective, proactive internal controls and investigative tools — in a word, good internal affairs systems. The reality is that even in the best of organizations, with well paid, highly educated and motivated officers, in the absence of good internal investigations and strong management controls,

officers can go astray. Organizations that rely simply on management controls and fear ("break the rules or the law and we will catch you and fire you"), some officers will stray from the expected behaviors and break both the law and the department's rules.

Most men and women who choose policing as a career do so for a noble purpose, to pursue a higher calling, rather than simply to obtain good wages and benefits. To maintain our integrity in a profession where we make decisions in a sea of grays rather than a world of black and white, we need to constantly remind and reinforce our members of their core reasons for signing up. We need to remind them of the nobleness of their job and the responsibilities to society that they agreed to carry out. And we need to ensure that police leaders exhibit the qualities we expect of those who follow us. Too often, there is a gap between the behavior that police leadership displays and that which we expect from our subordinates.

Finally, we need to struggle with the current conflict between our primary policing philosophy, community oriented policing, and the management controls we are using. Community policing is based on the concepts of employee empowerment, independent decision making, getting close to the communities that an officer serves, identifying problems within those communities, and then working to solve them. In contrast, overlaid on this policing philosophy, our management controls continue to demand strict supervision, log sheets detailing an officer's every move, rules that enforce keeping a distance from our citizens, and an oft-used philosophy of rotation designed to keep our officers from getting "too close" to our citizens. We must find a way to bring these conflicting philosophies into alignment. Otherwise, we will continue to send mixed messages to our officers, messages that in some cases will translate into ethical problems. ✦

Price (1996, 87) sums up the challenge confronting the police in her essay on the quest for professionalism.

> Eradicating the excessive use of force and the scourge of police corruption are the most critical internal issues police face if they are to continue the long and arduous course toward professionalism. There have been many successes of late for law enforcement, especially in communications technology, forensics, information systems, interagency cooperation, and the development of a commitment to their peers, if not to professional conduct. But until attitudes of the police towards those they serve can be changed, they will continue to make their own jobs more difficult and more dangerous—and professionalism for the police will not come to pass. (1996, 87)

Summary

Police accountability is concerned with controlling line-officer behavior. Two kinds of accountability mechanisms are oversight (internal and external) and standards (professional and ethical). Internal oversight mechanisms include bureaucratic procedure, internal investigation, and early-warning/early-identification systems. External mechanisms of accountability are citizen-review boards, police auditors, and legal controls. Officers are controlled primarily through the administrative procedure. Internal investigations are usually associated with internal-affairs units; external review is usually associated with civilian-review boards. The legal methods to control the police include criminal prosecution in both state and federal courts, the exclusionary rule, decertification, and civil suits.

Two primary sources of standards for police officers are professional and ethical training. The police professionalization movement has historically represented efforts to make the police occupation a profession. However, because of its preoccupation with the image of the department, it focused on controlling the behavior of line officers. Other trends in policing are consistent with ideas of professionalism at the individual level. These include community policing, efforts to expand and refine police discretion, and advances in functional research. The expansion of police professional organizations, state standards organizations, CALEA, and accreditation all indicate increasing levels of police professionalism.

By considering different ethical schools of thought, one can see how officers facing the same problem might come to quite different solutions. The "Dirty Harry" dilemma, for example, is commonly confronted by police officers and has no easy solution.

Critical Thinking Questions

1. Which is more effective for controlling police behavior, an internal-affairs unit or a civilian-review board? Why?

2. Should internal affairs be reactive or proactive? Which would be more effective? Why?

3. Which is a more effective method of external oversight of the police, a civilian review board or a police auditor? Why?

4. How effective is the exclusionary rule at deterring police from illegal searches and seizures? What are the pros and cons of excluding evidence that has been illegally obtained?

5. What will it take to make police work a profession?

6. How would each of the three ethical perspectives assess the "Dirty Harry" problem? As a citizen, how do you want the police to respond in "Dirty Harry" situations?

References

Alpert, G. 1989. "Police Use of Deadly Force: The Miami Experience." In R. Dunham and G. Alpert (eds.), *Critical Issues in Policing*, pp. 480–496. Prospect Heights, IL: Waveland Press.

Alpert, G., and Smith, W. 1999. "Developing Police Policy: An Evaluation of the Control Principle." In L. K. Gaines and G. W. Cordner (eds.), *Policing Perspectives: An Anthology*, pp. 353–362. Los Angeles: Roxbury Publishing.

Auten, J. 1988. "Preparing Written Guidelines." *FBI Law Enforcement Bulletin* 57: 1–7.

Barker, T. 1996. *Police Ethics: Crisis in Law Enforcement*. Springfield, IL: Charles Thomas Publishers.

Barker, T., and Carter, D. 1999. "Fluffing up Evidence and Covering Your Ass: Some Conceptual Notes on Police Lying." In L. K. Gaines and G. W. Cordner (eds.), *Policing Perspectives: An Anthology*, 342–350. Los Angeles: Roxbury Publishing.

Berg, B. 1994. "Education v. Training." In A. Roberts (ed.), *Critical Issues in Crime and Justice*. Thousand Oaks, CA: Sage Publications.

Bittner, E. 1970. *The Functions of Police in Modern Society*. Boston: Northeastern University Press.

Bobb, M. 2002. Los Angeles County Sheriff's Department: 15th Semi-Annual Report. Los Angeles, CA: Police Assessment Resource Center. Available at <http://www.co.la.ca.us/ bobbreports/ mbobb15.pdf>.

Caiden, G. E. 1977. *Police Revitalization*. Lexington, MA: D. C. Heath.

Carter, D. 1994. "Police Disciplinary Procedures: A Review of Selected Police Departments." In T. Barker and D. Carter (eds.), *Police Deviance*, 3rd ed., pp. 355–376. Cincinnati: Anderson.

Carter, D., and Barker, T. 1994. "Administrative Guidance and the Control of Police Officer Behavior: Policies, Procedures, and Rules." In T. Barker and D. Carter (eds.), *Police Deviance*, 3rd ed., pp. 13–28. Cincinnati: Anderson.

Cole, G. F. 1992. *The American System of Criminal Justice*, 6th ed. Pacific Grove, CA: Brooks/Cole.

Commission on Accreditation for Law Enforcement Agencies. 1995. *Standards Manual*, 3rd ed. Alexandria, VA.

Commission on Peace Officer Standards and Training. 1990. *POST Administrative Manual.* State of California: POST.

Cordner, G. W. 1989. "Written Rules and Regulations: Are They Necessary?" *FBI Law Enforcement Bulletin* 58, 7: 17–21.

——. 1996. "Community Policing and Accreditation: A Content Analysis of CALEA Standards." In L. T. Hoover (ed.), *Quantifying Quality in Policing,* pp. 243–261. Washington, DC: Police Executive Research Forum.

——. 1999. "Community Policing and Police Agency Accreditation." In L. Gaines and G. W. Cordner (eds.), *Policing Perspectives: An Anthology,* pp. 372–379. Los Angeles: Roxbury Publishing.

Cordner, G. W., and Williams, G. L. 1995. "The CALEA Standards: What Is the Fit With Community Policing?" *National Institute of Justice Journal* August: 39–49.

Crank, J. P. 1995. "The Community Policing Movement of the 21st Century: What We Learned." In J. Klofas and S. Stojkovic (eds.), *Crime and Justice in the Year 2010,* pp. 107–126. Belmont, CA: Wadsworth.

——. 1998. *Understanding Police Culture.* Cincinnati: Anderson.

Crank, J. P., and Caldero, M. A. 1991. "The Production of Occupational Stress Among Line Officers." *Journal of Criminal Justice* 19(4): 339–350.

——. 1999. *Police Ethics: The Corruption of Noble Cause.* Cincinnati: Anderson.

Crank, J. P., and Langworthy, R. 1992. "An Institutional Perspective of Policing." *Journal of Criminal Law and Criminology* 83: 338–363.

Croft, E. 1987. "Police Use of Force in Rochester and Syracuse, New York: 1984 and 1985." *Report to the New York State Commission on Criminal Justice and the Use of Force,* Vol. 3. New York.

Cullen, J. B. 1978. *The Structure of Professionalism.* Princeton, NJ: Princeton University Press.

D'Arcy, S. et. al. 1990. "Internal Affairs Unit Guidelines." San Jose, CA: San Jose Police Department.

Delattre, E. J. 1996. *Character and Cops: Ethics in Policing,* 3rd ed. Washington, DC: American Enterprise Institute.

Dugan, J. R., and Breda, D. R. 1991. "Complaints About Police Officers: A Comparison Among Types and Agencies," *Journal of Criminal Justice* 19: 165–171.

Fogelson, R. 1977. *Big-City Police.* Cambridge, MA: Harvard University Press.

Garrity v. New Jersey. 385 U.S. 483 (1967).

Geison, G. L. (ed.). 1983. *Professions and Professional Ideologies in America.* Chapel Hill: University of North Carolina Press.

Geller, W. A. (ed.) 1985. *Police Leadership in America: Crisis and Opportunity.* New York: Praeger.

——. 1991. *Local Government Police Management,* 3rd ed. Washington, DC: International City Management Association.

Goldman, R. and Puro, S. 1987. "Decertification of Police: An Alternative to Traditional Remedies for Police Misconduct," *Hastings Constitutional Law Quarterly* 15: 50–80.

Goldstein, J. 1998. "Police Discretion Not to Invoke the Criminal Justice Process: Low Visibility Decisions in the Administration of Justice." In G. F. Cole and M. G. Gertz (eds.), *The Criminal Justice: Politics and Policies,* 7th ed., pp. 85–103. Belmont, CA: Wadsworth.

Guerrero-Daley, T. 2003. *2002 Year End Report.* San Jose, CA: City of San Jose Independent Police Auditor. Available at <http://www.ci.san-jose.ca.us/ipa/reports/02ye.pdf>.

Hall, R. 1968. "Professionalization and Bureaucratization." *American Sociological Review* 33: 92–104.

Harmon, M. M. 1995. *Responsibility as Paradox: A Critique of Rational Discourse on Government.* Thousand Oaks, CA: Sage Publications.

Hayden, G. 1981. "Police Discretion in the Use of Deadly Force: An Empirical Study of Information Using Deadly Force Decision Making." *Journal of Police Science and Administration* 9: 102–107.

Independent Commission on the Los Angeles Police Department. 1991. *Report*. Los Angeles: California Public Management Institute. (Also known as the Christopher Commission.)

Iris, M. 2002. "Police Discipline in Houston: The Arbitration Experience." *Police Quarterly* 5(2): 132–151.

Klockars, C. 1991. "The Dirty Harry Problem." In C. Klockars and S. D. Mastrofski (eds.), *Thinking About Police: Contemporary Readings*, pp. 428–438. New York: McGraw-Hill.

Kuykendall, J., and Roberg, R. R. 1990. "Police Professionalism: The Organizational Attribute." *Journal of Contemporary Criminal Justice* 6: 49–59.

Lersch, K., and Mieczkowski, T. 1996. "Who Are the Problem-Prone Officers? An Analysis of Citizen Complaints." *American Journal of Police* 15(3): m23–44.

Manning, P. K. 1998. *Police Work: The Social Organization of Policing*. 2nd ed. Prospect Heights, IL: Waveland.

Manning, P. K. 1978. "Rules, Colleagues, and Situationally Justified Actions." In P. K. Manning and J. Van Maanen (eds.), *Policing: A View From the Street*, pp. 71–89. Santa Monica, CA: Goodyear.

Manning, P. K. and Redlinger, L. 1977. "Invitational Edges of Corruption: Some Consequences of Narcotic Law Enforcement." In P. Rock (ed.), *Drugs and Politics*, pp. 279–310. Rutgers, NJ: Society/Transaction Books.

Mastrofski, S. 1990. "The Prospects of Change in Police Patrol: A Decade in Review." *American Journal of Police* 9: 1–79.

McAllister, B. 1987. "Spurred by Dramatic Rise in Lawsuits, Police Agencies Warm to Accreditation." *Washington Post* March 17: A7.

McMullan, J. 1998. "Social Surveillance and the Rise of the Police Machine." *Theoretical Criminology* 2(1): 93–117.

Murphy, P. V., and Caplan, G. 1991. "Fostering Integrity." In W. A. Geller (ed.), *Local Government Police Management*, pp. 239–271. Washington, DC: International City Management Association.

National Advisory Commission on Civil Disorders. 1968. *Report*. Washington, DC: U.S. Government Printing Office.

National Commission on the Causes and Prevention of Violence. 1969. *To Establish Justice, to Ensure Domestic Tranquility*. Washington, DC: U.S. Government Printing Office.

Oettmeier, T. N. 1993. "Can Accreditation Survive the '90s?" In J. W. Bizzack (ed.), *New Perspectives on Policing*. Lexington, KY: Autumn House Publishing.

Perez, D. 1994. *Common Sense About Police Review*. Philadelphia: Temple University Press.

Petterson, W. E. 1991. "Police Accountability and Civilian Oversight of Policing: An American Perspective." In A. J. Goldsmith (ed.), *Complaints Against the Police: The Trend to External Review*, pp. 259–289. Avon, England: Bookcraft Limited.

Pollock, J. M. 1997. "Ethics and Law Enforcement." In R. G. Dunham and Alpert, G. P. (eds.), *Critical Issues in Policing*, 3rd ed., pp. 337–354. Prospect Heights, IL: Waveland.

Pollock-Byrne, J. M. 1998. *Ethics in Crime and Justice: Dilemmas and Decisions*, 3rd ed. Belmont, CA: West/Wadsworth.

President's Commission on Law Enforcement and Administration of Justice. 1967. *Task Force Report: The Police*. Washington, DC: U.S. Government Printing Office.

Price, B. R. 1996. "Police and the Quest for Professionalism." In J. Sullivan and J. Victor (eds.), *Criminal Justice: Annual Editions 96/97*, pp. 86–87. Guilford, CT: Brown and Benchmark.

Regoli, R., Crank, J. P., Culbertson, R., and Poole, E. 1988. "Linkages Between Professionalization and Professionalism Among Police Chiefs." *Journal of Criminal Justice* 16(2): 89–98.

Reuss-Ianni, E. 1983. *Two Cultures of Policing: Street Cops and Management Cops.* New Brunswick, NJ: Transaction Books.

Rhoades, P. W. 1991. "Political Obligation: Connecting Police Ethics and Democratic Values," *American Journal of Police* 10: 1–22.

Schein, E. H. 1985. *Organization Culture and Leadership.* San Francisco: Jossey-Bass.

Scogin, F., and Brodsky, S. L. 1991. "Fear of Litigation Among Law Enforcement Officers." *American Journal of Police* 10: 41–45.

Sherman, L. W. 1999. "Policing for Crime Prevention." In C. Eskridge (ed.), *Criminal Justice: Concepts and Issues,* 3rd ed., pp. 131–148. Los Angeles, CA: Roxbury Publishing.

Sherman, L., Gottfredson, D., MacKensie, D., Eck, J., Reuter, P., and Bushway, S. 1997. *Preventing Crime: What Works, What Doesn't, and What's Promising.* Washington, DC: U.S. Department of Justice.

Skolnick, J. 1994. *Justice Without Trial: Law Enforcement in Democratic Society,* 3rd ed. New York: John Wiley and Sons.

Skolnick, J., and Bayley, D. 1986. *The New Blue Line. Police Innovation in Six American Cities.* New York: Free Press.

Sparrow, M., Moore, M., and Kennedy, D. 1990. *Beyond 911: A New Era for Policing.* New York: Basic Books.

Sykes, G. W. 1994. "Accreditation and Community Policing: Passing Fads or Basic Reforms?" *Journal of Contemporary Criminal Justice* 10(1): 1–16.

Terrill, R. J. 1991. "Civilian Oversight of the Police Complaints Process in the United States." In A. J. Goldsmith (ed.), *Complaints Against the Police: The Trend to External Review,* pp. 291–322. Avon, England: Bookcraft.

Toch, H. 1995. "The 'Violence-Prone' Police Officer." In W. Geller and H. Toch (eds.), *And Justice for All: Understanding and Controlling Police Abuse of Force,* pp. 99–112. Washington, D.C.: Police Executive Research Forum.

Walker, S. 1977. *A Critical History of Police Reform.* Lexington, MA: Lexington Books.

——. 1985. "Setting the Standards: The Efforts and Impact of Blue-Ribbon Commissions on the Police." In W. A. Geller (ed.), *Police Leadership in America: Crises and Opportunity,* pp. 354–370. New York: Praeger.

——. 1998. *Sense and Nonsense About Crime and Drugs: A Policy Guide,* 4th ed. Pacific Grove, CA: Brooks/Cole.

——. 2003a. "Citizen Oversight, 2003: Developments and Prospects," *New York State Government, Law and Policy Journal* 5(2): 5–10.

——. 2003b. "Core Principles for an Effective Police Auditor's Office." Report of the First National Police Auditors Conference. Omaha, NE: University of Nebraska at Omaha, Department of Criminal Justice. Mimeo.

——. 2003c. *Early Intervention Systems for Law Enforcement Agencies: A Planning and Management Guide.* Washington, DC: Office of Community Oriented Policing Services.

Walker, S., and Bumphus, V. W. 1991. *Civilian Review of the Police: A National Review of the 50 Largest Cities.* Omaha, NE: University of Nebraska.

Walker, S., and N. Graham. 1998. "Citizen Complaints in Response to Police Misconduct: The Results of a Victimization Survey," *Police Quarterly* 1(1): 65–89.

Walker, S., and Kreisel, B. W. 1996. "Varieties of Citizen Review: The Implications of Organizational Features of Complaint Review Procedures for Accountability of the Police." *American Journal of Police* 15(3): 65–88.

Wallace, B. 1990. "S. F. Watchdog Upholds Few Charges." *San Francisco Chronicle.* May 29: 1: 4–6.

West, P. 1988. "Investigation of Complaints Against the Police." *American Journal of Police* 8: 101–121.

Williams, G. L. 1989. *Making the Grade: The Benefits of Law Enforcement Accreditation.* Washington, DC: Police Executive Research Forum.

Wilson, J. Q., and Kelling, G. 1982. "Broken Windows: The Police and Neighborhood Safety." *Atlantic Monthly* March: 29–38.

"Younger NYC Cops Comprise Bulk of Arrests for Misconduct." 1989. *Law Enforcement News* August 5: 1.

Suggested Websites for Further Study

Commission on Accreditation for Law Enforcement Agencies
http://www.calea.org
Police Accountability and Professionalism
http://www.policeaccountability.org/
Police Assessment Resource Center
http://www.parc.info/
National Association for Civilian Oversight of Law Enforcement
http://www.nacole.org/
National Internal Affairs Investigators Association
http://www.niaia.org/ ✦

Legal Issues

Chapter Outline

Key Terms

affidavit	intentional torts
arrest	interrogations
Carroll Doctrine	Miranda rights
color of law	negligent torts
Constitution or federally	open fields doctrine
protected rights	plain view doctrine
criminal procedure	pretextual stops
custody	probable cause
de-policing	protective sweep
exclusionary rule	reasonable suspicion
fruit of the poisonous tree doctrine	stop and frisk
hot pursuit exception	

Criminal Procedure

Criminal procedure is the process by which a person accused of a crime is processed through the criminal justice system (Zalman and Siegel 1997). It also consists of rules that the government must abide by to ensure that certain rights enjoyed by the public are not violated and ensures fairness in the processing of people accused of crimes. The most common rights related to policing that are addressed by the courts include arrest, searches, seizures, and interrogations. Criminal procedure is also related to the adjudication process, such as ensuring a fair trial, right to retain counsel, and various pretrial procedures.

Prior to 1937, there were few important procedural rulings by the Supreme Court. The individual safeguards found in the Bill of Rights had not yet been applied to the states. Between the 1930s and 1960s, the Court began to selectively incorporate some of these safeguards into the procedural requirements that local police had to follow. Not until the 1960s did the "due process revolution" begin. During this decade, the Supreme Court increasingly applied provisions of the Bill of Rights to the states. Table 1.1 (in Chapter 1) provides a list of amendments to the U.S. Constitution that apply to criminal procedure, and as we'll learn to civil liability.

The 1960s were characterized by widespread support for the protection of the civil rights of individuals. The Warren Court of this period, named for Chief Justice Earl Warren, was associated with a liberal political philosophy because the majority of judges supported more legal restrictions on the police. From a politically conservative point of view (which included the views of a majority of police officers), the police were "handcuffed" in their ability to fight crime. Hence, the process of criminal procedure is concerned with two competing values: the need to protect the freedom of citizens from government tyranny, while simultaneously ensuring a civil and ordered society that is free from disorder and crime.

A comprehensive overview of case law related to criminal procedure is beyond the scope of this chapter. Instead, we provide a description of laws and procedures related to common police practices of street level officers. This chapter will present an overview of rights related to searches and seizures of persons, and property, and rights citizens enjoy during custodial interrogations.

Searches and Seizures of Persons

The Fourth Amendment provides safeguards from unreasonable searches and seizures. Thus, it is this amendment that guides the Court in creating guidelines for when officers may stop or arrest citizens, for these actions constitute a seizure of that person. The two most common forms of seizure of a person are stops (and often "frisks" associated with the stop) and arrests, and the Court has provided roadmaps to ensure that these seizures are not unreasonable in scope or duration.

Before discussing "stop and frisks" or arrests, it is first important to understand the degree of certainty an officer must possess to avoid an unreasonable action. Stops and frisks must at a minimum be based on the legal standard of reasonable suspicion. This standard is difficult to quantify and perhaps explain, but del Carmen (2001) describes **reasonable suspicion** as that which is based on objective facts and logical conclusions that a crime has been or is about to be committed, and this is based on the circumstances at hand. Although the Court has not clearly defined this standard, in *Alabama v. White* (1990) it acknowledged that reasonable suspicion is a lower standard than probable cause and may arise from information that itself has questionable reliability. Since reasonable suspicion is somewhat less rigorous than other standards, the scope of officer behavior is necessarily limited to actions such as stopping a suspect or frisking a suspect. On the other hand, arrests must be based on the standard of **probable cause.**

Inside Policing 11.1   Selected Supreme Court Cases (1960 to Present)

Mapp v. Ohio, 367 U.S. 643 (1961): The "exclusionary rule" used in federal trials is applied to the states. Evidence obtained illegally cannot be used in a trial or in subsequent proceedings.

Escobedo v. Illinois, 378 U.S. 478 (1964): If the defendant requests an attorney, police must comply before interrogating the defendant.

Miranda v. Arizona, 384 U.S. 436 (1966): In order to prevent police from coercing confessions, the court established a rule that a defendant must be informed of Fifth and Sixth Amendment rights and that the defendant must waive those rights prior to any police interrogation.

Katz v. United States, 389 U.S. 347 (1967): Fourth Amendment requirements for search and seizure apply to electronic surveillance even if there is no actual physical intrusion into the property of a defendant.

Terry v. Ohio, 468 U.S. 1 (1968): Police officers are authorized to "stop and frisk" suspicious persons in order to conduct a proper investigation and to protect the officer from possible harm.

Chimel v. California, 395 U.S. 752 (1969): When making arrests, police officers are allowed to search the defendant and the immediate area under the defendant's control (which, in effect, means that only the area within an "arm's length" distance could be searched).

Harris v. New York, 401 U.S. 222 (1971): Statements taken from a defendant that were not coerced, but were obtained in violation of the Miranda ruling can be used to question the credibility of the defendant if he or she testifies in court.

Michigan v. Mosley, 423 U.S. 93 (1975): A second attempt to interrogate a defendant, after the defendant has refused to make a statement in the first interrogation, does not violate the Miranda ruling if the defendant waives his or her right to an attorney.

United States v. Ross, 456 U.S. 798 (1982): Where probable cause exists to believe that an automobile contains evidence in a criminal case, police may conduct a warrantless search, including searching any closed containers that may be in the automobile (e.g., luggage).

New York v. Quarles, 467 U.S. 649 (1984): Miranda rights do not apply when circumstances dictate to the police that "public safety" is an important and "immediate necessity." This means that under certain circumstances the police can ask incriminating questions of suspects prior to giving the suspect the Miranda warning. This is the "public safety" exception to the exclusionary rule.

Nix v. Williams, 467 U.S. 431 (1984): Illegally obtained evidence will not be excluded from a trial if it is "inevitable" that the evidence will be "discovered" anyway. This is the "inevitability of discovery" exception to the exclusionary rule.

United States v. Leon, 468 U.S. 897 (1984): Evidence obtained using a search warrant that a police office obtained from a "detached and neutral" judge can be used at trial even if it is later discovered that there was no probable cause to issue the warrant. This is one example of the good-faith exception to the exclusionary rule.

Moran v. Burbine, 475 U.S. 412 (1986): A request for an attorney must come from the defendant. If another party calls an attorney, and the attorney contacts the police about the defendant, the police are not obligated to delay or stop an interrogation of the defendant. This attempted contact has no bearing on the admissibility of the defendant's statement if the defendant waived his or her right to an attorney.

Maryland v. Garrison, 480 U.S. 79 (1987): When police officers conduct a warrant search at the wrong location, but their mistake is considered reasonable given the circumstances, there is no violation of the Fourth Amendment, and any evidence obtained will not be excluded in a criminal trial.

U.S. v. Sokolow, 490 U.S. 1 (1989): Sokolow was stopped by police as a possible "drug courier" when trying to smuggle drugs through the Honolulu airport. The Supreme Court ruled that probabilistic information describing characteristics of drug couriers provided a basis for an investigative detention in accordance with principles of reasonable suspicion.

Illinois v. Rodriquez, 110 S. Ct. 2793 (1990): If police enter a residence in good faith and observe drugs in plain sight inside the residence, the evidence thusly seized is acceptable in court.

Michigan Department of State Police v. Sitz, 110 S. Ct. 2481 (1990): This case upheld the constitutionality of a highway sobriety checkpoint.

Florida v. Bostick, 111 S. Ct. 2382 (1991): This case expanded the meaning of "consent" in consensual searches. If an officer's request is not coercive and the passenger was free to refuse, the search satisfies consent, even if the passenger—Bostick, in this case, being on a bus—is not free to leave.

Holland v. McGinnis, 763 F. 2d 1044 (1992): The police lied to a suspect, telling him that his car had been seen at the scene of a crime. The suspect confessed. The courts ruled that the confession was admissible evidence.

Minnesota v. Dickerson, 113 S. Ct. 2130 (1993): A police pat-down of a suspect on the basis of reasonable suspicion that reveals drugs is admissible evidence. An officer's sense of touch justifies seizing contraband even when no other reason to suspect the presence of narcotics exists.

Maryland v. Wilson, 117 S. Ct. 882, 137 L. Ed. 2nd 347 (1996): Is a police officer's order of a passenger to exit a vehicle after a valid stop a legal seizure? When a passenger, Wilson, exited, drugs fell from his pocket. The court ruled that the officer's order did not constitute an unreasonable seizure.

Whren v. United States, 116 S. Ct. 1769, 135 L. Ed. 2nd 89 (1996): Does a pretextual stop (a stop made for a legally valid reason such as a taillight violation but whose underlying purpose was altogether different, such as to examine the vehicle for drugs) made by a police officer invalidate a subsequent legal vehicular search for drugs? The court ruled that the subjective intentions of police officers do not invalidate an objectively reasonable action.

County of Sacramento v. Lewis, 118 S. Ct. 1708 (1998): The Supreme Court held that, in a high-speed chase, a police officer does not deprive an individual of substantive due process by causing death through actions that indicate a deliberate disregard or a reckless disregard for the rights of others. Only arbitrary conduct is actionable.

Chicago v. Morales, 527 U.S. 41 (1999): Chicago's ordinance, which prohibits suspected gang members from loitering in a public place and makes them subject to citation, violates the citizen's due process rights and is unconstitutionally vague.

Atwater v. Lago Vista, 532 U.S. 318 (2001): Texas law indicates failure of front seat passengers to wear a seat belt or properly secure children riding in the front seat to be a misdemeanor, punishable by only a fine. Officers who take citizens into physical custody pursuant to this law do not violate the Fourth Amendment's safeguard from unreasonable search and seizure.

Illinois v. McArthur, 531 US 326 (2001): Police officers may detain an individual from reentering his home in order to secure a search warrant if there is probable cause to believe he had hidden marijuana in the home and would destroy it upon reentry.

In *Brinegar v. U.S.* (1949), the Court indicated that "probable cause exists where the facts and circumstances within the officers' knowledge, and of which they have reasonably trustworthy information, are sufficient in themselves to warrant a belief by a man of reasonable caution that a crime is being committed." Hence, the officer has reason to believe that a particular individual has "more likely than not" committed a certain crime. Probable cause is the minimum legal standard necessary to make a custodial arrest of a person and it is a more rigorous standard than reasonable suspicion. In sum, the degree of certainty the officer has that criminal activity is afoot is inversely related to the scope, length, and intensity of the detention of the suspect.

Officers must have reasonable suspicion to believe a person is armed prior to conducting a frisk.

While the Fourth Amendment provides a right to be free from unreasonable searches and seizures, it does not address how this right should be enforced. The most recognized method for enforcing the reasonableness standard of the Fourth Amendment is called the **exclusionary rule.** This holds that evidence obtained by the government in violation of the Fourth Amendment's guarantee against unreasonable searches and seizures is not admissible in criminal prosecution to demonstrate guilt (Zalman and Siegel 1997). This rule is premised on the belief that excluding illegally seized evidence from court will deter police officers from acting improperly. While the birth of the exclusionary rule can be traced back to *Weeks v. U.S.* (1914), it was not until the decision in *Mapp v. Ohio* (1961) that the Court incorporated this rule to govern evidence collected by state and local police officers. Justice Clark, writing for the majority, stated that the Court previously acknowledged that the "criminal is to go free because the constable has blundered," but also noted, "The criminal goes free, if he must, but it is the law that sets him free. Nothing can destroy a government more quickly than its failure to observe its own laws, or worse, its disregard of the charter of its own existence."

An extension of the exclusionary rule is the **fruit of the poisonous tree doctrine,** which indicates that not only must evidence seized improperly be excluded from criminal court, but so, too, must any additional evidence seized after that police action. For example, assume the police improperly obtained a confession to a crime and that during the confession the suspect told the police where to find evidence (such as a knife). When the police locate the evidence, they find additional evidence (such as a handgun) of a different crime. In this hypothetical scenario, the confession and the knife would be excluded from court pursuant to the exclusionary rule. The handgun would also be excluded, as it was the "fruit" that was obtained from an initial improper confession.

Stop and frisk. An officer may *stop* a person, temporarily depriving him or her of freedom of movement, if the officer has reasonable suspicion that the person is involved in a crime. Furthermore, the officer may *frisk* the person if there is reasonable suspicion to believe the citizen is armed and poses a threat to the officer for the duration of the stop. The landmark case that outlined the parameters for stops and frisks was *Terry v. Ohio* (1968). In that case, the suspect (Terry) was observed engaging in suspicious behavior in front of a store in downtown Cleveland with others by a seasoned police officer. Based on the officer's experience, he indicated it was reasonable to believe they were "casing" the store for a robbery. Upon stopping the suspects to inquire of their intentions, the officer indicated that the suspects' mumbled responses to his questions led him to believe that the suspects were armed. He discovered a firearm on Terry after patting down his upper torso, and Terry was charged with carrying a concealed weapon.

Though the officer did not have enough information to elevate the legal standard to probable cause, he indicated there was reasonable suspicion to believe Terry was about to commit a crime and was armed at the time of the encounter. The Court indicated that a temporary stop of Terry, based on reasonable suspicion, did not violate the Fourth Amendment, and that a limited pat down or frisk of his outer garments was reasonable based on the circumstances. Since stops and frisks represent a limited intrusion on the citizen's liberty, these practices are permissible even if the officer does not have probable cause to believe a crime is about to be committed.

It is also important to understand that not all stops necessitate a frisk, and that these are separate activities (though the term "stop and frisk" often is confused so that people believe they are one continuous act). Frisks may only be conducted if there is reasonable suspicion to believe the suspect is armed and may pose a physical threat to the officer during the encounter (del Carmen 2001). Hence, the officer must articulate separately which factors led to the stop and which factors led to a frisk.

The purpose of the frisk is limited in scope to weapons or instruments that can injure the officer and may not be used as a "fishing expedition" for evidence or other contraband. For example, in *Minnesota v. Dickerson* (1993) the Court indicated that drugs found during a frisk must be excluded as evidence from trial. Dickerson was observed leaving a known "crack house," and he was frisked by an officer pursuant a stop. The officer felt a small object in Dickerson's pocket, and by manipulating it with his hands, believed it to be crack cocaine wrapped in cellophane. The officer retrieved the object and confirmed it was drugs. However, this evidence was not admissible in court because the purpose of the frisk was to discover weapons, and since the officer had to manipulate the object to determine what it was, this manipulation constituted a second search that was beyond what was reasonable.

In summary, stops and frisks are separate activities that must require reasonable suspicion. The purpose of a stop is to prevent criminal activity or to determine if a crime has taken place, and of a frisk is to ensure officer safety. The extent of intrusion permissible in a frisk is limited to a pat down of the suspect's outer clothing for weapons. The duration of the encounter is to be no longer than permitted to achieve its purpose, and no physical force is permitted, beyond that of the pat down (del Carmen 2001).

Arrest. An **arrest** is the act of depriving a person of his or her liberty by legal authority and is done for the purposes of interrogation or criminal prosecution (Zalman and Seigel 1997). Laws related to the reasonableness of an arrest also fall under the rubric of the Fourth Amendment, because arrest is the seizure of a person against his or her will by an agent of the government. Arrests are among the most critical activities police officers do within the criminal justice system, for an arrest must typically be made before other components of the system may act. Following an arrest, there are administrative procedures that are conducted, including fingerprinting, photographing, or "booking" the person into jail. Unfortunately, the public does not completely understand when and under what circumstances an arrest can be made, or the legal guidelines officers must follow when conducting a search for evidence during an arrest.

Prior to an arrest, officers must have probable cause to believe that a particular person has committed a specific crime. Since arrests are more intrusive than stops, it is necessary that the officer have a higher legal justification to deprive a person of his or her liberty. There is also a preference that arrests be made on issuance of an arrest warrant issued by a neutral and detached magistrate. In reality, though, the vast majority of arrests are made without an arrest warrant. Obtaining a warrant to make arrests in many situations would unduly limit the crime control function of the police. The courts have indicated that routine felony arrests made in public do not require a warrant, even if officers have ample opportunity to obtain one (*U.S. v. Watson* 1976). However, if officers wish to make a felony arrest in a private home, they must first secure a warrant if there is opportunity to do so or if exigent (emergency) circumstances are absent (*Payton v. New York* 1981). This demonstrates the expectation of privacy an individual enjoys in private places over public places.

It is not necessary to have reasonable suspicion to frisk an individual if that person is under arrest and taken into custody. Upon arrest, officers may perform a comprehensive search of the suspect and the possessions in their immediate control. This search incident to arrest may be for weapons but can also include any contraband discovered during the search. Further, officers may search the area in the suspect's immediate control to discover evidence or weapons without a search warrant (*Chimel v. California* 1969). The area in someone's "immediate control" has been understood to consist of the area within the person's wingspan or their "lunge and reach" area. The purposes of the *Chimel Rule* are to ensure officer safety as well as to prevent the destruction of evidence.

It is also permissible for officers to perform a limited **protective sweep** of a home to determine if there are others who could pose a safety risk for officers (*Maryland v. Buie* 1990). Buie and an accomplice were wanted for armed robbery, during which one of the men was wearing a red running suit. Officers obtained an arrest warrant for Buie, entered his house, and saw Buie emerge from the basement. After placing him under arrest, officers proceeded to the basement to determine whether anyone else was there who could pose a threat to officer safety. Once in the basement, officers observed a red running suit that matched the description of the one used during the course of the robbery. This running suit was seized (without a warrant) and used against Buie in court. The Supreme Court indicated that the search of Buie's basement was reasonable and that officers had reason to perform a cursory search of the area for protective purposes. However, a protective sweep is different from a full-blown search for evidence. This allows for only a cursory inspection of spaces where a person may be located. In this regard, protective sweeps are similar to frisks in that they must be limited in nature to discovery of weapons or people who could harm the officer and not to evidence of a crime. In contrast to frisks, evidence of a crime discovered during a protective sweep is permissible in court.

Searches and Seizures of Property

Similar to searches and seizures of persons, the courts have attempted to balance the need for public safety with adhering to expectations of privacy in regard to searches and seizures of property. Also, there is a preference for searches and seizures of property to be conducted pursuant to a search warrant. A *search warrant* is a "written order, issued by a magistrate, directing a peace officer to search for property connected with a crime and bring it before the court" (del Carmen 2001, 181). Search warrants must demonstrate that there is probable cause that evidence of a crime exists in a particular place and must fully describe the place to be searched, thus eliminating the possibility of a "general warrant." Probable cause must be supported under oath or affirmation, typically by a police officer, before a neutral and detached judge. During this oath (often called an **affidavit,** which is the same as an oath except that it is written), the officer describes exactly what is to be seized and exactly what is to be searched. The judge may then issue a search

Officers are often asked in court to explain how evidence is seized.

warrant commanding law enforcement to conduct a search by signing the warrant (del Carmen 2001).

There are many circumstances where searches without a warrant are reasonable in their scope. For example, the **plain view doctrine** falls beyond the warrant requirement. It is not unreasonable for the police to seize evidence of a crime if the evidence is in view of the officer. But the plain view doctrine contains several important caveats. First, the police must have prior justification for being present at the scene, or stated differently, the initial police intrusion must be lawful. Second, the evidence seized must be in plain view, and police may not take actions that expose to view concealed portions of the premises or its contents. Third, the objects seized must be immediately apparent as evidence or contraband.

The facts and circumstances in *Arizona v. Hicks* (1987) are instructive and provides an example of the plain view doctrine in action. The police responded to Hicks' apartment after a neighbor called complaining that someone had fired a bullet through the floor of the apartment. On arrival, the police entered the apartment and discovered several guns and a stocking mask. However, while in the apartment, an officer observed several new pieces of expensive stereo equipment that appeared out of place in the otherwise squalid apartment. Having reasonable suspicion that these stereos were stolen, the officer moved the pieces, recorded the serial numbers, and confirmed via radio that, indeed, the equipment was stolen. Hicks was charged and convicted of receiving stolen property. Later, the Supreme Court indicated the stereo equipment could not be used as evidence to prosecute Hicks because the act of moving the stereo constituted a second search in which the officers did not have probable cause. While the officers were legally present in the apartment and the stereo equipment was in plain view, it was not immediately apparent as evidence or contraband. Hence, the third criterion for the plain view doctrine was not present.

Another exception to the warrant requirement is items observed in open fields. The **open fields doctrine** indicates that "items in open fields are not protected by the Fourth Amendment's guarantee against unreasonable searches and seizures, so they can properly be taken by an officer without a warrant or probable cause" (del Carmen 2001, 259). In other words, people who leave items in public view do not enjoy a right to privacy, thus the Fourth Amendment does not apply to these places. In *Oliver v. U.S.* (1984), the police were acting on a tip that marijuana was being grown in a field on Oliver's farm. The police ignored the "No trespassing" sign at the edge of the property and, without probable cause, entered the field to observe the marijuana. The Court indicated that this type of trespass was permissible and that the marijuana could be used as evidence to convict Oliver.

Similarly, warrants are not required for property that is abandoned (such as garbage left on private premises). The police may seize garbage bags left for removal and search these bags for contraband (often receipts of illegal activity or drug paraphernalia). Once a person abandons property and makes it available for public scrutiny, that person no longer enjoys an expectation of privacy in relation to that property (*California v. Greenwood* 1988).

Another common exception to the warrant requirement is the **hot pursuit exception.** Police may follow a felon or otherwise dangerous criminal into a place typically protected by the Fourth Amendment, such as a home, or may cross jurisdictional boundaries. Hot pursuits must be based on probable cause, but the officer may develop probable cause via hearsay or direct observation. The gravity of the offense must be taken into consideration, and relatively minor offenses may not provide justification for warrantless pursuits. Once in a constitutionally protected area, the officer may search for the suspect and for weapons or evidence, but once the suspect is found, the search must cease. At this point, any search without a warrant must be based on other factors, such as those described previously in *Chimel or Buie*.

Another exception to the warrant requirement is when the citizen provides officers with *consent* to search. Officers may search property if a person *voluntarily* consents to the search; consent searches therefore do not require a warrant, and any evidence that is obtained during a consent search is permissible in court. Furthermore, officers do not need to advise citizens of their right to refuse consent (*Schneckloth v. Bustamonte* 1973); it must merely be demonstrated that consent was voluntarily given and not coerced by the officer.

Vehicle searches. Court doctrines related to search and seizure often rely on an individual's expectation of privacy when determining the reasonableness of police action. Generally, people enjoy a greater level of privacy in homes and private places than they do in public. But the lines between public and private spheres become difficult to disentangle when confronted with stops of citizens in motor vehicles. Are motor vehicles private places? Or because they are operated in public, do citizens enjoy a diminished expectation of privacy in vehicles? What can police do when making a traffic stop? Due to the unique nature of motor vehicle searches, it is important to consider these searches and seizures separately from other types of places.

The courts have recognized motor vehicles as having substantially less Fourth Amendment protections than fixed premises. This is because motor vehicles are highly mobile, allowing for evidence to be moved and suspects to flee police custody. The contents of motor vehicles (including drivers and passengers) travel in plain view, thus exposing them to public review. Furthermore, motor vehicles are highly regulated by the government (e.g., drivers' licenses, vehicle registration, insurance, etc.). Together, these characteristics have led the courts to adopt relaxed standards regarding searches and seizures and the necessity of obtaining warrants for searches of motor vehicles.

Police officers may stop motor vehicles if they have reasonable suspicion that a crime has been committed. Upon stopping a vehicle, officers may investigate to determine if there is probable cause to arrest a driver (or passengers) or issue a summons/ ticket. In fact, officers have a great deal of discretion pursuant to traffic stops. Inside Policing 11.2 provides an overview of what officers may do during traffic stops.

Inside Policing 11.2   What May an Officer Do After a Vehicle Is Stopped?

1. **Order driver and passengers to get out of the vehicle.** Officer safety is often cited as a primary rationale for having occupants exit the vehicle.

2. **Ask driver to produce driver's license and other documents (as required by state law).**

3. **Ask questions of driver and passengers. This may be done without providing Miranda rights, and while occupants have the constitutional right not to respond, nonresponse may be taken into consideration when determining probable cause.**

4. **Search passengers' belongings, if there is probable cause.** This is due to the fact passengers have a diminished expectation of privacy in a vehicle and the government's interest in effective law enforcement would be impaired due to the mobility of the vehicle.

5. **Require drunk driving suspects to take a breathalyzer test.** These tests may not be administered to all drivers, but only ones suspected of drunk driving.

6. **Locate and examine Vehicle Identification Number (VIN).** Officers may compare the VIN to the one registered to the plates of the vehicle, or to determine whether the car is stolen. A VIN is conveniently located on the dashboard on the driver's side, and is visible from outside the vehicle.

7. **Search vehicle if probable cause develops.**

8. **Search vehicle if consent is given.** If a person intelligently and voluntarily gives consent to search a vehicle, probable cause is not required.

9. **Search the passenger compartment for weapons if there is reasonable suspicion of a threat to officer safety.**

10. **Seize items in plain view.**

11. **Arrest with probable cause.**

Source: Adapted from: del Carmen, R. V., *Criminal Procedure: Law and Practice* (Stamford, CT: Wadsworth, 2001), 221–225.

May an officer stop a vehicle for a traffic violation under the pretext that the stop may elicit another, more serious violation? This was the question posed before the Court in *Whren v. U.S.* (1996). Two plainclothes officers observed Whren and another occupant driving a vehicle with temporary tags in an area of high drug activity. The

vehicle was stopped at an intersection for an unusually long period of time, and the driver was staring at the lap of the passenger. Suspecting the occupants to be involved with drug sales, the officers approached the vehicle at a red light, stopping them for a traffic violation. Whren was observed to be holding a bag of crack cocaine, for which he was arrested and subsequently convicted. Whren argued that the officers would not normally engage in traffic enforcement and were using the traffic violation merely as

The Supreme Court indicated that police may use traffic violations as a pretext to conduct searches of motor vehicles for other violations (such as drug possession).

a pretext to determine whether he was involved with drugs. The Supreme Court determined this practice to be permissible and that seizures incident to *pretextual stops* of vehicles are not unreasonable.

Circumstances exist where police officers may stop vehicles without reasonable suspicion. **Sobriety checkpoints** permit police officers to systematically stop vehicles without reasonable suspicion, because the nature of the stop is limited. This issue was addressed in *Michigan Department of State Police v. Sitz* (1990). The sobriety checkpoint in question was highly publicized prior to initiation, and officers' actions were set by guidelines developed by the Checkpoint Advisory Committee. Officers stopped 126 vehicles passing a set location over the course of 75 minutes. Motorists were stopped on average for 25 seconds so those officers could conduct preliminary investigations for intoxication. The Court determined that the stops were not unreasonable by adopting a balancing test of three factors: "the gravity of public concerns served by the seizure, the degree to which the seizure advances the public interest, and the severity of the interference with individual liberty" (del Carmen 2001, 221). The Sitz decision does not permit random stops for sobriety checks, and such stops absent reasonable suspicion are restricted to fixed checkpoints.

The *Carroll Doctrine* provides for warrantless searches of motor vehicles if the vehicle is, in fact, mobile and if there is probable cause. The Court's rationale in *Carroll v. U.S.* (1925) is that the inherent mobility of a vehicle may permit destruction of evidence, allow the occupants to flee the jurisdiction, and make obtaining a warrant in this situation impractical for law enforcement. The scope of the search may extend to the entire car, including the trunk and closed containers, if there is probable cause to believe these locations contain evidence or contraband (*U.S. v. Ross* 1982).

Recently, the Court determined that searches of passengers' belongings with probable cause are also reasonable (*Wyoming v. Houghton* 1999). Incident to a valid arrest, officers may search and seize evidence from the passenger's compartment of the vehicle, even if the officer lacks probable cause (*New York v. Belton* 1981). However, if the officers merely issue a citation (and the suspect is not taken into custody), a search of the vehicle absent probable cause is improper (*Knowles v. Iowa* 1998).

Interrogations and Confessions

Policing, at its core, involves personal contact between the officer and the public. Although these contacts occur millions of times a year, there are certain circumstances in which the police must advise citizens of their constitutional rights regarding answering questions. These procedures stem from perhaps one of the best known cases in the history of the Supreme Court, namely *Miranda v. Arizona* (1966). While most people can recite these *Miranda rights* verbatim (largely from their popularized use in television dramas), certainly far fewer people appreciate how these rights came about, when they must be used by police, and whether exceptions exist.

Ernesto Miranda, a poor Mexican immigrant, was arrested for rape and kidnapping. Police officers interrogated Miranda for two hours, while he was in custody, during which time he confessed to the crimes. After conviction, Miranda appealed, claiming his Fifth Amendment privilege from self-incrimination was violated. The U.S. Supreme Court agreed and indicated that the police must take appropriate safeguards to ensure that a defendant's rights are not violated during such procedures. Specifically, police must advise defendants that (1) they have the right to remain silent, (2) any statement made may be used against the defendant in court, (3) the defendant has the right to have an attorney present during questioning, and (4) if a defendant cannot afford an attorney, then the state will appoint one prior to questioning. The defendant must intelligently and voluntarily waive these rights prior to questioning, and while this waiver does not have to be written, many police organizations require a written waiver by the defendant.

The Court said that the police must advise defendants of these rights during all custodial interrogations. *Custody* occurs when a person is deprived of his or her freedom in a significant way, such as during an arrest. **Interrogations** are those circumstances when the police ask questions that tend to incriminate the citizen (del Carmen 2001). The Court required giving this advice because it recognized that custodial interrogations could be so psychologically coercive that responses during these encounters may not be completely voluntary. What makes this case so unique (and perhaps so memorable) is that the Court created active procedural safeguards for the police to follow, which are similar to a recipe for ensuring that a person's rights are not violated. But it is interesting to note that Miranda rights are not constitutional rights per se and that it is possible for a law to be created that would make these familiar rights a thing of the past. As the author of the majority opinion, Chief Justice Warren, indicated,

> We encourage Congress and the States to continue their laudable search for increasingly effective ways of protecting the rights of the individual while promoting efficient enforcement of our criminal laws. However, unless we are shown other procedures which are at least as effective in apprising accused persons of their right of silence and in assuring a continuous opportunity to exercise it, the following safeguards must be observed.

While Congress to date has been unable to rise to Chief Justice Warren's challenge, the Court has subsequently outlined several exceptions to the Miranda requirements.

Public safety exception. The police may ask questions of a suspect who is in custody if there is a concern for public safety, and this exception to the Miranda rights was outlined in *New York v. Quarles* (1984). In this case, officers were approached by a woman who claimed that she had just been raped by a man fitting the description of Quarles and that the man had a firearm. Officers found Quarles in a supermarket, placed him under arrest, and found him in possession of an empty holster. Before he was advised of his Miranda rights, the officer asked him where the gun was, to which Quarles responded by leading the officer to the gun. The Court indicated that while Quarles was clearly in custody, and while the officer's questions constituted an interrogation, there existed a significant, immediate threat to public safety that permitted the officer to ask these questions without first issuing Miranda rights. The rationale was that the threat to public safety outweighed the suspect's right to be free from self-incrimination.

Inevitable discovery. If the police do not advise suspects of their Miranda rights during custodial interrogations, then the information given during an interrogation may not be used in criminal court, according to the exclusionary rule. Furthermore, if the suspect provides information during the interrogation that leads to the recovery of physical evidence, this evidence, too, may not be used in court—unless the police can demonstrate that the physical evidence would have been inevitably discovered without the benefit of the information provided during the improper interrogation.

This exception was outlined in a series of cases before the Court. First, in *Brewer v. Williams* (1977), the Court indicated that the admission by the defendant would be excluded from court because the police engaged in what amounted to a functionally equivalent interrogation. On December 24, 1969, officers were driving the suspect (Williams, a religious man under arrest for kidnapping a little girl) to meet his attorney, and the suspect had previously indicated he wished to remain silent until speaking with his attorney. The officers engaged in what has been known as the "Christian Burial Speech," telling Williams that it would be nice if the girl's body could be recovered before Christmas so that the family could provide her with a proper Christian burial. Williams then led the police to the body, which happened to be only a few miles away from where a search party was actively looking for evidence of the crime.

Initially, the Court indicated that the admission was inadmissible in court, as the "speech" was likely to elicit an incriminating response from Williams, in violation of his Miranda rights. Since the discovery of the body was a "fruit" produced by an improper police action, it, too, must be eliminated from court. However, it was later argued in *Nix v. Willams* (1984) that the search party would inevitably have discovered the body, even if Williams had not led the police do the crime scene. The Supreme Court agreed, indicating that evidence that would have inevitably been discovered by the police is admissible in court. It is important to understand that the fact that an active search party was close to discovering the body was an integral component of the Court's rationale. Had the search party not been so close to the evidence, the ruling might have been different.

This chapter has thus far concentrated on issues related to criminal procedure, while highlighting current legal doctrines related to searches and seizures of persons, property, and the rights of the accused during police interrogations. To ensure compliance with criminal procedure, improperly obtained evidence is excluded from criminal court. However, there are other legal remedies available to ensure police compliance with criminal procedure as well as compliance with the substantive law or organizational procedure. A common remedy is civil liability.

Civil Liability

America is a litigious society, and certainly the police are not completely immune from such action. Civil liability is a growing concern in American policing, and this trend will not change in the foreseeable future. In many ways civil liability is inherent in the awesome power that police have in a democratic society, and civil lawsuits often arise when police officers abuse this power, engage in negligent behavior, or otherwise violate the civil rights of a citizen. The risk of being sued is part of the police presence, and officers, supervisors, managers, and other agents of government understand this. However, exactly *how, why,* and *under what circumstances* they may be held liable is not always as clear.

This section offers an overview of the laws that govern civil liability for police officers. It includes the actual (and potential) costs and pervasiveness of civil lawsuits against the police, various avenues for civil litigation (including state law and federal laws), emerging trends in police liability, and the unintentional cost litigation may have on officers. Police administrators must be cognizant of the law as it relates to policing innovation, and ultimately, "police executives of the future will have to sift innovations through a civil liability filter" (Kappeler 2001, 200).

Reginald T. Shuford, the American Civil Liberties Union Foundation's chief litigator in challenges to racial profiling, provides a discussion on how civil litigation has impacted policing in Voices From the Field. Shuford is leading national litigation efforts and consulting with state ACLU affiliates in cases of "driving while black or brown," airport profiling, and profiling related to the war on terror.

Voices From the Field
Reginald T. Shuford, J. D.
American Civil Liberties Union Foundation

Question: How has court litigation impacted policing in America?

Answer: At a general level, litigation against police departments has had a manifold effect. First, litigation helps to clarify the parameters of policing such that the balance between public safety and civil rights and liberties can be maintained. Court decisions and settlements provide officers with a roadmap of the boundaries within which they must operate in order to avoid running afoul of the Constitution and other laws. This result is beneficial to both police officers and civilians alike. Officers who adhere to these rulings are more likely to avoid being sued or disciplined, pro-

tecting their reputations and careers while at the same time saving their departments a significant amount of money and resources. The benefit to civilians is that they learn what their rights are and are therefore more empowered to ensure that those rights are protected and respected. Second, litigation—and the threat of litigation—promotes accountability. Litigation can be extraordinarily expensive and time-consuming. Accordingly, most responsible police agencies will seek to avoid litigation—or, if sued, will settle the case—by ensuring that their officers are trained to act within the bounds of the law and are disciplined when they do not; will devise systems to ensure that citizen complaints are properly processed and which provide managerial oversight; and will collect data to make sure that their officers are acting evenhandedly and not on account of an individual's race, national origin, or some other protected characteristic.

The case of *NAACP, et al. v. Maryland State Police* is instructive. Filed by the ACLU in 1998 on behalf of the NAACP of Maryland and a number of individuals, the lawsuit alleged that the Maryland State Police maintained a policy and practice of racial profiling carried out by some of its troopers. After years of contentious and costly litigation, the parties reached partial settlement of the case in May 2003, resolving everything but money damages for individual plain-

tiffs. The settlement includes a general prohibition against racial profiling; ongoing data collection, with personal data assistants and video and audio recording equipment in most cars; the creation of a Police-Citizen Advisory Committee; the appointment of a consultant who will oversee implementation of the settlement and issue regular progress reports; creation of a brochure with information about how to lodge a complaint or commendation; and development of new guidelines on the use of canines and consent searches. The settlement also contains oversight and monitoring mechanisms requiring the Maryland State Police to review information about racial profiling on a consistent basis and to investigate and take appropriate action in response to "red flags" that troopers may be profiling. ✦

Costs of Liability in Policing

There are many different costs associated with police civil liability. Beyond the obvious monetary costs, there are often other ancillary costs associated with retraining officers, purchasing new equipment, and personal costs for officers and supervisors who are targets of litigation. Civil litigation has increased, both in the frequency of lawsuits and in the amount of money paid to plaintiffs.

The number of civil lawsuits against the police continues to grow, and this trend will likely continue. An early report by the International Association of Chiefs of Police indicated there were 1,741 civil suits against the police in 1967. This estimate grew to 3,897 in 1971, an increase of 123 percent. By 1975, the number of suits nearly doubled again (del Carmen 1991). The frequency of such suits has continued to escalate since that time. Silver (1996) estimated that police face more than 30,000 suits per year. However, the true number of civil lawsuits filed against the police is largely unknown, and this has led some to call for the creation of a national, systematic data set to fully understand the dimensions of civil liability (Vaughn, Cooper, and del Carmen 2001). Kappeler (2001) estimated that the costs of liability could be as high as $780 billion annually.

What has changed in policing over the past three decades to warrant such profound increases in civil liability? One possible answer is "nothing"; instead, the propensity of the public and its lawyers to sue officers for their actions during encounters may have increased. The increase in lawsuits may be more a function of the publics viewing of the police (and government in general) as having abundant resources with which to compensate citizens for even the most meager of transgressions. And there may be some truth to this perception. Kappeler (2001) stated that the average jury award for litigation against municipal government is around $2 million. Awards resulting from civil litigation involving the police tend to be somewhat lower than this estimate. Ross (2000) conducted an analysis of federal lawsuits alleging failure to train between 1989 and 1999. He reported that the average award for the plaintiff was around $492,794, with an additional average of $60,680 in attorneys' fees. A survey of Texas police chiefs found the typical award in police civil liability cases was around

$98,100; however, these amounts are often significantly reduced on appeal (Vaughn, Cooper, and del Carmen 2001).

Of course, many of these cases are settled prior to court. Often the decision to settle out of court is a tactical decision designed to avoid potentially paying more money in a jury awarded decision. In their survey of Texas police chiefs, Vaughn and his colleagues (2001) asked chiefs about their motivations to "settle." Sixty percent reported that the decision was motivated by the desire to avoid paying more money later. Indeed, there was some truth to this motivation, in that the average settlement was around $55,411 per case (compared to $98,100 awarded by a jury). Other motivations included wanting to make the case "go away" (56 percent), to avoid losing in court (38 percent), to avoid embarrassment (37 percent), and to compensate for no police wrongdoing (22 percent). Only 17 percent of police chiefs indicated that their decision to settle was in part to compensate the plaintiff for some wrongful act by the police officer. In addition to paying less than if the case proceeded to court, the municipality would not have to devote scarce resources to other costs associated with the litigation, including attorney costs, costs associated with expert testimony, and officers' time testifying in court.

Though the number of lawsuits filed for improper police behavior has increased, what is seldom reported is the success rate for plaintiffs in their quests for compensation. The fact is, most police lawsuits are decided in favor of the officers, although the exact number varies considerably. Early research indicated that only about 4 percent of all claims against the police were found in favor of the plaintiff. More recent research places this figure at about 8 percent (Kappeler, Kappeler, and del Carmen 1993). In their survey of Texas police chiefs, Vaughn, Cooper, and del Carmen (2001) found chiefs reported losing about 22 percent of all civil suits. In his examination of federal lawsuits decided in federal district courts between 1980 and 2000, Kappeler (2001) reported that plaintiffs prevailed in between 45.7 percent and 53.4 percent of all cases. However, "prevail" does not necessarily mean the police were found liable, only that there were sufficient grounds to warrant a jury trial, since there was found to be a substantive issue before the court. Nonetheless, these civil suits can cause significant damage to the reputations of police officers and the police departments involved. Further, the cost associated with protecting officers and departments from lawsuits can be quite high, regardless of the final determination.

Avenues of Liability

Police may be defendants in two different ways: They may be sued in state courts for violations of state laws, or they may be sued in federal court for violations of constitutional or federally protected rights. However, it is important to understand that defendants may be held liable simultaneously in both arenas for the same action if the action violates both state torts and civil liberties. Recall that this discussion revolves around civil law; therefore, "double jeopardy" claims are irrelevant. In other words, if the officer's actions are negligent under state tort laws and are at the same time a violation of federal civil rights, the plaintiff may seek relief in both state courts and federal courts. To make matters more confusing, if the action by the officer is also in violation of criminal law, then prosecutors may seek indictments in criminal court as well. To understand these different procedures, we will now explore the basics of state tort law and federal liability, with particular emphasis on Section 1983 of the U.S. Code.

Civil Liability in State Courts

Officers and supervisors may be defendants in state courts when state torts are violated. Most suits in state court allege wrongful police conduct in which a person is injured because of actions conducted by another person. Generally there are three classifications of state tort laws, including strict liability torts, intentional torts, and negligent torts. Strict liability torts involves the creation of some condition that is so hazardous that the person engaging in such an activity can be reasonably certain a result of injury or damage will occur (Kappeler 2001). Strict liability torts rarely involve the police and thus will not be discussed in detail here.

Intentional torts. **Intentional torts** involve behavior specifically designed to cause some type of injury or harm. The key to intentional torts is the *culpable state of mind of the officer,* in that his or her actions were purposive and designed to bring about some type of injury or property loss. While numerous different activities may be classified as intentional torts, among the most common for police officers are excessive use of force, wrongful death, assault, battery, and false arrest.

Excessive use of force entails the application of physical force that is not in line with the level of resistance faced by the officer. In other words, the application of force was unreasonable. Officers are trained to match resistance by citizens with a certain level of force, but this must be *proportional* to the level of resistance by the citizen. If officers use force that is not proportional, they may be sued for intentional use of excessive force. Effective training, supervision, and documentation of use-of-force encounters between the police and the public are essential to reduce exposure to civil liability. Similarly, **wrongful death** suits may arise when an unjustified police action results in the death of a citizen. The victim's family levies a civil suit, and compensation is sought for pain and suffering, medical and funeral expenses, and loss of future earnings (del Carmen and Smith 2001).

Assault involves the "intentional causing of an apprehension of harmful or offensive conduct; it is the attempt or threat, accompanied by the apparent ability, to inflict bodily harm on another person" (del Carmen 1991, 18). Assault occurs when officers intentionally cause a person to fear for his or her safety. An example of this may be that during a custodial investigation, the officer grabs and threatens the suspect with serious physical injury, such as throwing him or her out the second floor window (Kappeler 2001). In contrast, **battery** is harmful or offensive body contact between two people, such as when an officer applies any force to an individual without justification. The basic difference between the two is that assault involves menacing conduct, whereas battery must involve actual contact (del Carmen 1991).

Claims of *false arrest* arise from intentional, illegal detention of an individual for prosecution. Typically, these suits arise from warrantless arrests, a very common event in modern policing. The legal standard for making an arrest is probable cause, that is, the facts and circumstances would lead a reasonable person to believe a specific person has committed a criminal act. If officers detain a person without sufficient probable cause, this may give rise to an allegation of false arrest.

Police officers, supervisors, organizations, and municipalities are often the targets of intentional tort violations, perhaps due to their very nature. The police occupy a unique role in society, whereby they are among the few government entities sanctioned to exercise control over the public through the use of force. Given the sheer number of encounters between the police and the public, coupled with the legitimate right to use coercion, it is not surprising that these civil suits occur with some frequency. However, actions only become problematic under intentional tort laws when the action is unreasonable.

Negligent torts. Where intentional torts focus on the mental state of an individual, **negligent torts** only require *inadvertent and unreasonable behavior resulting in damage or injury* (Kappeler 2001). Negligence is injury that is the result of a lapse of due care where the ingredients for injury were the result of some action or inaction on the officer's part. Thus, negligence provides liability for unreasonably creating a risk (Levine, Davies, and Kionka 1993). *To prove negligence, four criteria must be satisfied:*

First, there is *legal duty*, which involves those actions on the part of the defendant as prescribed by the courts that require some action. Thus, there must be a legal basis for the requirement of certain behavior or activity. Second, **breach of duty** (or failure to conform with duty), is more complex. It must be demonstrated that a reasonably prudent person would believe the officer breached his or her duty to a plaintiff. Third, this breach of duty must **cause** some type of injury, or in other words, but for the actions of the officer, the plaintiff would not have been injured or damaged. Finally, **actual damage or injury** must have resulted from this action, including mental, physical, or economic injury (del Carmen 1991; Hughes 2001a; Kappeler 2001).

Failure to arrest may be negligent behavior if the plaintiff can prove the *officer's inaction caused injury or damage.* Discretion involves the ability to choose between a course of action or inaction. Officers often do not make arrests even when there are sufficient legal grounds to do so. Whether discretion is a virtue or a vice is beyond the parameters of the current discussion; however, officers and supervisors should recognize liabilities associated with inaction. An example of negligence may be illustrated by the circumstances surrounding *Thurman v. City of Torrington* (1985). The plaintiff, Tracey Thurman, alleged that Torrington police officers failed to arrest her estranged husband for a pattern of domestic abuse, even though officers observed the abuse in question. After failing to arrest the suspect, Thurman sustained significant and debilitating injuries that persist to this day. Though this case was settled in federal court, the ingredients for negligent failure to arrest were also present. The *Thurman* case, along with other factors, gradually led to police departments taking a more legalistic approach to domestic abuse (Sherman 1992).

Civil Liability in Federal Courts

Recently, there has been a tremendous increase in the number of civil liability filings against the police in federal courts. The most typical avenue for redress has come through the "resurrection" of Title 42 of the U.S. Code, Section 1983 (Barrineau 1994). In §1983, citizens can seek relief from officials who violate their constitutional rights under the guise of their governmental positions. Title 42 USC §1983 reads in part:

> Every person who, under color of any statute, ordinance, regulation, custom, or usage, of any State or Territory or the District of Columbia, subjects, or causes to

be subjected, any citizen of the United States or other person within the jurisdiction thereof to the deprivation of any rights, privileges, or immunities secured by
the Constitution and laws, shall be liable to the party injured in an action at law,
suit in equity, or other proper proceeding for redress.

As such, 42 USC §1983 does not create any substantive rights. Instead, it outlines a
procedure individuals can follow to seek compensation for violations of their constitutional rights. There are two essential components of §1983, namely (1) the defendant must be acting under the color of law, and (2) there must be a violation of a constitutional or federally protected right.

Color of law. ***Color of law*** translates into the misuse of power possessed by an
individual who is a "state actor," and derives their power from the government. Police
officers are given authority and power by the state. Thus, if officers are performing
typical police duties (e.g., making arrests, enforcing traffic regulations, or conducting
searches and seizures of property), they are, for the purposes of liability, acting under
the color of law (Kappeler 2001). Worrall (1998) indicated the courts often define the
color of law by asking, "Was police power used?" or "Did the department authorize the
act?"

Is an officer who is working off-duty security acting under the color of law for the
purposes of liability? Can police organizations be liable under §1983 for their actions?
In other words, are there circumstances in which police officers may not act under the
color of law? Vaughn and Coomes (1995, 398) noted several important exceptions and
caveats to this prong of §1983 requirements for liability. In their review of contemporary case law on the topic, they concluded that officers act "under the color of law if they
invoke police power, if they discharge duties routinely associated with police work, or if
they use their authority to lure potential plaintiffs into compromising positions." Officers
are acting under the color of law if they perform certain activities typically associated
with policing, including wearing a uniform, identifying themselves as police officers,
placing people under arrest, and filing reports. This is subjective from the plaintiff's point
of view and depends on whether the plaintiff believed the defendant was acting as a public official.

However, if an officer, even if in uniform, acts as a private citizen and does not
invoke his or her police powers, then he or she is not acting under the color of law for
liability purposes. To answer the question posed above, if the officer is working an
off-duty assignment under the auspices and direction of the police department, then
his or her actions may be carried out under the color of law. In contrast, if the officer
is working off-duty security through a private contract with a private security firm,
then he or she is not acting under the color of law. Table 11.1 provides a series of situations where officers are considered to be acting under the color of law as well as when
they are not doing so.

Violations of constitutional or federally protected rights. The second prong of
§1983 involves rights protected by the **Constitution or federally protected rights.**
Therefore, rights provided by the states are not covered in §1983 actions. Typically,
plaintiffs will seek redress for violations in one of the amendments outlined in the Bill
of Rights or the equal protection clause of the Fourteenth Amendment.

An example of §1983 in action may be instructive. In *Graham v. Connor* (1989), the
plaintiff (Graham) asked a friend to drive him to a store to obtain orange juice for his
diabetic condition. Arriving at the store, Graham observed too many people in line, so

he hurried out and asked his friend to drive him to a friend's house instead. A police officer, observing Graham's suspicious behavior, stopped the car driven by Graham's friend and detained the plaintiff until he could determine what had happened in the store (even though Graham explained his medical condition). After the officer determined no crime had been committed, he released Graham. However, while Graham was in police custody, he was denied access to treatment for his medical condition and sustained injuries as a result. Graham sued the officer for violating his Fourth Amendment rights that protected him from excessive use of force. The Court held that officers might be liable pursuant to §1983 for excessive use of force. In doing so, they determined a standard of *objective reasonableness* is to be used in such cases, indicating the force must be considered from the view of the officer at the time of the event and not in 20/20 hindsight.

Table 11.1   Factors to Determine Whether an Officer Acted Under the Color of Law

Officers Act Under the Color of Law If. . .	Officers Do Not Act Under the Color of Law If. . .
They identify themselves as a law enforcement agent.	They do not invoke police power.
They perform duties of a criminal investigation.	Their inaction does not constitute state action.
They file official police documents.	They commit crimes in a personal dispute without invoking police power.
They attempt or make an arrest.	They act as federal agents.
They invoke their police powers outside their lawful jurisdiction.	They report the details of alleged crimes as private citizens.
They settle a personal vendetta with police power.	
They display or use police weapons/equipment.	They work for a private security company and do not identify themselves as law enforcement personnel.
They act pursuant to a statute or ordinance.	The department removes the officers' lawful authority.
The department policy mandates they are "always on duty."	
They intimidate citizens from exercising their rights.	
The department supports, facilitates, or encourages the off-duty employment of its officers as private security personnel.	

Source: Adapted from Vaughn, M. S., and Coomes, L. F. 1995. "Police Civil Liability Under Section 1983: When Do Police Officers Act Under the Color of Law?" *Journal of Criminal Justice* 23, 409.

Defenses to §1983. There are four instances when, confronted with suits under §1983, defendants can offer defenses for their actions, thus negating the federal lawsuit. First, *absolute immunity* is when a civil action is brought against those protected by this form of immunity that will be dismissed by the court. However, this form of immunity has little application on liability for police officers, and it is typically reserved for the judiciary. The lone exception to this rule is when an officer commits perjury in court. If the officer, while testifying in criminal court, gives incorrect information that violates a person's right, the officer may seek absolute immunity from lawsuits from §1983 lawsuits. However, though immune from civil lawsuits, the act of perjury is a criminal offense with which officers may be charged and convicted in criminal courts (Kappeler 2001). Second, **qualified immunity** extends to police officers performing duties that are discretionary in nature. This form of immunity addresses the question: Did the officer know his or her conduct was in violation of a constitutional right or a federally protected right? According to Kappeler (2001, 62), "If a court determined that the law was not clearly established or that the officer's conduct was reasonable, the officer is to be afforded immunity from liability."

Third, police officers may defend themselves from federal litigation if they can claim there was **probable cause** to believe their action was legal. This is particularly important for defenses of false arrest or improper searches and seizures. For example, if officers can demonstrate probable cause was present that either a person had committed a crime or that probable cause existed that justified a search, then redress in federal court is barred *(Hunter v. Bryant* 1991; Kappeler 2001). Even if it is later determined that probable cause did not exist, but the officer was acting on good faith, the officer is immune from liability. "Probable cause is so strong a defense in arrest and search and seizure cases that some courts have held that if probable cause is present, the officer is not liable even if malice is involved in the officer's act" (del Carmen 1991, 57). Finally, officers may be free from civil liability if they can demonstrate their actions were conducted in **good faith.** This means the officer could not have reasonably known that their actions were in violation of law or the Constitution, such as executing a warrant that they believed to be valid. The factors the court will consider regarding good faith actions include the following:

1. The officer acted in accordance with agency rules and regulations,

2. The officer acted pursuant to a statute that was reasonably believed to be valid, but was later declared unconstitutional,

3. The officer acted in accordance with orders from a superior that were reasonably believed to be valid, or

4. The officer acted in accordance with advice from a legal counsel that was reasonably believed to be valid. (del Carmen 1991, 55–56)

Emerging Liability Issues for the Twenty-First Century

Policing in the twenty-first century may present new challenges to police officers, supervisors, and municipalities in the civil liability arena. Changes in technology, information systems, data analysis, and society provide a dynamic environment to which police officers must adapt. As stated earlier, people may become plaintiffs in civil liability suits for violating constitutional or federally protected rights. As such, it is important for officers and police managers to remain current on changes in criminal procedure. This section does not present an exhaustive discussion of these issues, but provides an overview of contemporary issues confronting modern police organizations.

Community policing and zero-tolerance policing. Community policing is designed to increase the level of discretion of the line officer as well as the frequency of officer-citizen encounters. Officers will have more ability to make decisions, engage in problem-solving activities, and facilitate partnerships with citizens. The changing role of the police has caused some to wonder if community policing may alter the exposure of police officers and police managers to civil liability. Interestingly, Worrall (1998) found an organization's level of commitment was related to fewer civil liability lawsuits. Recalling the characteristics of community policing, the idea that may decrease liability makes sense theoretically, and Vaughn, Cooper, and del Carmen (2001) outlined these arguments: (1) an increase of women and minority voices in police organizations designed to reduce citizens' complaints, (2) there are improvements in attitudes toward the police, and (3) there are improvements in confidence in the police and the criminal justice system. In short, because the police and the public are working in partnership, there may be less antagonism and misunderstanding between them.

On the other hand, there are several reasons to believe community policing may increase civil liability for police. First, the number of contacts between the police and the public should increase; this may lead to more opportunities for civil liability. Community policing also exposes police to areas that were, prior to the community-policing model, not considered public matters. Hughes (2000), for instance, argues that increased contact with the public in new and diverse matters will logically lead to more opportunities for civil suits against the police.

Second, discretion and policy creation are shifted to the lowest level of the organization. Therefore, officers will have more opportunity and responsibility for creating and implementing policies or customs on behalf of the organization "under the color of law." This may suggest that control and accountability of police officers will decrease and make direct supervision of these officers more difficult. Indeed, direct supervision and control of officers runs coun-

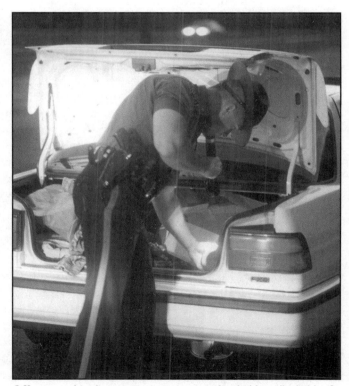

Officers and police organizations may be held civilly liable for behavior that violates a citizen's Constitutional rights, such as unreasonable searches and seizures.

ter to the community-policing philosophy. Similarly, police departments may have to relax the number of policies influencing the behavior of officers.

Increased liability may be demonstrated by considering New York City's experience with its Compstat (Compare Statistics) procedure. The NYPD has realized reductions in crime, and at least some of these benefits can be attributed to their aggressive zero-tolerance model of police services. This style encourages officers to be proactive in their problem solving and make arrests for relatively minor violations of the law. However, Greene (1999) also noted the number of legal filings alleging violations of civil rights have increased dramatically during the same time period. Many of these complaints involved police abuse of authority or brutality.

Impact on Officers

The potential for civil liability is a part of policing that officers and supervisors must accept. In a recent survey of police officers in Cincinnati, Hughes (2001b) found that 18.5 percent of officers had been sued for a job-related matter, and that 74.8 percent of officers personally knew of an officer who had been named in a lawsuit for a job-related matter. At the same time, 86.4 percent felt that officers are sued even when acting properly. This has led some officers to view public complaints and lawsuits as just another part of policing.

While the media tend to focus on plaintiff experiences, it is also important to consider the impact of a lawsuit from the officer's perspective. When officers and supervisors are sued for wrongdoing, there may be effects beyond the obvious loss of monetary resources. When named as a defendant in a civil lawsuit, officers may experience heightened levels of stress and anxiety. Pursuant to citizen complaints or civil litigation, officers are often interrogated regarding not only the act in question, but also past behavior and disciplinary records. Previously, we discussed the fact that officers often report administrative policies, discipline, and a perceived lack of support as important sources of stress. However, these organizational responses, at least in part, may be reactions by supervisors and municipalities to insulate themselves from litigation. Still, officers may interpret these reactions as the organization not "backing" them, citizens being out to "get rich" at the expense of officers, and "no one respecting what the police do." Not only does the stress of many officers increase, but these problems may also lead to increased cynicism among officers.

Even when not identified as a defendant, civil lawsuits can impact other officers in the police organization. In the wake of a lawsuit, officers may feel the need to engage in fewer interactions with the public, particularly officer-initiated encounters. Officers rationalize this as a normal response to what they feel is an unjust situation and rationalize that their own likelihood of being named as a defendant in a lawsuit decreases if they interact with fewer citizens. This phenomenon has been called **de-policing.**

There is some evidence that de-policing may have recently occurred in Cincinnati. In April 2001, a white Cincinnati police officer shot and killed an unarmed young black male. This shooting sparked several days of rioting resulting in injuries sustained by citizens and officers alike. In the months that followed, the officer was indicted and a civil lawsuit was filed in federal court alleging the police department engaged in racial profiling. After the riots, indictment, and lawsuit, there was evidence that officers engaged in a department-wide slowdown in activity. For example, in June 2000, officers made 5,063 arrests for nonviolent crimes (such as disorderly conduct and weapons violations). In June 2001 (after the riots, indictment and lawsuit), the department made half as many arrests (2,517). Additionally, arrests for violent crimes (such as murder and arson) declined to 487 from 502. This was despite a 20 percent increase from June 2000 in these crimes. Furthermore, traffic citations were down 35 percent. One police officer stated that officers were frustrated with the increase in crime rates, but also afraid of being labeled racial profilers whenever they arrested someone (Cloud 2001; McLaughlin and Prendergast 2001).

De-policing has implications for police managers. The most effective way to avoid this phenomenon is to maintain an environment that does not allow it to occur in the first place. Police managers who are confronted with subordinates engaged in de-policing will need to take additional steps to explain to officers that avoiding encounters with the public is not in line with organizational goals and is unethical behavior. Effective policing involves maintaining a healthy relationship with citizens. By engaging in de-policing, officers not only alienate citizens who are frustrated with the police, but also alienate citizens who support the police. Over time, it is likely de-policing will fade away and police officer activity will regress to the mean (or return to previous levels). In the meantime, the department may sustain irreparable damage to public trust, public support, and the department's reputation.

Recent empirical research suggests that the phenomenon of de-policing may be limited to post-traumatic events, such as those described above. Novak, Smith, and Frank (2003) examined whether officers who had experienced civil liability claims behaved differently than other officers. Their basic hypotheses were that officers will behave less "aggressively" (e.g., fewer proactive encounters with citizens, arrests, use of force, and searches) if they have previously been sued, known officers who have been sued, or are highly cognizant of liability during the course of their activities. In other words, officers who have more experience with litigation will subsequently avoid situations that increase their exposure to liability. However, the data did not support these hypotheses. It appeared that an officer's aggressive behavior was largely unaffected by that officer's experience with litigation. While it is important to not confuse "aggressive" and proactive behavior with "improper" behavior, it appears that officers may not allow fear of litigation to hamper them from engaging in proactive law enforcement activities. Relatedly, Hickman, Piquero, and Greene's (2000) analysis of officers in Philadelphia indicated that officers assigned to community-policing roles performed at parity with officers assigned to more traditional police roles regarding generation of citizen complaints. They found no difference between officers in proportion, type, or frequency of citizen complaints filed against them.

Summary

Criminal procedure is the process by which a person accused of a crime is processed through the criminal justice system and outlines the rules that the government must follow to ensure the civil liberties of citizens. Police officers may stop a citizen only if there is reasonable suspicion to believe criminal activity is afoot and may frisk that citizen only if there is reasonable suspicion to believe that the person is armed, posing a threat to officer safety. Arrests can only occur if the legal threshold is elevated to probable cause. Pursuant to an arrest, officers may search the person and the area within his or her immediate control or may perform a protective sweep for others who may pose a threat to officer safety. Like arrests, searches of property must be conducted only with probable cause. While there is a preference for obtaining a search warrant prior to engaging in a search of property, notable exceptions to this requirement include the plain view doctrine, the open fields doctrine, and the hot pursuit exception. The courts have indicated that persons in motor vehicles enjoy a diminished expectation to privacy, and searches of motor vehicles are more relaxed than those of private homes. Before questioning suspects who are in custody, officers must advise them of their Miranda rights, and these rights must be intelligently and voluntarily waived prior to questioning. Notable exceptions to the Miranda requirement include the public safety exception and inevitable discovery.

Civil litigation regarding police behavior has increased over time, both in the number of suits filed and the amount of money paid for damages or injury. People who initiate lawsuits (called plaintiffs) against the police (called defendants) may do so in either state courts or in federal courts. In state courts, torts may be brought for intentional as well as negligent behavior. In federal courts, plaintiffs may bring lawsuits against the police if there is a violation of constitutional rights or federally protected rights. Often, these lawsuits are filed under 42 USC §1983. To be successful in a §1983, the plaintiff must demonstrate that the officer acted under the color of law and that the act violated his or her civil rights. Acceptable defenses to §1983 lawsuits include absolute immunity, qualified immunity, probable cause, and good faith. While community policing may decrease the incidence of civil liability in policing, there is an equal chance that civil liability will increase. Regardless of whether plaintiffs prevail in their lawsuits against the police (and most do not), the process can cause negative consequences for police officers, including increased stress and cynicism.

Critical Thinking Questions

1. Discuss the difference between reasonable suspicion and probable cause as well as the permissible behaviors associated with these legal thresholds.

2. Compare and contrast the criminal justice system to the civil system of justice.

3. Discuss the ways the police must balance the need for public safety with the need to ensure the civil liberties of citizens.

4. Does requiring the police to advise suspects of their Miranda rights unduly handcuff the police? Support your answer.

5. What is more effective at controlling police behavior: the exclusionary rule or civil litigation? Why?

6. What types of claims may plaintiffs seek in state courts? In federal courts?

7. Describe 42 US §1983. What key components are necessary for a claim under §1983?

8. Under what circumstances do officers act "under the color of law," and why is it important to understand this?

9. Will community policing increase or decrease the number of civil liability claims? Support your answer.

References

Alabama v. White, 496 U.S. 325 (1990).

Arizona v. Hicks, 480 U.S. 321 (1987).

Barker, J. C. 1999. *Danger, Duty and Disillusion.* Prospect Heights, IL: Waveland.

Barrineau, H. E. 1994. *Civil Liability in Criminal Justice, 2nd ed.* Cincinnati: Anderson Publishing.

Brewer v. Williams, 430 U.S. 387 (1977).

Brinegar v. U.S., 338 U.S. 160 (1949).

California v. Greenwood, 486 U.S. 35 (1988).

Carroll v. U.S., 267 U.S. 132 (1925).

Chimel v. California, 395 U.S. 752 (1969).

Cloud, J. 2001, July 30. "What's Race Got to Do With It? Despite a Crime Wave, Cincinnati's Cops Pull Back, Underscoring Stakes in the Conflict Over Racial Profiling." Retrieved August 16, 2001 from the World Wide Web: <http://www.time.com/time/covers/1101010730/cover.html>.

del Carmen, R. V. 1991. *Civil Liabilities in American Policing: A Text for Law Enforcement Personnel.* Englewood Cliffs, NJ: Brady.

———. 2001. *Criminal Procedure: Law and Practice,* 5th ed. Belmont, CA: Wadsworth.

del Carmen, R. V. and Smith, M. R. 2001. "Police, Civil Liability, and the Law." In Dunham, R. G. and Alpert, G. P. (eds.), *Critical Issues in Policing,* 4th ed, pp. 181–198. Prospect Heights, IL: Waveland.

Graham v. Connor, 490 U.S. 397 (1989).

Greene, J. A. 1999. "Zero Tolerance: A Case Study of Police Policies and Practices in New York City." *Crime and Delinquency* 45: 171–187.

Hickman, M. J., Piquero, A. R., and Greene, J. R. 2000. "Does Community Policing Generate Greater Numbers and Different Types of Citizen Complaints Than Traditional Policing?" *Police Quarterly* 3: 70–84.

Hughes, T. 2000. Community Policing and Federal Civil Liability Under 42 USC §1983. Unpublished doctoral dissertation: University of Cincinnati.

———. 2001a. "*Board of the County Commissioners of Bryan County, Oklahoma v. Jill Brown*: Municipal Liability and Police Hiring Decisions." *Justice Professional* 13: 143–162.

———. 2001b. 2001. "Police Officers and Civil Liability: 'The Ties That Bind'?" *Policing: An International Journal of Police Strategies and Management* 24: 40–262.

Hunter v. Bryant, 502 U.S. 224, 112 S. Ct. 634 (1991).

Kappeler, V. E. 2001. *Critical Issues in Police Civil Liability,* 3rd ed. Prospect Heights, IL: Waveland.

Kappeler, V. E., Kappeler, S. F., and del Carmen, R. V. 1993. "A Content Analysis of Police Civil Liability Cases: Decisions in the Federal District Courts, 1978–1990." *Journal of Criminal Justice* 21: 325–337.

Knowles v. Iowa, 525 U.S. 113 (1998).

Levine, L., Davies, J., and Kionka, E. 1993. *A Torts Anthology.* Cincinnati: Anderson Publishing.

McLaughlin, S. and Prendergast, J. 2001, June 30. "Police Frustration Brings Slowdown: Arrests Plummet From 2000; Officers Seek Jobs in Suburbs." Retrieved August 16, 2001 from the World Wide Web: http://enquirer.com/editions/2001/06/30/loc_police_frustration.html.

Mapp v. Ohio, 367 U.S. 643 (1961).

Maryland v. Buie, 494 U.S. 325 (1990).

Michigan Department of State Police v. Sitz, 496 U.S. 444 (1990).

Minnesota v. Dickerson, 508 U.S. 366 (1993).

Miranda v. Arizona, 384 U.S. 436, 86 S. Ct. 1602, 16 L. Ed. 2d 694 (1966).

New York v. Belton, 453 U.S. 454 (1981).

New York v. Quarles, 467 U.S. 649 (1984).

Nix v. Willams, 467 U.S. 431 (1984).

Novak, K., Smith, B., and Frank, J. 2003. "Strange Bedfellows: Civil Liability and Aggressive Policing." *Policing: An International Journal of Police Strategies and Management* 26: 352–368.

Oliver v. U.S., 466 U.S. 170 (1984).

Payton v. New York, 445 U.S. 573 (1981).

Ross, D. L. 2000. "Emerging Trends in Police Failure to Train Liability." *Policing: An International Journal of Police Strategies and Management* 23: 169–193.

Schneckloth v. Bustamonte, 412 U.S. 218, 219 (1973).

Sherman, L. W. 1992. *Policing Domestic Violence.* New York: Free Press.

Silver, I. 1996. *Police Civil Liability.* New York: Mathew Binder.

Terry v. Ohio, 392 U.S. 1, 88 S. Ct. 1868, 20 L. Ed. 2d 889 (1968).

Thurman v. City of Torrington, 595 F.Supp. 1521 (1985).

U.S. v. Ross, 456 U.S. 798 (1982).

U.S. v. Watson, 423 U.S. 411 (1976).

Vaughn, M. S. and Coomes, L. F. 1995. "Police Civil Liability Under Section 1983: When Do Police Officers Act Under the Color of Law?" *Journal of Criminal Justice* 23: 395–415.

Vaughn, M. S., Cooper, T. W., and del Carmen, R. V. 2001. "Assessing Legal Liabilities in Law Enforcement: Police Chiefs' Views." *Crime and Delinquency* 47: 3–27.

Weeks v. U.S., 232 U.S. 383 (1914).

Whren v. U.S., 517 U.S. 806 (1996).

Worrall, J. L. 1998. "Administrative Determinants of Civil Liability Lawsuits Against Municipal Police Departments: An Exploratory Analysis." *Crime and Delinquency* 44: 295–313.

Wyoming v. Houghton, 526 U.S. 295 (1999).

Zalman, M. and Siegel, L. 1997. *Criminal Procedure: Constitution and Society,* 2nd ed. West Wadsworth: Belmont, CA.

Suggested Websites for Further Study

Supreme Court of the United States
http://www.supremecourtus.gov/
Collection of Supreme Court Opinions
http://supct.law.cornell.edu/supct/
ACLU and Police Practices
http://archive.aclu.org/issues/policepractices/hmpolice.html
Law Enforcement Liability Reporter
http://www.aele.org/lr.html ✦

Part IV
Contemporary Issues

## Chapter 12

Cultural Diversity

Chapter Outline

Key Terms

affirmative action plan	police*woman*
Civil Service, or merit, system	*police*woman
cultural diversity	quid pro quo harassment
defeminization	reverse discrimination
double marginality	sexual harassment
empirical evidence	structural characteristics
hostile-work-environment harassment	testimonial evidence
police culture	

P olicing in America remains a white male-dominated industry. This remains true after decades of calls from reformers to diversify policing in terms of race, ethnicity, and gender. Indeed, representation of females and racial/ethnic minorities has increased dramatically during the past 20 years; however, these groups remain underrepresented in most police organizations, particularly in smaller and rural police departments, which make up the overwhelming majority of departments in United States. Yet, as America continues to become more diverse, **cultural diversity** of police departments has again become important for both political and performance reasons. Although it is clear that diversity has widespread political support in many communities, the actual difference that diversification makes in police effectiveness is less clear.

In general, it is believed that a diverse police department is more effective than one that is not. In fact, diversity has become so important that it is often considered to be a significant strategy to reform departments with performance problems, particularly as they relate to use of force and community fear and distrust. The evidence regarding the impact of diversity on police effectiveness can be categorized as either testimonial or empirical. **Testimonial evidence** is based on the opinions of individuals who have strong political beliefs about the importance of diversity or whose experience (e.g., as citizens or police officers) has led them to believe that a diverse department is either more or less effective. In general, testimonial evidence about the effectiveness of diversity is usually favorable. **Empirical evidence** regarding the effectiveness of diversity based on data is derived from systematic study of one or more effectiveness criteria (e.g., crime rates, arrest rates, and citizen trust of police, or fewer complaints, civil suits, and confrontations). There is no empirical evidence that, in the long term, diversity makes a measurable, sustained difference in the effectiveness of the police. There is some short-term evidence, however, that diversity can make a difference in some areas of police effectiveness. For example, it has been shown that African American citizens in Detroit (Frank, Brandl, Cullen, and Stichman 1996) have a higher regard for the police than whites and that citizens in New York who came into contact with female officers (when they were first put on patrol) had a higher regard for the police department than they had before (Sichel, Friedman, Quint, and Smith 1978).

Given all the possible factors that can influence the relationship between police and citizens, it is unlikely that a police department that is a "perfect cultural match" for a community will necessarily be more effective *for that reason alone*. In the long term, the integrity, competence, and style of the officer, and the philosophy, strategies, and methods of the department have the greatest impact on effectiveness. However, diversity continues to have substantial political support because many persons believe that it is equitable to employ minorities and women, given the discrimination they have experienced in the past.

Historically, police departments have systematically discriminated against minorities and women in employment, assignments, promotions, and social acceptance. In addition, many white men have not, and do not, consider minorities and women to be their equals in terms of either capabilities or competencies. Beginning in the 1960s, governmental intervention was required to eliminate discrimination in employment and promotion. Legally, and in terms of government policy, this intervention became known as affirmative action (discussed in a later section).

As noted previously, during the early to mid-1960s there were ghetto riots and campus demonstrations that were often "sparked" by police actions. These events raised questions that went to the very core of the police role and operations in a democratic society: Are the police isolated from the community? How important is it to have community representation in police departments? How important to the community are the nonenforcement aspects of the police role? What type of individuals should be recruited as police officers? As has been discussed, several national commission reports, addressing these and other fundamental questions about the police, cited the need to increase especially minority but also female representation throughout the police field. The following is a brief discussion of the history of minorities and women in policing.

Minorities in Policing

Very little has been written about the early development of racial minority police officers in this country. Virtually all the literature that is available concerns African Americans and makes it clear that Blacks and other minority members, until recently, have had very little access to policing. For example, even though there were black police officers in Washington, D.C., as early as 1861 (Johnson 1947), by 1940 they represented less than 1 percent of the police population (Kuykendall and Burns 1980, 5). Since World War II, however, there has been a steady increase in the proportions of black officers, as well as other minorities, in policing. In general, although the proportions of blacks and other minorities reflect the available workforce in some communities, most departments do not have minority personnel equal to their numbers in the available workforce (see "Increasing Diversity in Police Departments," discussed later).

Minority representation of police grew in many cities only as a result of pressure from the black community. In Chicago, for instance, black citizens complained frequently of the "stupidity, prejudice and brutality" of white officers (Gosnell 1935, 245). After 1940, use of black police increased as a result of the emerging political participation of blacks. Liberal whites (Rudwick 1962) often supported organized movements. Often a church or civic group would become concerned over crime rates, law enforcement in black areas, or race relations because of either racial tension or a desire for integration. Believing that using black officers to patrol in black areas would substantially reduce black hostility toward the police, community leaders would usually agree to make a few experimental appointments (Johnson 1947).

Unequal Treatment

Even though African Americans were increasingly being hired into policing, they were not treated equally in the areas of powers of arrest, work assignments, evaluations, and promotions. Frequently, black officers were allowed to patrol only in black areas and to arrest only other black citizens. If a white person committed a crime in a black neighborhood, a black officer would have to call a white officer to make the arrest. In a 1959 survey of 130 cities and counties in the South, 69 required black officers to call white officers in arresting white suspects, and 107 cities indicated that black officers patrolled only in black neighborhoods (Rudwick 1962). Elysee Scott, associated with the National Organization for Black Law Enforcement Executives, who grew up in a small Louisiana town in the 1950s, remembers that the black police officers rode in cars marked "Colored Police" and were allowed to arrest only "colored" people (Sullivan 1989).

Black officers were frequently restricted in type and location of assignments, and superior officers negatively manipulated performance ratings. Dismissal because of race was also a possibility. In addition, black and white officers rarely worked together

(Gosnell 1935); even as late as 1966, squad cars were not totally integrated in the Chicago Police Department (National Center 1967). And promotions were rare for black officers. For example, Leinen (1984) found that in the mid-1960s, only 22 police departments had promoted blacks above the rank of patrol officer. Even when promotions did occur, blacks were not congratulated by whites nor given duties involving active command. In at least one instance, black lieutenants were assigned to walk a beat as patrol officers (Gosnell 1935). However, more recent research by Hickman and his colleagues (2001) found no direct effects of officer race on outcomes of internal department disciplinary procedures in their examination of Philadelphia police officers. This may suggest that the kinds of discrimination that did exist in the past are less common today.

A recommended strategy for increasing interest in policing careers among racial minorities (and women) is to involve minorities and female officers in the recruitment process. Voices From the Field provides a discussion of various ways police departments can engage in increasing minority and female representation within their organizations. Bob Stewart was most recently the Executive Director of the National Organization of Black Law Enforcement Executives (NOBLE) having served there between 1997 and 2001. Prior to his experience at NOBLE Bob was the Chief of Police in Ormond Beach (FL), and retired as a Captain from the Metropolitan Police Department in Washington D.C. after 22 years of service.

Voices From the Field
Policing and Cultural Diversity
Bob Stewart, Former Executive Director,
National Organization of Black Law Enforcement Executives

Question: Has cultural diversity changed policing?

Answer: While many forward-thinking agencies have taken steps that have improved their recruiting, hiring, assignment, and promotion practices, the primary delivery methodology for much of the last generation of policing has been through training. The thrust of this training has largely been devoted to making people conscious of potential biases that they might carry and generally appealing to the better person that resides in all of us.

The expansion of community policing and out enriched understanding through our discussions on racial profiling and biased-based policing have led to very different "best practices," both inside the agency and on the street. Both efforts are much more focused on defining courteous, professional agency-approved behavior, while also defining rude, discourteous, unprofessional, and unapproved behavior; modeling that behavior in recruit and in-service training; charging supervisors with

the responsibility of monitoring officer behavior; and a management system that identifies individual, unit, and agency warning signs before they become institutionalized.

The best outcomes are seen in agencies that are recognized for the courteous and professional demeanor of their officers, based on a very conscious effort on the part of the organization to value and reward this preferred behavior. These departments have used this to create trust and goodwill as they engage and partner in meaningful ways with community interests. We also find that those agencies have had no difficulty in their recruiting efforts. The best and most cost-effective means of doing that involve having current minority and female employees who are happy to tell recruits that they like the agency that they work for because they are treated well and that they have fair and equitable assignment and promotional opportunities. ✦

Performance of African American Police

As noted above, the ghetto riots of the mid-1960s were a major reason that increased emphasis was placed on the role of minorities in policing. Because a large number of these riots were triggered by incidents involving white officers patrolling black ghetto areas, many people thought that community relations would be improved if there were African American officers in these areas. Several national reports came to the same conclusion. For instance, the President's Commission on Law Enforcement and Administration of Justice stated:

> Police officers have testified to the special competence of Negro officers in Negro neighborhoods. The reasons given include: they get along better and receive more respect from the Negro residents; they receive less trouble . . . they can get more information; and they understand Negro citizens better. (1967, 162)

Historically, evidence to support the belief that black officers would perform more satisfactorily in black areas has been mixed. On the one hand, many black citizens wanted black officers because it would provide an opportunity for more public jobs, more understanding, less white police brutality, and more effective supervision of black criminals (Landrum 1947; Myrdal 1944). On the other hand, Rudwick (1960) has argued that blacks from lower socioeconomic classes preferred white to black officers. He found that poorer, uneducated blacks frequently asked for white officers when in need of help and were more likely to plead guilty to a charge made by a white officer (Rudwick 1962).

Some evidence indicates that black officers have actually been harder on black citizens than have white officers. In a study in Philadelphia in the 1950s, Kephart (1957) found that the majority of black officers believed it was necessary to be "stricter" with their "own" people than they were with nonblacks. Alex (1976) found that black officers were actually challenged more by young blacks and may have viewed themselves as protectors of the black community. In contrast, black officers needed to prove to the white officers that they were not biased and therefore treated black suspects the same as they treated white suspects, or even more harshly. In his influential book *Black in Blue* (1969), Alex termed this dilemma "double marginality."

This **double marginality** was evident by the mid-1960s, when the apparent desire of many black citizens for black police began to lose appeal. Studies conducted in San Diego and Philadelphia, for example, found that some black citizens felt that blacks who chose to become police officers were "selling them out." Of course, given the tenor of the times—police officers in general were viewed as enemies in minority communities—such a finding is hardly surprising. It is also interesting to note that while many still take the view that predominately minority neighborhoods need minority patrol officers, others view such an approach as a form of segregation. It is ironic that many of those same people who, during the riots of the 1960s, demanded that black officers be sent into black areas, are now condemning the same practice as racist (Sullivan 1989, 342).

Recent research indicated that the race of the officer might have less influence on citizens' perception of officer performance than conventional wisdom would assume. Weitzer (2000) analyzed surveys of three Washington, D.C. communities, where each community possessed different racial and class characteristics. He found that citizens in middle-class communities reported that black and white officers act similarly in their communities; however, citizens in lower-class communities were more likely to report perceived variations in officer behavior. However, when asked whether they would prefer to have mostly white or mostly black officers working in their neighborhood, black and white teams, or no preference, the majority of citizens indicated they would prefer racially mixed policing teams or indicated "no preference." This was true regardless of community racial characteristics or economic characteristics.

Weitzer (2000, 320) indicated that having racially mixed policing teams could have several benefits. First, the teams can have a moderating effect on officers of each race. This means that officers could "check and balance" or compensate for the behavior of their partners. Second, racially mixed teams can lead to socializing each officer in ways to interact with citizens of different races. Third, racially mixed teams serve a symbolic benefit for the police department, indicating unity and cohesion between officers of different races. Based on these results, there appears to be very little benefit from adhering to the old style of assigning officers to communities based on the race of the officer or makeup of the community (e.g., black officers in predominantly black communities, white officers in predominantly white communities).

Today, as African American officers become more self-assured and less likely to accept discriminatory practices , double marginality is less of a problem. On the one hand, in one study conducted in the aftermath of the Miami riots of the early 1980s, Berg, True, and Gertz (1984) found that black police officers were far less detached and alienated from the local community than were white or Hispanic officers. On the other hand, some police officials believe that black officers have trouble relating to the community because they tend to identify with their white colleagues, who often have a limited understanding of cultural differences (Felkenes 1990; Georges-Abeyie 1984). Because so little data exist in this area of study, it is difficult to know how large an issue double marginality remains for minority officers. One thing seems clear, however—as long as there is tension between minority communities and police departments, minority officers will be caught in the middle. It is anticipated that as the degree of discrimination lessens, both within and outside police departments, the problem of double marginality will lessen accordingly.

Women in Policing

Women remain significantly underrepresented in policing. This might be due in part to the fact that the crime-fighter image that is often portrayed in policing does not coincide with social perceptions of acceptable female behavior. Policing often involves male-attributed activities, such as aggression, physical competence, logic, and stable emotions. Common characteristics associated with women (e.g., compassion, empathy, and nurturing) are seen as less needed, if not undesired, in police work (Parsons and Jesilow 2001). Regardless of the reasons why women remain underrepresented in policing, it is often indicated that healthy and effective police organizations would benefit from a more integrated force.

The historical record for women in policing is even weaker than for minorities. The first woman to hold full police powers was Lola Baldwin in Portland, Oregon, who in 1905 was hired in a social-work capacity with the responsibility of protecting young girls and women. Such a crime-prevention role was viewed as separate from the traditional police role; as Walker notes, "Once the police began to think in terms of preventing juvenile delinquency, they responded to the traditional argument that women had a special capacity for child care" (1977, 85). Between 1905 and 1915, several police departments across the country copied Portland's example.

The policewoman idea achieved the status of an organized movement in 1910 with the appointment of Alice Stebbins-Wells to the Los Angeles Police Department. Like Baldwin, Stebbins-Wells had a background in social work and was assigned to care for young women in trouble with the law and to prevent delinquency among juveniles of both sexes (Walker 1977). Stebbins-Wells became the national leader for the policewomen's movement, which lasted into the 1920s. Her appointment led to the appointment of women to similar positions (as police social workers) in police departments in at least 16 cities by 1916 (Walker 1977). By 1925, 210 cities had women working in police positions, 417 as police social workers and 355 as jail matrons (Owings 1925).

Between 1925 and 1965, both the numbers and functions of policewomen increased, but only minimally. For example, a 1967 survey of police departments in the nation's largest cities indicated that there were only 1,792 women with police powers (Berkeley 1969). When they were represented on the force, policewomen typically comprised less than 2 percent of the personnel (Eisenberg, Kent, and Wall 1973; Melchionne 1967) and were excluded from patrol duties. During this period, most police departments had policies that not only discouraged the hiring of women but often included quotas as well, usually 1 percent or less (Simpson 1977).

A female police officer of the late 1940s.

Unequal Treatment

Prior to the 1950s, the role of women in policing was restricted primarily to social-welfare assignments, including dealing with juvenile and family problems; being prison matrons; detecting purse snatchers, pickpockets, and shoplifters; investigating sexual assault; and clerical work (Eisenberg, Kent, and Wall 1973). During the 1950s, their role was expanded to cover narcotics and vice investigations (Garmire 1978). In this period, it is ironic that the advocates for women in policing tended to argue that because of their "unique" contributions, including their skills with women and children, defusing domestic violence, and doing undercover work, they should be allowed to join the law enforcement profession (Melchionne 1967). Of course, such an argument most likely added to the prevailing view that women could handle specialist activities in "their areas" but were not suited for general police work. As Balkin notes, "It is an interesting if unanswered question why there was reluctance to demand simple equality for women in police work" (1988, 30). Undoubtedly, a large part of the answer lies in the strong tradition placed on the law enforcement, as opposed to social service, nature of the job. In addition, Wilson and McLaren, in their highly influential text,

Police Administration (see Chapter 4), were firmly against the equal employment of women. They argued that while women could be of some value in specialized activities and units, they were not qualified to head such units. Men, they noted, were more effective administrators and "were less likely to become irritable and overly critical under emotional stress" (1963, 334).

Although these stereotypic images of women and police work were soon to be challenged, the major breakthrough for the equal treatment of policewomen on the job was the passage of the 1972 amendments to the Civil Rights Act of 1964. After this date, police departments were required, often under the threat of a court order, to eliminate such discriminatory practices of hiring and job assignment. The changes that followed were drastic. For example, in 1971 there were fewer than 12 policewomen on patrol in the United States; by 1974, this number was approaching 1,000 (Garmire 1978).

In 1968, the first women were assigned to patrol work in the Indianapolis Police Department (Milton 1972). Within five years, many of the nation's largest police forces, including those of New York, Philadelphia, Miami, Washington, and St. Louis, had women working in patrol (Sherman 1973). By 1979, the percentage of policewomen assigned to patrol was approximately 87 in city departments serving populations over 50,000 (Sulton and Townsey 1981). In a comprehensive survey for the Police Foundation (1990) of municipal departments serving populations ranging from 50,000 to over a million, it was shown that the integration of women into all police assignments has continued to grow at a steady pace. The data indicated that by 1986, 98 percent of the responding departments assigned women to patrol, and women were being assigned to field-operations units (including patrol, special operations, and traffic assignments) in slightly greater proportion than their overall representation in policing (Martin 1989). Today, policewomen are assigned to virtually all police functions.

Performance of Women Officers

The evaluations of the first generation of women patrol officers found that they performed in a highly satisfactory manner. These findings are especially interesting because it was the argument that women could not handle the "physically demanding" job of patrol that had barred them from patrol work. The first study of women on patrol was conducted in Washington, D.C., in 1973 (Bloch and Anderson 1974). A matched pair of 86 newly trained policewomen and policemen were placed on patrol and evaluated for one year. The results indicated that men and women performed in a generally similar manner. Women responded to similar calls and had similar results in handling violent citizens. Some interesting differences were also found: Women made fewer arrests but appeared to be more effective than men in defusing potentially violent situations. Additionally, women had a less aggressive style of policing and were less likely to be charged with improper conduct. The unmistakable conclusion drawn from these results was that female officers can perform effectively on patrol.

Two additional major studies closely followed the Washington study, both with similar conclusions. In 1975, Sherman conducted an evaluation of policewomen on patrol in the St. Louis County Police Department; the first 16 women put on patrol in the county were compared with a group of 16 men who had been trained with the women officers. The results indicated that the women were equally as effective as the men in performing patrol work. Once again, some interesting differences were noted: Women were less aggressive, made fewer arrests, and engaged in fewer "preventive" activities, such as car and pedestrian stops. Citizen surveys indicated that women were more sensitive and responsive to their needs and handled service calls, especially domestic disturbances, better than men.

The second study, conducted in New York City in 1976 by Sichel, Friedman, Quint, and Smith (1978), was comparable to the Washington study in methodological rigor and sophistication. Once again, comparison groups of 41 women and men officers with similar background characteristics were evaluated. Based on 3,625 hours of observation on patrol, and some 2,400 police-citizen encounters, the results indicated that both groups of officers performed in a similar manner. Again, however, women officers were judged by citizens to be more respectful, pleasant, and competent; furthermore, citizens who came into contact with women officers tended to have a higher regard for the police department. Similar findings on the effectiveness of policewomen on patrol have been reported throughout the 1970s in departments of widely divergent sizes and geographical locations.

A review of these studies by Morash and Greene (1986) pointed out that despite the generally favorable evaluations, gender biases were inherent in the study designs. For example, there was an emphasis on traits stereotypically associated with "maleness" and policing, and approximately two-thirds of the policing situations observed were related to direct or potential violence, even though such incidents are not frequently encountered. Also important, although the studies found differences in men's and women's behavior, they did not consider the possibility that the women's policing style in resolving conflicts and disputes, rather than escalating incidents into unnecessary arrests, might have had a beneficial rather than a negative effect. Public policing may indeed benefit from police styles that play down the values of coercive authority, conflict, and interpersonal violence (Morash and Greene 1986, 249).

Today women perform virtually all police tasks, including bicycle patrol.

Another study of patrol teams in New York City (Grennan 1988) reported similar results with respect to male and female policing style differences: Women were found to be less likely to use a firearm in violent confrontations, less likely to seriously injure a citizen, no more likely to suffer injuries, and more emotionally stable. This study debunked another male stereotype, that because women have less strength and are less capable of subduing a suspect physically, they will be more likely to use their firearms.

Finally, Parsons and Jesilow (2001) argue that the attitudes and behavior of female police officers differ very little from their male counterparts. They attribute these similarities to a number of factors, including self-selection, department screening, and socialization. They posit that many women who are drawn to policing possess a propensity for the stereotypically masculine characteristics outlined previously (i.e., aggression, physical competence, logic, and stable emotions). Typically, police departments continue to select and train officers according to the traditional law enforcement orientation. They further find that occupational socialization contributes to similarities in values, beliefs, and behaviors for both men and women (though women often find this process more difficult and isolating than male officers). This has withdrawn male and female officers alike from the general population. The result, Parsons and Jesilow argue, is a collection of male and female officers who are more similar than many might believe.

Affirmative Action

The National Advisory Commission's *Report on Police* stated that "When a substantial ethnic minority population resides within the jurisdiction, the police agency should take affirmative action to achieve a ratio of minority group employees in approximate proportion to the makeup of the population" (1973, 329). The National Advisory Commission on Civil Disorders (1968, 316) suggested that police departments should not only intensify their efforts on minority recruitment but also increase the numbers of minorities in supervisory positions. Attempts to remedy past discriminatory employment and promotional practices are reflected in an **affirmative action plan.** In other words, the department tries to make an affirmative, or positive, effort to redress past practices and ensure equal employment opportunity. Such plans have been developed voluntarily, though often with political pressure or by court order following legal action.

In one study of the nation's 50 largest cities, Walker (1989) found that affirmative action plans appeared to play an important role in police employment trends. Nearly two-thirds (64 percent) of the departments reported operating under an affirmative action plan at some point during the five-year period. Interestingly, 23 of the affirmative action plans were court ordered, and only seven were voluntary. Clearly, much of the growth of both minorities and women in policing over the past several decades can be attributed to affirmative action plans and policies (see Inside Policing 12.l).

Inside Policing 12.1   **Dallas Police Department Reports Minority Officers Reflect City Makeup**

Long a target of protests over its racial makeup, the Dallas Police Department is making progress in its efforts to make the ranks of its sworn employees reflect the increasingly diverse population it serves. For the first time, the number of black employees at the officer rank is virtually proportionate to the city's black population, according to statistics kept by the departments. In the near future, the share of Hispanic officers also will be proportionate to the city's Hispanic population.

As of early 1998, 29 percent of the department's 1,145 officers were black and 18.8 percent were Hispanic. The 1990 census, which the city uses to set hiring goals, showed Dallas had 29.5 percent black residents and 18.8 percent Hispanics. Asian Americans make up less than 1 percent of officers and senior corporals. The department, however, has a way to go before minorities are proportionately represented in its upper ranks. Whites, who make up 55.3 percent of the city's population, account for about 75 percent of the 1,697 senior corporals, sergeants, lieutenants, captains, and chiefs. While the department acknowledges the imbalance, it continues to make headway in improving promotional opportunities for all officers.

The figures on the number of minority officers are heartening in light of the tenuous, nearly incendiary police-minority relations that were the norm less than 10 years ago, a period in which the racial dynamics of the department were a major issue. To remedy the scant numbers of minorities on the force, the City Council

> **Inside Policing 12.1   Dallas Police Department Reports Minority Officers Reflect City Makeup (continued)**
>
> adopted an affirmative action plan in 1988. Revised in 1993 and due to expire in September 1998, the plan stipulates that each new class of police recruits should be one-third black, one-third Hispanic, and one-third female. It also sets promotional goals for women and minorities in each rank.
>
> In 1992, protesters massed outside the department, charging that the effort was moving too slowly in hiring and advancing minorities. Two years later, an internal audit concluded that in the early 1990s the department had fired dozens of officers with questionable credentials. Critics of the affirmative action plan, including the Dallas Police Association, charged that standards had been lowered, leading to the firing of unqualified applicants. The DPA still opposes affirmative action, particularly the practice of "skip promotions" allowing minorities who score lower on tests to rank higher on promotion lists than whites with better scores. The apparent progress made by the department shows that the time is near to dismantle the controversial practice, said the DPA's president, Glenn White: "If you continue to hire minorities and get them in, having an affirmative action program with skip promotions is not necessary. They'll make it on their own."
>
> Other observers cautioned that progress does not mean police now can become complacent on the issue of minority representation in the upper ranks. "If we can reach the representation goal at the police officer level, why not at the senior corporal, sergeant, and lieutenant and above?" said Thomas Glover, president of the Texas Peace Officers' Association, a predominantly black organization.
>
> *Source:* Adapted from "Dallas PD Says Black Officers Mirror City Makeup." 1998, *Law Enforcement News*, March 7. Reprinted with permission from *Law Enforcement News*, John Jay College of Criminal Justice, New York City.

Equal Employment Opportunity

In general, the legal challenges to discrimination in employment are brought under either (1) the "equal protection of the laws" clause of the Fourteenth Amendment (which protects citizens of all states) or (2) the Equal Employment Opportunity Act of 1972 (which extended to public agencies the "anti-discrimination in employment" provisions of Title VII of the 1964 Civil Rights Act). Title VII prohibits any discrimination in the workplace based on race, color, religion, national origin, or sex. The Equal Employment Opportunity Commission (EEOC) was established in 1964 to investigate possible violations of the act.

Moran (1988, 274) suggests that much of the resistance to affirmative action litigation rests on the belief by many police executives that the **Civil Service, or merit system,** is a fair and effective means of producing a professional force. This system generally involves selecting in rank order those individuals who obtained the highest combined score on an objective, multiple-choice, written exam (many of which have been shown to be culturally biased and not job related) and an oral interview. Additionally, candidates must meet several physical, medical, and personal requirements to qualify for appointment to the department. The problem with this "fair" and "effective" system is that it has excluded women, except in some specialized positions, and many minorities from police work.

The federal courts began to recognize that many selection standards that appeared to be neutral in form and intent in fact operated to exclude minorities and women. In general, the courts have indicated (Moran 1988, 275–276) that a police department must: (1) establish that a selection procedure can be scientifically linked to job performance (i.e., "job validated"), or (2) restructure the selection process in a manner that does not discriminate against qualified minorities. The outcome of the affirmative action litigation has been that, from a scientific perspective, there was very little "merit" in the police-selection process. In fact, such standards as height, weight, age, and gender have not been correlated to job performance.

In the landmark decision in this area, *Griggs v. Duke Power Co.* (1971), the U. S. Supreme Court held that the use of a professionally developed examination (for intelligence) could not be used if it had a discriminatory effect. The Court pointed out that Title VII prohibited tests that are neutral in form but discriminatory in operation; that is, if a selection practice excludes minorities or women (even though not intended to do so) and cannot be shown to be job validated, it is prohibited. Griggs further found that once discrimination has been established, the burden of proof in establishing the validity of the practice shifts to the defendant (i.e., employer). In other words, once a police department has been judged to engage in a discriminatory practice, the department must indicate to the court that the practice (or requirement) is job related (Moran 1988).

In contrast, if a selection standard or requirement does not have a discriminatory impact, there is no need for validation. Furthermore, if a requirement can be shown to be a valid requirement for the job, even if it may have a discriminatory impact, it may be allowed to remain as a requirement. Chapter 14, for example, discusses how higher education may be shown to be a Bona Fide Occupational Qualification (BFOQ) for policing and thus allowed as a requirement for initial selection.

Reverse Discrimination

Increasing the proportional representation of ethnic minorities and women in policing is an extremely complex undertaking that has important social, ethical, and legal implications. Although there is undoubtedly a need for an increase, the question is how to do so fairly. When affirmative action plans for selection and promotion (which may include the use of quotas, separate lists, and "skip" promotions, although often temporary: see Inside Policing 12.1) are put into practice, individuals who are not part of that plan—usually white men—often feel they have been discriminated against. This situation has become known as **reverse discrimination.** As with affirmative action policies, there has been much litigation in this area.

The idea of reverse discrimination is important, because those who feel they are victims frequently develop resentment (known as "white backlash") toward those who are helped most by affirmative action. This reaction should not be too surprising when the immediate effect may be either rejection or lack of promotion for whites who believe they are more qualified for the position based on the merit system. Even though the criteria used may not have been job-validated, because the merit system has been used for so long it is often difficult to get this point across when careers are seriously affected. For example, a study by Jacobs and Cohen (1978) indicated that white police officers view affirmative action programs as a threat to their job security. Additionally, if new criteria (i.e., not based on the old merit system) are used to further increase minority representation in a department, veteran officers often view the new process as "lowering standards," and thus, the quality of police personnel.

Haarr (1997) described the resentment and bitterness white officers held toward many black supervisors due to perceived inequities associated with affirmative action and dual promotion lists. During her observations and interviews with officers in one city, white officers (both male and female) indicated that they believed that less qualified black officers were promoted over more highly qualified whites. Two-thirds of officers felt blacks had an unfair advantage in the promotional process. Conversely, blacks appeared to support the process as a mechanism for leveling the playing field due to culturally biased exams and the firmly entrenched "old boy network" of promoting white men. Regardless of whether the dual-list strategy in this department was fair, just, or achieved its designed goals, one fact is clear: The process contributed significantly to alienation and animosity between races within the department. Further, Haarr reported that social patterns of interaction were largely intraracial, and this might, in part, be due to these perceived inequities in the promotional process.

The litigation in this area is as complicated as the issue itself. In 1974, for example, the Detroit Police Department voluntarily adopted a policy of promoting one black officer to sergeant for each white officer promoted. The Detroit Police Officers Association filed suit against the department, claiming that the policy discriminated against white males. In *Detroit Police Officers' Association v. Young* (1978), the court ruled that preferential treatment had been granted to blacks solely on the basis of race and that the policy therefore discriminated against all others. In a similar suit, *U.S. v. Paradise* (1987), the U.S. Supreme Court upheld racial quotas as a means of reversing past discrimination. The Alabama Department of Public Safety was ordered to promote one black officer to corporal for each white officer promoted to rectify "blatant and continuous patterns of racial discrimination" (the department had only four of 66 black corporals and no blacks at the sergeant level or above). The Court justified the ruling saying that it did not impose an unacceptable burden on innocent third parties since the "one-for-one" requirement was temporary and would only postpone the promotion of qualified whites. Additionally, the promotion quota advanced blacks only to the level of corporal (not higher ranks) and did not require layoffs or dismissals of white officers.

As the above court interpretations indicate, rulings in this area are subject to changes by the judges who try the cases. Based on *Paradise*, however, it appears that the Supreme Court, in its attempt to balance equal employment opportunities, is equally concerned about blatant racial discrimination as well as unacceptable injuries to innocent third parties.

Increasing Diversity in Police Departments

The number of women and minorities in police departments has increased consistently since the 1960s, even though the increase has been uneven. For instance, a survey of municipal police departments serving cities of 50,000 or more (Martin 1989a) indicated that in 1978 women made up 4.2 percent of sworn personnel, and by 1986 they made up 8.8 percent. In local departments with 100 or more officers, about 99 percent have women officers, but fewer than 1 percent have 20 percent or more female representation. Furthermore, most of these departments are sheriffs' departments, where many women officers work in the jails (Carter, Sapp, and Stephens 1989). With respect to minorities, Walker (1989) reported that in the nation's 50 largest cities, between 1983 and 1988, nearly half (45 percent) made significant progress in the employment of black officers; however, 17 percent reported a decline in their percentage of African Americans. Forty-two percent of the departments reported significant increases in the percentage of Hispanic officers employed, while approximately 11 percent indicated a decline, and 17 percent reported no change.

The Bureau of Justice Statistics conducts regular surveys on the cultural changes taking place in policing. The increasing percentages of women and minorities can be readily observed in Figure 12.1. Women comprised 10.6 percent of all full-time local police officers in 2000, compared to 10 percent in 1997, 8.8 percent in 1993, 8.1 percent in 1990, and 7.6 percent in 1987. Black officers accounted for 11.7 percent of the total in 2000 (which is unchanged from 1997), compared to 11.3 percent in 1993, 10.5 percent in 1990, and 9.3 percent in 1987. Hispanic officers made up 8.3 percent of the total in 2000, compared to 7.8 percent in 1997, 6.2 percent in 1993, 5.2 percent in 1990, and 4.5 percent in 1987. All minorities made up about 22.6 percent of the total in 2000. This is a steady increase of minority representation compared to 1987, when minorities made up 14.6 percent of police personnel (Reaves and Goldberg 2000; Hickman and Reaves 2003).

The uneven increase of both women and minority officers in departments of varying size is shown in Table 12.1. Although women comprised 10.6 percent of all local police officers in 2000, their percentages were highest in large jurisdictions, with 16.5 percent of officers in jurisdictions of 1 million or more in population and 15.5 percent in jurisdictions with at least 500,000 residents but fewer than 1 million (see Table 12.1).

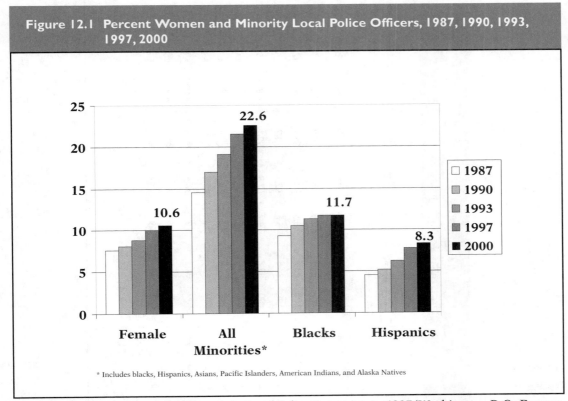

Figure 12.1 Percent Women and Minority Local Police Officers, 1987, 1990, 1993, 1997, 2000

* Includes blacks, Hispanics, Asians, Pacific Islanders, American Indians, and Alaska Natives

Sources: Reaves, B. A. and Goldberg, A. L. *Local Police Departments, 1997* (Washington, D.C.: Bureau of Justice Statistics, 2000), 4; Hickman, M. J. and Reaves, B. A. *Local Police Departments, 2000* (Washington, D.C.: Bureau of Justice Statistics, 2003), 4.

Table 12.1   Race and Ethnicity of Full-Time Officers in Local Police Departments, by Size of Population Served, 2000

Percentage of Full-time Sworn Employees Who Are:

Population Served	Total	Male	Female	White Total	White Male	White Female	Black Total	Black Male	Black Female	Hispanic Total	Hispanic Male	Hispanic Female	Other Total	Other Male	Other Female
All sizes	100	89.4	10.6	77.4	70.9	6.5	11.7	9.0	2.7	8.3	7.2	1.1	2.7	2.4	0.3
1,000,000 or more	100	83.5	16.5	63.5	55.7	7.8	16.1	11.0	5.1	17.3	14.2	3.1	3.1	2.6	0.4
500,000–999,999	100	84.5	15.5	62.4	54.7	7.7	25.2	18.6	6.5	6.8	6.0	0.8	5.6	5.1	0.5
250,000–499,999	100	85.8	14.2	67.9	59.1	8.8	19.0	15.0	4.0	10.7	9.5	1.1	2.4	2.2	0.3
100,000–249,999	100	89.3	10.7	76.2	68.7	7.5	12.2	10.1	2.1	8.0	7.2	0.7	3.7	3.3	0.4
50,000–99,999	100	91.8	8.2	85.2	78.8	6.4	7.3	6.1	1.1	5.7	5.2	0.5	1.8	1.7	0.1
25,000–49,999	100	93.0	7.0	87.8	82.1	5.7	6.1	5.2	0.8	4.6	4.2	0.4	1.5	1.4	0.1
10,000–24,999	100	94.3	5.7	90.6	85.8	4.8	4.6	4.1	0.5	3.4	3.2	0.2	1.4	1.2	0.2
2,500–9,999	100	94.5	5.5	90.1	85.5	4.6	4.5	4.1	0.4	3.9	3.5	0.4	1.5	1.4	0.1
Under 2,500	100	96.1	3.9	87.9	84.7	3.2	5.8	5.5	0.3	3.1	3.0	0.1	3.2	2.9	0.3

Source: Matthew J. Hickman and Brian A. Reaves, *Local Police Departments, 2000* (Washington, DC: Bureau of Justice Statistics, 2003), 4.

Minority officers, who made up approximately 11.7 percent of the total, also had the highest percentages in large jurisdictions, with black officers making up approximately 16 to 25 percent in jurisdictions over 250,000 residents; Hispanic officers were the most represented in jurisdictions with populations over 250,000, making up 10.7 to 17.3 percent. Each of these groups had the highest percentage of officers in jurisdictions with over 1 million population. Other minorities, including Asians, Pacific Islanders, American Indians, and Alaska Natives, represented 2.7 percent of the total, with 3.1 percent in jurisdictions with over 1 million population; all other jurisdictions were under 6 percent representation (see Table 12.1).

Three recent surveys of women in policing further point out their uneven development and continued gender-specific problems. The first survey of 800 police executives by the International Association of Chiefs of Police (IACP) reported that women make up 12 percent of the police officers but are not represented at all in nearly 20 percent of the departments ("Plenty of Talk. . ." 1999). Furthermore, the IACP found that 91 percent of the departments had no women in policy-making roles, and 10 percent reported that gender bias was one of the reasons women were not promoted. It was also found that women had more than one-third of the lawsuits filed against departments charged with gender bias and sexual harassment. Based on the findings, the IACP recommended that police departments should implement fairer screening procedures, institute more rigorous policies against sexual harassment, and increase recruiting drives designed to attract and retain more women in policing. The Albuquerque Police Department was identified by police executives in the survey as a possible model for other departments with respect to women in policing; Inside Policing 12.2 describes why.

Inside Policing 12.2 **Albuquerque Police Department Identified as Model for Policewomen**

The Albuquerque Police Department has been identified by police executives as a possible model for other departments regarding policewomen. In the past three years, women in the academy class have increased from just 8 percent to 25 percent. In the January 1999 class, the department reports, one-third of the recruits were women. Several years ago, however, despite participation in job fairs and a competitive salary, the department was still having problems recruiting female candidates. But significant changes seem to have turned the situation around. Those changes included (1) hiring a trainer to help women candidates pass the physical conditioning tests, (2) switching to weapons that were better suited to women's smaller hands, and (3) finding a body-armor manufacturer that was willing to construct bulletproof vests that accommodated bust sizes.

Officer Deedy Smith, an 18-year veteran of the APD, told *USA Today*: "For a long time, they tried their best to squeeze us into men. The uniforms, the vests, the whole thing. This has always been a man's job."

In addition, the department discovered that its in-house psychologists were disqualifying a disproportionate number of women whose employment histories did not include law enforcement experience or other work traditionally listed by male applicants. "We really don't know how many candidates we lost in that," said Lieutenant Vicky Peltzer, who assisted outside consultants in reviewing the APD's hiring practices.

Source: Adapted from *Law Enforcement News*. "Plenty of Talk, Not Much Action: IACP Survey Says PDs Fall Short on Recruiting, Retaining Women." 1999. January 15/31: 1, 14. Reprinted with permission from *Law Enforcement News*, John Jay College of Criminal Justice, New York City.

The second survey of some 700 state and local police departments with 100 or more full-time sworn officers by the Bureau of Justice Statistics (Reaves and Goldberg 1999) found that sheriffs' departments employed the highest percentage of female officers (15 percent)—although many of those worked in the jails rather than on patrol—followed by county departments (11 percent), municipal departments (9 percent), and State agencies (5 percent). The third survey, by the National Center for Women and Policing (2001), found that women held 12.7 percent of all sworn positions in 2001.

With respect to ethnicity and policewomen, Table 12.1 indicates that the proportion of minority women was related to city size—that is, as the size of the city increased, so, too, did the proportion of minority female representation. For example, black women constituted 5.1 percent of female officers in jurisdictions over 1 million and 6.5 percent in jurisdictions over 500,000. Furthermore, minority women made up a disproportionately large share of women in policing—approximately 35 percent in 2000. It has been suggested that this large proportion of minority female officers—who are mostly black (2.2 of the 3.0 percent)—may be related to several factors (Martin 1989a). First, black women may view policing as an attractive occupational choice because they have a narrower range of options to choose from due to racial differences in education and job discrimination. Second, black women have historically worked in occupations involving physical labor, and therefore may be less likely to be bothered by this aspect of the work than white women. Third, municipal departments may be disproportionately recruiting and hiring minority women in order to simultaneously meet affirmative action goals related to racial and sexual integration.

It is interesting to look at how the nation's largest jurisdictions and agencies are progressing with respect to diversity, since they tend to set the trends in policing. In 1997, full-time sworn officers in these departments, sometimes referred to as the "Big Six"—New York, Los Angeles, Chicago, Houston, Detroit, and Philadelphia—employed, on average, 17.8 percent female and 42.7 percent minority officers (Reaves and Goldberg 1999), up from 15.5 percent female and 36.8 percent minority officers in 1993 (Reaves and Smith 1995). Another way to view the progress of diversity is to look at those departments that have the largest percentage of women and minority representation. Table 12.2 presents the top five local police departments, with 100 or more officers, which have the largest percentage of women, blacks, Hispanics, Asians/Pacific Islanders, and American Indian/Alaska Natives.

The data from these tables indicate that many police departments are culturally diverse and becoming more so all the time. Even though this trend is uneven throughout the country, it is probable that within the next several decades, half or more of local police officers will be women and minorities. Such growth, however, assumes a continued emphasis on affirmative action and equal employment opportunity programs, which may be subsiding in some departments (see Chapter 14).

Promotional Opportunities

A comparison study of 290 police departments of female police supervisors (Martin 1989a) shows that women represented 2.2 percent of all municipal supervisory levels in 1978 and 7.6 percent in 1986 (including 3.7 percent at the sergeant level; 2.5 percent at the lieutenant level; and 1.4 percent above the lieutenant level).

Table 12.2 Top Five Local Police Departments with Percent Female/Minority Officers (Departments With 100 or More Officers)

Department	Number Female/Minority	Percent
Percent Female		
Orleans Parish Sheriff Dept (Louisiana)	308	45
Newport News Sheriff Office (Virginia)	54	34
Madison City Police Dept (Wisconsin)	121	32
Norfolk Sheriff Office (Virginia)	125	32
Terrebonne Parish Sheriff Dept (Louisiana)	100	31
Percent Black		
Jackson Police Dept (Mississippi)	294	70
Orleans Parish Sheriff Dept (Louisiana)	479	70
Richmond City Sheriff Dept (Virginia)	265	69
Riviera Beach Police Dept (Florida)	70	69
Greenville Police Dept (Mississippi)	68	67
Percent Hispanic		
Laredo Police Dept (Texas)	337	98
Mcallen Police Dept (Texas)	216	93
Brownsville Police Dept (Texas)	179	82
Harlingen Police Dept (Texas)	86	78
El Paso Police Dept (Texas)	762	72
Percent Asian		
Honolulu Police Dept (Hawaii)	663	37
Berkeley Police Dept (California)	28	14
San Francisco Sheriffs Dept (California)	107	14
San Francisco Police Dept (California)	281	13
Daly City Police Dept (California)	13	12
Percent American Indian		
Lawrence Police Dept (Kansas)	10	9
Tulsa Police Dept (Oklahoma)	66	8
Yakima Police Dept (Washington)	4	4
Minneapolis Police Dept (Minnesota)	30	3
Billings Police Dept (Montana)	4	3

Source: Bureau of Justice Statistics. *Law Enforcement Management and Administrative Statistics (LEMAS): 2000 Sample Survey of Law Enforcement Agencies.* United States Department of Justice.

A more recent study of departments with 100 or more sworn personnel by the National Center for Women and Policing ("Equality Denied" 2001) found higher percentages of women supervisors. The center evaluated the number of females in supervisory positions among large police departments as well as smaller and rural police departments. They found that for women, while underrepresented in police departments, the disparity is more pronounced at higher levels of the organizational chart. Women made up 9.6 percent of supervisory positions (lieutenant and sergeant) in large agencies, and 4.6 percent in smaller/rural agencies. Among top command positions (captain or above) women were represented at the rate of 7.3 percent and 3.4

percent. In sum, while the proportion of women in American police departments continues to experience modest increases, the proportion of females in positions of power and policy making in these organizations remains alarmingly low (see Figure 12.2).

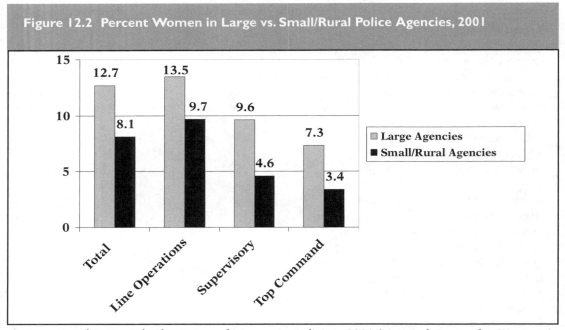

Figure 12.2 Percent Women in Large vs. Small/Rural Police Agencies, 2001

Source: *Equality Denied: The Status of Women in Policing, 2001* (National Center for Women & Policing), 7, 12, and 13.

Unfortunately, data on minority promotions are more limited than data on women. According to officials in African American and Hispanic national organizations, there is no agency that routinely and systematically gathers information about the promotion of

Females remain underrepresented in police organizations, particularly in high-ranking administrative positions.

minorities. Despite the lack of data, many affirmative action specialists claim that most minority officers are not promoted equally with white officers and remain essentially at the entry level (Sullivan 1989). As with female officers, however, it is also true that because minority members have not been well integrated into policing, until recently they have not had a sufficient amount of time in which to be promoted. The type of progress being made in Dallas (see Inside Policing 12.1) may be indicative of departments adopting affirmative action plans; approximately 48 percent of the department's officers are minority, and about 25 percent account for supervisory or command positions.

As might be expected, wide variation exists in promotion practices among police departments. In general, it appears as though the departments with the best records of promoting minority officers are those in cities that have large minority populations and minority leadership in the mayor's office or at the top levels in the police department. Thus, as Sullivan (1989) has noted, promotions tend to be more likely for black officers in Chicago and Atlanta (or Detroit) or for Hispanic officers in Miami (or Los Angeles) than for their colleagues in cities with larger white populations and power bases. This can be observed, at least to some extent, in Figures 12.3 and 12.4, which show the percentage of black and Hispanic officers in eight nationally representative large police departments and the percentage holding supervisory ranks.

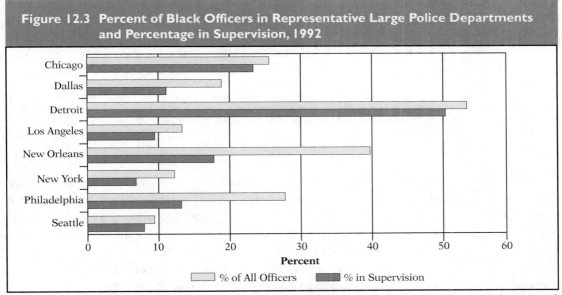

Figure 12.3 Percent of Black Officers in Representative Large Police Departments and Percentage in Supervision, 1992

Source: Adapted from S. Walker and K. B. Turner, 1993, *A Decade of Modest Progress: Employment of Black and Hispanic Police Officers, 1983–1992.* Omaha: University of Nebraska at Omaha. Reprinted with permission.

The Supreme Court's ruling in *Paradise* also appears to set the direction in attempting to balance the need to rectify past discriminatory practices, while protecting innocent third parties from discrimination. Rulings such as *Paradise*, along with continued emphasis on minority recruitment and affirmative action plans, should contribute substantially toward a higher percentage of minority personnel in supervisory positions in the near future. One interesting dilemma has developed, however, with respect to minority promotions at the local level—namely, "federal raiders," who recruit away top minority candidates (Sullivan 1989). Because federal agencies usually require some previous enforcement experience prior to employment, federal agents often recruit their personnel from local police departments. Furthermore, because federal agencies tend to be viewed as more prestigious and may pay more, it is easy to understand why they are often successful in recruiting the best-qualified personnel (especially minorities and women) that the local departments have to offer.

Such "raiding" results in the loss to local departments of the minority officers with the greatest potential for promotion.

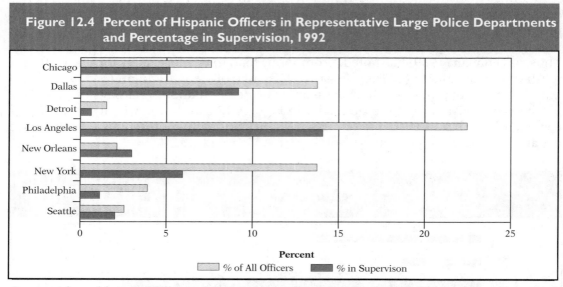

Figure 12.4 **Percent of Hispanic Officers in Representative Large Police Departments and Percentage in Supervision, 1992**

Source: Adapted from S. Walker and K. B. Turner, 1993, *A Decade of Modest Progress: Employment of Black and Hispanic Police Officers, 1983–1992.* Omaha: University of Nebraska at Omaha. Reprinted with permission.

As minority representation in policing has continued to increase, so has promotion of minorities to the highest position of police chief in major cities. In 1982 there were 50 black police chiefs, and in 1988 there were 130, an increase of 160 percent. At one point in the 1990s, six of the 10 largest cities in the country, including cities in the South, had a black chief (Narine 1988). For example, Lee Brown served as chief in Houston and New York City prior to his retirement and was appointed the nation's "drug czar." Beverly Harvard served as the nation's first African American female chief of a major U.S. police department in Atlanta. Such appointments are important because these chiefs serve as role models and will be sensitive to the recruitment and promotion of minority officers.

Employment Opportunities for Homosexuals

One of the more controversial issues facing police departments and equal employment opportunity is the employment of homosexual officers. Heterosexual police officers tend to be hostile toward homosexuals in general and especially hostile in a traditionally male-dominated occupation that values masculinity, machismo, and working-class morality. Opponents argue that gay police would lower the community's respect for the force, could not be counted on to come to the aid of fellow officers, contribute to disruptive work environments, and might force their sexual attentions on other officers. Additionally, hiring gay officers raises legal concerns in states where homosexual acts are still against the law (Shilts 1980).

Proponents of hiring gay men argue that homosexuality does not affect job performance, that gay police are not noticeably different, and that if they prove their worth as officers, gay recruits will gradually be accepted by their peers. Proponents further contend that a police force should reflect the composition of the community, and, in most major urban areas, homosexuals constitute a significant number of the population. While the Civil Rights Act does not specifically prohibit discrimination based on sexual identity, if gender is not a bona fide job-related requirement for police employment, then, proponents argue, it is also inconceivable to maintain that sexual orientation is a valid basis for exclusion. In any event, it is likely that homosexuals are already employed in most larger police departments throughout the nation, but they conceal their identities to avoid ridicule by their colleagues and job loss (Shilts 1980).

Belkin and McNichol (2002) conducted a qualitative investigation of the experiences of openly gay officers in the San Diego Police Department and explored the impact these individuals had on the organization over the past decade. Specifically, through interviews with numerous department employees, they examined issues of harassment, discrimination, work environment, morale, cohesiveness and recruitment, retention, and reputation. Overall, they reported that as the number of openly gay officers in the SDPD increased, few negative outcomes were experienced. In fact, they indicated that "a quiet but remarkable process of normalization has developed that has reduced much of the emotional and moral charge that the prospect of serving with gay colleagues generated originally" (Belkin and McNichol 2002, 89). They argued that by embracing openness and diversity in the workforce, the SDPD had developed into a higher performing organization than it might otherwise have been.

Integration of Minorities and Women Into Policing

From the preceding discussion, it is apparent that an increasing percentage and number of both minorities and women are entering the law enforcement field. Much of this increase, however, is due to the passage of the 1972 amendments to the Civil Rights Act of 1964. These amendments, and subsequent court decisions based on them, forced police departments to alter, rather radically in some instances, their selection and promotional practices. Hence, the question remains: How well are these "nontraditional" officers being treated once inside the department? This section looks at how well women and minorities appear to be integrating into the police work environment, as well as prospects for the future.

Because many male officers have been opposed to women in policing in general, and women on patrol in particular (see Bloch and Anderson 1974; Sherman 1975; Martin 1980; Charles 1981; Linden 1983), it is not surprising that women have had a particularly difficult time breaking into policing. Even though many departments are moving toward community policing, for the most part they remain tradition-bound and masculine. As Linden (1983) points out, men tend to object to women on patrol because they fear that women will not be able to cope with physical violence and that the image of the police will suffer. For example, a survey of police departments in the Northwest (Brown 1994) indicated that only one-third of male patrol officers actually accepted a woman on patrol and that more than half did not think that women can handle the physical requirements of the job as well as men. Martin (1980) further notes that women threaten to disrupt the division of labor, the work norms, the work group's solidarity, the insecure occupational image, and the sexist ideology that is contrary to the men's definition of the work as "men's work" and their identity as masculine men.

Police Culture

The major underlying dilemma confronting women in policing is the **police culture,** which has as its foundation a sexist and macho perception of the role of police. As Martin has noted:

> The use of women on patrol implies either that the men's unique asset, their physical superiority, is irrelevant (as it is, on most assignments) or that the man with a female partner will be at a disadvantage in a physical confrontation that he would not face with a male partner. (1989a, 11)

As emphasized previously, in general, the police role is not physically demanding and requires a much stronger mental than physical capacity. In addition, no research has ever indicated that strength is related to police functioning, nor has there been any research to suggest that physical strength is related to an individual's ability to successfully manage a dangerous situation (Charles 1981).

As the earlier review of the research on the performance of policewomen indicated, women not only perform satisfactorily on patrol but tend to be exemplary in the less aggressive, nontraditional aspects of the role (e.g., interacting with citizens, handling domestic disturbances). This suggests that in many respects, women may actually be better suited for police work than men. McDowell (1992) reports that the Christopher Commission (investigating the Los Angeles Police Department after the Rodney King beating) found that the 120 officers with the most use-of-force reports were all men and that civilian complaints against women were consistently lower. Policewomen, by contrast, tended to meet the public better, handled domestic violence better, and dealt with rape victims better.

Women face other hurdles in attempting to be accepted into the policing profession. For instance, the use of sexist language, sexual harassment, sexual jokes, and sex-role stereotyping all contribute to severe adjustment problems for women (Martin 1989a). Men frequently use language to keep women officers in their "place" by referring to them as "ladies" or "girls," suggesting that they need to be protected. Women who do not conform to sex-role stereotypes and are "tough" enough to gain respect as officers may be labeled as "bitches" or "lesbians" in an attempt to neutralize their threat to male dominance (Berg and Budnick 1986), a process referred to as **defeminization.** Men's cursing can also create problems for women, since men may feel inhibited—and resentful—about swearing in front of women, and yet men may lose their "respect" for women who swear.

Possibly due to the hurdles women face on entering policing, some research (Martin 1979) has suggested that two separate identities may develop: the **police*woman*** and the ***police*woman.** The former attempts to gain her male colleagues' approval by adhering to traditional police values and norms, with law enforcement her primary orientation; the latter attempts to perform her duties in a "traditionally feminine manner" by making few arrests, infrequently using physical activity, and placing strong emphasis on "being a lady." While Martin's research included only 32 female officers, seven of whom were classified as policewomen and eight as policewomen—with the rest in between—it is important that police departments promote policies and practices that allow female officers to be "themselves" and to utilize the particular strengths that many bring to the job. Some research (Belknap and Kastens Shelley 1992) suggests that in departments with a larger percentage of women officers (10 percent or more), women tend to view themselves as police officers first and women second; the opposite was found in departments with a smaller percentage of women officers. This finding suggests that peer support and familiarity may improve the working conditions of women officers. Different types of adjustments have been noted among black officers as well; some tend to align themselves with the black community, while others tend to align themselves with traditional police values (Alex 1969).

In general, research on policewomen suggests that they are still struggling for acceptance, believe that they do not receive equal credit for their work, and are often sexually harassed by their coworkers (Daum and Johns 1994). One study of over 500 women officers from nine western states (Timmins and Hainsworth 1989) revealed that open sexual discrimination and sexual harassment were far more common today than expected, especially by supervisors and commanders, who not only tolerate such practices by others but frequently engage in such practices themselves. The survey also indicated that duty assignments were often based on one's gender. Martin (1989a) further notes that frequent sexual jokes and informal harassment cause many women to avoid interaction with men that might be viewed as having a sexual connotation. To maintain their moral reputation, they may sacrifice the opportunity to build close interpersonal relationships that are so necessary for gaining sponsors and mentors (i.e., an influential person who provides guidance and assistance). Without backing from the informal political network within the department, women are likely to have a more difficult time being promoted or gaining specialized job assignments.

This lack of access to the informal political network within a department also applies to minority officers. Although there are many reasons why minorities may not be assigned to specialized jobs or promoted equally with whites, some of which were discussed earlier, Sullivan (1989) believes that the major reason is that minority networks usually do not reach the upper echelons of power and the existing white network. He suggests this is a "catch 22" situation—that is, minority promotions will increase only when more minority officers are promoted. Once again, it is important to recognize how important equal promotional opportunities are for both minority and female officers.

Structural Characteristics

Women also face problems relating to the **structural characteristics** or features of police departments (Martin 1989a). For example, most training academies place a strong emphasis on physical fitness. Once a certain level of fitness and performance has been achieved, however, it generally need not be maintained; that is, few departments require any testing of physical performance beyond that of the academy. Such an emphasis tends to magnify the importance of physical differences between the sexes, which, of course, tends to perpetuate the sex-role stereotype. This is not to suggest that police officers should not be physically fit but that fitness should be within the parameters of job related standards. Furthermore, if physical standards are job related, then they certainly should be maintained throughout an officer's career, at least in those jobs where such a requirement is necessary.

Training academies also often fail to place the proper amount of importance on the development of *interpersonal skills* that are essential to effective police work. Such skills are usually more highly developed in women than men, and their absence from the training curriculum deprives women of excelling in an important job-relevant area. Consequently, as Martin has observed: "New women recruits enter male turf on male terms with little recognition of their own problems or strengths" (1989a, 12). Associated with the problem of not recognizing the importance of interpersonal skills is the performance-evaluation process itself. Despite the favorable response to the effectiveness of women on patrol, internal performance-evaluation criteria tend to have a gender bias favorable toward males. Some research (Morash and Greene 1986) has discovered that such criteria tend to emphasize traits that are primarily associated with a male stereotype (e.g., forcefulness and dominance). Additionally, Lonsway (2003) reviewed research related to women's lack of physical prowess making them unsuitable for police work. She noted that while there are times when physical strength is advantageous for officers, these situations are relatively rare in everyday policing. Further, she notes that police departments have been unable to create valid tests that can predict successful performance of physical activities.

Pregnancy and Maternity

An important policy area concerning women officers is that of pregnancy and maternity or disability leave. As more women enter policing and become pregnant, their treatment becomes important not only to the officer and her family but also to the department and the community. Title VII of the Civil Rights Act was amended in 1978 to add the Pregnancy Discrimination Act, which outlaws discrimination on the basis of pregnancy, childbirth, or any medical condition they might cause. Employers are thus required to treat pregnancy as they would any other temporary disability (Rubin 1995a).

Although there is no law that requires a department to provide paid maternity leave to employees, if a department has a paid-leave policy for temporarily disabled officers, it must afford pregnant officers the same leave. Leave policies that favor pregnant woman, however, may not be discriminatory. In *California Savings & Loan v. Guerra* (1987), the U.S. Supreme Court upheld a California law that requires employers to provide a pregnant employee with up to four months' maternity leave and to permit her to return to her original job unless it has been eliminated due to business necessity. The Court reasoned that although the law appeared to favor women, employers also could give comparable benefits to employees with nonpregnancy-related disabilities. In addition, the Family Medical Leave Act of 1993 (FMLA) requires employers with 50 or more employees to provide 12 weeks unpaid leave for employees to care for a newborn child, adopted child, or foster child. This requirement applies equally to men and women and requires the employer to offer employees taking leave the same or an equivalent job when they return (Rubin 1995a).

Although the research is scarce with respect to policies on pregnancy and maternity, one survey of 73 of the largest departments in each of the 50 states and the District of Columbia (Watson 1995) provides some initial information. All but eight of the departments provided some form of pregnancy leave for women line officers. In general, the policies involved combining types of leave, including sick leave, then annual leave, and then unpaid leave of 180 days to a year or more. Only a few departments required pregnant officers to begin leave at a specific point in their pregnancy. Nine required women to leave only when advised to do so by their doctors. Fitness was the key for others; three required leaves to begin when women were unable to perform the full range of duties, and one when uniforms no longer fit. In general, in returning to work, officers were allowed to exhaust all permissible leave time, including unpaid leave to the limit available. If this occurred, and if the officer had to be terminated, then she was given preference in applying for a vacancy when it occurred. Although such a termination violates the FMLA, the survey was conducted prior to its implementation. However, since FMLA applies only to organizations with 50 or more employees, the act does not apply to a majority of the nation's police departments.

Although the FMLA of 1993 goes a long way toward establishing rights in pregnancy and maternity, it does not cover a majority of the nation's police departments; nevertheless, all departments should attempt to meet the FMLA requirements. In addition, based on *California Savings,* benefits for pregnant woman do not necessarily have to be equal—if departments wish to establish a favorable culture for women, they should establish maximum benefits in this area. For example, for many light-duty assignments, pregnant women may not need to wear their heavy belts (to be in uniform); this provision would allow them to work longer before initiating maternity leave. With the FMLA policies as a guide, a model policy needs to be developed to protect a woman officer's right to have children without damaging her career in policing. At the same time, policies regarding uniform and bulletproof vest sizes for women could also be addressed; most uniforms and vests are not made for women and fit improperly (Hale and Wyland 1993).

Sexual Harassment

The discussion on police culture above established that policewomen still face sexual harassment by their coworkers. If women officers are to gain equal treatment and status in police departments, sexual harassment must be taken seriously by the department and eliminated. Title VII of the Civil Rights Act prohibits sex discrimination. Sexual harassment is simply another form of sex discrimination. **Sexual harassment** in the workplace has been defined as

> Unwelcome sexual advances, requests for sexual favors, and other verbal or physical conduct that enters into employment decisions and/or conduct that unreasonably interferes with an individual's work performance or creates an intimidating, hostile, or offensive working environment. (Rubin 1995b, 1–2)

Sexual harassment applies to men as well as women and to same-sex harassment as well. In general, there are two forms of sexual misconduct:

> **Quid pro quo harassment** requires the employee to choose between the job and the sexual demands. Once equal access to employment opportunities are blocked for refusing the demands, Title VII has been violated (Rubin 1995a). This type of harassment usually occurs between a supervisor and subordinate. (Rubin 1995b)

Hostile-work-environment harassment occurs when unwelcome conduct is so severe or pervasive that it interferes with a person's job. Unlike quid pro quo harassment, which usually occurs as an isolated incident or single offending act, a hostile work environment usually includes repeated incidents or a series of events. (Rubin 1995a)

Some research confirms that sexual harassment continues to exist in American law enforcement organizations, and this has a negative outcome on female officers. Haarr (1997) conducted interviews and observations of officers in a midwestern police department. Every female participant in her study reported experiencing some degree of sexual harassment. Often this was done to marginalize women in the police department, providing symbolism that policing is not a legitimate occupation for women. Further, Morash and Haarr (1995) indicated that sexual harassment was a significant contributor to female officer workplace stress. Any sexual harassment, no matter how seemingly benign or harmless to the perpetrator, can have significant impacts on women with regards to stress, socialization, and patterns of interaction within the organization.

It is crucial that police departments have a policy that defines and prohibits sexual harassment, because failure to have such a policy may be construed as *deliberate indifference*, exposing the department to claims of liability. Employees who claim sexual harassment will not have to prove economic or psychological injury to win a claim. Even when such a policy exists, the department may still be held liable. Departments can also be held liable even, if they did not know of the offending behavior, if a court determines that they should have known of it. Departments are also generally liable for the acts of their supervisory personnel (Rubin 1995a). Accordingly, every complaint of sexual harassment should be taken seriously and acted on immediately with a follow-up investigation. Confidentiality should be maintained and every step of the investigation should be documented. Whenever harassment is found, swift remedial action—including warnings, reprimands, suspension, or dismissal—should be taken (Rubin 1995a). This action not only sends a message that sexual harassment will not be tolerated but indicates (to the courts) that the department is seriously attempting to control it. Inside Policing 12.2 provides a primer on how departments can prevent sexual harassment.

Future Prospects

Over the past three decades, substantial progress has been made in the recruitment and hiring of minorities and women in policing. However, although some departments have accomplished this voluntarily, others have been reluctant and were forced by the courts. This situation, combined with the traditional police culture, has created some serious problems for minorities and women with respect to integration and equal treatment within the field.

It is apparent that police departments will continue to struggle with the complex problems associated with minority hiring and promotion. If they are to increase or, in some instances maintain, their minority representation, they should pay particular attention to several areas (Sullivan 1989). First, agencies must continue to actively recruit among minorities while attempting to improve community relations and eliminating the reasons many minorities have had to distrust the police. Second, because studies have indicated that many of the entry-level paper-and-pencil tests are not job validated, it may be necessary to design a new series of tests that can more accurately measure potential police performance while ensuring they do not discriminate against racial or ethnic groups. Finally, because minority members may have been at a disadvantage prior to their police service, departments may need to initiate special programs to help these officers develop needed skills and knowledge in order to perform effectively on the job. This final suggestion applies equally well to female candidates, especially with respect to the physical requirements of the hiring process.

To improve the recruitment and retention of women in policing, departments must attempt to accelerate change in the traditional, militaristic, male-dominated, sexist police culture. Although some important strides have been made with respect to deemphasizing the highly militaristic and masculine approach to police organization and management, especially by those departments moving toward community policing, such traditions are firmly entrenched and difficult to overcome. Of course, as more women enter the field and move into supervisory positions where they can have an impact on policy, the more quickly change is likely to occur. As with minority personnel, police departments must continue to eliminate those aspects of the selection process that are discriminatory toward women and that cannot be job validated.

It is important for departments to implement policies and practices that are not discriminatory. It is crucial that minority and women personnel become fully integrated into police work. Only then can these officers become true role models and not merely tokens within their departments. Quite possibly the best recruitment device at a police department's disposal is its own personnel, who can act as sponsors and mentors for others who wish to enter the field.

Over the next decade, one important influence on minority and women recruitment is making police work attractive to them. Since these groups are recruited vigorously by other public-sector (including federal police departments) as well as private-sector agencies, the pool of qualified applicants may actually be shrinking. Accordingly, it may be even more difficult in the future to recruit qualified candidates. At least one study (Hochstedler and Conley 1986) has indicated that one major reason blacks tend to be underrepresented in municipal police departments is that they simply choose not to pursue a career in policing. One thing is clear: If departments are to remain competitive for minorities and women in the future, they must have an active and innovative recruitment strategy, promote a police culture that treats all employees equally and with respect, and if necessary, have a well-developed affirmative action plan regarding selection, duty assignment, and promotional opportunity.

Summary

The development of cultural diversity in policing was traced in this chapter. Included in this analysis was a look at how minorities and women, once they enter the profession, are treated unequally, even though their performance is, in general, satisfactory. There has been litigation regarding the impact of equal employment opportunity legislation and the use of the Civil Service, or merit, system. Reliance on the use of a nonjob-validated merit system for both selection and promotion in policing has led to the belief by many police traditionalists that a form of reverse discrimination and lowering of standards is taking place. Although implementing affirmative action plans in policing is complex, such plans have played an important role in police employment trends, in some cases significantly increasing the number and percentage of minorities and women. Once inside the department, however, these "nontraditional" officers have not always been well received—in large part due to the traditional police culture. As more minority and women officers enter policing and are promoted to higher ranks, their integration and acceptance into the field should become easier. Whether or not police departments can continue to attract qualified minority and women personnel depends on the public's interest in the police occupation, an active recruitment strategy, a departmental culture that treats members equally and with respect, and possibly a well-developed affirmative action plan.

Discussion Questions

1. Is cultural diversity important in policing? Explain why or why not.

2. Briefly discuss the types of unequal treatment received by minority and female officers when they first entered policing. Were their experiences essentially the same, or did they differ in significant ways?

3. What is the Civil Service System? Is it discriminatory? Why, or why not?

4. Discuss the importance of the Griggs and Paradise decisions by the U.S. Supreme Court regarding affirmative action plans.

5. In the push to diversify American police departments, some suggest the unintended consequence of reverse discrimination may occur. Discuss whether this perspective merits concern.

6. Briefly discuss the growth of diversity in police departments over the past several decades. What is the significance of this growth?

7. Briefly describe several problems confronting women and minorities in attempting to integrate into the police work environment. What are the prospects for the future?

References

Alex, N. 1969. *Black in Blue*. Englewood Cliffs, NJ: Prentice-Hall.

——. 1976. *New York Cops Talk Back*. New York: Wiley.

Balkin, J. 1988. "Why Policemen Don't Like Policewomen." *Journal of Police Science and Administration* 16:29–38.

Barker, A. M., and Heckeroth, S. E. 1997. "Deterring Sex-Harassment Liability: It Takes Proactive Policy and Commitment." *Law Enforcement News* April 15:14–15, 18.

Belkin, A., and McNichol, J. 2002. "Pink and Blue: Outcomes Associated With the Integration of Open Gay and Lesbian Personnel in the San Diego Police Department." *Police Quarterly* 5:63–95.

Belknap, J., and Kastens Shelley, J. 1992. "The New Lone Ranger: Policewomen on Patrol." *American Journal of Police* 12:47–72.

Berg, B., and Budnick, K. 1986. "Defeminization of Women in Law Enforcement: A New Twist in the Traditional Police Personality." *Journal of Police Science and Administration* 14:314–319.

Berg, B., True, E., and Gertz, M. 1984. "Police, Riots, and Alienation." *Journal of Police Science and Administration* 12:l86–190.

Berkeley, G. E. 1969. *The Democratic Policeman.* Boston: Beacon.

Bloch, P., and Anderson, D. 1974. *Policewomen on Patrol: Final Report.* Washington, D.C.: Police Foundation.

Brown, M. 1994. "The Plight of Female Police: A Survey of NW Patrolmen." *The Police Chief* 61:50–53.

California Savings & Loan v. Guerra, 479 U.S. 272 (1987).

Carter, D. L., Sapp, A. D., and Stephens, D. W. 1989. *The State of Police Education: Policy Direction for the 21st Century.* Washington, D.C.: Police Executive Research Forum.

Charles, M. T. 1981. "Performance and Socialization of Female Recruits in the Michigan State Police Training Academy." *Journal of Police Science and Administration* 9:209–223.

Daum, J., and Johns, C. 1994. "Police Work From a Woman's Perspective." *The Police Chief* 61:46–69.

Detroit Police Officers Association v. Young, 446 F. Supp. 979 (1978).

Eisenberg, T., Kent, D. A., and Wall, C. R. 1973. *Police Personnel Practices in State and Local Government.* Washington, D.C.: Police Foundation.

Felkenes, G. T. 1990. "Affirmative Action in the Los Angeles Police Department." *Criminal Justice Research Bulletin* 6:1–9.

Frank, J., Brandl, S., Cullen, F., and Stichman, A. 1996. "Reassessing the Impact of Citizens' Attitudes Toward the Police: A Research Note." *Justice Quarterly* 13:321–34.

Garmire, B. L., ed. 1978. *Local Government, Police Management.* Washington, D.C.: International City Management Association.

Georges-Abeyie, D. 1984. "Black Police Officers: An Interview with Alfred W. Dean, Director of Public Safety, Harrisburg, Pennsylvania." In D. Georges-Abeyie, (ed.), *The Criminal Justice System and Blacks,* pp. 161–165. Beverly Hills, CA: Sage.

Gosnell, H. F. 1935. *Negro Politicians: The Rise of Negro Politics in Chicago.* Chicago: University of Chicago Press.

Grennan, S. 1988. "Findings on the Role of Officer Gender in Violent Encounters With Citizens." *Journal of Police Science and Administration* 78–85.

Griggs v. Duke Power Co, 40l U.S. 432 (197l).

Haarr, R. N. 1997. "Patterns of Interaction in a Police Patrol Bureau: Race and Gender Barriers to Integration." *Justice Quarterly* 14:53–85.

Hale, D. C., and Wyland, S. M. 1993. "Dragons and Dinosaurs: The Plight of Patrol Women." *Police Forum* 3:1–8.

Hickman, M. J., and Reaves, B. A. 2003. *Local Police Departments, 2000.* Washington, DC: Bureau of Justice Statistics, p. 4.

Hickman, M. J., Lawton, B. A, Piquero, A. R., and Greene, J. R. 2001. "Does Race Influence Police Disciplinary Process?" *Justice Research and Policy* 3:97–113.

Hochstedler, E. and Conley, J. A. 1986. "Explaining Underrepresentation of Black Officers in City Police Agencies." *Journal of Criminal Justice* 14:319–328.

Jacobs, J., and Cohen, J. 1978. "The Impact of Racial Integration on the Police." *Journal of Police Science and Administration* 6:168–183.

Johnson, C. S. 1947. *Into the Mainstream: A Survey of Best Practices in Race Relations in the South.* Chapel Hill: University of North Carolina Press.

Kephart, W. M. 1957. *Racial Factors and Urban Law Enforcement.* Philadelphia: University of Pennsylvania Press.

Kuykendall, J. L., and Burns, D. E. 1980. "The Black Police Officer: An Historical Perspective." *Journal of Contemporary Criminal Justice* 4:4–12.

Landrum, L. W. 1947. "The Case of Negro Police." *New South* 11:5–6.

Leinen, S. 1984. *Black Police, White Society.* New York: New York University Press.

Linden, R. 1983. "Women in Policing—A Study of Lower Mainland Royal Canadian Mounted Police Detachments." *Canadian Police College Journal* 7:217–229.

Lonsway, K. A. 2003. "Tearing Down the Wall: Problems With Consistency, Validity, and Adverse Impact of Physical Agility Testing in Police Selection." *Police Quarterly* 6: 237–277.

Lonsway, K., Carrington, S., Aguire, P., Wood, M., Moore, M., Harrington, P., Smeal, E., and Spillar, K. 2002. *Equality Denied: The Status of Women in Policing: 2001.* National Center for Women and Policing.

Martin. S. E. 1979. "Policewomen and Policewomen: Occupational Role Dilemmas and Choices of Female Officers." *Journal of Police Science and Administration* 7:314–323.

——. 1980. *Breaking and Entering: Policewomen on Patrol.* Berkeley: University of California Press.

——. 1989. "Women in Policing: The Eighties and Beyond." In D. J. Kenney (ed.), *Police and Policing: Contemporary Issues,* pp. 3–16. New York: Praeger.

McDowell, J. 1992. "Are Women Better Cops?" *Time* 132:70–72.

Melchionne, T. M. 1967. "Current Status and Problems of Women Police." *Journal of Criminal Law, Criminology and Police Science* 58:257–260.

Milton, C. 1972. *Women in Policing.* Washington, D.C.: Police Foundation.

Moran, T. K. 1988. "Pathways Toward a Nondiscriminatory Recruitment Policy." *Journal of Police Science and Administration* 16:274–287.

Morash, M., and Greene, J. R. 1986. "Evaluating Women on Patrol: A Critique of Contemporary Wisdom." *Evaluation Review* 10:231–255.

Morash, M., and Haarr, R. N. 1995. "Gender, Workplace Problems and Stress in Policing." *Justice Quarterly* 12: 113–140.

Myrdal, G. 1944. *An American Dilemma: The Negro Problem and Modern Democracy.* New York: Harper & Brothers.

Narine, D. 1988. "Top Cops: More and More Black Police Chiefs Are Calling the Shots." *Ebony* May:130–136.

National Advisory Commission on Civil Disorders. 1968. *Report of the National Advisory Commission on Civil Disorders.* Washington, D.C.: U.S. Government Printing Office.

National Advisory Commission on Criminal Justice Standards and Goals. 1973. *Report on Police.* Washington, D.C.: U.S. Government Printing Office.

National Center on Police and Community Relations. 1967. *A National Survey of Police and Community Relations, Field Survey V.* Washington, D.C.: U.S. Government Printing Office.

Owings, C. 1925. *Women Police.* New York: F. H. Hichcock.

Parsons, D., and Jesilow, P. 2001. In the Same Voice: Women and Men in Law Enforcement. Santa Ana, CA: Seven Locks Press.

"Plenty of Talk, Not Much Action: IACP Survey Says PDs Fall Short on Recruiting, Retaining Women." 1999. *Law Enforcement News* January 15/31:1, 14.

Police Foundation. 1990. *Community Policing: A Binding Thread Through the Fabric of Our Society.* Washington, D.C.: Police Foundation.

President's Commission on Law Enforcement and Administration of Justice. 1967. *Task Force Report: The Police.* Washington, D.C.: U.S. Government Printing Office.

Reaves, B. A. 1996. *Local Police Departments, 1993.* Washington, D.C.: Bureau of Justice Statistics.

Reaves, B. A., and Goldberg, A. L. 1999. *Law Enforcement Management and Administrative Statistics, 1997: Data for Individual State and Local Agencies With 100 or More Officers.* Washington, D.C.: Bureau of Justice Statistics.

——. 2000. *Local Police Departments, 1997*. Washington, DC: Bureau of Justice Statistics.

Reaves, B. A., and Smith, P. Z. 1995. *Law Enforcement Management and Administrative Statistics, 1993. Data for Individual State and Local Agencies With 100 or More Officers*. Washington, D.C.: Bureau of Justice Statistics.

Rubin, P. N. 1995a. "Civil Rights and Criminal Justice: Employment Discrimination Overview." *Research in Action*. Washington, D.C.: National Institute of Justice.

——. 1995b. "Civil Rights and Criminal Justice: Primer on Sexual Harassment." *Research in Action*. Washington, D.C.: National Institute of Justice.

Rudwick, E. 1960. "The Negro Policeman in the South." *Journal of Criminal Law, Criminology and Police Science* 11:273–276.

——. 1962. *The Unequal Badge: Negro Policemen in the South, Report of the Southern Regional Council*. Atlanta: Southern Regional Council.

Sherman, L. J. 1973. "A Psychological View of Women in Policing." *Journal of Police Science and Administration* 1:383–394.

——. 1975. "Evaluation of Policewomen on Patrol in a Suburban Police Department." *Journal of Police Science and Administration* 3:434–438.

Shilts, R. 1980. "Gay Police." *Police Magazine* January: 32–33.

Sichel, J. L., Friedman, L. N., Quint, J. C., and Smith, M. E. 1978. *Women on Patrol—A Pilot Study of Police Performance in New York City*. New York: Vera Institute of Justice.

Simpson, A. E. 1977. "The Changing Role of Women in Policing." In D. E. J. MacNamara (ed.), *Readings in Criminal Justice*, pp. 71–74. Guilford, CT: Dushkin.

Sullivan, P. S. 1989. "Minority Officers: Current Issues." In R. G. Dunham and G. P. Alpert (eds.), *Critical Issues in Policing: Contemporary Readings*, pp. 331–345. Prospect Heights, IL: Waveland.

Sulton, C., and Townsey, R. A. 1981. *Progress Report on Women in Policing*. Washington, D.C.: Police Foundation.

Timmins, W. M., and Hainsworth, B. E. 1989. "Attracting and Retaining Females in Law Enforcement." *International Journal of Offender Therapy and Comparative Criminology* 33: 197–205.

U.S. v. Paradise, 107 U.S. l053 (1987).

Walker, S. 1977. *A Critical History of Police Reform*. Lexington, MA: Lexington Books.

——. 1989. *Employment of Black and Hispanic Police Officers, 1983-1988: A Follow-Up Study*. Omaha, NE: Center for Applied Urban Research, University of Nebraska at Omaha.

Walker, S., and Turner, K. B. 1993. *A Decade of Modest Progress: Employment of Black and Hispanic Police Officers, 1983–1992*. Mimeo. Omaha: University of Nebraska at Omaha.

Watson, P. S. 1995. "Maternity-leave for Cops—It's a Mother." *Law Enforcement News* December 15: 10, 15.

Weitzer, R. 2000. "White, Black, or Blue Cops? Race and Citizen Assessments of Police Officers," *Journal of Criminal Justice* 28: 313–324.

Wilson, O. W., and McLaren, R. C. 1963. *Police Administration*, 3rd. ed. New York: McGraw-Hill.

Suggested Websites for Further Study

Equal Employment Opportunity Act of 1972
http://www4.law.cornell.edu/uscode/42/2000e.html
Dallas Police Department
http://www.ci.dallas.tx.us/dpd/
The International Association of Chiefs of Police
http://www.theiacp.org/

Albuquerque Police Department
http://www.cabq.gov/police/
National Center for Women and Policing
http://www.feminist.org/welcome/police1.html
Law Enforcement Gays and Lesbians International
http://members.aol.com/legalint/index.html
Latino Peace Officers' Association
http://claraweb.co.santa-clara.ca.us/sheriff/lpoa.htm
National Asian Peace Officers Association
http://www.napoa.org/
National Organization of Black Law Enforcement Executives (NOBLE)
http://www.noblenatl.org/
Family and Medical Leave Act of 1993—U.S. Department of Labor
http://www.dol.gov/dol/esa/fmla.htm ✦

Chapter 13

Stress and Officer Safety

Chapter Outline

Key Terms

actual danger	physiological stress
acute stress	police stressors
chronic stress	post-traumatic stress disorder (PTSD)
critical-incident debriefing	potential danger
Crisis Intervention Team (CIT)	psychological stress
distress	sensitization training
eustress	situational danger
peer-counseling program	social-supports model
perceived danger	stressor-outcome model
person-initiated danger	suicide prevention training

Although negative effects of stress on society in general have been well documented by both the medical and social science professions, certain occupations, by their very nature, inflict more stress than others. Police work entails unique stressors (sources of stress) that are nonexistent or less prevalent in many other occupations. Some of these include departmental practices, shift work, danger, public apathy, boredom, and exposure to human misery. In addition, officers are expected to be in control at all times, yet they encounter people at their very worst, often on a daily basis. This demand of ongoing restraint, coupled with a set of unique job stressors, may lead to high levels of stress and, concomitantly, poor performance or dysfunctional behavior. This chapter will look at the concept of stress and stressors unique to police work, stress and emotional problems, policies and programs to help cope with stress, and officer safety.

The Concept of Stress

Stress is a highly complex concept because of the overlap of both physiological and psychological processes. **Physiological stress** deals with the biological effects on the individual, including such factors as increased heart disease, high blood pressure, ulcers, and so on. **Psychological stress** is much less clear and more difficult to evaluate. According to Farmer (1990), most psychologists prefer to use the term *stress* to refer to the physiological changes that can be determined and the term *anxiety* to capture the psychological effects. This book will use the more popular conception of stress, which includes anxiety within its scope.

Although stress is difficult to define, one of the more accepted interpretations comes from the pioneering work of Selye, who suggests that "the body's nonspecific response to any demand placed on it" can cause stress (1974, 60). In other words, a person can be considered under stress when he or she is required to adapt to a particular situation.

Selye further identifies two main types of stress: **eustress,** which is positive, and **distress,** which is negative. Some stress then, is considered to be positive or pleasurable—for example, the stress produced by a challenging sporting activity. Police stress, by contrast, relates to those aspects of police work that lead to negative feelings and consequences.

Basically, two forms of stress (distress) may affect police behavior (Farmer 1990). The first of these is **acute stress,** which represents high-order emergency or sudden stress, such as shootings or high-speed chases. The second type is **chronic stress,** low-level, gradual stress that includes the day-to-day routine of the job. Each type of stress is important to police work, but acute stressors require large amounts of physical and psychological adaptation; chronic stressors do not. In studying the possible effects of stress, there are several key concerns:

1. *Stress, like beauty, is in the eye of the beholder.* One person's experience of stress may have little or nothing in common with another person's.

2. *Stress is cumulative.* Minor stresses may pile up to produce major stress that leads to a heart attack or actual physical or mental breakdown.

3. *Prolonged emotional stress.* Stress that is a part of the everyday work environment can produce wear and tear on the body, with effects that may prove irreversible if not treated in time.

4. *When it comes to stress, there are no supermen or superwomen.* Stress tolerance levels may vary from person to person, but everyone is susceptible to the ravages of stress. (Territo and Vetter 1981, 7)

Occupational Stress

How stressful is police work? In general, there has been a tendency to give an alarmist answer, which is interesting in that existing research does not unanimously support this conclusion (Terry 1981, 1985). Terry has suggested that the reason for the push to support policing as a high-stress occupation may lie in an attempt to develop professional recognition and create a professional self-image. He says:

> The concept of stress . . . provides a tidy symbolic representation of the crime control and order maintenance functions of police work as well as providing a ready link to other professional occupations that bear responsibility for other people's lives. (1985, 509)

This perspective is interesting, especially in light of the fact that some of the earlier research does not support this view. For instance, in a comparative study of 23 white- and blue-collar occupations by French, it was discovered that "policemen . . . were not an extreme group, but they were higher than average on some stresses and lower than average on other stresses" (1975, 60). In another study of occupational groups, including skilled, semiskilled, and unskilled workers, Richard and Fell found that "police have an incidence of health problems which is somewhat greater than other occupations" (1975, 78).

Pendleton, Stotland, Spiers, and Kirsch (1989) compared the stress and strain levels of police officers, firefighters, and government employees and found that government workers experienced the greatest stress and firefighters the least, with police falling in the middle. Thus, they concluded that, contrary to popular belief, the police as a work group do not experience more health and social problems than all other occupations. The study urged caution, however, in that the research could not control for the possibility that police work could actually be more stressful but those officers selected for the job might simply be better able to manage stress and avoid strain. In a study of more than 500 officers in an Australian police department, Hart, Wearing, and Headey (1995) discovered that, compared with other groups, police display relatively high levels of psychological well-being and concluded that collectively, their findings indicate that policing is not highly stressful. This more recent research suggests that policing may not be as stressful as previously believed.

Nevertheless, policing can be a dangerous occupation. For example, officers are killed while on the job at a rate second only to taxi drivers, although the rate has been dropping steadily, from a high of 134 in 1973 to fewer than 80 per year in the 1990s (Fridell and Pate 1997; see the last section of this chapter). With respect to nonfatal violence, a Bureau of Justice Statistics survey from 1992 to 1996 found that police officers had the most hazardous job, with 306 nonfatal attacks per 1,000 officers, with private security guards second (218 per 1,000), and taxi drivers third (184 per 1,000)

(Lardner 1998). Not too surprisingly, on the one hand, the potentially dangerous nature of the job, especially in large urban departments, can be stressful. On the other hand, most fatal encounters are initiated by the police themselves and occur in situations that the police know to be dangerous. The implications suggest that while police work is sometimes dangerous, it could be considerably less so based on the officers' own actions.

Some research suggests that levels of stress vary by job assignments. Specifically, Wallace, Roberg, and Allen (1985), in a study of five police departments, found that narcotics investigators had significantly higher job-burnout rates than either former narcotics investigators or patrol officers. In another comparative study of job burnout and officer assignment, Roberg, Hayhurst, and Allen (1988) discovered that although narcotics investigators had the highest levels of burnout, civilian dispatch personnel exhibited significantly higher levels of occupational stress than did either former narcotics investigators or patrol officers. The conclusion is that although patrol work may be stressful, other job assignments (including civilian dispatchers) may actually be more stressful. Accordingly, while appropriate actions to prevent or reduce stress for patrol officers are certainly warranted, it should be recognized that all police personnel should be afforded appropriate stress-reduction programs.

Historical Overview of Stressors

In their review of the literature of police stress, Violanti and Aron (1995) discovered that two major categories of **police stressors** emerged: departmental practices and the inherent nature of police work. *Departmental practices* may include the authoritarian structure of the department, lack of administrative support, minimal participation in decision making affecting work tasks, and perceived unfair discipline. Stressors inherent in *police work* include rotating shift work, boredom, danger, public apathy, and exposure to human misery, including death or injury to fellow officers.

Police Stressors

Based on the above, Violanti and Aron ranked 60 police work stressors for 103 officers in a large police department in New York State. The top 15 stressors are ranked by their mean scores in Table 13.1. The top two stressors were "killing someone in the line of duty" and "fellow officer killed." Although these incidents occur infrequently, they have a significant psychological impact on the individuals involved. It is further interesting to note that eight of the top 15 (i.e., killing someone, officer killed, physical attack, chases, use of force, auto accidents, aggressive crowds, and felony in progress) are stressors related to potentially dangerous aspects of the work. Shift work was also reported as a major stressor because sleep patterns, as well as eating habits and family relationships, may be affected by rotating shifts. "Inadequate department support" (by supervisors) was another high-ranking stressor, due to the paramilitary structure of the department that minimizes interpersonal relationships between supervisors and subordinates. Other findings indicated that officers with work experience of six to 10 years had higher mean stressor scores than those with work experience of one to five years. This may be because newer officers with less work experience may remain challenged and still cling to idealism, whereas the more experienced officers may be less enchanted with police work and thereby find it more stressful and frustrating.

Table 13.1 Police Stressors Ranked by Mean Scores	
Stressor	**Mean score**
Killing someone in line of duty	79.4
Fellow officer killed	76.7
Physical attack	71.0
Battered child	69.2
High-speed chases	63.7
Shift work	61.2
Use of force	61.0
Inadequate department support	61.0
Incompatible partner	60.4
Accident in patrol car	59.9
Insufficient personnel	58.9
Aggressive crowds	56.7
Felony in progress	55.3
Excessive discipline	53.3
Plea bargaining	52.8

Overall mean score of 60 ranked stressors = 44.8

Source: Adapted from J. M. Violanti and F. Aron, 1995, "Police Stressors: Variations in Perception Among Police Personnel," *Journal of Criminal Justice,* 23: 290.

The most significant early study attempting to identify police stressors was that of Kroes, Margolis, and Hurrell (1974), whose research design was similar to the Violanti and Aron (1995) study. These researchers interviewed 100 male officers and asked them what they considered to be the most "bothersome" aspects about their job (it was assumed that "bothersome" and "stressful" were synonymous terms). Table 13.2 indicates the 12 categories into which the responses fell and the frequency of the responses.

Court leniency with criminals and the scheduling of court appearances on "off days" were the highest stressors. The second-highest stressors were administrative policies regarding work assignments, procedures, and personal conduct, and lack of administrative support. The third most significant stressor was the inadequacy and poor state of repair of equipment. The fourth stressor was poor community relations, including apathy and negative responses exhibited by the public toward officers.

The most striking difference between the 1974 and 1995 studies is the dangerous stressors of the job that are listed in the 1995 study but were not listed in the earlier study. Although society and the police may be more concerned about violent crime today, it is important to note that one of the reasons for these differences may be the ways the surveys were completed. The 1995 study used a 60-item check-off (listing potential dangerous stressors); the 1974 study asked officers to list those aspects of policing that were "bothersome" to them. In this 1974 study, crisis situations that might affect officer health and safety were categorized under "Other" because so few officers mentioned them. Kroes, Margolis, and Hurrell (1974) suggest there may have been two reasons for such a surprising finding. First, officers may not think of such situations as merely bothersome so much as threatening and dangerous. Second, officers may not consciously think about physical dangers at work so as to maintain their psychological well-being.

Table 13.2 Bothersome Aspects of Police Work

Category	Definition	Number of responses
Courts	Court rulings and procedures	56
Administration	Administrative policies/procedures; administrative support of Officers	51
Equipment	Adequacy/state of repair of equipment	39
Community relations	Public apathy/negative reaction to and lack of support of policemen	38
Changing work shifts	28-day rotating shift schedule	18
Relations with supervisor	Difficulties in getting along with supervisor	16
Nonpolice work	Tasks required of officer which are not considered to be police responsibility	14
Other policemen	Fellow officers not performing their job	8
Bad assignment	Work assignment that the officer disliked	6
Other	Stresses that did not readily fit into the above categories	5
Isolation/boredom	Periods of inactivity and separation from social contacts	3
Pay	Adequacy or equity of salary	2

Note: As officers may mention more than one stressor, the overall total can exceed 100.

Source: Adapted from W. H. Kroes, B. L. Margolis, and J. L. Hurrell, Jr., 1974, "Job Stress In Policemen," *Journal of Police Science and Administration* 2: 145. Reprinted by permission.

A similar finding was reported in the Crank and Caldero study discussed below, where concerns over occupational danger were among the least frequently cited stressors. As one officer commented, "The stress caused by work on the street is nothing compared to the stress caused by the administration in this department" (1991, 336). In addition, as the Crank and Caldero research also suggests, it is likely that larger, urban police departments contend with higher crime rates, and thus the perception of danger is most likely higher than in medium or small departments.

In contrast, the 1974 study by Kroes, Margolis, and Hurrell ranked court leniency as the highest stressor. Since the 1960s and early 1970s are known as the age of judicial activism (i.e., the Warren Court era), it is likely that the number of decisions expanding criminal "rights and procedures" influenced police stress as officers had to adapt their behavior accordingly. "Restrictive court decisions" and "court leniency" were not ranked in the top 20 on the 1995 study. Inadequate department or administrative support and shift work ranked very high in both studies; clearly, these issues need to be addressed. Lastly, equipment failure and poor community relations were high stressors in the 1974 study but much lower in the 1995 study: "inadequate equipment" ranked 18th and "public criticism" and "public apathy" were not in the top half. The state of repair of equipment may always be a problem to some degree in policing because of hard use, although it appears no longer to be the problem it once was. Since the improvement in community relations, especially through community policing, became a top priority in many police departments during the 1990s, poor community relations are viewed as less of a stressor today.

A survey conducted by Crank and Caldero (1991) studied 167 line officers in eight medium-size municipal departments in Illinois. Responses were categorized into five areas: organization, task environment, judiciary, personal or family concerns, and city government. More than two-thirds of those responding (68 percent) identified the department as their principal source of stress, especially problems relating to management and supervisors (42 percent), followed by shift changes (17 percent). The second most frequently cited source of stress (16 percent) was the task environment, with citizen contact as the primary source in this category (29 percent) and concerns regarding potential danger the second source (21 percent). The judiciary was the third ranked source (7 percent); the primary concern was related to the court's failure to prosecute criminals adequately. Personal or family concerns were ranked fourth (4 percent), while city government was ranked fifth (3 percent).

The findings of this 1991 study are similar to those of the 1974 and 1995 studies regarding stress relating to inadequate department support and shift work. The difference in the dangerousness of the work is most likely due to the size of the department; larger departments tend to be forced to contend with higher levels of crime. Interestingly, with respect to the courts or judiciary, both of the 1990s findings had relatively low rankings (third out of five in 1991, and 30 out of 60 in 1995) compared with the 1974 findings (first). It is likely that in the years since the study by Kroes, Margolis, and Hurrell (1974), officers have learned more about and adapted to court decisions with which they may not agree. It is also likely that departments have improved courtroom training to ensure that officers meet certain requisites when testifying in court. Such training should emphasize the importance of thorough reports and documentation, evidence, courtroom behavioral tactics, interface with the prosecution, case review, and prior mental rehearsal. And it is likely that improved courtroom demeanor and presentation by police officers can help to curtail "unfavorable" court decisions.

Emerging Sources of Stress

In their interviews with approximately 100 people, including law enforcement administrators, union and association officials, mental-health practitioners, and 50 line officers and family members from large and small departments, Finn and Tomz (1997) discovered that today's police are encountering new emerging sources of stress. As an example, although community policing has produced increased job satis-faction among many officers, others have found the transition to be stressful. Lord (1996) in her study of the Charlotte-Mecklenburg Police Department, which was attempting to move to community policing, also found increased levels of stress among officers and sergeants, particularly with respect to role conflict and role ambi-guity. Moreover, some officers felt that the higher expectations of solving community crime problems enhanced job pressure and burnout. Further, certain officers experi-enced reactions of disdain from those not involved in community policing. Commu-nity policing requires attributes that some officers may not possess and were not screened for: interpersonal, verbal, and problem-solving skills. Therefore, the transi-tion to community policing may be difficult and require training and communication to circumvent this emerging form of stress.

Many respondents thought that there had been a rise in violent crime and that they no longer had the upper hand; heavily armed criminals and increased incidents involving excessive violence and irrational behavior created added tension. Addi-tionally, they thought that the violent crime issue had been exacerbated because many departments had not increased the number of officers and in some instances had downsized. Thus, police employment had not increased commensurately with respec-tive rises in the population and crime rates in some locations. With respect to violent crime, these findings would appear to be consistent with the Violanti and Aron study (1995), where "killing someone in the line of duty," "fellow officer killed," "physical attack," "use of force," and "insufficient personnel" were ranked relatively high.

Dealing with large crowds, which may become aggressive, is one of the top stressors in police work.

A newer source of stress involves what officers perceive as negative media cover-age, public scrutiny, and prospective litigation. Many officers felt stressed by negative publicity such as that surrounding the Rodney King incident, the Abner Louima incident, the *Amadou Diallo* shooting in New York, police corruption scandals, and other dubious police incidents. Generally, the media focus attention on offenders' rights as opposed to victims' rights or officers' rights, which was resented by officers. More important, respondents demonstrated an increased fear of lawsuits, both civil and criminal, and consistently worried about the use of force endangering their lives.

Another emerging stressor was fear of both air- and blood-borne diseases (e.g., AIDS, hepatitis B, and tuberculosis). Cultural diversity and political correctness caused stress for some white officers, who perceived reverse discrimination in hiring, training, and promotional practices and excessive sensitivity to their behavior and language.

Finally, it has been recognized that stress may vary across gender and racial lines. As discussed in the previous chapter, women and racial/ethnic minorities often experience harassment, discrimination, and bias within the policing occupation. It follows that these experiences (coupled with the typical sources of stress) can result in higher levels of stress among females and people of color. He, Zhao, and Archbold (2002) reported that female officers had significantly higher levels of depression and somatization (e.g., physical reactions to stress such as headaches, nausea, and stomach pains) than their male counterparts. Morash and Haarr (1995) reported similar results in which women reported higher levels of stress than men. This difference was even greater for black female officers, possibly as a reaction to double stigmatization. They went on to note that women reported different sources of stress, specifically difficulties related to their outsider status in policing. Women reported stressors that included bias, language and sexual harassment, and stigma due to appearance. Minorities reported feeling "invisible" within the organization as a source of stress, and reported significantly higher levels of stress from "lack of advancement opportunity" as well as stigma due to appearance.

Eisenberg (1975) points out that minority officers face the additional stresses of rejection and skepticism by members of their own race and may not be accepted into the "police family," a source of support, camaraderie, and occupational identity. In support of Eisenberg, Haarr and Morash (1999) found in their national survey of over 1,000 officers in 24 departments that African American officers were significantly more likely than Caucasians to use as a strategy for coping with stress bonding with officers with whom they shared a racial bond.

Categories of Stressors

Based on the research findings presented above as well as on some earlier research (e.g., Grencik 1975; Roberts 1975; Stratton 1978), police stressors can be categorized into four major types, as indicated in Table 13.3.

Line-of-Duty and Crisis Situations

The continual potential for crisis situations in the line of duty is what tends to differentiate police work from most other occupations. On the one hand, the level of "routine" patrol activities can be extremely busy, emotionally draining, and potentially dangerous. On the other hand, the routine can become extremely boring and uneventful. The reason this situation may be so stressful is the idea of the "startle" response—that is, when the police officer must respond rapidly, at any point in time, to any number of extreme situations. The amount and type of activity on any particular patrol depends on many factors, including the type of city, beat, and shift. In some departments, especially in larger cities, officers are becoming more and more immersed in a continuous round of serious calls dealing with violence, drugs, and gang warfare. In such patrol areas there can be little doubt that the high workload, combined with intense emotional demands and potential physical harm, is conducive to high levels of stress and strain.

Table 13.3 Stressors in Police Work

External Stressors

- Frustration with the criminal justice system
- Lack of consideration in scheduling officers for court appearances
- The perception of inadequate public support and negative public attitudes
- Negative, biased, and inaccurate media coverage

Internal Stressors

- Policies and procedures that officers do not support
- Inadequate training and career development opportunities
- Inadequate recognition and rewards for good work
- Inadequate salary, benefits, and working conditions
- Excessive paperwork
- Inconsistent discipline
- Favoritism regarding promotions and assignments
- Politically motivated administrative decisions

Police Stressors

- The unhealthy consequences of shift work
- The potential role conflict between law enforcement and serving the public
- Frequent exposure to human suffering
- Boredom interrupted by the need for sudden alertness
- Fear and danger involved in certain situations
- Being responsible for protecting other people
- Too much work to do in time allotted

Officer Stressors

- Fears regarding job competence and success
- Fears regarding safety
- The possible need to take other jobs to support family or to pursue education
- Altered social status in the community

Source: Adapted from R. M. Ayers and G. S. Flanagan, *Preventing Law Enforcement Stress: The Organization's Role* (Washington, D.C.: Bureau of Justice Assistance, 1992), 4–5.

Anderson, Litzenberger, and Plecas (2002) conducted a research project in which they monitored the heart rates of individuals while on patrol. They noted that a particular indicator of physical stress is an elevated heart rate. Thus, their research attempted to monitor and categorize activities that produced the highest elevation in heart rates among police officers. They learned that heart rates begin to elevate prior to commencement of the shift. Officers, once in uniform, experienced anticipatory stress, resulting in a 23 percent increase in heart rates. In fact, they found that an officer's heart rate was 17 percent higher than at rest during the entire shift. This indicates that officers are experiencing physical reactions to policing, even absent critical incidents.

Not surprisingly, critical incidents resulted in even higher elevations in heart rates. Some critical incidents increase heart rates due to the fact they are physically demanding (e.g., tussling with suspects, wrestling, fighting, and handcuffing). However, they also found that heart rates are impacted by activities such as vehicle pursuits, being dispatched to calls for service, and talking to suspects. Further, heart rates remained high even after the critical incident was terminated. For most critical incidents, officer heart rates remained above average even 30 to 60 minutes *after* the incident occurred. This appears to indicate that even routine shift work has a significant physical impact on officers. The authors conclude by suggesting that debriefing officers after critical incidents and at the end of a shift can assist them in coping with the stress that is inherent to police work.

Post-traumatic Stress Disorder

The psychological stress caused by frequent or prolonged exposure to crises or trauma can lead to a condition known as **post-traumatic stress disorder (PTSD).** Although officers may not suffer physical injury, the emotional trauma may be catastrophic and could result in PTSD. While some officers recover within a few weeks, others may experience permanent trauma, which could adversely affect both the department and their personal lives. This disorder has been found in many Vietnam veterans who had been exposed to the stresses and violence of the war experience.

Martin, McKean, and Veltkamp (1986) conducted a study of a group of 53 officers and discovered that 26 percent suffered from post-traumatic stress. Stressors leading to PTSD included shooting someone; being shot; working with child abuse, spouse abuse, and rape cases; being threatened or having family threatened; and observing death through homicide (including colleagues being killed), suicide, or natural disaster. Another study of 100 suburban officers found a correlation between duty-related stress and symptoms of PTSD (Robinson, Sigman, and Wilson 1997). Thirteen percent of the sample met the criteria for PTSD; the best predictors for the diagnosis were associated with a critical event related to the job and exposure to a death-and-life threat. Sixty-three percent of the respondents stated that a **critical-incident debriefing** (i.e., counseling) would be beneficial following an extremely stressful crisis event.

Stephens and Miller (1998) examined the prevalence of PTSD among 527 police officers in New Zealand and further examined whether PTSD was related to on the job traumatic experiences or those experienced off the job. They found the presence of PTSD among police officers was similar to those in the civilian population who have experienced traumatic events. They also reported that as the number of traumatic events experienced by the individual officer increases, so, too, do the likelihood and frequency of PTSD symptoms. Traumatic events experienced on duty were more strongly related to PTSD. Among the most traumatic events were knowing of a police officer's death, a robbery/mugging or hold-up encounter, and chronic distress.

Loo (1986) found that officers experienced the most stress reactions within three days after a critical incident. The majority reported a preoccupation with the traumatic incident (39 percent) and anger (25 percent). Other reported symptoms of PTSD were sleep disturbances, flashbacks, feelings of guilt, wishing it had not happened, and depression (see Table 13.4). Many of the officers continued to report increased anger and lowered work interest one month after the incident. The course of recovery varied, but the average time for a return to "feeling normal" was 20 weeks after the critical incident.

Table 13.4 Common Reactions to Stress in Policing

Physical Reactions	Emotional Reactions	Cognitive Reactions	Behavior/Coping Reactions
✦ Headaches	✦ Anxiety	✦ Flashbacks	✦ Reduced motivation
✦ Muscle aches	✦ Fear	✦ Nightmares	✦ Reduced job satisfaction
✦ Sleep disturbances	✦ Guilt	✦ Slowed thinking	✦ Lack of job involvement
✦ Changes in appetite	✦ Sadness	✦ Difficulty making decisions & problem solving	✦ Absenteeism
✦ Decreased interest in sexual activity & impotence	✦ Anger	✦ Disorientation	✦ Premature retirement
✦ Heart disease	✦ Irritability	✦ Lack of concentration	✦ Poor relationships with nonpolice friends
✦ Ulcers	✦ Feeling lost or unappreciated	✦ Memory lapses	✦ Divorce
	✦ Withdrawal	✦ Post-Traumatic Stress Disorder	✦ Substance abuse
			✦ Suicide

Sources: Adapted from Kureczka, A. W., 1996, "Critical Incident Stress in Law Enforcement," *FBI Law Enforcement Bulletin* Feb./March: 15.; Lord, V. B., 1996, "An Impact of Community Policing: Reported Stressors, Social Support, and Strain Among Police Officers in a Changing Police Department," *Journal of Criminal Justice* 24(6): 503–522.; Lord, V. B., Gray, D. O., and Pond, S. B., 1991, "The Police Stress Inventory: Does it Measure Stress?" *Journal of Criminal Justice* 19: 139–150.

Martin and his colleagues (1986) concluded from their study that **sensitization training** regarding officers' work with victims, as well as their own victimization, should be conducted early in their careers. Such training may help to increase their empathy for crime victims and cope with their own reactions to the stress caused by dealing with such situations. Kureczka (1996) believes that officers will not ask for help for fear of being stigmatized. In other words, in an effort to preserve their "macho" image, officers remain reluctant to discuss their emotional responses to critical incidents.

In terms of cost, PTSD can also have an important impact on the department. It has been estimated (Vaughn 1991), for example, that 70 percent of police officers involved in deadly force incidents leave the department within five years. According to Kureczka, to replace a five-year veteran costs about $100,000, including retraining, benefits, testing for replacements, and overtime. In contrast, prompt treatment costs approximately $8,300, and delayed treatment costs about $46,000. Consequently, quick treatment for officers is not only professional but the most cost-effective option.

As a routine practice, department policy should mandate that officers visit a mental-health professional for evaluation and further treatment as needed, subsequent to any critical incident. Stress-management programs should be provided to all recruits and ongoing stress-education programs should be provided for all officers. As an added precaution, Kureczka advocates the use of officers who are specially trained to recognize problems and make referrals as deemed necessary. Such a **peer-counseling program** has been established in the Fort Worth Police Department, under the supervision of the Psychological Services Unit (Greenstone, Dunn, and Leviton 1995). Peer counselors are available 24 hours a day, seven days a week, and serve voluntarily and without compensation in addition to their regular police duties. The counselors receive basic training in crisis intervention and critical-incident debriefing.

Finally, counseling services or some type of stress-management program should also be made available to family members. In turn, family members might be able to understand and provide further nurturing and support (see social supports discussion below) to the officer involved. More important, intervention and treatment may circumvent suicide, the worst possible outcome of work-related stress.

Although little is actually known about the amount or effect of PTSD among police officers, it has been suggested that such a disorder might lead to increased brutality by the police. Kellogg and Harrison (1991), for instance, contend that much police brutality can be attributed to PTSD. Although they present no empirical evidence to support their claims, it seems likely that some officers suffering from post-traumatic stress could vent their anger and frustration on citizens through violence. Consequently, this is an important area for future study. It is important that scholars attempt to determine how widespread PTSD may be among the nation's police as well as its potential impact on police behavior.

Social Supports and Police Stress

Almost all research on police stress has been based on a **stressor-outcome model,** meaning that a stressful circumstance or stressor, leads directly to a negative outcome, such as psychological stress or a physical ailment. Another perspective to the study of stress, however, the **social-supports model,** suggests that an individual may be more or less insulated against the effects of stressors depending on whether he or she has a social-support network—friends, coworkers, and family members—in place. In other words, social supports may help people cope with stressful circumstances and thus lessen the potential negative effects. From this perspective, Cullen, Lemming, Link, and Wozniak (1985) studied police stress in five suburban police departments in a large midwestern city.

The researchers classified police stress along two different dimensions: that involving work and that affecting the officer's personal life. Work-related stressors were chosen that were not infrequent situations but ongoing parts of the police officer's job, such as role problems, court problems, potential danger, and shift changes. Social support measures included two work-related sources—peer support and supervisory support—and two nonwork sources—family support and community support. It was discovered that work stress was most significantly influenced by perceived danger, which could be counteracted by supervisory support. Life stress was influenced not only by perceived danger but also by court problems and shift changes. It was further found that family support counteracted stress in personal life.

It is interesting to note that danger was the only stressor significantly related to both dimensions of stress. Although the respondents worked in communities with relatively low rates of serious crime, and 86 percent disagreed with the statement, "A lot of people I work with get physically injured in the line of duty," the vast majority of the sample also felt that they had a "chance of getting hurt in my job." In other words, the *potential* of being physically injured was ever present and inherent in their work. Thus, even though policing may not be very dangerous in low-crime communities, the threat of injury is constant and may lead to stressful consequences. Another interesting finding was that both court problems and shift changes were significantly related to stress in personal life but not to work stress. This finding is important in that it "sensitizes us to the possibility that officers may adjust to the more strenuous features of their occupation while at work but nevertheless suffer deleterious effects on their general psychological health" (Cullen, Lemming, Link, and Wozniak 1985, 514).

In more recent research, Patterson (2003) reported that seeking social support reduced the impact of work stressors and emotional distress. However, he concluded that stress management programs should be expanded to consider a range of stressful life events, including off-duty stressors.

It was clear that supervisory support could mitigate work stress, while family support was helpful in lessening personal-life stress. These findings suggest that departments must establish programs and provide training adequate to deal with stress in both work and personal life, while taking into account various social supports.

Shift Work

Shift work not only adversely affects an officers' performance but puts an added burden on family and friends. While the rest of society orchestrates their leisure activities around a "day" schedule, officers reserve their activities for days off because on work days many find it difficult to do anything other than eat, sleep, and go to work. According to O'Neill and Cushing (1991), relationships with wives, children, and friends are disrupted, and many officers experience some or all of the following problems (i.e., intolerance to shift work):

Sleep alterations consisting of subjective self-ratings of poor sleep quality, difficulty in falling asleep, frequent awakenings, and insomnia.

Persistent fatigue, which does not disappear after sleep, weekends, or vacations, thus differing from physiological fatigue caused by physical and/or mental effort.

Behavior changes, including unusual irritability, tantrums, malaise, and inadequate performance.

Digestive troubles, ranging from dyspepsia to epigastric pain and peptic ulcers.

Some evidence indicates that many of the problems associated with shift changes, including sleep problems and fatigue, use of alcohol and sleeping pills, increased sick time, and accidents, can be substantially reduced if schedules are designed to accommodate the body's natural circadian rhythm, which controls sleep-wake cycles. For example, in Philadelphia, three major changes were made in officers' schedules in an attempt to reduce such problems:

- Shifts were changed every 18 days rather than every eight days, allowing more time to adjust to the change.

- The rotation shifted forward from day to evening to graveyard, rather than backward as had been the previous practice. Because the typical circadian clock runs on about a 25-hour day, the natural tendency is to shift to a later (rather than an earlier) hour.

- Consecutive work days were reduced from six to four, allowing officers to catch up on lost sleep and avoiding the cumulative sleep deprivation that night-shift workers often experience (Bain 1988).

After 11 months on the new schedule, officers reported significant declines in sleep problems and fatigue on the job. Automobile accidents while at work declined by 40 percent, sleeping pill and alcohol usage dropped by 50 percent, and sick time declined by 23 percent (Bain 1988).

There is little doubt that many departments could improve officers' job performance by redesigning traditional shift schedules to coincide more accurately with natural sleep patterns. In Voices From the Field, Bryan Vila, who directs crime control and prevention research for the Department of Justice, discusses the impact fatigue can have on police officers.

Voices From the Field
Unfit for Duty: The Impact of Fatigue
Bryan Vila, Ph.D.
U.S. Department of Justice

Question: What impact does officer fatigue have on stress and safety?

Answer: Police departments long have ignored one of the greatest threats to police officers' health, safety and ability to perform their jobs—fatigue. More than 100 years of research on the effects of fatigue in the work place have made it clear that excess tiredness arising from sleep loss, disruption of the body's natural rhythms (awake during the day, asleep at night) and working too many hours tends to decrease alertness, impair performance, and worsen mood. Yet most police departments routinely continue to allow officers work more hours in a day, week or month than would be legal for interstate truck drivers, pilots, train engineers or several other occupational groups. The most extreme examples I have found during the past decade include officers in several states who worked more than 3,000 hours of overtime on the job in a single year. This is roughly the equivalent of working 14 hours per day, 365 days in a row.

How fit can officers be when they work long hours? Two recent research studies found that being awake for 17 straight hours impaired hand-eye coordination, decision-making, and cognition as much as having a 0.05 percent blood-alcohol level. Being awake 24 straight hours was equivalent to a 0.10 percent blood alcohol—substantially higher than the level required in most U.S. states for DUI. Worse still, as NASA advised Congress in 1999, fatigue cannot "be willed away or overcome through motivation or discipline" because it is rooted in basic biology. It doesn't matter whether you're an Olympic athlete, a special operations commando or a cop on the beat, if you don't get enough good quality sleep, you will be less able to deal with people tactfully, or drive a vehicle safely. Nor will you be as able to analyze to what's happening in the world around you and choose the best, and safest, course of action.

The long-term consequences of repeatedly failing to get sufficient sleep are brutal. Too-tired officers are more likely to be injured, become ill, lose their tempers, and make bad decisions. They also are less able to handle stress constructively. It's easy to see how this set of problems can create a vicious cycle where worsening health or foul ups on the job cause more stress, more problems and stress make it harder to sleep well, and less sleep causes more health, safety and performance problems.

Fortunately, law enforcement agencies in the United States and Canada finally are starting to recognize fatigue as a serious threat. In the best departments, police executives and employee organizations are working together to assure that officers are alert and fit for duty. These fatigue management programs limit work hours and outside employment and minimize shift changes that disrupt officers' sleep schedules and family lives. They also educate officers about the dangers of fatigue and how to get enough sleep and stay healthy despite the challenges of overtime assignments, shift work, off-duty court appearances, and the emotional and physical demands of the job.

The opinions presented here are the author's and do not necessarily represent those of the U.S. Department of Justice or the National Institute of Justice. ✦

Other innovations in shift work might include allowing officers to determine the frequency of their shift rotation with an option to modify it at least annually or semiannually according to seniority. Further, permanent or semipermanent shifts as opposed to rotating shifts might be more desirable. The Michigan State Police, for instance, have instituted such modifications and have allowed individual work sites to make their own choices through majority vote (Finn and Tomz 1997). O'Neill and Cushing (1991) recommend that a minimum number of officers should work the early morning shifts (i.e., shifts that fall between 2:00 a.m. and 6:00 a.m.), with callbacks assigned to the day shift so that nonessential tasks are completed during the day. Additionally, they suggest that officers be allowed to bid for another shift at least twice a year and that midnight shifts be limited to four-day weeks. Although shift work cannot be eliminated, different and innovative approaches such as these above may mitigate its damaging impact on officers and their families.

Stress and Emotional Problems

There has been a limited amount of research on the relation between stress and emotional problems experienced by police officers. The research that has been done has been primarily concerned with alcohol and drug abuse, suicide, and marital and family-related problems, including divorce.

Alcohol Abuse

Hurrell and Kroes (1975) have suggested that police work may be especially conducive to alcoholism because officers frequently work in an environment in which social drinking is commonplace. "The nature of their work and the environment in which it is performed provides the stress stimulus" (241). They further contend that some police administrators have reported informally that as many as 25 percent of the officers in their departments have serious alcohol-abuse problems. It should also be noted, however, that other police administrators believe that alcohol-related problems are substantially lower.

In their survey of 852 police officers in metropolitan Sydney (Australia), Richmond, Wodak, Kehoe, and Heather (1998) reported relatively high rates of unhealthy lifestyles. They found that almost half of the respondents reported excessive consumption of alcohol, and that younger officers were particularly likely to consume. In fact, they reported that about two-fifths of male officers and about one-third of female officers reported binge drinking. They warned that excessive consumption of alcohol could have detrimental effects on officer performance, including slower reaction time, impaired performance, absenteeism, and liver problems. They reported that other research found alcoholic liver disease deaths among officers (1.2 percent) to be twice as high as in the general public (0.6 percent). They also noted a high level of other unhealthy behavior, including smoking, being overweight, and absence of exercise. Davey, Obst, and Sheehan (2000) found the frequency at which officers consumed alcohol was similar to the national averages; however, they did report that officers were more likely to engage in binge drinking. In their sample of 4,193 officers, 30 percent were classified as at-risk for harmful levels of consumption, while 3 percent were classified as alcohol-dependent. Consumption and substance abuse may not be limited to off-duty behavior. Perhaps most startling was the fact that 25 percent of their sample reported drinking alcohol while on duty.

Police departments have traditionally used the "character flaw" theory to deal with alcohol abuse (Hurrell and Kroes 1975). This theory calls for the denunciation and dismissal of officers with an alcohol problem because they will reflect badly on the department's reputation. What is not recognized is that "alcoholism may result from the extraordinary stresses of the job and that eliminating the officer does not do away with the sources of stress" (241). Today, however, many departments are attempting to deal with the alcoholic employee through in-house educational programs and admittance to outpatient programs designed to deal with such problems.

The following benefits are expected to accrue to those departments that develop procedures to help problem drinkers or alcoholics to recover from their illness:

1. Retention of the majority of officers who had suffered from alcoholism.

2. Solution of a set of complex and difficult personnel problems.

3. Realistic and practical extension of the department's program into the entire city government structure.

4. Improved public and community attitudes caused by the degree of concern for the officer and his or her family and by the eliminating of the dangerous antisocial behavior of officers.

5. Full cooperation with rehabilitation efforts from the police associations and unions that may represent officers.

6. The preventive influence on moderate drinkers against the development of dangerous drinking habits that may lead to alcoholism. In addition, an

in-house program will motivate some officers to undertake remedial action on their own, outside the scope of the department program (Dishlacoff 1976, 39).

Drug Abuse

Although there is little direct evidence about the amount of drug abuse among police officers, there is little doubt that, along with the general population, the problem is rising.

Narcotics. The principal category of illegal drugs is narcotics. Inside Policing 13.1 chronicles the growing concern with the use of illegal drugs in policing. In an attempt to reduce this problem, departments utilize drug testing to screen out police applicants who may have a drug-abuse problem (see later discussion). In addition, police administrators are increasingly testing officers on the job for illegal drug use. Because drug use is illegal, and officers are required to enforce laws against it, the usual result of a positive testing is dismissal from the force. Kraska and Kappeler (1988) examined on- and off-duty drug use by police officers in one police department. They reported that 20 percent of officers had used marijuana while on-duty. Use was actually higher among middle management (27.3 percent) than among line officers (21.9 percent). Further, the overall performance ratings of officers who used drugs on-duty were actually higher than officers who did not report on-duty drug use. While this study was largely exploratory and consisted of a relatively small sample of 49 officers from one jurisdiction, the results are reason for serious concern regarding the extent of illegal drug use by police officers.

Inside Policing 13.1   Drug Use by Cops Seen as Growing Problem

Top police executives say the use of illegal drugs by law enforcement officers is the biggest problem facing the profession today, and they see a growing trend toward the frequent use of urinalysis to detect drug use among recruits and officers.

"We didn't have this problem in law enforcement years ago," said Neil Behan, of the Baltimore County Department. "Our people, the young people were not using it to the degree that they are using it now," "Society continues to change in regard to narcotic drugs and it's been on the increase these many years." The people recruited 10 years ago, Behan said, were not likely to be drug users. However, he added, the young people that apply for police jobs now are very likely to have used them. "Ten years ago the number one problem in law enforcement was corruption; now the number one problem is the use of illegal drugs."

Richard Koehler of the New York City Police Department's personnel division sees the increased use of drug-detection tests on recruits as a mandate for police officials. "We have a responsibility under state law and the city's administrative code to maintain the fitness of the force. Illegal drug use requires someone to break the law and the use of drugs impairs somebody's ability to function." The department has been giving urinalysis tests to recruits for the past several years. Koehler said that three urinalysis tests are given to recruits: one as an applicant just prior to testing, another while the recruit is still in the training academy, and the last before the end of probation. "We set a tone, particularly up front. We think of it as a socialization process. People are coming from society in general to be police officers with 30 to 35 percent of the population using narcotics, particularly marijuana. So we make it clear in the department that you

Inside Policing 13.1   Drug Use by Cops Seen as Growing Problem (continued)

don't use drugs. If you do, you'll get fired."

The Chicago Police Department also gives urinalysis tests to recruits, as well as to selected in-service officers. As an officer moves up in rank or applies for assignment in a special unit, he or she must submit to a urine test. Over the past 20 months, 1,922 officers from different divisions have submitted to the drug tests. Of these, 81, or 4.2 percent, showed signs of illegal narcotics use. Chicago Police Department policy orders the reassignment to less sensitive positions for any officer who fails a drug test. Charges are then filed with the Police Board to have the officer dismissed from the force.

"Drug use is a crime," Koehler said. "In order to put the drugs in your body you must commit a crime. It's different from alcohol, which is protected under federal law." Because drug use is a crime, Koehler said, the department has no drug treatment program and no intention of starting one.

The 4.2 percent of the 1,922 Chicago officers who were found to be using drugs is a much lower proportion than the level found among the general population. Still, according to a representative of the Chicago Fraternal Order of Police, there is a problem. "The biggest problem is that many corporations that will identify alcoholism as a sickness have now identified chemical de-

pendency as a sickness and have programs to treat and retain those people in the workplace," he said. "I know of no police department in this country that will retain an officer who has been identified as having a chemical dependency."

Although none of the police officials questioned see a problem with substance abuse in their own departments, Behan said there is widespread concern within the law enforcement community. "We're concerned that drug abuse is out of control, especially cocaine, and we want to make sure that as we recruit and put people on special assignment that they are not drug users and do not become drug users after coming to us." At the NYPD, Koehler said, 3 percent of the applicants to the force are turned away because of narcotics use.

Koehler believes that the socialization process at the very beginning has led to the 3 percent hits. "Our objective is not to catch people who have ever used marijuana. Our objective is to make sure that they don't use marijuana as police officers. When you look at 3 percent hits, the message is out."

Source: Adapted from *Law Enforcement News*, 1985, "Drug Use by Cops Seen as Growing Problem," September 23, 1, 12. Reprinted by permission.

Anabolic steroids. Another area of growing concern is the abuse of anabolic steroids, which can lead to severe physical and psychological problems. This may become an increasingly important issue for police administrators, given that the culture of physical fitness and weightlifting often coexists with policing (*Law Enforcement News* 2000). Some of the potential adverse effects of these drugs include increased aggression (known as "roid rage"), increased risk of heart disease, acne, liver damage, and psychological dependence (due to improved strength, athletic ability, and physique). In men, sterility, impotence, and an enlarged prostate gland are also likely to develop from steroid abuse; in women, abuse may lead to menstrual and other irregularities, including increased body and facial hair, baldness, and a deepening voice.

Although little information is currently available on anabolic steroid abuse in policing, instances of unusual or violent police behavior associated with steroid use have been reported. For example, in 1989 *60 Minutes* reported several episodes of police violence and abuse of citizens attributed to the use of steroids. There have been other instances of the illegal use or sale of steroids by police. Personal interviews of administrators in 30 police departments across the country indicated that steroid use has been overlooked in policing and that the abuse of these drugs is beginning to become problematic (Swanson, Gaines, and Gore 1991). It should be noted that anabolic steroids are not detected in routine drug testing and therefore must be tested separately.

Besides the potential for violent and unusual police behavior, additional problems relating to steroid abuse include increased officer-to-officer conflicts and officer complaints about the department, its policies and procedures, or working conditions (Swanson, Gaines, and Gore 1991). Because of the potential harm that may accrue from abnormal behavior associated with steroid abuse, several police departments have implemented mandatory drug testing for steroids (*Law Enforcement News* 2000). Police departments must not only educate their officers about the use of steroids but must also develop effective policies and programs to eliminate the illegal use of steroids before it becomes a problem.

Suicide

Suicide has become the most dreaded result of a police officer under stress. Although it is difficult to obtain accurate data regarding whether police suicides are higher than those of the general population, it appears to be true, at least in some departments. Most of the early research suggests that it is higher than in the general population. In a comparison of police with 130 other occupations, Guralnick (1963) estimated the suicide rate to be 1.8 times that of the general population. Guralnick also found that police were more likely to commit suicide than be killed in a homicide. Richard and Fell (1975) ranked police as the third highest group in suicide among 130 occupations, and Violanti, Vena, and Marshall (1986) reported that police were three times as likely to commit suicide compared to other municipal workers.

Wagner and Brzeczek (1983) examined officer suicides of the Chicago Police Department from 1977 through 1979; they found 20 officer suicides during the period, including three retirees. They noted that if one looked only at the numbers, a Chicago police officer was five times as likely to take his life as a citizen of the city; the average suicide rate for Chicago police officers during this three-year period was 43.8 per 100,000. A follow-up study of the Los Angeles Police Department study by Josephson and Reiser (1990) from 1977 through 1988 found an average rate of 12.0 suicides per 100,000, which was up from the 8.1 rate found in the 1978 study. Once again, the rate for LAPD officers remained higher than those of the county, state, and nation (e.g., California's suicide rate was 14.8 per 100,000 in 1986, and since 1977 the national suicide rate has remained at approximately 12.0 per 100,000).

Data from a 40-year (1950–1990) study of 2,611 Buffalo police officers suggest that the frequency of suicides has increased in the last decade from an average of one suicide every 1.75 years to one every 1.42 years (Violanti and Vena 1995). This same study found that police were eight times more likely to commit suicide than to be killed in a homicide and three times more likely to commit suicide than to die in job-related accidents. The researchers looked at 138 deaths, all white males, including 39 police officers and 99 other municipal workers. Of the 39 police officer deaths, 29 were suicides (74 percent), three were homicides, six were accidental, and one was undetermined. Of the 99 municipal worker deaths, 14 were suicides (14 percent), four were homicides, 77 were accidents, and four were undetermined. According to these numbers, police officers were approximately five times more likely to commit suicide than city workers (74 percent of all deaths compared to 14 percent), a staggering difference and one that needs an explanation.

Data such as these in Buffalo and those in New York (Ivanhoff 1994), where there have been 66 suicides over the past decade (12 of them in 1994), suggest that police suicides are on the rise and may be a significant problem. The New York number is approximately four times that of the general population and compares with that found in Chicago in the late 1970s (Ivanhoff 1994). Part of the problem with making sense of disparate police suicide data is that they vary significantly across departments and may change significantly from year to year or over several years. Because most studies on police suicides focus on one department and are conducted in large cities, little is known about suicides in small or rural departments. Although most data indicate that police officers have a higher risk for suicide than the general population, such results may not hold for the entire country (Violanti 1995). Nevertheless, it appears that suicide may be a developing problem in policing, at least in larger jurisdictions.

The preliminary results of the Buffalo study indicated that police are at a higher risk for committing suicide for a variety of reasons, including access to firearms (95 percent of the suicides were by firearm), continuous exposure to human misery, shift work, social strain and marital difficulties, drinking problems, physical illness, impending retirement (i.e., separation from police peers and subculture), and lack of control over their jobs and personal lives ("What's Killing America's Cops?" 1996). Other research supports the general tenor of these findings. For example, Ivanoff (1994) found that 94 percent of police suicides in New York involved a firearm and that 57 percent were believed to be precipitated by relationship difficulties; Cronin (1982) and Wagner and Brzeczek (1983) found that the majority of police officers committing suicide abused alcohol; Loo (1986) found that 15 percent of police suicides in the Royal Canadian Mounted Police had been exposed to a traumatic work incident; and Gaska (1982) found a tenfold risk of suicide among police retirees.

However, the relationship between suicide and policing is far from consistent. For example, Stack and Kelley (1999) observed inconsistencies in the empirical research, and noted that most research on police suicide was limited to samples drawn from a few local police departments. To combat this apparent shortcoming, their analysis used the 1985 National Mortality Detail File, and included data from 12,000 local police departments, 3,000 sheriff's offices, 49 state police agencies, and various federal law enforcement agencies. Suicide rates for police officers were compared to those for other males in the population. Their analysis indicated that suicide rates for police officers (25.6 per 100,000) were only slightly higher than the suicide rate for nonpolice (23.8 per 100,000). Further, after controlling for socioeconomic status and other variables, *being a police officer was not significantly related with the odds of death by suicide.* This appears to indicate that while the policing occupation may be inherently stressful, occupational stress may not truly be related to suicide.

Interestingly, other findings (Ivanoff 1994) also found in New York that officers tend to kill themselves because of personal problems, substance abuse, and depression, not job-related stress. These are continuing life problems that people do not know how to solve. Ivanhoff's study, issued by the New York City Police Foundation, based its findings on surveys of 18,000 patrol officers between 1990 and 1993 and on studies of 57 suicides of officers from 1985 to 1994. These findings are noteworthy because they suggest that police suicides may not result from job stress, which, in turn, may suggest that different types of intervention strategies are necessary. It is clear that more research is needed to better understand the causes and effects of police suicides and prevention programs.

One of the primary problems of attempting to prevent police suicide is that, traditionally, officers refrain from asking for help. Often they do not want to appear weak in front of their peers and they see themselves as problem solvers, not persons with problems. In addition, officers fear the possible negative effects on their career if they come forward with a problem. To make it easier for officers to seek help, Ivanoff suggests that departments increase accessibility to confidential psychological services. Officers will be more likely to use such services if they do not have to go through a formal process.

Officers should receive training to help them recognize and avoid psychological factors leading to suicide. It is important to understand that suicide generally results not from a single crisis but from the accumulation of apparently minor life events. Training should begin at the academy before new officers are exposed to the police socialization process. Ivanhoff suggests that **suicide prevention training** include the recognition of psychological depression, communication skills, conflict resolution, and maintenance of intimate relationships. It is also important that departments train supervisors and managers to recognize the warning signs of suicide and suggest confidential referrals to those who are in need. As noted earlier in the chapter, supervisory support can be extremely helpful in mitigating work stress. In addition, as Violanti (1997) has pointed out, an organizational restructuring of the importance of the police role may be helpful. Recruits should be made aware that while the role of the police officer is important, it is not the only role in their lives. Sensitivity training could also be used to encourage officers to actively participate in family activities and establish friendships outside of policing; the narrow view of "we versus they" should be strongly discouraged.

Finally, based on the findings that over 90 percent of officers use a firearm to commit suicide, some suicides may be prevented by limiting access to firearms. Although many departments require their officers to carry their guns off duty, such a policy should be seriously reviewed. One way to reduce the availability of firearms, and thus impulsive suicide tendencies, is to eliminate the 24-hour off-duty carry regulation. Another would be to allow officers voluntarily to store their firearms at the station house or precinct on completion of their shift (Violanti 1996).

Marital and Family Problems

In the Kroes, Margolis, and Hurrell (1974) study on police stressors, officers (all men) were asked if being a police officer affected their personal lives. If the officer was married, he was asked about his home life; if he was single, he was asked about his social life. Of the 100 respondents, 81 were married, and 19 were single. Of the married officers, 79 felt police work affected their home life, and 16 of the single officers felt it affected their social life. Of the married officers, by far the most frequently cited complaint (48) was the difficulty of maintaining nonpolice friendships. Second was the problem of spending enough time with their children (25), and third was the problem of missing weekends and holidays with the family (19). For the single officers, the most cited problems were the fact that the unusual work hours made it difficult to date or attend important social events and, as with married officers, the lack of nonpolice friends.

A more recent study of over 400 spouses of police officers (Alexander and Walker 1996) found that police work also had an adverse impact on officers' lives, especially their social lives. The major problems were identified as long hours, shift work, and canceled leave. Surprisingly, dangerous duties and working with the opposite sex did not usually adversely affect officer spouses.

Finally, Roberts and Levenson (2001) reported that male officers are prone to take job-acquired stress home to their spouses. Both officers and spouses reported adverse reactions to the officers' on-the-job stress, and they concluded that stress and exhaustion probably has a negative impact on the family unit.

In view of these types of family problems, it has been assumed, as with alcoholism and suicide rates, that divorce rates for police officers are far higher than normal for the rest of the population. Some research has supported this view, but other research has indicated that divorce rates for police are no higher than for many other occupations (the divorce rate for the general population is approximately 50 percent). Davidson and Veno (1978), in their review of the literature, cite several weaknesses in the studies that support high divorce rates for police, including the failure to consider a number of factors that strongly influence divorce rates, such as age at marriage and number of children.

Whether police divorce rates are higher than those of the rest of the population is not critical because police stressors undoubtedly lead to family problems, which, in turn, affect on-the-job performance. It is important to keep in mind that marital discord appears to be the most significant problem for the suicidal officer. Factors that contribute to marital discord include the following:

1. *Overprotection of family members.* Due to the suspicious nature of the work and the trauma and degradation they observe daily, officers often become overly protective of their families, which can lead to resentment by the family members.

2. *Problems with children.* Children may encounter negative reactions from both peers and schoolteachers because of their father's occupation.

3. *Hardening of emotions.* To function adequately on the job, officers often find it necessary to suppress their feelings, which can lead to conflicts with spouses due to communication problems.

4. *Sexual problems.* The pressures and working hours of police work may lead to sexual problems, which, in turn, lead to frustration and anxiety and possibly to the search for release outside the marriage. (Territo and Vetter 1981, 218–222)

Because marital and family problems can have such a devastating impact on job performance, many police departments are developing programs aimed at helping family members understand and cope with the stressors inherent in police work. The Los Angeles County Sheriff's Department (Stratton 1976), for example, offers an eight-week spouses' training program, which includes an overview of departmental operations and the duties of law enforcement personnel. In Minnesota, the Couple Communications program (Maynard and Maynard 1980) helps officers and their spouses identify issues in their marriage that might produce additional on-the-job stress. The Kansas City (Missouri) Police Department implemented the Marriage Partner program (Saper 1980) to help involve spouses in an effort to reduce stress. In Indiana, the state police initiated an employee-assistance program (Lambuth 1984) designed to help employees and their families deal with emotional problems by referral to proper treatment agencies. Such programs should, in the long run, lead to improved job performance.

Policies and Programs

Based on the literature reviewed, there are a number of policies and programs that could be implemented by police management to help control the stressors encountered by police personnel. Of course, not every department can, or should, attempt to implement all the recommendations. Each department has different needs and budgetary constraints and therefore must decide what type of policies and programs best fit its particular needs. The following recommendations, however, provide a proper foundation for controlling police stress in both working and nonworking environments:

1. Establish quality-of-worklife activities designed to improve communication and increase participation in decision-making throughout the department.

2. Address workplace environmental issues, including quality of equipment, work space, compensation packages, and related aspects.

3. Develop training programs in stress awareness. Police should consider stress management as simply another skill to be learned, like criminal law or police procedure.

4. Establish specific stress programs. These can be part of a larger departmental psychological services, a health program, or a general employee-assistance program.

5. Establish operational policies that reduce stress. Consider the effects of shift assignments and scheduling, report writing, and so forth.

6. Improve management skills overall, especially in people-oriented aspects of supervision and management; include stress management skills in supervisory practice.

7. Utilize peer-counseling programs. Because peers may have already experienced many of the same problems, they can be of invaluable help to fellow officers.

8. Develop support groups by taking advantage of the natural groups that already exist informally and formally within the department.

9. Establish physical fitness programs that can strengthen the individual to withstand occupational stress. Such programs should also address stress-related dietary issues.

10. Encourage family activities as an important source of assistance to the officer. In particular, as spouses know more about police work and its stresses, they are in a better position to provide support (adapted from Farmer 1990, 214–215).

Officer Safety

Between 1992 and 2001, 643 police officers were feloniously killed on duty and another 670 were killed in duty-related accidents, for a total of 1,313. In addition, 597,277 officers were assaulted over the same 10-year period (FBI 2002). The data in Figure 13.1 cover nearly 30 years of felonious police killings and show that a significant drop occurred between 1976 and 1986. Since that time, the number of officers feloniously killed has leveled off, with the exception of 1999, when the number dipped to 42. This figure also indicates that the most frequently used method to kill officers was firearms, particularly handguns.

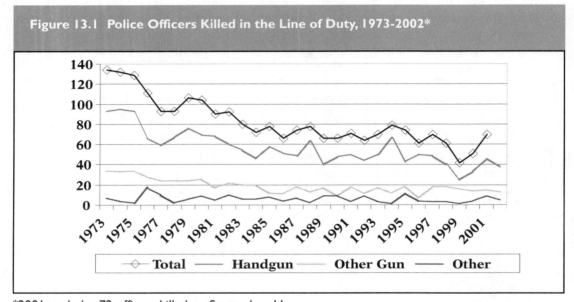

Figure 13.1 Police Officers Killed in the Line of Duty, 1973-2002*

*2001 excludes 72 officers killed on September 11

Source: FBI, *Law Enforcement Officers Killed and Assaulted, 1973–2000.*

Figure 13.2 depicts the various circumstances at the scene of the incident at which police officers were feloniously killed or assaulted. For officers killed, the primary circumstance was an arrest situation (e.g., during robberies or burglaries or pursuing suspects, drug-related matters, and other arrests); the second leading circumstance involved investigating suspicious persons or circumstances; the third circumstance was answering disturbance calls (e.g., bar fights, man with gun, family quarrels). The fourth circumstance involved traffic pursuits and stops.

For officers assaulted, the leading circumstance was responding to disturbance calls; this was followed by attempting to make arrests; handling, transporting, or maintaining custody of prisoners; investigating suspicious persons or circumstances; and traffic pursuits or stops. The remainder of the assaults took place while various other duties were being performed.

With respect to assault, in 2001 the rate of 12.2 per 100 law enforcement officers dropped 5.4 percent below the 2000 rate of 12.9, and was 12.7 percent lower than the 1997 rate (FBI 2002). The number of assaults that resulted in personal injury was 3.8

per 100 officers, which was lower than any other year since 1987. Geographically, the southern states had the highest assault rate at 13.6 per 100 officers, followed by northeastern states with 12.7 per 100, western states with 10.9 per 100, and midwestern states with 10.1 per 100. By population grouping, assault rates ranged from 17.9 per 100 officers in cities of over 250,000 inhabitants to 7.4 assaults per 100 officers in cities under 10,000 inhabitants. Clearly, there is a significant difference in assault rates depending on what part of the country and on the size of the city or county department in which the officer works.

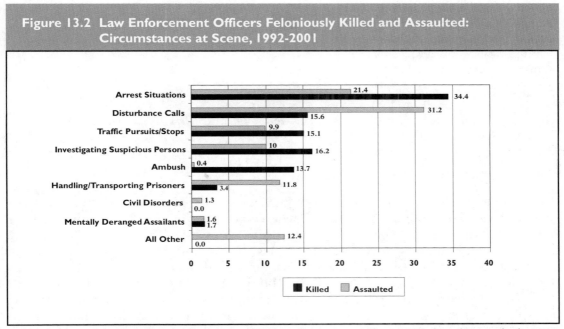

Figure 13.2 Law Enforcement Officers Feloniously Killed and Assaulted: Circumstances at Scene, 1992-2001

Source: Federal Bureau of Investigation, *Law Enforcement Officers Killed and Assaulted, 2001* (Washington, D.C.: U.S. Department of Justice, 2002), 31.

The final set of data reviewed involves police officers who are accidentally killed and the circumstances at the scene of the incident. As Table 13.5 shows, 670 officers were accidentally killed while on duty from 1992 through 2001. This number is almost half the total number of officers killed over the 10-year period. In addition, the leading circumstance of accidental death was automobile accidents, which accounted for slightly over half of all accidental police deaths (373 of 670). The second leading circumstance, accounting for nearly one-fifth of the total (110), was being struck by vehicles (i.e., the combination of directing traffic, assisting motorists, traffic stops, and roadblocks), followed by aircraft accidents, motorcycle accidents, and accidental shootings (e.g., crossfires, mistaken identities, and firearm mishaps). As we will discover in the following section, increased training and improved policies can significantly reduce officer fatalities.

Table 13.5 Law Enforcement Officers Accidentally Killed, Circumstances at Scene, 1992–2001

Circumstances at Scene of Incident	Total	1992	2001
Automobile accidents	373	34	38
Motorcycle accidents	47	5	7
Aircraft accidents	57	5	5
Struck by vehicles (traffic stops, roadblocks, directing traffic, assisting motorists, etc.)	110	11	19
Accidental shootings (crossfires, mistaken for subject, firearm mishaps, training sessions, self-inflicted, cleaning mishaps)	29	3	5
Other (falls, drownings, etc.)	54	8	4
Total	670	66	78

Source: Federal Bureau of Investigation, *Law Enforcement Officers Killed and Assaulted, 2001* (Washington DC: U.S. Department of Justice, 2002), 73.

Danger and Police Work

How dangerous is police work? Danger can be considered from three perspectives: perceived, potential, and actual. **Perceived danger** relates to the individual's or public's belief about danger in police work. It is influenced by a variety of factors, including media coverage, television, movies, books, and the actual and reported experiences of officers. In general, many people, including police officers, believe that police work is a very dangerous job. **Potential danger** relates to those situations that could become dangerous for an officer, for example, a felony car stop or investigating a suspicious circumstance. Potentially dangerous encounters are often characterized by a suspect's behavior that adds to the officer's concern (e.g., threats, shouting, challenges to police authority, name calling, and so on). **Actual danger** involves the actual number and rates of injuries and deaths that result from accidents and attacks from citizens.

Another useful way to analyze danger in police work is to categorize it in terms of how it is precipitated; that is, is it initiated by a person or is it a function of the situation? Few occupations include both the possibility and reality of **person-initiated danger,** that is, an attack by another person. **Situational danger** is a function of a particular problem, for example, a high-speed chase in policing, a taxi driver's risk of a traffic accident, the use of certain equipment, or the height at which a person has to work.

One of the more telling aspects of danger to police is that officers initiate a substantial number of the encounters in which they are injured or killed, and they often know that these situations are potentially dangerous. In one study on officer fatalities, Konstantin (1984) discovered that, contrary to popular belief, most police are not killed in citizen-initiated contacts. He found that approximately 75 percent of incidents resulting in officer deaths were initiated by the officers themselves. In addition, most officers are killed in the types of situations that they know are the most dangerous; the top three incidents were attempting arrests, situations involving robbery, and general car stops. Other situations, in order of occurrence, were assaults on officers, investigating suspicious persons, car stops of known offenders, responding to domestic disturbances, handling mentally deranged persons, and handling prisoners. Even with this knowledge, officers may fail to follow the training and procedures that would reduce the likelihood of injury or death.

Every year, many officers are injured during seemingly 'routine' traffic stops.

The general conclusions that can be reached from this study are important if officer fatalities are to be reduced. First, most fatalities occur in situations that the police know are dangerous; second, most of the incidents (approximately three-quarters) that lead to killings are *initiated* by the officers themselves. Such conclusions clearly suggest that the police are often not prepared to handle these potentially dangerous situations. It appears obvious that more thorough preparation and training in these areas could help officers to make better decisions about whether or not to intervene and, once the decision is made, how to handle the situation from the safest perspective. As Konstantin points out:

> Police training emphasis on the great majority of routine encounters that are citizen-initiated is well-meaning but insufficient. Such emphasis should not come at the expense of training officers to approach carefully situations where they themselves make decisions to intervene. (1984, 42)

However, the issue of proactive police behavior and dangerousness is a matter of debate. Police culture has supported the notion that traffic enforcement is extremely dangerous, in part due to the fear of the unknown. As such, the Supreme Court has over time relaxed civil liberties during traffic stops, in part, due to considerations of officer safety (see Chapter 11). But how dangerous, really, is traffic enforcement? Lichtenberg and Smith (2001) used the aforementioned FBI data to determine the "danger ratio" associated with traffic enforcement. They defined danger ratio as the number of harmful encounters (i.e., death or assault) divided by the total number of activities (i.e., traffic stops). They conclude that in fact, traffic encounters are really not all that dangerous. Examining data over a 10-year period, they found that officers are killed in about 1 in every 9.2 million traffic stops. Further, officers are assaulted at the rate of about 1 in every 20,512 traffic stops. Whether these estimates are alarmingly high or very low might be in part interpreted through the lens of the consumer, but the authors suggested that the Supreme Court overestimated the dangerousness of these encounters when determining legal precedent.

As discussed previously, 34.4 percent of officers who are killed are killed during arrest situations. These situations also result in 21.4 percent of all officer assaults. However, it is prudent to question under what circumstances suspects are most likely to resist or be combative during arrest encounters. Kavanaugh (1997) examined 1,108 arrests made over a one-year period in New York. He found that circumstances that increased the likelihood of force being used by either police or citizens included seriousness of the crime, suspect intoxication, whether other arrestees were present, and suspect disrespect. Like Konstantin, he found officer-initiated arrests increased the likelihood of violence. Interestingly, he found arrests that occurred during the daytime also had an increased likelihood of violence. Factors unrelated to violence included officer race, officer education, citizen race, and citizen gender. Hence, it appears that it is possible to determine situational factors in advance that increase the chances of violence during arrest encounters. Understanding these factors, with focused training on how to recognize and diffuse these encounters, can assist the police in reducing the number of assaults that occur during arrest situations.

Under what circumstances are officers injured during assaults? Kaminski and Sorensen (1995) examined 1,550 nonlethal police assaults in Baltimore County over a two-year period. They found the odds an officer was injured during an assault increased when certain situational characteristics were present. Officers were more likely to be injured during an assault when (1) more than one officer was assaulted, (2) suspects used bodily force rather than a weapon, (3) there was a single assailant, (4) suspects were under arrest, attempting to escape, or fighting upon arrival (rather than approaching or conversing with the officer), (5) the assailant was not intoxicated, and (6) officers were responding to disturbances or other legal situations (rather than domestic disputes).

The authors suggested that these final two findings may be due to the fact that officers perceive encounters with intoxicated citizens and domestic disputes to be dangerous and thus exercise greater caution when encountering these citizens. They found that officers were more likely to be injured during encounters with nonwhite suspects, indicating these encounters were characterized by greater hostility. They also reported characteristics of the officers themselves were related to injury. For example, short and tall officers were more likely to sustain injury when compared to "medium"-sized officers, and younger officers and officers without a college education were more likely to be injured than seasoned veterans or officers with a college education. Finally, they found some individual officers sustained injuries on multiple occasions. Based on their findings, they outline several policies police managers could initiate to reduce officer injuries:

1. Encourage greater proficiency with unarmed defensive tactics.

2. Provide additional in-service training for officers with less than five or six years of service.

3. Teach tailor-made defensive tactics for officers who are either short or tall.

4. Identify officers who are at risk for multiple injuries, and work with these officers to reduce the number of use-of-force encounters.

5. Train to assist officers in identification of high-risk assailants (e.g., hostile suspects who attempt to escape during arrest situations).

6. Offer community relations and awareness programs to reduce tension and hostility between police and nonwhite suspects.

7. Continue to hire officers with higher education levels.

8. Encourage greater caution when responding to nondomestic disturbance calls.

Are officers more likely to experience assaults in specific communities? Kaminski, Jefferis, and Gu (2003) researched the spatial distribution of aggravated assaults on Boston police officers over a seven-year period. Among other things, they found officers are more likely to be assaulted in areas characterized by economic distress and family disruption. They also reported that areas with high arrest rates had correspondingly higher rates of officer assaults. They remarked that high arrest areas present a greater risk level for officer-focused violence. This factor was the most important variable in their analysis of officer assaults.

How dangerous is policing compared with other occupations? A study by the California Department of Health Services (McLeod 1990) may provide some perspective. The data looked at the mortality rate of 56 occupations for males between the ages of 16 and 64 and compared it with the normal death rate for all working men. The California Occupational Mortality database considers the causes of death regardless of whether the deaths occurred on or off the job; thus, people in high-mortality occupations tend to die not only more often on the job but from physical or mental ailments (e.g., hypertension, stroke, cirrhosis, or suicide) that may cause death off the job.

Of the 56 occupations listed, deckhands and tankermen (on ships) had the highest mortality rating of 3.93 (i.e., a deckhand's death rate is 3.93 times the normal rate for all working men). The next highest mortality rates, in rank order, were as follows: (2) structural metal workers (3.17), (3) roofers (2.29), (4) industrial helpers (2.22), (5) foresters (2.19), (6) miners and drillers (2.17), (7) operating engineers (2.17), and (8) construction workers (2.13). Police officers and firefighters were ranked 31st, with a 1.07 mortality rating. In a separate study of police mortality, Hill and Clawson (1988) found that police officers' average age at death appears to be only slightly lower (by seven months) than that of individuals employed in 194 other occupations. Thus, it appears that police work is only moderately dangerous compared to other occupations.

Safety Issues in Special Populations

Throughout the past decade, several issues that have a vital impact on community health and safety have received increased attention. Below is a brief discussion of some of these special populations, including the mentally ill, public inebriates, the homeless and culturally diverse communities, and those with AIDS. Encounters with each of these populations are somewhat routine for street-level police officers and each brings to bear unique considerations regarding safety and stress.

Mentally ill and homeless. In recent years, requests for the police to assistance in handling people who are mentally ill have increased substantially. LaGrange (2000) indicated that 89 percent of officers in one city had contact with a mentally disordered citizen during the previous year. Interacting with these special populations often increased the actual or perceived risk to officer safety, as many officers believe they are not adequately trained or prepared to intervene with citizens suffering from mental illness (Finn and Sullivan 1987). As a result, police often rely on the use of force or make arrests during encounters with these citizens. Teplin (1984) indicated that police make arrests in 46.7 percent of encounters with mentally ill citizens, compared to 27.9 percent of other citizens. But recently Engel and Silver (2001) found that mentally ill citizens are no more likely to be arrested by the police after taking into consideration other important situational factors (including being under the influence of drugs, verbal resistance, seriousness of offense, victim wishes, and whether a weapon was present).

To help police lessen the burden of handing these special populations, some jurisdictions have implemented programs to share responsibility by creating formal networks between law enforcement and social-service agencies. A National Institute of Justice study of such network arrangements indicated that benefits accrue not only to the agencies involved but also to individuals who need help (Finn and Sullivan 1988). Networks that focus on the mentally ill have special units, on call 24 hours a day, that screen individuals for the most advisable disposition, identify the most appropriate facility to refer them to, and provide on-the-scene emergency assistance when necessary. These units consist either of specially trained police officers or social workers hired by the department to perform these functions; in addition, some networks utilize social service agencies to provide the special unit.

One successful **Crisis Intervention Team (CIT)** can be found in Memphis. Following a police shooting of a mentally ill citizen, a CIT was created that consisted of the police officers (with special crisis intervention training), emergency medical/psychiatric services, hospitals, and families of people with mental illness. These partners are more effective in determining nonconfrontational outcomes of encounters with the mentally ill and more effective in determining whether evaluation of citizens taken into custody is necessary. For example, if citizens are identified as displaying mental illness, they may be taken to the hospital for evaluation, rather than being taken to jail and placed in the general population there. This program has had beneficial results, including reduced use of deadly force, fewer injuries to both officers and citizens, lower arrest rates, and reduced stigma and perception of danger attached to mental illness (Vickers 2000). Other programs have experienced similar success in New Orleans (Wellborn 1999) and Albuquerque (Bower and Pettit 2001).

With respect to the homeless and public inebriates, most networks have made arrangements directly between the police department and one or more detoxification facilities or homeless shelters. The parties involved have typically agreed to strict referral and admission procedures (Finn and Sullivan 1988).

AIDS. As the number of people who have Acquired Immunodeficiency Syndrome (AIDS) has increased, so too have the concerns of police officers who have the most exposure to individuals with AIDS. Some levels of fear regarding contracting AIDS may be helpful in that officers would more likely take precautions when engaging in encounters with those suspected to be infected. AIDS involves high-risk behavior and is transmitted through unprotected sexual contact, sharing of needles, or any activity that includes the exchange of vaginal secretions, semen, or blood. Although it may be possible for AIDS to be transmitted through other means (e.g., bites, urine, feces), research indicates that this is highly unlikely and no such cases have been reported. However, unrealistic levels of fear can be related to added stress, inhibiting officers from effectively performing their jobs (Flavin 1998) or providing unbiased services to all populations.

Thompson and Marquart (1998) conducted a survey of 142 Texas police officers regarding their exposure to AIDS and reactions to confronting special populations. Over half of officers surveyed indicated they interact with high-risk populations every month (i.e., IV drug users, known prostitutes, and known homo- or bisexuals). High proportions of officers indicated they were very or extremely concerned they would contract AIDS while interacting with high-risk people. Police departments should give training in this area, develop necessary procedures, and provide proper equipment that will lessen officers' concerns for their safety. They recommended that future training curricula should include information about:

1. The known means of HIV/AIDS transmission and the relative risk involved with each.

2. The appropriate use of alternative methods for minimizing risk of exposure in differing law enforcement situations.

3. Proper handling of contaminated evidence.

4. Procedures for decontamination following suspected exposure. (Thompson and Marquart 1998, 660)

Improving Safety and Reducing Fatalities

From the research presented here, it is clear that more training and new or clearer policies are needed in several key areas of police officer safety. There appears to be a need for continual retraining in safety procedures as well. For instance, arrest situations, traffic stops, investigation of suspicious persons or situations, and disturbance calls all need more attention. Since approximately half of all police killings are accidental, departments should review the circumstances in which they occur and review the level of training and policies they provide in these areas. One study of police killings in drug situations (Sherman et al. 1989), for instance, advised that rehearsing each drug raid could substantially reduce the danger to police.

The FBI, in its in-depth studies of officers killed in the line of duty (1992) and officers who survived a serious assault (1997), has also made a number of training and policy recommendations. The researchers found that in a significant number of incidents, officers made tactical errors, such as improperly approaching a vehicle or suspect, or failed to conduct a thorough search of a suspect. Increased training was recommended in those areas as well as in the handling of traffic stops, weapons retention, handcuff use, and waiting for backup. With respect to traffic stops, department regulations should include sections on officer safety, including the proper selection of a safe stop location, dispatcher notification, and wearing of soft body armor. Body armor, or bulletproof vests, has been credited with saving more than 2,000 officer lives since 1980; FBI statistics indicate that about 42 percent of police officers killed with guns since 1980 could have been saved if they had been wearing vests ("Congress OK's . . . Body-Armor Fund" 1998).

Funerals for officers killed in the line of duty are often attended by many within the 'police family,' including officers from other departments.

Weapons retention is another serious problem, where some 16 percent of officers are murdered with service weapons wrested from them or a fellow officer. Part of the solution to this problem may lie in technology. The Colt company is developing a personalized gun that uses radio signals that allow the weapon to recognize and respond to a transponder worn by the officer so that it can be fired only by that officer (Witkin 1998).

In addition, the FBI recommends that citizens be advised of the proper response when stopped by a marked police unit (i.e., they should remain in the vehicle, keep hands in plain view, and wait for further directions from the officer). Finally, since a large number of officers are killed while off duty (approximately one out of every seven), departments should provide a well-defined policy for off-duty performance (e.g., carrying or not carrying firearms, how to act when observing an offense, and so on).

Police managers, especially first-line supervisors and midlevel managers (i.e., sergeants and lieutenants), can also contribute to the reduction of the number of injuries and deaths (Roberg, Kuykendall, and Novak 2002). They must be ever-vigilant to make sure that officers follow departmental safety and response guidelines. In addition, all incidents involving the use of force and citizen resistance should be reported and used by a department not only to assess the officer's style and discretion but also as a basis for improving future police responses. Any time a police officer or citizen is injured or killed, the department should undertake an immediate and comprehensive reassessment of all related programs, policies, and personnel. This type of response is necessary because police managers need to reduce the fear level of officers if they hope to modify some of the behavior resulting from irrational fear, including verbal abuse of citizens, overreliance on the use of force, unnecessary and excessive force, and brutality. Police managers must convince officers that officer safety, next to integrity, is the most important priority in the department (332).

Roberg and colleagues (2002) further suggest that departments undertake an extensive community-education program to instruct citizens how to behave when interacting with officers; this goes beyond the FBI's recommendation about citizens' behavior in traffic stops. Essentially, citizens need to understand that they must cooperate with the police and follow police orders and that citizen grievances should not and cannot be resolved "in the streets," but rather, if necessary, in the courts or through some other formal mechanism. Unfortunately, some people believe that it is their right to challenge police authority at the very moment that authority is being exercised. The police will have problems with such individuals until there is a change in citizen attitudes. Just as the police must modify their behavior in some situations to secure public respect and cooperation, citizens must also modify their behavior to reduce officers' fear.

Summary

Stress and danger confront the police, but there are methods to reduce both. There are two major categories of police stressors: departmental practices and the inherent nature of police work. The first may include authoritarian structure, lack of administrative support, or minimal participation in decision-making; the second may include rotating shift work, boredom, danger, public apathy, and exposure to human misery, including death or injury to fellow officers. In addition, some new forms of stress include efforts toward community policing, especially role conflict and role ambiguity, increased levels of violence with which the police must deal, perceived negative news media coverage, fear of air- and blood-borne diseases, and for some white officers, cultural diversity and political correctness. In addition, the psychological stress caused by frequent or prolonged exposure to crises or trauma can lead to post-traumatic stress disorder, which can have serious adverse affects, including increased levels of brutality.

Police stress can also lead to alcohol and drug abuse, suicide, and various family problems. Social-support systems (e.g., supervisory and family support) can mitigate against work stress and general life stress. There are numerous policies and programs designed to reduce police stress. Finally, although police fatalities have lessened over the past two decades, policing is a potentially dangerous occupation. Most officer fatalities occur in situations that the police know to be dangerous, and the officer typically initiates them. Research has demonstrated that situational and community level factors are significantly related to the likelihood that an officer will be assaulted sustain injury from the assault. More and better training is needed about managing dangerous situations. Policy review, management's insistence on adhering to departmental safety and response guidelines, and community education can all play roles in reducing danger to the police.

Critical Thinking Questions

1. Briefly define the concept of stress; differentiate between the two forms of stress that may affect police behavior.

2. Describe the two major categories of police occupational stressors and provide several examples of each.

3. Discuss at least three types of new sources of stress for today's police. Will police work become more or less stressful in the future? Discuss.

4. What is post-traumatic stress disorder and how does it apply to the police?

5. Describe the social supports for the study of stress and their implications for policing.

6. Discuss the common methods officers use to cope with occupational stress (e.g., alcohol abuse, drug abuse, suicide). Are officers more prone to these coping mechanisms than other occupations? What can police organizations do about this?

7. Discuss at least three aspects of police stress that influence the quality of family life. What are some programs that attempt to deal with such problems?

8. Is policing a dangerous occupation? What factors are commonly associated with officer assaults and injuries? Discuss why this is the case.

References

Alexander, D. A. and Walker, L. G. 1996. "The Perceived Impact of Police Work on Police Officers' Spouses and Families." *Stress Medicine* 12: 239–246.

Anderson, G. S., Litzenberger, R., and Plecas, D. 2002. "Physical Evidence of Police Officer Stress" *Policing: An International Journal of Police Strategies and Management* 25: 399–420.

Ayers, R. M. and Flanagan, G. S. 1992. *Preventing Law Enforcement Stress: The Organization's Role.* Washington, DC: Bureau of Justice Assistance.

Bain, L. J. 1988. "Night Beat." *Psychology Today* June: 10–11.

Bower, D. L. and Pettit, W. G. 2001. "Albuquerque Police Department's Crisis Intervention Team: A Report Card." *FBI Law Enforcement Bulletin* 70: 1–6.

"Congress OK's $75M Body-Armor Fund." 1998. *Law Enforcement Journal* May 15: 1.

Crank, J. P. and Caldero, M. 1991. "The Production of Occupational Stress in Medium-Sized Police Agencies: A Survey of Line Officers in Eight Municipal Departments." *Journal of Criminal Justice* 19: 339–349.

Cronin, T. J. 1982. "Police Suicides: A Comprehensive Study of the Chicago Police Department." Master's Thesis, Lewis University.

Cullen, F. T., Lemming, T., Link, B. G., and Wozniak, J. F. 1985. "The Impact of Social Supports on Police Stress." *Criminology* 23: 503–522.

Davey, J. D., Obst, P. L., and Sheehan, M. C. 2000. "Developing a Profile of Alcohol Consumption Patterns of Police Officers in a Large Scale Sample of an Australian Police Service." *European Addiction Studies*. 6: 205–212.

Davidson, M. J. and Veno, A. 1978. "Police Stress: A Multicultural, Interdisciplinary Review and Perspective, Part I." *Abstracts on Police Science* July/August: 190–19l.

Dishlacoff, L. 1976. "The Drinking Cop." *Police Chief* 43: 34–36, 39.

"Drug Use by Cops Seen as Growing Problem." 1985. *Law Enforcement News*, September 1, 12.

Eisenberg, T. 1975. "Job Stress and the Police Officer: Identifying Stress Reduction Techniques," In W. H. Kroes and J. J. Hurrell, Jr. (eds.), *Job Stress and the Police Officer: Identifying Stress Reduction Techniques*, pp. 26–34. Washington, D.C.: Department of Health, Education, and Welfare.

Engel, R. S. and Silver, E. 2001. "Policing Mentally Disordered Suspects: A Reexamination of the Criminalization Hypothesis." *Criminology* 39: 225–252.

Farmer, R. E. 1990. "Clinical and Managerial Implications of Stress Research on the Police." *Journal of Police Science and Administration* 17: 205–218.

Federal Bureau of Investigation. 1988. *Law Enforcement Officers Killed and Assaulted, 1987.* Washington, DC: Department of Justice.

——. 1992. *Killed in the Line of Duty: A Study of Selected Felonious Killings of Law Enforcement Officers*. Washington, DC: Department of Justice.

——. 1997. *Law Enforcement Officers Killed and Assaulted, 1996*. Washington, DC: Department of Justice.

——. 2002. *Law Enforcement Officers Killed and Assaulted, 2001*. Washington, DC: Department of Justice.

——. 1998. "Law Enforcement Line-of-Duty Deaths and Assaults." *Law Enforcement Bulletin* September: 5.

Finn, P. and Sullivan, M. 1987. "Police Handling of the Mentally Ill: Sharing Responsibility With the Mental Health System." *Journal of Criminal Justice* 17: 1–14.

——. 1988. "Law Enforcement and the Social Service System: Handling the Mental Ill." *Research in Action*, Washington, DC: National Institute of Justice.

Finn, P. and Tomz, J. E. 1997. *Developing a Law Enforcement Stress Program for Officers and Their Families*. Washington, DC: National Institute of Justice.

Flavin, J. 1998. "Police and HIV/AIDS: The Risk, the Reality, the Response." *American Journal of Criminal Justice* 23: 33–58.

French, J. R. P. 1975. "A Comparative Look at Stress and Strain in Policemen." In W. H. Kroes and J. J. Hurrell (eds.), *Job Stress and the Police Officer*, pp. 60–72. Washington, DC: Department of Health, Education, and Welfare.

Fridell, L. A. and Pate, A. M. 1997. "Death on Patrol: Killings of American Law Enforcement Officers." In G. G. Dunham and G. P. Alpert (eds.), *Critical Issues in Policing: Contemporary Readings*, 3rd ed., pp. 580–608. Prospect Heights, IL: Waveland Press.

Gaska, C. W. 1982. "The Rate of Suicide, Potential for Suicide, and Recommendations for Prevention Among Retired Police Officers." Ph.D. dissertation, Wayne State University.

Greenstone, J. L., Dunn, J. M., and Leviton, S. C. 1995. "Police Peer Counseling and Crisis Intervention Services Into the 21st Century." *Crisis Intervention and Time-Limited Treatment* 2: 167–187.

Grencik, J. M. 1975. "Toward an Understanding of Stress." In W. H. Kroes and J. J. Hurrell, Jr. (eds.), Job *Stress and the Police Officer: Identifying Stress Reduction Techniques*, pp. 163–181. Washington, DC: Department of Health, Education, and Welfare.

Guralnick, L. 1963. "Mortality by Occupation and Cause of Death Among Men 20–64 Years of Age." *Vital Statistics Special Reports* 53. Bethesda, MD.: Department of Health, Education, and Welfare.

Haarr, R. N. and Morash, M. 1999. "Gender, Race, and Strategies of Coping with Occupational Stress in Policing." *Justice Quarterly* 16: 303–336.

Hart, P. M., Wearing, A. J., and Headey, B. 1995. "Police Stress and Well-being: Integrating Personality, Coping and Daily Work Experience." *Journal of Occupational and Organizational Psychology* 68: 133–156.

He, N., Zhao, J. and Archbold, C. A. 2002. "Gender and Police Stress: The Convergent and Divergent Impact of Work Environment, Work-Family Conflict, and Stress Coping Mechanisms of Female and Male Police Officers." *Policing: An International Journal of Police Strategies and Management* 25: 687–708.

Hill. K. Q. and Clawson, M. 1988. "The Health Hazards of 'Street Level' Bureaucracy: Morality Among the Police." *Journal of Police Science and Administration* 16: 243–248.

Hurrell, J. J., Jr. and Kroes W. H. 1975. "Stress Awareness," In W. H. Kroes and J. J. Hurrell, Jr. (eds.), *Job Stress and the Police Officer: Identifying Stress Reduction Techniques*, pp. 234–246. Washington, DC: Department of Health, Education, and Welfare.

Ivanoff, A. 1994. *The New York City Police Suicide Training Project*. New York: Police Foundation.

Josephson, R. L. and Reiser, M. 1990. "Officer Suicide in the Los Angeles Police Department: A Twelve-Year Follow-Up." *Journal of Police Science and Administration* 17: 227–229.

Kaminski, R. J. and Sorensen, D. W. M. 1995. "A Multivariate Analysis of Individual, Situational and Environmental Factors Associated with Police Assault Injuries." *American Journal of Police* 14: 3–48.

Kaminski, R. J., Jefferis, E., and Gu, J. 2003. "Community Correlates of Serious Assaults on Police" *Police Quarterly* 6: 119–149.

Kavanagh, J. 1997. "The Occurrence of Resisting Arrest in Arrest Encounters: A Study of Police-Citizen Violence." *Criminal Justice Review* 22: 16–33.

Kellogg, T. and Harrison, M. 1991. "Post-traumatic Stress Plays a Part in Police Brutality." *Law Enforcement News* April 30: 12, 16.

Kraska, P. B., and Kappeler, V. W. 1988. "Police On-Duty Drug Use: A Theoretical and Descriptive Examination." *American Journal of Police* 7: 1–28.

Kroes, W. H., Margolis, B. L., and Hurell, J. L, Jr. 1974. "Job Stress in Policemen." *Journal of Police Science and Administration* 2: 145–155.

Konstantin, D. N. 1984. "Homicides of American Law Enforcement Officers, 1978–1980." *Justice Quarterly* 1: 29–45.

Kureczka, A. W. 1996. "Critical Incident Stress in Law Enforcement." *FBI Law Enforcement Bulletin* 65: 10–16.

LaGrange, T. 2000. "Distinguishing Between the Criminal and the "Crazy": Decisions to Arrest in Police Encounters with Mentally Disordered." Paper presented at the annual meeting of the American Society of Criminology, San Francisco, CA.

Lambuth, L. 1984. "An Employee Assistance Program That Works." *Police Chief* 51: 36–38.

Lardner, G. Jr. 1998. "Crime at Work Often Unreported." *San Jose Mercury News* July 7: A3.

Law Enforcement News. 2000. "The Strong Arm of the Law: Steroid-Using Cops—A Problem for Policing?" 26(527): 1, 6.

Lichtenberg, I. D., and Smith, A. 2001. "How Dangerous Are Routine Police-Citizen Traffic Stops? A Research Note." *Journal of Criminal Justice* 29: 419–428.

Loo, R. 1986. "Suicide Among Police in a Federal Force." *Suicide and Life-Threatening Behavior* 16: 379–388.

Lord, V. B. 1996. "An Impact of Community Policing: Reported Stressors, Social Support, and Strain Among Police Officers in a Changing Police Department." *Journal of Criminal Justice* 24: 503–522.

Lord, V. B., Gray, D. O., and Pond, S. B. 1991. "The Police Stress Inventory: Does it Measure Stress?" *Journal of Criminal Justice* 19: 139–150.

Martin, C. A., McKean, H. E., and Veltkamp, L. J. 1986. "Post-Traumatic Stress Disorder in Police and Working with Victims: A Pilot Study." *Journal of Police Science and Administration* 14: 98–101.

Maynard, P. E. and Maynard, N. W. 1980. "Preventing Police Stress Through Couples Communication Training." *Police Chief* 47: 30, 31, 66.

McEwen, J. T. 1995. "National Assessment Program: 1994 Survey Results." *Research in Action.* Washington, DC: National Institute of Justice.

McLeod, R. G. 1990. "Who Has California's Deadliest Jobs?" *San Francisco Chronicle,* January 22.

Morash, M. and Haarr, R. 1995. "Gender, Workplace Problems, and Stress in Policing." *Justice Quarterly* 12: 113–140.

O'Neill, J. L. and Cushing, M. A. 1991. *The Impact of Shift Work on Police Officers.* Washington, DC: Police Executive Research Forum.

Patterson, G. T. 2003. "Examining the Effects of Coping and Social Support on Work and Life Stress Among Police Officers." *Journal of Criminal Justice* 31: 215–226.

Pendleton, M., Stotland, E., Spiers, P., and Kirsch, E. 1989. "Stress and Strain Among Police, Firefighters, and Government Workers: A Comparative Analysis." *Criminal Justice and Behavior* 16: 196–210.

Richard, W. and Fell, R. 1975. "Health Factors in Police Job Stress." In W. W. Kroes and J. J. Hurrell, (eds.), *Job Stress and the Police Officer,* pp. 73–84. Washington, DC: U.S. Government Printing Office.

Richmond, R. L., Wodak, A., Kehoe, L., and Heather, N. 1998. "How Healthy Are the Police? A Survey of Life-Style Factors." *Addiction* 93: 1729–1737.

Robinson, H. M., Sigman, M. R., and Wilson, J. R. 1997. "Duty-Related Stressors and PTSD Symptoms in Suburban Police Officers." *Psychological Reports* 81: 835–845.

Roberg, R. R., Kuykendall, J., and Novak, K. 2002. *Police Management,* 3rd ed. Los Angeles: Roxbury Publishing Co.

Roberg, R. R., Hayhurst, D. L., and Allen, H. E. 1988. "Job Burnout in Law Enforcement Dispatchers: A Comparative Analysis." *Journal of Criminal Justice* 16: 385–393.

Roberts, M. D. 1975. "Job Stress in Law Enforcement: A Treatment and Prevention Program." In W. H. Kroes and J. J. Hurrell, Jr. (eds.), *Job Stress and the Police Officer: Identifying Stress Reduction Techniques.* pp. 226–233. Washington, DC: Department of Health, Education, and Welfare.

Roberts, N. A. and Levenson, R. W. 2001. "The Remains of the Workday: Impact of Job stress and Exhaustion on Marital Interaction in Police Couples," *Journal of Marriage and Family* 63: 1052–1067.

Robinson, H. M., Sigman, M. R., and Wilson, J. R. 1997. "Duty-Related Stressors and PTSD Symptoms in Suburban Police Officers." *Psychological Reports* 81: 835–845.

Saper, M. 1980. "Police Wives: The Hidden Pressure." *Police Chief* 47: 28–29.

Selye, H. 1974. *Stress Without Distress.* Philadelphia: Lippincott.

Sherman, L. W., DeRiso, D., Gaines, D., Rogan, D., and Cohn, E. 1989. *Police Murdered in Drug-Related Situations, 1972–1988.* Washington, D.C.: Crime Control Institute.

Stack, S. and Kelley, T. 1999. "Police Suicide" In D. J. Kenney and R. P. McNamara (eds.), *Police and Policing: Contemporary Issues* 2nd ed., pp. 94–107. Westport, CT: Praeger.

Stephens, C. and Miller, I. 1998. "Traumatic Experiences and Post-Traumatic Stress Disorder in the New Zealand Police." *Policing: An International Journal of Police Strategies and Management* 21: 178–191.

Storch, J. E. and Panzarella, R. 1996. "Police Stress: State-Trait Anxiety in Relation to Occupational and Personal Stressors." *Journal of Criminal Justice* 24: 99–107.

Stratton, J. G. 1976. "The Law Enforcement Family: Programs for Spouses." *Law Enforcement Bulletin* March: 16–22.

Swanson, C., Gaines, L., and Gore, B. 1991. "Abuse of Anabolic Steroids. " *FBI Law Enforcement Bulletin* August: 19–23.

Teplin, L. A. 1984. "Criminalizing Mental Disorder: The Comparative Arrest Rates of the Mentally Ill." *American Psychologist* 39: 794–803.

Territo, L. and Vetter, H. J. (eds.) 1981. *Stress and Police Personnel.* Boston: Allyn and Bacon.

Terry, W. C. 1981. "Police Stress: The Empirical Evidence." *Police Science and Administration* 9: 61–75.

——. 1985. "Police Stress as a Professional Self-Image." *Journal of Criminal Justice* 13: 501–512.

Thompson, R. A. and Marquart, J. W. 1998. "Law Enforcement Responses to the HIV/AIDS Epidemic: Selected Findings and Suggestions for Future Research." *Policing: An International Journal of Police Strategies and Management* 21: 648–665.

Vaughn, J. 1991. "Critical Incidents for Law Enforcement Officers." In J. Reese, J. Horn, and C. Dunning (eds.), *Critical Incidents in Policing*, p. 148. Washington, D.C.: U.S. Government Printing Office.

Vickers, B. 2000. "Memphis, Tennessee, Police Department's Crisis Intervention Team." *Bulletin From the Field.* Washington, DC: Department of Justice, Office of Justice Programs.

Violanti, J. M. 1995. "The Mystery Within: Understanding Police Suicide." *FBI Law Enforcement Bulletin* 64: 19–23.

——. 1996. "Police Suicide: An Overview." *Police Studies* 19: 77–89.

——. 1997. "Suicide and the Police Role: A Psychosocial Model." *Policing: An International Journal of Police Strategies & Management* 20: 698–715.

Violanti, J. M. and Aron, F. 1995. "Police Stressors: Variations in Perception Among Police Personnel." *Journal of Criminal Justice* 23: 287–294.

Violanti, J. M. and Vena, J. E. 1995. "Epidemiology of Police Suicide." *Research in Progress*, NIMH Grant MH47091-02.

Violanti, J. M., Vena, J. E., and Marshall, J. R. 1986. "Disease Risk and Mortality Among Police Officers." *Journal of Police Science and Administration* 14: 17–23.

Wallace, P. A., Roberg, R. R., and Allen, H. E. 1985. "Job Burnout Among Narcotics Investigators: An Exploratory Study." *Journal of Criminal Justice* 13: 549–559.

Wagner, M. and Brzeczek, R. J. 1983. "Alcoholism and Suicide: A Fatal Connection." *FBI Law Enforcement Bulletin* 52: 8–15.

Wellborn, J. 1999. "Responding to Individuals with Mental Illness." *FBI Law Enforcement Bulletin* 68: 6–8.

"What's Killing America's Cops? Mostly Themselves, According to New Study." 1996. *Law Enforcement News* November 15: 1.

Witkin, G. 1998. "Childproofing Guns." *U.S. News and World Report* June: 25–26.

Suggested Websites for Further Study

Police Stress
http://www.theroad.com.hk/policestress.html
Police Psychology
http://www.heavybadge.com/
The Central Florida Police Stress Unit, Inc.
http://www.policestress.org/
Memphis Police Department Critical Intervention Team
http://www.memphispolice.org/communit.htm

Texas Commission on Law Enforcement Officers' Standards and Training
http://link.tsl.state.tx.us/tx/TCLEOSE/
FBI's Uniform Crime Reports (includes Law Enforcement Officers Killed
and Assaulted)
http://www.fbi.gov/ucr/ucr.htm
New York Police Officers Killed September 11, 2001
http://www.nyc.gov/html/nypd/html/memorial_01.html
National Law Enforcement Officers Memorial Fund
http://www.nleomf.com/ ✦

Higher Education

Chapter Outline

Key Terms

BFOQ	Omnibus Crime Control and Safe
COPS	Streets Act
Davis v. City of Dallas	PERF
educational incentive policies	Police Corps
LEAA	President's Commission, *The Challenge*
LEEP	*of Crime in a Free Society*
National Advisory Commission on	scholarship and recruitment program
Higher Education for Police	Violent Crime Control and Law Enforce-
National Advisory Commission on Crim-	ment Act (Crime Control Act)
inal Justice Standards and Goals	

There has been a longstanding debate over whether a college education for police officers is necessary or even desirable. In present-day society, with the ever-expanding complexity of the police role and the transition toward community policing, this question is more significant than ever. Interestingly, the initial requirement of a high school diploma to enter the field of policing occurred at a time when most of the nation's population did not finish high school. Thus, a requirement of a high school education actually identified individuals with an above-average level of education. Statistics from the Department of Health, Education and Welfare, for instance, indicates that immediately after World War II, less than half of the 17-year-old population had earned a high school diploma in 1946 (National Advisory Commission 1973). Although it is difficult to determine precisely when the high school diploma, or its equivalent, the general education diploma (GED), became a standard requirement for a majority of the country's police departments, it was a well-established trend after World War II.

Today, of course, the high school diploma has essentially been replaced by a college degree as the above-average level of educational attainment in the United States. Consequently, those police departments that have not raised their educational requirements for entry have failed to keep pace with their tradition of employing people with an above-average education. It should be noted, however, that most police departments with minimum educational requirements have employees who exceed that minimum. Additionally, police forces at different governmental levels have traditionally required different levels of education for employment. For example, most federal agencies such as the ATF, DEA, or FBI have required at least a college degree for quite some time, but only a minimal number of city and state police and sheriff's departments require one. Many others require a minimum two-year degree, or its equivalent in college units. Baro and Burlingame (1999) noted that an increasing number of officers are completing college units even without a formal degree requirement. However, they argue that this could represent "degree inflation" as an associates degree (two-year) today may only be the equivalent of a high school diploma in the 1960s (Baro and Burlingame 1999, 60).

The debate over higher education, however, is much more complicated than determining whether or not police requirements are above or below national population norms. The development of higher education programs and the ensuing debate is the focus of this chapter.

The Development of Higher Education Programs for Police

The debate over higher educational requirements for police officers is not new. Starting in the early 1900s, Berkeley, California, Police Chief August Vollmer called for the recruitment of officers who were not only trained in the "technology of policing" but who also understood "the prevention of crime or confrontation through [their] appreciation of the psychology and sociology of crime" (Carte 1973, 275). Contrary to traditional practices of the time, Vollmer felt that such skills must not only be learned through on-the-job experience, but first be taught in the classroom.

Calling for the "very best manhood in the nation" to join the police profession (Carte 1973, 277), Vollmer campaigned strongly for police courses in higher education and the need for college-educated personnel throughout the police ranks. He was primarily responsible, along with the faculty, for the establishment of the first police school in higher education at the University of California, Berkeley, which he joined part time in 1916, and full-time in 1932 after his retirement from the Berkeley Police Department (Caiden 1977). For his efforts to reform and professionalize the police, Vollmer eventually gained a reputation as the father of modern American policing.

Following Berkeley's lead, other programs emphasizing police education were developed at major universities. Between the early 1920s and mid-1930s, a number of schools established programs of study for criminal justice professionals, primarily the police. Although the majority of these programs lasted only a few years, several continue to this day, including those at the University of Chicago, Indiana University, Michigan State University, San Jose State University, and Wichita State University.

These early programs laid the foundation for higher education in criminal justice, which was typically labeled police science, police administration, or law enforcement. Such curricula were developed in selected four-year institutions and many community colleges through the mid-1960s. The focus of these programs was usually on administration and supervision issues in policing, as well as on the practical applications of the "science" of policing, including such topics as patrol procedures, traffic enforcement, criminalistics, criminal investigation, and report writing. It is interesting to note that during these years, most police departments had no formalized training programs; many of these programs were designed to fill this "training gap."

Even with the development of academic police programs, the concept of the college-educated police officer was strongly resisted by the majority of rank-and-file officers. Those who either had a degree or were attending college, the so-called college cops, were often viewed with suspicion and distrust. Goldstein aptly describes their plight during this era:

> The term itself implied that there was something incongruous about an educated police officer. College graduates, despite their steadily increasing number in the general population, did not seek employment with the police. The old but lingering stereotype of the "dumb flatfoot," the prevalent concept of policing as a relatively simple task, the low pay, and the limitations on advancement—all of these factors made it appear that a college education would be wasted in such a job. And the tremendous difference between the social status accorded a college graduate and the status accorded an officer made an anomaly of the individual who was both (1977, 284).

The reasons listed by Goldstein—including (1) viewing the police role in simplistic terms; (2) the need to hire only low-quality personnel to perform the job; (3) low pay; (4) lack of advancement opportunities; and (5) low status—all continued to play a role in discouraging the concept of advanced education for the police. Two significant and interrelated events, however, took place in the mid-to-late 1960s that required the country to take a hard look at the level of professionalism and quality of U.S. police forces as well as the rest of the criminal justice system. These two events played a major role in ushering in the "golden age" of higher education for the police (Pope 1987).

The first event was the enormous increase in the crime rate that began in the early 1960s, leveled off in the early 1980s, and started moving upward again in the mid-1980s. In 1968, for the first time in three decades of opinion sampling, the Gallup poll found crime ranked as the most serious national issue (ahead of civil rights, the cost of living, and poverty), as well as the most important local issue (ahead of schools, transportation, and taxes). Furthermore, Gallup found that three persons in 10, and four in 10 for both women and residents of larger cities, admitted that they were afraid to go out alone at night in their own neighborhoods (Saunders 1970).

The second event was the ghetto riots, which occurred in the mid-1960s. The burning, looting, and general turmoil in many of the nation's major cities was the catalyst that spurred the public and the government into action. At this juncture, the "war on crime" began (Pope 1987).

"Crime in the streets" thus became a national issue in the 1964 presidential campaign. The following year, Congress passed the Law Enforcement Assistance Act of 1965, a modest grant program that expressed a national concern about the adequacy of local police departments. Two years later, the **President's Commission on Law Enforcement and Administration of Justice** issued a comprehensive report titled *The Challenge of Crime in a Free Society* (1967) documenting the serious impact of crime on U.S. society. Although the report issued over 200 specific proposals for action involving all levels of government and society, a majority of the recommendations—either directly or indirectly—dealt with the police as the "front line" of the criminal justice system.

Serious and continuing problems between the police and the community, especially minority-group members, were a major concern of the commission. It was thought that without respect for the police or community participation in crime prevention, there could be little impact on the crime rate. Because much of this problem was associated with the low quality of police personnel, many of the commission's recommendations dealt with the need for "widespread improvement in the strength and caliber of police manpower. . .for achieving more effective and fairer law enforcement" (President's Commission 1967, 294). The commission thought that one of the most important ways to upgrade the quality of police personnel would be through higher education. Consequently, one of their most significant, and controversial, recommendations was that the "ultimate aim of *all* police departments should be that *all* personnel with general enforcement powers have baccalaureate degrees" (109, emphasis added). Perhaps just as important, the commission further recommended that police departments should "take *immediate* steps to establish a minimum requirement of a baccalaureate degree for all supervisory and executive level positions" (110, emphasis added).

The President's Commission in 1967 recommended that all officers should possess college degrees. Here an officer is awarded his diploma in a graduation ceremony.

Federal Programs and Support for Higher Education

Shortly thereafter, Congress passed the **Omnibus Crime Control and Safe Streets Act** of 1968, which created the **Law Enforcement Assistance Administration (LEAA).** Through LEAA, the federal government poured literally billions of dollars into the criminal justice system—focusing on the police—in an attempt to improve their effectiveness and reduce crime. This money was initially earmarked for the research and development of "innovative" programs in policing, but was instead used primarily to purchase additional hardware (e.g., cars and communications equipment, weapons) that departments could not afford on their own and secondarily for training. The result was that most police departments, rather than introducing new programs, instead operated from a perspective of "more of the same."

Under LEAA an educational-incentive program, known as the **Law Enforcement Education Program (LEEP),** was established in the late 1960s. It provided financial assistance to police personnel, as well as to others who wished to enter police service, to pursue a college education. The impact of LEEP on the growth of law enforcement programs in both two-year and four-year schools was nothing short of phenomenal. For example, it has been reported that in 1954 there was a total of 22 such programs in the country (Deutsch 1955), but by 1975 the numbers had increased to more than 700 in community colleges, and nearly 400 in four-year schools (Korbetz 1975).

In 1973, a highly influential *Report on Police* (1973) by the **National Advisory Commission on Criminal Justice Standards and Goals,** further advanced the higher-education recommendations made by the president's commission. The report included a *graduated timetable* that would require all police officers, at the time of initial employment, to have completed at least two years of education (60 semester units) at an accredited college or university by 1975, three years (90 semester units) by 1978, and a baccalaureate degree by 1982. In the same year, the American Bar Association issued another influential report, *Standards Relating to the Urban Police Function*, which recognized the demanding and complex nature of the police role in a democracy. The ABA further elaborated on the need for advanced education in order to meet the professional skills required by such a role:

> Police agencies need personnel in their ranks who have the characteristics which a college education seeks to foster: intellectual curiosity, analytical ability, articulateness, and a capacity to relate the events of the day to the social, political, and historical context in which they occur (ABA 1973, 212).

More recently, the **Violent Crime Control and Law Enforcement Act (Crime-Control Act)** of 1994 became the most comprehensive federal crime legislation since the Omnibus Crime Control and Safe Streets Act of 1968. The Crime-Control Act allocates approximately $30 billion to various criminal justice agencies, with almost $11 billion for state and local law enforcement, including almost $9 billion to hire an additional 100,000 police officers under the **community-oriented policing services (COPS)** program (U.S. Dept. of Justice 1994). These new officers are to be used by local departments to help further their community-policing efforts. In addition, the legislation provides for federal funds to be used to establish a police corps and a scholarship and recruitment program for local police departments. This is the largest federal investment in education for law enforcement personnel since the creation of the Law Enforcement Education Program ("Dissecting the Crime Bill" 1994).

The **Police Corps** and the **scholarship and recruitment program** were established under Title XX of the Crime-Control Act of 1994 and are administered through the Office of the Police Corps and Law Enforcement Education, under the auspices of the Justice Department. Under the Police Corps program, full-time college students are eligible for up to $10,000 annual tuition reimbursements, but they must agree to work in a state or local police force for at least four years after graduation (see Inside Policing 14.1). Participants who fail to meet service requirements will be required to repay all of the tuition reimbursements plus 10 percent interest; however, a community service commitment can be substituted for police work if there is a physical or emotional disability or a "good cause" reason the participant cannot fulfill the original commitment ("Dissecting the Crime Bill" 1994).

Inside Policing 14.1   The Federal Police Corps

With Police Corps programs in operation in Maryland and Oregon, more programs are beginning to recruit college students who are willing to serve as police officers for four years in exchange for tuition reimbursement. The program is administered by the Justice Department's Office of Community Oriented Policing Services (COPS), which disburses funds to localities by states, which have broad discretion to develop the programs to meet the specific needs of local police departments. The nation's first class of 19 Police Corps Cadets took a 16-week training course at the Oregon State Police Academy. Once the cadets completed training, they went to work for the Portland Police Department and began receiving $10,000 annual tuition reimbursements up to a total of $40,000. In Maryland, the Police Corps program recruited up to 120 participants, who eventually went to work for the Baltimore Police Department. "It's very exciting,"

said Lieutenant Governor Kathleen Kennedy Townsend. "It's an innovative way to recruit a number of young people into police work, some of whom will stay and be excellent police officers, while others will go out and be supporters of the police in their communities."

New cadets will be selected from high school seniors and current college students. Cadets must complete the same selection process as regular officers, including a written exam and oral interview, on which they are scored on an overall point system.

Source: Adapted from "Surprise! The Police Corps Is Back—Not That It Ever Left." 1997a. *Law Enforcement News*, January 31: 1, 10. Reprinted with permission from *Law Enforcement News*, John Jay College of Criminal Justice, New York City.

The scholarship and recruitment program provides scholarships for higher education to in-service law enforcement personnel and to students who are juniors or seniors in high school or enrolled in an institution of higher learning (who do not currently hold a law enforcement position), and interested in pursuing a career in law enforcement. Priority is given to racial, ethnic, or gender groups whose representation in police departments is substantially less than in the population eligible for police employment in the state. Participants are required to work in a law enforcement position for one month for each credit hour for which funds were received, for a period of not less than six months or more than two years. If participants fail to meet program guidelines, they will be required to repay the entire scholarship ("Dissecting the Crime Bill" 1994).

Quality of Higher Education Programs

The meteoric, unregulated rise of programs in police science or law enforcement led to serious questions about their academic rigor and viability. The increase coincided with the infusion of federal moneys distributed through LEEP. In order to capture their fair share of the federal funds, many schools hurriedly spliced together programs to study the police. Due to a lack of qualified faculty, many part-time instructors, frequently selected from the local police or sheriff's departments, were employed to teach classes. Because instructors generally lacked proper academic qualifications, little attempt was made to introduce current research or critical analysis of contemporary issues and practices. Instead, instructors focused on training, using readily available models from their own experience. They concentrated on their department's operating policies and procedures and offered "war stories" from their street experiences as examples of the "way things are." The students taking these courses were overwhelmingly in-service, that is, full-time police or criminal justice employees returning to school through the provision of LEEP funds. Because they are narrowly focused, training-oriented programs are not traditionally found in a university setting, so it is not surprising that they encountered stiff opposition from the well-established, academic disciplines. For example, the picture of police science majors depicted below wearing uniforms enhances the image of a training environment rather than an academic one.

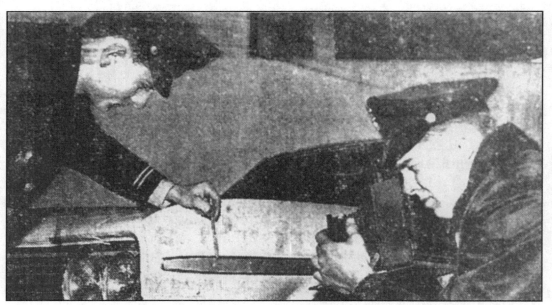

Uniformed San Jose State University Police Science students collecting evidence in the early 1960s. Notice that the students wore uniforms.

In the late 1960s and early 1970s, many programs began to broaden their focus, emphasizing criminal-justice–related topics rather than technical police training. The titles of the programs began to change to reflect this broader approach; common new titles were Departments of Criminal Justice, Criminology, or Administration of Justice. Reflecting on these changes, Pope comments:

Curriculums became much less practice oriented (at least in the four-year institutions) and more academically based. Some criminal justice programs even took a more critical stance toward the criminal justice system, adding courses based on a radical perspective. Many programs eliminated courses on patrol, traffic and the like, or at least expanded offerings to include race, gender, victims and related issues. It was a period when criminal justice attempted to gain academic respectability and institutional support. (1987, 4)

A policy decision by LEAA to spend more money for research on crime and justice issues and less on police hardware indirectly helped advance the respectability of these programs. Scholars entering the field now had a chance to receive grants to study and evaluate criminal justice programs. Accordingly, the criminal justice faculty could more easily expand its research efforts and develop a research orientation (i.e., advancing knowledge of the field) similar to the more traditional disciplines. Another important development during this period was the emergence of doctoral programs in criminal justice developed to supply faculty for the new criminal justice departments. At the same time, the nature of the student body was also changing from in-service students to pre-service students (Terry 1980).

Following a decade of tremendous growth, accompanied by severe criticism of police programs in higher education, the Police Foundation put together a commission of noted educators, police administrators, and public officials to evaluate the quality of these programs. Known as the **National Advisory Commission on Higher Education for Police Officers,** the commission spent two years conducting a national survey and documenting the problems of police education (Sherman and the National Advisory Commission 1978). The report was extremely critical of the state of the art of police education at the time. It recommended significant changes in virtually all phases of police higher education, including institutional, curriculum, and faculty. Among the more crucial recommendations, the commission proposed the following:

1. The majority of federal funds for police higher education should go to programs with broad curriculums and well-educated faculty rather than to narrow technical programs.

2. No college credit should be granted for attending police department training programs.

3. Community colleges should phase out their terminal two-year degree programs in police education.

4. Colleges should employ primarily full-time police-education teaching staffs, seeking faculty members with Ph.D. degrees in arts and sciences.

5. Prior employment in criminal justice should be neither a requirement nor a handicap in faculty selection.

6. Government policies at all levels should encourage educating police officers before they begin their careers.

These recommendations struck at the heart of many police programs throughout the country and consequently were not well received by many. However, as discussed above, improvements had already begun.

The commission's call for eliminating terminal two-year degree programs in police education further emphasized the importance it attached to a broad-based education, enhanced by a campus setting where "greater student interaction with diverse kinds of people" could take place (Sherman and National Advisory Commission 1978, 115). According to the commission, the two-year terminal-degree programs, which focused on vocational training, produced a "paraprofessional caste" system, since they were often housed in the same academic units as programs in cosmetology and auto mechanics.

Criminal justice curriculums (and textbooks) are more broadly based and scholarly than in the past, allowing for the rapid development of this emerging field of study.

The changing nature of the criminal justice student was also significant, as the commission recommended that police should be educated *prior* to employment; this argument attacked the very basis of the LEEP program, which provided an overwhelming amount of its funds to in-service personnel only. This recommendation started a serious debate on whether police departments should place more emphasis on "recruiting the educated" or on "educating the recruited." The commission thought that the "occupational perspective" of full-time police work "probably reduces the impact of college on students" (Sherman and National Advisory Commission 1978, 13).

As the LEEP program was eventually phased out, so too were many of the weaker police programs in higher education. The stronger programs continued to recruit Ph.D.s trained in criminal justice and other social sciences for their faculties, thus establishing a more scholarly approach toward teaching and research. The emphasis on a broader-based curriculum became firmly established, and the students became less vocationally and in-service oriented.

These changes in higher education in criminal justice, including faculty quality, student body makeup, and curricular content, have allowed the field to mature quite rapidly and gain academic respectability; students of such programs are no longer viewed as second-class citizens of the university community. Today, on most college campuses where degree programs have become firmly established, program quality and student interest continue to increase.

Higher Education Requirements for Police

Advances in raising educational requirements for police have been slow and sporadic. Until the 1980s, in many police departments, an officer with a college degree was often viewed with contempt or resentment; it was not understood why anyone with a degree would want to enter policing. Indeed, a college degree requirement is still virtually nonexistent. A national study conducted by the Bureau of Justice Statistics (BJS) (Hickman and Reaves 2003a) of approximately 3,000 state and local law enforcement agencies, serving communities of all sizes, indicates that only 1 percent of departments required a college degree for employment in 2000 (see Table 14.1).

Table 14.1 Minimum Educational Requirement for New Officer Recruits in Local Police Departments, by Size of Population Served, 2000

Population Served	Total With Requirement	Percent of Agencies Requiring a Minimum of:			
		High School Diploma	Some College*	2-Year College Degree	4-Year College Degree
All sizes	98%	83%	6%	8%	1%
1,000,000 or more	100	67	33	0	0
500,000–999,999	100	71	18	6	6
250,000–499,999	98	65	18	10	5
100,000–249,999	99	71	18	9	2
50,000–99,999	99	65	17	16	1
25,000–49,999	99	73	11	13	2
10,000–24,999	99	78	8	12	1
2,500–9,999	99	85	4	9	1
Under 2,500	97	86	4	6	—

Note: Detail may not add to total because of rounding.
*Non-degree requirements.
—Less than 0.5%

Source: Hickman, M. J., and Reaves, B. A., *Local Police Departments 2000* (Washington, D.C.: Bureau of Justice Statistics, 2003a), 6.

Table 14.1 also indicates that in some jurisdictions the figure is considerably higher than 1 percent; for example, it is 6 percent for departments in cities serving more than 500,000 residents but fewer than 1,000,000. Interestingly, 0 percent of departments serving more than 1,000,000 residents require either a four-year or even a two-year degree. However, 33 percent of departments serving more than 1,000,000 residents do require some college. Fifteen percent of departments had some type of college requirement, usually a two-year degree (8 percent). For sheriffs' offices, the BJS survey (Hickman and Reaves, 2003b) reports that 12 percent of offices serving more than 1,000,000 residents require some college, and that 6 percent of all offices required a 2-year degree. Fewer than 1 percent require a degree.

The BJS survey (Hickman and Reaves 2003a) further reported that the percentage of officers employed by a state or local department with some type of college require-ment for new officers in 2000 was 32 percent, or about three times that of 1990 (10 percent). For sheriffs' offices (Hickman and Reaves 2003b), the percentage of officers with some type of college requirement also increased about three times, from 4 per-cent in 1990 to 13 percent in 2000. Additionally, from 1990 to 2000 the percentage of officers employed by a state or local department with a degree requirement increased from 3 percent to 9 percent; for sheriffs' offices, the percentage with a degree require-ment increased from 3 percent to 5 percent. These trends are encouraging, but there is clearly room for improvement.

Even though the development of formal educational requirements has been slow, some research suggests that approximately one-quarter of officers in the field have a baccalaureate degree, most likely due to the increased number of colleges and univer-sities offering criminal justice/criminology degrees. For instance, a 1994 national study of departments with more than 500 sworn officers (Sanders, Hughes, and Langworthy 1995) found that approximately 28 percent of the officers were college graduates. Another study indicated that 65 percent of police officers have completed at least one year of college and an additional 23 percent possess a four-year degree (Carter and Sapp 1990a).

Police Chiefs, Promotion, and Higher Education

Just as the percentage of police officers holding college degrees has increased, so too has the number of police chiefs holding degrees. A study conducted by PERF ("Survey Says Big-City Chiefs Are Better-Educated Outsiders" 1998) of 358 city and county police chiefs in jurisdictions of 50,000 or more residents discovered that 87 percent held bachelor's degrees, almost 47 percent had master's degrees, and nearly 5 percent had law or doctoral degrees. In comparison, a 1975 International Association of Chiefs of Police (IACP) survey found that about 15 percent had bachelor's degrees and only about 4 percent had advanced degrees. This is an important finding because it suggests that with highly educated police chief executives as role models, higher education may now be emerging as an important part of the police culture. It is likely that these chiefs will begin to emphasize, and even require, higher education as part of their overall strategy to improve their departments, including promotional and hir-ing practices.

The continuing increase in college-educated officers suggests it will become increasingly difficult to earn a promotion without a college education in the years to come. One study, for example, of 51 sheriffs' departments and municipal police agencies in Colorado indicated that 22 percent had a written policy requiring a col-lege degree for promotion (Nees 2003). The PERF survey by Carter and Sapp (1992) found a growing trend for departments to tie educational requirements to promotion. Some 20 percent of those responding indicated that they had either a formal or informal policy requiring some level of advanced education for promo-tion; only 5 percent required a college degree. In addition, a notable number of police chiefs said they believed a graduate degree should be required for officers in command ranks. In a Texas survey of 72 departments (Garner 1998), only five reported that they had an educational requirement for promotion; however, this number may be similar to the PERF results, since it does not include informal policies or practices.

The Arlington, Texas Police Department is an example of what the relationship between promotion and higher education requirements may look like in the future. Arlington, with approximately 600 sworn and 180 nonsworn personnel, began phasing in college degree requirements in 1986; currently, about 75 percent of Arlington officers hold a bachelor's degree (Bowman 2002). Table 14-2 chronicles the development of the Arlington Police Department's emphasis on higher education.

Table 14.2 Development of Higher Education Requirements in the Arlington, Texas, Police Department

For Entry

✦ 1986: Bachelor's degree required for new recruits with no prior police experience. Associate's degree required for recruits with a minimum of two years experience.
✦ 1999: Bachelor's degree required of all new recruits, regardless of experience.

For Promotion

✦ 1991: Bachelor's degree required for deputy chiefs.
✦ 1995: Bachelor's degree required for lieutenants.
✦ 1999: Master's degree required for assistant chiefs.
✦ 2000: Bachelor's degree required of officers seeking promotion.

Source: T. Bowman, 2002, "Educate to Elevate," *Community Links*, August, 11.

As Table 14.2 indicates, by 1999, all new recruits in Arlington were required to hold a bachelor's degree. With respect to promotion, by 1991 a bachelor's degree was required for deputy chiefs, in 1995 for lieutenants. A master's degree requirement was instituted in 1999 for assistant chiefs; and in 2000, at least a four-year degree was required of officers seeking promotion. In Voices From the Field, Arlington's Police Chief Theron Bowman discusses the advantages he sees in requiring a college degree for all police officers.

The Impact of Higher Education on Policing

If college is going to become a requirement for policing, it will be necessary to indicate to the courts the relevance of such a requirement to on-the-job performance. Over the past three decades, research on higher education and police officer behavior has focused on two major areas: the relationship between education and police attitudes, and the relationship between education and police performance. Although the quality of the research and the consistency of the findings have varied tremendously, it appears that some important general trends and conclusions can be drawn.

Voices From the Field
Theron Bowman
Chief of the Arlington, Texas, Police Department

Question: What impact on performance have you noticed since raising the department's educational standards to a college degree for new recruits and for promotion?

Answer: Since the Arlington Police Department raised educational standards to a college degree, we have noticed that officers more readily and more routinely make very good decisions in difficult situations independent of supervisory oversight and direction.

Our officers have a broader understanding of society and an improved ability to communicate. The ability to connect with residents while understanding big-picture sociological problems leads to innovative solutions to crime-related problems. This allows supervisors the opportunity to focus on the department's mission rather than micro-managing officers' response to calls for service. The overall effect is enhanced problem-solving skills, which leads to a higher level of service to citizens. ✦

Police Attitudes and Performance

Early research on the impact of college on police attitudes centered on comparing levels of authoritarianism of college-educated police to police with little or no college. For instance, it was shown that police with some college (Smith, Locke, and Walker 1968) and those with college degrees (Smith, Locke, and Fenster 1970) were significantly less authoritarian than their noncollege-educated colleagues. Guller (1972) found police officers who were college seniors showed lower levels of authoritarianism than officers who were college freshmen and of similar age, socioeconomic background, and work experience; this indicated that the higher the level of education, the more flexible or open one's belief system may be. Dalley (1975) further discovered that authoritarian attitudes correspond with a lack of a college education and increased work experience; he suggested that a more liberal attitude is more conducive to the discretionary nature of law enforcement.

Other researchers have found college-educated officers to be more flexible and less authoritarian (Parker, Donnelly, Gerwitz, Marcus, and Kowalewski 1976; Trojanowicz and Nicholson 1976; Roberg 1978). Further, some evidence indicates that college-educated officers are not only more aware of social and ethnic problems in their community but also have a greater acceptance of minorities (Weiner 1976), are more professional in their attitude (Miller and Fry 1978), and more ethical in their behavior (Tyre and Braunstein 1992).

College-educated officers are thought to be more understanding of human behavior, more sensitive to community relations, and to hold a higher service standard (Miller and Fry 1976; Regoli 1976). This suggests that such individuals are more "humanistic" police officers. Humanism is a valuable trait in departments that practice community policing because an officer's ability to empathize and communicate with local citizens is vital to its success (Meese 1993). Carlan and Byxbe (2000) conducted a study of undergraduate college students (235 criminal justice majors and 428 noncriminal justice majors) at three large southern universities in which subjects were asked to specify the prison sentence for a convicted felon in one of two hypothetical scenarios, randomly assigned. One scenario involved a car theft and the other a homicide. The race of the offender in each scenario (either black or white) was randomly varied. The authors concluded that no significant differences in sentencing preferences separated the aspiring police officers from their noncriminal justice counterparts—demonstrating that higher education appears to deliver a more humanistic candidate for police work—a good sign as the nationwide trend toward community policing continues to build.

Because police departments are so diverse, it is difficult to define performance measures; that is, what is considered to be "good" or "poor" performance may vary from department to department. The criteria used to measure police performance, then, are not clear-cut and are often controversial. Accordingly, research findings on police performance will usually be more useful if they are based on a wide variety of performance indicators. The research described next, on the relationship between higher education and police performance, is based on a number of different indicators, or measures, of performance.

Several studies have indicated that officers with higher levels of education performed their jobs in a more satisfactory manner than their less educated peers, as evidenced by higher evaluation ratings from their supervisors (Finnegan 1976; Roberg 1978; Smith and Aamodt 1997; Truxillo, Bennett, and Collins 1998).

The Smith and Aamodt (1997) study, which consisted of 299 officers from 12 municipal departments in Virginia, found that the benefits of a college education did not become apparent until the officers gained some experience; this finding is not surprising and suggests that higher education is simply another tool, along with training and experience, that allows officers to become more effective performers.

Truxillo, Bennett, and Collins (1998) studied a cohort of 84 officers in a southern, metropolitan police department over 10 years and found that college education was significantly correlated with promotions as well as with supervisory ratings of job knowledge.

Roberg (1978) examined the relationship between attitudes and performance (as measured by supervisory ratings) and found that "patrol officers with higher levels of education had more open belief systems (were less authoritarian) and performed in a more satisfactory manner on the job than those patrol officers with less education"; in addition, patrol officers with "college degrees had the most open belief systems and the highest levels of job performance, indicating that college-educated officers were better able to adapt to the complex nature of the police role" (344). It was shown that age, seniority, and college major had no impact on the results, lending support to the notion that the overall university experience is important in broadening one's perspectives. It is important to note that all the college graduates in this research were from a major land-grant state university that could be considered to have high-quality academic programs. Thus, the quality of the educational experience may also be an important variable in determining the impact of higher education.

Other researchers have found college to have a positive effect on numerous individual performance indicators. For example, several researchers have found college-educated officers to have fewer citizen complaints filed against them (Cascio 1977; Cohen and Chaiken 1972; Finnegan 1976; Trojanowicz and Nicholson 1976; Sanderson 1977; Wilson 1999; Lersch and Kunzman 2001). Additional research has indicated that college officers tend to perform better in the academy (Sanderson 1977), have fewer disciplinary actions taken against them by the department, have lower rates of absenteeism, receive fewer injuries on the job, and are involved in fewer traffic accidents (Cohen and Chaiken 1972; Cascio 1977; Sanderson 1977). There is even some evidence that better-educated officers tend to use deadly force (i.e., fire their weapons) less often (Fyfe 1988).

In a more recent study, citizen encounters involving inexperienced and less-educated officers resulted in increased levels of police force (Terrill and Mastrofski 2002). A study conducted in the state of Florida ("For Florida Police" 2002) reported that police officers with just a high school diploma made up slightly more than 50 percent of all sworn law enforcement personnel between 1997 and 2002, yet they accounted for nearly 75 percent of all disciplinary actions issued by the state. Based on these findings, the International Association of Chiefs of Police (IACP) has commissioned a two-year national study on the correlation between higher education and disciplinary action against officers ("For Florida Police" 2002). The goal of the national study is to provide empirical support to police administrators who want to implement college requirements in their departments.

Some interesting findings with respect to the future development of police departments indicate that college-educated officers are more likely to score better on written exams and attain promotions (Cohen and Chaiken 1972; Sanderson 1977; Roberg and Laramy 1980; Whetstone 2000; Polk and Armstrong 2001), tend to be more innovative in performing their work (Trojanowicz and Nicholson 1976), and are more likely to take leadership roles in the department and to rate themselves higher on performance measures (Cohen and Chaiken 1972; Trojanowicz and Nicholson 1976; Weirman 1978; Krimmel 1996). Kakar (1998) indicates that those officers with higher education rated themselves higher in leadership, responsibility, problem-solving, and initiative-taking skills in comparison to less-educated officers.

There is also developing evidence that college-educated officers become involved in cases of "individual liability significantly less frequently than noncollege officers" (Carter and Sapp 1989, 163), and that college-educated officers tend to have a broader understanding of civil rights issues from legal, social, historical, and political perspectives (Carter and Sapp 1990b). Because lawsuits claiming negligence on behalf of police departments are on the increase (along with the amount of damages being awarded—often between $1 million and $2 million per case)—this is an important area for future research. If a correlation between higher education and reduced liability risk can be established, the availability and cost of such insurance to police departments could be affected.

Finally, studies have indicated that police legitimacy (i.e., belief that police are fair and equitable) among the public is highly correlated to a willingness to obey the law (Tyler 1990) and that community policing facilitates police legitimacy (Skogan 1994). The superior communication and problem-solving skills derived from higher education, implicitly required by community policing, would seem well suited to fostering legitimacy among citizens for law enforcement officers.

When viewed together, these findings suggest that, in general, a college education has a positive impact on police attitudes and behavior. Essentially, college is related to less authoritarian beliefs, greater tolerance toward others, a more humanistic approach, and a greater acceptance of minority groups. Additionally, there is evidence to suggest that college-educated officers tend to perform better than their noncollege-educated colleagues, are less likely to be involved in civil liability complaints, and are more likely to be promoted.

Job satisfaction. Does higher education lead to increased job satisfaction for officers? The number of job satisfaction studies related to policing is surprisingly small. Early research in this area suggested that officers with a college education would be more frustrated and less satisfied because of unmet expectations for promotion (Niederhoffer 1967). There is some evidence that highly educated officers are more likely to terminate their careers in policing (Levy 1967; Cohen and Chaiken 1972; Stoddard 1973; Weirman 1978), and to hold differing and more negative views of job satisfaction (Griffin, Dunbar, and McGill 1978; Mottaz 1983). It is possible, however, that such results may be related to the traditional bureaucratic nature of police departments. Since it appears that higher education affects authoritarian attitudes, it would follow that college-educated police would be less willing to work in, and be less satisfied with, authoritarian departments and managerial practices. For example, Kakar (1998) indicates that with respect to job satisfaction, college-educated officers self-reported lower scores, coupled with higher scores of levels of frustration as a result of not feeling rewarded and/or feeling understimulated by the duties of traditional patrol work. In addition, officers with higher levels of education felt unrewarded and expressed frustration due to their inability to use their professional knowledge. Although this may appear to be a negative finding, it most likely simply indicates that college-educated officers prefer challenging and stimulating jobs. Dantzker (1998) also reported findings of lower levels of job satisfaction with higher education.

Interestingly, Griffin, Dunbar and McGill (1978) found that as education increases, sources of satisfaction may be more related to internal factors, such as control. Sherwood (2000) suggested that all officers—regardless of education level—are interested in job satisfaction, and departments that are more advanced in instituting community policing may hold an advantage over more traditional departments in providing it to their personnel. He further states that job satisfaction may be linked to the "use of a variety of skills, the ability to follow the task through to a conclusion, freedom to make decisions, and knowledge of the effectiveness of one's efforts" (2000, 210). Similarly, Griffin, Dunbar, and McGill (1978) recommended that structural changes (i.e., decentralization) be implemented in police departments to allow for more control among lower-level officers. Significantly, this is consistent with the less hierarchical structure and more autonomous style of community policing that, logically, should be most appealing to officers with higher education. As noted by Baro and Burlingame (1999, 64), "the community-policing movement indicates that police organizations and the police role could change in ways that require more education."

Police executives' views on higher education. In Table 14.3, the advantages and disadvantages of college-educated officers, as reported by police executives throughout the country, are summarized. The findings of the PERF study (Carter, Sapp, and Stephens 1989), where nearly 500 police executives were surveyed with respect to their opinions on higher education and policing, are consistent with most of the research findings discussed thus far. Citing the study, a resolution was passed by the members of PERF (college-educated police chief executives) calling for all police applicants to possess 30 semester units from an accredited college or university. This requirement was to be increased in increments of 15 units until the minimum requirement for employment in policing was the baccalaureate degree (PERF 1989).

Table 14.3 Police Executives' Opinions: Advantages and Disadvantages of Police Officers With Higher Education

Advantages	Disadvantages
College-educated officers are more likely to:	*College-educated officers are more likely to:*
Communicate better with the public	Leave policing
Write better reports	Question orders
Perform more effectively	Request reassignment
Receive fewer citizen complaints	
Show more initiative in work performance	
Be more professional	
Use discretion more wisely	
Be promoted	
Make better decisions	
Show more sensitivity to racial or ethnic groups	
Have fewer disciplinary problems	

Source: Adapted from D. L. Carter, A. D. Sapp, and D. W. Stephens, *The State of Police Education: Policy Directions for the 21st Century* (Washington, DC: PERF, 1989), xxii–xxiii. Used by permission.

Reflecting on the advantages of higher education described above, the police chief of Tulsa, Oklahoma, pushed through a policy requiring all police recruits to have a college degree. Inside Policing 14.2 describes the reasoning behind Tulsa's degree requirement.

Validating Higher Education for Police

Given the increasing number of college-educated officers in the field, such slow progress in developing higher-education standards is perplexing, especially considering the evidence that, in general, college education has a positive effect on officer attitudes, performance, and behavior. With such support for higher education, why have standards not been significantly raised by most police departments? Carter, Sapp, and Stephens (1989) identified two common reasons: (1) fear of being sued because a college requirement could not be quantitatively validated to show job relatedness, and (2) fear that college requirements would be discriminatory against minorities. Each of these important issues warrants discussion.

Higher Education as a BFOQ

As the PERF study of police executives reported (Carter, Sapp, and Stephens 1989), one of the primary reasons departments had not embraced higher-educational requirements more vigorously was the dilemma of not being able to validate such a requirement for the job, thus opening the department to a court challenge. Establishing higher-educational requirements as a **bona fide occupational qualification (BFOQ)** for police work could be an important step in facilitating the use of advanced education as a minimum entry-level selection criterion. A brief discussion of higher education as a BFOQ for police work follows.

Inside Policing 14.2   **No BS: Tulsa PD Rookies Required to Have Four-Year Degree**

Beginning with the January 1998 class, recruits entering the Tulsa, Oklahoma, police academy will have to have a four-year college degree after the City Council unanimously endorsed a proposal by Police Chief Ron Palmer to increase the police department's college requirement from the current 108 credit hours. The department is used to being on the cutting edge of higher education for police, having required 108 credit hours since 1981. "It wasn't a quantum leap for us but it's certainly something that's unusual for a city of our size, and it's unique among major cities," observed Palmer, who has a master's degree.

Chief Palmer believes that college-educated officers are better grounded to meet the demands of the job and are less likely to be the subjects of citizen complaints or engage in misconduct. He also believes that officers with college degrees "come to you a bit more mature, they're a little more aware of diversity issues, and they're more prone to use their minds to problem-solve than one that doesn't have that type of background."

Currently, about 73 percent of the department's 794 officers have college degrees, while an additional 20 percent have 60 hours or more of college credit. More than 40 sworn members have master's degrees, and the department has one member with a Ph.D. and three officials with law degrees.

At the same time, he points out, the requirement has not hampered the department's efforts to attract more minority recruits, as some thought might happen. "That doesn't appear to be the case," said Palmer. "We've hired [minorities] at the same level for the past two or three years, which was the result of a multicultural recruiting task force that partnered with the community. Coupled with this, we do a fairly strong recruiting effort not only in Tulsa, but outside the state, to get the numbers we feel will satisfy our goals."

Source: Adapted from *Law Enforcement News,* 1997b, "Men and Women of Letters: No BS: Tulsa PD Rookies to Need Four-Year Degrees." *Law Enforcement News,* November 30: 1.

Interestingly, the courts in this country have continuously upheld higher educational requirements in policing to be *job-related*. In *Castro v. Beecher* (1972), the requirement of a high school education by the Boston Police Department was affirmed, citing the recommendations of the President's Commission on Law Enforcement and Administration of Justice (1967) and the National Advisory Commission on Civil Disorders (1968). *Arnold v. Ballard* (1975) supported the notion that an educational requirement can be quantitatively job validated in stating that such requirements "indicate a measure of accomplishment and ability which . . . is essential for . . . performance as a police officer" (738). And in ***Davis v. City of Dallas*** (1985), the court upheld a challenge to the Dallas Police Department's requirement of 45 semester units (equivalent to one and one-half years of college) with a minimum of a C average from an accredited university.

In *Davis,* the court's decision was based partially on the complex nature of the police role and the public risk and responsibility that are unique to it. Such a decision indicates that higher standards of qualification can be applied to the job because police decision-making requires an added dimension of judgment. This logic has been applied by the courts to other occupations, such as airline pilots and health-related professions. Thus, the *Davis* decision can be viewed as the next logical step in increasing police professionalism and may provide further support for police executives to require higher education (Carter, Sapp, and Stephens 1988).

To validate the need for higher-education requirements, possibly the best approach, one that has withstood the scrutiny of the courts, is to use national studies and commission reports (e.g., National Advisory Commission on Criminal Justice

1973, President's Commission on Law Enforcement 1967, and others cited in this chapter), and the opinion of experts (including both police scholars and police executives). The PERF study recommended a preventive approach for a department that is going to require higher education for employment. This can be accomplished by having an expert prepare a policy support paper citing the "benefits and need of college-educated officers" (Carter, Sapp, and Stephens 1988, 16). The study further suggested that, although general studies and reports should be used, the policy support document should be specific to the individual department. The probability of litigation should be substantially lessened with such a document, and the educational program can also be based on the policies developed in the document.

Higher Education and Discrimination

A second area of concern reported to PERF by police executives was the potential impact the higher-education requirement might have on the employment of minorities. If minority-group members do not have equal access to higher education, such a requirement could be held to be discriminatory by the courts. Not only that, but there are also obvious ethical and social issues raised. Any educational requirements for policing, then, must not only be job-related but also nondiscriminatory. In the Davis case, the suit contended that higher-education requirements were discriminatory in the selection of police officers. According to Title VII of the Civil Rights Act, there cannot be employment barriers (or practices) that discriminate against minorities, even if they are not intended to do so. However, in *Griggs v. Duke Power Co.* (1971), the U.S. Supreme Court held that if an employment practice is job related (or a "business necessity"), it may be allowed as a requirement, even though it *has* discriminatory overtones. Thus, courts must base decisions on the balance between requirements that are necessary for job performance and avoiding discriminatory practices. In *Davis,* the city of Dallas conceded that the college requirements did have a "significant disparate impact on blacks" (1985, 207). As noted above, the court held that the complex requirements of police work (e.g., public risk and responsibility, amount of discretion) mitigated against the discriminatory effects of a higher-education requirement.

It would appear, then, that if certain requirements for the job can be justified, even though they may discriminate against certain groups, the benefits of such requirements may be judged to outweigh the discriminatory effects. Following this line of reasoning, if higher-educational requirements can be shown to be a BFOQ, such a requirement would be considered a business necessity and thus a legitimate requirement for successful job performance.

With respect to higher educational levels in policing and minority representation, the PERF study of some 250,000 geographically dispersed police officers throughout the nation reported some interesting findings. For instance, as indicated in Table 14.4, the average educational levels of the various racial and ethnic groups (12.0 years = a high school degree), as well as the overall minority representation, are not significantly different. Furthermore, the percentage of black and Hispanic officers with some undergraduate work, and also with graduate degrees, is greater than for white officers.

Table 14.4 Educational Levels by Race/Ethnicity and Minority Representation in Police Organizations

Group	Mean Yrs. Graduate Work	% in Police Degree	National %	No College	Some College	Under-Graduate
Black	13.6	12.3	12.1	28	63	9
Hispanic	13.3	6.4	8.0	27	68	5
White	13.7	80.3	76.9	34	64	4
Other	13.8	1.0	3.0	19	73	8

Sources: Adapted from D. L. Carter, A. D. Sapp, and D. W. Stephens, 1988, "Higher Education as a Bona Fide Occupational Qualification (BFOQ) for Police: A Blueprint," *American Journal of Police*, 7: 20; D. L. Carter and A. D. Sapp, 1992, "College Education and Policing: Coming of Age," *FBI Law Enforcement Bulletin*, January: 11.

Some recent data suggest, however, that requiring a bachelor's degree may have an impact on race. Decker and Huckabee (2002) explored the effect of raising educational requirements to a bachelor's degree by analyzing recruit information from the Indianapolis Police Department over four years. They concluded that almost two-thirds (65 percent) of successful candidates overall would have been ineligible, and 77 percent (30 of 39) of African American applicants did not have degrees. The researchers also looked at raising the age requirement to 25, and found that 25 percent of the traditionally successful applicants would not have been eligible; however, the age requirement would not have a disproportionately high effect on minorities as it would have eliminated only 18 percent of black applicants. While the research did not discuss whether any recruitment efforts were made to increase the pool of college-educated minority applicants, it is worth noting that nine of the 39 African American applicants did possess baccalaureate degrees.

While it appears, at least in this instance, that a college degree requirement had an impact on race, it also had an impact on the overall applicant pool, which is likely to occur when departments are attempting to improve the quality of their personnel by raising standards. There is little doubt that departments that raise their educational requirements will also need to significantly enhance their recruitment efforts, as other professional organizations have done. For example, in Tulsa (see Inside Policing 14.2), a multicultural recruiting task force was developed, coupled with a strong recruiting effort outside the state. It appears that if strong recruitment efforts are made to attract college educated minorities, a college degree requirement should have little impact on minority hiring.

Another PERF finding, reported in Table 14.5, indicates that the average educational level of female officers was a full year higher (14.6 years compared to 13.6 years) than that of their male colleagues, with almost one-third (30.2 percent) possessing graduate degrees. This extreme difference may exist for at least three reasons: (1) women tended to believe that they must have stronger credentials to compete effectively for police positions; (2) police departments may have been more rigid in their screening of female applicants; and (3) many women entering law reinforcement tended to come from other occupations that required a college degree, such as teaching (Carter and Sapp 1992). Interestingly, any significant movement toward requiring a college degree has significant implications for women in policing.

Table 14.5 Educational Level of Police Officers by Gender

	Male	Female
Mean years	13.6 years	14.6 years
No college	34.8%	24.1%
Some undergraduate work	61.7%	45.7%
Graduate degree	3.3%	30.2%

Source: Adapted from D. L. Carter and A. D. Sapp. 1992. "College Education and Policing: Coming of Age." *FBI Law Enforcement Bulletin*, January: 11.

The preponderance of data indicates that a trend toward higher education exists in policing and appears not to have had the negative impact on minority-officer recruitment that was initially feared. The fact that the proportion of minorities employed by state and local departments is approximately equal to the proportion in the national population is also encouraging. As Carter and Sapp (1992) suggest:

> It appears that a college requirement is not impossible to mandate as evidenced by both the legal precedent and empirical data. . . . A college educated police force that is racially and ethically representative of the community can be achieved. This only serves to make a police department more effective and responsive to community needs. (1992, 11, 13)

As discussed above, those departments that wish to establish higher-education requirements need to develop a sound policy support document. Inside Policing 14.3 shows how the framework for such a policy might look.

Inside Policing 14.3   Developing a Higher-Education Policy for Police Departments

Each department should have a written policy defining college education as a BFOQ as it uniquely relates to the department, regardless of the requirements adopted. The department can then be fully prepared for any questions concerning the validity of any new educational requirements.

Policy development should include input from all levels of the department, particularly the local collective-bargaining organizations. This provision will lead to a common understanding of the rationale for the policy, enhance its acceptance, and expedite its implementation.

Promotional Requirements. If the entry-level educational requirements are raised, then the educational requirements for promotion should also be reviewed. As more highly educated officers enter policing, more highly educated supervisors, managers, and police executives will be needed.

Policy Standards. Educational policies should specify standards, especially that college

---

Inside Policing 14.3   **Developing a Higher-Education Policy for Police Departments (continued)**

credit and degrees be awarded from an accredited college or university. Acceptable credit should be based on a minimum grade average of "C," or 2.0 on a 4.0 scale. Other standards could include the requirement that college credits earned be directly in pursuit of a degree. This rule ensures that the student has a liberal arts background in addition to courses in a major area.

Women and Minority Candidates. Attracting qualified women and minority candidates continues to be a concern for police departments. It is increasingly evident, however, that there is no need to limit entry or promotional educational requirements for these groups so long as innovative and aggressive recruiting programs are in place.

Source: Adapted from D. L. Carter and A. D. Sapp. 1992. "College Education and Policing: Coming of Age," *FBI Law Enforcement Bulletin*, January: 12.

College Education Standards for Employment

If college education is to become an entry-level requirement for policing, it is important that supporting policies also be established. As noted above, it is possible to offset the possible discriminatory effects of a higher-education requirement through an aggressive recruitment strategy (see also Chapter 12). Additionally, of course, it is helpful to have a competitive salary scale, good employment benefits, and high-quality working conditions. It is important to point out that over the past decade, most medium and large police departments have implemented highly competitive salary structures, in line with, and often substantially above, the starting salaries for college graduates in most public- and many private-sector jobs. In addition, health benefits and retirement packages are generally very good.

The PERF study found that most of the departments had developed one or more **educational-incentive policies** to encourage officers to continue their education beyond that required for initial employment. As Table 14.6 indicates, some of these include tuition assistance or reimbursement, incentive pay, shift or day-off adjustments, and permission to attend classes during work hours. Another study of 72 Texas police departments, representing more than half of the police officers licensed in the state (Garner 1998), indicated that 52 departments (72 percent) offered some type of incentive for obtaining a college education. Forty-two reported various forms of tuition reimbursement, while 32 provided higher pay for those with degrees. Other educational incentives offered by numerous departments included the use of vehicles for transportation to classes, time off to attend courses, and scheduling preferences to accommodate the college semester. Various departments used one or more of these incentives.

In the final analysis it appears as though enough evidence (both empirical and experiential) has been established to support a strong argument for a college-degree requirement for entry-level police officers:

1. The benefits provided by a higher education, combined with the increasing complexity of police work, suggest that a college degree should be a requirement for initial police employment.

2. If educational and recruitment policies are appropriately developed, a higher-education requirement should not adversely affect minority recruitment or retention.

Table 14.6 Higher Educational Incentive Policies for Sworn Officers

College Incentive Policy	Number*	Percentage
Tuition assistance or reimbursement	302	62.1
Educational-pay incentive	261	53.7
Adjustments of shifts or days off	207	42.6
Permission for class attendance while on duty	115	23.7
Other programs or policies**	57	11.7
No educational incentives	43	8.8

*Based on sample of 486 departments.
**Includes tuition for POST-approved course only; leaves of absence for college; fellowship and scholarship programs; in-service training programs for college credit. Most agencies have more than one incentive.

Source: Adapted from D. L. Carter and A. D. Sapp, 1992, "College Education and Policing: Coming of Age," *FBI Law Enforcement Bulletin*, January: 13.

Recognizing that there are diverse types of police departments throughout the country, with differing styles of operation, levels of performance, and community needs, it is apparent that some can adapt to a college-degree requirement more readily than others. Consequently, perhaps some type of *graduated timetable* for college requirements—similar to those found in the National Advisory Commission's *Report on Police* (1973)—would be appropriate (the commission recommended that all officers be required to have a baccalaureate degree by 1982). A graduated timetable could again be set up for phasing in first, a two-year degree requirement, and second, a baccalaureate degree for initial selection purposes. At the same time, requirements could be established for supervisory and executive personnel, first at the baccalaureate level, and then, at least for executives, at the master's level. These requirements could also be adjusted to account for different types of agencies; for example, larger agencies serving larger and more diverse populations could have the requirements phased in earlier. The bottom line would ultimately require any officer with general enforcement powers to have a degree, regardless of location or type of agency. Those departments or cities that feel they could not comply with such a requirement could contract with a nearby agency that can meet the requirements. Such an arrangement is not without precedent, as many small and/or rural cities that feel they cannot afford to support their own police departments contract for local police services through their county law-enforcement agency.

The quickest way for a police department to require higher education is for the chief to get squarely behind it, as highlighted in the Arlington and Tulsa departments. This, however, has occurred in only a very small number of departments over the past four decades, and it is clear that something more is needed. It is likely that in order for higher education to become entrenched throughout the field, a serious push will be needed from the federal government, perhaps along the lines of the Justice Department's COPS (Community Oriented Policing Services) program, which has provided funds nationally to promote community policing. With respect to higher education, initial funding could be provided to those departments for adopting college degree requirements and for developing recruitment programs to target educated personnel; for example, through recruitment incentives, use of task forces, broadening the scope of the search (i.e., to college campuses and beyond city limits), and perhaps, working to eliminate residency requirements.

Although some "growing pains" are to be expected, the advantages of such a requirement in today's ever-changing, more highly-educated society, outweigh any potential disadvantages of waiting for additional "evidence" of its importance to accrue (see Inside Policing 14.4). The time has arrived to upgrade American policing and service to the community, through higher-education requirements, moving the occupation closer to a professional status.

Inside Policing 14.4   Support for College-Education Requirement for Entry-Level Police Officers

At least three significant changes support a college degree requirement for initial selection of police.

Organizational Changes. Today's police departments are very different from those that existed when LEAA and LEEP were begun in the 1970s. Many more police officers and managers have college degrees (and advanced degrees), and the police cultural bias against "college cops" has significantly declined. The challenges of community policing require officers to use more discretion in problem solving and decision making. At the same time, officers must be aware of cultural differences in, and sensitivity to the needs of, the community. Research has suggested that successful community policing is dependent on the quality of educated police officers.

Because of these changes, departments can now recruit college-educated officers and provide them with salaries commensurate to other entry-level occupations requiring degrees. Most police departments throughout the country provide incentives to officers to continue their education or to pursue a college degree.

Societal Changes. Today's police officers need to be culturally sensitive and willing to value ethnic differences. Most college degree programs offer courses in such areas as cultural diversity, ethics, and cross-cultural comparisons, and some even require a foreign language. In addition, courses in sociology, psychology, and other human-behavior courses (including criminal justice and criminology) all contribute to a better understanding of the complex society in which we live. Research has demonstrated that officers who are exposed to such an educational experience deal better with diverse community groups.

Police departments must also recognize that as members of the community are becoming more educated, their expectations of police service will also increase. Thus, police departments need to raise their educational requirements in order to represent the populations they serve.

Technological Changes. Today's police officer is faced with more modern technology than ever before. The field notebook has been replaced by the laptop computer. The Internet, World Wide Web, and e-mail have greatly expanded resources and data-collection techniques, and the emphasis on solution-oriented policing has placed greater demands on crime analysis, problem solving, and computer sophistication.

As innovative programs are developed to address crime and disorder, departments must have officers who can evaluate their impact with methodologically sound techniques. Most college-degree programs require coursework (e.g., computer science, research methods, and math and statistics) that is beneficial in today's technologically sophisticated environment.

Source: Adapted from R. Garner, 1998, "Community Policing and Education: The College Connection," *Texas Law Enforcement Management and Administrative Statistics Program,* January: 7–9.

Finally, it is worth noting that even if the above scenario were to develop, including federal funding and the recruitment and hiring of college-educated officers, the question of how to retain such officers would still remain. If policing is ever to become a true profession where higher education is required and respected, ultimately, the traditional paramilitary structure and authoritarian managerial style will need to be significantly altered or abandoned. Police departments will need to be designed and run more like private organizations, where employees are treated more professionally and allowed more decision-making powers, which in turn should lead to higher levels of job satisfaction. The movement toward community policing should, at least theoretically, help promote such changes. But, as we have discovered, departments that have adopted a community-policing approach (at least from their own perspective) have generally not significantly altered their military structures or managerial styles. Such structural changes take many years, if not decades, to accomplish. It is hoped that, in the long run, the movement toward community policing can have an important impact in these areas, and thus lead to an atmosphere where college graduates feel comfortable and can flourish. As Moskos (2003, 8), a former Baltimore City police officer, has observed:

> But too many potentially good police won't join an organization filled with Marine haircuts, snappy salutes and a six-month boot camp. Too few people with four-year degrees and liberal upbringing want a job in a conservative organization with archaic grooming codes. . . .What other civilian profession hides behind a conservative faux-military facade? What other occupation demands that you stand at attention every time a boss enters the room? If police departments treated their employees more like professionals, more professionals would join the police.

Summary

Berkeley Police Chief August Vollmer began a campaign for higher education for police that has continued to the present. Major universities developed programs for police education, despite the resistance of many street officers. Research has indicated that higher education can be job-validated for police entry and that such a requirement should not have an adverse impact on minority recruitment or retention, if appropriate recruitment policies and efforts are developed. To this end, police departments would be wise to develop a written policy defining college education as a BFOQ as it relates to the department.

The Police Corps and the scholarship and recruitment program established under the Crime Control Act of 1994 appear to expand further the importance and availability of higher education to both in-service and preservice students. In general, college education for entry-level police officers can also be supported based on ongoing changes, including organizational, societal, and technological changes. In the final analysis, enough evidence has been established to support the requirement of a college degree for policing. A graduated timetable for development and federal funding for support will most likely be necessary for national recognition and implementation.

Critical Thinking Questions

1. Why were the President's Commission on Law Enforcement and Administration of Justice and the National Advisory Commission on Criminal Justice Standards and Goals important to higher education for police?

2. In your opinion, was LEAA successful? Why or why not?

3. Briefly describe what you believe the impact the Violent Crime Control and Law Enforcement Act of 1994 has had on policing.

4. Briefly describe what you believe to be the important empirical research on the impact of higher education on policing. What areas are in need of further research?

5. In your opinion, can higher education be supported as a BFOQ in policing? State specific reasons why or why not.

6. Do you think that the field of policing can ever be regarded as a "profession" if higher-educational requirements are not ultimately adopted? Give several specific reasons why or why not.

7. If you were a police chief, would you attempt to require higher education for entry-level positions or for promotion? Discuss your reasons for both positions.

References

American Bar Association. 1973. *Standards Relating to the Urban Police Function.* New York: author.

Arnold v. Ballard 390 F. Supp. (N.D. Ohio 1975).

Baro, A. L. and Burlingame, D. (1999). "Law Enforcement and Higher Education: Is There an Impasse?" *Journal of Criminal Justice Education* 10(1): 57–73.

Bowman, T. 2002. "Educate to Elevate." *Community Links,* August, 11–13.

Caiden, G. E. 1977. *Police Revitalization.* Lexington, MA: D. C. Heath.

Carlan, P. E. and Byxbe, F. R. 2000. "The Promise of Humanistic Policing: Is Higher Education Living up to Societal Expectation?" *American Journal of Criminal Justice* 24(2): 235–245.

Carte, G. E. 1973. "August Vollmer and the Origins of Police Professionalism." *Journal of Police Science and Administration* 1: 274–281.

Carter, D. L. and Sapp, A. D. 1989. "The Effect of Higher Education on Police Liability: Implications for Police Personnel Policy." *American Journal of Police* 8: 153–166.

——. 1990b. "Higher Education as a Policy Alternative to Reduce Police Liability." *Police Liability Review* 2: 1–3.

——. 1992. "College Education and Policing: Coming of Age." *FBI Law Enforcement Bulletin,* January: 8–14.

Carter, D. L., Sapp, A. D., and Stephens, D. W. 1988. "Higher Education as a Bona Fide Occupational Qualification (BFOQ) for Police: A Blueprint." *American Journal of Police* 7: 1–27.

——. 1989. *The State of Police Education: Policy Direction for the 21st Century.* Washington, D.C.: Police Executive Research Forum.

Cascio, W. F. 1977. "Formal Education and Police Officer Performance." *Journal of Police Science and Administration* 5: 89–96.

Castro v. Beecher, 459 F.2d 725 (lst Cir. 1972).

Cohen, B. and Chaiken, J. M. 1972. *Police Background Characteristics and Performance.* New York: Rand Institute.

Dalley, A. F. 1975. "University and NonUniversity Graduated Policemen: A Study of Police Attitudes." *Journal of Police Science and Administration* 3: 458–468.

Davis v. City of Dallas, 777 F.2d 205 (5th Cir. 1985).

Dantzker, M. L. 1998. "Police Education and Job Satisfaction: Educational Incentives and Recruit Educational Requirements." *Police Forum* 8 (3): 1–4.

Decker, L. K. and Huckabee, R. G. 2002. "Raising the Age and Education Requirements for Police Officers: Will Too Many Women and Minority Candidates Be Excluded?" *Policing* 25: 789–801.

Deutsch, A. 1955. *The Trouble With Cops.* New York: Crown Publishers.

"Dissecting the Crime Bill: New Era for Law Enforcement and Higher Education." 1994. *Law Enforcement News* October 15: 1, 7.

Finnegan, J. C. 1976. "A Study of Relationships Between College Education and Police Performance in Baltimore, Maryland." *The Police Chief* 34: 60–62.

"For Florida Police, Higher Education Means Lower Risk of Disciplinary Action." 2002. *Law Enforcement News* October 31: 1, 10.

Fyfe, J. J. 1988. "Police Use of Deadly Force: Research and Reform." *Justice Quarterly* 5: 165–205.

Garner, R. 1998. "Community Policing and Education: The College Connection." *Texas Law Enforcement Management and Administrative Statistics Program Bulletin* January.

Goldstein, H. 1977. *Policing a Free Society.* Cambridge, MA: Ballinger.

Griffin, G. R., Dunbar, R. L. M., and McGill, M. E. 1978. "Factors Associated With Job Satisfaction Among Police Personnel. " *Journal of Police Science and Administration* 6: 77–85.

Griggs v. Duke Power Co. 401 U.S. 432. 1971.

Guller, I. B. 1972. "Higher Education and Policemen: Attitudinal Differences Between Freshman and Senior Police College Students." *Journal of Criminal Law, Criminology, and Police Science* 63: 396–401.

Hickman, M. J. and Reaves, B. A. 2003a. *Local Police Departments, 2000.* Washington, DC: Bureau of Justice Statistics.

——. 2003b. *Sheriffs' Offices, 2000.* Washington, DC: Bureau of Justice Statistics.

Kakar, S. 1998. "Self-Evaluation of Police Performance: An Analysis of the Relationship Between Police Officers' Education Level and Job Performance." *Policing: An International Journal of Police Strategies and Management* 21: 632–647.

Korbetz, R. W. 1975. *Law Enforcement and Criminal Justice Education Directory, 1975–1976.* Gaithersburg, MD: International Association of Chiefs of Police.

Krimmel, J. T. 1996. "The Performance of College-Educated Police: A Study of Self-Rated Police Performance Measures." *American Journal of Police* 15: 85–96.

Levy, R. J. 1967. "Predicting Police Failures." *Journal of Criminal Law, Criminology, and Police Science* 58: 265–276.

Lersch, K. M. and Kunzman, L. L. 2001. "Misconduct Allegations and Higher Education in a Southern Sheriff's Department." *American Journal of Criminal Justice* 25(2): 161–172.

Meese, E. 1993. "Community Policing and the Police Officer." *Perspectives on Policing* 15, National Institute of Justice and Harvard University, Washington, DC.

"Men and Women of Letters: No BS: Tulsa PD Rookies to Need Four-Year Degrees." 1997. *Law Enforcement News* November 30: 1.

Miller, J. and Fry, L. 1976. "Reexamining Assumptions About Education and Professionalism in Law Enforcement." *Journal of Police Science and Administration* 4: 187–196.

Miller, J. and Fry, L. J. 1978. "Some Evidence on the Impact of Higher Education for Law Enforcement Personnel." *The Police Chief* 45: 30–33.

Moskos, P. 2003. "Old-School Cops in a New-School World." *Law Enforcement News* Oct. 15/31: 8.

Mottaz, C. 1983. "Alienation Among Police Officers." *Journal of Police Science and Administration* 11: 23–30.

National Advisory Commission on Criminal Justice Standards and Goals (1973). *Report on Police*. Washington, DC: U.S. Government Printing Office.

Nees, H. 2003. "Education and Criminal Justice Employees in Colorado." *Police Forum* 1: 5–9.

Niederhoffer, A. 1967. *Behind the Shield: The Police in Urban Society*. Garden City, NY: Doubleday.

Parker, L. Jr., Donnelly, J., Gerwitz, J., Marcus, J., and Kowalewski, V. 1976. "Higher Education: Its Impact on Police Attitudes." *The Police Chief* 43: 33–35.

Police Executive Research Forum. 1989. *A Resolution of the Membership of the Police Executive Research Forum*. Washington, DC: PERF.

Polk, E. and Armstrong, D. A. 2001. "Higher Education and Law Enforcement Career Paths: Is the Road to Success Paved by Degree?" *Journal of Criminal Justice Education* 12(1): 77–99.

Pope, C. E. 1987. "Criminal Justice Education: Academic and Professional Orientations." In R. Muraskin (ed.), *The Future of Criminal Justice Education*, Brookeville, NY: Long Island University.

President's Commission on Law Enforcement and Administration of Justice 1967. *The in a Free Society*. Washington, DC: U.S. Government Printing Office.

Regoli, R. M. 1976. "The Effects of College Education on the Maintenance of Police Cynicism." *Journal of Police Science and Administration* 4: 340–345.

Roberg, R. R. 1978. "An Analysis of the Relationships Among Higher Education, Belief Systems, and Job Performance of Patrol Officers." *Journal of Police Science and Administration* 6: 336–344.

Roberg, R. R. and Laramy, J. E. 1980. "An Empirical Assessment of the Criteria Utilized for Promoting Police Personnel: A Secondary Analysis." *Journal of Police Science and Administration* 8: 183–187.

Sanders, B., Hughes, T., and Langworthy, R. 1995. "Police Officer Recruitment and Selection: A Survey of Major Departments in the U.S." *Police Forum*. Richmond, KY: Academy of Criminal Justice Sciences.

Sanderson, B. B. 1977. "Police Officers: The Relationship of College Education to Job Performance." *The Police Chief* 44: 62–63.

Saunders, C. B. 1970. *Upgrading the American Police*. Washington, D.C.: The Brookings Institution.

Sherman, L. W. and the National Advisory Commission on Higher Education for Police Officers. 1978. *The Quality of Police Education*. San Francisco: Josey-Bass.

Sherwood, C. W. 2000. "Job Design, Community Policing, and Higher Education: A Tale of Two Cities." *Police Quarterly*, 3 (2), 191–212.

Skogan, W. 1994. "The Impact of Community Policing on Neighborhood Residents: A Cross-Site Analysis." In D. Rosenbaum (ed.), *The Challenge of Community Policing: Testing the Promises* pp. 167–181. Thousand Oaks, CA: Sage.

Smith, A. B., Locke, B., and Fenster, A. 1970. "Authoritarianism in Policemen Who Are College Graduates and Noncollege Graduates." *Journal of Criminal Law, Criminology, and Police Science* 61: 313–315.

Smith, A. B., Locke, B., and Walker, W. F. 1968. "Authoritarianism in Police College Students and Nonpolice College Students." *Journal of Criminal Law, Criminology, and Police Science* 59: 440–443.

Smith, S. M. and Aamodt, M. G. 1997. "The Relationship Between Education, Experience, and Police Performance." *Journal of Police and Criminal Psychology* 12: 7–14.

Stoddard, K. B. 1973. "Characteristics of Policemen of a County Sheriff's Office." In J. R. Snibbe and H. M. Snibbe (eds.), *The Urban Policemen in Transition*, pp. 281–297. Springfield, IL: C. Thomas.

"Surprise! The Police Corps Is Back—Not That It Ever Left." 1997. *Law Enforcement News* January 31: 1, 10.

"Survey Says Big-City Chiefs are Better-Educated Outsiders." 1998. *Law Enforcement News* April 30: 7.

Terrill, W. and Mastrofski, S. D. 2002. "Situational and Officer-Based Determinants of Police Coercion." *Justice Quarterly* 19(2): 215–248.

Terry, W. C. 1980. "Criminal Justice Faculty and Criminal Justice Students." *Journal of Criminal Justice* 8: 287–298.

Trojanowicz, R. C. and Nicholson, T. 1976. "A Comparison of Behavioral Styles of College Graduate Police Officers v. Noncollege-Going Police Officers." *The Police Chief* 43: 57–58.

Truxillo, D. M., Bennett, S. R., and Collins, M. L. 1998. "College Education and Police Job Performance: A Ten-Year Study." *Public Personnel Management* 27(2): 269–280.

Tyler, T. 1990. *Why People Obey the Law.* New Haven, CT: Yale University Press.

Tyre, M. and Braunstein, S. 1992. "Higher Education and Ethical Policing." *FBI Law Enforcement Bulletin* June: 6–10.

U.S. Department of Justice. 1994. *The Violent Crime Control and Law Enforcement Act of 1994.* Washington, DC: U.S. Government Printing Office.

Weiner, N. L. 1976. "The Educated Policeman." *Journal of Police Science and Administration* 4: 450–457.

Weirman, C. L. 1978. "Variances of Ability Measurement Scores Obtained by College and NonCollege Educated Troopers." *The Police Chief* 45: 34–36.

Whetstone, T. S. (2000). "Getting Stripes: Educational Achievement and Study Strategy Used by Sergeant Promotional Candidates." *American Journal of Criminal Justice* 24: 247–257.

Wilson, H. (1999). "Post-Secondary Education of the Police Officer and Its Effect on the Frequency of Citizen Complaints." *Journal of California Law Enforcement* 33: 3–10.

Suggested Websites for Further Study

Berkeley Police Department
http://www.BerkeleyPD.org/
Michigan State University, School of Criminal Justice
http://www.cj.msu.edu/
San Jose State University, Administration of Justice
http://www.sjsu.edu/depts/casa/aj/index.html
University of California—Berkeley
http://www.berkeley.edu/
Office of Community-Oriented Policing Services
http://www.usdoj.gov/cops/
Police Executive Research Forum
http://www.policeforum.org
National Archive of Criminal Justice Data
http://www.icpsr.umich.edu/NACJD/
Sourcebook of Criminal Justice Statistics
http://www.albany.edu/sourcebook/
Canadian Police College
http://www.cpc.gc.ca/home_e.htm
Police Association for College Education (PACE)
http://www.police-association.org/ ✦

## Chapter 15

Contemporary and Emerging Issues

Chapter Outline

Key Terms

baby boom	information technology
cyber crime	in-migration
deinstitutionalization	interoperability
eyewitness identification	migration
federalization	militarization
geographic information systems	poverty rate
globalization	privatization
global positioning systems	racial profiling
homeland security	terrorism
immigration	unemployment rate
income inequality	

Predicting the future is a perilous task. The soothsayer is inevitably wrong on key points and may be embarrassed if the future fluctuates wildly from expectations. There is tremendous variety in the police forces of the United States with respect to size, structure, and overall quality; which will be trendsetters for the future remains to be seen. Further, the importance of often-uncontrollable environmental influences cannot be overestimated. Something unexpected always occurs to undermine even the most reasonable forecasts, reminding us that the future will be predictable in the same way as the past—in retrospect.

Thoughtful observers have noted that police in the United States are in the midst of profound changes. Within police departments, shifts in role, function, technology, and philosophy are important trends. Outside departments, changes in the character of those being policed, along with changes in government, the academic world, the criminal world, and technology may lead to changes even more fundamental and far-reaching than those seen in the last 25 years. There are so many things going on affecting the American police that trying to make sense of its "present" is already difficult; delineating its "future" is virtually impossible. Nevertheless, this chapter will try to identify trends in present-day society and policing that indicate directions the police might take in the future.

A central argument of this chapter is that to understand the police and their future, one must look at the environments in which they work and the way those environments affect them—after all, this is a book about police *and society*. These environments, which themselves are changing, can lead to many different possibilities for the police. What the future holds for policing will say as much about Americans as a people as about the police.

Police departments are *institutionalized organizations*—that is, they are responsible for acting on behalf of the values a society holds dear. Unlike economic organizations (businesses), which prosper through their own technical efficiency, police organizations prosper by successfully supporting and reproducing society's sense of right and wrong. To do this, they must look beyond themselves to the groups that make up society. Because they serve society, they must respond to pressures from those groups.

Who are these groups? Police departments have to deal with criminals and provide assistance to citizens. They also must address the concerns of mayors, city councils, organizations such as Mothers Against Drunk Driving (MADD), business groups, and police unions. They have to deal with prosecutors and the courts, and they must always be sensitive to changes in the law. They have to deal with hostile relations between different ethnic groups. They have to contend with rebellious youth and youth gangs. They always have to keep an eye on the media, which can support or embarrass the police with printed or televised news. Increasingly, they are linking with the military to deal with such problems as drug smuggling and international terrorism. In short, the police have to deal with an environment of great complexity. The police have the ethical responsibility to help all these groups get along, to help solve their problems, and to intervene when citizens get into conflicts or hurt one another.

In addition, the police have to respond to technological changes. Consider the ways technology has changed the police over the past century. Installing a two-way radio in a police car in the first third of the twentieth century profoundly changed the delivery of police service. The linkage of these two technologies (car and radio) with the telephone made it possible for citizens to call the station house and for the station house to dispatch a police car. This style of patrol, based on random preventive patrol and rapid response, remains the dominant style today. It would have been an unlikely prediction 100 years ago.

Changes in American Society

One set of factors that is likely to influence the future of policing involves changes in society. This section reviews some ongoing demographic, economic, and geographic changes in American society that seem likely to affect policing (also see Table 15.1 for a summary of demographic changes in the United States during the twentieth century).

Table 15.1 Demographic Changes in the United States During the Twentieth Century

- The U.S. population more than tripled from 76 million people in 1900 to 281 million people in 2000. The growth of 32.7 million people in the 1990s represented the largest numerical increase of any decade in U.S. history.

- The U.S. population grew increasingly metropolitan each decade, from 28 percent in 1910 to 80 percent in 2000. Suburbs rather than centralized cities accounted for most of the metropolitan growth. By 2000, half of the U.S. population lived in suburban areas.

- The population of the West grew faster than the population in each of the other three regions of the country in every decade of the twentieth century.

- The Northeast was the most densely populated region and had the highest percentage of its population living in metropolitan areas throughout the century.

- At the beginning of the century, half of the U.S. population was less than 22.9 years old. At the century's end, half of the population was more than 35.3 years old, the country's highest median age ever.

- Children under age 5 represented the largest 5-year age group in 1900 and again in 1950. By 2000, the largest 5-year age groups were people ages 35 to 39 and 40 to 44, large segments of the baby-boom generation.

- The United States' gender composition shifted from a majority male population to a majority female population around mid century.

- From 1980 to 2000, the Hispanic population more than doubled.

- By the end of the century, three states—California, Hawaii, and New Mexico—and the District of Columbia—had majority "minority" populations (including Hispanics).

Table 15.1 Demographic Changes in the U.S. During the 20th Century (continued)

- Prior to 1950, over half of all occupied housing units were rented. By 1950, home ownership became more prevalent than renting.

- In 1900, the most common household contained seven or more people; from 1940 to 2000, it contained two people.

- In 1900, nearly half of the U.S. population lived in households of six or more people; by 2000, more than half lived in households of one, two, or three people.

- Between 1950 and 2000, married couple households declined from more than three-fourths of all households (78 percent) to just over one-half (52 percent).

Source: U.S. Census Bureau, *Demographic Trends in the 20th Century* (Washington, DC: author, 2002). Available at <http://www.census.gov/prod/2002pubs/censr-4.pdf>.

The Aging Population

The United States has a graying population. The past century has seen the average lifespan greatly increase, from under 50 years in 1900 to close to 80 years today (see Figure 15.1). In 1900, those over 65 years old—considered elderly—constituted 4 percent of the population; today this group accounts for 13 percent of the population (Federal Interagency Forum on Aging-Related Statistics 2003). The over-65 group numbered less than 5 million in 1900, but will grow to about 40 million in 2010 and 80 million in 2050 (see Figure 15.2).

The new elderly pose unique dilemmas for criminal justice. First, among those over 85, three-fourths of the men are still married, but fewer than four of 10 women are (Roberts 1994). Why? Men die younger than women, leaving many widows. This longevity does not mean that the quality of life for surviving women is high. On the contrary, they are one of the populations most highly vulnerable to victimization. Also, one in five of those over 85 (both genders) are institutionalized. As this institutionalized population dramatically increases over the coming decades, there are likely to be sharp increases in white-collar crime in the health-care industry against the elderly.

Second, the elderly, usually dependent on fixed budgets, tend to mobilize in order to vote against tax increases to support social infrastructure. They particularly tend to oppose property tax increases needed to support school budgets. The growing elderly population will likely strain the Social Security System and Medicaid as well as the resources of their adult-age children. The grandchildren of these elderly, then, may encounter poorer schools and recreational opportunities, as well as over-burdened parents. If these conditions materialize, one might anticipate increases in juvenile crime to accompany the growing elderly population.

The post-World War II period has been characterized as the **baby boom** for the large numbers of children born to returning veterans. Yet this population's growth has

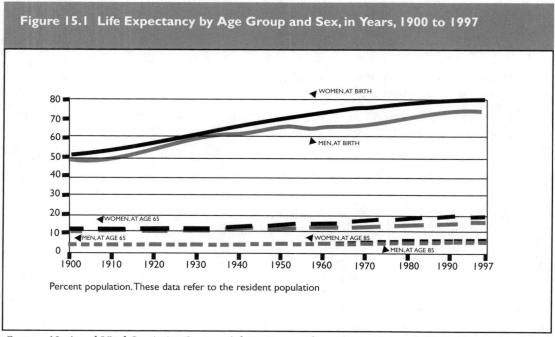

Figure 15.1 Life Expectancy by Age Group and Sex, in Years, 1900 to 1997

Source: National Vital Statistics System (<http://www.efmoody.com/estate/lifeexpectancy.html>).

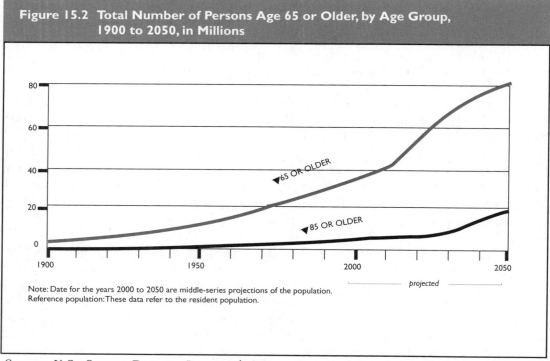

Figure 15.2 Total Number of Persons Age 65 or Older, by Age Group, 1900 to 2050, in Millions

Source: U.S. Census Bureau, *Decennial Census Data and Population Projections* (<http://www.agingstats.gov/chartbook2000/population.html>).

not continued but has instead reversed. Baby boomers were the first population in U.S. history not to replace itself in population numbers. This phenomenon has been called the *baby bust*. The slowed growth in the numbers of young people in the 1990s was a symptom of the baby bust; at the end of the twentieth century, growth rates reached only replacement levels. The numbers of young, unlike the numbers of elderly, are not expected to increase over the coming decades.

The most crime-prone population is widely regarded by criminologists to be those between the ages of 18 and 24. Judging by population forecasts, this population will not increase at high rates for many years. The number of Americans in the 18–24 age group is not expected to exceed the 1980 level for at least 50 years (Roberts 1994).

Diversity

The United States is in the midst of a dramatic population transformation. Migration from abroad, large-scale internal migration, and the way in which these migration patterns are distributed across the landscape will profoundly change the face of the U.S. population.

Consider the changing pattern of foreign migration into the country. In the 1980s, half as many people emigrated from Europe to the United States as in the 1960s; more than five times as many came from Asia, twice as many from Mexico, the Caribbean, and Central America, and nearly four times as many from Africa. Even these groupings mask important regional and local differences. The 1990 census counted 179 ancestry groupings for the Latino category alone. In the 1990s, the number of Asians more than doubled. The long-term implications are clear. By the middle of the twenty-first century, no racial or ethnic group will constitute a majority in the United States (Roberts 1994).

Growth and change involve the relocation of many kinds of people. People tend to think of migration in terms of foreign immigration. Yet this is a proportionally small aspect of overall migration. Blue-collar workers in search of jobs tend to migrate at a much higher rate than their white-collar counterparts. City dwellers in search of a better lifestyle move to the rural hinterland or to the *ex-urbs*, the semirural areas just beyond a city's suburbs. This region is increasingly popular to well-off members of the middle and working classes, who commute to the city to work. Religious groups seek divine meaning though rural settlement. All these are groups on the move. All of them carry the potential for conflicts that the police will have to deal with.

Dynamic changes in ethnicity will confront Americans in the twenty-first century. Diversity is already remarkable in some areas. In Los Angeles, for example, more than 80 distinct languages are spoken (Kaplan 1998). These changes may profoundly affect police services. Consider Asians. In Minnesota, a state seemingly distant from the impact of migration, Asians tripled in number from 1980 to 1990, then almost doubled again by 2000, to a total of almost 145,000 residents (U.S. Census Bureau 2003a). Their in-migration creates unique police problems. The prone-out position many officers use to effect an arrest, for example, is the same position Vietnamese police use when they execute citizens. Vietnamese are sometimes terrified when "proned-out" and thus are more likely to run from the police (Taft 1991). How can police deal with public-order problems if they do not even share a common language with the citizens they serve? Language is, after all, the most fundamental element of culture, from which common ideas of order arise.

As the United States becomes a truly international society, there is a great demand for police to help people work together, to mediate ethnic frictions, and to find common ground. History books sometimes portray U.S. society as a *melting pot,* where different kinds of people blend together in harmony. Yet, there is little evidence that Americans "melt together," or that we ever have, for that matter. On the contrary, some scholars warn that increased contact among different kinds of peoples contributes to increased group identity, particularly group religious identity (Huntington 1996).

Religious differences are an aspect of cultural differences. Demographic changes consequently are closely tied to religion. Religion has the capacity to become the basis of cultural friction across the United States, as was discovered in the aftermath of September 11, 2001, when some Americans turned their anger toward followers of Islam, as well as toward people of Middle Eastern descent. In the world of tomorrow, police will increasingly take on the responsibility of managing conflicts among religious groups, finding common order among them, and facilitating their coexistence.

Economics

Economic conditions affect crime, disorder, and the demand for police services. Economics change over time, and it is risky to predict them, as stock market investors know quite well. Certainly, one long-term trend in the nature of employment has been from hunting and gathering to farming to manufacturing jobs to service jobs and on toward the information-based economy. In 2000, about 75 percent of American workers were in management, professional, service, sales, or related jobs, whereas only about 25 percent were in construction, transportation, manufacturing, farming, and related jobs (U.S. Census Bureau 2003b). Employment today is more likely to be indoors, in an office, and white-collar than in the past.

Employment markets are much more global today than in the past, as textile workers, steel workers, and others have learned the hard way. The promotion of free trade over the last decade, as exemplified by NAFTA (the North American Free Trade Agreement), has created more opportunities for companies to move part, or all, of their operations to countries with lower labor costs, weaker environmental protections, less concern for workplace safety, and so forth. Until recently, this trend has mostly affected blue-collar employment and has helped account for the decline in manufacturing jobs in the United States. Currently, though, the same forces are also starting to affect white-collar and creative employment (Florida 2004). If these types of jobs, the very ones expected to take up the slack from declining manufacturing, also go "offshore," then the United States may face some serious unemployment challenges in the future.

Another big economic change has been in the participation of women in employment. In 2000, 58 percent of women aged 16 years and older were in the labor force (U.S. Census Bureau 2003c). By comparison, in 1900 less than 20 percent of adult women were in the labor force (Infoplease 2003). This has changed the characteristics of the workforce that the police encounter, helped empower women economically, and affected whether parents are present or absent from home with their children after school and at other times.

> Seven and a half million children in the United States between the ages of 5 and 14 are latch-key kids, according to the National Institute on Out-of-School-Time. Research confirms that kids are less likely to get into trouble when a responsible adult is watching them. In a study published by the American Academy of Pediatrics, researchers found that eighth graders who are unsupervised more than 10 hours a week are about 10 percent more likely to try marijuana, and twice as likely to smoke cigarettes or drink alcohol, as eighth-graders who are unsupervised 0 hours per week. (National Youth Anti-Drug Media Campaign 2003)

The **unemployment rate,** which is measured as the percentage of adults seeking work who are not successful in gaining employment, is one of the most important measures of economic well-being. Since 1948, the monthly unemployment rate in the United States has varied between 2.5 percent (in May and June, 1953) and 10.8 percent (in November and December, 1982). In recent years, the U.S. unemployment rate has generally ranged between 4 percent and 6 percent (U.S. Bureau of Labor Statistics 2004). This is considered to be a low rate of unemployment, since some degree of joblessness is inevitable in a dynamic economy.

This unemployment rate can be deceiving, though. In December 2003, for example, the official unemployment rate was 5.7 percent. If marginally attached workers are included (those who are not working and are not actively looking for a job, but say they want one and have had one within the past year), however, the rate goes up to 6.7 percent. Then, if workers who have only part-time employment, but would like full-time jobs, are included, the "real" unemployment rate climbs to 9.9 percent as of December 2003 (U.S. Bureau of Labor Statistics 2003). In other words, one out of every 10 adult Americans is either unemployed or employed for fewer hours than they would prefer.

Another important economic measure is the **poverty rate.** In 2002, 9.6 percent of families in the United States had incomes below the poverty level, up from 8.7 percent in 2000. The family poverty rate was 12.3 percent in 1993, but 18.5 percent in 1959. Similarly, 12.1 percent of individuals fell below the poverty level in 2002, up from 11.3 percent in 2000, but down from 22.4 percent in 1959. So the long-term trends have clearly been positive, with ups and downs and a worrisome recent increase in poverty since 2000 (U.S. Census Bureau 2003c).

Yet another key economic measure is **income inequality,** which indicates how much range there is between low-income and high-income individuals or families. In the United States, income inequality decreased from 1947 to 1968, but it has been increasing since 1968 (Weinberg 1996). In other words, since 1968 the rich have been getting richer. How much of a problem this represents is a matter of opinion, of course. Democrats and liberals tend to see income inequality as a serious social and economic problem, and generally push for income redistribution remedies, such as progressive income, estate, and inheritance taxes, and higher unemployment and welfare payments. Republicans and conservatives, on the other hand, do not necessarily regard income inequality as a problem, seeing it instead as a natural consequence of capitalism (market forces) and differences in peoples' abilities and willingness to work hard.

In sum, the U.S. economy has thrived for several decades, and Americans are better off economically than most other people in the world. However, long-term trends in income inequality and short-term trends in unemployment and the poverty rate are worrisome. Also, globalization, the changing nature of jobs, and the much greater participation of women in the workforce all have ripple effects for social relations, families, and other aspects of modern society. Collectively, these are likely to affect the nature of crime, disorder, and the demand for police services in the future, albeit in unpredictable ways.

Migration and Geographic Variation

Americans are becoming older and more diverse, and they face a challenging economic situation. One additional factor to consider is population **migration** and its result—large demographic variations among different states and regions. For example, Figure 15.3 shows the concentration of elderly residents in different states. The high level of over-65 residents in Florida (17.6 percent of all citizens, compared to the national average of 12.4 percent) is not much of a surprise, given that state's reputation as a retirement haven. Also not surprising is the state with the lowest proportion of over-65 residents—Alaska, with only 5.7 percent. But one might expect other warm-weather states such as Texas (9.9 percent) and California (10.6 percent) to have high levels of elderly, yet they do not. This is probably due to higher levels of **in-migration** (from other states) and **immigration** (from other countries) of younger as well as older persons into Texas and California.

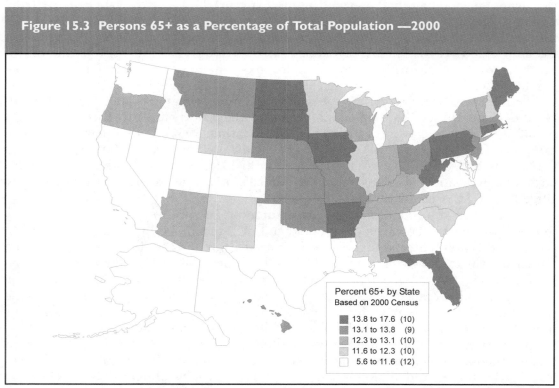

Figure 15.3 Persons 65+ as a Percentage of Total Population —2000

Percent 65+ by State
Based on 2000 Census

■ 13.8 to 17.6 (10)
■ 13.1 to 13.8   (9)
▨ 12.3 to 13.1 (10)
▨ 11.6 to 12.3 (10)
□ 5.6 to 11.6 (12)

Source: Based on Census 2000 Data from the U.S. Bureau of the Census as presented in *A Profile of Older Americans: 2002* (Administration on Aging, U.S. Department of Health and Human Services), available at <http://www.aoa.gov/prof/Statistics/profile/2002profile.doc>.

Migration patterns within the United States lead to differences in the proportion of the population living in a state that was born in that state (see Figure 15.4). The states with the highest levels of "native-born" residents (born within the state) are Louisiana, Pennsylvania, and Michigan. The states with the lowest levels of residents born in the state are Nevada, Florida, and Arizona. These latter states are among the most transient in the country, and perhaps not coincidentally, all have higher-than-average reported crime rates, with Arizona's the highest in the United States (Federal Bureau of Investigation 2003).

Figure 15.4 Population Born in State of Residence: 2000

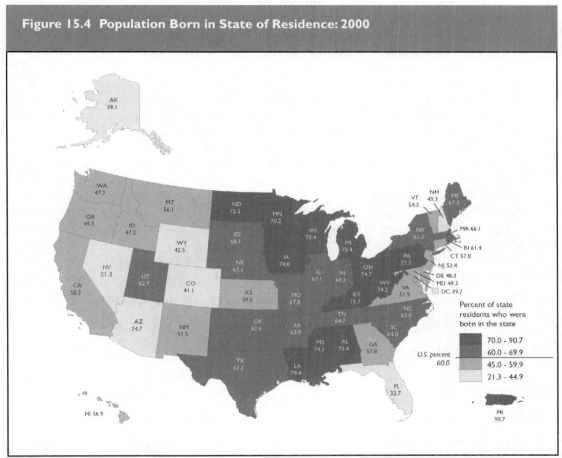

Source: U.S. Census Bureau 2003, *Geographic Mobility: 1995 to 2000* (Washington, D.C.: author, 2002), available at <http://www.census.gov/prod/2003pubs/c2kbr-28.pdf>.

One of the more dramatic demographic changes has been in the rural areas of America. In the nineteenth and twentieth centuries, population became heavily concentrated in metropolitan regions, as farm people moved to the cities to find work. This trend has changed in the last 20 years, as in-migration into cities has balanced and sometimes been overshadowed by out-migration. Growth has dispersed from the cities to outlying regions. Decentralization has given rise to edge cities, strip cities, ex-urbs, and rural sprawl. This centrifugal trend is characteristic of growth at the beginning of the twenty-first century. The states recording the fastest growth in rural areas are Nevada, Alaska, and Idaho. As new people arrive, the rural areas tend to lose many of their traditional elements.

The idea of rural communities conjures two related ideas for most people. First, we imagine small towns with a main street, a town square, and farmland or woodland on the outskirts. Second, we think of old-fashioned farm folk, sharing common customs and a common identity, rooted in American traditions. Today, both these images are rapidly disappearing from America's rural landscapes, as they are transformed into ex-urbs inhabited by working commuters, retired people, and others seeking to escape big-city pressures.

Weisheit and Kernes (1997) identified several changes in rural areas. One is substantial growth in service industries. Another is that satellite communications have opened rural areas to many occupations that in the past were only practical in the cities. A third is that companies are drawn to rural areas by lower crime, lower taxes, lower wages, and a more peaceful lifestyle. There are also "modern cowboys," who include industrial engineers, shopping-center planners, software designers, and others. They can live and work any place and are linked by fiber-optic cables and modems (Margolis 1993).

These changes herald new directions in the way rural police do their work. Increasingly, they are developing ways to deal with their new, not-so-rural residents. Drug couriers are using rural areas as principal routes (Weisheit, Falcone, and Wells 1996). Rural police increasingly use citizen surveys to assess the opinions of their constituencies (McGarrell, Benitez, and Gutierrez 2003). Departments are confronting increasing problems with extremist groups (Corcoran 1990). Order-maintenance problems are expanding, requiring a new breed of rural officer, one trained in problem-solving techniques and skilled in modern technologies. Weisheit and Kernes (2003) envision several changes in rural policing to cope with these changes:

- The most remote areas will see the rise of live interactive "video justice."

- Technology will play an important role in rural crime prevention.

- Improvements in automobiles and highways will be particularly important for rural police.

- There will be dramatic improvements in police communications.

- Technology will play an important role in training rural police.

Inside Policing 15.1 discusses one new phenomenon in rural policing—the need for SWAT teams. It seems increasingly likely that the Mayberry RFD model of rural policing, in which Andy and Barney handle whatever comes their way with old-fashioned common sense, and at most, one or two bullets in their pockets, is destined to give way to a more high-tech, legalistic, and professionalized style of small-town and rural policing, with few characteristics that distinguish it from urban and suburban policing.

Modern Problems

Besides the kinds of social and demographic changes described above, it is likely that the specific problems facing the police will change over time. These are quite difficult to forecast, so in this section we simply discuss four problems that exist today but are not

Inside Policing 15.1   SWAT in Small-Town America

Rainbow City is a small community of less than 20,000 people, policed by a force of 19 officers. Only two or three cars are fielded per shift. Unlike many small towns, the department had a small tactical team, but the team was equipped only with handguns and shotguns. A Rainbow City detective, Gary Endrekin, was working an overtime patrol shift when Chris McCurley, the head of the Etowah County Drug Task Force, asked Endrekin to be part of a warrants service the following day. McCurley had personally worked up the case on Ezra George Peterson, the suspect and a 50-year-old probationer, and did not expect any problems.

Officers went to Peterson's house; Detective Endrekin and another officer approached the back while McCurley and others knocked on the front door. They were initially met with silence. When they tried to force entry, they encountered every officer's worst nightmare—a well-armed suspect opening up with an AK-47 assault rifle.

"I was around back with another officer and I heard the door crash in," Endrekin said. "I heard the sound of a high-powered rifle and it sounded like it was fully auto. I ran around to the front and was hit in the legs. Endrekin crawled behind a van on the property, but the suspect seemed specifically to target the wounded detective. He just kept shooting, ricocheting the shots off the ground," said Endrekin.

Without warning, the suspect came out of the house, moving directly toward Endrekin. "He was yelling, 'I'm going to finish you, you son-of-a-bitch'." The experienced detective thought his life was over until his partner, Sergeant Tommy Watts, shot the suspect several times with a shotgun. The suspect went down, but he was not seriously injured because he was wearing body armor.

When the smoke cleared, the suspect had fired more than 200 rounds. Chris McCurley was dead. Gary Entrekin's legs were so badly torn up by the AK-47 rounds that he spent more than two months in the hospital and ultimately had to have one leg amputated. After this tragic incident, Rainbow City purchased H&K MP-5s and Colt AR-15s. The department also provided training with the weapons and upgraded the capabilities of its tactical team.

Should small towns have SWAT teams? Or is a SWAT team an unnecessary move toward militarization, as some critics claim? In Handcock County, Mississippi, Major Matt Karl is the commander of the Special Operations division, a joint-department, special-weapons team. About three years ago, he became concerned that the law enforcement departments in his area did not have the ability to respond properly to a tactical incident. Karl took the initiative to contact managers in two small, adjacent departments, Waveland and Bay St. Louis, and developed a plan for a multi-department tactical team. Three years later, the team consisted of 26 officers, who handled any situation beyond the capabilities of patrol officers. The unit even assisted an adjacent county that did not have a tactical team after a barricaded suspect held the local police at bay for hours.

Source: Adapted from D. Stockton. 1998. "SWAT's Small-Town Question: How Prepared Are You?" *The Law Enforcement Magazine* 22 (4), 20–24.

likely to disappear any time soon. Two of these are chronic problems rooted in police work itself—racial profiling and eyewitness identification. The other two are problems in the community that police must deal with—persons with mental illness and cyber crime.

Racial Profiling

Racial profiling, or "driving while black," emerged in the 1990s as perhaps the most serious and sensitive issue facing police departments in the United States (Buerger and Farrell 2002). It was the subject of lawsuits, civil rights investigations, and consent decrees. It was discussed and debated in the U.S. Congress and in the 2000 presidential election. Many states mandated new police policies and data collection systems, and even more local communities did so. Only the events of September 11, 2001, deflected attention away from racial profiling, and when the issue reemerged, it was focused more on the profiling of potential terrorists and the effects this might have on the rights of Middle Eastern and Moslem persons.

Two aspects of the racial-profiling phenomenon merit its identification as one of the most important contemporary issues in American policing, despite its lower profile immediately following the terrorist attacks against the United States. One is that it underscores the continued salience of race for policing. Given the emphasis on community policing throughout the 1980s and 1990s, with its focus on community engagement and the improvement of police-community relations, it might have been expected that police-minority relations would have been greatly improved. During the same period, however, the Rodney King incident occurred in Los Angeles, the Amadou Diallo and Abner Louima incidents occurred in New York, and many other instances of questioned police use of force against people of color occurred in other cities and states. Understandably, uneasiness and suspicion continued to characterize race and policing, creating the conditions for the dramatic rise of the racial profiling issue.

The racial-profiling issue clearly struck a strong chord in minority communities and among those most concerned about civil rights and civil liberties in America (American Civil Liberties Union Foundation of California 2002). While most police have ardently denied that they use, or support the use of, any such profiles, 40 percent of African Americans believe they have been profiled by police, and a majority of whites believe the problem is widespread (The Gallup Organization 1999). It seems likely that the term "racial profiling" has gradually expanded in the public mind and come to signify larger issues of racial bias and discrimination by police. For this reason, the Police Executive Research Forum has encouraged police departments to address "racially biased policing," not just the narrower problem of racial profiling (Fridell, Lunney, Diamond, and Kubu 2001).

As racial-profiling-inspired data collection has continued around the country, it has frequently been discovered that minority drivers are overrepresented, in comparison to the population, in vehicle stops by the police. They are also typically more likely to have their persons and vehicles searched subsequent to vehicle stops (Schmitt, Langan, and Durose 2002). Whether this overrepresentation of minorities in stops and searches is the result of police profiling (discrimination), or alternatively, a reflection of police deployment in lower-income neighborhoods, police efforts to address crime- and gang-related problems, or even differential driving habits, is currently not empirically known (Engel, Calnon, and Bernard 2002). It is the subject of much discussion and debate, though. In the most promising scenario, police and citizens will work together to collect and analyze these data, interpret the results, discuss their implications, and fashion appropriate responses (Farrell, McDevitt, and Buerger 2002). This approach employs the themes of community engagement and collaboration within the framework of community policing to encourage open conversation about a very thorny and complex issue, something that has not happened often enough with respect to race and policing in America.

Eyewitness Identification

Two relatively recent developments have brought the practice of **eyewitness identification** to the forefront. One is the spate of death penalty cases in the United States in which after-the-fact DNA analysis has led to convicted persons being exonerated. According to one account, mistaken identification was a factor in 61 of the first 70 such DNA exonerations, the most common factor by far (Innocence Project 2001).

Of course, police and the courts have long known that eyewitness identifications can be mistaken. As safeguards, police have developed systematic methods for conducting photographic and in-person line-ups to make sure that eyewitness identifications are valid. In particular, police are careful to show witnesses several (typically six) similar-looking photos simultaneously in one display or several similar-looking live suspects simultaneously in a line, and to refrain from any suggestive remarks that might point the witness toward any one suspect. However, recent research has revealed that this simultaneous method inadvertently leads to some number of false identifications because witnesses often believe that the perpetrator *must* be among the suspects displayed (why else would the police be showing me these pictures?). Thus, witnesses have a tendency, conscious or not, to select the suspect who seems closest to their recollection, instead of limiting themselves to a certain or positive identification, as instructed (Wells and Seelau 1995).

As a result of this research, sequential rather than simultaneous line-ups are now recommended (National Institute of Justice 1999). Using this technique, witnesses are shown one photo or person at a time, with strict instructions to decide whether that person is or is not the person they saw committing the offense. The difficulty, though, is in changing a well-established practice in 17,000 police departments supported by years of training, procedures, and policies. To compound the problem, thousands of prosecutors, defense lawyers, and judges are also more familiar with the old simultaneous method and unlikely to be aware of more recent research and best practices. Thus, it will take some years for the law enforcement and criminal justice systems to change course, even though the need for the change is compelling and well supported.

This situation is emblematic of the failure of policing to fully professionalize. A genuine profession takes its knowledge base seriously, including new knowledge, and especially new information that directly affects the lives of innocent people. There should be an all-out effort underway in American policing today (already five years after these recommendations were published), but there is not. As research into police practices becomes more common and more authoritative, it will be incumbent on police executives to develop better mechanisms to incorporate new knowledge into police practice.

Persons With Mental Illness

Police problems related to persons with mental illness are not new. American society adopted **deinstitutionalization** of the mentally ill during the second half of the twentieth century, mental hospitals were closed or downsized, and thousands of people with mental illness were brought back into the community. Deinstitutionalization was supposed to be paired with a major increase in community-based services for people with mental illness, but these services have always been underfunded. As a consequence, society has come to rely on the police more and more for dealing with people who have severe mental health emergencies and for handling people whose mental health problems lead to substance abuse, homelessness, and similar public order problems (Perkins, Cordner, and Scarborough 1999).

What makes this particular longstanding problem current and likely to remain vexing for the police is that (1) American society shows no signs of improving the provision of social services or health care for people with mental illness; (2) mental health problems are increasingly entangled with substance abuse problems (so-called dual-diagnosis issues); and (3) police encounters with people suffering severe mental health crises continue to have tragic consequences. All too often, police use standard techniques, such as "command voice," when trying to calm people experiencing psychotic episodes, the techniques fail, the person makes what is interpreted as a threatening move with a knife or other weapon, the police shoot, and the person dies (Fyfe 2000).

Some police departments have developed alternative tactics for handling persons exhibiting serious mental health problems that are demonstrably more effective than the standard approach of dispatching a regular patrol officer to handle the call (Borum 2000). The most common approach is to prepare some patrol officers to be specialists and to give them on-scene authority whenever they can respond to such calls (Dupont and Cochran 2000). This approach has great promise, although it works best in metropolitan areas with nearby mental health professionals, and is a much bigger challenge in a small town or rural area miles away from the nearest hospital. Perhaps the bigger problem, though, is figuring out how to police the chronic alcoholics, drug addicts, and homeless people who live on the streets in many of our cities, a large proportion of whom also have serious mental health problems. American society has largely abandoned these people—abandoned them to the police, who are clearly ill equipped to really help them. This is an example of a present-day chronic problem that will continue to exasperate the police unless they can find a way to convince the public to support the kinds of social services and health services that can actually address the real needs of people with mental illness.

Cyber Crime

One obvious new form of criminal activity is **cyber crime,** or computer crime. The three categories involve (1) the computer as a target; (2) the computer as a tool for the commission of a crime; and (3) the computer as incidental to the crime itself, or simply put, as evidence. Crimes in which the computer is the target involve individuals breaking into or attacking a victim's system and may include activities such as hacking, cracking, sabotage, or so-called denial of service (overwhelming a Website). Crimes in which the computer is used as a tool are typically traditional crimes, such as fraud, theft, forgery, embezzlement, and even stalking committed in new ways. Finally, crimes in which the computer is incidental to the criminal activity could include using a computer to keep financial records of illegal business activities or sending a threatening email message to someone (Brenner 2001).

Although numerous efforts have been undertaken to provide a better description of the incidence and prevalence of cyber crime, what we know is still limited. The National Crime Victimization Survey has recently added questions to examine fraud, identify-theft, and stalking among its respondents, though, and the FBI has included a question in the National Incident-Based Reporting System to indicate whether an offender used a computer in the commission of a crime. In other efforts, a recent Bureau of Justice Statistics national survey of state prosecutors found that 42 percent of these offices prosecute computer-related crimes under their state's computer statutes. As one might expect, in larger cities, prosecution of these crimes is even more likely, with 97 percent of full-time large offices indicating that they prosecute computer-related crimes. The most frequently prosecuted type of computer-related crime is child pornography, with three in 10 offices reporting prosecuting this type of offense. Credit- and bank-card fraud were the next most frequently prosecuted cases (Bureau of Justice Statistics 2002).

The National Institute of Justice (NIJ) recently conducted an assessment of the needs of state and local law enforcement in combating electronic crime and cyber terrorism. In this survey, respondents indicated what they perceived as the 10 most critical needs (Stambaugh et al. 2001):

- Public awareness.

- Adequate data and reporting.

- Uniform training and certification courses.

- Onsite management assistance for electronic crime units and task forces.

- Updated laws.

- Cooperation with the high-tech industry.

- Special research and publications.

- Management awareness and support.

- Investigative and forensic tools.

- Structured computer crime units.

Today, most large police agencies have established computer crime units, while smaller agencies typically rely on assistance from federal agencies, state agencies, or multijurisdictional task forces (for links to a large number of units and task forces, visit the Electronic Evidence Information Center at http://www.e-evidence.info/index.html). Federal law enforcement agencies have taken a lead role in providing computer crime investigation assistance to local and state agencies over the past decade; however, their focus has shifted more toward counterterrorism since September 11, 2001. As a result, local and state agencies have an even greater need to develop their own capabilities in this area.

Cyber crime is an interesting "future issue" for several reasons. One is the growing ubiquity of computers—in cell phones, cars, trucks, appliances, home security systems, and so on. Another is the severe lag time for police in developing sufficient technical expertise to compete successfully with high-tech offenders. It seems likely that the police will always be at least a few technology steps behind serious hitech offenders, guaranteeing that police will continue to need a lot of assistance from outside experts. This reliance on civilian experts generally makes police uncomfortable, but is probably a long-term necessity in such technical areas as cyber crime.

Also, cyber crime and white-collar crime are more and more closely related. Major fraud is often committed with a computer today, or at the least, the evidence of these financial transactions is stored on computers. Recent scandals and exposés concerning the Enron Corporation and questionable practices in the accounting and mutual fund industries are reminders that the biggest thefts are committed by men and women in suits, not by armed robbers or shoplifters. Most police agencies have never really accepted the prevention and investigation of white-collar crime as an important part of their mission, in part because there is little public clamor for them to do so—community groups tend to complain about speeders and rowdy kids, not pension fund fraud. However, as state and federal law enforcement agencies refocus their missions more toward counterterrorism, it may become necessary for local police agencies to give white-collar crime more serious attention.

Significant Trends

An important part of forecasting is to identify significant trends that are likely to have future consequences. Some demographic and economic trends were identified earlier in the chapter, such as aging and diversification of the population, increased participation of women in the labor force, and the changing nature of jobs. Also noted above was the trend toward more high-tech crime. In this section, we briefly discuss four other trends directly connected to modern policing—privatization, federalization, militarization, and globalization.

Privatization

Private policing is not new—in fact, private police preceded the formation of public police in London in 1829, and private detectives like the Pinkertons provided most criminal investigation in the United States throughout much of the 1800s. Nevertheless, Americans are accustomed to thinking about the police as a public agency. Their public responsibilities, to represent the government and enforce the law, are central to the way most citizens believe the police should behave in a democratic setting. The public role played by the police today, however, may be shrinking in the face of **privatization.** Over the past 30 years, the traditional monopoly of the government over police services has diminished. Today in the United States there are three times more private security agents than public police officers (Bayley and Shearing 1998).

The trend toward private security is likely to continue, for several reasons. First, the police, by themselves, can only do so much about crime. Their behavior is constrained by due process in a democracy, as well as by social and economic variables outside their control. Yet, the public's fear of crime is not likely to decline and may increase. Private security has already begun to fill the gap for those who can afford to pay the price for extra protection.

Second, there is a change in the way in which we use physical space. The latter half of the twentieth century witnessed what Bayley and Shearing (1998) call the rise of *mass private property*—facilities that are privately owned but used by the public.

These include shopping malls, college and school campuses, residential communities, high-rise condominiums, banks, commercial facilities, and recreational complexes. To that list could be added the increasing popularity of gated communities separated from their surrounding areas by tall walls and gates staffed by security guards. Private security specialists are the most likely form of policing for these kinds of facilities. Market-based private security will follow a market-based private economy. The outcome will be policing stratified by class and race.

Western democratic societies are moving inexorably, we fear, into a "Clockwork Orange" world where both the market and the government protect the affluent from the poor—the one by barricading and excluding, the other by repressing and imprisoning—and where civil society for the poor disappears in the face of criminal victimization and governmental repression (Bayley and Shearing 1998). This vision of the future raises important questions. Can we avoid a system where public crime control is acted out primarily against the poor?

Bayley and Shearing contend that we can, but only if we make two conscious policy choices. First, poor people need to participate in the market for security. Society should provide poorer communities with the ability to fund their own security. Such funding can only happen with the financial assistance of the federal government, interceding to prevent the continued split of American society into two camps, one well off and mostly Anglo, the other poor and mostly everyone else.

Second, community policing has to become the organizing principle of public policing. Since safety is fundamental to the quality of life, coproduction between the police and the public legitimates government, lessening the corrosive alienation that disorganizes communities and triggers collective violence. Community policing is the only police strategy that incorporates the problems encountered by the poor into decision-making by the police. If society does not make a conscious effort to implement community policing and reinforce federal investment in local communities, it is possible that the character of policing could shift to private enterprise for the rich, and public social control for the poor.

Federalization

A strong trend throughout the second half of the twentieth century, and one that seems to be gaining increasing momentum, is the **federalization** of crime control and law enforcement (see Figure 15.5). In recent years, the U.S. Congress has passed more and more federal criminal laws, giving wider jurisdiction to federal prosecutors and police. Many crimes today, especially those involving guns or drugs, can be investigated and prosecuted federally as well as by state and local law enforcement. One might think that this would be an unmitigated positive trend, but an American Bar Association study (Task Force on the Federalization of Criminal Law 1998, 50) concluded differently:

- It generally undermines the state-federal fabric and disrupts the important constitutional balance of federal and state systems.

- It can have a detrimental impact on the state courts, state prosecutors, attorneys, and state investigating agents who bear the overwhelming share of responsibility for criminal law enforcement.

- It has the potential to relegate the less glamorous prosecutions to the state system, undermine citizen perception, dissipate citizen power, and diminish citizen confidence in both state and local law enforcement mechanisms.

- It creates an unhealthy concentration of policing power at the federal level.

- It can cause an adverse impact on the federal judicial system.

- It creates inappropriately disparate results for similarly situated defendants, depending on whether their essentially similar conduct is selected for federal or state prosecution.

- It increases unreviewable federal prosecutorial discretion.

- It contributes, to some degree, to costly and unneeded consequences for the federal prison system.

- It accumulates a large body of law that requires continually increasing and unprofitable congressional attention in monitoring federal criminal statutes and agencies.

- It diverts congressional attention from a needed focus on that criminal activity that, in practice, only federal prosecutions can address.

- Overall, it represents an unwise allocation of scarce resources needed to meet the genuine issues of crime.

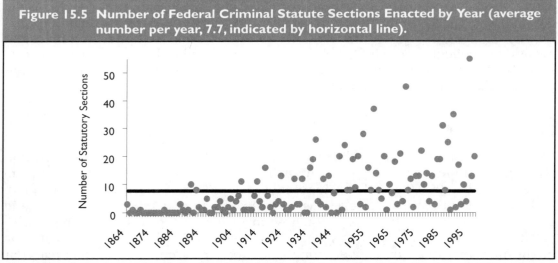

Figure 15.5 Number of Federal Criminal Statute Sections Enacted by Year (average number per year, 7.7, indicated by horizontal line).

Source: Task Force on the Federalization of Criminal Law, *The Federalization of Criminal Law* (Washington, D.C.: American Bar Association), 8, available online at <http://www.abanet.org/crimjust/fedcrimlaw2.pdf>.

It is particularly significant that the ABA Task Force reached these conclusions well before September 11, 2001. Since then, the nation's heightened concern about international terrorism and weapons of mass destruction has led to an even greater tendency to rely on federal laws and federal law enforcement.

The biggest problem with this trend toward federalization is that it undercuts the very police officers and police agencies who are in the best position to deal with most crime—local and state police. It undercuts them in part because law enforcement resources are limited; more resources for federal law enforcement inevitably means fewer resources for state and local police. It also undercuts state and local police by sending a subtle message that they must not be effective or professional enough to deal with serious crime, thus the need for a bigger federal role. And finally, federalization undercuts effective policing because it "puts more distance between law enforcers and local community residents—in direct conflict with community-policing objectives" (Police Executive Research Forum 1997).

Militarization

The **militarization** trend is similar to the federalization trend. Traditionally, the regular military has been very restricted in its role in crime control and policing within the U.S. borders (the National Guard and Coast Guard are somewhat less restricted). Military police have had jurisdiction on military bases and with respect to military personnel, of course, but otherwise, the military has generally only been used for law enforcement or order-maintenance duties in serious emergencies, such as natural disasters or mass civil disorder, when martial law is declared. These limitations on the domestic-police role of the military were enacted in The Posse Comitatus Act of 1878, which generally "prohibits U.S. military personnel from interdicting vehicles, vessels and aircraft; conducting surveillance, searches, pursuit and seizures; or making arrests on behalf of civilian law enforcement authorities" (U.S. Northern Command 2004).

While Americans have historically viewed the separation of the police and the military as an essential characteristic of their democratic heritage, this view may be changing. Kraska (1994) has observed a heightened level of activity linking the military to the police in the United States. He argues that the traditional separation of the police and the military is eroding today.

> Changes in the post-cold war world and in the influence of contemporary militarism—the reliance on military-style force to solve problems—are eroding the separation between police and military activity, resulting in a military involved in law enforcement, and the police at times operating "militarily," all under the guise of ameliorating "social problems." (Kraska 1994, 1)

Kraska cites several examples of military involvement in domestic affairs:

- The Washington, D.C., National Guard has used soldiers to assist federal and local police in air and ground transportation, lending military equipment, demolishing crack houses, and flying aerial surveillance missions.

- Portland, Oregon, in 1991 became the first municipality to deploy armed National Guard soldiers to assist local police in drug-related operations.

- Under the auspices of training, the U.S. military in southern Florida and Louisiana is conducting Andean-type exercises using military helicopters. Once the military locates a suspected operation and secures the area, the local police actually search and arrest suspects.

Military involvement in domestic law enforcement had been most common in conjunction with the so-called war on drugs until the terrorist attacks of September 11, 2001. Since then, it has become more common to see military personnel guarding airports and other critical facilities, and there have been calls for military participation in other types of counterterrorism efforts. In some citizens' minds, it is a fairly easy and comforting segue from U.S. Army Special Forces chasing terrorists in Afghanistan to U.S. Army units chasing terrorists in New York or California. For other citizens, though, the specter of U.S. soldiers patrolling the streets or knocking on doors in the middle of the night is frightening and antithetical to the American way of life.

Globalization

Another trend in modern policing is **globalization.** Developments in business, finance, trade, travel, communications, and computers really have "shrunk the world" in the last decade or two. It is far more likely now than 20 years ago that a local criminal investigation might involve international transactions and foreign individuals. These foreign individuals might have traveled to the local jurisdiction or they might have played their roles (as witnesses, victims, or suspects) from afar.

Many traditional crimes can have international features today, such as drug distribution and theft. Much has also been made in recent years of international organized crime, especially that involving Russians. Crimes committed with computers, including frauds, thefts, vandalism, and hacking, really know no boundaries. Then there are newer crimes (or perhaps crimes that are simply getting more attention today), such as human smuggling of women and children and illegal smuggling of immigrants, weapons, and even nuclear material. The term "transnational crime" has been coined to describe the increasingly international nature of crime.

Of course, international terrorism has become a huge concern for local, state, and federal law enforcement since September 11, 2001. Americans, and people all around the world, saw the death and destruction that could be caused by a relatively small group of terrorists from the Middle East who had trained in Afghanistan. These were far from the first acts of international terrorism committed against the United States, of course, and in fact, other countries had been more seriously plagued by these kinds of attacks than the United States. The attacks of September 11 galvanized national and world attention, however, and drove home the new reality that crime and terrorism emanating from halfway around the globe could threaten American communities and American citizens.

Another aspect of globalization that has affected American policing has been the participation of local and state police in international policing missions in places like Haiti, Bosnia, and Kosovo (Perito 2002). As the United States, the United Nations, the European Union, and other bodies have accepted peacekeeping roles in war-torn countries around the world, it has become evident that a key element in the restoration of order and civil society is effective policing. Typically, police and military forces in these countries were previously aligned with repressive regimes. Once the initial military phase of peacekeeping has been accomplished, the country needs reliable, professional policing to maintain order and reassure the citizenry of their safety. While a policing system is being rebuilt along democratic lines, police officers are brought in from around the world to provide police service and help train the country's new police.

U.S. and international officials presenting donated equipment to a police station in Kacanik, Kosovo.

Many American police officers have now had the experience of serving in such international missions, and many American police departments now see that part of their responsibility is to support the development of more professional and democratic policing in other countries. This is a relatively new awareness for American police, and contributes to their sense of being part of a global police community. It is also a fairly new realization for those in the U.S. government responsible for foreign relations that "security is important to the development of democracy and police are important to the character of that security. Assisting in the democratic reform of foreign police systems has become a front-burner issue in American foreign policy" (Bayley 2001, 5).

It is difficult to predict all the future ramifications for policing of this trend toward globalization. Clearly, though, international issues and considerations once thought irrelevant for local American policing have become relevant and even significant. This trend can only continue.

Technology

Technology has clearly changed policing in the past. Patrol cars, two-way radios, 911 telephone systems, and in-car computers have changed the way police do their work and interact with the public. Similarly, automobiles, televisions, air conditioning, computers, and a host of other technologies have changed American society, patterns of social behavior, and consequently the police-community relationship. As technological change speeds up in the twenty-first century, these changes in society and policing are likely to occur even faster, as emphasized by Captain Thomas Cowper of the New York State Police in this chapter's Voices From the Field.

One entity that tries to help police agencies adapt new technologies successfully is the National Law Enforcement and Corrections Technology Center system (see Inside Policing 15.2).

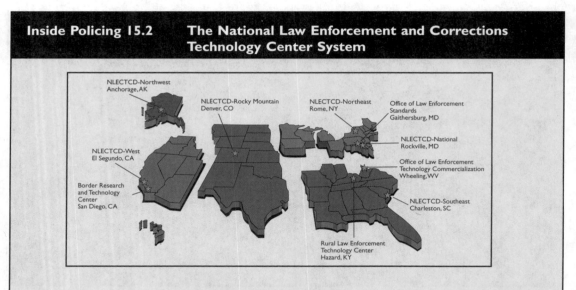

Inside Policing 15.2   The National Law Enforcement and Corrections Technology Center System

Created in 1994 as a component of the National Institute of Justice's (NIJ's) Office of Science and Technology, the National Law Enforcement and Corrections Technology Center (NLECTC) system serves as the "honest broker" offering support, research findings, and technological expertise to help State and local law enforcement and corrections personnel perform their duties more safely and efficiently. The NLECTC system is assisted in its work by a national and regional advisory councils.

The NLECTC system consists of facilities across the country that are co-located with an organization or agency that specializes in one or more specific areas of research and development. Although each NLECTC facility has a different technology focus, they work together to form a seamless web of support, providing technology assistance, support, and information.

New technologies are not always as beneficial as expected and sometimes have unanticipated consequences. Putting police in cars, for example, certainly improved their response time to calls from the public and allowed them to patrol wider areas, but it also made patrolling less personal and interactive. Putting computers in police cars has given officers much quicker access to critical information, but it also tends to focus their attention on the computer instead of on the community outside of the car. Table 15.2 presents one perspective on some of the best and worst technology developments in policing over the past 50 years.

Suspect Control and Officer Safety

Since the use of force is at the heart of police work, technology that helps officers control violent suspects and combatants more effectively is of utmost importance. Closely related is technology that better protects officers from offenders who might try to harm them. In the suspect control category, police today have less-than-lethal weapons and equipment, such as pepper spray, stun guns, and rubber bullets, that often help them disarm or capture offenders without having to resort to the use of deadly force. The dream for the future is a weapon akin to Captain Kirk's *Star Trek* phaser—a device that would immediately disable and stop a violent person without causing any permanent harm. The beauty of the phaser would be that it is a signal that could be carried easily on the person, instead of the current situation in which officers have several items on their persons, and several more in the trunk of the patrol car.

Table 15.2 Best and Worst Police Technologies of the Past 50 Years (Based on a Survey of 30 Law Enforcement Agencies).

Ten Best

- Soft body armor
- Less-than-lethal weapons
- Portable 2-way radios
- Semi-automatic pistols
- Computerized databases
- Portable and in-car computers
- Improved patrol vehicles (safety and performance)
- DNA identification
- Video cameras
- Cell phones

Five Worst

- Downsized, front-wheel drive patrol cars
- Sticky foam
- Direct-contact stun guns
- Capture nets
- Multi-function equipment (e.g., baton/flashlight)

Source: Law and Order, 2003, "Best and Worst Technologies: Law Enforcement Products From 1953–2003," (Special Issue): 26–32.

The other suspect control situation that may eventually be solved by technology is the high-speed pursuit. The need in this regard is for technology that can stop a car as opposed to stopping a person. A few technologies are already available, including portable spike strips, but police are hopeful that some kind of electronic solution will be developed that can be activated from the pursuing police car. One need only consider the dangerousness of pursuits for police officers and the public to understand how beneficial a technological solution to this problem could be.

Voices From the Field
Thomas Cowper
Captain, New York State Police
Treasurer, Society of Police Futurists International

Question: In what ways will technology have the greatest impact on policing in the next 25 years?

Answer: We are living in an era of accelerating change driven by technological advancement. Artificial Intelligence is allowing advanced robots to have increasing autonomy within our world to accomplish many tasks once

performed exclusively by humans. Genetic engineering and stem cell research hold the potential to cure many of our worst diseases and extend human lifespan. Nanotechnology will allow us to create components at the molecular scale and weave computers, wireless devices, and their associated power sources directly into our clothing and embed them directly into our bodies. Augmented Reality technology will make information flow faster and farther, directly to the people who need it, wherever they are at exactly the right time. All of these technologies are converging to make our world more complex and dynamic. Policing that 21st Century world effectively will be a growing challenge.

Emerging technologies will allow for a Network-Centric police organizational model that abolishes rigid hierarchies, decentralizes decision making and fosters self-synchronization from the bottom up without close and direct control of individual officers. The resulting increase in real-time situational and organizational awareness will al-low for quick adaptation to rapidly changing circumstances, an organizational flexibility unheard of today. Indeed, Net-Centric policing will be a requirement if police departments are to be effective participants within an increasingly Net-Centric world, but the transition from today's paramilitary model and associated militaristic culture will not be easy.

The improvements in policing that will be possible within a few short years are staggering and filled with controversy, but will be absolutely necessary to maintain public safety and ensure economic prosperity in a networked world filled with terrorists and criminals with access to the same technologies. Police will have new ways to solve problems, new ways to gather and share information, new methods to track down and stop those who strive to do harm within our communities, thereby destroying liberty by creating fear. Dramatically improved police capabilities however can also have severe consequences for Constitutional freedom when used ignorantly or unethically. The greatest impact that technology will have upon policing and police officers in the next 25 years will be the absolute requirement that they use it with wisdom and understanding to foster freedom and not destroy it. ✦

The most important technological contribution to officer safety has been soft body armor, which has saved the lives of many officers who have been shot or involved in automobile crashes. Modern body armor (often called a bulletproof vest) is much lighter and more comfortable than in years past, contributing to the willingness of officers to wear it regularly, even in hot weather. As noted in Inside Policing 15.3, there have been some recent concerns about the effectiveness of some varieties of body armor. Nevertheless, body armor is likely to become even more comfortable and effective in the future, contributing still more to police officer safety.

Crime Detection and Crime Solving

Another category of technological change pertains to crime detection and crime solving. Crime detection technology includes devices to detect weapons and drugs, cameras that can record illegal behavior (including traffic violations), listening devices that can intercept illicit conversations, and biometric techniques (such as retinal scanning) that can identify wanted persons. Needless to say, each of these types of technology raises concerns about privacy and civil liberties, since what they do is increase the level of surveillance in society. Most people would support additional surveillance that helps prevent serious crime, but they do not want their own lives subjected to more government prying. It is not clear that we can have one without the other, however, making these modern crime detection technologies quite controversial.

Inside Policing 15.3   Once Protective, Now Defective?

"States, Feds Up in Arms Over Shortcomings in Police Body Armor." Data showing that the fabric used to some police body armor could lose as much as 20 percent of its strength after just two years had led to a flurry of lawsuits by states against the manufacturer.

Massachusetts Attorney General Thomas Reilly filed a suit in November against Second Chance Body Armor, Inc., of Central Lake, Michigan, asking that a judge halt the sale of its vest in the state, and the company replace defective products or return officers' money.

A similar action was brought by Arkansas Attorney General Mike Beebe, who has demanded that Second Chance refund more than $200,000 for body armor bought for the Arkansas State Police and the state Capital Police. In Arizona, Attorney General Terry Goddard has also demanded a refund or replacement. And in Pennsylvania, the state police have struck a tentative deal for close to $1 million in free bulletproof vests.

"The level of outrage is very, very high," said Andy Swann, president of the Arizona Police Association.

An intensive review of body armor reliability has also been launched by U.S. Attorney General John Ashcroft.

In a letter, Senators Patrick Leahy (D-Vt.) and Ben Nighthorse Campbell (R-Colo.) said the review should also look into whether companies knowingly sold defective vests and if so, whether they should be barred from participating in federal grant programs.

"Close doesn't count when the lives of police officers are on the line," said Leahy.

The Justice Department's initiative includes a study by the National Institute of Justice on how the vests are certified by the government, a summit meeting of law enforcement organizations, vest manufacturers, and testing groups to review the study and determine whether body armor remains suitable for police, and financial assistance to law enforcement agencies and state in replacing defective body armor.

Although the vests are covered by a five-year warranty, Second Chance notified police agencies in September that a material made the vests, called Zylon, deteriorate fast than expected. In June, Forest Hills, Pennsylvania, Officer Edward Limbacker was injured when a .40-caliber bullet pierced his vest and lodged in his stomach. The vest had been made less than a year before.

The company that makes Zylon, Corporation Toyobo of Japan, found that the synthetic fiber loses 15 percent of its strength when exposed to 104-degree heat and 80 percent humidity for 150 days.

Second Chance began selling the Ultima and Ultimax vest with Zylon about four years ago. It discovered problems with the material during tests performed over the past two years on 200 used vests. The company has since stopped selling those models.

Other vest makers use Zylon, but Second Chance is the only one that has gone public with the problem, said Gregg Smith, a company spokesman. The vests, he said, have helped save the lives of 35 officers struck by gunfire.

One of the deals offered by Second Chance to departments is the fortification of the Zylon layers with Kevlar panels. It also offers trade in discounts on Monarch Summit vests, made with a different protective material, or a "warranty adjustment" that gives police discounts on any Monarch vest.

The Arkansas attorney general has rejected those alternatives. "We can't take chances with officers' lives," Beebe told the Arkansas Demo-

Inside Policing 15.3   Once Protective, Now Defective? (continued)

crat-Gazette. "That's just not something we even mess around with."

But police organizations called on the nation's police to continue wearing the body armor, noting that wearing no vest is worse that wearing one that might be ineffective.

"I want to strongly encourage police officers everywhere to continue wearing their vests—even if it is a Zylon vest—until this investigation is completed . . . and corrective measures are taken," said Craig W. Floyd, chairman of the National Law Enforcement Officers' Memorial Fund.

Source: Law Enforcement News, January 2004, 5.

Crime-solving technologies create fewer privacy issue problems since they tend to focus on crimes that have already occurred. Improved techniques for finding latent fingerprints at crime scenes and linking them to suspects have helped solve many crimes in recent years. Similar improvements in finding other types of evidence (hairs, fibers, fluids, etc.) have been made, as well as in linking that evidence to suspects (most notably through DNA identification). The use of technology and science to solve crimes in the real world is not nearly as systematic or effective as portrayed in the popular *CSI* television series, mainly because most police departments cannot afford the latest equipment, and most crime labs do not have sufficient staff to analyze all the evidence submitted to them. Nevertheless, science and technology have improved police crime-solving effectiveness and are likely to improve it even more in the future.

Crime solving does raise privacy and civil liberty issues, though. Fingerprints and DNA evidence are most productive when they can be compared against large databases—however, most Americans do not favor the creation of universal fingerprint or DNA registries, so available databases tend to be limited to previously convicted offenders and military personnel. Similarly, although current polygraph (lie detector) techniques are not considered completely reliable, there is little doubt that more effective techniques will be developed in the future. When that time comes, how comfortable will we be with a

Crime-solving technology continues to improve.

device that allows the police (or anyone else) to tell for certain whether we are telling the truth or lying?

Information Technology

It is widely accepted that police work is all about gathering and using information. In previous eras this meant that good police officers had to be persuasive interviewers and needed to develop informants and other human sources of information about crime and criminals. These skills are still crucial, of course, but technology has added an entirely new component to the quest for information. Today, a tremendous amount of information is stored in computer databases (criminal records, arrest records, tax records, business license records, telephone records, etc.), and tools exist that allow police and others to access such information quickly and with ease.

Information technology (IT) refers to the whole system of information collection, storage, retrieval, and analysis that allows officers to check driving records from the side of the road, review previous calls at a particular address to which they are responding, positively identify arrestees during booking, and base their patrol tactics on up-to-date crime analysis information. This system is mostly comprised of electronic (computer) hardware and software, along with analytical techniques that usually still require a degree of human judgment and expertise. The hardware elements of IT keep getting smaller and faster, so that PDAs (personal digital assistants) will soon be standard equipment for police officers in the field. When PDAs can be successfully and reliably combined with cell phone and radio capabilities, police officers will then have the IT and communications equivalent of the phaser—one small IT device that meets all their information and communication needs.

One of the most popular IT developments of recent years has been crime mapping (Vann and Garson 2003) and **geographic information systems** (GIS). Mapping relevant police data (crimes, calls for service, traffic crashes) in a timely manner makes the data more user-friendly for most police officers, as well as for the public (see Inside Policing 15.4 for an example of crime mapping available to the public). When a patrol officer is specifically responsible for a particular geographic area, maps can help identify crime hot spots, stolen car drop-off locations, repeat call locations, residences of parolees, locations covered by domestic violence emergency protective orders, and lots of other useful pieces of information that might otherwise go unrecognized or be forgotten.

The important role that IT might play in solving serious crimes was illustrated in the Washington, DC-area sniper case in the fall of 2002 (Sink 2002). This case illustrates a situation in which information about several crimes and one or more unidentified offenders was tucked away in different databases, maintained by different agencies, some of which were not even aware that they were part of a larger pattern. IT could have efficiently search different databases and pulled together disparate pieces of information that might have helped the investigators identify their suspects more quickly, possibly saving additional lives. Unfortunately, in this case, as in so many others, many pieces of the puzzle did not fall into place until well after the suspects were identified and captured through more traditional means. It will be very interesting to see whether modern IT can fulfill the high expectations that law enforcement currently has for it.

Inside Policing 15.4   **Crime Map for Zone 11, Port St. Lucie, Florida for December, 2003**

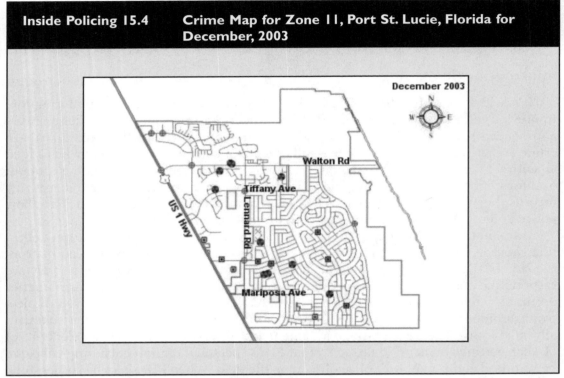

Source: Port St. Lucie Police Department Web Page.

Communications and Interoperability

Since the introduction of two-way radios in police cars many years ago, police communications equipment has gotten smaller, more powerful, and more reliable. Nevertheless, police in many rural and remote areas still sometimes lack reliable communications between cars and with the communications center, and police in metropolitan areas sometimes have dead spots caused by massive buildings or access problems caused by heavy radio traffic on too few channels. These problems can be solved, of course, but at an expense that not every community can easily afford.

A bigger contemporary issue with respect to police communications is **interoperability,** which refers to the capacity of different units and different agencies to communicate between each other and also share digital information (computerized data). In many communities, the police department and the fire department have such different radio systems that they cannot communicate directly, for example. This was the case in New York and at the Pentagon on September 11, 2001. Also, it is frequently the case that town police and sheriff's deputies, or local and state police, cannot communicate directly. It is even more likely that local and federal authorities cannot communicate "car to car." This widespread lack of interoperability is sometimes just a nuisance, but in emergency situations it can be a significant impediment to effective response and incident management. Efforts are currently underway at the federal level to find technology solutions to this problem, such as a so-called software radio that would allow officers to "dial" any frequency they needed to use (Vanu Inc.

2003). This solution faces opposition, though, from military and commercial interests that currently own the rights to most of the communications spectrum.

Police communications also play an important role in command and control—the police department's ability to deploy, manage, and maneuver its units in the field. The modern development of **global positioning systems** (GPS) has made it possible for police departments to keep closer track of officers and patrol cars. When AVL (automated vehicle locator) systems based on earlier technology were first introduced about 20 years ago, they were resisted by police officers who did not want their bosses keeping such close track of them, but in the current era these systems have become more acceptable because of their role in promoting officer safety. In the future, command and control potential will be greatly enhanced by miniature video cameras that officers can wear, which could transmit real-time video and audio back to the station. In this scenario, commanders really will be able to control their officers in the field. This could reduce individual officer discretion and make operational decisions more consistent and predictable. Time will tell whether it would lead to policing that is more fair and just, though.

Terrorism and Homeland Security

Massachusetts Public Safety Secretary Ed Flynn recently called terrorism "the monster that ate criminal justice" (Rosen 2003, 1). Since the events of September 11, 2001, **terrorism** and **homeland security** have dominated nearly every discussion about public safety in America, led to new legislation and to a significant reorganization of the federal government, and dramatically changed national funding priorities. It is important to give these new priorities their due, and yet, at the same time, to remember that policing has many other responsibilities and concerns. Just to illustrate, every month in the United States there are about 1,300 murders, 8,000 rapes, and 35,000 robberies (Federal Bureau of Investigation 2003). Also, every month about 3,500 people die in fatal traffic crashes (National Highway Traffic Safety Administration 2004). To say the least, there are a lot of very serious crimes and incidents demanding police attention besides those associated with terrorism.

The attack of September 11 demonstrated, though, that a weapon of mass destruction could be delivered in the United States with catastrophic results. It also demonstrated that a small group of individuals from halfway around the world could have both the hatred and the determination to plan and carry out such an attack on American soil. As so many commentators have said, nothing will ever be the same again. For police, the fact that these individuals lived in American cities and towns for an extended period before the attack, taking flying lessons and making other preparations, raises the possibility that they might have been identified in advance, if neighbors, patrol officers, and intelligence analysts had only been a bit more observant. Whether local police could possibly have anticipated the intentions of these terrorists has not been established, more than two years after the attack, but certainly police are now trying very hard to identify any individuals or groups who might have similar intentions.

One of the clearest lessons from the September 11 attack is the need for local, state, and federal authorities to improve intelligence analysis and sharing (Hoover 2002). At the local level, few police departments had sophisticated intelligence operations of any type, much less ones focused on international terrorism. At the national level, in the aftermath of the attack, it became evident that the FBI, in particular, had a very weak intelligence analysis capacity (Marshall 2003). For many reasons, but mainly its historic focus on criminal investigation, the FBI never developed a strong intelligence capacity in the counterterrorism arena, especially after the end of the cold war. This shortcoming might not have been as serious if there was a strong tradition of information-sharing among the federal agencies with intelligence responsibilities, such as the FBI, CIA, and National Security Agency, but unfortunately, these agencies have historically behaved more like competitors than partners.

The federal government reorganization that created the new Department of Homeland Security (see Inside Policing 15.5) was designed to improve information-sharing and coordination among the various federal agencies with counterterrorism and law enforcement responsibilities. Time will tell whether the reorganization will succeed at these objectives. None of the major intelligence-gathering agencies, including the FBI, CIA, and NSA, were moved to the Department of Homeland Security, though, clearly indicating that interagency relations will still be key, even at the federal level. When it comes to information-sharing from federal agencies to state and local agencies, it appears that the traditional "one-way street" is still largely intact—federal agencies expect local agencies to send them information, but they provide little in return (Johnson 2002).

Inside Policing 15.5   The Department of Homeland Security

The agencies slated to become part of the Department of Homeland Security will be housed in one of four major directorates: Border and Transportation Security, Emergency Preparedness and Response, Science and Technology, and Information Analysis and Infrastructure Protection.

The Border and Transportation Security directorate will bring the major border security and transportation operations under one roof, including:

- The U.S. Customs Service (Treasury)

- The Immigration and Naturalization Service (part) (Justice)

- The Federal Protective Service (GSA)

- The Transportation Security Administration (Transportation)

- Federal Law Enforcement Training Center (Treasury)

- Animal and Plant Health Inspection Service (part) (Agriculture)

- Office for Domestic Preparedness (Justice)

The Emergency Preparedness and Response directorate will oversee domestic disaster preparedness training and coordinate government disaster response. It will bring together:

- The Federal Emergency Management Agency (FEMA)

- Strategic National Stockpile and the National Disaster Medical System (HHS)

- Nuclear Incident Response Team (Energy)

- Domestic Emergency Support Teams (Justice)

- National Domestic Preparedness Office (FBI)

The Science and Technology directorate will seek to utilize all scientific and technological advantages when securing the homeland. The following assets will be part of this effort:

Inside Policing 15.5   The Department of Homeland Security (continued)

- CBRN Countermeasures Programs (Energy)

- Environmental Measurements Laboratory (Energy)

- National BW Defense Analysis Center (Defense)

- Plum Island Animal Disease Center (Agriculture)

The Information Analysis and Infrastructure Protection directorate will analyze intelligence and information from other agencies (including the CIA, FBI, DIA and NSA) involving threats to homeland security and evaluate vulnerabilities in the nation's infrastructure. It will bring together:

- Critical Infrastructure Assurance Office (Commerce)

- Federal Computer Incident Response Center (GSA)

- National Communications System (Defense)

- National Infrastructure Protection Center (FBI)

- Energy Security and Assurance Program (Energy)

The Secret Service and the Coast Guard will also be located in the Department of Homeland Security, remaining intact and reporting directly to the Secretary. In addition, the INS adjudications and benefits programs will report directly to the Deputy Secretary as the U.S. Citizenship and Immigration Services.

Source: http://www.dhs.gov/dhspublic/display?theme=13

New federal legislation addressing terrorism and homeland security is primarily to be found in the USA Patriot Act of 2001, enacted less than two months after the September 11 attacks. This act contains numerous provisions that can be summarized as follows (Doyle 2002):

- The act gives federal officials greater authority to track and intercept communications.

- It vests the Secretary of the Treasury with regulatory powers to combat corruption of U.S. financial institutions for foreign money-laundering purposes.

- It seeks to further close our borders to foreign terrorists and to detain and remove those within our borders.

- It creates new crimes, new penalties, and new procedural efficiencies for use against domestic and international terrorists.

The Patriot Act has been very controversial since its enactment. Critics have been concerned about invasions of privacy, including the much-celebrated authority to examine library records, the authorization of "sneak and peek" search warrants, and the expansion of government access to confidential information. By the same token, few if any serious abuses have been alleged so far, no provisions have been found to be unconstitutional, and much of the investigative and intelligence-gathering authority in the act had previously been authorized for drug and organized crime investigations, and was merely extended to counterterrorism (Olson, 2003). It should be noted that several of the act's provisions are slated to sunset at the end of 2005, and that Congress has so far shown little real enthusiasm for enacting any further expansions of law enforcement authority.

The American people want to be safe and free. Over time, and especially in response to crime waves, drug epidemics, and most recently, terrorism, the immediate concern for safety often gets stronger, leading to new laws like the Patriot Act and more funding for police and public safety. Usually, though, the countervailing desire for freedom helps check increases in government power and authority. Also, new laws and practices are subject to constitutionality questions, and sometimes the courts tell the executive or legislative branches that they have gone too far. Whether the Patriot Act went too far is a political and legal question that has been debated hotly since it was enacted, and that debate will no doubt continue. In the meantime, it will be up to law enforcement officials to implement the act with professionalism and restraint in order to maximize both safety and freedom. Balancing the public's twin desires for safety and freedom is something that local and state police have a great deal of experience with, and we must hope that they draw on that experience in this new era of terrorism and homeland security.

All four significant trends discussed earlier in this chapter—privatization, federalization, militarization, and globalization—have large impacts on counterterrorism and homeland security. Private corporations have some of the information that law enforcement might like to include in intelligence analysis, and private security has a major interest in protecting commercial assets from terrorist attack. Despite some rhetoric about hometown security, America's initial approach to homeland security has been further federalization of law enforcement. Counterterrorism and protection against weapons of mass destruction seem inevitably to give the military a larger domestic role and to further militarize local, state, and federal policing. And despite our longer experience with domestic terrorism, the more recent emergence of international terrorism dramatically demonstrates the global nature of the problem and the necessity for a global response.

Police Strategies Post-9/11

Terrorism and homeland security are not the only important issues facing police agencies in the twenty-first century, but they are such serious concerns that it is necessary to contemplate whether existing police strategies are still up to the job. Because terrorists are so violent and so determined to commit dreadful acts on behalf of their causes, some commentators have suggested that policing strategies based on openness, consent, and cooperation need to be reconsidered (de Guzman 2002). While understandable, this point of view seems shortsighted and ultimately a concession to those who use terror to achieve their ends. We are more inclined to argue that community policing (COP) and problem-oriented policing (POP) represent the most promising approaches to homeland (and hometown) security (Burack 2003). Neither of these approaches, of course, precludes the use of supplementary and specialized responses to terrorism. But COP and POP still constitute the most effective police strategies for controlling crime and disorder and reducing fear while protecting the legitimacy of the police institution in a free and open society (see Inside Policing 15.6 for a resolution adopted by the International Association of Chiefs of Police in support of a community-policing approach to homeland security).

The threat of biological terrorist attack is of increasing concern.

Inside Policing 15.6   Resolution Adopted by the International Association of Chiefs of Police in 2002

Homeland Security

Community Policing—A Valuable Tool in the Fight Against Terrorism

Submitted by Community Policing Committee

WHEREAS, the IACP recognizes that in the aftermath of the September 11th atrocities, there is a clear danger to the public of additional terrorist attacks; and

WHEREAS, the IACP recognizes that while technology plays an important role in countering terrorism, there is a recognition that human intelligence is a key factor in both the prevention of and response to these acts; and

WHEREAS, the IACP maintains that it is imperative that law enforcement maintains the trust and support of the citizens as partners in the co-production of public safety; and

WHEREAS, the IACP maintains that this partnership has been established through the successful implementation of community policing initiatives; and

WHEREAS, the IACP maintains that community policing efforts have fostered those partnerships that are aimed at supporting and facilitating the prevention of terrorist acts and the response to handling these acts when they do occur; and

WHEREAS, the IACP maintains that community policing should be an integral part of the measured response to the threats to homeland security; and

WHEREAS, the IACP recognizes that the principles of community policing are even more important post-September 11th than ever be-

Inside Policing 15.6	Resolution Adopted by the International Association of Chiefs of Police in 2002 (continued)

fore. The philosophy it represents, the principles for which it stands, and the strategies it offers, should further enhance the capabilities of law enforcement agencies, public safety agencies, social service agencies, and the corporate community to improve public safety in connection with potential terrorist attacks as well as non-terrorist criminal activity; now, therefore, be it

RESOLVED, that the IACP will strongly support and employ community policing as a valuable tool to provide the best possible readiness, response and handling of terrorist incidents; and that the IACP encourages governments of the free world to actively promote, support and fund community-policing philosophies and initiatives in an effort to prevent terrorist activity and ensure the safety and security of their citizens.

In policing, as in many other fields, practitioners and observers strive to anticipate "the next big thing." We all hope, of course, that the next big incident will be prevented or at least less tragic than the events of September 11, 2001. As for the next big development in police strategy, we hope and expect that it will represent further refinement of community policing, or better yet, some kind of a quantum leap forward in democratic policing, rather than any retreat from the significant improvements made in policing over the last 25 years. This is based on the view that terrorism, while certainly a frightening threat, is best dealt with according to proven principles and practices, as eloquently articulated by Charles Ramsey, Chief of Police in Washington, D.C. (2002, 6–7):

> While many U.S. law enforcement agencies have adopted community-policing strategies in recent years, traumatic events like the 9/11 attacks can cause organizations to fall back on more traditional methods of doing business. Some police departments may abandon community policing for seemingly more immediate security concerns. Community policing, however, should play a central role in addressing these issues.

As law enforcement is only one of many entities that respond to community problems, partnering with other agencies and community groups is central to community policing. Community policing encourages law enforcement officials to develop partnerships with civic and community groups to help address community needs and to involve the public in problem-solving efforts.

While the fear of terrorism may be different from the fear of other types of crime, many of the same responses still apply. For example, law enforcement can conduct surveys to determine the extent and nature of citizen fear and tailor their responses accordingly. Awareness campaigns can inform citizens about local police and government activities to prevent and prepare for possible terrorist events, and crisis response plans can be made public. Citizens can be informed about what they can do to prepare for possible terrorist events, such as preparing emergency survival kits for their homes, reviewing evacuation routes, and learning to identify suspicious activity. Encouraging citizens to partner with law enforcement and other community groups in prevention and preparedness efforts may significantly increase citizens' feelings of efficacy and security.

The burden placed on local law enforcement is great. Since 9/11, in addition to traditional responsibilities, America's law enforcement agencies have provided a visible security presence at potential terrorist targets, partnered with federal intelligence agencies, responded to an increasing number of hate crimes, and investigated a large number of terrorism related leads. Community policing can be an effective strategy for conducting and coordinating these and other terrorism prevention and response efforts.

Summary

American society has always been very dynamic and the current situation is no different. Consideration of police *and society*, then, must take into account the changing nature of that society. A few important facets of ongoing societal change include the aging of the population, the increasing diversity of the American people, shifts in jobs and other economic conditions, and migration of the population from cities to rural areas and between regions and states. Among the most obvious factors affecting policing are the different cultures and languages they now encounter, increasing income inequality, and a vast increase in the proportion of families with both parents working outside the home, leaving more children unsupervised after school and at other times.

Changing times create new challenges and issues. Among the contemporary issues facing policing that seem likely to remain salient are racial profiling, eyewitness identification, persons with mental illness, and cyber crime. The first two of these are examples of problems with police practice, while the latter two are problems in the community that are particularly challenging. Police practices need continuous refinement in order to ensure that policing is done in an efficient, effective, and equitable manner. Crime and disorder problems in the community need careful analysis and attention, whether they are of a longstanding nature such as dealing with mental health emergencies or newer problems such as computer crime.

Significant trends that seem likely to affect policing in the future include privatization, federalization, militarization, and globalization. Together, these trends have the potential to radically change the distinctive nature of American policing—public, local, fragmented, and civilian. Whether the momentum behind these trends is inexorable or more temporary is open to debate. The increasingly complex and transnational nature of crime and the sudden emergence of international terrorism suggest that these trends can only increase in momentum. However, everyday crime and disorder are still much more common than sophisticated international crime and more of a threat to the average American, suggesting that our local police may not become an endangered species anytime soon.

There is probably no surer forecast than that technology will continue to change, and change ever faster, affecting society and policing. Improvements in less than lethal weapons, soft body armor, crime scene investigation and forensic science, information technology, and communications are likely to make tremendous contributions toward more effective and efficient policing. It is harder to predict the unintended consequences that will follow from these new technologies, except to say that there will be some.

Terrorism and homeland security have dominated the police agenda since September 11, 2001. As a result, the authority of the police has been expanded, federal law enforcement has been reorganized, and state and local police have accepted new high priority missions. Exactly what these new missions are, at least at the local level, is still being worked out, as are the very sensitive and controversial matters of intelligence analysis and intelligence sharing. While counterterrorism and homeland security will undoubtedly spawn new police tactics and specialties, it is anticipated that community policing will prove to be the right foundation on which to build twenty-first century policing.

Critical Thinking Questions

1. The American people are becoming, on average, older. How will this make your life different from what your parents experienced? What impact will this have on policing in the future?

2. The U.S. economy was once based heavily on farming, and later on manufacturing. Now, most jobs are in the service, information, or creativity sectors. What are the implications of these fundamental economic changes for social relations, crime, and policing?

3. Cyber crime and other types of electronic and white-collar crime are very complicated and technical. Do you think the average small police department will ever have any personnel competent to investigate them? If not, and if state and federal police become more and more focused on counterterrorism, who will investigate these types of crime in the future?

4. Which of the four significant trends discussed in the chapter (privatization, federalization, militarization, and globalization) do you think will have the biggest impact on future policing? Why? Which of the trends concerns you the most, and why?

5. Police commanders will soon have the technical capability to sit in the police station and monitor what all of their officers are doing in the field, thanks to miniature video cameras that can be worn by officers. What effect do you think this will have on police work? As a police officer, would you welcome this new technology? Would you welcome it as a member of the public?

6. The USA Patriot Act is a controversial law. What liberties and freedoms do you think Americans should be willing to give up to help prevent major terrorist acts? What additional powers do you think police need in order to be successful at counterterrorism?

References

American Civil Liberties Union Foundation of California. 2002. *Driving While Black or Brown: The California DWB Report.* San Francisco: author.

Bayley, D. 2001. *Democratizing the Police Abroad: What to Do and How to Do It.* Washington, D.C.: National Institute of Justice.

Bayley, D. and Sheaning, C. 1998. "The Future of Policing." In G. Cole and M. Gertz (eds.), *The Criminal Justice System: Politics and Policies*, 7th ed., pp. 150–167. Belmont, CA: West/ Wadsworth Publishing.

"Best and Worst Technologies: Law Enforcement Products from 1953–2003." 2003. *Law and Order* (Special Issue): 26–32.

Borum, R. 2000. "Improving High Risk Encounters Between People with Mental Illness and the Police." *The Journal of the American Academy of Psychiatry and the Law* 28(3): 332–337.

Brenner, S. W. 2001. "Defining Cybercrime: A Review of State and Federal Law." In R. D. Clifford (ed.), *Cybercrime: The Investigation, Prosecution and Defense of a Computer-Related Crime*, pp. 11–69. Durham, NC: Carolina Academic Press.

Buerger, M. and Farrell, A. 2002. "The Evidence of Racial Profiling: Interpreting Documented and Unofficial Sources," *Police Quarterly.* 5(3): 272–305.

Burack, J. 2003. "Community Policing in a Security-Conscious World: Working to Prevent Terrorism in Rural America." *Subject to Debate* 17(8): 1, 3, 7. Washington, D.C.: Police Executive Research Forum.

Bureau of Justice Statistics. 2002. *Prosecutors in State Courts*. Washington, D.C.: author.

Corcoran, J. 1990. *Bitter Harvest: Gordon Kahl and the Posse Comitatus*. New York: Penguin Books.

de Guzman, M. C. 2002. The Changing Roles and Strategies of the Police in Time of Terror." *ACJS Today* 22(3): 8–13. Greenbelt, MD: Academy of Criminal Justice Sciences.

Doyle, C. 2002. "The USA Patriot Act: A Sketch." Library of Congress, Congressional Research Service. Available on-line at <http://www.fas.org/irp/crs/RS21203.pdf>.

Dupont, R. and Cochran, S. 2000. "Police Response to Mental Health Emergencies—Barriers to Change." *The Journal of the American Academy of Psychiatry and the Law* 28(3): 338–344.

Engel, R. S., Calnon, J. M., and Bernard, T. J. 2002. "Theory and Racial Profiling: Shortcomings and Future Directions in Research." *Justice Quarterly* 19(2): 249–273.

Farrell, A., McDevitt, J., and Buerger, M. 2002. "Moving Police and Community Dialogues Forward Through Data Collection Task Forces." *Police Quarterly* 5(3): 359–379.

Federal Bureau of Investigation. 2003. Uniform Crime Reports: 2002. Washington, D.C.: author. Online at <http://www.fbi.gov/ucr/02cius.htm>.

Federal Interagency Forum on Aging-Related Statistics. 2003. "Older Americans 2000: Key Indicators of Well-Being." Online at <http://www.agingstats.gov/chartbook2000/population.html>.

Florida, R. 2004. "Creative Class War." *The Washington Monthly* 36(2): 31–37.

Fyfe, J. J. 2000. "Policing the Emotionally Disturbed." *The Journal of the American Academy of Psychiatry and the Law* 28(3): 345–347.

Hoover, L. T. 2002. "The Challenges to Local Police Participation in the Homeland Security Effort." *Subject to Debate* 16(10): 1, 3–4, 8–10. Washington, D.C.: Police Executive Research Forum.

Huntington, S. 1996. *The Clash of Civilizations and the Remaking of World Order*. New York: Simon and Schuster.

Infoplease. 2003. Women in the Labor Force, 1900-2002. Online at <http://www.infoplease.com/ipa/A0104673.html>.

Innocence Project. 2001. Causes and Remedies of Wrongful Convictions. Online at <http://www.innocenceproject.org/causes/index.php>.

Johnson, K. 2002. "Police 'Infuriated' Over FBI Program." *USA Today* (August 19). Available on-line at <http://www.usatoday.com/news/washington/2002-08-01-fbi-police_x.htm>.

Kaplan, R. 1998. "Travels Into America's Future." *Atlantic Monthly* August: 37–72.

Kraska, P. 1994. "The Police and the Military in the Cold-War Era: Streamlining the State's Use of Force Entities in the Drug War." *Police Forum* 4(1): 1–7.

Margolis, J. 1993. "The Computer Cowboys." *Chicago Tribune* November 18: Sec. 2, 1.

Marshall, J. M. 2003. "The FBI: The Nineties and 9/11." *Understanding Government.* Washington, D.C.: American University. Available on-line at <http://www.understandinggovt.org/marshall.html>.

McGarrell, E., Benitez, S., and Gutierrez, R. 2003. "Getting to Know Your Community Through Citizen Surveys and Focus Group Interviews." In Q. C. Thurman and E. F. McGarrell (eds.), *Community Policing in a Rural Setting,* 2nd ed., pp. 113–120. Cincinnati: Anderson Publishing Co.

National Highway Traffic Safety Administration. 2004. *Traffic Safety Facts 2002.* Washington, D.C.: author. Available on-line at <http://www-nrd.nhtsa.dot.gov/pdf/nrd-30/NCSA/TSFAnn/TSF2002Final.pdf>.

National Institute of Justice. 1999. *Eyewitness Evidence: A Guide for Law Enforcement.* Washington, D.C.: author.

National Youth Anti-Drug Media Campaign. 2003. Keeping Latch-Key Kids Off of Drugs. On-line at http://www.theantidrug.com/news/news_latchkey.asp.

Olson, R. 2003. "Responding to the USA Patriot Act." *Subject to Debate* 17(8): 2. Washington, D.C.: Police Executive Research Forum.

Perito, R. 2002. *The American Experience with Police in Peacekeeping Operations.* Clementsport, Nova Scotia: Canadian Peacekeeping Press.

Perkins, E. B., Cordner, G. W., and Scarborough, K. E. 1999. "Police Handling of People With Mental Illness," in L. K. Gaines and G. W. Cordner (eds.), *Policing Perspectives: An Anthology,* pp. 289–297. Los Angeles: Roxbury Publishing Co.

Police Executive Research Forum. 1997. Position on Federalism. Washington, D.C.: author. Cited in Task Force on the Federalization of Criminal Law. 1998. *The Federalization of Criminal Law.* Washington, D.C.: American Bar Association, p. 41.

——. 2001. *Racially Biased Policing: A Principled Response.* Washington, D.C.: author.

Port St. Lucie Police Department Web Page. Available on-line at <http://pslgis.cityofpsl.com/Starcom/zone11.asp>.

Ramsey, C. 2002. "Community Policing: Now More Than Ever." *On the Beat* 19: 6–7. Washington, D.C.: Office of Community Oriented Policing Services.

Roberts, S. 1994. *Who We Are: A Portrait of America Based on the Latest U.S. Census.* New York: Random House/Times Books.

Rosen, M. R. 2003. "2003: A Year in Retrospect." *Law Enforcement News* December: 1, 4.

Schmitt, E. L., Langan, P. A., and Durose, M. R. 2002. *Characteristics of Drivers Stopped by Police, 1999.* Washington, D.C.: Bureau of Justice Statistics.

Sink, M. 2002. "An Electronic Cop That Plays Hunches." *New York Times* November 2: A1, A19.

Stambaugh, H., Beupre, D. S., Icove, D. J., Baker, R., Cassaday, W., and Williams, W. P. 2001. *Electronic Crime Needs Assessment for State and Local Law Enforcement.* Washington, D.C.: National Institute of Justice.

Taft, P. 1991. "Policing the New Immigrant Ghettos." In C. Klockars and S. Mastrofski (eds.), *Thinking About Police: Contemporary Readings,* pp. 307–315. New York: McGraw-Hill.

Task Force on the Federalization of Criminal Law. 1998. *The Federalization of Criminal Law.* Washington, D.C.: American Bar Association.

The Gallup Organization. 1999. *Racial Profiling Is Seen as Widespread, Particularly Among Young Black Men.* Princeton, NJ: author.

U.S. Bureau of Labor Statistics. 2003. The Employment Situation: December 2003. Online at <ftp://ftp.bls.gov/pub/news.release/empsit.txt>.

——. 2004. Labor Force Statistics From the Current Population Survey. Online at <http://data.bls.gov/servlet/SurveyOutputServlet>.

U.S. Census Bureau. 2002. Demographic Trends in the 20th Century. Washington, D.C.: author. Available at <http://www.census.gov/prod/2002pubs/censr-4.pdf>.

——. 2003a. Quick Facts. Online at <http://quickfacts.census.gov/qfd/states/27000.html>.

——. 2003b. American Fact Finder. Online at <http://factfinder.census.gov/servlet/GCTTable?_bm=y&-geo_id=01000US&-_box_head_nbr=GCT-P13&-ds_name=DEC_2000_SF3_U&-_lang=en&-format=US-9&-_sse=on>.

——. 2003c. Historical Poverty Tables. Online at <http://www.census.gov/hhes/poverty/histpov/hstpov13.html> and <http://www.census.gov/hhes/poverty/histpov/hstpov2.html>.

U.S. Northern Command. 2004. Posse Comitatus Act. Online at <http://www.northcom.mil/index.cfm?fuseaction=news.factsheets&factsheet=5>.

Vann, I. B. and Garson, G. D. 2003. *Crime Mapping: New Tools for Law Enforcement.* New York: Peter Lang Publishing.

Vanu, Inc. 2003. "The Software Radio Solution to Public Safety Interoperability." Available on-line at <http://www.vanu.com/publications/TheSoftwareRadioSolutionto-PublicSafetyInteroperability.pdf>.

Weinberg, D. H. 1996. "A Brief Look at Postwar U.S. Income Inequality." Washington, D.C.: U.S. Census Bureau. Online at <http://www.census.gov/prod/1/pop/p60-191.pdf>.

Weisheit, R., Falcone, D., and Wells, L. E. 1996. *Crime and Policing in Small-Town and Rural America.* Prospect Heights, IL: Waveland Press.

Weisheit, R. and Kernes, S. 2003. "Future Challenges: The Urbanization of Rural America." In Q. Thurman and E. McGarrell (eds.), *Community Policing in a Rural Setting,* 2nd ed., pp. 137–147. Cincinnati: Anderson Publishing Co.

Wells, G. and Seelau, E. P. 1995. "Eyewitness Identification: Psychological Research and Legal Policy on Line-Ups." *Psychology, Public Policy & Law* 1: 765–791.

Suggested Websites for Further Study

U.S. Census Bureau
www.census.gov
U.S. Bureau of Labor Statistics
www.stats.bls.gov
National Law Enforcement and Corrections Technology Center System
http://www.nlectc.org/
U.S. Department of Homeland Security
www.dhs.gov
Pearson Peacekeeping Centre
http://www.peaceoperations.org/en/home.html ✦

Photo Credits

Chapter 11   Page 397—Mark C. Ide; page 402—Mark C. Ide; page 405—Corbis; page 408—Mark C. Ide; page 417—Mark C. Ide.

Chapter 12   Page 427—Judith Calson/*San Jose Mercury News*; page 434—San Francisco Police Museum; page 436—Mark C. Ide; page 446—Judith Calson/*San Jose Mercury News*.

Chapter 13   Page 461—DigitalStock; page 469—The Feminist Majority Foundation; page 489—DigitalStock; page 494—Mark C. Ide.

Chapter 14   Page 503—Don Gottfredson; page 507—Dale Stockton; page 510—Spartan Daily.

Chapter 15   Pages 533 and 545—DigitalStock; page 555—U.S. State Department; page 560—Mark C. Ide; page 567—U.S. Department of Defense. ✦

Glossary

Abuse of Authority
Misuse of power by police that tends to injure a member of the police constituency. It can take the form of excessive physical force; psychological abuse; or violation of civil rights.

Accreditation
A process by which police departments are assessed in terms of standards of competency and professionalism. Accreditation typically involved a rigorous process of self-study followed by external review by an accreditation team made up of an official body of organizations. See CALEA.

Actual Danger
Strong likelihood of harm in a situation based on the actual number and rates of deaths and injuries that resulted from similar situations.

Acute Stress
A form of high-level distress caused by sudden emergencies such as shootings of high-speed chases.

Affidavit
A written oath establishing probable cause to obtain a search warrant; an officer describes exactly what is to be seized and exactly what is to be searched.

Aggressive Law Enforcement
Strict police practices in a given area where as many arrests as possible are made, numerous citations are given, and many field investigations are conducted.

Andragogy
An instructural method promoting the involvement of students and instructors in the learning process, stressing analytical and conceptual skills. See also *pedagogy*.

Announcement Effect
Initial modification of people's behavior when publicity surrounds a crackdown; behavior returns to normal when publicity subsides.

Apprehension
An arrest.

Arrest
The act of depriving a person of his or her liberty by legal authority and is done for the purposes of interrogation or criminal prosecution.

Arrest Rates
The number of persons arrested in relation to all crimes known to the police.

Assessment Center
A process that attempts to measure a candidate's potential for a particular position using multiple strategies, including job-related simulations and possibly interviews and psychological tests.

Avoiders
Officers who tend to sidestep or ignore problems.

Baby Boomers
Originally children born to returning veterans of World War II, now those born between 1947 and 1964. Baby boomers were the first population in U.S. history not to replace themselves.

Baby Bust
The failure of the baby boomers to replace themselves, reversing the usual trend in populations.

Balance of Power
The autonomy, authority, power, or status of groups or units compared with each other within an organization or a community.

Beat
A geographic division used by a department to distribute the workload.

Beat Teams
In order to develop partnerships with the community and to learn about the neighborhood, officers in these teams were dispatched less frequently on service calls in order to have time to work instead on community projects.

Bertillon System
A method to identify suspects, including physical measurements, a detailed description, a photograph, and fingerprints.

BFOQ
Abbreviation for Bona Fide Occupational Qualification, a job-related standard that is permissible under Title VII of the Civil Rights Act. If a particular characteristic (such as the ability to lift heavy weights or run a computer) can be shown to be needed for successful job performance or a "business necessity," it may be allowed as a requirement even though it may discriminate against some protected groups of people.

Bias Crime
A crime that is racially or sexually motivated, a hate crime.

Bow Street Runners
The first police investigators, a special section of the Bow Street Station developed in London between 1749 and 1750 and made up of carefully selected personnel who would move swiftly to the scene of a crime to begin an investigation.

Broken Windows Theory
A theory of crime that emphasizes the influence of the quality of community life. It suggests that once a neighborhood is allowed to run down, it can be a short time before it becomes inhospitable and infested with crime.

Bureaucracy
A term coined by Max Weber at the end of the nineteenth century to identify characteristics that an organization needed to operate on a rational basis.

CALEA
Acronym for **Commission on Accreditation of Law Enforcement Agencies**, developed as a result of the combined efforts of the International Association of Chiefs of Police, National Organization of Black Law Enforcement Executives, National Sheriffs' Association, and Police Executive Research Forum. The commission established specific standard that a police department meet before it can become accredited.

CAPS
Chicago Alternative Policing Strategy, began in 1993, remains the best big-city example of department-wide community policing, with sustained implementation and measurable effects on crime, public opinion, citizen involvement, problem solving, and African Americans' views about neighborhood problems.

Career Path
The direction one's chosen profession takes, including broadening of one's position, new assignments, and promotions.

Carroll Doctrine
Provides for warrantless searches of motor vehicles if the vehicle is, in fact, mobile and if there is probable cause.

Case Law
Written rulings of state and federal appellate courts that define when and how a procedure is to be used.

Centralization
Retention of authority and decision making by the top levels of a police department.

Certification
A document (license or certificate) that states that a department of individual has met professional standards. It is typically given by a state-level organization.

Chain of Command
Levels in an organizational (departmental) hierarchy; the higher the level, the greater the power, authority, and influence.

Change Strategies
Management methods used by a department to facilitate change.

Chronic Stress
A form of low-level, cumulative distress that includes the day-to-day routine of the job.

Citizen Input

Community-policing belief that citizens should have open access to police organizations and input to police policies and decisions. Individual neighborhoods and communities should have the opportunity to influence how they are policed, legitimate interest groups in the community should be able to discuss their views and concerns directly with police officials, and police departments should be responsive and accountable.

Civil Law

Laws concerned with relationships between individuals (contracts, business transactions, family relations) as distinct from *criminal laws*.

Civil Liability Suit

A legal action against a police officer, supervisor, chief, or police (or at least the city) for recovery of monetary damages for the negligent behavior of one or more of the above.

Civil Service, or Merit, System

A selection method for filling government jobs determined by rank order based on the highest combined score on a written exam; oral interview; and physical, medical., and personal requirements; these requirements have often been not job related and therefore discriminatory.

Civilian Review Board

Group of citizens charged with investigating allegations of police misconduct.

Class-Control Theory

One of four theories to explain the development of police departments: to dominate the working class for the benefit of the industrial elite.

Classical Principles

Rules governing a bureaucracy including specialization of work, assigning of authority and responsibility, discipline, unity of command, scalar chain of authority, centralization of decision making, and small spans of control.

Clean-Beat Crime Fighters

Officers who are *Proactive* and *legalistic* but not selective.

Closed System

System (organization or department) that does not interact with or adapt to its environment, as distinct from *open system*.

Coactive Policing

Strategies in which the police form a partnership with the community. Examples are neighborhood watches and citizen patrols.

Code of Silence

The secrecy that line officers maintain about their work-related activities, both from the public and from police administrators. A part of line-officer culture, it is particularly associated with covering up wrongdoing committed by colleagues.

Coercion

See *force*.

Coercive Approach
Using authority to obtain an appropriate outcome.

Cognitive Learning
Training that goes beyond learning a specific skill or task and instead focuses on the process that establishes correct and valid thinking patterns.

Color of Law
The misuse of power possessed by an individual who is a "state actor," and derives their power from the government.

Command Voice
Firmly spoken order.

Commission Approach
Use of commissions (groups) of appointed citizens and experts to effect the police reform.

Community Crime Prevention
An approach to crime based on the assumption that by changing a community, both through appearance and preventive activities, the behavior of residents can also be changed.

Community Policing
See *community policing model*.

Community Policing Model
An approach to the relationship between the police and the community that attempts to be responsive to individuals, groups, and the neighborhood without engaging in preference or discrimination. In includes both a working partnership with the community and a capacity to identify and to help solve community problems.

Community-service Officer (CSO)
A nonsworn position that is assigned support duties that generally do not require a weapon.

Compstat
A process that utilized current crime data to analyze crime patterns on which to base appropriate responses, also known as an anti-crime program.

Computerized Crime Mapping
A computer generated map of crime information matched to a geographic area to help officers know where to concentrate their patrol activities.

Consolidation
The integration of two or more police departments (also called regional police departments).

Constable
Official in medieval England appointed to assist the *sheriff*; later a British police officer.

Constable-nightwatch System

A system of law enforcement that began in England and prevailed in cities in the northeastern United States from the 1600s to the early 1800s; the constable provided limited daytime police services while the night watch patrolled after dark.

Constitutional or Federally Protected Rights

Title 42 USC §1983 established that these rights need to be violated for plaintiffs to seek redress against police officers or departments; these rights are outlined in the Bill of Rights or the equal protection clause of the Fourteenth Amendment.

Contingency Theory

Management based on the recognition that many internal and external factors influence police behavior and there is no one best way to run a department.

Continuum of Force

A range of possible responses police officers use; from mere presence to deadly force; according to the intensity of resistance of suspects. The continuum provides officers with a standard for training in the use of force.

Contract Law Enforcement

A kind of policing that involves an agreement (contract) between two units of government in which one provides law enforcement services for the other.

Controlling

The process by which managers determine how the quality or quantity of departmental systems and services can be improved if goals and objectives are to be accomplished.

Co-production of Public Safety

A process in which the police and the public become partners in determining the police role and identifying solutions to problems such as crime and disorder.

COPS

Acronym for **community-oriented policing services**; a program created by the Crime Control Act of 1994 to hire 100,000 new officers to be used by local departments to help further their community policing efforts. It is administered by the Justice Department's Office of Community Oriented Policing Services.

Corporate Strategy

A private-sector process,that suggests that, like private-sector managers, police managers should define the principal financial and social goals the organization will pursue, and the principal products, technologies, and production processes on which it will rely to achieve its goals.

Covert patrol

Patrol officers or detectives working under cover in order to blend into the community.

CPTED
Abbreviation for **crime prevention through environmental design**, a strategy by which police and the community work together to control neighborhoods and buildings in order to reduce opportunities for crime. It includes target hardening and territorial reinforcement.

Crackdown
An intensive, short-term increase in officer presence and arrests for the specific types of offenses or for all offenses in specific areas.

Crime Clearance Rates
The number of Part I Crimes reported to the police divided by the number of crimes for which the police have arrested a suspect.

Crime Control Act
See *Violent Crime Control And Law Enforcement Act*.

Crime-control Theory
One of four theories to explain the development of police departments: to prevent or suppress criminal activity.

Crime Index
See *Uniform Crime Reports (Part I Crimes)*.

Crime Repression
The control of crime through the omnipresence of patrol activities, traditionally regarded ad the most important patrol function.

Criminal Laws
Laws concerned with the relationship between the individual and the government, especially in the areas of public safety and order (driving licenses, theft, rape, and murder), as distinct from *civil laws*.

Criminal Procedure
The process by which a person accused of a crime is processed through the criminal justice system.

Crisis Intervention Team (CIT)
Units consisting of either specially trained police officers or social workers hired by the department to deal with the homeless and the mentally ill.

Critical-incident Debriefing
Counseling services provided to officers after and extremely stressful event.

Cultural Diversity
A wide variation in racial, ethnic, and gender makeup of a police department, also of a community of society.

Culture
See *police culture*.

Custody
Situation where a person is deprived of his or her freedom in a significant way, such as during an arrest.

Cyber Crime
Computer crime, involving the computer as a target, the computer as a tool for the commission of a crime, or the computer as incidental to the crime itself.

Danger Signifiers
Warnings of trouble that include a person's behavior, language, dress, area, age, sex, and ethnicity.

Davis v. City of Dallas
The Supreme Court upheld the Dallas Police Department's requirement of 45 hours of college credit, even though it discriminated against minorities, because of the professional and complex nature of police work.

Deadly Force
Coercion used with the intent to cause bodily injury or death.

Decentralization
Delegation of authority and decision making to lower organizational levels.

Decertification
Suspending a police officer or putting the officer on probation.

Defeminization
The process whereby women who do not conform to sex-role stereotypes and are "tough" enough to gain respect as officers may be labeled as "bitches" or "lesbians" in an attempt to neutralize their threat to male dominance.

Deinstitutionalization
The closing or downsizing of mental hospitals during the second half of the twentieth century, bringing thousands of people with mental illness back into the community.

De-policing
Phenomenon where, in the wake of a lawsuit, officers may feel the need to engage in fewer interactions with the public, particularly officer-initiated encounters. Officers rationalize this as a normal response to what they feel is an unjust situation and rationalize that their own likelihood of being named as a defendant in a lawsuit decreases if they interact with fewer citizens.

Detective
A specialist who responds to crimes serious enough to warrant a follow-up investigation.

Deterrence
The ability to halt an adversary by force rather than threats or reason.

Discretion
The decision-making latitude of the police on whether to invoke legal sanctions when circumstances are favorable for them.

Disorder-control Theory
One of four theories to explain the development of police departments: to prevent or suppress mob violence.

Disparate Impact
A selection method can be considered to have a legally disparate impact when the selection rate of a group is less than 80 percent of the most successful group, also knows as the four-fifths rule.

Distress
Negative stress.

Domestic Violence
An assault on or battery of a domestic partner; traditionally handled by the police through arrest.

Double Marginality
The situation in which minority police officers are not fully accepted by either the police or members of their own racial or ethnic group.

Due-process Revolution
Important changes in procedural laws that had occurred by the 1960s.

Early-Warning (Early-Identification) System
A modern approach to police officer accountability that combines the bureaucratic and internal investigation methods; these systems track specific types of officer behaviors and then alert management when individual officers exceed the threshold for such behavior.

Economic Corruption
The breaking of the law by officers in order to seek personal financial gain, for example, keeping drug money confiscated from dealers.

Education
Instruction in a general body of knowledge on which decisions can be based as to *why* something should be done on the job; concerned with theories, concepts, issues, and alternatives. See also *training*.

Educational-incentive Policies
Departmental policies that encourage officers to pursue a college degree; such incentives may include tuition assistance or reimbursement, more pay, shift or day-off adjustments, and permission to attend class during work hours.

Empirical Evidence
Proof based on systematic study of data.

Enforcers
Officers who use coercion when the chance arises.

Enticement
A police activity that purposely encourages someone to commit a crime.

Entrapment
Police activity that purposely provides a person with the opportunity and intent to commit a crime.

Ethical Formalism
Idea of the absolute importance of doing one's duty. An officer who believes that police should "go by book" is an ethical formalist.

Ethical Relativism
Idea that what is considered good varies with the particular values of groups and individuals.

Ethical Utilitarianism
Idea that it is good results of one's actions that determines whether the action itself is good. For example, telling a lie (generally an unethical act) might save a life (a good result).

Eustress
Positive stress.

Event Analysis
A patrol approach that suggests that the police should be aware of important celebrations, ideologies, and anniversaries of known activists, terrorists, or groups and attempt to determine whether these events may be connected to a possible terrorist act.

Exceptional Clearance
Situation when the police claim to know who committed a crime but cannot make an arrest; the crime is considered to be solved.

Excessive Force
More violence that is needed to carry out a legitimate police task.

Exclusionary Rule
A legal means for controlling officer behavior. All evidence obtained unconstitutionally is not admitted in a state court.

Exigent Circumstances
Unusual situations, for example, when an officer or someone else might be harmed or when the police are chasing a suspect (in "hot pursuit").

Exoneration
Clearing an officer of blame when an investigation finds a complaint is essentially true, but the officer's behavior is considered to be justified, legal, and within departmental policy.

Expectation-integration Model
An approach to police work that illustrates how compatible and conflicting concerns of the law, the community, and the police department determine the police role.

External (Citizen) Review
Efforts by individuals and groups outside the department to control the police.

Eyewitness Identification
Practice where an eyewitness identifying a suspect, often from a line-up, is considered convincing evidence in court.

False Complaints
Unfounded allegations of misconduct.

Federalization
A strong trend throughout the second half of the twentieth century, the federalization of crime control and law enforcement means that the U.S. Congress has passed more and more federal criminal laws, giving wider jurisdiction to federal prosecutors and police. Many crimes today, especially those involving guns or drugs, can be investigated and prosecuted federally as well as by state and local law enforcement.

Field-training Officer
An experienced, well-qualified officer selected and taught to act as a mentor to a new recruit by providing on-the-job training.

Flat Structure
Organization design that has few levels with many employees per supervisor, as distinct from *tall structure*.

Fleeing-felon Rule
Guideline for use of deadly force in pursuit of someone hastening from the scene of a suspected grave crime.

Follow-up Investigation
An official inquiry generally conducted by a detective to develop a case; includes identifying and locating a suspect, possibly obtaining a confession, and disposing of the case.

Foot Patrol
Patrol strategy using officers on foot rather than in patrol cars. Foot patrol officers are considered in a better position to relate more intimately with citizens than officers driving by in cars, to understand what constitutes threatening or inappropriate behavior, and to observe and correct it.

Fourth amendment
Amendment to the Constitution with the "right of the people to be secure in their persons, houses, papers, and effects, against unreasonable searches and seizures.

Four-fifths Rule
See *disparate impact*.

Frankpledge System
A system for keeping order in medieval England based on tithings (10 families) and hundreds (10 tithings).

Fraternal Organization
An association that seeks chiefly recognition and benefits for its members, generally organized along ethnic lines.

Fruit of the Poisonous Tree Doctrine
An extension of the exclusionary rule which indicates that not only must evidence seized improperly be excluded from criminal court, but so, too, must any additional evidence seized after that police action.

Garrity Interview
Compelled testimony for internal investigations; routing practice but not protected by the fifth amendment and cannot normally be used in a criminal proceeding.

General Deterrence
A police strategy where the goal is to maximize motor vehicle stops as a sign of increased police presence.

Generalist
A police officer who performs a variety of activities, some of which could be assigned to a specialist.

Geographic Focus
A community-policing strategy emphasizing the geographic basis of assignment and responsibility by shifting the fundamental unit of patrol accountability from time of day to place. Seeks to establish 24-hour responsibility for smaller areas, rather than responsibility for wide areas for 8 to 10 hour shifts; also seeks permanency of assignment for officers so they will know their community better.

Globalization
Developments in business, finance, trade, travel, communications, and computers have "shrunk the world," so now it is far more likely that a local criminal investigation might involve international transactions and foreign individuals. Many traditional crimes have international facets today, such as drug distribution and theft. International organized crime, cyber crime, and terrorism are also concerns.

Goals
Purposes, objectives, or aims, general statements of big-term purpose.

GPS
Abbreviation for **geographic positioning system**, a system of 24 tracking satellites belonging to the Department of Justice. GPS scan can locate persons within millimeters of their true position. It is used to establish longitude and latitude by surveyors, hikers, the U.S. Coast Guard, and a host of other organizations.

Grass Eaters
Police officers who accept graft when it comes their way but do not actively solicit opportunities for graft, as distinct from *meat eaters*.

Gratuity
Something of value, such as free or reduced-cost beverages or meals, discount buying privileges, free admission to athletic events or movies, gifts, and small rewards. Most commonly it is beverages or meals. Some officers accept such gratuities from the public.

Grievance Arbitration
In unionized agencies, this is an option for officers appealing recommended disciplinary action they believe is inappropriate.

Group Norms
Expected behavior from group members, which can be a powerful factor in resistance to organizational change.

Highway Patrol
A state police force whose duties are generally limited to enforcing traffic laws and dealing with accidents on state roads and highways. See also *state police*.

Homeland Security
In addition to traditional duties, local police are now seeking to identify any individuals or groups who might have terrorist intentions, and to share information with federal agencies.

Hostile Work-Environment Harassment
A situation in which unwelcome conduct by other workers is so severe or pervasive that it interferes with a person's work performance.

Hot Pursuit Exception
A common exception to warrant requirements. Police may follow a felon or otherwise dangerous criminal into a place typically protected by the Fourth Amendment, such as a home, or may cross jurisdictional boundaries. Hot pursuits must be based on probable cause and the gravity of the offense must be taken into consideration. Once in a constitutionally protected area, the officer may search for the suspect and for weapons or evidence, but once the suspect is found, the search must cease.

Hot Spots
Locations that have a greater amount of crime or disorder than other areas.

Hot Times
Periods in which a greater amount of crime or disorder occurs than in other periods.

ICAM
Acronym for **information collection for automated mapping,** a program of the Washington, D.C., police department.

Income Inequality
A key economic measure which indicates how much range there is between low-income and high-income individuals or families.

Individual Expectations
The degree to which police employees' needs are met by the organization and their working environment.

Inertia
A condition of doing things as they have always been done before; it is a strong influence in resisting change in police departments.

Information Technology
The whole system of information collection, storage, retrieval, and analysis that assists officers in having ready access to information (such as driving and criminal records) and to base their patrol tactics on up-to-date crime analysis information. This system is mostly comprised of electronic (computer) hardware and software, along with analytical techniques that require a degree of human judgment and expertise.

In-group Solidarity
A closeness and loyalty among officers brought about by the perceived danger of police work, the close-knit working relations among officers, concerns that outsiders cannot be trusted, and a common basis of patrol activity.

In-migration
Movements of population within a country (from state to state).

Innovation
The development and use of new ideas and methods.

In-service Training
A program to update all department members regularly on a wide variety of subjects.

Intentional Tort
A tort (wrong) that an officer plans to cause some physical or mental harm. See also *tort*.

Internal Affairs
Section in a police department to respond to complaints.

Internal (Departmental) Review
Efforts by police to control their own behavior.

Interoperability
The capacity of different units and different agencies to communicate between each other and also share digital information (computerized data).

Interrogations
Circumstances when the police ask questions that tend to incriminate the citizen.

Investigators
Specialists in crimes serious enough to warrant inquiry.

Iron Fist
The use of aggressive police strategies, particularly those carried out by police paramilitary units.

Job Analysis
Validating selection and testing methods by identifying the behaviors that are necessary for adequate job performance.

Job Redesign
An effort to enrich police work by broadening the role in order that the job will its own reward.

Job Related
Affecting on-the-job performance, the standard by which job requirements are measured so that they are not discriminatory.

Jurisdiction
The geographic area or type of crime for which a police force is responsible.

Kin Policing
In early or nonindustrial societies, enforcement of customary rules of conduct by family, clan, or tribe.

Lateral Entry
The ability of a police officer, at the patrol or supervisory level, to transfer from one unit to another, usually without losing seniority.

Law Enforcement Assistant Act (1965)
A modest grant program that expressed a national concern about the adequacy of local police departments; the act in turn spawned the President's Commission report, which focused attention on police behavior and departmental practices.

LEAA
Acronym for **Law Enforcement Assistance Administration**, an agency through which the federal government poured literally billions of dollars into the criminal justice system—focusing on the police—in an attempt to improve effectiveness and reduce crime; LEEP, the Law Enforcement Education Program, was established under LEAA.

Leading
Motivating others to perform various tasks that will contribute to the accomplishment of goals and objectives.

Learning organization
An organization that benefits from, and adapts to, its own and others' experiences.

LEEP
Acronym for **Law Enforcement Education Program**, established under *LEAA* to provide financial assistance to police personnel, as well as to others who wished to enter police service, to pursue a college education; it significantly increased police programs in higher education in the mid-1970s.

Legalistic Model
An approach to police work that makes the standards of law and departmental policy, not politics or personal considerations, the basis for decision making. It emphasizes crime control.

Legalistic Style
Policing that insists on enforcing the law in maintaining order.

Less-Than-Lethal Weaponry
Weapons that increase the ability of the police to resolve violent encounters where use of deadly force has traditionally been standard. They include bean bags and capstan (pepper) sprays.

Macho Orientation
Traditional training outlook that has underrepresented order maintenance and social-service aspects of the police role while overrepresenting law enforcement activities.

Management
Directing individuals to achieve departmental goals efficiently and effectively.

Management Training
Instruction of officers promoted to managerial or executive-level positions; usually involves increased knowledge of management's role, long-range planning, policy development, and allocation of resources.

Manager's Culture
Emphasis on both the ends and means of policing; concerned with departmental priorities, policies, and procedures.

Marshal
A federally appointed official to keep order in federal territories (U.S. marshal); also a federally appointed local police officer (deputy marshal) and a locally appointed official (town marshal).

Meat Eaters
Police officers who actively solicit opportunities for financial gain and are involved in more widespread and serious corruption than *grass eaters*.

Mere Presence
An officer's being in view in a situation, the mildest level of force.

Militarization
Involvement of the military with law enforcement. Traditionally kept separate, these two bodies now frequently work together in the so-called war on drugs and in antiterrorism efforts.

Miranda Rights
Based on Fifth Amendment privilege from self-incrimination, police must take appropriate safeguards to ensure that a defendant's rights are not violated during arrest. Specifically, police must advise defendants that (1) they have the right to remain silent, (2) any statement made may be used against the defendant in court, (3) the defendant has the right to have an attorney present during questioning, and (4) if a defendant cannot afford an attorney, then the state will appoint one prior to questioning. The defendant must intelligently and voluntarily waive these rights prior to questioning.

National Advisory Commission on Higher Education for Police Officers
A commission to study the problems of college and graduate education for police in the 1970s; a report in 1978 called for significant changes in virtually all phases of police higher education, including institution, curriculum, and faculty.

National Advisory Commission's *Report on Police"*
Report stating that when a substantial ethnic minority population resides within the jurisdiction, the police agency should take affirmative action to achieve a ratio of minority group employees in approximate proportion to the makeup of the population.

NCVS
The National Crime Victimization Survey is the most widely used and extensive victim survey, asking a national sample of approximately 120,000 individuals over 12 years of age specific questions regarding criminal victimizations.

Negligent Tort
A tort (wrong) resulting from a breach of lawful duty to act reasonably toward an individual whom a police officer might harm.

NIBRS
The National Incident-Based Reporting System is the FBI's redesign of the UCR program, helping improve the quantity, quality, and accuracy of the crime offense statistics. NIBRS includes 52 data elements on 22 offense categories in the Part A classification and 11 offenses in a Group B category, for which only arrestee data are to be reported. It distinguishes between attempted and completed crimes, provides additional information on victim/offender relationships and characteristics, and includes the location of crimes.

Nightwatch
In olden times, group of citizens who patrolled at night looking for fires and other problems.

Noble-cause Corruption
The abandonment of ethical and legal means in order to achieve good ends. Police may use both violence and subjugation of rights if they are more concerned about the noble-cause—getting bad guys off the streets, protecting victims and children—than about the morality of technically legal behavior.

Occupational Deviance
Illegal behavior by an officer in the course of work or under the clock of police authority.

Officer Survival
Major risks faced by police officers—officer stress, suicide, and threats— are countered through officer survival training.

Old-style Crime Fighters
Officers who are aggressive and selective, concentrating on felonies.

Omnibus Crime Control and Safe Streets Act (1968)
A major piece of legislation to deal with the national concern over crime; it created the Law Enforcement Assistance Administration.

Open Fields Doctrine
A search doctrine indicating that items in open fields are not protected by the Fourth Amendment's guarantee against unreasonable searches and seizures, so they can properly be taken by an officer without a warrant or probable cause.

Open System
System (organization or department) that interacts with or adapts to its environment, distinct from *closed structure*.

Order Maintenance
Patrol goal that may or may not involve a violation of the law (usually minor), during which officers tend to use alternatives other than arrest.

Organization Chart
Diagram that depicts the functions, relationships, and flow of communication among designated groups with a police department.

Organization Design
The formal patterns of arrangements and in relationships developed by police management to accomplish departmental goals.

Organizational Change
A department's adoption of new ideas or behavior; a term often associated with community policing.

Organizational Culture
The values, beliefs, and norms that evolve both formally and informally within a police department.

Organizational Expectations
The formal and informal concerns of the department about how officers should behave and what they should do.

Organizing
The process of arranging personnel and physical resources to carry out plans and accomplish goals and objectives.

Paramilitary Model
Formal pattern where the police are organized along military lines, with emphasis on a legalistic approach.

Particularistic Perspectives
Views of the police that emphasize difference among police officers, as distinct from *universalists perspectives*.

Patronage System
Unofficial practice in which public jobs are given as rewards for supporting the political party in power.

Pedagogy
An instructional method involving a one-way transfer of knowledge, usually facts and procedures, from the instructor to the student, distinguished from *andragogy*.

Peer-counseling Program
A program in which police officers who are specially trained to recognize problems associated with stress from critical incidents provide support to colleagues and make referrals as deemed necessary.

Peer Group
Officers of the same rank in the department

Perceived Danger
Harm that an officer of the public believes to be potential in a situation.

PERF
Acronym for **Police Executive Research Forum**, an association made up of college-educated police chief executives; it passed a resolution calling for all police applicants to possess 30 semester units of college, increasing to a minimum requirement of a bachelor's degree for employment in policing.

Person-initiated Danger
An attack against a police officer by another person.

Physical Force
Use of physical means to control or apprehend citizen suspects.

Physiological Stress
A state resulting from physical, chemical, or emotional factors that can cause biological disease such as high blood pressure and ulcers.

Plain-view Doctrine
The principle that what police discover during the performance of their normal duties can be seized. For example, if a police officer stops a person who committed a traffic violation, and the officer sees illegal items in the back seat of the car, then that contraband is in plain view and can be legally taken.

Planning
The process of preparing for the future by setting goals and objectives and developing courses of action for accomplishing them.

Police
Nonmilitary persons or organizations that are given the general right by government to use coercion to enforce the law and respond to conflict involving illegal behavior.

Police-Auditor Systems
Developed more recently than civilian review boards, these systems do not usually investigate or monitor individual citizen complaints—that is left to the internal affairs. Instead, the auditor model focuses on the police organization and its policies and practices, ensuring that legal requirements are being met and that the most efficient and effective practices are being followed.

Police Brutality
Excessive force, including violence, that does not support a legitimate police function.

Police Cadet Corps
Recruitment program designed to increase applicants with college degrees, and possibly increase the number of women and minority applicants. College recruits receive scholarship money and work part-time as police cadets.

Police-Community Relations
Philosophy emphasizing the importance of communication and mutual understanding between the local police department and the surrounding community.

Police Corruption
Any forbidden act that involves misuse of an officer's position for gain.

Police Culture
The informal, but important relations among police officers and the values they share. Police work is characterized by its own occupational beliefs and values, which traditionally include a perception of the police as sexist and macho.

Police Deviance
Activities of officers that inconsistent with their legal authority, the department's authority, and standards of ethical conduct.

Police Image
The favorable representation of the department and the police role, especially to aid recruitment.

Police Legitimacy
Public confidence in the police as fair and equitable; it may help to prevent crime through citizens's increased willingness to obey the law.

Police Misconduct
Actions that violate departmental guidelines (policies, procedures, rules, and regulations) that define both appropriate and inappropriate conduct for officers.

Police Power
The authority given to government to regulate health, welfare, safety, and morality.

Police Pursuit
Chasing a suspect who is trying to avoid arrest.

Police Stressors
Sources of stress for police, including departmental practices (e.g. authoritarian structure) and the inherent nature of police work (e.g., shift work, boredom, exposure to human misery).

Police Union
Association of police officers to represent the police in collective bargaining with the employer to gain recognition, improved wages and benefits, clear disciplinary procedures, and better job conditions.

Police Violence
Use of force to obtain confessions.

*Police*woman
Female officer who tends to emphasize the traditional police culture, especially its law enforcement aspects.

Police*woman*
Female officer who attempts to maintain a "feminine manner" while performing police duties.

Political Model
An approach to the relationship between the police and the community that sees the police primarily as serving the interests of politically powerful groups. It leads to preferential treatment for some citizens and discrimination against others, that is, corruption.

Posse Comitatus
Group in medieval England called out to pursue fleeing felons.

POST
Acronym for **peace officers' standards and training**.

Potential Danger
Harm that could exist in a situation.

PPU
Abbreviation for **police paramilitary unit**, group of police that functions as a military special-operations team, primarily to threaten or use collective force.

President's Commission's *Challenge of Crime in a Free Society*
A comprehensive 1967 report documenting the serious impact of crime on U.S. society. Although the report issued over 200 specific proposals for action involving all levels of government and society, a majority of the recommendations —either directly or indirectly—dealt with the police as the "front line" of the criminal justice system.

Predispositional Theory
The idea that the behavior of a police officer is primarily explained by the characteristics, values, and attitudes of that person before he or she was employed.

Preliminary Investigation
An initial inquiry conducted by patrol officers of the purpose of establishing that a crime has been committed and to protect the scene of the crime from those not involved in the inquiry.

President's Commission's *Challenge of Crime in a Free Society*
A comprehensive 1967 report documenting the serious impact of crime on U.S. society. Although the report issued over 200 specific proposals for action involving all levels of government and society, a majority of the recommendations —either directly or indirectly—dealt with the police as the "front line" of the criminal justice system.

Pretextual Stops
Officers stopping a suspect for a minor violation with the goal of eliciting another, more serious violation?

Prevention Emphasis
Community-policing strategy that emphasizes a more proactive and preventive orientation, encouraging better use of police officers' time by devoting the substantial resource of free patrol time to directed enforcement activities, specific crime prevention efforts, problem solving, community engagement, citizen interaction, or similar kinds of activities. Officers are encouraged to look beyond individual-incident calls for service and reported crimes in order to discover underlying problems and conditions.

Private Police
Police employed and paid by an individual or nongovernmental organization.

Private World of Policing
Police work characterized as politically conservative, close, or secretive and emphasizing loyalty and solidarity.

Proactive Approach
Initiated by the police; it applies to the activities of both the officer, such as proactive arrest, and the department.

Proactive Arrests
Arrests initiated by the police, focusing on a narrow set of high-risk targets. The theory is that a high certainty of arrest for a narrowly defined set of offenses or offenders will have a greater deterrent effect than will a low certainty of arrest for a broad range of targets.

Probable Cause
According to the Supreme Court, probable cause exists where the facts and circumstances within the officers' knowledge, and of which they have reasonably trustworthy information, are sufficient in themselves to warrant a belief by a man of reasonable caution that a crime is being committed. Hence, the officer has reason to believe that a particular individual has "more likely than not" committed a certain crime. Probable cause is the minimum legal standard necessary to make a custodial arrest of a person and it is a more rigorous standard than reasonable suspicion.

Problem Analysis Triangle
The problem analysis triangle (sometimes referred to as the crime triangle) provides a way of thinking about recurring problems of crime and disorder. This idea assumes that crime or disorder results when (1) likely offenders and (2) suitable targets come together in (3) time and space in the absence of capable guardians for that target.

Problem-Oriented Policing (POP)
An approach to police work that is concerned primarily with identifying and solving community problems, with or without input from the community.

Problem Solving
Techniques to gain deeper insight into the issues that police are called on to address and to develop tailored solutions that have a longer-lasting impact on the problem.

Procedural Laws
Criminal laws that govern how the police enforce *substantive laws*.

Professional-style Officers
Police who are somewhat proactive but not selective, believing their work is to serve people. They use coercion if necessary but seek other means first.

Professionalization
Movement to help the police be more objective and effective in their decisions by forming a code of ethics, developing a scientifically derived body of knowledge and skill, and providing extensive education and training. These are all means to turn police work from an occupation into a profession.

Protective Sweep
A limited examination of a home to determine if there are others who could pose a safety risk for officers.

Psychological Force
Limited nonphysical interrogation methods.

Psychological Stress
A state resulting from physical, chemical, or emotional factors that can cause deterioration of mental health.

PTSD
Abbreviation for **posttraumatic stress disorder**, a psychological state caused by frequent or prolonged exposure to crises or trauma.

Public Police
Police who are employed, trained, and paid by a government agency.

Public Safety
The partial or complete integration of police and fire services.

Public World of Policing
Police work presented to the public that tries to avoid controversy and sometimes may involve cover-up of illegal or inappropriate behavior.

Quality Circle
A management technique by which a group of employees from the same work area volunteer to meet on a regular basis to identify an solve common work problems.

Quality Leadership
A department-wide management philosophy which includes principles of teamwork for planning and goal setting, data-based problem solving, a customer orientation, employee input in decisions, policies to support productive employees, encouragement for risk taking and tolerance for mistakes, and the manager as facilitator rather than commander.

Quality Management
See *TQM*.

Quality-of-Life Crimes
Part of zero-tolerance policing, these crimes are minor public violations (e.g., panhandling, public urination, rowdy behavior) whose enforcement, it is theorized, will improve the quality of life in an area.

Quality-of-Life Policing
Police strategy which targets the reduction of physical and social disorder so that community members will work together to promote neighborhood safety, and concomitantly reduce crime.

Quid Pro Quo Harassment
A situation requiring the employee to choose between the job and meeting a supervisor's sexual demands.

R & D
Research and development; a proposed unit to help police departments to become learning organizations by going beyond mere statistical descriptions of departmental inputs and outputs and trying to develop new ideas.

Racial Profiling
Proactive police actions that rely on race or ethnicity rather than behavior that leads the police to identify a particular person as being, or having been, engaged in criminal activity.

Random Patrol
Police officers patrolling their beats at random (by chance) when not otherwise on assignment.

Reactive Approach
Responsive to the request of the citizen for police action, such as an arrest made in response to citizen complaints, generally for a minor offense.

Reactive Arrests
Arrests made in response to citizen complaints, are random, and are generally for minor offenses.

Reasonable Suspicion
Suspicion based on objective facts and logical conclusions that a crime has been or is about to be committed, and this is based on the circumstances at hand.

Reciprocators
Officers who use persuasion if possible.

Recruitment Strategies
The various methods used to attract applicants, particularly women and minorities, to become police officers.

Reinventing Government
Strategy for improving organizational performance through reorganization, downsizing, and TQM.

Reliability
The consistency of a measure in yielding results over time. If other observers conducted the same research in the same setting, they would probably come to similar conclusion.

Reno Model
A type of field-training program emphasizing aspects of community policing, based on andragogical (versus pedagogical) learning methods, and placing heavy emphasis on problem-based learning exercises.

Reoriented Operations
An aspect of community policing which recommends less reliance on the patrol car and more emphasis on face-to-face interactions, replacing ineffective or isolating operational practices with more effective and more interactive practices, and finding ways of performing necessary traditional functions more efficiently in order to save time and resources that can then be devoted to more community-oriented activities.

Resident-officer Program
A plan whereby a department provides officers with rent-free or low-rent housing or low-interest loans to purchase rehabilitated homes in low-income or high-crime areas.

Residual Deterrence
Continued reduction of crime even after a crackdown is ended.

Retrenchment
Cutting back to the minimal level of activity needed for highly aggressive police work.

Reverse Discrimination
The charge made by a group—usually white men—who feel that an affirmative-action plan in the selection and promotion process shows bias in favor of minorities and women.

ROP
Acronym for **repeat offenders project** of the Washington, D.C., police department.

Rotten-apple Theory of Corruption
The idea that corruption is limited to a small number of officers who were probably dishonest prior to their employment. The term stems from the metaphor that a few rotten apples will spoil the barrel; in other words, a few bad officers can spoil a department.

Rule of Law
A principle of constitutional democracy whereby the exercise of power is based on laws, not on an individual or organization.

SARA
Acronym for **scanning, analysis, response, and assessment**, a four-stage problem-solving process.

Scholarship and Recruitment Program
A program established under the Crime Control Act of 1994 that provides scholarships for higher education to in-service police personnel and students (juniors or seniors in high school or college students) who do not currently work in law enforcement and are interested in pursuing it as a career.

Screening In
Process of identifying police applicants who are the best-qualified candidate for the applicant pool.

Screening Out
Process identifying police applicants who are unqualified and removing them from consideration.

Sensitization Training
Instructing an officer to be aware of the problems of victims as well as their own victimization; it should be conducted early in their careers.

Service Style
Approach to policing that intervenes frequently but often informally in maintaining order.

Service-style Officers
Officers who do the minimum to get by, who are not aggressive but are selective.

Sexual Harassment
Unwelcome sexual advances that unreasonably interfere with a person's work or create a hostile working environment.

Sheriff
Originally an English official appointed to levy fines and keep order in a county; later in the United States an official, usually elected, who enforces the law in rural areas. In addition to patrol and investigations, a sheriff's duties often include managing a jail and providing services for courts.

Shift
A working period.

Situational Crime Prevention
Crime prevention approach emphasizing the necessity of tailoring crime prevention responses to the specific characteristics of the crime problem being addressed, rejecting any one-size-fits-all thinking. It also focuses primarily on reducing opportunities for crime by, for example, increasing the effort required to commit offenses, increasing the risk of being detected, and reducing the reward should the offense be consummated.

Situational Danger
A particular problem on the job, for example, a high-speed chase, that threatens an officer's safety.

Slippery Slope Theory
The idea that corruption at a lower level can easily lead to corruption at a higher level.

SMART
Part of a multistrategy approach to drug control, a Specialized Multi-Agency Response Team is a special unit made up of Beat Health officers which coordinates site visits by a group of city inspectors (such as housing, fire, public works, and gas and electric) to inspect a problem location and enforce local safety codes.

Social Services
Police responsibilities that involve taking reports and providing information and assistance to the public, everything from helping a stranded motorist to checking grandma's house to make sure she is all right.

Social-supports Model
An approach to police stress based on the premise that individuals are insulated against stressors when they have a support network of friends, family, and co-workers.

Socialization
Process by which recruits learn values and behavior from experienced officers.

Socialization
Process where recruits learn the values and behavioral patterns of experienced officers.

Special-jurisdiction Police
Police who function within a particular type of organization (e.g., college police) that is not part of the basic structure of the police department.

Specialist
A police officer who performs a particular kind of activity such as investigation, as distinguished from a *generalist*.

Specialization
The division of labor of personnel; the fewer kinds of tasks a person performs, the greater the level of specialization.

Specialized Training
Instruction to prepare officers for particular categories of tasks or jobs.

Specific Deterrence
Patrol strategy to reduce firearm violence, where the goal was to focus on the seizure of illegal weapons from targeted offenders (i.e., suspicious-looking pedestrians and motorists),

State Police
A state force that has bored law enforcement power, conducts criminal investigations, patrols roads and highways, and frequently has forensic science laboratories.

Sting Operation
An undercover activity in which police set up fencing outlets and encourage thieves to sell them stolen merchandise.

Stop and Frisk
Practice where an officer may stop a person, temporarily depriving him or her of freedom of movement, if the officer has reasonable suspicion that the person is involved in a crime. Furthermore, the officer may frisk the person if there is reasonable suspicion to believe the citizen is armed and poses a threat to the officer for the duration of the stop.

Strategic Management
An approach to police work that involves identifying departmental goals and the most effective and efficient way to achieve them; this approach suggests that departments should experiment with alternative police methods.

Strategies
Broadly conceptualized plans or activities that affect the attitudes and behavior of individual officers.

Street Cop's Culture
Emphasis primarily on achieving results, concern with "street wisdom" and survival.

Stressor-Outcome Model
An approach to police stress based on the premise that circumstances of strain or tension lead to psychological or physiological stress.

Structural Characteristics
The features that police departments emphasize or do not emphasize, which may be discriminatory, especially against women.

Subculture
Police culture as part of a broader societal culture.

Subjugation of Defendant's Rights
Overriding a citizen's civil rights in order to obtain a confession.

Substantive Laws
Criminal Laws that identify behavior and punishment, distinct from *procedural laws*.

Suicide Prevention Training
Instruction aimed at reducing police suicides by recognizing depression, developing communication skills, resolving conflicts, and maintaining close relationships.

Supervision
The management function that focuses primarily on leading and controlling.

Supervisory Training
Instruction for officers promoted to first-line administrative positions; it usually includes leadership, specific job requirements, and policies and procedures.

Sustained Complaints
Allegations of misdeeds by police that an investigation finds to be justified.

SWAT
Special Weapons and Tactics units function as military special-operations teams—often gaining expertise and training from the Navy's Seals and the Army's Rangers—and have as a primary function the threat or use of collective force, not always as a function of last resort.

Symbolic Assailant
Type of person the police officer thinks is potentially dangerous or troublesome, usually because of the way the person walks, talks, and dresses.

Systematic Theory of Corruption
The idea that police corruption arise from the nature of police work and if anti-corruption protocols are inadequate, corruption will spread throughout the department.

Systems Theory
The idea that all parts of a system (organization) are interrelated and interdependent.

Tall Structure
Organization design that has many levels with few employees per supervisor, as distinct from flat structure.

Target Hardening
Crime prevention strategy that seeks improvements in doors, windows, locks, alarms, lighting, and landscaping to make illegal entry into homes and businesses more difficult and time-consuming.

Target Oriented
Concept used by officers to assess likely targets in their districts; that is, they should not only be watching over obvious places and persons who might be of danger but also where disruption in "safe places" might occur.

Task Analysis
Course content criteria where the subject matter should be based on the jobs to be performed by the recruits; such analysis, however, still tends to be more the exception than the rule, with training based more on legal requirements and experience.

Task-Force Approach
Using a team of officers from two or more police agencies to work together to solve a particular problem that transcends jurisdictional limits (e.g., a drug task force).

Team Policing
A group of officers, working as a unit, who are stationed in a neighborhood and are responsible for all police services there.

Terrorism
Strategy whereby a group tries to influence a society's direction through acts of extreme violence against targeted groups, random citizens, or both.

Testimonial Evidence
Proof based on the opinions of others.

Thief Catcher
In olden times, a person hired to secure return of stolen property.

Third Degree
Coercive police methods including both physical and psychological force.

Tort
A civil wrong (not concerned with a contract) in which one person, in violation of a legal duty required by law, causes an injury to another person or damage to that person's property.

TQM
Abbreviation for **total quality management**, a customer-oriented approach that emphasizes human resources and quantitative methods in an attempt at continuous improvement.

Training
Instruction of an individual in how to do a job; concerned with specific facts and procedures. See also *education*.

Tribal Police
Law enforcement bodies on Native American (Indian) reservations.

Unfounded Complaints
Allegations of police misdeeds that an investigation finds did not occur as stated.

Uniform Crime Reports (Part I Crimes)
An index of the crime rate per 100,000 population of eight major crimes: murder and nonnegligent manslaughter, forcible rape, robbery, aggravated assault, burglary, larceny, motor vehicle theft, and arson.

Universalistic Perspectives
Views of police behavior that look for the ways officers are similar, as distinct from *particularistic perspectives*.

Unsubstantiated Complaints
Allegations that in the opinion of those making the decision cannot be sustained as either true or false.

Urban-Dispersion Theory
One of four theories that explain the development of the police department: to provide an important part of government.

Use Corruption
Illegal use of drugs by officers.

Validity
Justifiability of a measure as an accurate assessment of the attribute it is designed to assess. Other people are likely to see the same thing the observers sees.

Values
Fundamental assumptions that guide a police department and individual members in the exercise of discretion.

Velvet Glove
A metaphor for community policing, based on the idea that a less aggressive approach to crime is more effective than hard-edged methods.

Verbal Force
Persuasive use of words to control a situation.

Victim Survey
A study in which scientifically selected samples of the population are asked about being victims of crime.

Vigilante
Member of a voluntary band (usually men) who organize to respond to real or imagined threats to their safety; to protect their lives, property, or power; or seek revenge. Characteristic of the old West, they are also active today.

Violent Crime Control and Law Enforcement (Crime Control Act) (1994)
The most comprehensive federal crime legislation since the Omnibus Crime Control and Safe Streets Act of 1968; it included the *COPS* program to hire 100,000 police officers.

Watchman Style
Policing that allows great latitude in maintaining order.

WHAM
Winning the Hearts and Minds of the rank-and-file members of a department, in order to secure their cooperation in implementing organizational change.

Zero-Tolerance Policing
A strategy of proactive arrests, based on the broken-windows theory of crime causation. In practice, this theory suggests that if police aggressively pursue minor quality-of-life crimes the improvement in the quality of life in an area will indirectly lead to a lower rate of serious crime. ✦

Author Index

Subject Index